# welcome greece

TO ENTER GREECE IS TO STEP INTO A LAND WHERE YOU HEAR THE LAP OF WAVES ON HONEY-COLORED BEACHES. YOUR EYES LOOK UPON THE SUN-BLANCHED RUINS OF ANCIENT TEMPLES. YOUR NOSE TAKES IN THE AROMA OF AGED OLIVE GROVES AND THE PERFUME OF CAPER BLOSSOMS. AND BEST OF ALL, YOU ARE INVITED TO SAVOR AN ARRAY OF DISHES THAT HAVE WELCOMED VISITORS FOR COUNTLESS CENTURIES.

central

THE GREEK FRIED EGG, PAGE 217

# olives

You have entered the heart of Greece. Paths that have been trod for thousands of years take you from the tip of Attica, where famed Athens stretches along the coast, to Mount Hymettus, known for honey, to the wild fennel—covered battlefield of Marathon, and on to the hillside reaches of Delphi. You wander past Mesolongi, where Lord Byron died, and come to Thebes, home of Oedipus. The region is now called Sterea Ellada, "Solid Greece." Around old temples and monasteries are wheat and vegetable fields. Towns hum with age-old activities—the buying and selling of food—and fresher food cannot be found.

sizzled in the greenest olive oil, no egg in the world can top a newly laid egg, fried in the Greek style.

ancient ladders lead to the monasteries tucked into the meteora rocks. below lies thessaly, greece's breadbasket.

from central greece come hymettus honey, olives from spata, and time-honored piney attica retsina.

# greece

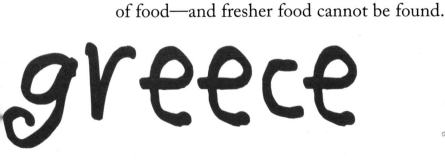

the creamy marble ruins of the temple of demeter, goddess of the harvest, greet you at eleusis.

# Peloponnesos

GIANT BEANS PLAKI-STYLE WITH HONEY AND MINT, PAGE 286

If Central Greece is the country's heart, the Peloponnesos, across the isthmus of Corinth, is its marrow. Some of the most ancient Greek settlements lie here. Warriors and heroes sailed for Troy from Mycenae. Jason launched his fabled ship from Argos. Sparta, to which soldiers returned with their shields or on them, sits halfway down. For over one thousand years, Olympia drew athletes from all over the world to test their skills.

a bowl of greece's unique giant beans simmered tender in a sauce of tomato, onion, and mint satisfies heart and soul.

a mosaic floor from ancient corinth features the head of dionysos surrounded by an intricate pattern.

the ruins of the temple of apollo at corinth.

# citrus

every greek avidly awaits the late-winter ripening of peloponnese lemons and oranges, followed by the spring appearance of early-ripening apricots.

The fortress town of Monemvasia, connected to the mainland by only a spit of land, produced a wine so famous it was known to Shakespeare as "Malmsey." The Peloponnesos is home to Nemean wines, Kalamata olives, and the cheese, goats, and cakes of Arcadia.

# northern

smiling in the sun, a thracian woman walks daily to her fields with the help of a cane.

S tretching across the top of Greece lie Epiros, Macedonia, and Thrace, all three jigsawed with jagged mountains, deep gorges, inlet beaches, and lush river valleys. Epiros is studded with stone and slate villages, reed-lined lakes, and the slim minarets from the reign of Ali Pasha. Macedonia is the proud birthplace of

right: a triple-crusted filo pie of leeks, potatoes, and olives is a typical epiros dish.

below: lake arta is surrounded by breathtaking mountains and plains.

# capers

straight from northern high mountain pastures come the majority of greece's incomparable curdy, tangy, crumbly sheep and goat cheeses.

Alexander the Great and of Aristotle. Thrace holds unexplored forests and hidden Byzantine ruins. All are home to Greece's wandering shepherds. The rich cuisine—tangy cheese, crusty pies, broth-plumped grains, simmered meats, and root vegetables—is tinged with spices.

# greece

LEEK, POTATO, AND OLIVE PIE, PAGE 97

*watching what passes for rush-hour traffic in kefalonia.*

*behind scrolled gates, flower-filled gardens scent the corfu air.*

# ionian

The Ionian islands are as close to Eden as one can find. Jade-green hillsides, cobalt waters, pink and ocher houses, and peach-colored beaches invite all comers. Corfu has grottoes and delicious quince preserves. Kefalonia boasts *tavernas* serving spicy fish. Paxi has famed grassy olive oil. Lefkada's verandas burst with pots of purple-flowered basil. And as for Ithaca, it's easy to see the truth in Homer's verses about fruit-filled gardens and orchard-filled fields, and why Odysseus loved his island home.

*right: in zakinthos, a boat will take you, a picnic basket, and a bottle of island wine to an otherwise unreachable beach.*

*below: a baked swordfish swims in a sauce of ionian kumquats and blood oranges, page 330.*

*the olive oils of paxi range in color from amber gold to jade green and are famous throughout greece.*

islands

# cyclades
## fish from the

left:
red mullet is a much-praised specialty of the fishermen of the cyclades.

The Cyclades decorate the Aegean Sea like a string of pearls. Yet each pearl has a different shape and character: Tinos with its miraculous

positioned to catch every breeze, the few working thatch-roofed windmills of milos stand quiet at day's end.

# aegean

shrine and castle-topped Naxos; Milos's underwater ruins and the gaiety of Mykonos; the hallowed isle of Delos and dazzling Santorini, hanging like a pendant at the bottom of the string. There are octopus and fritters and wine from ancient grape varieties. No wonder fleets of boats steam to the island.

below:
just arrived at the docks of ios, today's fresh fish will be tonight's soup.

right:
tiny thirasia looks across the water-filled volcanic caldera at its famous sister island, thira (santorini).

It's hard to say which is thicker or more flavorful: creamy cretan yogurt or herb-tinged honey.

# crete

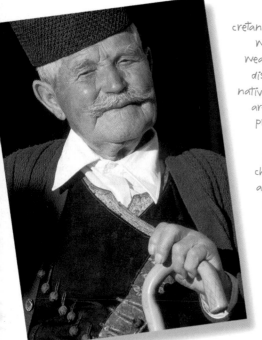

cretans, many who still wear their distinctive native dress, are justly proud of their resolute character and rich history.

People have lived on Crete for more than four thousand years, and the palimpsest of that history is there for the visitor to relish—along with an astounding variety of landscape and color and food. Crete staggers the senses, from the complex Minoan ruins at Knossos, Phaistos, and Kato Zakros to the lazy harbor of Nikolaos, the deep Samarian Gorge, the Roman carved caves, and the Medieval and Renaissance sites of Rethymno. The island is sometimes gracious, sometimes austere, always bold. Little is ethereal about Crete; it is tangible, substantial, authentic, vital, and sometimes shrewd. Logic rules, discourse reigns. The *tavernas* are the best in Greece, the spicy ouzos the biggest, the *mezedes* the most generous. This is the land of Zorba, of passionate dances and heartrending dirges.

juicy lamb shanks, tangy greens, and a glass of robust brusco red wine make up a perfect cretan meal.

behind the aged doors of narrow winding streets in iraklion and hania, family-run cafés offer the best of crete's abundant foods.

ROASTED LAMB SHANKS WITH GARLIC AND THYME, PAGE 387,
WARM GREENS, PAGE 267

L ying at the eastern edge of the Aegean Sea is the proud Dodecanese archipelago. Though each is different from the others, its twelve-plus tiny

above: rose petals, pears, and saffron come to the banquet table from the gardens, orchards, and fields of rhodes.

# preserves

islands have forever shared a common fate of threats from and invasions by others. To visit them is to see temples, castles, mansions, and hideouts. Rhodes is the largest, with a rich history, but wave-bouncing *kaikis* will take you from one island to the next, including Kalymnos, with its famous death-defying sponge divers.

why settle for a single sea-born morsel? kalymnos fisherman's catch stew offers fillets of numerous fish, a collection of shellfish, and baby octopus.

left: looking west to mainland greece, the red-tile-roofed houses of karpathos drink in the sunset.

# dodecanese

*FISHERMAN'S CATCH STEW, PAGE 180*

Although Cyprus is an independent country, its long Greek heritage on its southern half remains unfaltering. Stretches of beach miles long ascend to the high Troodos Massif. Magnificent mosaic floors from Greek and Roman villas make you feel as if you are walking on diamonds. Churches painted with breathtaking murals centuries old grace every vineyard.

dates, grapes, and almonds fresh from the tree are some of the treasures of cyprus.

# cyprus

left: cherry, apricot, and eggplant spoon sweets surround a lemon-ouzo yogurt cake.

Lemons scent the air and meals consist of a run of thirty to forty small, delectable dishes. The goddess Aphrodite claimed the island as her home, and you can still visit her beach and dip your toes in her bath.

left: who can resist a walk on the beach where sea-born aphrodite came ashore?

*YOGURT CAKE WITH OUZO-LEMON SYRUP, PAGE 520*
*SPOON SWEETS, PAGES 535 TO 547*

... THAT HUNGER
MAY HATE YOU, AND
VENERABLE DEMETER,
RICHLY CROWNED,
MAY LOVE YOU AND
FILL YOUR BARN
WITH FOOD ...

—HESIOD, CA. 700 B.C.E.

# ADVENTURES IN GREEK COOKING

the **Olive**
**and**
the **caper**

## SUSANNA HOFFMAN

IN COLLABORATION WITH VICTORIA WISE

WORKMAN PUBLISHING · NEW YORK

Library of Congress Cataloging-in-Publication Data

Hoffman, Susanna.
The olive and the caper: adventures in Greek cooking / by Susanna
Hoffman; in collaboration with Victoria Wise.
Includes index.
ISBN-13: 978-1-56305-848-6 (alk. paper)—
ISBN-13: 978-0-7611-3468-8 (hc)
ISBN-10: 1-56305-848-0 (alk. paper)—ISBN-10: 0-7611-3468-9 (hc)
1. Cookery, Greek. 2. Food habits—Greece. 3. Greece—Social life
and customs. I. Wise, Victoria. II. Title.
TX723.5.G8H64 2004
    641.5945—dc22                2004040862

Cover design by Paul Hanson
Book design by Paul Hanson and Lisa Hollander with Lori Malkin
Color photographs by Susan Goldman
Food styling by Victoria Granof
Prop styling by Sara Abalon
New illustrations by Meredith Hamilton

Workman books are available at special discounts when purchased in
bulk for premiums and sales promotions as well as for fund-raising or
educational use. Special editions can also be created to specification.
For details, contact the Special Sales Director at the address below.

Workman Publishing Company, Inc.
225 Varick Street
New York, NY 10014-4381

Printed in the U.S.A.
First printing July 2004
10 9 8 7 6 5 4 3

The sanctuary of Athena Pronaia looms among the wild herbs and caper vines of Delphi.

Time for a sweet, foamy afternoon coffee in a Cyclades island coffeehouse.

In a clay pot unchanged in shape since Homer's time, the flowers of Macedonia flourish.

A Maniot woman of the Peloponnesos offers a double handful of plump olives from her orchard.

TO VICTORIA
WITHOUT WHOM
I WOULD NEVER HAVE PLUCKED
THIS BOOK
FROM THE EMBERS,
WITH LOVE AND ENDLESS THANKS

AND TO THE ELEVEN OTHERS
OF THE OPTIMISTS CLUB
WHO HELPED ONE ANOTHER RISE AGAIN

ARLEEN, CLARA, CAROL, ELLIE
INJA, JOAN, JUDITH
KATHY, MARILYN, ROBBIE, SANDY

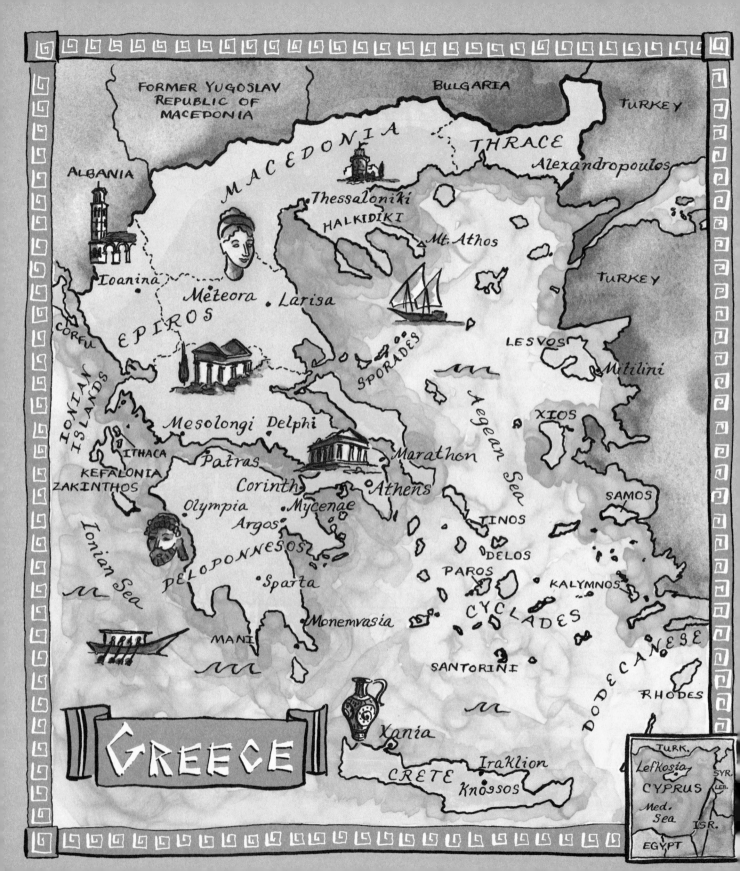

# acknowledgments

I HAVE NOT COUNTED WHETHER THIS BOOK DEMANDED EXACTLY TWELVE MOMENTOUS LABORS, BUT IT ENTAILED MANY, AND, CONSIDERING ITS TWOFOLD HISTORY, COULD SURELY BE CALLED A HERCULEAN EFFORT. (THE GREEKS WOULD SAY ERAKLEAN.) I DID NOT ACCOMPLISH IT ALONE. AT MY SIDE WERE MANY HEROES, AND MY GRATITUDE GOES TO THEM ALL.

Tryfon Tzifas kept my Greek alive, joyously discussed with me the curiosities that arose, and helped me untangle enigmatic words and translate passages. John Pardales must be Dionysos's agent with his impeccable knowledge of Greek wine. Jan Brukman, friend and fellow, while lending his ear to the anthropology, kept his eye directed to the food. Bob DeBarge helped me trim a love of history and detail that would have turned many of the chapters' tales into tomes. Martha Casselman, my wonderful agent, had the patience of Hestia while letting the book bake and rebake.

Suzanne Rafer, divine editor, metamorphosed the work into a whole with a goddess's touch and the Olympian help of Ann Ffolliott and Kathie Ness. Thanks, too, to Paul Hanson and Lisa Hollander for a beautiful cover and interior design, Leora Kahn for finding photos that perfectly capture the food and spirit of Greece, and photographer Susan Goldman, food stylist Victoria Granof, and prop stylist Sarah Abalon for making the dishes in the color section so luscious. My diadem is also off to Kate Tyler and Katie Workman, who wonderously sport the winged sandals of message-bearing Hermes, along with all the other miracle-makers in Workman's publicity, sales, and marketing departments. Above all, a special bow to the Zeus of this whole pantheon, Peter Workman.

Over the long and double history of this book, a Greek chorus of supporters include Cielo Arango de Luzarraga, Sandy Ashton, Deborah and Levi Bendele, Suzanne Bohning, Larry Bolder, Jim Botsakos, Craig Brock and David Ramirez, Dawn Bryan, Argene Klonaris Carter, Bill Chambers, Joe Cooley, Richard Cowan and Kathy Collins, Rena Down, Gale Hayman, Marida Hollos, Gordon Jacobs, Michelle Kodis, Karin and Tim Knowles, Aglaia Kremezi, Gail and Stuart Lake, Jake Linzinmeir, Robert Mandel, Susan Mitchell, Paula Moss, Alan Petraske, Lisa Rich and Robbie Greenberg, Susanna Smith, Bernie Weintraub, Marshall Whiting, Deborah Wolf, Paula Wolfert, Mary Woods, and a true legion of Greek village and city friends, especially Markella Damigos, her daughter, Maria, and her sisters, Paraskevi and (in memoriam) Koko; Tousa Damigos and her parents, Markos and Theodosia; Markos M. Damigos; Eirini Kafouros; Stelios Vougioucalos, and my many friends at the Greek Fulbright Foundation.

My deepest gratitude also goes to my many compassionate colleagues at the 1991 Symposium on The Foods and Wine of Greece who succored me when calamity struck. Though many people helped me recover, and I am grateful to you all, two steadfast Titans especially carried me through: Karen Joffee and above all, Stephen Hettenbach. The Gaia of this travail was and is, of course, Victoria Wise, who not only helped me recover, but helped recover this book.

My son, Jesse Aratow, my ever valiant champion, remains a constant source of strength. Like an Artemis with arrows of clean writ, my daughter, Gabriella Aratow, put tremendous time, effort, and talent into polishing the work. Heracles means "Hera's Glory." Gabriella is mine.

# contents

**PART ONE**

## HONORED DRINKS, SMALL DISHES, AND SAVORY PIES

## from water to wine

Of utmost importance in Greece, each drink is special, from glasses of crystal clear water and fruitade to anise-flavored ouzo and piney retsina; from cups of rich, freshly ground coffee to fragrant tea.

## meze
### THE GRAND ARRAY

A lavish gallery of little foods to go with drinks, *mezedes* appear at all times of the day as well as at the start of the meal. They can be as simple as a piece of cheese or a few olives, or more complex—tasty meatballs, Russian salad, marinated shrimp, stuffed grape leaves, *taramasalata*, and *houmus*. All tease and appease the appetite.

## savory Pies
### FROM FILO PASTRY

Flaky, fragrant, filled savory filo-crusted pies are served both as *mezedes* and as main courses throughout Greece. It is easy to re-create the big filo pies baked in square or round pans, as well as the little pies shaped like cigars or snails.

# the vegetable parade

Plates of warm fresh greens, broad beans with toasted bread crumbs, crispy fava croquettes, zucchini flower fritters, and eggplant-stuffed bell peppers—vegetables play a starring role in the Greek kitchen. . . . . . . 263

# fish and shellfish

In a country surrounded by the sea, it's no wonder that the freshest fish and shellfish frequently adorn the Greek table. Grilled with lemon juice and olive oil, baked *plaki*-style in a sauce of tomatoes and garlic, accompanied by zesty *skordalia*, they show up in many delicious guises. . . . . 323

# meat
## OF EVERY SORT

Often reserved for the most festive occasions, in Greece, meat symbolizes good living, celebration, fulfillment, and gratitude. When it comes to Beef with Olives and 100 Cloves of Garlic, spring lamb stewed in a light lemon egg broth, or hearty pork stew with plenty of savory white beans, it's easy to be grateful. . . . . . . . 361

# birds
## FROM THE COOP

Chicken baked with exotic spices or sautéed with fruit; duck marinated in ouzo or simmered in wine and broth; turkey stuffed with chestnuts and figs—all are delectable and enticing combinations that make for special meals. . . . . . . . . . 407

# Wild game
## FROM THE WOODS AND SKY

The hunt for wild game was a fixture of ancient Greek lore and game continues to play its role on the Greek table. Grilled Rabbit seasoned with savory and juniper, Grilled Quail on a Bed of Butter-Braised Cabbage, and Grilled Venison with Sour Cherry Sauce are just a few of the mouthwatering dishes offered up in this chapter. . . . . . . . . . . . . . . . 437

# sauces, toppings, and marinades

From egg and lemony *avgolemono* to white *saltsa besamel,* garlickly *skordalias,* and yogurt-based *tzatzikis,* here are sauces, plus savory toppings and marinades, that vitalize Greek dishes of yesterday and today. . . . . . . 455

# fruit as the finale

To refresh the palate at the end of a Greek dinner, only fruit will do. Cakes, pastries, and other sweets are treats for other occasions. . . . . . . . . . . . . . . . 489

## PART THREE
## CONFECTIONS DULCET AS AMBROSIA

# sweets
## IN PROFUSION

Greek sweets—served with afternoon coffee, with late-night drinks, to celebrate a special occasion, or because you just have to have one—are seductive. Filo-crusted *baklava, kadaifi,* and other cakes; fried pastry ribbons; rice, semolina, and milk puddings; pine-nut cookies; the jewel-like spoon sweets—all help make any occasion feel special. . . . . . . 499

# The olive, The caper,

# AND THE LEGACY OF GREEK FOOD

Baked by a stark and crystal sun, enhanced by mineral-laden soils and buoyant salty seas, parched into the highest concentration by summer's long drought, the foods of Greece are the richest in the Mediterranean. Every morsel explodes with flavor.

Grinning up at me,
The casserole boils and chatters to itself
And fishes leap up in the frying pans.

—EUBOULOS, *GIANTS*, 385 B.C.E.

From the majesty of their bounty, over millennia the Greeks have spun a cuisine of sublime and captivating dishes.

*Weighing out, with pride, 3 kilos of white eggplant destined for moussaka.*

Great weavers that they are—plaiting wool into tapestry, ideas into philosophy, stone into monuments—the Greeks have done the same with food. Greek fare intertwines ingredients and tastes until preparations blaze with an intermingling of flavor, hue, and texture. Greek cooks marry savory meats with juice-absorbent vegetables in long-simmered stews laced with mountain herbs. They rub birds of every sort with native bay leaf and roast them until delicate meat falls from delicate bone. They simmer lentils until they are thick as pudding, add wild greens, and serve the dish with chunks of pungent goat cheese. The next day, frugal and imaginative cooks chop in scallions and tomatoes and fry the lentils into crisp croquettes. Greeks stuff peppers with eggplant, sultana raisins, mint, basil, and nutmeg. They braise rabbit with tiny onions and black-red, thick-as-custard tomato paste. Fish joins shellfish, all just pulled from the sea, in soups reminiscent of legendary voyages. Greek cooks turn their prodigality of sun-blessed vegetables—artichokes, beans, beets, cabbage, lettuce, okra, spinach, squash—into mixtures and casseroles so fine and filling that there's no need to look farther than the fields for sustenance. They fold nuts and fruit in sheets of paper-thin dough and bathe the winsome pastries in syrups of honey, muscat, citrus, and brandy.

Their repast is simply and utterly glorious.

Throughout time, from morning's first meal to evening's soporific finale, Greeks have studded the tapestry of their marvelous cuisine with two particular native foods: the olive and the caper. The one was domesticated on Greek shores so many eons ago that the story of its earliest cultivation is lost. The other sprouts wild from almost every cliff and rock outcropping.

## THE OLIVE AND THE CAPER

Farmers of the first civilization in Greece, the Minoans, began the cultivation of the olive. By the time of classical Greece, the tree was held in such sacred esteem that no one was allowed to fell a single silvery, fruit-bearing bough. People ate olives as breakfast, to quiet the hunger that rose throughout the day, as enticement to a feast, as an ingredient in preparations, and as a late-night repast. The oil of the fruit produced such a lucrative trade that Greek empire after empire thrived. Meanwhile, the wily caper bush produced a bud that could be gathered like a precious gift. Cured in much the same way as the olive, the caper, too, offered lasting larder, one that could be stored in great clay vessels or glass jars.

The caper enlivened bread and pottage, awakened the appetite, and sated the yen for salt and savory. Today the same green-to-purple-to-ebony olives and jade-bright capers continue to embellish the montage that is Greek food. They launch festivals, feasts, and simple dinners, ornament a profusion of wild greens and fresh salads, offer nipping contrast to fundamental hunks of bread, and enhance a mélange of stews and spreads. They represent the union of hard work and nature, so very Greek in essence, and speak to the largesse of small offerings, a Greek credo.

The ancient Greeks divided their meals into two sections: the *siton,* the filling grains that made up the majority of any meal, along with the *opson,* the bits of flavorful foods—vegetables, meats, fish, sauces—that spark up the cereal mainstay; and the *poton,* the drinking course after the meal, accompanied always by liquor-tempering snacks.

Greeks today also have those two sections in their dining along with a third, though the divisions are somewhat different than in earlier times. Drinking is still a separate activity from dining, although nowadays it often precedes a meal, in the dwindling afternoon. Still, like the ancients, Greeks often enjoy drinks and conversation late in the evening, long after the meal. Early or late, they never drink without some tidbits of food, and these tidbits are some of the most delightful dishes in the cuisine. The foods that go with drinks are not appetizers per se, nor openers, nor the first course

to the meal, but a separate category of taste treats that act as beverage sops and hunger appeasers. Some of these cross over into snacks or dinner-table dishes. They are called *mezedes* or *oretakia* and in this book appear, along with the distinguished drinks of Greece, in "Honored Drinks, Small Dishes, and Savory Pies."

The second portion of Greek dining involves the true meal. Rather than featuring a series of courses or a large and filling entree, a Greek meal consists of a number of small offerings presented all at once—the way many Americans now also like to eat. The various plates on a Greek table—and there can be many—cover almost every nutritional element in a proper diet while at the same time providing a rainbow of flavors. A bowl of soup, a platter of chicken, some stewed zucchini with garlic paste, a sparkling village salad of tomatoes, olives, cheese, and capers, perhaps a plate of herbed pilaf, all bedeck the table. Should the cook feel that the foods are not sufficient or appropriately well rounded, she will add a plate of fried eggs, potatoes, or fish to the collection. Family and guests partake of all selections. "The Banquet of Dishes" celebrates the many sorts of preparations that make up the meal.

Then comes the third aspect of Greek fare: the sweets. These, once more, are an entirely separate event—not ending a meal, as we would have a dessert. A main meal always ends with fresh fruit. The sweet treats of Greece are eaten as a delightful pickup and sweet-tooth satisfier whenever the fancy hits, often in the late afternoon or late evening. Some are special holiday and ceremonial dishes

*Stringing orange peel to turn into a syrupy spoon sweet.*

designed to honor occasions and guests. All these treats are featured in "Confections: Dulcet as Ambrosia."

Greek food has long had the reputation of being heavy. In reality it is lighter, more modern, and more to current taste than the fare of almost any other culture—and it is remarkably healthful. Greeks have the lowest rates of heart disease and cancer in Europe. Their food is based on the freshest of pickings. At the heart of it lie vegetables, salads, and fruits. There are fish dishes galore. Meat is eaten only occasionally; many Greeks so prefer the vegetable dishes that highlight their daily meals that they eschew meat almost completely. The cooking medium and sauce base is almost exclusively the venerated olive oil, so long a part of Greek cuisine. With the exception of yogurt, milk is rarely used, and cheeses are from sheep and goats.

## REGIONAL VARIATIONS

The many dishes differ somewhat from area to area. In regions with wood for fuel, people do more grilling and traditional wood-oven baking. Those with no wood used to rely on alcohol- and gas-fueled stovetop heating as their main cooking method, although more and more now have electric ovens. Barren areas support more herding, so they offer more meat and cheese dishes. Garden spots produce more vegetable concoctions.

Greeks have also long used a wide range of spices and flavorings, some familiar to us, some seemingly exotic. They span a range from garlic to geranium leaves, cinnamon to gum mastic, savory to chamomile, fish roe, and retsina. Modern Greeks use many of the same flavorings that the ancient Greeks employed, as well as some that are different.

## A DOUBLE LIFE

As both chef and anthropologist, I have lived and worked in Greece for thirty years. I have simmered soup over a single butane burner in a village kitchen, gathered snails after a rainstorm, baked black barley rings, bitten the coin in the Saint Basil's Day cake, and bargained for fish in the *agora*. In the village where I live when I am in Greece, the women welcome me to the day with bottles of fresh goat's milk at the crack of dawn. Wood for fuel is rare and precious, so all the women bake together. Each of us brings an armful of grape twigs to fire the communal oven. We make Easter cakes and fig sandwiches,

*My friend Kyria Markezina with a tray of* koulouria *ready for the oven.*

and if it is autumn and the chickens have finally stopped laying, we roast a hen.

I have also gathered many stories, so while there are recipes galore in this book, surrounding them are tales that reflect my other vocation. I talk about the origins of Greek food, the people who settled the land, the eating customs, and the Greek words that have crept—often in amusing ways—into our language. I divulge food lore from ancient to Byzantine to modern times, and recount the sagas of my life in Greece. Many of the foods in Greek cuisine have been gathered and prepared for millennia. The olives that drop from shimmery branches onto waiting blankets do so from aged trees.

Women in babushkas still drive small flocks of sheep and goats along rocky trails where gnarly old caper brambles send forth their blossoms. Tweed-capped men, proud as Hector, harvest garlic and almonds. Village boys spear fish and pick peaches and melons. Other foods, like rice, tomatoes, potatoes, and even spinach, entered Greek cooking pots later—some quite recently—as arrivals from far-off continents. As the new foods took to the sun-soaked land, the Greeks melded them so thoroughly and compellingly to their old repertoire that they are now as fundamental to the daily cooking as foods from Plutarch's time.

This book has a two-part saga of its own. The first version burned to ashes when my home, office and all my work and possessions were destroyed in the Oakland-Berkeley Firestorm of October 20, 1991. Ironically, I was at a Greek food conference in Halkidiki at the time and able to save not a page nor a frying pan.

Thankfully none of my loved ones was hurt. I was ready to abandon what seemed an overwhelming task of retrieval when my best friend, Victoria Wise, with whom I had co-authored three cookbooks and owned a restaurant, gently urged me not to let the endeavor fade away. As well as helping me rally

## IT'S ALL GREEK

Transforming Greek words to English presents a difficult spelling dilemma. I prefer a more modern orthography that reflects how Greek really sounds, rather than the old system that overwhelmed the words with extra consonants and vowels. But this choice can create confusion when applied to the familiar ancient names for people and places (Hristoforos for Christopher, Kriti for Crete). As a result you will find references to familiar history and sagas written in the old spelling, but some spellings reflect more recent ideas of transliteration—for example, Epiros for Epirus.

in every other way, she offered to reconstitute much of the cooking when the thought of any flame, even one beneath a stewpot, was dismaying to me, leaving me to concentrate largely on reclaiming the narrative. To her I owe an immeasurable debt of gratitude and unending thanks.

As I reacquired the books of my calling, the pots of my kitchen, and the fabric of my life, I was also part of a wonderful band of women, all of whom had also lost everything. We gave one another incomparable aid and abiding support during our recovery. To them I also owe much appreciation and with

them I share much jubilation.

The untoward event also allowed me to transform the book, which began as a volume of traditional dishes, into one that more represents the way I really cook Greek food—with the same remarkable ingredients and style, but with the food elements often reimagined and differently combined than is strictly customary in Greece. The reader familiar with Greek cooking will find that while I include many classic preparations (some works simply cannot be improved upon!), most of the recipes present new variations based on a Greek foundation.

As much as the foods of Greece are foods of the past, they are foods of the future. The tradition, the style, the ingredients, and the way Greeks have dined since time immemorial are once again rising to the forefront, especially as the world turns back to more grains, more vegetables, more fish, to smaller portions, and to a wider variety of edibles. As the well-worn saying goes, we can learn much from history, and in the Greek case, especially from a people who honor their history in their continuing customs.

The ancient Greeks believed that the cook was no different from the poet, and the Greeks today believe much the same. So indulge your lyricism and enjoy.

# honored drinks, small dishes, and savory pies

TWO FRIENDS ARRANGE TO MEET IN THE LATE AFTERNOON. THEY HAVEN'T SEEN ONE ANOTHER FOR A WHILE . . . OR PERHAPS THEY SAW EACH OTHER ONLY YESTERDAY. THEY SIT DOWN AT AN OUTDOOR CAFE AND ORDER DRINKS. THEY ARE GREEK. FOR THE TALK TO FLOW AS THEY DESIRE, THEY REQUIRE THE PRESENCE OF SOMETHING LIQUID. THE LIQUID ARRIVES, BUT NOT ALONE—THIS IS GREECE. THE DRINK IS ACCOMPANIED BY A SMALL MORSEL OF FOOD DESIGNED BOTH TO ROUSE AND TO SATIATE THE APPETITE.

olives. On a name day a party takes place. There is much to drink—brandy, sweet liqueur, and wine—and with it much to eat—tiny meatballs, fish roe salad, singed peppers, assorted pickles.

Beverages and their serving are essentials in the Greek way of socializing. To receive a brother into your *saloni* (living room), is to offer him water; to invite a wandering traveler from a far-away country into your *kypos* (garden) is to sit her down to coffee; to throw a party is to ply the guests with flowing ouzo; to host

Four friends meet at a tavern in the late hours of the night, long after they have eaten their evening meal. They joke and discuss the weather, crops, theater, and always politics. Such discourse—and discourse it is—never takes place without a potable to "loosen" it. Yet to drink and not eat is also unthinkable. Along with the drinks come a number of plates laden with zesty appetizers.

Three sisters visit in the morning. They make coffee, and

*An exchange of ideas over a cool drink on a warm afternoon.*

the hosting sister puts out a plate of tidbits. As the day dwindles a guest arrives, and immediately the greeter brings out a glass of water, a cup of coffee, a fruitade, a brandy. To go with the drink comes a spoon sweet, a slice of cheese, some

a dinner is to decant a *stamna* (pitcher) of wine from the barrel; to invite a comrade to play *tabli* (backgammon) is to order a round of *tsikoudia* (grappa). But equally essential are the accompanying

nibbles. The brother receives a soupcon of the rabbit *stifado* from the stew pot bubbling with the evening's dinner, a greens-filled *dolma* is urged upon the traveler, a tray of filo *bourekakia* immediately greet the party guests, the dinner honoree is offered herbed olives with the first sip of wine, the *tabli* players receive a handful of dried almonds around their narrow glasses of crystal spirit. In consequence, a wide range of pleasurable drinks and huge array of foods are enjoyed outside and around the actual meal in Greek cuisine.

These are the *poton*, the drinks, and the *meze* or *oretakia*, the appetizers. The tradition goes back to the dawn of Greek culture, when the drink was usually wine. The ancients believed, as Greeks today still believe, that a person should be refreshed with a beverage, and yet a person should never drink without eating. To do so was uncivilized and not duly communal.

The great reward of this ancient custom today is that while Greek drinks are many, the accompanying edibles are myriad. The drinks range from wines to ouzo and other alcoholic beverages, to coffee, tea, wild herbal tisanes, and fruit concentrates. The treats served alongside may be simple bread, cheese, and olives, savory spreadlike salads, piquant stuffed leaves, small tidbits of juicy meat, salty fish, pickles, or a whole world of flaky pastries. On top of this, we moderns enjoy a munificence in this long-standing tradition that the ancients didn't. Greeks of old lounged on separate couches to drink and dine, and beverages and treats were brought out to them on trays by circulating servants. They complained about the custom: the drink was over there while they were over here; the snack passed them on the left, making it unreachable with their right hand (and they ate with only the right hand). They missed a lot, said one noble ancient, who claimed he needed five mouths and five right hands. Greeks today, like us, sit together around a table, so as all get their drinks, each gets the *meze* at the same time, or should a dozen different *mezedes* come, they are placed in front of the entire *parea* (company)—and Greeks love company—for all to indulge in together.

According to the Greeks, if you aren't thirsty and don't feel hungry, when presented with beverage and *meze* you will instantly kindle a want for a refreshing sip and a rumble for a satiating snack. The drinks are heavenly. The *meze*—meant to inspire hunger and also to assuage it—constitute some of the best of Greek dishes.

# from water to wine

MAGNANIMOUS WINE, BURNT ROSE, CARMINE RED, AND, WHITE GOLD IN COLOR, TASTING OF HONEY-SWEET GRAPES FROM AGE-OLD VINES; GALLANT LIQUEURS AND SPIRITS, COLORLESS TO PEARL TO AMBER; COFFEE AS BRONZE AS ANCIENT WEAPONS; TISANES OF HERBS, CHAMOMILE YELLOW, SAGE GREEN; OPALESCENT FRUIT WATERS SHIMMERING AND THIRST-QUENCHING; AND THE MOST FAVORED OF ALL—WATER, CRYSTALLINE CLEAR.

One may hide all else . . . but not these two things—that he is drinking wine and that he has fallen in love. Both betray him through his eyes and through his words, so that the more he denies, the more they make it plain.

—ATHENAEUS,
SECOND CENTURY B.C.E.

These are the beverages of Greece. On the arid hills of the country and by the frothy coasts, drinks to douse thirst, rouse joy, reenergize, cure, and fuel the ever-flowing conversation are omnipresent. Greeks believe in beverages. They believe they give health, satisfy the soul, and vitalize the body. Drinks are served to you instantly in cafés, brought to you on thresholds of homes, offered to you as you stroll dusty paths, urged on you as you rest or recline.

Some—water and wine—have been Greek signature and symbol since the people first arrived. Some reveal the path of history: the coming of new fruits, the discovery of spirits, the creation of aperitifs, the arrival of aromatic beans. Along with water and wine, the ancients drank honey water, barley water, and honeyed vinegar. They quaffed fermented grain; sipped the juice of fruits, celery, garlic, clover, fennel, leek, mint, and parsley. Later Greeks added brandy, ouzo, and coffee. In Greece today, water remains as esteemed, wine as idolized, the liquors of grain and greens as savored, the taste of beer as pleasing, the juices of fruits as dreamy. In short, the potations —from the Greek for "drink," *poton*—remain much the same as from time immemorial.

# THE SPICES OF GREECE

In ancient to modern times, ouzo, brandy, *tsikoudia*, fruit drinks, and even wine have been spiced with many of the same spices used in food. The list of ones used then, as now, is long.

**ALLSPICE**—*bahari*

**ANISE SEEDS**—*glykaniso*

**CARAWAY**—*karo*, used more in ancient days

**CARDAMOM**—*kardamomon, koriandroto,* or *koliantros,* also used more in earlier times

**CHOCOLATE**—*sokolata*, used more by candy and pastry cooks, but increasingly in the home

**CINNAMON**—*kanella.* In Greece it is almost always true cinnamon, but they also have cassia *(akakia).*

**CITRON**—*kitron*

**CLOVE**—*garyfallo*

**CORIANDER**—*koliandro* or *koriandro*

**CUMIN**—*kimino*

**GINGER**—*ziggibero,* used in ancient times more than now, probably dried

**JUNIPER BERRY**—*iouniperos* or *agriakuparissi* "wild cypress"

**LIME BLOSSOM**—*tilis*

**MAHLEPI**—*maxlepi*, the seed of a small flowering cherry tree

**MASTIC**—*mastixa,* from the resin of the lentisk bush, grown on the island of Xios

**MUSTARD SEED**—*sinapi* or *sinaposporos*

**NUTMEG** and **MACE**—*moskokarido*

**PEPPER**—*piperi,* white and black; also dried powdered or flaked mild to hot chile pepper, called *boukovo,* used constantly in Thessaloniki, Macedonia, and other northern places

**ORANGE-BLOSSOM WATER**—*anthonero*

**ORANGE JUICE** and **PEEL** (and occasionally tangerine)—*portokali*

**LEMON JUICE** and **PEEL**—*lemoni*

**ROSE WATER**—*rothonero*

**SAFFRON**—*zafora* or *krokos*

**SESAME**—*sesami*

**VANILLA**—*banilia,* which in Greece comes as crystals or as a white gum

# Water

N o word can describe what water is to the Greeks more than *osios*, "blessed." It is the word from which we derive "pious." To Greeks water is life. Water is so important, as both drink and symbol, that no guest is ever greeted in a Greek home without being presented a glassful. No meal is ever served without water. No pause in the day is complete without a glass of water.

In ancient times many villages had a central well or spring, where communal cups hung on the rim so all could partake of the liquid. Today still, Greeks flock around gushing streams and crystal springs. Cups still hang from the taps at fountains. As in ancient times, when children brought ewers of clear water to pour over guests' hands before eating, Greek hosts admonish their guests to do so now. And today as then, Greeks compare the water of different towns and fountains, describing in detail

*Alone, with food, or with another drink, water is the most sacred of beverages.*

the taste and clarity as they would wine.

## A DRINK AND A SACRAMENT

I n the ancient days water was thought so blessed that gods were born from it. Today it is still used during the church service and at baptism. In fact, every Greek Orthodox church has two types of water: the *agiasmos*, or "blessing," water, flicked upon the celebrants with

sprigs of basil during the liturgy, and the *agiasma*, or "blessed," water, the running water at a spring or faucet in the church, monastery, or convent courtyard, which people drink to absorb its benediction.

When offered a glass of water in Greece, it behooves the drinker to treat it with the reverence the pure, clear liquid of life has always provided.

# wine

*Checking the first sample from a barrel of aging sweet wine.*

Greeks began to make wine long before their written history, but they were not the first. Archaeologists have found a clay jar containing wine residue from about 5400 B.C.E., soon after the first farming and settled life, in the Zagros Mountains of ancient Persia. Along with the wine traces, the jar contains evidence of resin. This means the ancient winemakers put the wine in pine casks or, more probably, put the resin in the wine as a preservative, and that the wine most likely tasted much like Greece's present-day retsina. Wax, pitch, or resin was also used to seal wine amphorae. Wine was also kept in hollowed trees, the open end covered with skins.

Wine arrived in Greece soon after. Wild grapes thrived in stretches from Spain and France across all of Italy and Greece to beyond the Caspian Sea. People in Greece were eating wild grapes as early as 11000 B.C.E. The communication between the Greeks and the Persians, while hostile at times, was continuous. The first winemakers lived near well-traveled trade routes connecting the two groups, so the cultivation of the grape and the making of the drink no doubt readily traveled to Greece.

Wine was an essential part of Minoan civilization. Pre-Greek and Minoan vases, drawings, and writings depict the importance of grapes and wine. Houses and palaces had storerooms filled with wine jars. By Mycenaean times wine was clearly an even more integral element of Greek culture. Winemaking installations were abundant; cups and jugs existed by the thousands. Indeed wine, winemaking, and wine drinking became the signature of Greek life. As Greeks emerged into the classical age they brought grapes and made wine wherever they went—to Cyprus, to Dalmatia, to the Crimea, to France, to Sicily, to Tarentum (modern Taranto) and Neapolis (modern Naples), and to rich Sybaris in the arch of Italy's boot. Sicily and the toe of Italy were, in fact, called Oenotria, "The Land of Staked Vines."

Greeks made many sorts of wines—white and red, dry and sweet—and were discerning drinkers of it. Early on they began to name wines for the region of their origin—Samian, Thracian, Hian—a custom adopted in other lands and reaffirmed in 1969 by national legislation. Dying Aristotle asked for Rhodian wine, then wine from Lesbos to anoint his successor. Regions of origin were stamped on the handles of amphorae and *pithoi*. Greeks recognized the value of aging wine and stamped the dates on the jars. They also made wine from apples, dates, figs, pears, pomegranates, raspberries, blackberries, wild grapes, and wild strawberries.

## GRAPES ANCIENT AND MODERN

At first Greeks grew only a few types of wine grapes, but they quickly developed many more. Some were prized for their color, their rosiness, rich red, or "blackness," others for their tiny berries, their "coolness" or "heat." Many ancient varieties—*agiorgitiko, asertiko, athiri, moshofilero, roditis, hynomavro*—are still grown in Greece, along with more contemporary sorts. All in all, today more than three hundred varietals of wine grapes are grown. In ancient times—and to some extent in villages today—Greeks preferred sweet wine, which then, as it is today, was generally made from very ripe or partially dried grapes. Some seems to have been much like today's sherry; others like vin santo. Honey was mixed with dry wine, though the practice was expensive. Other wines, both sweet and dry, were flavored with flowers, herbs, and spices.

Wine today is part of the main meal, but in ancient times wine was reserved for the second part of the dinner, called the *symposion*, the time when conversation, games, and entertainment took over. There, after a first sip of undiluted wine taken as libation to the gods, the wine was always diluted with water. Drinking undiluted wine was considered dangerous, with possible dire consequences.

The water/wine formula was a matter of much discussion. Usually wine was diluted one half to one fourth with water. It was also considered preferable to mix the water into the wine rather than the wine into the water. They were mixed together in a bowl called a *kratir*, and the word for mixing was *krasis*—from which derives the modern Greek word for wine, *krasi*.

By Byzantine times Greeks were beginning to drink undiluted wine, sometimes alternating wine with glasses of water. They began to dislike the taste left by the resin seals long used on the amphorae. As befit the Byzantine predilection for complex food, wine flavored with a variety of herbs and spices—aniseed, mastic, spikenard, violet, pepper, and clove—gained greatly in popularity. Byzantines preferred sweet wine made from Greece's many varieties of *muskatos*, or Muscat, and especially from the *monemvasios* grape. The Byzantines were also the first Greeks to "cook"

The wine spurted up in the
grape-filled hollow,
the rivulets becoming purple:
pressed by the
alternating tread,
the fruit bubbled out red
juice with white foam.
They scooped
it up with oxhorns.

—NONNOS, *DIONYSAICA*, FIFTH CENTURY C.E.

*A hand-painted sign announces Nikodemos's Mediterranean wine shop.*

time passed, the heavy taxes they imposed suppressed the wine industry, and soon many Greek farmers stopped cultivating their vines. When Greece then battled to reclaim independence, the country faced many problems more dire than the return of wine production. The world lost track of Greek wines, with the exception of the resinated wines that lingered from the old methods of preservation.

wine and to fortify wine with sugars—such as is done with port—which made the wine more transportable for trade.

As the Byzantine era faded, however, Greek wine production entered a long decline. With the spread of feudalism, farmers increasingly had to work for landlords, turn over their produce to pay the taxes, or sell their acreage. Many of the landlords were monasteries, and they, acquiring many of Greece's finest vineyards, took over much of the winemaking. As Ottoman control later spread, at first the new overlords protected Greek winemaking. Wine crops were lucrative and local officials could monopolize the sales. But as

Slowly but surely, though, in the past fifty years Greek wine has witnessed a return to its former glory. Grapes again flourish all over Greece, and magnificent wines are made. To this day wine remains an elemental part of Greek life, an essential aspect of Greek Orthodox ritual, and a joyous part of the Greek meal. Most wines of Greece are still pressed from ancient and indigenous varieties, each prized for its individuality. Many forgotten grapes and wines have been recovered and revived. Today, as before, the wines taste of rocks and bushes, of mountain and coast, of forest and plain, of pumice and loam, of wild

herbs and berries. Many of them—white and red, dry and sweet—are stupendous.

## THE WINE REGIONS OF GREECE

Greek wines, produced in several quite diverse parts of the country, have been classified by appellation, as French wines are, since 1971. By law they are divided into three categories: *specific-appellation wines,* which come from particular geographic areas and are made in particular ways as defined by the European Union, allowing them to be labeled "Quality Wine"; *local wines,* which may be made in any of a number of designated areas; and *table wines,* which are not restricted geographically and are generally sold under a producer's or winery's brand name. Retsina is given a "traditional appellation" designation that refers to a production technique, not a geographical zone.

The wine labels also bear three aging distinctions: A wine designated "cava" is aged two years for white and three for red, the first six months for both in the barrel. When labeled "reserve," the wine has aged two years in cask and bottle for white and three for red. And "grand reserve" signifies an appellation wine aged one year in cask and two in bottle for white, two years in cask and two in bottle for red. As well, vintage wines must be at least 85 percent from the year indicated. For resinated wine, no more than 1,000 grams per hectoliter of resin from the *Pinus helepensis* pine may be added, and the alcohol content must be between 10 and 13.5 percent.

Because the grape varietals of each region are quite specific, knowing the region of the wine also indicates the sort of grape from which the wine is made.

The northernmost wine-producing area of the country is Macedonia, with three appellations: Naoussa, Goumenissa, and Amynataion. Each area produces dry reds, and Amynataion also produces a dry rosé and a sparkling rosé. The wines of Naoussa tend to be light to medium in body, with good tannin and acid and a nose of black olive, ripe fruit, and blackberry. The wines of Goumenissa are similar but softer; they are often a blend of grape varieties. Amynataion, a cool region, produces wines that are lighter than those of Naoussa. The Côtes de Meliton in Macedonia also turns out fine dry red and white wines.

Epiros, in the northwest corner of mainland Greece, also produces wine, though the quantity is small. Only Zitsa is a recognized appellation. In this region, the fruit does not ripen as fully as elsewhere. The wines are light, but with good acid and balance. Zitsa wines—dry, dry sparkling, and semi-dry sparkling—have a nose of citrus and lemon zest.

Within Thessaly lie two appellations: Rapsani and Ankialos. Rapsani's dry red wines come from older vineyards and as a result are concentrated, with good color. Their nose hints of chocolate and tobacco. The wines are earthy, rustic, big, and chunky. The dry white and rosy-tinted wines of Ankialos must be from unstaked vines.

## RETSINA AND MORE

Attica has the largest wine production of Greece, with the area dominated by one type of wine, retsina, both dry white and red-tinged. The region has only one appellation that makes non-resinated wine, Kantza. The retsinas have good acid and are piney and woody.

The Peloponnesos, in the warmer half of Greece, contains three appellations: Nemea,

## THREE BOWLS FULL

At the *symposion*, the wine part of the banquet, three *kratirs*, or mixing bowls, were thought the proper, moderate amount of wine to imbibe. The host was in charge of the pace of drinking, and since rituals accompanied the first three bowls, he could even force guests to finish the number of bowls served. At some gatherings a wine watcher was in charge to see that all received an equal amount of wine.

In a play by a writer named Euboulos, the god Dionysos describes the bowls: The first bowl, he says, is for health, the second for love and pleasure, the third for sleep. At this point wise drinkers go home. Should guests drink onward, the fourth bowl belongs to hubris, which in Greek means "boastful talk among males." The fifth leads to shouting, the sixth to revelry, the seventh to black eyes, the eighth to court summonses, the ninth to bile, and the tenth to madness and people throwing the furniture about.

Sounds about right.

All the while, though, Greeks applied certain preventives to avert drunkenness. Guests at *symposia* wore wreaths of parsley and marjoram on their heads, for the two herbs were believed to thwart inebriation. Greeks also believed that a certain purple gemstone would prevent drunkenness, and so wore jewelry containing the stone to meals. That belief remains in the word we use for the gem today: amethyst, or *a* ("not") *methys* ("drunk").

Mantinia, and Patras. Nemea has three districts: The lowest elevation produces a light-bodied rosé tasting of cherry and strawberry. The wines from the middle section have soft tannin, but can lack acidity. The nose is of strawberry and cherry with tobacco overtones. The high region produces super-premium fruit. The wines are more concentrated, with more tannin and acid, which brings their fruit up to the surface. Nemean reds are both dry and sweet. Mantinia is very high and grows a very versatile muscat-type grape called *moshofilero*. The region produces a sparkling wine and a rosé and is especially known for its dry white, whose bouquet is of apple, rose and other flowers, melon, lemon zest, and pear. Fermented in stainless steel, the wines are nicely acid and give off lazy bubbles. Patras's wines, both red and white, are light in body with a great deal of fruit. The Peloponnesos also produces three noteworthy dessert wines: Mavrodaphne of Patras, Muscat of Patras, and Muscat of Rion.

## ISLAND WINES

In the Ionian islands there is only one appellation, Kefalonia. It is famous for its *robola,* a white grape variety. The wines have good acid and fruit and bear a nose of lemon peel, orange peel, and citrus. The strong dry white wines were once called "Wines of Stone." Kefalonia also makes two sweet wines, Mavrodaphne and Muscat.

A number of Aegean islands are noted winegrowing regions. In the eastern Sporades, Limnos wines are all produced by a co-op, and the island is famous for its sweet wine, a light style of Muscat, though a dry white is also made. The wines have a luscious nose of apricot, peach, and marmalade.

In the Dodecanesos, Rhodes was recognized in ancient times for both dry red and white wines, as well as a sweet white wine, and these are undergoing reestablish-ment. Samos was famous in ancient times for its wine, and exceptional wines continue to be produced there today. Samos's wines are from late-harvest fruit, very ripe. They are very concentrated, with good acid and residual sugars. Their nose is of ripe fruit, of apricot and pear.

In the Cyclades, Paros grows two varietals. The white Monemvasia is light-bodied, lacks acid, and is light of alcohol. The bouquet is floral, or of pears, green apples, and plum, making a great aperitif wine. The varietal red produces a wine so dark that it is almost black, so the law of the island dictates that the reds be a blend of 50 percent red and 50 percent white, fermented together. The result is a light-bodied, light-colored wine, similar to pinot noir in color and on the palate. It is big, ripe red, stony, and delicate. To the south, Santorini's fertile pumice soils produce renowned dry and sweet whites. The main grape is the ancient *asertiko*. The island's wines have never experienced the phylloxera blight and so are very old. They have naturally high acidity and are pressed from fruit that ripens early. Santorini's wines have a glorious nose of melon, honey, and honeysuckle.

Crete contains four appellations: Arhanes, which makes a dry red; Dafnes, producing dry and sweet reds; Peza, producing both red and white dry wine; and Sitia, which makes a dry and a sweet red. The wines of Crete are light-bodied and taste of very ripe fruit.

In addition there are at least seventy-five areas throughout the country producing local table wines. Few of these are exported, but they are a delight to sample when traveling about the country. Just ask the restaurant or tavern owner for the local wine.

# OUZO

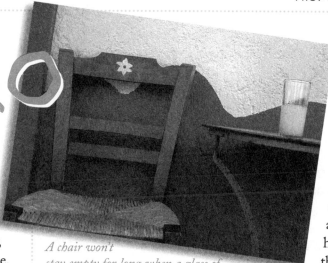

*A chair won't stay empty for long when a glass of ouzo awaits.*

**A**ll across Greece, people sip an anise-flavored aperitif called *ouzo*. A latecomer on the beverage scene, ouzo was developed late in the nineteenth century, but it has deep roots in Greece. Hippocrates drank a similarly flavored beverage called *anisum* on special occasions.

What exactly is this mysterious yet compelling beverage?

Ouzo is distilled from grapes, figs, or raisins, and various sugars. It is then flavored, according to each maker's secret recipe, with an assembly of spices and herbs. Among the predominant flavorings are such Greek favorites as anise, coriander, mastic, and lime. Even more than coffee, ouzo is the beverage of community and conversation. It mediates the lazy afternoon chat, eases the late evening repose when friends gather, refreshes the summer afternoon, and warms the winter get-together. It is served most commonly in outdoor cafés and in special *ouzeria,* where appetizers accompany each glass. The nibble might be a gift that goes with the glassful, or one that can be ordered from the *meze* menu.

The cafés and bars sometimes reflect social classes; there are the workers' *ouzeria,* the after-business *ouzeria,* and the elegant *ouzeria* of the wealthy connoisseurs. Ouzo bottles range from water-clear to mysterious black; the spicings range from strong yet subtle to sweet yet complex. The mix of flavoring is always hard to discern. Some ouzos bite, some glide; some are saccharine, most aromatic. And somehow, no matter what the collage of tastes, the drink is both fortifying and refreshing.

As well as being taken as a wonderful drink, ouzo can flavor many dishes. It gives an exotic touch to a sauce for fish and snails, makes pungent a bath of steaming mussels, renders heady the syrup over honey cake,

## ANISE SEEDS

**I**n every culture, certain settings and holidays bear the fragrance of particular spices. In the United States, relaxed evenings are often marked by the aroma of coffee and liqueur, or the loamy scent of bourbon or scotch, or the perfume of cognac. Thanksgiving smells of the mélange of spices that go into pumpkin pie. Ginger and nutmeg, the duo in so many of its sweets, accompany Christmas.

In Greece, mastic goes with Easter, and evenings in the Aegean breezes are redolent of anise.

Anise, *glykaniso*, is indigenous to the Greek islands. Slow growing but tenacious, it bears white flower clusters and feathery leaves. You can stroll about the countryside and pick it, and it has long been used both as a flavoring and as a medicine. A tea of anise is thought to soothe childbirth pains, and it is the spice that gilds Greek Christmas cakes and cookies to celebrate the birth of Christ.

I always bring back some wild dried anise seeds from my trips to Greece to use in stuffings, rich sauces, and sweets. And since a little goes a long way, it lasts for many a Greek-inspired repast or festive occasion.

## MASTIC LIQUEUR

Greeks have another aperitif that changes from clear to milky. *Mastiha* is made from the same sort of grape or other fruit base as ouzo, but it is strongly flavored with Greece's famous mastic from Hios.

*Mastiha* is not only a noteworthy beverage for guests, but it can be used to flavor sweet sauces and spoon sweets. And, aromatic far beyond vanilla, it makes a great splash—with the required dollop of whipped cream—in after-dinner coffee.

custard, or ice cream, and turns the sugared medium of spoon sweet from mere jam to something quite adult.

In Greece there are many brands of ouzo. For a long time only a few brands were available in the United States, but now in good Greek markets and restaurants the selection is wide and delightful.

To serve it, pour an ounce of clear ouzo into a tall narrow glass. Accompany it with a tall glass of water. Nowadays, the drink is often also accompanied by a small bowl of ice.

Unadulterated, ouzo remains as crystal clear as water. Add water or ice, and it becomes as frosty white as milk.

# Tsikoudia

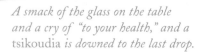

The early Greeks were not only the first Europeans to turn the juice of grapes into wine, they were also the first to embark on the art of distilling. First a liquid is heated to boiling, and vaporizes. When cooled, the vapor recondenses into drops of liquid. The liquid reclaimed this way—distilled—comes out very concentrated, and if it is an alcoholic liquid, turns into a very powerful spirit. The ancient Greeks definitely applied the process to pine resin to make turpentine, and Aristotle claimed that distilled seawater turned into sweet water. Whether the ancients made a distilled beverage is unknown, but they certainly had them by the end of the sixteenth century, probably using knowledge acquired from the Arabs by way of the Ottomans.

*Tsikoudia* (also called *tsipouro* in many areas of Greece and on Cyprus) is Greece's primary distilled beverage. It is usually made

*A smack of the glass on the table and a cry of "to your health," and a* tsikoudia *is downed to the last drop.*

from grapes, both red and white, but it can also be made from figs and berries. But rather than being made from the juice, it is a "pomace brandy," made from the pulp, skins, and seeds left over after the juice is pressed out to make wine.

*Tsikoudia* is what the Italians call *grappa* and what many Balkan and Near Eastern people—and Macedonian Greeks—call *raki*. It is a sort of water-clear brandy, not aged or put in wood where it would develop color and refinement, but rather left young, raw, and fiery. *Tsikoudias* range from intensely grapey or fruity to coarse, almost varnishlike in taste, with a host of nuances in between. Their aromas tell instantly of their strong alcohol content—not much top note— but they can have an intriguing medley of flavors from the earth, the herb, the grape.

I am very fond of the *tsikoudias* of Greece. Drinking them—little sips is the best process—brings on a brassy camaraderie rather than an all-too-civil ouzo suaveness. *Tsikoudia* is a country drink, a worker's and tiller's drink, and the drink that often sets Greek men to dancing.

*Dionysos, accompanied by a maiden, a flute player, and a satyr, carries a vessel of his beloved wine.*

# DIONYSOS, GOD OF THE GRAPE

While other Greek gods were famous, one perhaps was infamous: Dionysos, the god of grapes and wine.

Dionysos was the youngest of the Greek gods. According to one legend, his mother was Semele, a daughter of Cadmus of Thebes and Harmonia, a princess not of Greek origin. Zeus appeared to Semele in Thebes, wanting to be her lover. He came as a mortal man, but he told her he was Zeus. She fell in love with him and conceived a child, but Hera found out. Jealous Hera disguised herself as Semele's nanny and put it into Semele's mind that her lover's claim might be braggadocio. To find out for sure, she suggested that Semele ask her lover to appear in his true state. When Semele demanded that Zeus appear in his full splendor, his lightning bolts burned her to a cinder. Zeus called on Hermes to rescue her unborn child, which he sewed into his thigh. Three months later Dionysos was born.

In other legends Dionysos arrives from somewhere else. One famous painting shows him coming on a boat, the mast of which has sprouted clusters of grapes. Perhaps he came with grapes themselves from Asia Minor, perhaps from the great winegrowing island, Crete, where his mother was said to be Persephone, the daughter of grain goddess Demeter.

At first Dionysos was not an important god—Homer hardly makes note of him—and he was persecuted early on by those who refused to accept his divinity. But in later times a cult devoted to Dionysos swept so strongly across Greece that he rose to importance far above other Olympians. After all, how could a god of something as important as the grape, and the glorious beverage extracted from it, not rise to prominence?

Dionysos's followers were generally women, not men, who abandoned themselves to frenzied dances on the hillsides. They wore fawn skins and carried torches wrapped in grapevines. Their behavior left the bounds of propriety and slipped into the ecstatic. Dionysos punished those who did not follow him by taking their women into his cult or by driving the naysayers mad. Plays were written about the god, and two huge festivals celebrated him. At one, people dressed in erotic costumes and portraying satyrs packed into the theater of Athens to see a sacrifice of bulls, then, while drinking from wineskins, to watch dancers and tambourine players. A second festival took place in February, when the newly fermenting jars of wine were opened for a first taste. Near an ancient shrine, water was mixed with the new wine and an actor dressed as Dionysos was carried from the seashore on a wheeled boat. Drinking competitions took place to determine who could drink the longest or the most. His cult was so widespread that it flourished well into the age of Christianity.

So important was Dionysos and his wine that no other Greek god has been portrayed so often. We see old Dionysos everywhere—on museum walls and restaurant walls, on wine bottles and wine magazines, and even in Disney cartoons.

# THE NAME DAY

**I**T WAS ST. NIKOLAOS DAY, AND THEREFORE, ALL OVER GREECE, THE NAME DAY OF EVERYONE NAMED NIKOLAOS.

I prepared myself. It was a day of many brandies—sweet drinks for me, unless, as a foreigner, I could place myself somewhat among the men—and therefore a day to be faced with a full stomach and plenty of water. Every Nikolaos I knew must be visited, and there are many.

The day passed as always, with breakfast, work, midday dinner, and more work. After the evening's small repast, as darkness crept in, I began my travels. I went to the farthest Nikos first. That would be Niko tou Louka, the son of Loukas, commonly called "Kouis"—"goat with trimmed ears," also his father's nickname, to distinguish him from other Nicks. At their house his wife and daughters were ready and waiting. I was immediately served a sweet liqueur and a cake. I toasted Nikos "Xronia polla," "Many years," and chatted for a while. Then I was off to Niko tou Ioanni, called "Bekris," meaning "drinker," which he isn't, but some great-grandfather must have been. I drank and ate again and was off to Niko tou Georgiou, Niko tou Ioanni's cousin. I whispered to his wife, "Please a *koniak*," though it was inappropriate, for I was sugared out. Working my way closer to home, I was off to Nikoses four and five. By now I was only sipping my drinks and eating half a cake, but everyone understood. Nikoses six and seven followed.

At the home of the final Nikolaos, an ardent Greek fascinated with his country's history and culture, I looked around at my surroundings and noted how much of the decor had to do with the tale of Greek beverages. The night had slowed and the last of us were sitting on couches covered with *flokati* rugs, which are woven of long sheep's wool in northern Greece. On a shelf, Nikolaos has an amphora that popped out of a field he plowed with his father. It is a late one, not important as an antiquity, yet still marked with the region of its origin, the island of Paros. Next to it sit two crude and broken but recognizable *kantharoi* (goblets) and one *kylix*, a two-handled drinking cup. There's a set of *denekakis*, the containers Greeks used for measuring out and buying wine from the barrel until about thirty years ago. We drank from the small but sturdy nonstemmed glasses Greeks serve wine in, which we pinched between thumb and forefinger on the far, not the near, side as we toasted, so the two glasses banged together in a ripple of touches rather than a single clink. I felt as Greeks must often feel, wine-washed in history.

Now I had only to face what lay ahead as the months turned: St. George's Day, St. Mark's, St. Spiros's, St. Vasilis's, St. Eleuterios's, St. Antonio's, St. Petros's, St. Pavlos's, and even St. Nikiforos's, whose name means "victory carrier." After vanquishing all those name days, I'd need him to carry me off.

# brandy

**T**hough the Greeks knew early about flavoring wine with wooden casks and aging it to refinement and, later, about making spirits from grape pulp, only recently have they put the two ideas together to make elegant aged brandy, which they call by the French term *koniak*. As with so many things, they knew a good union when they saw it. Today, in areas throughout the mainland, the Peloponnesos, and the islands, brandy production is widespread.

Many local *koniaks* are available in Greece, but the largest-selling one is Metaxa. Exported to over a hundred countries around the world, Metaxa is, however, not quite a pure brandy. While the spirit of Metaxa is grape brandy, sweetening and spices are added, so it might be called a kind of "brandy liqueur." There are four grades of the drink, each containing progressively older blends of brandy, but even in the finest Metaxa, the "grande fine," the added flavorings are as much a part of the drink as is the age. The company first began to

# and sweet liqueurs

*A drink is always accompanied by a well-received toast.*

## HYDROMELI, THE ANCIENT HONEY "BRANDY"
······················

**N**othing that can serve as the basis for the transformation of sugar into alcohol has escaped the attention of Greeks, beginning with honey. The ancient Greeks had a drink called *hydromeli*, which was nothing other than honey and water fermented to ten to twelve times its original volume. It wasn't actually a "honey brandy," such as sweet Metaxa and other Greek brandies, but rather a "honey beer," the original mead. Still, it must have been a good hot toddy when an old soul had a cold.

produce the brand in 1888 and now makes three-star, five-star, seven-star, and twenty-year-old "grande fine" or "private reserve." The three- and five-star are fruit-flavored, with a citrus-apricot-brandy mix and aroma, light in body, and with only minimal sweetness. The seven-star adds older brandies, the "grande fine" still more aged brandies and less fruit.

Greeks also make sweet liqueurs of almond, apricot, arbutus, cherry, coffee, mulberry, orange, prune, rose, and various berries. At home these are concocted by combining grape *tsikoudia* or *katharo*

*oinopnevma* ("clean alcohol" or "grape spirit") with the almond or other flavor. Commercial liqueurs tend to be saccharine sweet, much like the honey drinks of old, and are made in a large range of colors and flavors.

More than as after-dinner drinks, Greeks serve brandies and sweet *potons* for a number of ritual occasions—engagement parties, weddings, baptisms, name days, and in the cemetery on funerary memorial days. Strict gender rules mark the drinking: Only men are served *koniak;* women are generally given sweet *poton.* However, at times of

mourning no sweet beverages are served; only a swallow of wakeful, strong drink, such as brandy, properly acknowledges the dead.

Before such occasions, there is a rush to the store to purchase the liqueurs, and along with them cakes, for these drinks are more often offered with celebration sweets than with savory *mezedes.*

# beer

Beer has been known to the Greeks for millennia, but only recently has it gained enough in popularity to compete with wine. Beer, in fact, probably came before wine, for the simple fermentation of grains was known early. Some say Dionysos reigned first as the god of beer, not wine.

In ancient Greece beer, called *bryton*, was made from barley and rye and was drunk at *symposia* along with *hydromeli*. Aristotle compared the intoxication caused by beer to that of wine: Wine, he said, caused a drunk to pass out and fall face down, whereas beer caused one to fall belly up. Generally, though, the ancient

## WHO WERE THE BEER DRINKERS?

Athenaeus, discussing drink, had a different opinion about who drank beer, and what he voiced may have started a tradition that continues today. Rather than the drink of the rustic, he claimed that beer was the drink of the poor. "A way was found," he said, "to help those who could not afford wine—namely to drink wine made of barley."

Greeks considered beer a barbarian drink, drunk by people who didn't have access to the civilized intoxicant derived from the grape.

Today beer is firmly accepted as civilized. It has become a popular drink at home, at cafés, and especially at seaside tavernas on hot summer nights. The nation brews some excellent beers, most quite strong. Some employ quantities of the country's fine barley. Others, following the global fad, are brewed from lighter mixtures. Rather than calling it *bryton*, modern Greeks have adopted the Germanic name for the drink: They call it *biera*.

# coffee

*Several small coffees fuel the day and its camaraderie.*

According to legend, coffee was discovered by an Arab in Abyssinia who noticed that his goats became quite lively after chewing the fruit of a tall evergreen shrub. The seeds or beans were carried by caravan to Persia, and, starting in the ninth century, a drink was made from them. Ottoman Turks introduced the drink to Constantinople in 1453. The beverage was already popular in the lands they had passed through, though many believers of the new religion in those areas, Islam, disapproved of it.

Although some Muslims persecuted coffee drinkers, because Mohammad had not known the brew, in 1475 the world's first coffeehouse opened in Constantinople. Coffeehouses soon became such centers of socializing and talk that Sultan Amurat III closed them in order to end political chatter. The next sultan, who liked his pleasures, soon opened them again.

By now the Greeks had coffee, too, and it quickly became their most indulged-in drink. Today it is downed by every adult in every home, where it is made in a special coffeemaker called a *briki*. *Brikia* come in many sizes, from tiny, for one cup, to huge. Homemakers and coffeehouses have graduated sets of them. Coffee is brought on a tray—always along with a glass of water—to every visitor. It is brewed up and served in coffeehouses in every city, town, and village to clients by the thousands, some of whom spend a good part of their day in the establishments. The coffeehouses, *kafenions*, are men's domain (women go to sweet shops for coffee), and in them men drink coffee,

smoke cigarettes, talk—still most fervently about politics—and play backgammon and cards. Coffee is also brought on trays to offices and workshops, for Greeks never go to a coffee machine—they order up the real stuff from nearby coffeehouses. At home women taking a break share coffee with their sisters and neighbors. Coffee is also the drink of courtship: In the days of arranged marriages, young suitors hoped to be invited for a coffee. If his coffee had foam on it, the girl liked him; no foam, no hope. And today it is the drink of the first date.

The coffees are small—only demitasse or espresso-cup size. The beans are roasted

medium to dark and are ground powder-fine. Coffee is made by putting spoonfuls of the powdered beans in the *briki* along with water and sugar. The *briki* is placed over a flame and the coffee boiled up to a froth, removed from the flame, and placed back on the heat; this is repeated two more times. Then it is quickly poured into a cup, where the grounds settle to the bottom and the liquid rises to the top. It is important that a little froth float on top. The coffee is sipped and savored, not gulped, down to where the grounds begin. When I was first in Greece, you could still buy green coffee, roast it yourself, then grind it to suit. Now

## FORTUNE COFFEES

Some cultures have their palm readers, some their zodiac charts, runes, or tarot cards, some their fortune cookies. Greeks have their coffee grounds. Many Greeks claim they can read the future from the dregs left behind in a person's cup. After finishing the coffee, the one to be "read" turns the cup over on the saucer until the grounds fall out. The "reader" then looks into the cup at the pattern left behind and tells the fortune.

One year at a Greek church festival in mid-August, my friend Argine's husband read my coffee cup. "That's very strange," he said. "I see absolutely nothing at all in your cup except one big lump of money." Six weeks later my house burned down in a fire so hot that only eighteen inches of ashes remained. It took more than a year, but finally the insurance company paid me. When I received the check, I remembered: In my lap was one big lump of money, and all around me—nothing else. At the time of the reading, the prediction was as enigmatic as a prophecy from the Delphic oracle, but, skeptic that I was, Greek coffee had indeed told my fortune!

## MASTIC-FLAVORED COFFEE

The world lately has taken a fancy to flavoring coffee. Some of the most popular flavorings, such as hazelnut and cinnamon, echo the essences used by the ancient Greeks, from the long-trodden spice routes. One spice has been missed, however, and the bouquet it adds to coffee is truly exquisite: mastic from the Greek island of Hios.

To flavor 2 espresso cups of coffee, add 1/8 teaspoon finely ground mastic just as the coffee is removed from the flame and at its hottest. If the coffee is not really hot, dissolve the mastic in 1/2 tablespoon boiling water and add that to the coffee.

coffee everywhere comes already roasted and ground, and the coffee grinders of older folks stand silent on the shelves.

Most Greeks drink their coffee very sweet, called *vari glyko*. Besides the super sweet, three other variations are made: *glyko*, "sweet," *metrio*, "semisweet," and *sketo*, "plain with no sugar." I have always been a rarity in drinking mine *sketo*. Greeks often slip in a teaspoon of sugar since it's clear to them that I don't know what I'm asking for.

## TO MAKE GREEK COFFEE

In a *briki*, or if you don't have one, in the smallest and narrowest saucepan

you have, for *vari glyko* mix 1 rounded teaspoon of Greek coffee (available at good coffee stores, delis, and groceries), 1 espresso cup of cold water, and 3 teaspoons of sugar. Bring to a boil until the froth rises to the *briki* rim. Remove from the heat. Do this boiling and removing a total of three times. Then immediately pour the coffee into an espresso-size cup and let it rest until the grounds settle. Serve right away, accompanied with a glass of water.

For *glyko*, use only 2 teaspoons sugar. For *metrio*, use 1 teaspoon sugar. And for *sketo*, add no sugar.

# fragrant tea

"Tea" is an infusion of leaf or seed or berry steeped in very hot water and served as a beverage. As such, Greeks have had tea for a very long time. The tea we think of—the pekoe, or oolong, or Darjeeling of China and India—came to

Greece only recently. (When Asian teas arrived in Greece, they were distinguished as "European tea.") Rather, Greek tea has always been a brew of herb or flower meant to heal an illness or disorder. The list is long: a brew of one

herb to ease pain, another for a cough, another just to ease the day. Hippocrates enumerated many such hot curatives. The one of barley water he called *ptisane*, which is the root of the word "tisane"—and that is what a true Greek tea is.

*Sprigs of sage gathered from the hills make a "mountain tea," a favorite drink and curative.*

boil, remove from the heat, and let steep for 2 to 3 minutes. Strain into a cup. Stir in ½ to 1 tablespoon honey.

Some Greeks squeeze in a dash of lemon, add a sprinkling of cinnamon, or drop a clove into the boiling brew before straining it.

Should you ask for tea in most rural areas—other than in some tourist restaurants—you will still be served an herbal tea. All are called *tsai;* all are aromatic and made with honey, and sometimes lemon. All are wonderfully soothing.

## TO MAKE TEA THE GREEK WAY

Place 1 teaspoon of the herb of choice and 1 cup of water in a saucepan. Bring to a

## WHICH TEA TO CHOOSE

With hills full of a mad variety of wild plants, Greeks, both ancient and modern, have always had a plethora of roots, seeds, flowers, and berries from which to make teas. In times past, some were thought to have healing properties for certain disorders, and some were simply brewed for overall goodness:

**Asafoetida:** for digestion

**Wild celery leaf:** to calm the nerves and a nervous stomach

**Chamomile:** to treat wounds

**Clove:** as a diuretic

**Garlic and leek:** also a diuretic

**Germander:** for weight loss

**Mallow:** for digestion

**Mint:** as anti-purge

**Poppy:** for sleep

**Stinging nettle:** for bronchitis and as anti-purge

Today Greeks brew teas of more familiar plants:

**Anise seeds:** for the pain of childbirth, mild sedation, or to aid digestion

**Chamomile:** for nerves, upset stomach, croup, and colic

**Cinnamon:** for warmth

**Elder blossom:** for the skin

**Lime blossom:** a cure-all

**Mint:** for stomachaches, sore throats, and colds

**Oregano, marjoram, thyme, or savory:** as a diaretic and to invigorate

**Sage:** for the stomach

**Salepi (an orchid root):** to fight chronic illness

# fruitades and other drinks

According to Herodotus, the ancient historian, the Scythians (neighbors northeast of Greece) lived beneath their cherry trees in order to help protect them from winter frost, which they also accomplished by wrapping the trees in blankets. In summer they made a thick juice from the fruit of the tree, and from the leftover fruit pulp they made cakes.

The Greeks of the time also made a similar thick cherry syrup and fashioned a beverage from it. The Greeks of today still prepare the sweet, crimson syrup, from which they create *vissinada,* cherryade. They also make fruit syrups from the juice or pulp of apricots, various berries, figs, lemons, peaches, plums, oranges, and raisins, into which they stir water, add a bit more sugar if needed, and sometimes ice. Greeks make other fruit drinks from fresh fruit juice. Many sorts of fruit beverages have

*A woman invites passersby to quench their thirst with fruit from her own trees.*

long been on the Greek table. On a hot day—and a summer day in Greece can grow very hot—the tall, fruity, sweet liquid hydrates, cools, and renews. Never is one imbibed without producing a great sigh and an ear-to-ear smile. Among the most popular are:

■ almondade—called *soumada,* made from chopped almonds, almond flavoring, or almond syrup combined with sugar and water. Some Greeks add some almond extract or rose water.

■ cherryade—*vissinada*

■ lemonade—*lemonada*

■ orangeade—*portokolada*

■ pomegranate-ade—*granita*

■ tamarind-ade—*tamarinti*

Greeks also drink:

■ the water left over from boiling greens or beets

■ the water left over from boiling the wheat for *kollyva* (page 559), to which they add sprinklings of chopped almonds, toasted sesame seeds or anise seeds, chopped toasted walnuts, raisins, parsley, salt, and sometimes a bit of coconut. This resembles *kykeo,* the ancient drink, in which sage, mint, or thyme was added to barley water

■ honey water (the ancient *hydromeli*) and honied vinegar water. Both are sometimes enhanced with mint or other herbs

■ *gazoza,* or mineral water, and a selection of soda pops

Greek children love a drink called a "submarine," *ypobryxio.* Submarines are made by sinking a large heaping spoonful of mastic or vanilla paste—much like our marshmallow "creme"— into a tall glass of water. The drinker slowly drinks the water as the mastic or vanilla dissolves into it and flavors it, then when the liquid is gone, nibbles away at the paste. Spoon licking is required. Without spoon sweets at hand, many a hostess will offer guests a submarine.

## TO MAKE FRUIT SYRUP

Boil 2 cups of fruit liquid with 2 cups of sugar until the syrup heavily coats a spoon. Some Greeks add a clove or a pinch of cinnamon for a touch of spice.

The almond syrup is made with ¾ cup finely chopped blanched almonds, 3 cups water, 2 cups sugar, and a drop of almond extract if desired.

To turn it into a drink, place 1 or 2 tablespoons syrup,

or ½ to ¾ cup fresh juice, in a tall drinking glass. Add water, extra sugar to taste, and ice if

# DRINKING WITH THE NEIGHBORS

During the Greek dark ages, about the eighth century B.C.E., a mysterious tribal people from Central Asia rode into the region the Greeks themselves had once come from, the area north of the Caspian Sea and to the west of the Ural Mountains. They were Indo-European and spoke a language related to Iranian, though they had previously wandered into Asia. Greeks called them "Scythians" and conducted a lively trade with them. The great Greek historian Herodotus learned much about them on his visit to Olbia, a Greek city at the confluence of the Bug and Ingul rivers. Six centuries later the Scythians disappeared, their demise as much a riddle as their appearance, and Herodotus remains the major source of information about them, along with the extraordinary treasures they left in their graves.

The Scythians were accomplished horsemen, moving so fast on their steeds that both Greeks and Persians were stunned at how suddenly they appeared and conquered the Cimmerians, who had occupied the land before them. They were keen hunters and fisherman, skilled at curing hides, adept at working metals, and good farmers as well. They quickly became extremely prosperous, and their royalty lavished much wealth on art, ornament, and jewelry.

Their art was unique and astonishing. The Scythians created many carvings of animals, large and small, in a realistic yet impressionistic style. They especially idolized deer and elk, which they represented with antlers reaching high as towers or sweeping back in swirling curves toward the animal's tail. They shaped masks of horses that had horns like ibexes, molded fantastic creatures attacking horses, deer, sheep. All these magnificent figures were carved of wood, then encased in gold leaf. They also crafted gold necklaces and bracelets adorned with the same array of wild animals.

Most numerous among their golden objects were drinking cups, some with one handle, some two, some with animal figures as handles, some with no handles at all. Many of these, too, were carved of wood, then encased in gold leaf that slipped over cup rim and handle in a perfect fit. Many were round bottomed and could not be set down, though some had cup mounts to hold them. What did the cups contain? What was the drink of choice? No one knows, but they lived in a land where grapevines and fruit trees grew by the orchardful, and they had many Greek friends. In fact, they hired Greek craftsmen to fashion many of their baubles.

I can see them now, Scythian and Greek, in the forerunner to the coffeehouse, drinking, perhaps, cherryade instead of coffee.

desired. For the almond drink, milk is sometimes used instead of water.

# meze
# THE GRAND ARRAY

THE DIVERSITY IS INFINITE: A SMALL PORTION OF WHATEVER IS COOKING FOR DINNER; A TUMBLE OF TINY MEATBALLS; A SCHOOL OF LITTLE FISH; SMALL PLATES OF VEGETABLE PUREES, AND SEED AND ROE SPREADS. TWO ARE KNOWN ROUND THE WORLD: RICE-STUFFED GRAPE LEAVES, *DOLMADAKIA*, AND CRISP RINGS OF FRIED SQUID, *KALAMARI*. WITH THEM ARE TIDBITS OF ORGAN MEAT, LITTLE SKEWERS OF BEEF, FRIED CHEESE, CHILLED OCTOPUS, REFRESHING PICKLES, A FILLED FILO TRIANGLE OOZING SALTY CHEESE.

Dress your hair with fine extracts of perfume . . . and while you are drinking let these tasty dishes be brought to you.

—ATHENAEUS, SECOND CENTURY B.C.E.

These are the vast complement of little foods to go with drink, the "appetizers." Each is delectable, rousing, provocative, and satisfying. In Greece today, they are called *meze* (for a single one), *mezedes* (for a proliferation of two or ten or twenty), or because they often come in tiny bits, *mezetakia* ("little middles"). And that is what the word means: "middle." It comes from the Italian for "middle," *mezzano*, which was borrowed from the Genovese spice buyers who at one time swarmed about the Mediterranean. Whether the tidbits were named for the "middlemen" or the middlemen's habit of eating between meals remains a topic to discuss while munching a *meze*. For certain, the custom of having small morsels of food with drinks was already an ancient one in Greece before the pirates of Genoa sailed in. The little go-with-drinks, snack-on-at-midday, serve-party-guests taste treats are also still known by their ancient name, *oretakia*, from *orexi*, meaning "appetite,"

## APPETIZING CROSSOVERS

Some Greek *mezedes*, such as Eggplant Salad (page 32), Russian Salad (page 36), *tarama* salad (page 43), meatballs (page 52), fried small fish, *marides* (page 59), and especially the large-pan filo pies (pages 85 to 106), often appear among the dishes that traditionally grace the dinner table in Greece. In turn, certain dinner dishes, in particular Big Beans salad (page 208), Giant Beans *Plaki*-Style (page 286), and any and all croquettes and fritters (pages 292 to 298), frequently come out on plates as appetizer treats.

just as we call the savory fare "appetizers."

But with a major difference. *Mezedes* in Greece are not meal starters, so they are not appetizers in the "first course" sense. Rather *mezedes* are counterpoints taken with drinks in late afternoon, at galas, or in a café's late-night afterglow. As drink companions, they are meant to mitigate the effects of alcohol, satisfy any stirring hunger, and hold the social verve in bounds. Gatherings feature whole tableaus of *mezedes* ranging from flaky filo pies to pickled onions. At home, hosts offer little things, each different, for each drink. In tavernas, where conversation becomes more avid by the glass, boisterous dances might break out, and plate breaking once occurred, tables are heaped with them.

Ancient Greek writings speak of the appetizer tradition: so many plates of little things to eat—from peas to grasshoppers —that guests hardly knew what to sample next. People were admonished never to drink "dry hammer" (strange, we still say "get hammered"), but always to temper any drinking with small bites of foods.

Luckily for Greeks, for us, and for anyone partaking of the Greek way with food, the custom produced a lavish gallery of delectables. *Meze* is one of the most enjoyable aspects of the Greek diet. *Mezedes* inspire a panegyric!

# THE SIMPLEST MEZEDES

## bread as meze

### SERVES 6

SIMPLE AS IT MAY BE, THE OFFERING OF BREAD WITH A GLASS OF WATER, A SIP OF WINE, A DEMITASSE OF COFFEE, IS NOT A SMALL MATTER. BREAD IS PRIDE. BREAD IS HONOR. BREAD IS WELL-BEING. WHEN IT IS ALL THERE IS TO TREAT GUESTS, IT IS THE CORE OF HOSPITALITY, THE EMBRACE INTO CAMARADERIE, THE GIFT OF SUSTENANCE. GREEKS CRY HUNGER ONLY WHEN THEY ARE WITHOUT BREAD. I HAVE BEEN OFFERED AS MEZE FRESH BREAD, OLD BREAD, TOASTED BREAD, WATER-REFRESHED BREAD, OIL-SOAKED BREAD. I AM ALWAYS GRATEFUL.

*A glorious homemade bread already has one slice cut out for some guest's meze.*

*1/3 pound good Greek or other crusty bread (see pages 121 to 124)*
*3 tablespoons olive oil*

Cut the bread into 1-inch cubes and place on a plate. Drizzle with the olive oil and serve right away.

In a Greek kitchen, whether the cupboard is filled to abundance or is as bare as a Greek cupboard ever gets, a crock of shiny olives always sits in the darkest corner. On the draftiest shelf will air at least one round of cheese. And a loaf of bread, crusty and dense, invariably rests in a breadbox.

These three foods—staples in Greek cuisine since the dawn of their culture—comprise the simplest, and in many ways the most magnanimous, *meze* a Greek might place before a guest. They represent the sharing of the giver's own provisions. With these three elemental foods nearby, no second-cousin-once-removed who shows up unannounced, nor any forlorn patron who strays into the tavern, ever goes without a welcoming morsel.

The tiny plate—often a demitasse saucer—to the side of the water, wine, or ouzo will feature five or six perfect olives with perhaps a bit of brine or oil surrounding them and maybe a sliver of lemon rind or a sprinkling of herb on top. Or it will hold a slice of ordinary cheese (never really "ordinary" when it's the sharp, curdy, often homemade cheese of Greece). Or, if worse comes to worst and the cupboard is *truly* empty, cubes of earthy bread, possibly drizzled with green-gold olive oil, will be set out.

Who could ask for anything better?

# THE GLORIOUS CHEESES OF GREECE

Greece has marvelous cheese. True, they are often somewhat crude and inconsistent; the texture, quality, density, and intensity vary from round to round. But this is a feature to value.

It means the cheeses are still made in authentic ways where fickle circumstance—the weather, the grass that season, the thickness of the milk—alters the product. Greek cheeses are genuine and artless in the best of ways. They are modest and undeceptive. Because almost all the milk produced is from goats and sheep, it follows that almost all the cheeses are goat and sheep cheese, and since every region and individual village produces different cheeses, many are not commercially available. Described here are the main sorts of cheese found all over Greece. Most of these are also available internationally.

**ANTHOTYRI:** a fine-textured sheep's-milk cheese, like a smooth, hard cream cheese. One of the milder cheeses. Most comes from Crete. The name sometimes applies to dilled cheese.

**FETA:** Greece's most famous cheese, so common the name simply means "a slice." Feta is a moist, crumbly sheep's- or goat's-milk cheese. Although the density ranges from very soft to hard, generally it comes medium-soft. While lively, it is also milky in flavor, making it a wonderful appetizer cheese, complement to salads, or addition to cheese mixtures. Feta is a brined cheese. Shortly after firming, it is placed in a salt-water solution to stop its ripening, and it retains its young, curdy qualities. Feta is available in almost any supermarket. In square tins, it is also called *telemes*.

**GRAVIERA:** Greece's rendition of Gruyère. A medium-hard, yellow sheep's-milk cheese, it is homier than Gruyère and piquant enough to make a good grating cheese.

**HALOUMI:** originally from Cyprus. It is made from the curd of sheep's or goat's milk and is moist, sharp, and crumbly like feta. Haloumi is sometimes flavored with mint.

**KASSERI:** a Cheddar-style cheese made from goat's milk. It is yellow, medium-hard, and tangy, but with a certain mellowness. It is the main cheese of *saganaki*, the fried-cheese appetizer (page 40). Since it both crumbles and melts like Cheddar, it works well in *kleftico* dishes (see page 389) and nicely crusts the tops of *pastitsio*, *moussaka*, and other casserole dishes.

**KEFALOTYRI or KEFALOGRAVIERA:** translated literally, a "head" cheese, such as is common across all of Europe. It is hard and sharp, an excellent grating cheese that all Greeks lavish over their *makaronada*. At its best, it is as good as or better than Romano or aged Asiago. It is a goat's-milk cheese.

**KOPANISTI:** a blue cheese that is ripened in earthenware pots, from which the cheese gets its name. The curd is wrapped in a cloth and dried until blue-green mold develops. The mold and added salt are then pressed into the cheese and it is potted to ripen more.

**LATHOTYRI:** an oil-cured cheese made on Zakinthos and Mitilini (Lesbos). It is made from sheep's milk, is semisoft, and because of its curing medium, is grassy in flavor. It is formed into balls and ovals and, after several months' aging, is stored in olive-oil vats. When removed, the balls or ovals are sealed in wax.

*Rounds of homemade* mizithra *are proudly displayed on a kitchen table by their makers.*

**MANOURI:** a silken, white, unsalted cheese, so fine-textured it looks and breaks like snowy marble. It is made from the whey of sheep's or goat's milk and is increasingly available internationally. It is milder than many Greek cheeses, though still lemony sharp.

**METSOVO:** the province of Metsovo produces two distinct and special types of cheese: One is a fetalike goat's-milk cheese flavored with whole black peppercorns. The other is a semihard sheep's-milk cheese that is smoked.

**MIZITHRA:** comes two ways, as an unsalted, softly firm cheese, and as a lightly salted, semihard grating cheese. Greek shepherds make it from the whey that remains after the curd is removed from goat's or sheep's milk to use for other cheese. At home, it is made from whole goat's milk. Either way, it is in essence the Greek cotter's (cottage) or farmer's cheese. It is crude and homey, often quite strong, and at the least sharp and tangy, not at all like cottage cheese or ricotta. Nor, since it is well drained of liquid, is it curdy or spreadable. It is made wherever Greek women milk goats and make their own cheese, and in different areas it bears different names. It is called *hlorou* on the Cycladic islands. There is also a dry sort of *mizithra* that is made commercially and makes a fine rustic topping cheese when grated.

**TOULOMOTYRION:** a sheep's-curd cheese, originally made by the Greeks of Asia Minor, then from Crete, and now widespread. It is similar to feta but less salty. It is pressed and cured in goat hide, hair side in, aged, and sold from the hide. It is soft but firm. *Megithra*, from the Cycladic islands, is similarly aged in hide but is flavored with oregano or other herbs before ripening.

# cheese as meze

**SERVES 6**

YOU WANDER INTO THE FIELDS TO PASS THE TIME OF DAY WITH A LOCAL FARMER. OUT OF HIS PACK COME A BOTTLE OF WATER OR WINE AND A PAPER-WRAPPED PACKAGE OF SOMETHING FROM WHICH WAFTS A MILKY PUNGENCY. OUT FROM HIS POCKET COMES HIS SHORT, CURVED PRUNING KNIFE. HE UNWRAPS THE PACKET TO REVEAL A PORTION OF WHITE OR GOLDEN CHEESE AND CUTS A HUNK TO OFFER YOU. THERE IS NO SAYING NO.

You enter your neighbor's courtyard to see what she is up to. She whisks you inside, reaches into the cheesecloth hanging in the window, and pridefully pulls out her drying cheese. With her serrated kitchen knife, she slices you a wedge.

Off-hours in an empty café, you order a *tsikoudia* (grappa). The owner brings with it a slice of shepherd's kasseri, drizzled with a dram of olive oil or a squeeze of lemon and sprinkled with a pinch of fresh oregano.

Any way, you have a *meze* to satisfy both taste buds and hunger.

*6 ounces kasseri, feta, kefalotyri, mizithra, or any other good Greek cheese*
*1 tablespoon extra-virgin olive oil, or 1/2 tablespoon fresh lemon juice (optional)*
*Pinch of fresh or dried oregano (optional)*
*Bread, warmed or toasted, for serving (optional)*

Cut the cheese into bite-size slices or cubes. Place them on a plate and serve plain, or drizzle with the oil or lemon juice and sprinkle with oregano.

Accompany with hunks of fresh warmed or toasted bread, if using.

# THE MANY AND VARIED GREEK OLIVES

THE NUMBER AND VARIETIES OF GREEK OLIVES SEEM COUNTLESS. MOST ARE NAMED FOR THE REGION FROM WHICH THEY COME—SOME OF THE REGIONS ARE VAST AND THE OLIVE WELL KNOWN, SOME REGIONS ARE TINY AND THE OLIVES RARE AND PARTICULAR.

Some names refer to how ripe the olive is, how it is picked, or whether it falls from the tree. Other names describe whether the olives are left whole, slit, cracked, dried, brined, or cured to a wrinkle. There are also a number of grades of olives, reflecting their size, quality, and type of cure.

Here are some of the more commonly available ones:

**AGRINION:** plump, medium to very large, oval, ripe black olives from Agrinion in central Greece.

**AMFISSA:** ripe, large, soft, purple to black round olives from near Delphi, in central Greece.

**ATALANTI:** large, spotted, green to brown, brine-cured olives from the northeastern mainland of Greece.

**CRACKED GREEN:** not a variety, but rather large, oval, unripe green olives from across the country that are stone cracked to pick up more flavor from the brine.

**ELITSES:** not a variety, but rather tiny purple and brown olives, most grown on Crete. Their name means "little olives."

**IONIAN:** green brine-cured olives from the western shore of the Peloponnesos.

**KALAMATES:** the famous plump, large, fleshy oval olives originally from the Kalamata region in the Peloponnesos, now widely grown. They are black, green, or purple depending on the stage of ripeness when they are picked; the blacker, the riper. They are slit and soaked in a number of freshwater baths, then packed in salt brine. The most commonly available Greek olives, they come in bulk, bottles, with pits or pitted. In Greece they are also sometimes called *xydates*.

**KERKYRES:** plump and glossy black olives from the Ionian island of Kerkyra (Corfu).

**MEGARES:** long, dun to black wrinkled olives from around Megara in Attica.

**NAFPLION:** small green, unripe, dense olives, from the eastern shore of the Peloponnesos.

**ROYAL:** very large, red to brown, slit olives, similar to and widely grown like Kalamata; brined first in salt, then in vinegar and oil.

**SALONES:** medium, round, brown to purple, fleshy olives, widely grown.

**SPORATHES:** particularly meaty, round olives from the Sporathes islands, near Athens.

**THASSOS:** dry and oil-cured olives from the northern Aegean island of Thassos.

**THROMBES:** not a variety or from a special region, although many are from Samos; rather they are olives that have been left on the trees until they wither and fall. They are dark black, wrinkled, strongly flavored, and salty.

**TSAKISTES:** crushed green olives from Crete.

**XOURMADES:** the name means "dates"; very large, brown, wrinkled olives from Hios that look like dates.

## CURING OLIVES

Fresh off the tree, olives are inedible, acrid beyond belief. The ancients could not have just picked the fruit and nibbled away at the flesh. Olives must be "cured"—that is, leached of their glucosides—to be edible, and how that was discovered (the process takes days if not months) is anyone's guess.

Most Greek olives are brine-cured (soaked in salt water) for several weeks to six months, some with vinegar added. Greeks also dry-cure, oil-cure, and water-cure olives. Two of these ancient methods are still used by Greeks at home:

**HOME SALT- (OR DRY-) CURING METHOD:** Rinse the fresh olives and place them in a wicker basket or another container with numerous airholes. Cover the olives with coarse sea salt and cover the container with a thin tea towel or with cheesecloth. Set the basket in the sun. Two times a day for 7 days, toss the olives with a spoon or with your hands, bringing the olives on the bottom up to the top. Take the olives indoors at the end of the day to protect them from the moist night air. In 6 or 7 days, black ripe olives will be largely cured. You might want to stop the curing process at this point and leave some bite in the olives. Green unripe olives will be cured in 3 to 4 weeks; turn them once a week. If you want olives with no bite at all, cure them for another 3 weeks in each case. Take those you wish to use, rinse them, and if you desire, coat them in oil. Leave the others in the salt for up to 6 months.

## HOME WATER-CURING METHOD:

Wash the olives and place them in a glass container or pottery crock. Cover them with a solution of salt water—about 1 cup salt for every 4 cups water. Place a plate on top of the olives and weight it with a rock or other object to keep them submerged. Change the water solution once a week. In 3 to 4 weeks, most of the bitterness will be leached from the olives. Leave the olives in the solution longer if they are still too bitter. When the taste is as desired, drain off the salt water and put the olives in fresh water, where they will keep for up to 2 months.

Adding 1 cup white wine vinegar to 1 quart of the home water-curing solution produces a brine cure.

To either of the home cures you can add oregano, thyme, chile pepper, bay leaf, cumin, coriander seeds, garlic cloves, strips of lemon zest, or minced orange zest. Removed from their curing solutions, the olives can be kept in oil and the same flavoring can be added then, to produce a marinade.

In Greece, when the olives are done curing, they emerge in many colors. Some of the color is determined by the ripeness of the olives when they were picked. Most of the homemakers I know who have their own olive trees still cure their own olives for home use. Others who have no trees often buy uncured olives from a local orchard owner in order to cure a crock at home.

One caution: Olives must be cured right after they are picked. Use only unbruised fruit. Olives bruise easily, and when they are bruised, they do not cure successfully.

# the olive as meze

## ELIES

### SERVES 6

ACCORDING TO SOCRATES, THE GREAT ELDER OF THE GREEK PHILOSOPHERS, GREEKS ADAPTED THE ORIENTAL STYLE OF RECLINING AT BANQUETS AS THEY PICKED AND CHOSE AMONG RIPE AND UNRIPE, WRINKLED AND SMOOTH, PLAIN AND SPICED OLIVES ALONG WITH THE OTHER FOODS THAT WERE SERVED. OLIVES WERE UNDOUBTEDLY THE MOST COMMON, MOST ADMIRED, MOST DESIRED FLAVOR TREATS TO GO BEFORE AND ALONGSIDE ALL MEALS.

Today, as in ancient times, the spectrum of colors Greek olives come in invites description. They are dun and green, black and khaki, brown and purple. Some are a single hue, some are speckled, mottled, spotted, or dappled. They grow from tiny to colossal, lean to fat, and emerge from their brines satiny to wrinkled, mild to sharp. When a guest comes for diversion or dinner, the olives are scooped out and placed on a side dish to accompany a drink or bedeck a table. Greeks sometimes spark up a crock of olives with bits of chopped onion, herbs, bay leaf, pimento, or lemon zest.

As *meze* to go with a drink, place six to eight olives on an individual plate. For the dinner table, set them out in a single bowl.

*1 cup good Greek olives, such as Kalamata, Amfissa, Thassos, Nafplion, or Atalanti*
*1/2 teaspoon coarsely chopped lemon zest*
*Chopped fresh basil, oregano, or parsley leaves*

Drain the olives and toss them with the zest and herbs. Set aside at room temperature until ready to serve.

# THE SALADS AND SPREADS

# eggplant salad

## TWO WAYS

### MELANZANOSALATA ✳

SMALL WHITE ONES, LONG GREEN AND MAUVE ONES, GREAT TEARDROP PURPLE ONES—THE LOVE AFFAIR BETWEEN GREEKS AND *MELANZANA*—EGGPLANT—IS SENSUOUS AND SAVORY. GREEKS FRY EGGPLANTS, BAKE THEM, STEW THEM, AND STUFF THEM. THEY MATCH THEM UP WITH CHOPPED MEAT OR LIVER. AND WITH OTHER VEGETABLES, THEY MIX THEM INTO A LUSTY APPETIZER SALAD.

The salad is contrived in two ways: one more urbane and smoothly suave, one more rustic and punched with relish. City-style, the eggplant is roasted smoky, then pureed into an unadulterated eggplant spread. It has no distractions, only a dram of oil and a splash of vinegar. It exalts eggplant to an aristocratic stratum; it's for purists. Country-style eggplant salad is full of coarsely chopped vegetables and stands out brusquely gustatory with mustard, mint, and oregano. It's a bucolic gem for lovers of vegetable medleys and cold ratatouille. Both are culinary prizes, and both have adorned countless appetizer tables I have prepared.

## EGGPLANT SALAD
### CITY-STYLE
**MAKES 1³/₄ CUPS** ✳

*1 large eggplant (about 1 ¹/₂ pounds)*
*¹/₄ cup olive oil*
*¹/₂ teaspoon salt*
*2 teaspoons red wine vinegar*
*Lemon slices or sprigs of fresh*
*    mint or parsley, for garnish*
*Bread, pita, or crackers, for serving*

When it comes to teasing and appeasing the appetite, the Greeks are a cunning and frugal lot. What has more allure than a mix of vegetables, each with a different flavor? And why waste even a smattering of one? What completes a glass of wine more than a salty paste of fish roe? And why not glorify such a treasure of a sea catch?

Some of the most creative, tasty, and adored appetizers in Greek cuisine are purees or mixtures of vegetables, handsomely oiled and herbed, or smooth concoctions of seed or roe, resplendently emulsified. Greeks label them "salads." We might call them spreads. The distinction makes little difference when delighting in them. They are eaten by the forkful or scooped upon bread, enjoyed with drinks among friends, among family, around the room and at the table.

1 Preheat the oven to 450°F.

2 Prick the eggplant once with a knife. Place it on a baking sheet in the oven and roast until the skin is wrinkled and the eggplant has collapsed, about 1 hour. Remove and set aside until cool enough to handle.

**3** Slit the eggplant open length-wise and scrape the pulp from the skin. Finely chop the pulp and transfer it to a medium-size bowl.

**4** Add the oil, salt, and vinegar to the eggplant, and stir until thoroughly blended. Leave in the bowl, or transfer to a platter and shape into a loaf. Cover the salad and refrigerate for several hours or overnight.

**5** To serve, garnish with the lemon slices or herb sprigs, and accompany with bread.

# EGGPLANT SALAD
## COUNTRY-STYLE

### MAKES 2 CUPS

1 medium eggplant (about 1 pound)
1/4 medium onion
2 to 3 cloves garlic
1 small tomato (3 ounces)
2 tablespoons chopped fresh
    flat-leaf parsley leaves
1/2 teaspoon chopped fresh
    mint leaves
1/2 teaspoon chopped fresh oregano
    leaves, or 1/4 teaspoon dried
1/8 teaspoon dry mustard, or
    1/2 teaspoon prepared mustard
1 1/2 tablespoons red wine vinegar
1 1/2 teaspoons fresh lemon juice
1/4 cup olive oil

1/2 teaspoon salt
Pinch of freshly ground black pepper
Bread, pita, or crackers, for serving

**1** Preheat the oven to 450°F.

**2** Prick the eggplant once with a knife. Place it on a baking sheet in the oven and roast until the skin is wrinkled and the eggplant has collapsed, about 50 minutes. Remove and set aside until cool enough to handle.

**3** Slit the eggplant open length-wise and scrape the pulp from the skin. Coarsely chop the pulp and transfer it to a large bowl.

**4** Coarsely chop the onion, garlic, and tomato. Add to the bowl, along with the parsley, mint, oregano, mustard, vinegar, lemon juice, oil, salt, and pepper. Stir to blend. Serve right away, accompanied by the bread, or cover and refrigerate for up to 1 week.

### NOTES:

■ Like so many Greek food mixtures, Eggplant Salad gains in flavor if the ingredients are allowed to sit together overnight.

■ Because this is a country-style salad, lively and unrefined, the ingredients should be chopped into small chunks and pieces, not minced.

## THE FIVE CURES

Five methods of curing are used for commercially available olives. The Greeks use the first four, the last—lye-cured—is used by U.S. canning companies.

**BRINE-CURED** olives are soaked in a salt water brine for several weeks to six months. Sometimes vinegar is added to the brine at the start or the brine is thinned with vinegar in the final weeks.

**DRY-CURED**, also called salt-cured, olives are sprinkled with quantities of salt, much as capers are cured. When black ripe olives are salt-cured, they can be ready to eat in about a week. Green unripe olives take several weeks. Sometimes dry-cured olives are also finished in an oil cure.

**OIL-CURED** olives are soaked in vats of olive oil for many months.

**WATER-CURED** olives are soaked in vats of water, then drained and rinsed, then submerged in water again and soaked for many months.

**LYE-CURED** olives are soaked in a solution made alkaline with lye, wood ash, or alkaline soda. The lye method of curing is fast—it takes only a few days. The disadvantage is that it removes much of the olive's taste. For that reason, lye-cured olives are usually seasoned with herbs and spices.

# THE EGGPLANT URBANIZATION OF MILTIADES

I WAS SITTING ON THE BALCONY WITH MILTIADES, THE FATHER OF MY ATHENIAN FRIEND PETROS. WE WERE WATCHING EGGPLANT WRINKLE OVER HOT COALS AS IF AGED BY KRONOS, THE GOD OF TIME, RIGHT BEFORE OUR EYES. MILTIADES, AT AGE EIGHTY, TOLD ME THAT HE AND KRONOS WERE FRIENDS, AND SMILED WITH THE GLEAM IN HIS EYES THAT ONLY A MAN FROM CRETE COULD MUSTER.

Despite many years in Athens, Miltiades—named for a general at the battle of Marathon—remained a true specimen of his island. A strapping, rough-hewn, keenly cunning man, he sported a magnificent mustache and wore tall Cretan riding boots. He insisted his vegetables be freshly grown and so kept on his Kolonaki Square terrace a garden as resplendent as any in his native village. He produced beans, okra, tomatoes, onions, and herbs, but his prize was his eggplant. He was mad for the sleek white or purple orb, especially when it was turned into a salad, and he told me how his eggplant salad came to be.

As a young man new to the city, sent by his family to acquire what Greeks value most, an education, Miltiades clung to his island ways. He liked boisterous backgammon games in a coffeehouse, and ate hunks of bread and cheese which he clamped in his teeth and cut off at the entrance to his mouth with his curved pruning knife. Lacking a kitchen in his rented student room, he patronized neighborhood Cretan restaurants where the proprietors served eggplant oozing oil and goodness one way

*Never fainthearted, a Cretan would jump a wall to court a fair maiden.*

or another, and especially the ones where they created eggplant salads with roughly chopped mint, onion, tomato, and the punch of pungent mustard and wild oregano. From one of these eateries, Miltiades spied a petite young woman walking near the first Olympic stadium, and he could think of nothing else but meeting her.

In due time he did exactly that and more. He not only met her; he married her. Trouble was, it was a Jack Sprat match. Delicate Fotini was a high-born lass who had lost her wealth, position, and home when her family was forced out of Turkey in 1922. But Fotini never lost her refinement. She was patrician. She collected lace embroideries, liked "European" music, read the Greek poets, and knew all the ins and outs of drawing-room etiquette. Miltiades liked *stifado* (see page 374), raw red wine, and *galaktoboureko* (see page 510). Fotini preferred Parisian-style roast meats, white bread, cakes, and tea.

In order to please his bride, Miltiades knew some compromise was called for, and he decided to begin with eggplant. He couldn't cease his love for the vegetable, but he could change how he ate it. Miltiades saw that in the fine city restaurants, the eggplant salad was made in a more "haute" manner. He determined he would learn to reproduce the smooth, uncorrupted spread tasting only of luscious eggplant. He roasted the eggplant on a small outdoor grill, village-style, to ensure a smoky flavor, then split the collapsed vegetable, scraped out the pulp, and pureed it with pestle and mortar, adding only a dollop of oil and vinegar.

The salad, he laughingly told me, was to Fotini's rarified taste, as well as to his. Over it, Fotini let Miltiades into her heart and, more important, into her kitchen.

# eggplant and yogurt spread

## WITH RED ONION AND OLIVES

### MAKES 2½ CUPS

IN NORTHERN GREECE AND IN CRETE, WONDROUS THICK, SAVORY-SOUR YOGURT IS READY AT HAND, AND ITS USE AS AN INGREDIENT IN DISHES, NOT JUST ON ITS OWN, IS COMMON. IN BOTH AREAS, SOFT, PULPY, TRACTABLE EGGPLANT IS SOMETIMES COMBINED WITH YOGURT TO YIELD A TANGY, SMOKY SPREAD.

Often a little dill or oregano is added to the blend, and the preparation is then served with chunks of thick country bread. I find the spread a perfect foundation for the basil that every Greek grows but rarely uses in cooking; and since the dish is almost inevitably served with a few olives on the side, I also take the liberty of chopping in some olives. The basil adds both an alluring perfume and an herby greenness, the olives contribute a briny shadow, turning the simple spread into a more complex and intriguing compound. With the yogurt, neither lemon nor oil is necessary.

*1 small eggplant (12 ounces)*
*1 cup plain yogurt, or Thickened*
*   Yogurt (see Notes)*
*1 ½ tablespoons finely chopped*
*   fresh basil leaves*
*6 tablespoons chopped Kalamata*
*   olives (see Notes)*
*½ small red onion, finely*
*   chopped*
*2 cloves garlic, minced or pressed*
*1 teaspoon salt*
*Whole fresh basil leaves,*
*   for garnish*
*Bread, for serving*

1 Preheat the oven to 450°F.

2 Prick the eggplant once with a knife. Place it on a baking sheet in the oven and roast until the skin is wrinkled and the eggplant has collapsed, about 1 hour. Remove and set aside until cool enough to handle.

3 Slit the eggplant open lengthwise and scrape the pulp from the skin. Finely chop the eggplant and transfer it to a large bowl. Stir in the yogurt, chopped basil, olives, onion, garlic, and salt, blending well. Cover and refrigerate for several hours, until thoroughly chilled.

4 To serve, garnish with the basil leaves and accompany with slices of bread.

## NOTES:

■ The dense and creamy yogurt of Greece is very thick. To achieve a similar consistency, use the firmest yogurt you can find or substitute Thickened Yogurt (page 471).

■ To dot the dip with red instead of black, substitute chopped sun-dried tomatoes for the olives.

## THE "EGG" IN EGGPLANT

In summer, when a Greek farmer comes home from the fields, he always carries with him an armload of ripe fruits and vegetables. He may grow fields of wheat and tiers of tomatoes, have grapevines and pistachio trees for commerce, but he and his wife also plant a patch of melons, onions, peppers, for home use. Invariably the patch includes eggplants, which take to almost any soil as long as there's sun to ripen them—and in Greece, the sun matures them to brilliance. But not necessarily purple brilliance.

The first time Markos, my then landlord, brought a load of eggplants up from the fields—some to sell in his shop and some for his wife to cook—I finally understood what their name was about. The eggplants were small and snowy white, some round as goose eggs, some dented like their relatives the sweet pepper. Markos didn't know exactly what his wife would do with the eggplants; he only knew they would show up the next day in a stew or salad, or maybe stuffed, or fried in slices.

As it was, Sofia made an eggplant spread with yogurt (see page 35). She understood that after a long day, many of the other men home from the fields would stop by to chat with Markos in the store. They would have a sip of last year's wine right from the barrel, smoke cigarettes, tell tales, and while away the evening in the intimacy of each other's long-established company. And nothing would go better with their repose than a store's last loaves of daily bread and a tangy eggplant spread.

# russian salad
## WITH CAPER MAYONNAISE
### SALATA ROUSSIKI

**MAKES 3 CUPS**

DURING THE LATE 1800S, AS GREECE WAS SLOWLY WRESTING TERRITORY BACK FROM THE OTTOMAN RULERS, THE URBAN EDUCATED WERE TURNING NORTH TO THE COUNTRIES WHOSE CULTURE GREECE HAD INSPIRED. AT THE TIME, THE FRENCH, THEIR LANGUAGE, AND THEIR FOOD WERE CONSIDERED THE PARAGONS OF EUROPEAN CULTURE. ALSO MANY EUROPEAN COUNTRIES WERE UNDERGOING A RAGING FAD FOR ALL THE THINGS ETHNIC ABOUT THEIR LAND. ALTHOUGH THE GREEKS HAD FROM TIME ETERNAL EATEN DISHES OF VEGETABLES, A NEW DISH HAD ARRIVED FROM THE NORTH. IT WAS CALLED A "SALAD," AND SOON ALL SORTS OF "SALADS" NAMED FOR ALL SORTS OF NATIONALITIES APPEARED.

The most popular was a medley of diced cooked vegetables smoothed by a novel French sauce called "mayonnaise." For some reason—perhaps the borschtlike miscellany—the dish received the tag "Russian Salad," and it quickly appeared as an appetizer on Greece's European-inspired menus.

And there it remains. *Salata Roussiki* is a mainstay

*Bags of freshly dug potatoes are delivered for the day's meze.*

of the Greek *meze*. Like a smattering of many-colored beads, a mixture of lightly cooked fresh vegetables is held in tow by a *saltsa mayoneza*—here, a very lemony version. The mix is patted into a loaf or roll, and in the most polished presentation, iced over with mayonnaise until white-coated, like a savory frosted cake.

4 ounces fresh green beans, trimmed
    and cut into ¼-inch lengths
½ cup fresh shelled peas
1 medium carrot, trimmed and
    cut into ¼-inch dice
½ cup fresh or frozen baby lima beans
1 medium red or white potato,
    peeled and cut into ¼-inch dice
½ cup Lemony Mayonnaise
    (page 470)
½ tablespoon capers, minced
½ teaspoon salt
1 large egg, hard-cooked and
    cut into 6 wedges
1 lemon, cut into 6 wedges

1 Bring a medium-size pot of water to a boil over high heat. Drop in the green beans and cook until the beans are barely tender and still bright green, about 2½ minutes. Lift out the beans from the water with a slotted spoon, and transfer them to a colander. Let them drain thoroughly, then transfer to a large bowl and set aside.

2 Bring the water back to a boil. Drop in the peas and cook until they are bright green and most have floated to the top, about 1 minute. Remove with a slotted spoon, drain, and transfer to the bowl with the beans.

3 Bring the water back to a boil, add the carrot, and cook until barely tender, about 3 minutes. Remove, drain, and transfer to the bowl with the other vegetables.

## THE RUSSIAN CONNECTION

When I first arrived on Santorini, a very elderly spinster lived atop the island's spectacular cliff in a whitewashed mansion. She was the daughter of a wealthy, landowning, Catholic family—inhabitants since the days when Venice held the island. As with all educated girls of her day, she spoke French and Italian, but "Miss Vera" also spoke Russian, and apparently, now in her dotage and as yet unwed, she was still waiting for the return of her Russian fiancé.

How did her life take such a twist, I wondered? It turned out that Miss Vera's story was the story of the island itself.

Like many places in Greece, Santorini, tiny dot in the sea that it is, has a history far more complex and global than one might think. From its early days, Santorini's merchant farmers peddled their main product, their heavenly wine, to whatever thriving center the shippers could reach by sea. The Minoans, who first occupied the island, ferried their amphorae of wine to Egypt. By classical Greek times, Santorini was a Spartan possession and the wine was shipped to that capital. When the Romans took the island—the Ptolomaic princes of Roman Egypt were educated at Santorini's *gymnasium*—the wine was traded to Alexandria. By the Middle Ages the port of choice for the wine was powerful Venice. After the Middle Ages, another thriving city, also reachable by sea but this time through the Dardanelles and Bosphorus, quietly became the island's main wine buyer: Odessa, the busy hub on the Black Sea. With their shared religion and alphabet, Greece and Russia have always felt a certain kinship.

When did Miss Vera last see her lover? 1917. The year of the Russian Revolution is the year Santorini lost its trade with Odessa and Vera lost Ivan.

Now, after almost eighty years of hardship, Santorini has at last found a new client eager for its wine, and business has resurged. For the first time the customer is Greece's own capital, Athens; and from Athens, Santorini wine, perfect to serve with any *meze*, has reached North America.

4 Bring the water back to a boil and cook the lima beans— 5 minutes for fresh, 1 minute for frozen. Remove with a slotted spoon, drain, and add to the bowl.

## DURABLE MEZE
..............

I n the springtime, Greece's nut trees bedeck the landscape with a profusion of white and pink blossoms, for nut trees of one sort or another—most commonly almond and pistachio— ornament almost every province. As summer passes the blossoms give way to a bountiful crop. As always not wasting a morsel, Greeks preserve their generous bounty of nuts to last until the next year or even longer. (Nuts four or more millennia old have been found in Greece.) Though they sometimes pickle the nuts, Greeks most often dry and then bathe them in a salt bath. A small offering of these also often accompany a drink. The most common are pistachios, both green and dyed pink, still in the gaping shell, or almonds, shelled but still sheathed in their brown jackets.

5 Add the potato to the same pot of water and boil until the pieces are cooked through but still holding their shape, about 6 minutes. Remove with a slotted spoon, drain as above, and add to the bowl. Set the bowl aside until all the vegetables are cool.

6 When you are ready to dress the salad, whisk together the mayonnaise, capers, and salt in a small bowl. Toss the vegetables together and stir in half the mayonnaise mixture. Transfer the salad to a platter and shape into a long rectangle or log. Spread the remaining mayonnaise mixture over the top to cover completely, like a frosting.

7 Set aside in the refrigerator until chilled, 30 minutes to several hours. Then decorate with the egg and lemon wedges, and serve.

## OTHER RUSSIAN ADDITIONS

In this lively miscellany of a salad, the range of possibilities is almost as varied as the Russian people.

■ For the vegetable mixture, as well as or in place of the ingredients above, Russian Salad can feature almost any diced cooked vegetable. Some common ones are: beets (a very popular addition, which turns the entire dish lush pink), bell pepper, broccoli, cauliflower, celery, and tomato (diced fresh, not cooked).

■ You can also add a tablespoon of finely diced sweet or dill cucumber pickles, Sweet Zucchini Pickle, or Pickled Red Onions (pages 72 and 75).

■ Russian Salad can be made with an olive instead of caper mayonnaise: Simply replace the capers with finely chopped Kalamata or other Greek olives. A few chopped fresh basil leaves offer an aromatic dash to the dressing.

# roasted sweet pepper salad

**SERVES 6 TO 8**

WITH THEIR PIQUANT BITE—AND EVEN THE SWEET BELL PEPPERS OF GREECE HAVE A BIT OF A BITE—AND THEIR CHEWY TEXTURE, PEPPERS ARE SERVED GRILLED, ROASTED, OR SAUTEED WHOLE OR IN STRIPS, TO SPARK AND ALSO TO ASSUAGE THE APPETITE. AS SUCH THEY ARE PRESENTED PLAIN, USUALLY WITH SOOTHING OLIVE OIL, OR THEY MIGHT BE TOPPED WITH CHOPPED MINT, OREGANO, OR SCALLION.

Peppers are also tossed together with sausage slices, heated, and served hot or lukewarm, or are marinated like mushrooms (page 50) or pureed into a spread with herbs and feta cheese. Greeks also like to pickle peppers and present them as *meze* called *onsini*. The Macedonians enjoyed a mix of peppers with garlic, oil, and vinegar.

*6 large bell peppers (about 3 pounds total), preferably a mixture of red, yellow, and green*
*4 cloves garlic, coarsely chopped*
*2 tablespoons olive oil*
*2 teaspoons red wine vinegar*

1 Heat a grill to high or preheat the oven to 450°F.

2 Rinse the peppers and roast them on the grill or in the oven, turning once, until the skins are charred and blistered all around, 25 to 30 minutes. Transfer the peppers to a plate and cover them with a cloth. Set aside until cool enough to handle, at least 20 minutes.

3 With your fingers, peel the peppers and pull out the stems. Cut the peppers in half and scrape away the seeds. Cut the halves lengthwise into 1-inch-wide strips, and arrange the strips, along with any juices, on a serving platter.

4 Sprinkle the garlic over the pepper strips, then pour the oil and vinegar over all. Serve right away, or set aside for up to several hours. The dish can also be covered and refrigerated for up to several days.

## GREEK VINEGAR

Vinegar was an integral part of daily cooking from early times. In later Greek times it was sometimes mixed with water and drunk as wine, called *fouska*, when true wine was too far beyond the budget to buy.

The copious use of vinegar remained throughout the history of Greek cuisine and continues on today. From earliest times and still, the vinegar of Greece has almost entirely been wine vinegar, made from the same grapes—almost always red—that have provided their timeless wine. Practically never are cider vinegar, distilled vinegar, or balsamic vinegar used on salads, or added to any other Greek dishes.

# fried cheese cubes

## TOPPED WITH OREGANO AND CAPERS

### SAGANAKI

**MAKES 24 PIECES**

Olive oil, for frying
10 ounces Greek kefalotyri, or
    other hard grating cheese,
    such as Parmesan, aged
    Asiago, or Romano, cut into
    $3/4$-inch cubes
24 whole or $1/2$ tablespoon coarsely
    chopped fresh oregano leaves
24 (about 2 tablespoons) large
    capers, rinsed
2 tablespoons fresh lemon juice
Bread, for serving

BESIDES SERVING PLAIN CUBES OF CHEESE AS A DRINK COMPANION, GREEKS ALSO PREPARE A TANTALIZING DISH OF FRIED CHEESE CUBES THEY CALL SAGANAKI. THE TERM DERIVES FROM THE NAME OF THE SMALL, OFTEN COPPER, TWO-HANDLED FRYING PAN IN WHICH IT IS PREPARED.

The cozy, curdy dish is such a popular favorite that it has made its way to the United States . . . more or less. I have found that in most American restaurants, the cooks melt a mass of cheese into a single pool, decorate the dish with lemon wedges, serve it with bread for dipping, and unabashedly call the concoction *saganaki*, proclaiming it "Greek fondue."

That is not *saganaki*. True *saganaki* consists of individual cubes that are fried until they have a crisp crust on all sides, but never melted. Yes, crisp! As each cube is carefully turned in the pan, it becomes a crunchy-on-the-outside, soft-in-the-center morsel to serve with wine or a malty beer. If cheese could become candy, *saganaki* is it. An especially zesty rendition adds a sprinkling of heady Greek oregano and a studding of capers. While not technically a spread, once past the crisp crust, *saganaki* oozes onto the bread like a cheesy mantle.

## SAGANAKI SAVVY

To make the *saganaki* properly, you need to use a good hard grating cheese, preferably Greek kefalotyri. Most recipes for the dish call for kasseri cheese, which has the right salty, arid taste, but beware, for it collapses more easily in the frying pan. Others call for Jack, Cheddar, Edam, or Bel Paese—but they collapse far too readily. Should you use them, you will indeed get Greek fondue! Kefalotyri holds its shape, readily develops a crunchy brown crust, and has a wonderfully keen flavor like Parmesan.

1 Pour oil to a depth of ⅛ inch in a small, heavy skillet. Heat over medium-high heat until very hot.

2 Add the cheese cubes in a single layer and fry until the bottoms begin to brown, 45 seconds to 1 minute. Turn and continue to fry until all the sides of the cubes are lightly browned, about 3 minutes more. Remove with a slotted spoon and drain on paper towels.

3 To serve in a city manner, place an oregano leaf on each cheese cube. Top each leaf with a caper and spear through the caper, leaf, and cheese with a toothpick. Douse all the cubes with the lemon juice. Place the cheese cubes on a plate and surround with wedges of bread.

To serve in a country manner, place the cheese cubes on a plate. In a small bowl mix together the oregano, capers, and lemon juice. Pour the mixture over the cheese and serve, accompanied with a loaf or slices of bread.

## TIME AND SAGANAKI

Different people use time differently and pace their lives at different rates. One of the most slippery aspects for an American to adjust to when first living in Greece is that things move . . . not so much slower, but the time frame required to accomplish, say, an errand is "larger." An American might call it "longer." As a result, you cannot do all the things in a single Greek day that you would do in a single American day.

Countless frustrations eventually taught me what I grew to call Greek Rule Number One: "Try to accomplish more than three things in a day and the gods will kick you." Inevitably, if I attempt a fourth errand or chore, something will go wrong: A tire will go flat, the shopping bag will break, the bus will have left, the store will be out of stock, a pipe will burst as I walk out the door.

I have grown to prefer the Greek pace of life, and every time I return from there, I try to keep my Greek time frame and not fall back into the American frenzy of doing twenty things a day. Eventually I succumb. I go native again and begin to run around like a mad person. Making *saganaki*, though, reminds me of Greek time. I must cut each cube of cheese nice and even. I must use a heavy skillet, not sizzle or zap the cubes in some time-saving appliance, and I must turn each piece from side to side to side until gently browned—never blackened, never melting—all around. And although the dish cooks in a jiffy, I must give it all my concentration—not answer the phone or write another list. If I don't take my time, the gods kick me in a special way: I won't have perfectly fried, crunchy bites of delectable cheese.

## NOTES:

■ Not everyone has a small two-handled frying pan, and they can be hard to find. Instead, you can use a cast-iron or other sturdy, heat-conducting skillet. A lightweight pan will not crisp the cheese cubes without their sticking and melting.

■ Unless your block of cheese is nicely rectangular, it is difficult to cut it into regular ¾-inch cubes. Irregular shapes make fine *saganaki* bites too, but keep the cubes—or trapezoids or rhombuses—about ¾ inch on each side. Any smaller and they will melt away in the frying pan.

# chickpea and sesame spread

## ASIA MINOR–STYLE

### HOUMUS ME TAHINI

**MAKES 1¾ CUPS**

IN THEIR SUN-WARMED COUNTRY, WHERE THE PEAS IN PODS AND THE SEEDS IN FLOWERS BURST FORTH WITH TOASTED ESSENCE RIGHT FROM THE VINE, THE GREEKS COMBINE TWO ANCIENT PUREES MADE FROM SEEDS: CHICKPEA AND SESAME SEED. THE TAVERN OWNER WHO PUTS OUT A PLATEFUL WITH A GLASS OF WINE KNOWS THAT DRINKERS WILL DIP THEIR BREAD AGAIN AND AGAIN, AND WILL BUY ANOTHER GLASSFUL AND ANOTHER.

Greeks of mainland descent make the *meze* spread plain, with only vinegar, lemon, and onion. Those of Asia Minor ancestry add more of the pungent spices indigenous to the region. The spread is often served on lettuce or ripe tomato slices, as well as on bread or pita.

*On the sidewalk "deck" of a taverna named for a famous ship, diners enjoy an afternoon snack.*

1 cup dried chickpeas
¾ teaspoon salt
3 teaspoons tahini
2 tablespoons fresh lemon juice
⅓ cup water
¼ cup olive oil
2 to 3 cloves garlic, minced or pressed
½ teaspoon ground cumin
½ teaspoon coriander seeds, or
   ⅛ teaspoon ground coriander
¼ cup fresh flat-leaf parsley leaves
Bread or pita, for serving

1 Place the chickpeas in a medium-size pot and cover with water by 1½ inches. Bring to a boil, cook for 2 minutes, and remove from the heat. Set the chickpeas aside to soak for 1 hour.

2 Drain and rinse the chickpeas. Return them to the pot, add fresh water to cover by 1½ inches, and bring to a boil again. Reduce the heat and simmer until they are tender and the skins are breaking open, 50 minutes to 1¼ hours, depending on the size and age of the peas. Remove from the heat, stir in ½ teaspoon of the salt, and set aside to cool to room temperature.

3 In a small bowl, whisk together the tahini, lemon juice, water, and oil. Set aside.

4 Drain the chickpeas, reserving ½ cup of the liquid. Transfer the peas to a food processor or food mill, add the reserved liquid and the garlic, and puree as fine as possible. Slowly drizzle in the tahini mixture. Add the cumin, coriander, and remaining ¼ teaspoon salt and process thoroughly.

5 Transfer the mixture to a bowl and garnish with the parsley. Serve at room temperature or chilled, accompanied by bread or pita.

# taramasalata

SOMETIMES IT'S MADE WITH THE ROE OF THE MEDITERRANEAN'S PLUMP MULLET. NEAR GREECE'S TRICKY SHORE IT'S THE ROE OF LOBSTERS OR CRAB. A PALE PINK VARIETY, WHICH THE GREEKS CALL "WHITE," COMES FROM CARP. SOMETIMES IT'S COD'S ROE, IMPORTED FROM ICELAND AND OTHER NORTHERN REALMS. WHICHEVER THE ROE, IT'S CALLED TARAMA, AND SALTY, APPETITE-ALLURING, AND MIXED IN A SPREADABLE "SALAD," IT IS ONE OF GREECE'S MOST FAMOUS *MEZEDES*.

In cosmopolitan bars, patrons order it to accompany their ouzo or their *ouiski* (whiskey). In country homes it's featured as an engagement or wedding banquet hors d'oeuvre. Traditionally the salad is served along with onions and lemons on Clean Monday, the first day of Lent.

Greeks make two versions, one based on soaked bread, the other on mashed potato. With bread, the salad is saltier and more textured. With potato it is sweeter and smoother. Some cooks combine both starches. Substituting shallots for onions and cilantro for parsley offers a bright twist. Some recipes include vinegar, but vinegar can overwhelm delicate fish roe, and that would defeat the purpose!

## TARAMASALATA WITH BREAD

### MAKES 2 TO 2½ CUPS

8 slices (½-inch-thick) Greek or Italian-style white bread (about ½ loaf), preferably stale, crust removed
4 ounces tarama (about ½ jar), preferably carp or codfish roe
1 tablespoon minced shallot
3 tablespoons fresh lemon juice
½ cup olive oil
½ cup fresh cilantro leaves, for garnish
Olives, for garnish
Bread, for serving

1 Place the slices of bread in a bowl and add water to cover. Set aside to soak for a few minutes. When the bread is saturated, squeeze out the water.

2 Using a food processor, mixer, or mortar and pestle, blend together the bread, roe, shallot, and lemon juice while gradually drizzling in the oil until thoroughly combined.

3 Transfer the mixture to a serving dish and shape it into a loaf or mound. Sprinkle the cilantro over the top, and arrange the olives around the edges. Serve accompanied by the bread.

## TARAMASALATA WITH POTATO

### MAKES 2 TO 2½ CUPS

1 large (about 10 ounces) russet potato, peeled and cut into ½-inch pieces
4 ounces tarama (about ½ jar), preferably carp or codfish roe
1 tablespoon minced shallot
3 tablespoons fresh lemon juice
¾ to 1 cup olive oil
½ cup fresh cilantro leaves, for garnish
Olives, for garnish
Bread, for serving

# THE CYCLADES AND THE SCENT OF LEMON

SCATTERED IN A ROUGH CIRCLE TO THE EAST OF THE MAINLAND LIE WHAT HAS BECOME THE PICTURE IMAGE OF THE GREEK ISLANDS: WHITEWASHED HOUSES LOOKING OUT OVER A PEACOCK-BLUE SEA—THE CYCLADES. SOME STORIES SAY THE ISLANDS WERE THROWN INTO THE SEA BY THE EARLY GODS AND LANDED LIKE BOULDERS IN A HAPHAZARD RING. SOME SAY THEY WERE NAMED FOR SEA NYMPHS WHOM POSEIDON TRANSMOGRIFIED INTO ROCKS WHEN THEY DEFIED HIM. BUT IN TRUTH, THEIR NAME COMES FROM THE WAY THEY CIRCLE THE HOLY ISLAND OF DELOS, WHERE APOLLO AND ARTEMIS WERE BORN.

All the Cyclades are stunningly beautiful, romantic, and alluring; most fetching of all, each one is unique. All but the southernmost, Santorini, are the tops of an underwater mountain range; Santorini instead is a dramatic, cliff-rimmed volcano. All were far more the centers of commerce, government, arts, and learning than one would believe of such tiny specks lying in such a small sea. Some were inhabited as early as 6000 B.C.E., and the earliest Greek art—the stark and elegant Cycladic kouros statues that have so strongly influenced modern artists—come from them. Minoans populated some. Mycenaeans came to many. In classical times Athens ruled a number of them; Sparta others. Egyptian kings sought their education on them. Throughout every era their fabulous wines and sun-browned grains were shipped to faraway ports. Fertile and strategic as they are, they have long been coveted by conquerors.

Near sacred Delos—as always, uninhabited by mortals—lies dashing Mikonos. Loaf-shaped houses, rows of windmills, and beaches of breathtaking beauty have for decades made it a glitzy destination of tourists. Close to Mikonos hovers Tinos, the holiest island of present-day Greece. Tinos and its shrine of the Virgin draw a yearly religious pilgrimage equal to that of ancient Eleusis. On northernmost Andros, rather than white or blue domes, the blazing white houses sport red tile roofs. Kea, Kithnos, Serifos—the "barren one," where the hero Perseus, son of Zeus and Danae, brought the head of terrible Medusa—and Sifnos harbor hidden beaches, flaunt wild hills, and feature sea views from every acre. Folegandros's lunar terrain is carved with terraces that give purchase to both orchards and houses. Milos, where lodes of ore attracted prehistoric miners, is home to inlets where some of the Aegean's clearest water swirls. Paros and its shadow, Andiparos, are covered in vineyards and fruit trees. Ios, shaped like a dot, looks east to misty Anafi; both rise to peaks where animals find pasture on wild herbs and grasses. Syros, in the center, is the capital. It is wealthy, commercial, home of a thriving city, and bustling with many textile factories. But in many respects, Naxos is the queen of the archipelago. Biggest of the Cyclades, its port spirals up in layers like a wedding cake, topped by an old Venetian castle. Theseus abandoned Ariadne on Naxos after she helped him kill the Minotaur. Dionysos came to her rescue, married her, turned her bridal crown into stars, and fathered her six children. Sweet, soft Naxos is the most fertile of the islands, lush with lemon orchards, fig and peach trees, melons, grapevines, wildflowers, garden crops, and herds of sheep.

The Arabs and others after them sailed to all the islands, bringing Greece's new boon: lemon trees. Now the scent of the blossoms wafts the aroma throughout the Cyclades. The people gather the fruit from early spring into the summer. They splash the juice on fish caught from the surrounding waters. They grate the rind into biscuits unique to the Cyclades. And for the evening's pleasure, when an ouzo or a lemonade brings the workday to a close, if you are a lucky visitor, they will sometimes serve you a salty lemon pickle with your hors d'oeuvre.

*A reburbished Cyclades windmill is now a place where visiting wayfarers can idle time away.*

1 Place the potato in a small saucepan, cover with water, and bring to a boil over high heat. Reduce the heat and simmer until cooked through, about 8 minutes. Drain the potato and set aside to dry for a few minutes, until cool enough to handle.

2 Using a food processor, mixer, or mortar and pestle, blend together the potato, roe, shallot, and lemon juice while gradually drizzling in the oil until thoroughly combined.

3 Transfer the mixture to a serving dish and shape it into a loaf or mound. Sprinkle the cilantro over the top, and arrange the olives around the edges. Serve accompanied by the bread.

**NOTES:**

■ If you don't care for cilantro (fresh coriander), use parsley.

■ Whether you use a food processor, mixer, or mortar and pestle, puree the roe thoroughly with the other ingredients. The more fish eggs that are broken and blended, the better the *taramasalata*. Some Greeks contend that *taramasalata* is good only when mashed and melded with a wooden spoon in a wooden bowl.

## APOTSOS

Around the corner from Constitution Square—I don't remember whether it was on Stadium or University Street—Apotsos, the most famous *meze* bar in Athens, lay hidden. The doorway leading to the smoky interior was without distinction. No blaring sign announced the drinks and delicacies within. You had to be "in the know" to find Apotsos—and many were.

Once inside, you found a barroom that was long, narrow, and high-ceilinged, dingy from the smoke of Hellas cigarettes and echoing from many years of clamorous talk. The walls were lined with old posters, and each waiter, though clad in a modern white jacket, looked as though he might have served Socrates and Plato. Of course the tavern held mostly men—an ouzo bar in Apotsos's day was for serious talk about politics and business—but women did stray in and were well treated. The list of ouzos available was as long as a leg, but the list of appetizers to go with them was even longer.

They cost extra money, the *mezedes*. Free with a drink were only a few olives, but the few drachmas extra for the appetizers were very worth the while. Apotsos had the creamiest *taramasalata* in Greece. The overstuffed cheese pies were half the size of the ones on the street, twice as flaky, and one hundred times richer. There was cold octopus in lemon juice, Russian Salad with each tiny potato cube intact, and long before others had it, fried zucchini so lightly battered and crunchy it beckoned you daily. Among the some twenty-plus brands of ouzo available, some were peppery, some sweet. There were also wines, beers, coffees, teas, *tsikoudia* (grappa), and a dozen brandies. Then, to make way for a modern office building, Apotsos was demolished, leaving nothing but a memory.

Until . . . a new Apotsos opened several blocks away.

I hear that it is wonderful, but I admit I haven't made the lady-or-the-tiger choice yet. Try the new Apotsos and be disappointed? Not try it and never find out if the cheese pies, the octopus, the Russian Salad, or the *taramasalata* are the same?

## TARAMASALATA WITH BREAD AND POTATO

**MAKES 2 TO 2½ CUPS**

*2 slices (½-inch-thick) Greek or Italian-style white bread, preferably stale, crust removed*
*1 medium russet potato, peeled and cut into ½-inch pieces*
*4 ounces tarama (about ½ jar), preferably carp or codfish roe*
*1 tablespoon minced shallot*
*3 tablespoons fresh lemon juice*
*¾ cup olive oil*
*½ cup fresh cilantro, for garnish*
*Olives, for garnish*
*Bread, for serving*

1 Place the slices of bread in a bowl and add water to cover. Set aside to soak for a few minutes. When the bread is saturated, squeeze out the water.

2 Place the potato in a small saucepan, cover with water, and bring to a boil over high heat. Reduce the heat and simmer until cooked through, about 8 minutes. Drain the potato and set aside to dry for a few minutes, until cool enough to handle.

3 Using a food processor, mixer, or mortar and pestle, blend together the bread, potato, roe, shallot, and lemon juice while gradually drizzling in the oil until thoroughly combined.

4 Transfer the mixture to a serving dish and shape it into a loaf or mound. Sprinkle the cilantro over the top, and arrange the olives around the edges. Serve accompanied by the bread.

## JASON AND THE ARGONAUTS

One of the most famous Greeks who sailed to lands unknown was the legendary Mycenaean hero Jason. He commanded the ship *Argo* and its sailors, the Argonauts, venturing all the way up Asia Minor and across the Black Sea.

Jason was born in Iolkus, a city near Argos. He was due to become king, but his half-brother usurped the throne. Fearing that the evil brother might assassinate her son, Jason's mother sent him to a cave where the centaur Chiron (a creature with the body of a human and the legs of a horse) reared him to adulthood. Chiron gave the boy his name, which means "healer."

As Jason grew big and strong, the goddess Hera fell in love with him. When he reached adulthood, she helped him return to Iolkus, where his brother attempted to get rid of him without exactly killing him: He offered Jason succession to the throne if Jason would sail to the kingdom of Colchis—present-day Georgia—where rumor said there was a valuable object, the fleece of a golden ram.

Jason gathered a band of the noblest Greeks, each one with a special skill; but like all Mycenaean heros, Jason bore a twisted fate and made a few disastrous mistakes. For one, he met the sorceress Medea. That was well and good, but in his gratitude for her help, he promised to marry her.

Still, Jason succeeded. After a long journey, he made off with the fleece. He gathered up Medea and returned to Iolkus, where his brother, as one would expect (after all, this is a Greek saga), reneged on the promise. Undaunted, Jason moved on to Corinth and stayed there for ten years. Then he made his next mistake: He tried to divorce Medea.

Medea, as we all know, exacted a rather infamous punishment: She killed their children. After that, Jason died sitting in the shade of his old ship, *Argos*.

# TWO FAMOUS VEGETABLE MEZEDES

## grape leaves stuffed

### WITH PINE NUTS, CURRANTS, AND GOLDEN RAISINS

### DOLMADAKIA

**MAKES 30 TO 40 PIECES**

T UCKED TIGHTLY TOGETHER IN CONCENTRIC CIRCLES IN THEIR PAN, OR ARRAYED ON A GALA APPETIZER PLATTER, LITTLE GRAPE LEAF *DOLMADES*—FILLED WITH RICE, NUTS, HERBS, AND DRIED FRUIT—GLISTEN LIKE GEMS; NOT FOR THE WEARING, BUT FOR THE PALATE!

Greeks have been wrapping foods in tender grape leaves since antiquity, and still today *dolmadakia* are perhaps their most famous snack. They make hot *dolmades* as a main dish, too (page 311), but it is the cool, rice and raisin–filled ones that enhance festive occasions. The stuffing is even more alluring if the currants and raisins have been plumped with piney retsina wine (see page 49) and if short-grain rice is used to keep the filling moist and chewy.

2 tablespoons dried currants
2 tablespoons golden raisins
1/4 cup retsina wine
30 to 40 fresh or bottled grape leaves, stems cut off (see Grape Leaf Tricks, page 48)
1/3 cup olive oil
1/2 cup short-grain rice, preferably Arborio
1 small onion, finely chopped
1 clove garlic, minced or pressed
1/4 cup pine nuts
2 tablespoons finely chopped lemon zest
3/4 teaspoon salt
2 tablespoons chopped fresh dill, stems reserved
2 tablespoons chopped fresh mint leaves, stems reserved
1 1/2 tablespoons fresh lemon juice
Lemon slices, for garnish

I n ancient times Greeks were very concerned with the *gaster*, which meant the "gnawer," or the stomach. How to satisfy that rumbling pest— thought to be different for men (easy to fill) and women (endlessly voracious)—was a matter of ceaseless discussion among philosophers and scholars. From the *gaster* and those discussions we get "gastronomy," the term for the art of good eating.

Fortunately the hills, fields, and gardens provided tidbits to quell the *gaster*, and many of the vegetables the ancients collected are still served as *mezedes*.

Two of those *mezedes* are famous. One has changed through time but its essence remains the same: tender leaves of the grapevine filled with grains and a smattering of other ingredients. In times past the leaves were used to encase barley or wheat sparked with all sorts of sweet sharp morsels; today it is rice with raisins.

The other *meze* was created from the harvest of wild mushrooms, tasting of smoke, loam, forest, and dew. These were simmered with oil, dotted with garlic, tossed with herbs, and bathed in wine vinegar much as they are today.

Both deserve their fame, for both are fabulous.

1 Combine the currants and raisins with the retsina in a small bowl and let stand for at least 1 hour, or preferably overnight.

2 *If using fresh grape leaves,* bring a large pot of water to a boil over high heat. Drop in the leaves, pressing down to submerge them, and blanch until they are no longer bright green, about 2 minutes. Drain immediately, rinse in cool water, and gently squeeze out the excess liquid. Set aside.

## GRAPE LEAF TRICKS

S ince bottled grape leaves come in stacks with the leaves cupped together facing the same direction, you can cut off the stems from an entire stack at one time before separating the leaves for filling. For fresh grape leaves, you need to trim each leaf individually, either before or after blanching.

When filling and rolling the *dolmadakia,* work around any minor holes or tears by overlapping or tucking the leaf in a creative way as you go. Use leaves with major tears, or ones that are too small to roll easily, for lining the pan.

Every now and then, you will have a leaf that tears completely or just won't cooperate as you roll it. Shake out the filling and use the rascal along with the other torn leaves to line or top the pan.

*If using bottled grape leaves,* remove them from the jar gently to avoid tearing, and squeeze out the excess liquid. Set aside.

3 Heat the oil in a medium-size skillet over medium-high heat. Add the rice, onion, garlic, pine nuts, zest, and salt, reduce the heat to medium, and sauté until the onion is transparent, about 5 minutes. Add the currants and raisins, with their liquid, and sauté until the liquid has mostly evaporated, about 3 minutes. (The rice will not be cooked through.) Remove from the heat and stir in the dill and mint leaves.

4 Line the bottom and sides of a medium-size pot or sauté pan with torn or extra grape leaves and some of the reserved dill and mint stems.

5 On a counter, lay out as many grape leaves, veined side up, as you have room for. Place about $1/2$ tablespoon of the rice mixture near the stem end of each leaf. Roll the bottom of the leaf up over the stuffing. Then fold in the sides of the leaf to partially enclose the filling. Continue rolling to completely enclose the filling, forming a stubby cylinder.

6 As you fill and roll the leaves, tightly pack the *dolmadakia,* leaf tip down, in the pan, forming concentric circles until the bottom is completely covered. When one layer is complete, make a second layer.

7 Continue stuffing, rolling, and tightly packing the leaves until all the stuffing is used. Try to keep the top layer as even and flat as

**FOLDING A GRAPE LEAF**

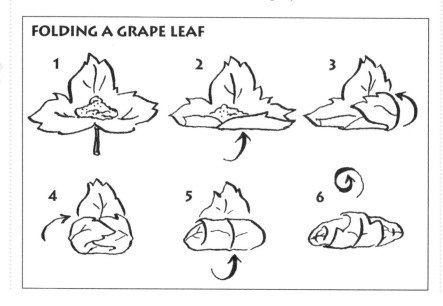

possible, even if it is not complete. Cover the top layer with the remaining dill and mint stems and any extra grape leaves.

8 Fill the pan with enough water to barely cover the leaves. Pour the lemon juice over all. Weight down the *dolmadakia* with a heavy plate or a slightly smaller pan partially filled with water. Set the pan on the stove and bring to a boil over medium heat. Reduce the heat and simmer until the rice is tender, 1 hour. Remove, taste a *dolma* to make sure the rice is done, and allow to cool.

9 When the *dolmadakia* are cool enough to handle, carefully pour off the liquid, pressing down on the leaves slightly to extract the excess liquid. Chill until completely cool.

10 Present the *dolmadakia* in their cooking pan if it is attractive, or arrange them nicely on a platter. Garnish with the lemon slices and serve.

## NOTES:

■ You can produce equally fine *dolmadakia* in less time by precooking the rice. Add the cooked rice to the sautéed ingredients, mix well, and set aside until cool enough to

### KEEPING WINE-INFUSED CURRANTS AND RAISINS AT HAND

Wine-enhanced currants and raisins add an extra dash of flavor, and in Greek cooking I use lots of them, so I keep a supply soaking in the refrigerator. Generally I have on hand a container of currants, one of golden raisins, and one of dark raisins, all in tart retsina, for appetizer and entree dishes. I also keep a set of the three soaking in a sweet muscat-style Greek wine, such as Mavrodaphne, for dessert dishes. They can be soaked in regular dry and sweet white wines as well. The process could not be simpler: Place a cupful or two of the fruit in a glass or plastic container that has a good lid. Pour in enough wine of choice to cover the fruit by 1/4 inch or so, seal with the lid, and refrigerate.

The wine-soaked fruit will store for months. As I scoop out the currants or raisins I need for a recipe, I add more dried fruit. In due time, I use the very fruity wine collected at the bottom of the container as a dessert flavoring.

handle. Fill, roll, and pack the *dolmadakia* as described above, using 1 tablespoon of the rice mixture instead of 1/2 tablespoon. Weight and cook as described, simmering for 10 minutes only.

■ Though using a round pan and placing the grape leaves in concentric circles is both traditional and most amenable to weighting down with a heavy plate, you can use a rectangular or square pan and layer the leaves in rows if you have a slightly smaller, similarly shaped object to place on top of the leaves to hold them down during cooking.

■ If you don't have enough *dolmades* to completely fill a second or third tightly packed layer, a partial one will do as long as the plate or pan you use for weighting covers the top layer well enough to keep individual *dolmades* from floating up and breaking apart during cooking.

■ Rice and raisin–filled appetizer *dolmadakia* keep well for several days, so you can successfully make them ahead of time for a big party. After cooling and pouring off the liquid, cover them well with plastic wrap so they don't dry out, and store in the refrigerator until ready to serve.

# a mix of mushrooms

## MARINATED IN WINE, FENNEL, AND THYME

### MAKES 2½ CUPS

THE APPEARANCE OF MUSHROOMS POPPING UP IN THE WOODS AND HILLS PERPLEXED THE ANCIENT GREEKS. HOW COULD SOMETHING THAT WAS GATHERED UP SO FAST THAT IT HAD NO TIME TO FLOWER STILL ARISE AGAIN YEAR AFTER YEAR? DIOSCORIDES, A GREEK DOCTOR AND PHARMACOLOGIST WHO LIVED IN THE FIRST CENTURY C.E., DECIDED HE HAD THE ANSWER: MUSHROOMS, HE MUSED, ARISE FROM SPONTANEOUS GENERATION; JUST BOOM, AND THERE THEY ARE, NO BLOSSOMS AND NO SPORES.

While Dioscorides's musings were a bit amiss, his speculation reveals just how interested the early Greeks were in succulent fungi, especially truffles and certain rare mountain mushrooms. The devotion lasts. The Greeks are so famous for their mushroom cooking that one preparation crept into French cuisine

*A hilltop village in Mani, where mushrooms spring up beneath the olive trees.*

## PICKLED MUSHROOMS

To keep the bounty on hand all year, taverns, shops, and households in Greece often pickle the mushrooms. It's a treat to walk into a store and see mushrooms displayed in rustic crocks or big glass jars, or to have a host or hostess bring you some with a glass of ouzo. With the dots of fennel and thyme, equally pickled, they are indeed a *meze* to offer your favorite guest. They are best using commercial button mushrooms, rather than delicate wild ones.

Replace the wine in the marinated mushrooms recipe with 1 cup white wine vinegar, and mix together all the ingredients except the mushrooms in a small saucepan. Bring to a boil over high heat, add the mushrooms, lower the heat, and simmer, stirring occasionally, until just softened, about 5 minutes. Allow to cool to room temperature; place in jars and refrigerate for 1 week before serving. They will keep for 2 weeks in the refrigerator.

as *Mushrooms à la Grecque.* No reason to stray from a simple treatment that garnered such an international laurel. When sautéed in what becomes their marinade—oil, wine, lemon, and garlic, touched with fennel and thyme—the mushrooms can be served hot or cold.

*¹/₂ cup olive oil*

*1 pound fresh porcini, cremini, or
commercial button mushrooms,
stemmed, rinsed, and patted dry*

*2 tablespoons fresh lemon juice*

*2 large cloves garlic, coarsely
chopped*

*¹/₄ cup dry white wine*

*¹/₄ cup thinly sliced fresh fennel
stalk and fronds, or ¹/₄ cup thinly
sliced celery plus 2 small pinches
of anise seeds*

*¹/₂ teaspoon fresh thyme leaves,
or ¹/₄ teaspoon dried*

*¹/₄ teaspoon salt*

*¹/₄ teaspoon freshly ground
black pepper*

**1** Heat the oil in a large non-reactive skillet over medium-high heat. Add all the remaining ingredients and cook, stirring from time to time, until the mushrooms are slightly collapsed, 6 to 8 minutes, depending on the size. Remove from the heat and allow to cool.

**2** Transfer the mixture to a bowl or jar and refrigerate for at least 1 hour, or as long as overnight, for the flavors to blend. Serve cold or reheat for a hot hors d'oeuvre.

**NOTE:** Some Greek cooks add a little chopped tomato to their marinated mushrooms.

## ONE WHO DIDN'T EAT *MEZE* WHILE DRINKING . . .

**. . . A**nd one who did. Alexander the Great and his father, Philip, came from Macedonia, and presumably both loved to eat the wild mushrooms that still proliferate in that rugged region.

They also both loved wine—Philip perhaps overly so. It seems he didn't temper his drinking with little nibbles of food as Greeks believe one should. Alexander once described his father as a man who was able to peregrinate to Persia and conquer it, but who got lost making his way from couch to couch at a banquet.

Later, some of Alexander's followers said he too drank prodigiously—especially after he too peregrinated to Persia, where he took up Persian dress and courtly manners. But Plutarch says no: Alexander was not so much a wine drinker as a talker whose pursuit of conversation led him to spend protracted lengths of time dining. With each cup it was his habit to start a new topic of discussion, so it was really the talk more than the potable that poured on. Possibly he sampled the mushrooms that grew in his homeland as he chatted. If so, Alexander was, indeed, very Greek, for no people have so perfected combining the art of conversation with a sip of drink and a little morsel to munch.

# INVITING MEAT MEZEDES

# little herbed meatballs

## KEFTEDAKIA

### MAKES 50 WALNUT-SIZE MEATBALLS

TWO WORDS DESCRIBE THE APPETIZER MEATBALL IN GREECE: "UBIQUITOUS" AND "DELICIOUS." MEATBALLS, OR *KEFTEDES*, ROLL ONTO APPETIZER PLATES FROM COAST TO MOUNTAIN, ISLAND TO MAINLAND, PARTY TO TAVERN, DAILY DINNER TO GALA FEAST. *KEFTEDES* DISAPPEAR FROM THE PLATTERS IN THE BLINK OF AN EYE.

Made of *kima,* or ground meat, they may be lamb, though beef is more common and is a meat almost any *tsepi,* or "pocket," can afford. *Keftedes* are sometimes the only meat on the *meze* table, and they are relished. Of course, being Greek meatballs, they are never made of just plain meat. Rather, the meat is keenly flavored with dashes of herb rounded out with onion and oil-soaked bread. Here a touch of sharp and milky Greek cheese adds extra relish, and as a special finish the meatballs are spun in one of three Greek-style coatings, all ancient: blanched almonds, crunchy bulgur, woody hazelnuts or walnuts.

*1/2 large onion, minced*

*1 1/2 tablespoons water*

*1/2 tablespoon olive oil*

*3 slices (1/2-inch-thick) good Greek or other crusty bread, crust removed*

*12 ounces ground beef or lamb*

*1 1/2 tablespoons good grated cheese, such as kefalotyri, kefalograviera, or kasseri*

*1/4 cup chopped fresh mint leaves*

*1/4 cup chopped fresh flat-leaf parsley leaves*

*1 teaspoon chopped fresh oregano leaves, or 1/2 teaspoon dried*

*1/2 tablespoon red wine vinegar*

*3/4 teaspoon salt*

*1/4 teaspoon freshly ground black pepper*

To the Greek mind, there is no treat quite like meat. It is of the highest order when the meat is roasted whole on a spit; it is prized in a stew; or when strung, tender pieces one by one, upon a skewer and grilled; or when rolled into patties, loaves, and balls. Meat is the most esteemed of foods, a luxury, and often a rarity.

And so, when even a bit of meat is offered as companion to a drink, the honoree—duly flattered—sighs in exclamation, breaks into a smile, and takes the treasure to mouth.

Because meat signifies sumptuousness in Greece and is so highly prized, no *meze* pleases quite the way a meat *meze* does. The portion needn't be much—indeed, shouldn't be. Just a tender meatball, a few slices of piquant sausage, a delicate bit of liver, will do.

To offer a meat *meze* is to say to your guest, your customer, your friend, "I value you—please have a taste of my appreciation."

*1/2 cup finely chopped blanched almonds, or 1/2 cup fine or coarsely ground bulgur wheat, or 1 cup finely crushed hazelnuts or walnuts*

*1/2 cup flour (see Notes)*

*Oil, for frying*

*Fresh mint or flat-leaf parsley leaves, for garnish*

1 Place the onion, water, and the ½ tablespoon oil in a small saucepan and bring to a boil over high heat. Reduce the heat and simmer until the water has evaporated, about 5 minutes.

2 Place the bread in a bowl, add water to cover, and let soak until soft. Remove the bread and squeeze it dry.

3 Mix together the onion mixture, bread, meat, cheese, chopped herbs, vinegar, salt, and pepper in a large bowl. Cover with plastic wrap, patting it down to seal out the air, and refrigerate for at least 4 hours or up to 2 days.

4 When ready to cook, roll the meat mixture with your hands into balls the size of large walnuts. Spread the almonds or bulgur on one plate and the flour on another. Roll the meatballs in the almonds or bulgur, then in the flour. If you are using hazelnuts or walnuts, spread them on a plate and roll the meatballs in them.

5 Pour oil to a depth of ½ inch into a large skillet and heat over medium-high heat. Sauté as many meatballs as will fit in one uncrowded layer until lightly browned all over, about 4 minutes. Transfer them to a paper towel to drain, and repeat until all the meatballs are cooked.

6 Place a toothpick in each meatball and arrange them on a plate. Garnish with the mint leaves, and serve.

## NOTES:

■ If using hazelnuts or walnuts, omit the flour.

■ Meatballs are almost always cooked ahead and served later at room temperature.

■ Meatballs are often also served as part of the selection of dishes for the main meal.

# MENU
## AN EXCELLENT MEZE TABLE

CRUSTY BREAD, OLIVES, AND CHEESE

ANCHOVIES

ROASTED SWEET PEPPER SALAD
(page 39)

SANTORINI FAVA CROQUETTES SUSANNA-STYLE
(page 292)

A MIX OF MUSHROOMS MARINATED IN WINE, FENNEL, AND THYME
(page 50)

LITTLE HERBED MEATBALLS
(facing page)

MARINATED SHRIMP CRETAN-STYLE
(page 64)

FIELD GREENS, FENNEL, AND OUZO PIE
(page 93)

CHICKPEA AND SESAME SPREAD
(page 42)

# little skewers of meat

## WITH GRILLED BREAD

### SOUVLAKIA

#### MAKES SIX 4½-INCH SKEWERS

THESE ARE THE SIGHTS AND SOUNDS OF A SUMMER SUNDAY EVENING IN A GREEK VILLAGE: CHILDREN, COINS IN HAND, RUN UP TO THE KITCHEN WINDOW OF THE *TAVERNA* TO BUY THEMSELVES A *SOUVLAKI*. FATHERS, OFF FROM WORK, SIT ON THE *TAVERNA* PORCH, LAUGHING AND BANTERING. DICE CLICK ACROSS THEIR BACKGAMMON BOARDS. MOTHERS, THEIR COOKING DONE FOR THE WEEK, HAVE GATHERED AT THE CORNER OF THE SQUARE AND SOON THEY, TOO, DRIFT TO THE *TAVERNA* VERANDA. A FEW BEERS ARE ORDERED, MAKING A *MEZE* NECESSARY. ONE OR TWO MEN ORDER PLATES OF A DOZEN OR SO *SOUVLAKI* FOR ALL TO SHARE.

In the *taverna* kitchen, the owner and his wife string bits of marinated meat on short metal or bamboo skewers. They place the skewers on a grill, sizzle the meat juicy, stick a grill-toasted piece of bread on the end of the *souvla*, squirt on a brisk spurt of fresh lemon, and hand them over. The sun takes forever to set, fading away in slowly softening pinks and azures. Electric lights switch on or the kerosene lamp is pumped and lit. A tape of popular tunes is snapped into a tape deck. Children sidle onto laps, and life is good.

While big skewers of meat on long metal *souvla* swords come with bravado to the dinner table, little ones—here with bay leaf as well as oregano—make for satisfying snacks. Served as such, they make any day a summer Sunday in Greece.

## LITTLE SWORDS

When ancient Greeks sacrificed animals to the gods, those animals met their end with a sword, assuming the man slaughtering the beast was any sort of warrior. Knives were for butchers; swords were for soldiers, cavaliers, or kings.

To consume the sacrifice, the ancient Greeks then divided the animal into *ostrea*, the bones, and *krea*, the meat. They used the bones for fuel and sectioned the meat into the *meria*, the "fatty thigh," and the *splankhna*, or viscera. The viscera were eaten first; the organ meats were put on swords and roasted over a fire. The *meria* was placed on an altar to be consumed by the altar fire. Without swords for the viscera part of the ceremony, no sacrifice could take place (which is one way the ancient Greeks determined that the Scythians were barbarians—they didn't use their swords as skewers). Placing the sacrificial meats on a sword also made the apportioning egalitarian: Slipping bits off the sword, all those attending received a portion.

Meat sacrifice is long gone, but the tool used has, in somewhat changed form and diminished size, stayed on. The Greek word for skewer, *souvla*, means "sword," and to eat a *souvlaki* means to eat a "little sword."

12 ounces lean beef, lamb,
or pork
1/4 cup olive oil
2 tablespoons fresh lemon juice
1 teaspoon chopped fresh oregano
leaves, or 1/4 teaspoon dried
(see Notes)
1 bay leaf, crumbled
1/2 teaspoon salt
1/4 teaspoon freshly ground
black pepper
3 thick (1-inch) slices good Greek or
other crusty bread, or 3 pitas
Olive oil, for moistening the bread
6 lemon wedges

**1** Cut the meat into 3/4-inch
cubes, trimming off most—but
not all—of the fat (see Notes).
String enough meat on each
of six small skewers to stretch
4 1/2 inches, leaving an inch
or two of space at the
pointed end of the skewer.

**2** Mix together the
1/4 cup oil, the lemon juice,
oregano, bay leaf, salt, and
pepper in a nonreactive dish
that is large enough to hold
the skewers. Place the skewers
of meat in the marinade and
turn to coat. Cover and set
aside in the refrigerator for
1 hour, or up to overnight,
turning occasionally.

**3** When ready to cook, heat a
grill to medium-high or heat a
griddle. Cut each slice of bread
into 6 pieces, or if using pitas,
cut each one into 6 triangles.

**4** Place the skewers on the grill
rack directly above the coals, or
on the griddle. Cook for 3 to
4 minutes, turn, and cook until
done, 3 to 4 minutes more,
taking care not to overcook the
meat.

**5** While the meat is cooking,
moisten the bread or pita lightly
with oil and place it on the grill
or griddle. Toast until brown
all around, about 30 seconds
per side.

**6** To serve, spear 2 to 3 pieces
of bread or pita on the tip of each
skewer. Squeeze the juice from
1 lemon wedge over each skewer,
and offer it to awaiting hands.
Or place the *souvlakia* on plates
and garnish with lemon wedges.

## NOTES:

■ Many Greeks make their
*souvlaki* marinade very strongly
flavored with oregano. To do so,
use dried oregano.

■ Good *souvlaki* meat has a little
fat left from the trimming so that
it sizzles. In fact, some *souvlaki*
makers string 1 or 2 bits of fat
between meat chunks to add
flavor.

*Old signs from a seaside
restaurant that offered up an array
of* souvlakia.

# ZEUS, KING OF THE GODS

AS THE GREEKS STREAMED INTO THE LAND THAT WAS TO BECOME THEIRS, THEY BROUGHT WITH THEM A DEITY ALL THEIR OWN, A GOD WHOSE NAME MEANT "SKY," AS IN "THE DAY" OR "DAYLIGHT."

He was Zeus, powerful and mighty, patriarch and protector of his followers, and he soon took his seat as master of all the divinities. He overthrew his tyrannical father, Kronos, god of the Titans, set free his brothers and sisters, and though they were as mighty as he, took over their command.

On his breast Zeus wore a goatskin shield called the Aegis. Its border was entwined with serpents, its center set with a horrible Gorgon's head, which killed all who looked upon it. To this day Zeus's shield remains a symbol of protection and majesty. His bird was the eagle, his tree the oak. He was also called the Rain God and Cloud Gatherer. He came with the Greeks from a land where storms were violent, and he remained a weather god. From his aerie atop cloud-shrouded Mount Olympus, he rained thunderbolts upon the world. Lightning still shoots out from his peak.

Zeus was both idol and image of the Greeks. He was a demanding god, a warrior, and fierce. He could mete out cruel punishments. Yet he was a family man, ever sorting out the intrigues among his kin, ever arbitrating fights among deities and men. As a king himself, he was the special defender of rulers and fought on their behalf. Yet he defended cities and their populations as well. He safeguarded strangers and travelers and harshly punished those who broke the law of hospitality—a law that Greeks still heed. He watched over property and held households to be havens, and should a man ask for immunity from crime or sanctuary at a temple, his pursuers met the wrath of Zeus. He was called "savior."

But, like the men he guarded, he had foibles. In particular he was a terrible womanizer. He married three times—Greeks never were polygamous, but they could marry again and again, and Zeus certainly did. And when finally united with his sister Hera, he could not keep his eyes off nubile maidens divine and mortal. In the form of a bull, Zeus chased the fair Europa, who fled up the continent that now bears her name. He slept with one of the Pleiades. He dallied with his sister Aphrodite. He chased Niobe, the princess of Argos, and seduced Io, who bore him Epaphus, the ancestor of the kings of Egypt. He bedded Leda, mother of Helen of Troy, and Leto, who gave him the twins Apollo and Artemis. He fathered Herakles, the hero who saved the gods, and trifled with Semele, who bore him Dionysos.

Still, despite his peccadillos, Zeus was just too awesome not to worship, and as the god of herding folk, the best way to worship him was to give him meat, that tastiest, most esteemed of foods. (Because his mother had grown tired of his arrogant ways and tried to poison him with an herb, Zeus was rather disinclined toward vegetables.) He was partial to the fat loin of beef, but he didn't look askance at delicacies like liver. He was, in fact, quite aware of how tender liver is. He punished Prometheus for giving mankind fire with an eternity of having his liver pecked by birds. Better to have the liver delicately sautéed and served with an ouzo.

*Zeus, whose usual symbols were the eagle, the oak tree, and thunderbolts, sometimes carried Winged Victory— Nike.*

# marinated lamb's liver

### SERVES 6

THE EARLIEST GREEKS, ARRIVING FROM THE NORTH WITH THEIR SKY GOD, CHARIOTS, AND HERDS OF CATTLE, HAD A REVERENCE AND TASTE FOR MEAT. CERTAIN PIECES WERE CONSIDERED PARTICULARLY SUBLIME, BOTH TO OFFER TO THE GODS, ESPECIALLY ZEUS, AND TO EAT. ONE WAS THE SUCCULENT LIVER. THE FAVORED MEAT OF GREECE EVENTUALLY BECAME LAMB, AND TODAY GREEKS, MUCH AS IN THE PAST, DEEM LAMB'S LIVER A TRUE DELICACY—SO MUCH SO THAT THEY ALMOST ALWAYS PREPARE IT SIMMERED IN WINE TINGED WITH GARLIC AND OREGANO, AND SERVE IT IN LITTLE PIECES AS *MEZE*.

You can order a lamb's liver from almost any good butcher with a day's notice. To make it ambrosial, it can be marinated two different ways, one more subtle with white wine, the other sharper with vinegar. Cooking the piece whole and cutting it after cooking also keeps the liver more succulent.

*2 tablespoons olive oil*
*3 cloves garlic, minced or pressed*
*1 teaspoon chopped fresh oregano leaves, or 1/4 teaspoon dried*
*1/4 cup white wine plus 2 tablespoons fresh lemon juice, or 1/4 cup red wine vinegar*
*1/2 teaspoon salt*
*1/4 teaspoon freshly ground black pepper*
*12 ounces lamb's liver, sliced 1/2 inch thick*
*Olive oil*
*1 1/2 teaspoons chopped fresh marjoram leaves, or 1/2 teaspoon dried (optional)*
*1 lemon, cut into 6 wedges*

1 Combine the 2 tablespoons oil, the garlic, oregano, wine and lemon juice mixture, salt, and pepper in a bowl that is large enough to hold the liver. Add the liver and turn to coat it all over. Marinate, covered, in the refrigerator for several hours or up to overnight, turning once or twice.

2 When ready to cook, lightly oil a large nonreactive skillet, and heat over medium-high heat. Add the liver, reduce the heat to medium, and sauté for 2 1/2 minutes. Turn and cook 1 1/2 minutes more. Add the marinade to the pan, turning the liver to coat both sides, and cook 1 minute more. Remove from the heat and let sit for 5 to 10 minutes.

3 Cut the liver into bite-size pieces. Transfer to a serving plate and pour the juices from the pan over the pieces. Sprinkle the marjoram, if using, over the top. Serve right away, accompanied by lemon wedges.

## NOTES:

■ The amount in this recipe makes enough for an appetizer. To serve as a main dish, use the entire lamb's liver, 1 to 1 1/2 pounds, and double the marinade.

■ Bite-size pieces of lamb's liver can also be wrapped in a package of flaky filo, as in meat *bourekakia* (page 108), to make a *meze* that is doubly notable.

# sausage slices

## TOPPED WITH OLIVE AND CAPER TAPENADE

### LOUKANIKA

**SERVES 6**

THE MODERN GREEK WORD FOR SAUSAGE, *LOUKANIKA*, REFERS TO THE LUGANO REGION OF ITALY, FROM WHEN LATIN AND GREEK OFTEN SHARED NOT ONLY FOODS BUT ALSO FOOD WORDS. THE WORD "SAUSAGE" ITSELF DERIVES FROM THE SHARED ANCIENT GREEK AND LATIN WORD *ISICIA* (THE NAME OF A SORT OF GRECO-ROMAN HAMBURGER), WHICH, WITH THE ADDED PREFIX FOR SALT, BECAME *SALSICIA* AND REFERRED TO A SPECIAL "SALT SAUSAGE." THERE IS A POPULAR FAVORITE SAUSAGE TODAY THAT STILL SHOWS THE ADORATION OF THE ZESTY TREAT: SALAMI. THOUGHT TO BE ITALIAN, SALAMI ACTUALLY GETS ITS NAME FROM THE GREEK ISLAND IN THE SARDONIC GULF FAMOUS FOR ITS SALT MINE: SALAMIS.

*10 ounces uncooked loukanika (page 400), or other good sausage (see Note)*

*1/4 cup Olive and Caper Tapenade (page 477)*

*4 thick slices good Greek or other bread*

1 Heat a grill to high (or use the stove).

2 Cook the sausage on the grill, or on the stove in a lightly greased skillet over medium heat, turning once, until done, 12 to 20 minutes depending on the kind and thickness of the sausage.

3 Cut the sausages into 1/4- to 1/2-inch-thick slices and arrange them on a serving plate. Spread about 1/2 teaspoon of the tapenade on each slice and spear each with a toothpick. Cut the bread slices into 6 to 8 bite-size pieces each. Arrange on the plate around the sausage, and serve.

**NOTE:** Greeks also serve sliced salami-type sausage as

## WHAT WAS SAUSAGE FOR THE SPARTAN . . .

The tradition of mixing meats and fat with sharp flavorings goes way back in Greek cooking, though apparently with less tasty results than today's versions. The Spartans, famed for their rigorous austerity and unflinching bravery, were reputed to mix together such a concoction almost daily. It was called *melas zomos*, or black broth, and it was as famous—or in this case infamous—as they were. Plutarch said it tasted terrible. Still, the valor of the Spartans was so illustrious that many thought it might be due to the famous dish.

In order to taste *melas zomos* and hopefully gain valor from it, Dionysius, king of a Greek colony in Sicily, imported a Spartan cook to prepare it. The stuff was so vile he spat it out. Reprimanded for serving such a travesty, the cook explained that the two main seasonings were missing, the very ones that made the concoction taste so good to the Spartans. What were they? asked Dionysius, thinking to redeem the dish. Hunger and thirst, the cook replied. Dionysius decided to forgo the preparation and, especially, the necessary ingredients.

*mezedes.* They can be served plain, but a topping of olive and caper spread gives the palate still more to enjoy.

# MEZEDES FROM THE SEA

# little fried fish

## IN A LEMON AND RETSINA BATH

### MARIDES

**SERVES 6**

THE MEDITERRANEAN, AEGEAN, AND IONIAN SEAS ARE AS WARM AS INCUBATORS. THEY ARE ALSO QUITE SHALLOW AND BUOYANTLY SALTY. LIKE THREE NURTURING MOTHERS, THEY FOSTER A STUPENDOUS ARRAY OF FISH: FLOUNDER, SOLE, TURBOT, WHITING, CONGERS, CROAKERS, RED MULLET, GOBIES, GUNNARDS, LIZARD FISH, REDFISH, SEA BASS, GROUPERS, COMBERS, SEA BREAMS, JACKS, SHARKS, RAYS, AND SKATES. THE FISHERMEN'S NETS ALSO PULL IN MANY SMALL FISH, CALLED COLLECTIVELY *MARIDES*, WHAT WE CALL "WHITEBAIT."

The aroma of the sea pervades Greece. You can smell the water, the salt, and the kelp even on the most remote mountaintop. And everywhere you can sample the fruits of the sea—the fish and the shellfish.

It follows that Greeks have long considered even a single taste of these briny treats an epicurean delight: one perfectly fresh, finger-long fried fish, one salty anchovy, one urchin or periwinkle, a ring or two of *kalamari*, a slice of pink-and-white octopus. A little munch of any such sea creature to partner a glass of *tsikoudia*, ouzo, wine, beer falls among the most praiseworthy of appetizers.

Not to waste these little fish, Greeks fry them up and eat them, bone and all, as *mezedes*. Virtually tons of the battered little fish swarm across the appetizer plates of the land, to be popped in the mouth whole. Some people eat the heads; some leave them. In some places three are held together at the tail, battered together, and fried in the shape of a fan. Greeks use a flour batter, but I prefer a semolina or cornmeal crust for extra crispness. A bath of lemon combined with retsina wakes them up and gives them a fragrance of the Greek hills. The fish must be very fresh; otherwise they lose flavor. Most American fishmongers

*A catch of sardines awaits the frying pan.*

carry fresh whitebait or can easily get it. For a card game, a sports final, a party, I suggest frying up and serving a batch piled as high as Mount Ossa.

*1 pound tiny fish, such as smelt
   or whitebait*
*¹/₂ cup cornmeal or fine
   semolina flour*
*¹/₂ teaspoon salt*
*Olive oil, for frying*
*2 tablespoons fresh lemon juice*
*2 teaspoons finely shredded
   lemon zest*
*3 tablespoons retsina wine*
*1 teaspoon chopped fresh oregano
   leaves, or ¹/₄ teaspoon dried*

1 Rinse the fish and pat them dry. (There is no need to gut them.) On a plate, mix together the cornmeal and salt. Dredge the fish in the mixture, coating each one well.

2 Pour oil to a depth of ¹/₄ inch into a large skillet and heat it over high heat until hot. Add enough fish to fit in one uncrowded layer, reduce the heat to medium-high, and fry for 1¹/₂ minutes. Turn and fry on the other side until lightly golden and crisp all over, 1¹/₂ minutes. Transfer the fish to paper towels to drain, and repeat with another batch until all the fish are fried.

3 In a small bowl, mix together the lemon juice, zest, retsina, and oregano.

4 Place the fried fish on individual plates or on a platter. Pour the lemon-retsina mixture over them and serve right away, while still warm and crisp.

## NOTES:

■ While in Greece little fish are frequently cooked ahead of time and served at room temperature, they are better served crisp and hot. If you must cook them early, don't dress them with the lemon-retsina bath until just before serving.

## WHERE TO GET THE BEST MARIDES, THEN AND NOW

• • • • • • • • • • • • •

V alue as "trash" all small fry except the Athenian kind. . . . Get it when fresh and caught in the beautiful Faleron bay, in its sacred arms. . . . And if you should desire to taste it, you should buy at the same time sea nettles, the ones with long locks. Mix them together and bake them in a frying pan, grinding the fragrant flowers of the greens in oil.

**—ARCHESTRATOS,
FOURTH CENTURY** B.C.E.

■ Heaping plates of *marides* are also served among dinner offerings.

## SALTING THE APPETITE

**S**alt, the seasoning that makes anchovies so smackingly desirable, is without a doubt the most widely used taste accent of all time. Worldwide it is sprinkled abundantly on all sorts of edibles, as both taste enhancer and preservative. No one knows when or why the taste for it began, but by Neolithic times people were mining salt deposits. Greeks were certainly using it early, although at first salt was a minor seasoning in Greece. Honey, rather, was the primary flavoring. At some point, however, Greeks and others discovered the effects of salting olives and certain other foods, and then salt became a much-used seasoner. The taste for salt also spread with the use of *garos,* the sauce made from fermented, and very salty, fish, probably often anchovies. On the heels of both olive and *garos,* the mining of salt for a condiment expanded steadily throughout Greek times.

By the fifth century the salting of whole fish was widespread. Still, Socrates mentions salt as a luxury, to go with grains, as if it were a bit of meat or vegetable. And indeed, salt was not easy to get. Much came from the island of Salamis, whose name to this day implies how once it was a major source of the substance. Galen later describes fry cakes that were sometimes dusted with salt, as the Greeks still do, making what might have been the first pretzel.

Today we consider the taste of salt an appetite awakener, and we look to our snacks and hors d'oeuvres to stand out with salt's indescribable influence.

# anchovies

## IN OIL AND VINEGAR

### ANTZOUGIA

**✳ SERVES 6**

**H**OW LONG HAVE GREEKS SNACKED ON SALTED ANCHOVIES? WHEN KING NIKOMEDES OF BITHYNIA, NEAR THE PONTOS, WAS TOO FAR FROM THE SEA AND HIS STOCK OF THE BRINY APPETIZER DIMINISHED, HIS CREATIVE CHEF, SOTERIDES, PERHAPS IN FEAR OF LOSING HIS HEAD, CARVED A TURNIP IN THE SHAPE OF THE LITTLE FISH, BOILED IT, DUNKED IT IN OIL, THEN DUSTED IT HEAVILY WITH SALT AND PRESSED EXACTLY FORTY POPPYSEEDS ALL OVER IT TO MIRROR SPINE, FIN, AND GILLS.

Soterides went on to become a famous chef, although no legend of his other, no doubt equally brilliant, innovations remains. Apparently Nikomedes, like other Greeks, so adored anchovies with his drinks that fake ones were better than none.

Luckily, anchovies are still abundantly available. They can be purchased salt-packed or canned in oil; for a *meze,* the salt-packed ones, with their crystal coating, are preferable. Rinse them well, revitalize them in a sea of oil,

*For millennia, silvery anchovies have been caught, salted or oiled, and sent to near and far shores.*

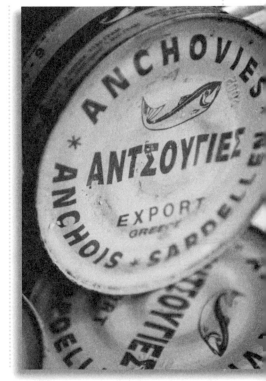

lemon, and vinegar, and they will be great with a glass of retsina or anise-flavor ouzo. No diner of Greek sensibility need settle for sculpted turnip again.

*18 whole salt-packed anchovies (see Note)*
*2 1/2 tablespoons olive oil*
*1 teaspoon fresh lemon juice*
*1 teaspoon red wine vinegar*
*2 teaspoons chopped fresh flat-leaf parsley leaves*
*Crusty bread, for serving*

1 Rinse the anchovies well, rubbing off the salt with your fingers. Gently pull the anchovies apart lengthwise, removing the head and backbone as you go, to make two fillets out of each. Rinse the fillets and pat them dry.

2 Arrange the anchovies on a small platter. Drizzle the oil, lemon juice, and vinegar over them, and sprinkle the parsley on the top. Serve with hunks of bread.

**NOTE:** Salt-packed anchovies are available in many gourmet food shops. If you can't find them, you can substitute anchovy fillets packed in olive oil. Depending on your taste, use the oil in the tin or drain the anchovies and dress them with fresh olive oil.

# fried squid
## IN PARSLEY AND LEMON BATTER
### KALAMARAKIA
**SERVES 6**

THE ITALIANS SERVE THEM WITH MARINARA SAUCE. IN CALIFORNIA THEY COME WITH FLAVORED MAYOS AND TARTARS. IN THE SOUTHWEST A CORNMEAL BATTER BEDECKS THEM. IN THAI RESTAURANTS THEY ARRIVE WITH A SWEET DIPPING SAUCE. NO SNACK, NO APPETIZER, NO *MEZE* HAS MOVED AROUND THE WORLD QUITE LIKE *KALAMARI*, BUT THE BEST *KALAMARI* APPETIZER IS STILL THE ORIGINAL—THE GREEK.

*Kalamari* are one of the most populous of seafoods, and the Mediterranean and its inlet seas teem with their own variety. They have been caught in the fishnets and served in Greece since the earliest times. Minoan and Mycenean vases and plates picture the tentacled sea creatures swimming against red and black backgrounds. In classical times, they were sizzled as a treat for celebrants at family rituals, such as baby namings. Cooks mixed and fried them up with small fish, *marides* (page 59), in heaping plates of "small fry." And while Greeks today have added a splash of lemon, they honor the forefathers with a treatment that echoes time: Batter them lightly, cook them quickly, serve them fresh, and add to them only a dash of brightener, for why alter a taste so delicate? Here lemon zest is added to the batter, complemented by a touch of parsley.

*3 pounds small squid, cleaned and bodies cut into narrow rings, tentacles left whole*
*1 cup all-purpose flour*
*1 cup chopped fresh flat-leaf parsley leaves*
*2 tablespoons coarsely chopped lemon zest*
*1/2 teaspoon salt*
*1/8 teaspoon cayenne pepper, or 1/4 teaspoon freshly ground white pepper*
*Olive or peanut oil, for frying*
*2 lemons, each cut into 6 wedges*

1 Rinse the cleaned squid and pat very dry. Mix the flour, parsley, zest, salt, and cayenne together in a large bowl. Add the squid and toss to coat well.

2 Pour oil to a depth of ½ inch into a large skillet and heat over medium-high heat until hot. Place as much squid in the pan as will fit in one uncrowded layer and fry until beginning to turn golden, about 30 seconds. Turn and fry on the other side until golden all over, about 30 seconds more. Transfer to paper towels to drain, and repeat until all the squid are fried, adding more oil and reheating to the smoking point as necessary.

3 Mound on a platter or individual plates, garnish with the lemon wedges, and serve right away.

## WHERE TO SHOP 'TIL YOU DROP IN ON SQUID

The central market of Athens, though it offers a vast array of fruit, vegetables, and meat, is modest in comparison to other famous city markets. It's not as enormous as Les Halles, not as intense a whirligig as the bazaar in Tangiers, and lacks the awesome scope of Guadalajara's free market. Nor is it a magnet for crowds. It lies not far from Omonia square, rather hidden, devoid of notoriety, and untramped by tourists.

The market is shaped somewhat like a concentric grid. Lining the perimeter, a ring of bargain clothiers sell housecoats, sweaters, baby bibs, denim work shirts, and the like. Within that loop comes the girth of butchers, where carcasses of cattle and sheep swing from overhead hooks and boisterous men shout jibes as they grind *kima*. Next come the vegetable stands, displaying a colorful paean to whatever the season may be, and beyond them sit banks of shiny fish, large and small, strewn upon ice-covered trays.

Inside all that hubbub there is yet another ring—a quiet courtyard sitting in the midst of it all—where you discover the cordon of *kalamari* vendors. It's tradition in the Athens market to take a pause and have a snack while in the whirlwind of shopping. And that snack is—must be—Greece's spectacular fried *kalamari*. Little marble-top round tables sparkle in sun-dappled shade. Each vendor has his deep-fryers sizzling. Waiters bring out plate after plate of the freshest *kalamari* possible, each scattered with handfuls of lemon wedges. Tasting circlet after circlet, the well-tempered shoppers heed a favorite Greek saying: Never be in a hurry to spend your money. Certainly not where *kalamari* beckons.

# marinated shrimp cretan-style

## IN SALTY LEMON DIP

### SERVES 6

## STILL GOOD ADVICE

Find the fattest shrimp in the market. Do not bother to haggle with the fishmongers. They are too independent and will ignore you. Order your cooks to boil the shrimp with salt, leaves from the bay tree, and marjoram. Serve hot on a fig leaf.

—ANANIOS, SIXTH CENTURY B.C.E.

THE ZEPHYRS OF CRETE ARE THE GENTLEST IN ALL GREECE. IN THE SUMMER THEY RISE NIGHTLY TO COOL THE PATRONS IN THE MANY OUTDOOR TAVERNS OF IRAKLION, HANIA, FAISTOS, AND AGIOS NIKOLAOS. NOWHERE IN GREECE IS THE TRADITION OF AN EVENING STOP AT THE *TAVERNA* FOR A DRINK AND A *MEZE* AS DEFINITIVE. AND NOWHERE ARE THE *MEZEDES* AS ORNATE, EXTRAVAGANT, AND SURPRISING.

I have never forgotten the taste of the huge pink shrimp that was nonchalantly served to me in a tiny *taverna* in Iraklion. How could the owner afford this? But his next *meze* was octopus, and his next liver. At other *tavernas,* the *mezedes* have been equally stunning, each a triumph for the *taverna* owner and a trophy for the customer. To duplicate that first fat shrimp is to harken back to Crete and its delights, both edible and climactic—whether you have been there or merely dreamed of it.

*1 cup dry white wine*

*¼ cup olive oil*

*4 cloves garlic, minced or pressed*

*¼ cup fresh flat-leaf parsley leaves, chopped or left whole*

*¾ teaspoon chopped fresh oregano leaves, or ¼ teaspoon dried*

*2 teaspoons fresh lemon juice*

*1 pound medium to large raw shrimp, shells on, deveined and rinsed (see Note)*

*2 tomatoes, each cut into 6 wedges*

*18 Kalamata, Amfissa, cracked green, or other good olives*

*⅓ cup Salty Lemon Dip (recipe follows)*

1 Place the wine, oil, garlic, parsley, oregano, and lemon juice in a nonreactive skillet or saucepan and bring to a boil over high heat. Add the shrimp, reduce the heat, and simmer, stirring, until the shrimp begin to turn pink, 1 ½ to 3 minutes, depending on the size. Transfer the shrimp and the cooking liquid to a bowl and refrigerate, covered, until well chilled, up to several hours.

2 When ready to serve, drain the shrimp. Divide them among individual plates, placing them tail up. Arrange the tomato wedges and olives around the shrimp. Drizzle the lemon dip over all, and serve right away.

**NOTE:** To clean shrimp in the shell, make a slit through the shell into the top of the shrimp from the head end down to the tail. Ease the shell apart with your fingers and remove and discard the dark vein.

## SALTY LEMON DIP

### MAKES 1/3 CUP

Joining salt and lemon doubles the relish of each alone, and gives restrained shrimp a bit of attitude.

*2 tablespoons fresh lemon juice*
*1/4 cup olive oil*
*1/2 teaspoon salt*
*1/2 teaspoon chopped fresh oregano leaves, or 1/4 teaspoon dried*
*1/4 teaspoon freshly ground white pepper*
*2 teaspoons chopped capers (optional)*

Whisk all the ingredients together in a small bowl, making sure to blend the salt thoroughly. Use right away or store, covered, in the refrigerator for up to 3 days.

# lemon-dressed chilled octopus or squid

### SERVES 6

A LIVELY OCTOPUS APPEARS ON A JAR FROM KNOSSOS, CIRCA 1500 B.C.E. IT HAS WILDLY FLOWING TENTACLES THAT SPLAY OUT ACROSS THE ENTIRE ROUND BELLY OF THE POT, SUCKERS LIKE BUTTONS RUNNING DOWN EACH, AND GREAT CARTOONLIKE EYES. IT IS PORTRAYED AS A FRIENDLY, AMIABLE BEAST, NOT AT ALL FEARSOME FOR A SEAMAN TO ENCOUNTER, AND CLEARLY A CATCH FOR THE CAULDRON.

Squid, the cousin of the friendly octopus, are rapturously described by ancient writers, who liked them salted, wined, dried, and pickled. Still today, when a kaïque pulls up on the sand with a windfall of octopus or squid, or when young boys out spearfishing nab either treasure from a rocky hideout, there's no hesitation. Immediately cooks relay the creature to the pot. Many do not make the journey to the main dinner course. They are too much savored as appetizers, especially when dressed simply but elegantly with lemon and oil.

*The octopus features prominently in Greece's meze as well as its art.*

*FOR THE OCTOPUS*

2 small fresh octopus
(1 to 1½ pounds each),
pounded and cleaned
(see sidebar), or 1½ pounds
precooked octopus, or
1½ pounds uncooked
squid steaks (see Notes)

*FOR THE SIMMERING
LIQUID*

2 tablespoons fresh lemon juice
2 tablespoons olive oil
1 teaspoon fresh oregano leaves,
or ½ teaspoon dried
½ teaspoon salt
1½ cups water

*FOR THE DRESSING*

2 tablespoons fresh lemon juice
2 tablespoons red wine vinegar
⅓ cup olive oil
½ cup chopped fresh flat-leaf
parsley leaves
1 teaspoon fresh oregano leaves,
or ½ teaspoon dried
½ teaspoon salt
¼ teaspoon freshly ground
white pepper
Parsley sprigs, olives, or capers,
for garnish

1 *If using uncooked octopus or
squid steaks,* place them in a large
pot. Add the ingredients for the
simmering liquid and bring to a
boil over high heat. Reduce the
heat and simmer, covered, until
tender, 45 minutes to 1 hour
for octopus, 2 to 3 minutes for
squid steaks. Drain in a colander
and set aside until cool enough
to handle.

*If using precooked octopus,*
go directly to Step 2.

2 Cut the octopus into ¼-inch-
thick slices. Cut squid steaks into
1-inch-wide strips.

3 In a large bowl, mix together
all the ingredients for the dressing. Add the octopus or squid,
tossing to coat thoroughly.
Refrigerate, covered, for several
hours or as long overnight.

4 To serve, transfer the octopus
or squid and dressing to a platter
or individual plates. Garnish with
parsley, olives, or capers.

## NOTES:

■ Many Japanese fish markets sell
cooked octopus by the tentacle.
When pressed for time or unable
to find fresh octopus, you can
substitute precooked octopus.

■ Juicy squid steaks, cut from
large squid, have recently become
available at many fish markets.

## PREPARING OCTOPUS

T hough readily available in
Greece, uncooked octopus
can be difficult to find in the United
States. The best sources are docks
where fishermen sell their catch directly,
seafood markets near piers, or Chinese
markets, which almost always have a
supply, fresh or frozen.

To prepare fresh or defrosted
frozen octopus for cooking, first pound
it with a mallet until it becomes pearly
gray, slightly translucent, and frothy,
about 5 minutes. Remove the head.
(Some cooks add the head, but be aware
that its texture and flavor are different
from the tentacles; if not removing the
head, clean it and remove the beak.)
If saving the ink sac for a stew or
pigment, remove it and rinse it well;
otherwise discard it.

Place the remaining body, with
tentacles, in a large pot and cook as
directed.

They usually come ¼ to ½ inch
thick. If yours are thicker, simmer
them a little longer. If you are
using large whole squid, clean
them, then tenderize them by
pounding as you would octopus.

# retsina-pickled octopus or squid

### SERVES 6

THOUGH LONG ILLEGAL, IN PRIOR YEARS THERE WAS MUCH DYNAMITING OF FISH IN GREECE, A PRACTICE THAT SEVERELY HARMED THE SEA LIFE. THERE WERE ALSO FISHING VESSELS CALLED *GRI-GRIS* THAT BADLY DAMAGED THE OCEAN'S ECOLOGY: A LARGE BOAT WOULD REEL OUT A STRING OF TINY DINGHIES BEHIND, LIKE A MOTHER GOOSE LEADING A LINE OF GOSLINGS. EACH OF THE SMALL VESSELS CARRIED A BRILLIANT LIGHT TO STUN THE FISH THAT SWAM NEARBY.

*Gri-gris* looked lovely from the shore, but their take was excessive. Greeks are far more aware now and have taken steps to ensure that all in the future will have the sorts of fish that

*Racks of octopus drying on the quay.*

past generations have enjoyed. Luckily for *meze* tables, squid and octopus have been among the first to return to their prior teeming numbers. To ensure that plenty would be available even when the fishermen didn't go out, Greeks have long pickled both octopus and squid. Retsina pickles with a special essence, the same one used to preserve wine long ago, that gives the treat a distinctive piney-ness.

*2 small fresh octopus*
*(1 to 1 1/2 pounds each), pounded and cleaned (see sidebar, page 66), or 1 1/2 pounds precooked octopus, or 1 1/2 pounds uncooked squid steaks*

### FOR THE SIMMERING LIQUID
*3/4 cup water*
*2 tablespoons olive oil*
*3/4 cup white wine vinegar*

### FOR THE PICKLING SOLUTION
*1/2 cup retsina wine*
*2 cloves garlic, chopped*
*1 small bay leaf, crushed*
*1 teaspoon chopped fresh fennel frond*
*1/2 teaspoon mustard seeds*
*1/4 teaspoon salt*
*1/8 teaspoon freshly ground black pepper*
*Parsley sprigs, olives, or capers, for garnish*

1 *If using uncooked octopus or squid steaks,* place them in a large pot. Add the ingredients for the simmering liquid and bring to a boil. Reduce the heat and simmer, covered, until tender, 45 minutes to 1 hour for octopus, 2 to 3 minutes for squid steaks. Drain in a colander, reserving the liquid, and set aside until cool enough to handle.

*If using precooked octopus,* go directly to Step 2.

2 Cut the octopus into 1/4-inch-thick slices. Cut squid steaks into 1-inch-wide strips. Place in a bowl or dish that is large enough to hold the reserved liquid.

3 In a medium-size pot, combine the reserved liquid and the ingredients for the pickling solution and bring to a boil. Let boil 1 minute, then pour over the octopus or squid. Cover and chill overnight, or as long as 3 days. To serve, transfer the octopus or squid to a platter or individual plates, and garnish with the parsley, olives, or capers.

**NOTE:** Meaty white fish can be pickled the same way to make a buoyant hors d'oeuvre.

# mussels

## IN WHITE WINE WITH SHALLOTS AND BASIL

### SERVES 6

GREEKS ARE FERVENT ABOUT SHELLFISH. THEY GATHER THEM FROM ROCKS, TIDEPOOLS, AND BEACHES AFTER A STORM, AND EAT THEM RAW THEN AND THERE. THEY FRY THEM, ESPECIALLY MUSSELS AND CLAMS, AND BATTER THEM LIKE FRITTERS. THEY ALSO TAKE A CATCH OF FRESH MUSSELS STRAIGHT FROM THE FOAMY WAVES—THE ONES NEAR THESSALONIKI AND THE HELLESPONT ARE ESPECIALLY PRIZED—AND STEAM THEM IN WHITE WINE. IN BYGONE TIMES, THE FISHERMAN MADE GLOVES OUT OF MUSSEL BEARDS. KEPT IN TUBS OF SEAWATER, THE GLOVES LASTED LIKE IRON.

*3 pounds mussels*
*1 cup dry white wine*
*3 shallots, coarsely chopped*
*2 cloves garlic, minced or*
  *pressed*
*1/3 cup chopped fresh flat-leaf*
  *parsley leaves*
*1/2 teaspoon fresh thyme leaves,*
  *or 1/4 teaspoon dried*
*1/4 teaspoon salt*
*1/4 teaspoon freshly ground*
  *black pepper*
*2 tablespoons thinly shredded*
  *fresh basil leaves*
*Crusty bread, for serving*

1 Scrub the mussels and pull off any exposed beards. (Removing the beards kills the mussels, so do not do it until you are ready to prepare the dish.)

2 Place the wine, shallots, garlic, parsley, thyme, salt, and pepper in a large pot and bring to a boil over high heat. Add the mussels, cover, and cook until the mussels open and are slightly firm, 8 minutes.

*A small* kaïque, *with a rowboat in tow, ferries a load of shellfish to shore.*

3 Transfer the mussels to a large serving platter, or divide them among individual plates or bowls. Discard any that have not opened. Spoon the cooking liquid over the mussels, and sprinkle the basil over all. Accompany with bread for dipping into the liquid.

**NOTE:** Many fishmongers now find it convenient to wrap mussels, clams, and the like in plastic bags for transporting home; but left in the bag, they will suffocate. As soon as you are home, remove them from the bag, transfer them to a bowl, loosely cover with a dish towel so they can breathe, and refrigerate until ready to cook.

# lobster

## IN TOMATO MAYONNAISE

### SERVES 6

IN THE WARM SEAS SURROUNDING GREECE, THE MOST COMMON LOBSTER, THE SPINY LOBSTER, SPROUTS FIVE SETS OF LEGS AND NO CLAWS. FOR THIS IT ACQUIRED ITS GREEK BIOLOGICAL NAME, *DECAPOD*, OR "TEN-FOOT." SPINY LOBSTERS HAVE NUMEROUS QUILLS, OR SPINELIKE PROTUBERANCES, ALL OVER THEIR BODIES, AND HORNS COVER THEIR EYES. THEIR SHELLS ARE DARKLY COLORFUL, A DEEPWATER RAINBOW OF BLUE, BROWN, GREEN, AND YELLOW-ORANGE. THEIR MANY-JOINTED TAIL CAN CURL UP UNDER THEIR TORSO AND PROPEL THEM BACKWARD. LACKING CLAWS AND THICK SWIMMERETTES, THEIR MEAT LIES IN THEIR TAILS. THE MEAT IS COARSER THAN THAT OF A MAINE LOBSTER, BUT TASTY ENOUGH TO DRIVE GREEK COOKS—AND EATERS—QUITE CRAZY.

Fresh spiny lobsters are difficult to find in the United States, though freshwater crayfish are similar, but any lobster meat can take on a Greek-style preparation with elegance. In Mikonos, Cyclades, they are sometimes presented with a lemony mayonnaise that is topped with a few intense, almost sun-dried Cyclades tomatoes.

*2 large or 3 small live lobsters (about 3 pounds total), or 6 small frozen lobster tails, defrosted*
*1 cup Lemony Mayonnaise (page 470)*
*1 tablespoon finely chopped sun-dried tomatoes*
*Parsley sprigs or olives, for garnish*

1 Bring a large pot of water to a boil over high heat. Drop in the lobsters, and cover the pot. Bring to a boil again, reduce the heat, and simmer just until the meat is pink and firm but still moist, 11 minutes for live lobster, 6 minutes for tails (the small legs of the whole lobster will pull off easily). Drain in a colander and set aside until cool enough to handle.

## DANGEROUS DELIGHT
.....................

I sometimes think Greeks go to the beach not for the lobster or octopus *mezedes* at the nearby tavern, not for salt air or the pleasure of swimming, but in the hope of stepping on a sea urchin. It's not that they are seeking the pain of those nasty black spikes impaled in their feet; it's that they are hungry for the coral insides of the sea hedgehog.

Mussels are nice, clams quite congenial, periwinkles and cockles proffer sweet bites—but urchins are a beach wader's caviar. Greeks so love them that they open them up and devour them right by the rock where they lay hidden—no herbs, no lemon, no ceremony. They teased me into trying them, and now I, too, risk peril for the morsel. Then I do as the Greeks do: Break off the top, exposing the clamlike interior, and simply suck the meat out with its own juice and saltwater for seasoning.

**2** *If using fresh lobsters,* pull off the small legs and the large front claws. Crack the claws with a hammer or nutcracker, and pull out the meat. Reserve the small legs to decorate the platter. Set aside.

*If using lobster tails,* go directly to Step 4.

**3** Break the bodies apart at the joint between the tail and the torso. Remove the green liver, white marrow, and pink coral, and transfer them to a separate bowl to serve separately for those who like them.

**4** For fresh or frozen lobster, split the tails in half by cutting lengthwise through the soft part of the shell on the underbelly with the point of a heavy knife. Pull out the meat and cut it into bite-size pieces. Set it aside with the claw meat, if you have it.

**5** When ready to serve, blend together the mayonnaise and the sun-dried tomatoes. Spoon some dressing onto each plate, arrange several bites of lobster on top, and drizzle a little more dressing over the lobster. Garnish with parsley or olives, and the reserved legs, if you have them.

## VARIATION:

**Lobster in Oregano Dressing:** In Kefalonia, lobster is often offered as an afternoon *meze* in a lemony dressing topped with a sprig of wild oregano. I blend the herb right into the sauce: In a small bowl, combine 1 cup olive oil, 2 tablespoons fresh lemon juice, and 2 teaspoons chopped fresh oregano leaves or 1 teaspoon dried. Prepare, cook, and serve the lobster as described above.

## THE PERIWINKLE DAY TRIP

Markella, my best friend in the village on Santorini where I often live, was three years into young widowhood and feeling low. Every year I had taken her and a troop of village women—laughingly referred to as the "Drunken Mothers Club," because none drank at all—on some excursion across the island. This time, Markella ventured a wilder idea. "Let's go to another island," she said, "and come back that night."

"Fine with me," I said, and we picked Paros. I was excited. We planned actually to *leave* the island (almost unheard of), take a morning boat to Paros, tootle around the whole day, and return by night steamer. Markella gathered up three of her sisters while I planned our outing. I had in mind all the sorts of things I think of when it comes to an excursion: I would rent a car. We would enter an ancient temple and contemplate the early Greeks. We would visit an old church and admire Byzantine icons. We would swing around the island and view the landscape.

We did swing about the island, but little did I know that the trip would turn into what my friends considered the happiest of excursions—a food extravaganza!

At the dock on Paros we were joined by their cousin in her car. We must have been quite a sight—four very short Greek women dressed in black, and string-bean me in white Bermuda shorts and visor—but despite the quizzical looks we piled into the car and roared off. No sooner had we gotten to the first beach than the women called for a halt, piled out of the car, and dashed into the sea. The beaches of Paros skirt the island like an ecru-colored petticoat. They are also, it turns out, home to many shellfish. Soon all my companions were plucking periwinkles from the rocks and devouring them then and there.

We proceeded onward. I knew of a castle to see, but they knew of a town that is famous for its cheese. There we went, where they bought kilos of curd. Heading farther around the island, they had inside information on a village where butter was churned. They bought packs of it.

As the day dwindled, they called for one more beach to sample yet more shellfish, and then we were back to port, where the final goal was the candy shops. Boxes and boxes were purchased to bring back to waiting children, brothers, more sisters, and a couple of husbands.

And that is how I learned the Greek idea of a joyful junket. I sought to show them history; they sought to live the moment. I wanted to feast my eyes; they wanted to feast their palates. And feast we did.

# TART AND TANTALIZING PICKLES

# sweet zucchini pickle

**MAKES 8 CUPS**

VINEGAR WAS AN INGREDIENT IN GREEK COOKING FROM EARLY ON. IT WAS USED WITH VARIOUS FOODS PLAIN, MIXED WITH HONEY, MIXED WITH OLIVE OIL, MIXED WITH FISH, AND USED IN A VARIETY OF SAUCES. THEY PICKLED WHOLE FISH, SHELLFISH, VEGETABLES, EGGS, CERTAIN MEATS, AND EVEN THE YOUNG TENDRILS OF GRAPEVINES.

Most Greek pickles are sharp, not sweet like these zucchini pickles, but their pickling follows in the ancient tradition of *oximeli* (see sidebar, this page). Brown sugar is a sweetener the ancients didn't have, but it imparts a near-to-honey taste without darkening the vegetables or leaving a cloying consistency.

3 pounds (12 to 15) small to medium zucchini, ends trimmed, sliced into 1/4-inch-thick rounds (see Notes)

2 medium onions, quartered, then sliced 1/8 inch thick

2 teaspoons kosher or fine sea salt

1 tablespoon dry mustard powder

1 tablespoon mustard seeds

1 1/2 teaspoons ground turmeric

1/2 teaspoon whole cloves

1 1/2 cups packed dark brown sugar

1 1/2 cups white wine vinegar

What we would call "pickling" has been a part of Greek cuisine since very early days. Many olives are cured by pickling in vinegar or brine. Ancient Greeks exclaimed about pickled fish and shellfish and the satisfying smack of vinegared roots and onions. *Oximeli*, the used-on-almost-everything vinegar and honey sauce of ancient Greece, no doubt also produced something very like a sweet-and-sour pickle. The Romans, who took their culinary lessons from Greece and hired legions of Greek chefs, pickled everything from cucumbers to thistles.

By Arabic-influenced Ottoman times, shops and stalls in many Greek cities presented barrels of various kinds of pickled vegetables, fruits, and often fish and shellfish, each vessel flavored with different spices and herbs—cumin, cinnamon, clove, anise, mustard, dill, fennel, pepper.

The sprightliness of a pickle placed it from early on in the category of treat. Pickles are among the most extolled *mezedes*, and they also add to the dinner table as an enlivening relish.

1 Place the zucchini and onions in a large colander. Add the salt and toss to mix. Set aside until the zucchini starts to sweat and wilt, 10 to 15 minutes.

2 Meanwhile, mix together the dry mustard, mustard seeds, turmeric, cloves, brown sugar, and vinegar in a large pot. Bring to a rolling boil over high heat, stir, and remove from the heat.

3 Transfer the zucchini and onions to the pot, stir, and set aside to cool. When cool enough to handle, transfer to a glass or plastic container. Cover and refrigerate overnight before serving. The pickles will keep for up to 2 months, covered, in the refrigerator.

## NOTES:

■ For the best pickles, use slightly underripe zucchini or other vegetables, and ones that have not been waxed.

■ Honey, with or without some white sugar, can be substituted for the brown sugar. Bring the ingredients to a boil without the honey; then add the honey just before you remove the pot from the heat.

■ Use whole spices for pickling; ground spices will darken the vegetables.

## SOCRATES, THE PRICKLY PHILOSOPHER

Socrates, the most venerated philosopher of classical Greece, was born in Athens in 469 B.C.E. and died in that same city in 399. He received the typical Athenian education in his youth, studying literature, music, and mathematics, and upon reaching adulthood became a sculptor in his father's workshop. But troubled by what he viewed as disturbing trends, he soon gave up his occupation and determined instead to reform the moral and intellectual reasoning of his time.

In short order he provoked the ire of the Athenian state and the leading philosophical school of his time, the Sophists. Like a bit of vinegar in the system, he relished the vexation. The Sophists taught that there was no objective standard on which to judge what is true and what false; only what seemed true was true and what seemed false was false. Socrates said that such a view meant that anyone could get away with anything and that would lead to moral anarchy. So he undertook to determine the nature of universally valid moral principles. Self-awareness was a first step, to which he applied perhaps his most famous aphorism:

The unexamined life is not worth living. He believed in continuously seeking knowledge, for humans failed to realize how little they knew about anything. He became a renowned—if unconventional—teacher, initiating a kind of student-teacher dialogue called to this day the Socratic Method. In it he approached the student with an attitude of assumed ignorance and proceeded to ask questions until the pupil taught himself. He exclaimed that knowledge was gained through concepts and the examination of human behavior. Ignorance was the true vice. No evil, he said would befall a good man, and life's difficulty lay not in avoiding death but in avoiding unrighteousness.

Socrates' teachings and principles last to this day, but in the end he got himself in quite a pickle. He was accused of impiety and subversion. He met the accusations with defiance instead of defense. He refused to retract any of his teachings or to apologize. He was condemned to death and made to drink a tea of a deadly hemlock—and died in his favorite place in the Agora, ancient Athens's great marketplace.

# green tomato pickle

### MAKES 4 QUARTS

WHEN THE YEAR ROUNDS TOWARD OCTOBER AND GREECE'S BLAZING SUN BEGINS TO FADE, SMALL GREEN TOMATOES AND TINY EGGPLANTS OFTEN REMAIN IN THE GARDEN. DEPLORING THE NOTION OF LETTING THEM GO TO WASTE, GARDENERS TURN THEM INTO A REFRESHING PICKLED RELISH FOR THE COMING WINTER. HARDLY A KITCHEN EXISTS WHERE CROCKS OF BRINING LATE GARDEN VEGETABLES DO NOT SIT IN A FAR CORNER.

To the usual vinegar, garlic, coriander, and dill, I add pimento for color. The grape leaves help the pickles keep their crunch. If little eggplants are to be found, I use them, too, adding them to the mix.

*4 pounds green tomatoes, stemmed, rinsed, and cut into 1-inch wedges*

*1 large pimento or red bell pepper, stemmed, seeded, and cut into $^1/_4$-inch-wide strips*

*8 whole fresh grape leaves*

*12 large sprigs fresh dill*

*4 cloves garlic, sliced*

*3 cups white wine vinegar*

*5 cups water*

*$^1/_4$ cup kosher or fine sea salt*

*$^1/_2$ tablespoon coriander seeds*

1 Divide the tomatoes, pimento, grape leaves, dill, and garlic evenly in layers in sterile quart glass jars, beginning with the tomatoes, followed by a layer of pimento strips, then 2 grape leaves, 3 sprigs of dill, and the garlic slices. Set aside.

2 Mix the vinegar, water, salt, and coriander seeds in a large nonreactive pot and bring to a boil over high heat. Immediately pour this over the vegetables, filling the jars to the top. Make sure an equal amount of coriander seeds are added to each jar. Set aside to cool completely; then cover and refrigerate overnight before using. The pickles will keep in the refrigerator for several months.

**NOTE:** Save any extra liquid to top off the jars after the ingredients have cooled and settled, so the jars are filled right to the top.

## THE PHOENIX PICKLED IN MYRRH

According to Greek mythology, the phoenix lived in the east, near the crimson rising sun. It was as large as an eagle, bloodred and gold like the ascending sun (the word "phoenix" means "bloodred"), and had a melodious cry. Only one phoenix lived at a time, and it thrived a very long while—500 years, according to the Greek historian Herodotus. As the end of its era approached, the legendary bird would fashion a nest of boughs and spices, sit within, and set the nest on fire until it was consumed in the flame. From out of the fire, the bird would then arise anew, refeathered and reborn. It would gather up the ashes of its old incarnation, embalm them in an egg of myrrh, and fly them to Heliopolis, the ancient city of the sun. The legendary phoenix became a symbol of resurrection, immortality, and Greek identity, reflecting the country's survival during war, invasion, and natural disasters.

# pickled red onions

### MAKES 3 CUPS

ONIONS HAVE BEEN EATEN—AND PICKLED— FOR SO LONG IN GREEK CUISINE THAT THEIR ANCIENT NAME, *KERMYION*, THE ROOT OF OUR "ONION," HAS CHANGED LITTLE IN MODERN LANGUAGE, *KREMIDI*.

Onions were employed as the food enhancer that was most at hand, and most common to grow in gardens and fields *pandou* (everywhere). Their tangy slices traditionally were spread across grain pilafs or placed atop hunks of bread. They were munched as a snack and used to enhance soups and stews. They were cut or sliced, sometimes dried in the sun, sometimes parboiled and then preserved in vinegar. Sometimes they were spiced with mustard, grape must (another ancient flavoring), or crushed raisins—or with silphium, an herb that was wildly popular and is now extinct.

Though small pickled onions are served as a *meze* alone, perhaps with some bread, the larger sliced ones are used as a relish with other dishes.

*2 medium red onions, halved and very thinly sliced*
*1 cup red wine vinegar*
*1 cup water*
*2 tablespoons sugar*
*1 bay leaf*

1 Place the onions in a medium-size bowl and set aside.

2 Combine the vinegar, water, sugar, and bay leaf in a small nonreactive pot and bring to a rapid boil over high heat to dissolve the sugar. Stir, and pour over the onions. Set aside to cool and marinate for at least 30 minutes. Use right away, or cover and store in the refrigerator for up to several weeks.

## OTHER GREEK PICKLED VEGETABLES

The swiftness of the pickling depends on the density of the vegetable, the thickness of the slices you cut, and the amount of salting used to start the process (be careful of oversalting, because the pickles can become inedible). To pickle all sorts of vegetables, use 3 pounds of your vegetable of choice and the amounts of dill, garlic, vinegar, water, salt, and coriander seeds from the Green Tomato Pickle recipe on the facing page. Follow the recipe using:

**BEETS**, small whole ones or pieces, parboiled until barely able to be pierced, 15 to 20 minutes

**CAULIFLOWER FLORETS**

**CUCUMBERS**, sliced or whole, especially small ones

**EGGPLANT** in 1-inch pieces or slices

**MELON RIND** in 1-inch pieces, simmered in salted water to soften

**ONIONS**, small whole ones (also see Pickled Red Onions, this page)

**PEPPERS**, bell and hot, halved if small or quartered if large

**RADISHES**, small whole ones or halves

**TOMATOES**, small red or green

# THE PEOPLE, PROVINCES, AND CULINARY SPECIALTIES OF GREECE

WHILE THE PEOPLE OF GREECE RELISH THEIR SINGLE LANGUAGE AND CULTURE, THOSE FROM DIFFERENT REGIONS— NORTHERN EPIROS TO SOUTH-LYING MANI, FORESTED THRACE TO BARREN ARCADIA, COOL SAMOS TO ROASTING SANTORINI, CIVILIZED THESSALONIKI TO WILD CRETE—DISPLAY A COLORFUL DIVERSITY OF FOLKWAYS, COSTUMES, DANCES, AND DIALECTS.

Likewise, while they share one cuisine and most of the same foods can be found everywhere, from region to region, mainland to island, city to village, they cook up a profusion of dishes based on local tradition and products. Grape leaves are stuffed much the same everywhere, but the pies of Macedonia are different from the pies of Kefalonia, and the pilafs of Thrace are different from the porridges of Milos.

## A GEOGRAPHY LESSON

The land the Greeks occupy consists of a single two-part peninsula and some 1,400 islands, of which only about 170 are inhabited. Four fifths of the nation is mountainous. The

temperature can rise to 108°F in the summertime. In the winter it snows on the mountains and sometimes on the plains and islands as well. Trimming the land with a stunningly jagged coastline are three azure seas and many gulfs. Not one spot in Greece is more than fifty miles from water.

Within the country are a number of distinct regions: starting at the north, Epiros (Ipiros), Macedonia (Makedonia), and Thrace (Thraki).

## THE NORTHERN REGIONS

Epiros, in the northwest corner near Albania, is the most mountainous region of Greece, and its rugged peaks have from ancient times given shelter to

*Horse racing around a hippodrome called for light togas or no clothing at all.*

fiercely independent tribes and rustic settlements. Even so, Ioanina, the capital, became a major commercial and intellectual center during the Ottoman rule (fifteenth to twentieth century). Near Ioanina lie forty-four villages known together as the Zagorohoria, where the houses are built of mountain slate. Below Epiros's majestic hills stretch romantic beaches. Epiros is known for its corn-crusted vegetable pies and its lamb stews, rivers running with trout, and fresh shepherd's cheese.

Macedonia, in the central north, is a broad extension of rolling hills and fertile reaches. It contains the three-fingered peninsula of Halkidiki (Chalcidice) where austere, men-only Mount Athos (an autonomous state) perches. Nearby lies Greece's second-largest city, Thessaloniki. Over time a varied array of people with different dress, customs, crops, and foods have settled in Macedonia's fruitful expanse. There are the winegrowers of Naoussa, the vegetable growers of waterfall-kissed Edessa, the gold and fur merchants of Thessaloniki, the pepper growers of Florina, the musicians of Kastoria, the peach pruners of Veria. Lakes filled with waterfowl lie to the west at Prespa, and no

city in Europe offers the palimpsest of history that Thessaloniki presents. Among the special dishes of the region are a distinct syrup cake called *revani*, a spicy *fasolada* (bean soup), red peppers of every heat, mussels sautéed in a *saganaki* pan, and acclaimed wild hare.

*Pantokratoras is one of the Athonite monasteries on Mount Athos.*

Thrace lies like a long arm to the east of Macedonia. Of the once-powerful ancient region, only part now lies in contemporary Greece. Stretching like an arm toward Asia, Thrace has ever served as a road for conquerors moving in either direction. As a result, amid a jumbled landscape crisscrossed with rolling hills and speeding rivers, Thrace houses a bright hodgepodge of Greek ethnicities. The majority of Greece's

Muslims live here, along with Greeks of mixed Slavic descent and many Gypsies, all adding their flavors to Thrace's cultural and culinary stew. Orpheus came from Thrace, and the province is still known for its music and poetry. The region is also the center of Greece's tobacco industry.

Much produce is grown here, especially root crops and bulgur wheat and barley, both cold-weather grains. Zesty leek pies, bulgur-stuffed birds, pilafs, goat's milk, and sour noodles made with yogurt are among the area's gastronomic specialties.

## GREECE'S BREAD-BASKET

Below Macedonia on the east stretches Thessaly (Thessalia), the breadbasket of Greece. Thessaly contains the largest expanse of flat land in Greece, and extending across that plain are great fields of wheat and other crops. Yet to each side of the plain ascend dramatic mountain ranges, one home of Mount Olympus, the other Mount Pelion. The bustling agricultural cities of Volos and Larisa lie in Thessaly, as do stark monasteries clinging to black cliffs. The apples and peaches of the district are famous, as are the yogurt cakes. Thessaly also shimmers with olive groves, and the region produces barrels of fine wine.

## STEREA ELLAS

Central Greece spans from below Thessaly to the Gulf of Corinth and includes the country's second-largest island, Euboea (Evia). Noble Attica (Attika), where Athens lies, was also a part of Central Greece, but its huge population recently brought about its administrative separation. Thebes (Thiva), home of Oedipus; Delphi (Delfous), the site of the enigmatic oracle; Marathon (Marathonos); and Mount Parnassos are all in what Greeks call *Sterea Ellas,* or "Solid Greece." Deep inlets and lakes, high mountains, tiny port towns, and two major cities notch the region. At the west lie the gulf ports of Vonitsa and Mytikas, with their calm waters. In the middle are the mountain towns of Lamia and Karpenision. Celebrated Attica extends along an eastern peninsula of the cen-tral core, and running along that spit sprawls the megalopolis of Athens and its connected port city, Piraeus. The dual cities house people from every part

> ... and there, in beautiful Nafplio, one can delight in ouzo and fish roe while looking at the tiny island in the bay.

of Greece. Thousands of boats leave Piraeus daily for the islands. Trains and buses from the cities' stations reach every corner of the country. To the south of the cities lies Eleusis and the magnificent coastline of the Saronic Gulf, where abruptly Greece is cut almost in half at the Isthmus of Corinth. Foods of Central Greece range from the periwinkles of the west near Vonitsa, the wine stews of Mesalongi, where Lord Byron died, the seafarer's stew of Galaxidi, a town whose name means "vinegar milk," the spit-roasted lamb of Lamia, the honey from Attica's Mount Hymettus, European-style salads and cakes cooked in Athens, and every sort of fish imaginable at the harbor in Piraeus.

## PELOPS'S ISLAND

Across the isthmus of Corinth you enter the lower half of the Greek peninsula, the Peloponnesos, "Pelop's Island," named for King Pelops, grandfather of Agamemnon. The Peloponnesos is home to regions whose names are familiar from the works of Homer: Akaia, with its major city Patras; Elia, where in graceful Olympia the ancient games took place; Argos, home to Jason and where the citadel of Mycenae flourished; Arcadia; Corinth; Messinia; and Kalamata and its olive groves. Toward the bottom of the Peloponnesos on the east, Sparta still stands. At the southernmost coast, the three long appendages swim into the sea. On them are located old Pylos; the strange tower-filled, feud-filled region of Mani; and the legendary wine capital of Monemvasia. From the many citrus and other fruit orchards near Corinth city come spoon sweets of every sort. Arcadia, famous for the god Pan, is equally renowned for roasted goat, rustic bread, and cheese. Argolida holds the mulberry trees that once gave the whole Peloponnesos the name *Morea*, and there, in beautiful Nafplio, one can delight in ouzo and fish roe while looking at the tiny island in the bay.

## ISLANDS OF THE ADRIATIC

And then come the islands. Across from Epiros on the western side of the Greek mainland, lying almost in a line are the Ionian islands: Corfu (Kerkira); Paxi and Antipaxi; Lefkada; Ithaca (Ithaki), beloved home of Odysseus; Kefalonia; numerous small islands; and the island once called Zante, original home of Zante currants, now called Zakinthos. The Ionian islands have always projected a somewhat different aura than other parts of Greece because of their desirable position. Throughout history they were battled over as stepping-stones to Italy and invaluable Sicily. As Byzantium's strength waned and Italy's grew, Venice took the islands one by one. Many Greeks

on the islands intermarried with Italians. When Venice fell, the islands were annexed by France until a joint Russian-Turkish force drove the French out. After Napoleon was defeated, the British moved in. Today the Ionian islands display squarishly northern architecture and rather Parisian streets. Corfu's cafés sell ginger beer. Kefalonia offers a spicy meat, potato, and carrot pie—not unlike an English pub's shepherd's pie, but with a filo crust. From Corfu to barren Lefkada, tangy wild-greens pies are baked. Paxi produces esteemed olive oil, and Corfu esteemed olives. Small birds are stewed in wine, and the spicy *kapama* is a signature Ionian dish.

## ISLANDS OF THE AEGEAN

In the Aegean Sea to the east of the mainland jut up several distinct island groupings. To the north, just skirting Turkey, are Thasos, Samothrace, Limnos, Lesbos (Mitilini), Chios (Hios), Samos, Ikaria, and a number of others. Some, like Mitilini, are arid; others, like Samos, are thickly forested with pine and cypress. For a time Genoa held some of the

*Every spiritual spot throughout the country has been honored with a church or chapel.*

*A fisherman of Crete with eels and octopus.*

islands and on them built castles, such as the lofty one in Molyvos on Mitilini. Eventually the nearby Turks conquered the northern islands. Yet throughout their history, many of their particular foods never changed. With their northern coolness, the islands feature beets along with wild bulbs in their vegetable compotes. Cheese pies are fried, stuffed fowl is roasted, and spit-roasted chickens spin in every town. The ancients raved about Samos's wine, and it is still stellar.

Farther south, still following the Asia Minor coastline, stretch the Dodecanese, the "Twelve Islands," although there are more than twelve. Among them repose the lauded islands of Patmos, Kos, Kalymnos, Astypalea, far-reaching Karpathos, and famed Rhodes.

The complex and unusual history of the Dodecanese gives Greece yet another area with a unique legacy. The islands were settled early because of their fertile soils, many trees, and minerals. The Byzantines highly valued them, but when the Ottomans moved west, the islands were taken, first by the Ottomans, then the Crusaders, then by the Ottomans again. Later some fell to the control of Fascist Italy. Though grouped as a region, each of the islands is different. Ancient Greeks prized the quince of Kos as well as the saffron and rose-perfumed wines of Rhodes. Today the people of Astipalaia continue to make saffron bread, and Kos still produces quince and spoon sweets flavored with rose geranium. The sponge divers of Kalymnos make a hearty fish chowder. The wines of Rhodes remain spectacular, as do their cherry drinks and cakes, Byzantine-style nut sauces, stuffed Turkish-style eggplant, and a menu of Italian-style pasta dishes. Karpathos has lobster to nibble.

Closer to the Greek mainland, scattered like the beads of a broken necklace, rise the Cyclades (Kyklades). Among them are Andros, Tinos, Siros, Kea, Kithnos, Mikonos, Sifnos, Milos, Paros, Naxos, Amargos, Ios, Thira (Santorini), Anafi, and many more. Delos, where Apollo and Artemis were born, glimmers—legend says it floats—

across the water from Mikonos. Here on these sun-shimmering islands sit the whitewashed houses and blue-domed churches featured on countless Greek travel posters. Twisted pathways through the villages are painted to look as if they were paved with stone, not concrete. Again, each island is distinct. Tinos is the site of religious pilgrimages. Mikonos has reigned as a jet-set favorite for decades, although the island women still weave colorful shawls as Greek women have for generations. Naxos, over which looms a Venetian castle, is so large that it contains both planted valleys and high barren hills. Most of the Cyclades islands are the tops of underwater mountains that wink above the sea and are arid with limited agriculture. Santorini, though, is a volcano whose eruptioms have produced a topsoil of pumice ash so fertile that virtually every inch of the island is terraced for growing crops and vineyards. The Cyclades cuisine features dishes from both land and sea. Aegean eel is topped with heavenly garlic paste; red mullet is exquisitely grilled. The islands' tomatoes have such an intense flavor that sauces and salads made with them taste as if honied. Santorini is famous for its dense, rich yellow lentil soup, Naxos for its grape-must cookies, Paros for its plethora of pastries and candies. All give habitat to enough wild birds to produce sage-sautéed woodcock and quail.

Even closer to the mainland, lying just east of Attica, the Sporades islands are anchored. Their name comes from the word for "seeds," and means "here or there," or "sporadic." They include Skiathos, Skopelos, Alonnisos, and Skyros, while south of Attiki sit the islands of the Saronic Gulf: Aegina, Poros, Hydra, and Spetses. The wines of the Sporades have long been savored. No cars befoul Hydra, and the gardens there are lush. Special foods include vegetable fritters, pickled garlic, bread rings. On Hydra's neighboring islands you can eat watercress and kale salads, grape leaf–wrapped fish, and lamb chops.

## APHRODITE'S ISLAND

By itself, just below the Peloponnesos, lies the island of Kythera. In ancient times Kythera had such an abundance of murex shellfish that the Phoenicians settled there to extract the purple dye from the mollusks. After her foam birth, Aphrodite washed ashore on the island and made it her own. Now many flock to the charming island, with its humming ouzo bars and *meze* appetizers, still including a wealth of shellfish.

## THE HOME OF THE MINOTAUR

Most southern of all is Greece's biggest island, Crete. Practically no place in Greece boasts such antiquity and variety of foods. A mountain chain connected to Cyprus runs across the island. Dotted between the mountains are plateaus where herds feed and crops grow. Inlets and harbors serrate the coastline. All these features have separated sections of the island so that each has developed its own distinction. Crete has long been known for a certain wildness, fierce men, strong women, and self-reliance. Its songs and dirges speak of love, liberty, and tragedy. The island was first settled in prehistoric times, snatched up by the incoming Minoans. Among their ruins are labyrinthlike palaces, spirited murals, and earthen jars still containing olives, barley, and wine. The present capital, Iraklion, borders the once-powerful and mysterious Minoan city of

Knossos. Grotyna, in the south, was the Roman capital of Cyrenaica. Crete's second-largest town, Hania, is edged with a fortress and seawalls left from Venetian days. The cornucopia of the island's foods, many of them particular to the island, is as abundant as its history. From their herds, the people of Crete make yogurt thick as cake. They sizzle up snails, make unique meat pies, simmer a botany book's worth of wild greens, and are hailed for their deep-fried sweet pastries.

Vital and vibrant Greece is the home of great modern writers such as Seferis, Elytis, and Kazantzakis, and magnificent musicians including Hadjidakis and Theodorakis. As well as incomparable antiquities and legacy, Greece beckons with rich and vivid people, multifarious folkways—and incredible food.

*Ancient Greek chariots were two-horse vehicles used mainly for racing and processionals.*

# savory pies

# FROM FILO PASTRY

Beyond the Parthenon, more than the exquisite statues of Phidias and Praxiteles, equal to the acclaim of Mount Parnassos, Greece is famous for its flaky filo-crusted pastries and pies. In square or diamond-shaped pieces, folded in triangles, coiled, or pinched into boats, they entice. How could they not? On the bottom lie four to six to twelve or more crinkling layers of tissue-thin pastry.

Sometimes pie with a flask of wine
Sometimes pie alone.

—GREEK PROVERB

*A filo maker with his mound of dough, ready to start rolling.*

And four to six to twelve or more sheets cap the top. In between rests an inch or two of sumptuous filling, sometimes oozy, sometimes sturdy, always stirring. Filo pastries and pies are a "transitional" food of the Greek diet, a food betwixt and between. They constitute the biggest, probably most captivating *mezedes*, yet they—

especially the large pies—also appear as entrees on the dinner table.

It seems that the ancient Greeks had pies. In his lavish poem "Banquet" (fifth century B.C.E.), Philoxenos states that in the final drinking course of a meal, suave hosts served a cheesecake made with milk and honey that was baked like a pie. Other writers speak of pastry dough. Sadly, though, the ancients left no hint of how their pies were made.

The fabulous pies of today's Greece—those crusted with the thinnest of filo dough—first appear in Byzantine times, and from then on their savory lusciousness fixed their place in Greek cuisine.

Greek pies can be found wherever Greeks dwell. In Greece itself, vendors hawk them from carts where the buttery, crisp treats bask under warming lights. Towers of pies stand stacked in bakery windows. They arrive with

beverages in ouzo bars, patrician to plebeian.

The pies are also cooked at home, and easily so. For those who care to make it, filo dough is easy to blend, though rolling it truly thin does take practice. Commercial filo dough, however, is widely available. Already mixed and rolled, no dough is as fast and facile to work with, even when forming what might look like complicated shapes. Most Greeks now use commercial filo dough. Making the tantalizing filling for the pies is almost effortless. Usually only one sumptuous layer goes between the crusts, so the assemblage of what looks like mysteriously multilayered pies is in fact almost slapdash. A very short span in the oven, and *oopah*, the filo crust turns golden and flaky. Big pies baked in square or round pans, little pies shaped like cigars and snails, all come out of the oven with the speed of Zeus's thunderbolts.

# homemade filo dough

**MAKES 4 TO 6 SHEETS;
ENOUGH FOR A 12- X 9-INCH PAN**

THE ALLURE OF ANY PIE IS THE CRUNCHY PASTRY ENVELOPING THE FOOD. THE SPECIAL ALLURE OF GREEK PIES IS THAT THE CRUST COMES AS A STACK OF PASTRY SHEETS, THIN AS MICA AND PILED ONE ATOP THE OTHER. WHEN BAKED, THE LAYERED CRUST IS AS FRAGILE AS PAPYRUS.

Not so long ago, every Greek cook made her own thin sheets of filo dough. Some still do. The dough is the simplest sort, calling merely for flour and water, perhaps oil, maybe a dash of baking powder or a splash of vinegar. It need only be exceedingly elastic. To turn the dough into filo sheets, the pie maker rolls out the dough with a straight, untapered stick, rather than a tapered rolling pin. The slim sticks range from 10 inches to 4 feet long and are no thicker than a broomstick. Adept filo makers can roll their dough hairbreadth thin, almost as thin as commercial filo, although many stop when the dough is about $1/16$ inch thick.

Homemade dough is more tender and has better flavor than the commercial type, no question.

A bit thicker than machine-rolled filo, homemade filo sheets encase the filling in a wrap that has more crunch and more density than the store-bought sort.

For those who would like to try their hand at it, here is a recipe for homemade filo dough, with four variations. Note that fewer sheets of dough—only two to four on bottom and top—are layered together when making crusts from homemade dough. The recipe below is enough for one pie or a batch of little *pitakia*. Should you want more layers or more little pies, double the recipe.

*Olive oil, for the bowl*
*3 cups all-purpose flour, plus more*
*    for the work surface*
*1 teaspoon salt*
*1/2 to 3/4 cup warm water*

1 Lightly oil a large bowl and set it aside. Mix the flour and salt together in a second large bowl. Make a well in the middle and slowly blend in the warm water, using an electric mixer or a fork, until a stiff dough has formed.

2 Lightly sprinkle a work surface with flour, and transfer the dough to it. Knead and fold the dough until it is elastic and shiny, about 10 minutes. Pat the dough into a ball, place it in the oiled bowl, and turn to coat it all over with the oil. Cover with a cloth or plastic wrap and set aside in a warm place to rest for 2 hours.

3 Dust the work surface again with a light layer of flour. Divide the dough into four pieces. With a $1^1/2$-inch-diameter dowel, roll each piece out to form a 10-inch circle. Lay the dough circles out on a dry surface that has been dusted with cornstarch, cover them with a cloth, and allow to rest for 30 minutes.

4 Dust the rolling surface again. With the dowel, roll each circle as thin as you can. This dough is very elastic, and you will probably have to use your hands to stretch it as well as roll it. You can roll the whole circle of dough

around the rolling stick, and holding up the stick let the dough slowly unroll so that gravity helps stretch it. After rolling and stretching each circle as thin as you can, place a clean, smooth cloth over your table. Dust the cloth with flour and lay the rolled pastry in the center. With both hands, stretch the dough until it is as thin as a dime and at least 14 x 12 inches in size. Don't worry about any holes; you can work around them later.

5 When the dough is stretched thin, cut sheets the size you desire. Save any trimmings to roll again. Continue with the other circles until all the filo is rolled and cut. Keep the rolled-out sheets covered until ready to use.

6 Use the filo sheets right away, or sprinkle them with flour and stack them one on top of another. Loosely roll the stack up into a log. Wrap in plastic wrap and refrigerate for up to 2 weeks, or freeze for up to 6 months.

## VARIATIONS:

■ **Filo with Carbonated Water, Beer, or Baking Powder** Some Greeks substitute carbonated water or beer for the plain water, or add a little baking powder, to get a bit of rise in their dough.

When using carbonated water or beer, simply replace the water with the liquid of choice.

When adding baking powder, include 2 teaspoons baking powder when you mix together the flour and salt in Step 1. Include 2 tablespoons olive oil along with the first $1/2$ cup water; then add up to $1/4$ cup more water, as needed, to form a stiff dough.

■ **Filo with Vinegar or Lemon Juice** Vinegar and lemon juice, in some opinions, add a little sparkle and elasticity to the dough. Vinegar in the dough goes particularly well with pitas filled with spinach, leeks, or various greens.

To use, include 1 tablespoon white wine vinegar or lemon juice and 2 tablespoons olive oil along with the first $1/2$ cup water. Add up to $1/4$ cup more water, as needed.

■ **Filo with Egg, Milk, or Yogurt** Occasionally a dough maker will enrich filo dough with an egg, or will use milk or yogurt instead of the water. The resulting dough is yellower and creamier.

When adding egg, you will need to use a little less water or a little more flour to achieve a stiff dough. It takes approximately 4 cups of flour to make the dough stiff enough when using 2 eggs.

To use milk, simply substitute the same amount of milk for the water.

When replacing water with yogurt, use either less flour or add a few extra tablespoons of water to achieve a stiff dough.

■ **Filo with Oil** Many Greeks use oil in their filo dough. Oil makes the dough even more elastic, though a bit less flaky. Use $3/4$ cup warm water, $1/3$ cup oil, and $1/2$ cup more flour. The oil can be olive oil, a flavorful nut oil, or for a very Mediterranean touch, sesame oil. You can also use part oil and part melted butter. Work the dough as little as possible; stop when it holds together.

# FILO FINESSE

**W**orking with filo can at first seem daunting, but if certain little tricks are followed, the results are the fastest, easiest pies you'll ever bake.

◼ The dough dries out fast, so place a damp cloth over the sheets you aren't working with.

◼ Each sheet of filo dough must be oiled as it is placed in the pan.

◼ Have the filling ready if you are using commercial filo, or prepare it while the dough rests if you are making homemade dough. You don't have to be terribly accurate about the amount of filling for a filo pie. Logically, the larger or thicker the pie, the more filling it can hold.

◼ Decant the olive oil or melt the butter, depending on which you wish to use to slick the filo, and place it in a large-mouthed container or bowl so you can easily dip your pastry brush into it. Butter is generally used for sweet pies, olive oil or a combination of olive oil and butter for savory pies. When using butter, allow a few minutes for the butter solids to settle after melting; then dip your brush only in the clarified butter at the top.

◼ Cut the filo sheets to the size you need before assembling the pie, remembering that dough shrinks a bit while baking. Cut the sheets for the bottom crust just slightly larger than the pan's dimensions for pies with a stiff filling, such as chicken pie. For pies with a runny filling, such as *galaktobouriko* (page 510), cut the bottom sheets a good 1 inch larger than the container so that you can slightly extend the edges up the sides of the pan. For the top crust, cut the sheets to pan size.

When using thicker homemade filo, Greek pie makers generally layer only two to four sheets of dough for both bottom and top crust for a savory pie. When using machine-rolled (thus gossamer-thin) commercial dough, six to as many as twelve sheets are stacked for both bottom and top of the pastry shell. Sweet pies often have more layers; certain pies and pastries, such as *baklava,* traditionally have generous crusts. In the recipes here, I assume the pie maker is using commercial dough and call for six to eight sheets of filo for both top and bottom. You may prefer to use more—or less, especially if using homemade dough or thicker sorts of commercial filo.

For small shaped filo pies, cut the strips, rectangles, or squares into the size you need (see page 90). You can use the cut filo singly, or oil and stack two or three cut sheets together for a thicker crust.

◼ Make sure your work surface is dry, then dust it with flour before placing the filo on it. Otherwise the filo will stick. Place the whole stack you are working in front of you, with the pan or baking sheet you are filling next to the filo.

◼ Using a pastry brush, dip only the tip in the butter or oil. *Working as quickly as you can,* lightly brush the butter or oil completely over the first sheet, particularly covering the edges. Don't oversaturate. Too much oil and the pie will be greasy; too little and it will be doughy. Use only a natural-bristle brush that is in good condition, and don't put your pastry brush in the dishwasher.

◼ Oil the bottom of the baking pan or sheet. For a pie baked in a pan, as each filo sheet is buttered or oiled, *carefully* lift the sheet and lay it in the pan. As you build up the sheets, gently smooth each down over the sheet below. Continue adding layers until the bottom is completely built. Then pour in

*A filo maker counts out sheets of dough for sale. She also sells* kadaifi *and other Greek pastry doughs.*

the filling and spread it out evenly. Make the top crust in the same manner as the bottom, laying the first filo sheet directly over the filling. For festive occasions, you may want to divide the filling into two parts and add a third, center layer of crust between two layers of filling.

When making small pastries, place the required amount of filling in the cut strip or square, fold or roll the dough into the shape you want, and place it on the baking sheet. Continue until all the filo is used.

■ If the filo sheets tear or have holes, don't worry. Using a little butter or oil, overlap tears and patch holes with scraps. If your batch of filo is dry or ragged, save the best sheets for the top crust, or the best parts of the sheets for strips and squares.

■ If the filo sheets have become stuck together before you've used them, gently try to separate them. If you can't, use them together, brushing the top with a little extra oil. Work out of the direct sunlight and away from the heat, or the filo will dry out too quickly.

■ Keep the filo moist. If you need to walk away, cover the filo stack you are using with plastic wrap or a slightly damp towel. Rewrap any leftover filo right away before it dries out.

■ Be sure to butter or oil the top sheet on pan pies and small pastries. In a pan, tuck down the sides and corners, perhaps with oiled fingertips, so that the layers won't flake apart when baking. For some pies you might want to use the milk trick (see below). To give a glaze to smaller *bourekia* or triangle pies for parties, some pie makers brush the top with a mix of egg yolk and water.

■ Before baking a pan pie, score the top crust with a paring knife—almost all the way to the filling. After scoring a pie or folding a shaped pastry, dampen or oil your fingers and run them along the scoring or the exposed dough edges, to keep the sheets from flaking up during baking.

■ Cook filo pastries only until golden brown in a 350° to 400°F oven. At a lower temperature the pie will be soggy on the bottom; at a higher temperature the bottom will burn.

## A BUSY COOK'S SECRET

I find store-bought filo dough so handy that I also use it for non-Greek pies, fruit tarts, and cinnamon cookies. The flavor of the dough is generally quite lemony or nutty, far better than store-bought American-style piecrust, and with some oil or melted butter and a pastry brush, I can turn a pie out in virtually minutes. Since I find the premade filo so usable, I keep several boxes in my freezer. The only caution is, don't thaw it and freeze it again. The dough is delicate, and any rough treatment like this causes it to crumble into an unusable mess.

## COMMERCIAL FILO— THE THICK AND THE THIN

Commercial filo dough comes in a number of thicknesses, but stores usually carry only the thinnest (Athenian #7, for example). Some Greek cooks think the slightly thicker commercial filo is better—you use fewer layers but get a richer flavor. You might experiment with thicker varieties if you can find them. Commercial filo is usually found frozen, to preserve its pliability. Be sure to thaw the dough to room temperature before using it, and do not take it out of its plastic wrapper until ready to use.

## THE MILK TRICK

My friend Sandy's mother-in-law, Soula, who came from the Pontos, taught Sandy how to keep the edges of her leek pie from rising upward untidily. After the pie is put together and the top crust laid down and scored, dip your pointer and middle fingers into 2 to 3 tablespoons of milk and gently spread it around the outside edges and along the scored lines of the top crust. Then gently press the edges down. With the milk trick, the corners of a filo pie won't curl up in the baking. This trick is particularly useful on leek, spinach, and horta pies to keep the crust crisply surrounding the soft vegetable centers.

# cheese pie

## WITH LEMON AND NUTMEG

### TYROPITA

**MAKES 48 PIECES**

FRESH, HOT CHEESE PIES APPEAR SO EARLY EVERY DAY IN GREECE THAT IT SEEMS THE *NYKTIMENES*, THE "NIGHT BIRDS," MUST BAKE THEM. COME MORNING, ROLLING CARTS AND BAKERY SHELVES DISPLAY TOWERING STACKS OF THE PIES. EVEN SO, EVERY VENDOR IS SURE TO SELL OUT. JUST THE SIGHT OF A CHEESE PIE IS ENOUGH TO CAUSE PEOPLE EXITING THE TRAIN, SHOPPING THE BAZAARS, OR AWAITING THE BOAT TO SCRAMBLE TO BUY ONE.

Some cheese pies have fillings that ooze out. Some have crusts so puffy they spread open like petals. Traditionally cheese pies are made in a triangle shape, giving the eater the triple delight of three flaky corners. The pies are composed of one or a combination of cheeses, depending on the area's custom and the baker's prerogative. As a consequence, the pies are always a taste adventure. The recipe here follows a traditional vein, with the cheeses tripled to match the triangle's three corners and the filling humming with lemon and a grating of fresh nutmeg.

*1 pound crumbled manouri or mizithra cheese, or 8 ounces crumbled feta and 8 ounces cream cheese*
*1/2 cup (3 ounces) coarsely grated kefalotyri or other hard grating cheese*
*1/2 cup (3 ounces) coarsely grated kasseri cheese*
*2 large eggs*
*1/2 teaspoon freshly grated nutmeg*
*1/4 teaspoon freshly ground white pepper*
*1/2 teaspoon finely chopped lemon zest*
*1/2 teaspoon fresh lemon juice*
*16 sheets commercial filo dough, or 12 sheets homemade*
*Olive oil or melted butter, for oiling the filo*
*1 egg yolk beaten with 1/2 tablespoon water (optional)*

1 Preheat the oven to 400°F. Brush two baking sheets with olive oil.

2 Mix the cheeses together in a large bowl. Break the 2 eggs into a small bowl and beat until frothy. Add the eggs, nutmeg, white pepper, zest, and lemon juice to the cheese mixture and blend thoroughly.

3 Cut the filo sheets into strips 3 inches wide by 12 inches long (you should get 6 strips per commercial sheet; 4 strips per homemade). If working with homemade dough, use just one strip; if working with commercial dough, oil one strip and stack a second strip on top of it. (Cover the rest with a damp cloth or plastic wrap.) Brush the top of the strip with oil. Place about 1/2 tablespoon of the cheese mixture at one corner. Fold the strip over and up flag-style (see page 90). Seal the flap down with oil. Brush oil lightly over the top, and place the pastry on a prepared baking sheet. Continue until all the cheese mixture is used, making sure the pastries are not touching each other on the baking sheets. Brush them all with the egg wash, if using.

# THE SHAPES OF FILO PIES AND PASTRIES

**F**ILO PIES SERVED AT FAMILY GATHERINGS IN GREECE ARE USUALLY BAKED IN DEEP RECTANGULAR PIE PANS OR IN GREAT CIRCULAR *TAPSI*, THEN CUT INTO SQUARE OR DIAMOND-SHAPED PIECES FOR SERVING. PIECES CAN ALSO BE CUT LIKE PIE WEDGES.

Pies for snacks are commonly turned or rolled into triangular shapes, like three-cornered hats.

Party pies are often twisted into cigar, snail, or other fanciful shapes.

For individual pies you can also shape them in a muffin pan. Or, for a very pretty rendition, arrange long snakes of stuffed filo around the inside of a pie pan, forming a spiral; then cut the baked rolls into wedges, squares, or diamonds. The top crust will look like curling waves.

With filo dough's great versatility, all these shapes are easy.

## TRIANGLES

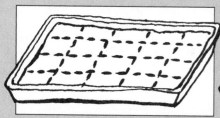

For small triangles, cut filo sheets lengthwise into 2¹/₂- to 3-inch-wide strips (or into 5-inch-wide strips for larger triangles). Stack the strips in a pile.

Oiling each strip—you can use them singly, or for a flakier crust, use two or three layered strips at a time—place a dollop of filling at one narrow end. Then fold the bottom edge of the strip to the left side, forming a triangle. Oil the top. Fold the triangle up along the left side, then across to the right side, as if folding a flag, triangle upon triangle. Oil each fold, and then oil and tuck in the edge and top.

## SQUARES AND DIAMONDS

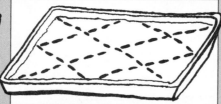

To cut a pan of pastry into squares, make evenly spaced score marks in the pie both horizontally and vertically. To cut it into diamonds, first score the pie from the upper left corner to the lower right. Make parallel and evenly spaced score marks to the top, then to the bottom of that center mark. Then cut a score mark from the upper right corner to the lower left. Make parallel and evenly spaced score marks above and below it. Following the score marks, cut the pieces through after baking. Two- to 3-inch squares or diamonds are typical.

## CIGARS

Cut the filo lengthwise into 4-inch-wide strips. Oil and stack the strips. Oil the top strip, and spread a dollop of filling along one narrow end, leaving about ¹/₂ inch at either side. Fold the unfilled edges over the filling and up the length of the strip. Then roll the filo up tightly from the filled end, forming a cylinder. Oil the tucked-in "cigar tips" and the top of the "cigars."

For larger tube shapes, use 5-inch-wide strips and more filling.

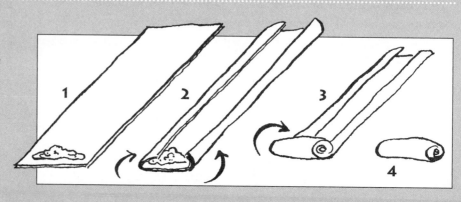

## SNAILS OR COILS

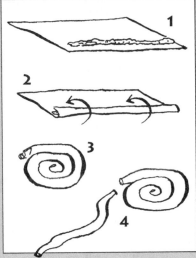

*Oil a whole rectangular sheet of filo dough. Spread the filling in a narrow line 1/2 inch in from the edge along the entire long side of the sheet. Roll the 1/2-inch edge over the filling, and continue rolling, forming a long thin cylinder. Starting at one end, and tucking the tip down as you come around, coil the row around itself. Continue until the roll is completely coiled. Oil and tuck the end tip under.*

## HALF-MOONS

*Use thicker filo or several oiled and stacked sheets together. Cut the filo into 5-inch-wide strips. With a 2 1/2- to 3-inch round cookie cutter or jar lid, cut out circles from the strips. About 1/2 inch in from the bottom of each circle, dollop a spoonful of filling. Fold the top of each circle over the filling, then oil the tops, and press or pinch the edges of the semicircles together.*

4 Place the baking sheets in the oven and bake until the pastry is golden and the cheese has melted, about 25 minutes. Remove and set aside until cool enough to handle. Serve warm or at room temperature.

### NOTES:

■ The triangles called for here are small, hors d'oeuvre size. To make cheese pies the size of those sold on the streets of Greece, cut the filo strips 5 inches wide and use twice as much filling in each. You will get 25 to 30 pieces.

■ If using mizithra, which is strong and salty, place a little less filling in each triangle.

■ For speed, you can make a cheese pie in a single 11- x 9-inch baking pan, using 6 sheets of filo on the bottom and 6 on top. Score the pastry into squares or diamonds.

### FILLING INNOVATIONS

**The Tarragon Touch:** Add 1 teaspoon chopped fresh tarragon, or 1/2 teaspoon dried, to the cheese mixture.

**Olive Version:** Add 1/2 cup chopped Kalamata olives to the cheese mixture (rinse them before chopping so they're not too salty).

**Tangy Picnic Version:** Add 1/3 cup finely chopped jarred grape leaves. (Use the tender parts of the leaves, removing the thicker, tough veins.)

**A Racy Version:** Add 1 tablespoon chopped fresh fennel to the cheese mixture. ("Fennel" is *maratho* in Greek.)

**Cheese and Rice Pie:** In many parts of Greece, cheese pies are made with rice, which stretches the cheese, makes the filling chewy, and renders the pie more substantial. Usually the pie is baked in a pan rather than in individual triangles, and it makes a distinctive side dish as well as a *meze*. Mix together 1 cup cooked arborio rice, 8 ounces crumbled manouri cheese, 3/4 cup combined grated kasseri and kefalotyri cheeses, 1/2 cup chopped flat-leaf parsley, 2 eggs, and 1/4 cup yogurt.

# classic spinach pie

## SPANAKOPITA

**MAKES ONE 13- X 9-INCH PIE;
SERVES 12 AS AN APPETIZER**

DARK GREEN SPINACH ORIGINATED IN THE MIDDLE EAST. ARABS WHO FOUND PEOPLE AVIDLY MUNCHING ON IT THERE INTRODUCED IT TO SPAIN IN THE EIGHTH CENTURY, AND FROM SPAIN THE VERDANT LEAF SPREAD TO THE REST OF EUROPE AND BYZANTIUM. LIKE TOBACCO, IT SPED SO RAPIDLY ACROSS NATIONS AND INTO CUISINES THAT PEOPLE EVERYWHERE THINK THE PLANT IS NATIVE TO THEIR LAND. CERTAINLY THE GREEKS DO. ALREADY GREAT EATERS OF GREENS, THEY WERE DELIGHTED TO OBTAIN ONE THEY COULD READILY GROW AND NOT FORAGE FOR, AND ONE SO RICHLY FLAVORFUL.

In Byzantine towns and villages, Greeks stirred the new edible into a pie, and the pie quickly became a signature dish. Parsley, dill, and scallions stir the appetite yet further. Otherwise the rendition is true to the original. Why trifle with a classic?

*2 pounds (about 2 bunches) fresh spinach, stems removed, leaves coarsely chopped, well rinsed, and drained*
*2¹/₂ tablespoons olive oil*
*8 scallions, trimmed, white and light green parts finely chopped*
*¹/₃ cup chopped fresh flat-leaf parsley leaves*
*¹/₂ tablespoon chopped fresh dill*
*10 ounces feta cheese, crumbled*
*3 large eggs, lightly beaten*
*¹/₂ teaspoon salt*
*12 to 16 sheets commercial filo dough, or 4 to 6 sheets homemade*
*Olive oil or melted butter, for oiling the filo*
*2 to 3 tablespoons milk, or 1 egg yolk beaten with ¹/₂ tablespoon water (optional)*

1 Preheat the oven to 375°F. Lightly oil the bottom of a 13- x 9-inch baking dish or equivalent round pan.

2 Place the moist spinach in a large nonreactive pot or skillet over medium heat, and stir until wilted but still bright green, 3 to 4 minutes. Drain in a colander, pressing down lightly to extract most of the water.

3 Place the 2¹/₂ tablespoons oil and the scallions in the same pot and stir over medium heat until the scallions begin to wilt, 3 to 4 minutes. Stir in the spinach, mix well, and then transfer the mixture to a large bowl.

4 Add the parsley, dill, cheese, eggs, and salt to the bowl and mix well.

5 Following the tips in Filo Finesse (page 87), cut the filo sheets to size. Oil and layer 6 to 8 sheets of commercial filo (or 2 to 3 sheets of the homemade filo) in the bottom of the prepared baking dish. Spread the spinach filling over the filo, and top with the remaining layers of oiled filo. Oil the top sheet. Tuck the filo in around the edges, and score the pastry to make 12 pieces. Brush the top with the milk or egg wash if using.

6 Place the pie in the oven and bake until the top is golden and

crisp, 45 minutes. Serve right away, or keep for up to 2 days in the refrigerator. Reheat or serve at room temperature.

## GATHERING

As small children following their mothers, Greek girls in the countryside learn which wild plants and herbs are edible or aromatic, which to gather for food or flavoring. I can recognize the kinnikinnick of my native Rocky Mountains, but I was a blank page when I first arrived in Greece. Taking me by the hand, my Greek companions slowly began to show me the leaves and roots, the stalks and flowers that I could add to my larder.

I am now almost accomplished when it comes to Greek herbs. I can spot all the obvious—oregano, marjoram, sage, and definitely dill, fennel, and anise—but I still miss the rarer varieties, and will never master all the greens. When pouncing on a carpet of chicory, my eyes bypass the salsify. When scooping up amaranth greens, I never notice the chenopodium. My companions jump upon a thicket of some chartreuse shoot—I see nothing but weed. My knowledge grows with each visit, but I am resigned to remaining botanically challenged. The good side is that I don't have to master total recognition because my friends are so generous. Whether I pick the greens or they do, I get to enjoy them all—pennyroyal mint to sow thistle to burdock.

# field greens, fennel, and ouzo pie

## HORTOPITA

**MAKES ONE 13- X 9-INCH PIE; SERVES 12 AS AN APPETIZER**

WHILE DEVOTED EATERS CAN NOW FIND THE SPINACH PIE, WITH ITS GREEN, ITS CHEESE, AND ITS EGG, ALL AROUND THE WORLD, THAT PIE IS A MERE DERIVATIVE OF THE PARENT: FILO *PITA* MADE WITH WILD GREENS. THE BEAUTY OF THE PROGENITOR IS THAT ALMOST ANY LEAFY GREEN CAN GO IN—SWEET GREENS, TANGY GREENS, SHARP GREENS, WOODY GREENS. THE GREEKS USE TENDER PICKINGS OF DANDELION, GRAPE HYACINTH, WILD MUSTARD, SORREL, CHICORY. THEY ALSO FILL PIES WITH THE YOUNG GREEN LEAVES OF THE POPPY PLANT, GATHERED FROM BELOW THE BLOOMS, LEMON BALM, AND FENNEL AND DILL FRONDS.

*Filo making is a family affair: He kneads and punches down the dough, she rolls it out.*

With equal aplomb, less wild greens such as chard, turnip greens, and sturdy lettuces, can be turned into a fine foliage pie. *Horto* pie is truly field- and market-based: What goes in is what's in season. To give the greens the wild scents of Greece, combine them with feathery fennel and dash them with ouzo.

2 pounds leafy greens, preferably
    a mix of sharp and buttery,
    such as dandelion, cress, turnip,
    spinach, and chard, well rinsed,
    drained, and chopped
3 tablespoons olive oil
1 onion, finely chopped
2 tablespoons chopped fresh fennel
    fronds with some of the
    tender stalk
2 tablespoons chopped fresh
    dill
2 tablespoons chopped fresh flat-leaf
    parsley leaves
3 tablespoons uncooked rice
3 large eggs, well beaten
6 ounces feta cheese, crumbled
1 tablespoon ouzo
1/2 teaspoon salt
1 tablespoon chopped capers
    (optional)
12 to 16 sheets commercial filo dough,
    or 4 to 6 sheets homemade
Olive oil or melted butter,
    for oiling the filo
2 to 3 tablespoons milk, or 1 egg yolk
    beaten with 1/2 tablespoon water
    (optional)

## THE SAGA OF THE CISTERN

Water is a necessity. You need it to drink, to wash your face and hands, to live. But during my early days in a Greek village, I was having a little water problem: I couldn't get any of the precious stuff.

The matter came to a crisis one day when I needed water to wash the wild greens I had gathered in the company of several other women. The leaves were dusty with Santorini's dry volcanic soil. Like others in the village, my house had no well, but rather sat over a deep rainwater-collecting cistern. City person that I was, however, I could get my bucket down into the cistern, but I simply couldn't make it dip into the glassy water. Try as I might, the bucket sat on the surface of the water. When I jiggled it, I could possibly get about two cups to splash in, but never more. Weeks had passed by now, and I was stretching my precious water as if I were lost at sea.

Then on this lucky day, old Marketousa happened to spy me bouncing my bucket on the water's unrelenting surface. "You poor baby," she said, scurrying over and patting me on the head. "Let me show you." She let the bucket down the channel, rested it for a short second on the water, then gave the rope a quick jerk, causing the bucket to turn over and dip its lip into the water. It sank and filled. Hand over hand, she pulled up the bucket, full to the brim and splashing water out on its way. She then bustled into my house, dropped my greens in a basin, and submerged them in the crystal fluid. But that was not all. She pulled down a sack of flour, took more of the water, and kneaded them together in an old battered pot to make dough—at which point she hustled out to attend to her abandoned chores. Two hours later she returned with her roller and rolled out filo. She drained my *horta* and chopped it into a mix of egg and lemon and dill. Like a master architect, she constructed a pie, then walked over to Marousi's (who had her oven lit) and baked me a *hortopita*.

I had many a teacher in Greece, and Marketousa was among the best of them. It's because of her that I can now make an ovenful of wild or tame— and well washed!—Greek greens pies.

1 Preheat the oven to 375°F. Lightly oil the bottom of a 13- x 9-inch baking dish or equivalent round pan.

2 Bring 3 quarts salted water to a boil in a large pot over high heat. Add the greens, cover, and cook until the greens are tender, 4 to 10 minutes depending on the age and type of green. Transfer the greens to a colander and set aside to drain for 10 to 15 minutes.

3 Heat the 3 tablespoons oil in a large skillet over medium heat.

Add the onion, fennel, dill, parsley, and rice and sauté until the onion is well wilted and the rice is milky white, 6 minutes.

4 Transfer the drained greens to a large mixing bowl. Add the skillet ingredients, and mix in the eggs, cheese, ouzo, salt, and capers, if using.

5 Following the tips in Filo Finesse (page 87), cut the filo sheets to size. Oil and layer 6 to 8 sheets of commercial filo (or 2 or 3 three sheets of the home-made filo) in the bottom of the prepared baking dish. Spread the filling over the filo and top with the remaining layers of oiled filo. Oil the top sheet. Tuck the filo in around the edges, and score the pastry to make 12 pieces. Brush the top with the milk or egg wash, if using.

6 Place the dish in the oven and bake until the pastry is golden and crisp, 45 to 50 minutes. Remove and let rest for 5 minutes. Serve hot or at room temperature.

# epiros cornmeal and greens pie

**MAKES ONE 13- X 9-INCH PIE;
SERVES 12 AS AN APPETIZER**

RATHER THAN USING FILO, IN EPIROS COOKS OFTEN MAKE A CORNMEAL CRUST FOR *HORTA* OR LEEK PIE. THOUGH GREEKS ARE NOT TERRIBLY FOND OF CORN, I, AMERICAN THAT I AM, AM MAD FOR IT AND ALSO FOR THE VERY AMERICAN COMBINATION OF GREENS AND CORNBREAD.

The pie, with its succulent mess of greens and its crunchy biscuit top, is a true intercontinental enchantment. I serve it with southern food and at barbecues. Why not? There are plenty of Greeks in Birmingham, Atlanta, New Orleans, and Dallas.

2 pounds leafy greens, preferably
    a mix of tangy and buttery,
    such as dandelion, cress, turnip,
    spinach, and chard, well rinsed,
    drained, and chopped
3 tablespoons olive oil
1 onion, finely chopped
2 tablespoons chopped fresh fennel
    fronds, including some of the
    tender stalk
2 tablespoons chopped fresh dill
2 tablespoons chopped fresh
    flat-leaf parsley leaves
3 large eggs, well beaten
4 ounces feta cheese, crumbled
1 tablespoon ouzo
$1/2$ teaspoon salt
1 tablespoon chopped capers
    (optional)
1 cup cornmeal or polenta

*An Epiros baker with a well-tempered pan sells warm pies through a street-level window.*

## AN ODE ON MY GRECIAN WATERWORKS

I had a container shaped like a half-
    barrel with a flat back.
It had a lidded opening on top, and
    a spigot on the rounded front.
It hung on a wall.
Beneath the container, attached to the
    same wall, I had a basin made of
    concrete.
It had a hole in the middle that could
    not be plugged.
Under the hole, on the floor, sat a
    bucket.

I would fill the water holder with
    water I collected from the cistern
    by the bucketful. (On bath days,
    I would heat the water.)
I would turn the spigot open, and
    water from the container would
    run over my hands, my hair,
    and if I'd been foraging, over
    the *horta* I'd gathered,
Into the basin,
Through the hole,
Into the bucket below.
I would pick up the bucket filled with
    the water that had run from the
    container through the basin,
Carry it out of the house, and dump
    the water on the garden near the
    cistern.

Running water, immediate drainage,
    effective plumbing.
Gravity flow for two years of living.

1 Preheat the oven to 375°F. Lightly oil the bottom of a 13- x 9-inch baking dish or equivalent round pan.

2 Bring 3 quarts salted water to a boil in a large pot over high heat. Add the greens, cover, and cook until the greens are tender, 4 to 10 minutes.

3 Transfer the greens to a colander, reserving the liquid, and set them aside to drain for 10 to 15 minutes.

4 Heat the oil in a large skillet over medium heat. Add the onion, fennel, dill, and parsley and sauté until the onion is well wilted, 6 minutes.

5 Transfer the drained greens and the skillet ingredients to a large mixing bowl. Mix in the eggs, cheese, ouzo, salt, and capers, if using.

6 Evenly spread half the cornmeal over the bottom of the prepared baking dish. With your fingers, sprinkle 1 to 2 tablespoons of the reserved greens liquid over the cornmeal (as you would when dampening laundry to be ironed) until the entire bottom of the pan is evenly sprinkled.

7 Gently spread the filling evenly over the cornmeal.

8 Spread the remainder of the cornmeal over the greens, and sprinkle it again three or four times with some of the reserved liquid, until the top is evenly dampened.

9 Place the dish in the oven and bake until the top and bottom crusts are golden and crunchy, about 1 hour. Remove and let rest for 5 minutes before serving. Serve hot or at room temperature.

### OTHER CORN CRUST "FILL-INS":

Instead of leafy greens, use coarsely shredded zucchini, squeezed dry. In place of fennel, you can use chopped leeks.

And as a stand-in for dill, you can use 1 tablespoon chopped fresh chervil.

# leek, potato, and olive pie

## PRASSOPITA

**MAKES ONE 13- X 9-INCH PIE;
SERVES 12 AS AN APPETIZER**

LEEKS GROW SO WELL IN GREECE'S HOUSEHOLD GARDENS THAT THEIR NAME SIMPLY MEANS "GREEN." EVERY HOUSEWIFE KNOWS EXACTLY WHEN THE UPRIGHT LEAVES HAVE STRETCHED TALL ENOUGH TO INDICATE THAT THE WHITE OF THE LEEK IS THICK AND READY. WITH A HANDFUL OF FAT ONES, SHE CAN MAKE *PRASSOPITA*, THE CHEAPEST OF PIES AND ONE OF THE BEST.

## TWO ANCIENTS AND THE LEEK

Aristotle claimed that the clear cry of the partridge could be attributed to its diet of leeks.

When Herodotus was scribing an account of his country's war with Egypt, he asked for a translation of the heiroglyphs of the great pyramid at Cheops. It said sixteen hundred silver talents had been spent on radishes, leeks, onions, and garlic for the workers. Since Greek eating habits were similar to the Egyptians', and onions were not even considered true food at the time, he queried how much their *actual* vittles, clothing, and tools had cost.

Two unusual touches bring a leek pie to new heights: potato, such a good companion to any sort of onion, and olives, whose ebony dots add a salty accent. While black olives have a better color contrast, green olives offer more astringency: The choice is yours. An extra layer of filo in the center graces the soft filling with satisfying crispness.

*3 tablespoons olive oil*
*3 to 4 medium leeks (1 1/2 pounds total), white and light green parts well rinsed, drained, and chopped*
*1 large egg*
*1 tablespoon milk*
*2 medium potatoes (10 ounces), peeled and coarsely grated*
*3 tablespoons chopped Kalamata or other good black or green Greek olives*
*1/3 cup grated kefalotyri or Parmesan cheese*
*2 tablespoons chopped fresh dill*
*3/4 teaspoon salt*
*Dash of cayenne pepper*
*12 to 15 sheets commercial filo dough, or 6 to 9 sheets homemade*
*Olive oil or melted butter, for oiling the filo*
*2 to 3 tablespoons milk, or 1 egg yolk beaten with 1/2 tablespoon water (optional)*

1 Preheat the oven to 375°F. Lightly oil the bottom of a 13- x 9-inch baking dish or equivalent round pan.

2 Heat the 3 tablespoons oil in a nonreactive skillet over medium heat. Add the leeks and sauté until they are well wilted but still bright green, 10 minutes. Set aside to cool slightly.

3 While the leeks are cooling, lightly beat the egg together with the 1 tablespoon milk.

# THE TRAIL OF THE OLIVE

A SPINY, INDIGENOUS VARIETY OF OLIVE WAS ALREADY GROWING IN GREECE WHEN THE FIRST PEOPLE BEGAN TO LIVE THERE. THE TREE WAS NATIVE TO THE LEVANT AS WELL, AND PEOPLE IN BOTH PLACES WERE QUICK TO REALIZE THE VALUE OF THE FRUIT AND, SOON, TO CULTIVATE IT. EVIDENCE EXISTS THAT INHABITANTS OF SYRIA AND PALESTINE WERE PLANTING THE TREE BY 4000 B.C.E., AND OLIVE PITS ARE FOUND IN MANY NEOLITHIC AND BRONZE AGE SITES. THE BIBLE MENTIONS OLIVES AND OLIVE OIL MANY TIMES. SOON GROWERS OF THE TREE WERE SELLING OLIVE OIL TO EGYPT TO REPLACE THE RADISH SEED AND MORINGA FRUIT OIL EGYPTIANS HAD USED. ORCHARDS OF OLIVE TREES WERE QUICKLY THICK ENOUGH FOR RAIDERS TO USE THE WOOD TO BURN DOWN BESIEGED TOWNS, AND EXCAVATIONS AT UGARIT, IN SYRIA, HAVE REVEALED LARGE STORES OF OLIVE OIL VESSELS, APPARENTLY READY AND WAITING FOR TRADE WITH OTHER LANDS.

cereal grains. Orchards of olive trees were grown wherever Greeks spread, and where the Greeks spread is quite possibly explained by the olive tree. Olives need coastal semi-arid land, and that is where Greeks settled—in places where the tree could grow. From harbor to harbor, with sea breezes and dry soil, the Greeks brought the trees and the fruit they depended upon to the shores of Italy and Sicily, the Iberian peninsula, and the coast of France. In all these lands where the olive thrived, the people claim the olive as their own. Each developed new olives and pressed fine oils, and each now alleges to have the best olives and the finest olive oil in the world.

King Minos did have the golden touch, after all, and left behind a wealth of treasure—only it was green-gold trees, black to green-gold olives, and vats of golden oil.

## THE MINOANS

The people who settled Crete were quick to realize the virtues of the olive as well. Though the wild olive yields little oil, the Minoans developed the domestic olive quickly enough for the unctuous liquid to play a vital part in their economic command of the eastern Mediterranean. They had the plant under cultivation by 2500 B.C.E. and by late Minoan times had invented oil presses. They also had settling vats for extracting the oil from the olive fruit, much like those still used in Crete. Virtually every Minoan site reveals vast quantities of jars used to store olives and olive oil, and storerooms of oil jars in palaces indicate that the fruit and the oil were considered part of the treasury. Minoans contrived and

peddled perfume oils as well, and these were olive oil–based. For their perfumes, it seems, they preferred the unguent of wild olives and continued to gather these.

## A LEGACY OF OLIVES

When the Greeks came upon the Minoans—if the myth of Theseus, King Minos, and the Minotaur be based on fact—first as subjects, then as conquerors, they took over the Minoans' olive legacy. By the classical period, from about 800 to 300 B.C.E., Greeks were breeding many new varieties of olives, now combining their cultivation with many sorts of grapevines and

*A long-haired Minoan woman carries a heavy swirl-handled pitcher of ruby wine or amber oil.*

**4** Place the potatoes, olives, cheese, dill, salt, and cayenne in a mixing bowl. Add the leeks and the egg mixture and stir together.

**5** Following the tips in Filo Finesse (page 87), cut the filo sheets to size. Oil and layer one third of the filo in the bottom of the prepared baking dish. Add half the filling, spreading it out evenly. Oil and layer another one third of the sheets over the filling. Spread the remaining filling evenly over the filo. Oil and layer the remaining sheets of filo on top. Oil the top of the pie. Tuck the filo in around the edges, and score to make 12 pieces. Brush the top and around the edges with the milk or the egg wash, if using.

**6** Place the dish in the oven and bake until the top and the edges are golden and crisp, 1½ hours. Serve right away, or at room temperature.

**NOTES:**

▪ You can also make the pie with simply a top and bottom crust and one layer of filling.

▪ The milk trick (see page 86) is particularly good for leek pie.

## FOOD: GREEK TO ROMAN TO BYZANTINE

Ancient Greeks had a preference for finely chopped food. They ground meats, vegetables, grains, and herbs in mortars or reduced them to purees, all of which led to the development of many a stuffing. They served their mashes wrapped in grape and other leaves, packed inside birds, and stuffed in doughs—the beginnings of *bourekakia*. The Romans followed this predilection, but their appetite tended toward the lavish. They favored extreme spicing, elaborate preparation, and pungent sauces on their chopped foods and complex stuffings.

The Byzantines carried on from there, hungering for highly wrought salmagundis, flamboyant flavorings, sauces, and extravaganzas. They also continued, with the panache that only they could display, the habits of mincing and filling. Foods in Constantinople, at least for the courtiers and the wealthy, involved ambitious and ostentatious dishes with a great many ingredients, sometimes one food placed inside another, often over imbued with exotics. Breads were filled. Cakes were filled. Pies were filled. The presentations became as wildly highfalutin as the preparations. Some dishes grew as tall as a chef's hat; others were crafted as tiny and delicate as the jewelry created by fellow artisans.

Still, much about the food was essentially Greek and Roman. The use of fish sauce, *garum*, continued in Byzantium long after it was deemed exceedingly unpleasant in the Western world. A certain Bishop Liutprand of Cremona visited Constantinople in the mid-900s as the ambassador from Germany. He writes that he was served kid goat that was stuffed with onions, leeks, and garlic—all, however, completely saturated in fish sauce. Though red wine was no longer watered as the Greeks and Romans had done, the poor bishop found that the wine still was flavored with resin as in ancient Greece. He couldn't drink it any more than he could stomach the fish sauce.

# mushroom and retsina pie

**MAKES ONE 13- X 9-INCH PIE; SERVES 12 AS AN APPETIZER**

IN THE DAMP AREAS OF GREECE, WHERE RAINS FALL AND THE EARTH GETS LOAMY AND MOIST, MUSHROOMS RISE UP IN GREAT COLONIES. THEIR SEASON FOLLOWS THE DRIZZLE AND FOG—MID-FALL THROUGH LATE WINTER. THE MOST COMMON MUSHROOMS, AS IN NEIGHBORING ITALY, ARE PORCINI, BUT GREAT NUMBERS OF OTHERS ALSO APPEAR TO THE ELATION OF EVERY COOK IN THE VICINITY.

Wild mushrooms are still known as *manites,* not the diminutive *manitaria,* used for commercial ones. These earthy morsels are thought of as "mountain" or "forest" food, and evoke sylvan images. Since the primary mountain and forest tree of Greece is the venerated pine, a piney retsina suits them well. Here the filling is baked in a large pie, but it can also be wrapped in small shaped filo pies—as snails, half-moons, or *bourekia.* The succulent treats will disappear as mysteriously as mushrooms among the mountain ferns.

*2 pounds mixed mushrooms, such as porcini, chanterelle, or oyster*
*2 tablespoons olive oil*
*1 medium leek, trimmed, white and light green parts thinly sliced, well rinsed, and drained*
*4 large cloves garlic, coarsely chopped*
*1 teaspoon paprika, preferably hot Hungarian*
*1 teaspoon fresh thyme leaves, or scant 1/2 teaspoon dried*
*1/2 cup retsina wine*
*1 tablespoon fresh lemon juice*
*3/4 teaspoon salt*
*12 to 16 sheets commercial filo dough, or 4 to 6 sheets homemade*
*Olive oil or melted butter, for oiling the filo*
*2 to 3 tablespoons milk, or 1 egg yolk beaten with 1/2 tablespoon water (optional)*

## A ROSTER OF NYMPHS

In Greek mythology, the nymphs were minor divinities of nature, and there were almost as many of them as there were mushrooms. Like mushrooms, they could pop up almost anywhere. Also like mushrooms, they thrived in clusters, often circles, and preferred shadow and shade. Some were good; some very, very bad. The good ones you had to treat delicately or they spoiled. The others, the potentially harmful ones, you learned to avoid. In addition to the ones below, almost every local geographic feature—a river, a spring, a meadow, a beach—had its own nymphs who were named for the place.

**DRYAD:** a wood nymph. Some say more specifically a tree nymph. There were also *hamadryads,* who lived in individual trees and died with them.

**THE MAENADS:** the frenzied women who followed the drunken Dionysos, the god of wine.

**NAIAD:** a nymph that lived in lakes, rivers, springs, and fountains; in short, a water nymph.

**NEREID:** a sea nymph, one of the fifty to one hundred daughters of Nereus and Doris who attended Poseidon. Some also lived in springs and trees.

**OCEANID:** a nymph of the ocean, a daughter of Oceanus and Tethys.

**OREAD:** a mountain nymph (for *oros,* meaning "mountains").

1 Preheat the oven to 375°F. Lightly oil the bottom of a 13- x 9-inch baking dish or equivalent round pan.

2 Wipe the mushrooms clean, and trim the stem ends. Cut the mushrooms into slices about ¼ inch thick and set them aside.

3 Heat the 2 tablespoons oil in a large skillet over medium heat. Add the leek and garlic and sauté until beginning to wilt, 3 minutes. Add the paprika, thyme, retsina, lemon juice, salt, and mushrooms. Stir over high heat until the juices have evaporated but the mushrooms are still moist, 6 to 7 minutes. Set aside to cool.

4 Following the tips in Filo Finesse (page 87), cut the filo sheets to size. Oil and layer 6 to 8 sheets of commercial filo (or 2 or 3 sheets of homemade filo) in the bottom of the prepared baking dish. Add the filling, spreading it out evenly. Oil and layer the remaining sheets of filo over the top. Oil the top of the pie. Tuck the filo in around the edges, and score to make 12 pieces. Brush it with the milk or the egg wash, if using.

5 Place the dish in the oven and bake until the top is golden and crisp, 30 minutes. Serve right away or at room temperature.

# squash and cardamom pie

**MAKES ONE 13- X 9-INCH PIE; SERVES 12 AS AN APPETIZER**

FROM THRACE TO THE PELOPONNESOS, GREEKS ENJOY TOWERING PITAS FILLED WITH THE GARDEN SQUASH THEY GROW SO ABUNDANTLY. IN THE NORTH, THE SQUASH PIE TENDS TO BE SWEET. STRAY TOWARD THE PELOPONNESOS AND THE PIE IS MORE SAVORY. THE VERSION BELOW HOLDS THE MIDDLE GROUND, USING CARDAMOM, A SWEET SPICE KNOWN SINCE ANCIENT TIMES, BUT NO SUGAR.

And while the squash the Greeks use most often is zucchini, the filling can come from any squash. Using yellow winter squash creates a pie that is more autumnal and more richly flavored. Almost all squash pies use a little rice or bulgur. The choice is yours: The former is chewier; the latter crunchier.

*2 tablespoons olive oil*
*¼ cup pine nuts or chopped walnuts*
*1 small onion, finely chopped*
*2 pounds pumpkin, Hubbard, butternut, or acorn squash, peeled, seeded, and coarsely grated (5 cups)*
*½ cup cooked rice, or ¼ cup cooked bulgur*
*½ cup chopped fresh flat-leaf parsley leaves*
*¼ teaspoon ground cardamom*
*1½ teaspoons salt*
*1 teaspoon freshly ground white pepper*
*2 large eggs, lightly beaten*
*2 tablespoons fresh lemon juice*
*12 to 16 sheets commercial filo dough, or 4 to 6 sheets homemade*
*Olive oil or melted butter, for oiling the filo*
*2 ounces (about 2 tablespoons) crumbled feta cheese*
*2 to 3 tablespoons milk, or 1 egg yolk beaten with ½ tablespoon water (optional)*

1 Preheat the oven to 375°F. Lightly oil the bottom of a 13- x 9-inch baking dish or equivalent round pan.

2 Heat the 2 tablespoons oil in a small skillet over medium-high heat. Add the nuts and the onion and sauté gently until the nuts begin to turn golden, 2 to 3 minutes. Transfer to a large mixing bowl.

3 Add the pumpkin, rice, parsley, cardamom, salt, white pepper, eggs, and lemon juice to the bowl and mix well.

4 Following the tips in Filo Finesse (page 87), cut the number of filo sheets you are using to size. Oil and layer 6 to 8 sheets of commercial filo (or 2 to 3 sheets of homemade filo) in the bottom of the prepared baking dish. Add the filling, spreading it out evenly. Sprinkle the cheese over the filling. Oil and layer the remaining sheets of filo on top. Oil the top of the pie. Tuck the filo in around the edges, and score to make 12 pieces. Brush with the milk or the egg wash, if using.

5 Place the dish in the oven and bake until the top and the edges are golden and crisp, 1½ hours. Serve right away or at room temperature.

**NOTES:**

■ Zucchini, which Greek kitchen gardens provide in abundance, can be used instead of winter squash. But remember that all squash, and especially an overgrown zucchini, can be watery. You might need to squeeze water from the grated squash, or add more rice or bulgur.

■ To make a sweet squash pie in the style of Thrace, follow the recipe using winter squash, and add ¼ to ½ cup honey.

## CARDAMOM

The Greeks probably first learned of cardamom from the swashbuckling Phoenicians, who were avidly sailing and trading throughout the Mediterranean when Greeks first arrived and continued to do so throughout the flowering of Greek civilization. In particular, the Phoenicians ferried large cargos of spices to and from Egypt. The Egyptians utilized great quantities of Indian spices, not only to flavor their food but also to mummify the dead.

Cardamom, from the ancient Greek word *kard*, made its way to Greece from the cardamom hills of the southern tip of the Malabar Coast in western India. Eighty percent of the world's cardamom still comes from there. Along with clove, cinnamon, ginger, and pepper, cardamom poured into Byzantium, the terminus of the overland trade routes. From that key trading city, the spices were loaded onto ships ferried to Thessaloniki and other Greek cities, to Rome, and on to Venice and northern Europe.

Nowadays Greeks use the spice almost exclusively in sweet pastries. My own love of cardamom comes not only from its use in Greek cooking, but also from my Swedish ancestry. Like Swedes and Greeks both, I sometimes put a tiny dish of partially crushed cardamom seeds on my kitchen counter just to perfume the air. To use it in squash pies or sweet filo pastries, I crush fresh seeds more finely.

# shrimp-filled filo rolls

## BYZANTINE-STYLE

### PSAROPITES

**MAKES 18 TO 20 PIECES**

SURROUNDED AS IT IS BY WATER—THE SEA OF MARMARA AND THE DARDANELLES BELOW, THE BOSPOROS AND THE BLACK SEA ABOVE—BYZANTIUM WAS (AND ISTANBUL STILL IS) RENOWNED AS A CENTER OF THE SEAFOOD TRADE. ITS TUNA WAS ACCLAIMED THROUGHOUT THE EASTERN MEDITERRANEAN BEFORE CONSTANTINE SETTLED THERE; THE BREAM WAS LAUDED; THE OFFSHORE WATERS PRODUCED ABUNDANT SHELLFISH, AMONG THEM TEEMING SHRIMP, AND STILL DO. HERE, IN A NOD TO THAT WATERY WORLD, IS A *BOUREKAKIA* COILED AROUND A HEART OF PLUMP, PINK SHRIMP. WITH DILL AND CHIVE ADDING A FLICKER OF GREEN, THESE LITTLE SHRIMP *PITES* ARE A BYZANTINE JEWEL.

1 1/2 cups Saltsa Besamel
   (page 459)
3 tablespoons Muscat wine
1/3 cup fresh lemon juice
12 ounces uncooked shrimp,
   shelled, deveined, and
   coarsely chopped
3 tablespoons chopped fresh
   dill
1/4 cup chopped fresh chives

9 to 10 sheets filo dough,
   commercial or homemade,
   quartered to make 9- x 7-inch
   rectangles for commercial
   dough or 7- x 6-inch for
   homemade
Olive oil or melted butter,
   for oiling the filo
1 egg yolk beaten with
   1/2 tablespoon water (optional)

1 Place the *saltsa besamel*, wine, lemon juice, shrimp, dill, and chives in a medium-size bowl and stir to mix.

2 Preheat the oven to 400°F. Very lightly oil a baking sheet.

3 Brush a rectangle of filo lightly with oil. Place about 1 1/2 tablespoons of the shrimp mixture in a narrow strip along the long side of the rectangle, and spread it out the full length. Roll the filo once over the shrimp, then continue rolling until the filled dough is in one long roll. Starting from one end of the roll, turn the roll into itself, continuing round and round to make a coil. Place the coil on the prepared baking sheet, seam side down. Lightly oil the top of the roll with oil, and brush it with the egg wash, if using. Repeat with the remaining filo sheets until all the mixture is used.

4 Bake until crisp and golden on top, 20 minutes. Serve right away or at room temperature.

# chicken pie

## WITH ONIONS, NUTMEG, AND SAFFRON

### KOTOPITA

**MAKES ONE 13- X 9-INCH PIE; SERVES 12 AS AN APPETIZER**

GREECE'S ENTIRE LINEUP OF LUSCIOUS FILO PIES IS CROWNED BY A REIGNING TRIUMVIRATE: CHEESE PIE, SPINACH PIE, AND AN INCOMPARABLE CHICKEN PIE.

There hardly exists a nation where the mere mention of chicken pie doesn't evoke homage and stir hunger. Greece is no exception. The chicken pie of Greece, though, doesn't arrive sunk in a deep pot and crusted on top (France) or crusted both under and over (America). Rather, its dense stuffing lies between sheets of golden, crunchy filo. A rendition where the stewed chicken is infused with saffron and mixed with a wealth of amber-hued sautéed onions especially tantalizes. On top of that, a dash of nutmeg, combined with the usual dill and lemon, opens up all the flavors.

*4 cups chicken stock, preferably homemade (page 170)*
*12 chicken thighs (about 3 1/2 pounds total), skinned*
*2 tablespoons plus 1 teaspoon olive oil*
*3 tablespoons butter*
*2 medium onions, quartered and thinly sliced*
*2 tablespoons all-purpose flour*
*3 large eggs, well beaten*
*2 1/2 tablespoons fresh lemon juice*
*1/2 cup chopped fresh dill leaves*
*Dash of nutmeg, preferably freshly grated*
*1/2 teaspoon saffron threads, or 1/4 teaspoon ground*
*3/4 teaspoon salt*
*12 to 16 sheets commercial filo dough, or 4 to 6 sheets homemade*
*Olive oil or melted butter, for oiling the filo*

**1** Place the stock and the chicken thighs in a large heavy pot and bring to a boil over high heat. Reduce the heat, partially cover, and simmer until the meat is very tender and no longer pink around the bone, about 25 minutes. Set aside to cool completely in the stock.

**2** Heat the 2 tablespoons oil and 1 tablespoon of the butter in a large heavy skillet over medium heat until the butter melts. Add the onions, stir to coat, and sauté, stirring occasionally, until they are thoroughly soft and golden brown, 20 to 25 minutes. Set aside.

**3** When the chicken and stock are cool, lift out the thighs, reserving the stock, and cut or pull the meat off the bones. Tear or coarsely cut the meat into large pieces. Set aside.

4 In a medium-size nonreactive saucepan, heat the remaining 2 tablespoons butter over medium-high heat until foaming. Whisk in the flour and stir until beginning to turn golden, about 2 minutes. Slowly, in 1/2-cup amounts, whisk in the reserved stock, allowing the mixture to thicken slightly each time before adding more. When all the stock has been added, remove the pan from the heat and whisk in the eggs, lemon juice, dill, nutmeg, saffron, and salt.

5 Preheat the oven to 375°F. Lightly oil the bottom of a 13- x 9-inch baking dish or equivalent round pan.

6 Following the tips in Filo Finesse (page 87), cut the filo sheets to size. Oil and layer 6 to 8 sheets of commercial filo (or 2 to 3 sheets of the homemade filo) in the bottom of the prepared baking dish. Spread the onions evenly over the pastry. Spread the chicken over the onions, and pour the sauce over all. Oil and layer the remaining sheets of filo over the top. Oil the top of the pie.

Tuck the filo in around the edges, and score to make 12 pieces. Drizzle the remaining 1 teaspoon oil over the top.

7 Place the dish in the oven and bake until slightly golden on top, bubbling on the bottom, and crisp around the edges, about 50 minutes. Remove and let sit for 10 minutes or so, then serve.

## CONSTANTINOPLE QUAIL PIE

While there is no detailed recipe for the pies of ancient Greece, Byzantine texts indicate that the savory pies of that later empire were brought to crusty new heights and that abundant sorts of foods were placed in them. Saffron, used mostly in wine in classical Greece, now became a culinary ingredient, and nutmeg took over as a preferred spice. Feta, under its medieval name *prosfatos*, began to resemble the feta of today. The Byzantines raised so many fowl—pigeons, chickens, geese, pheasants, peacocks—that no doubt these birds found their way between sheets of pie dough.

The Byzantines also wrote of the small birds they liked to catch and eat. Of these, they particularly relished quail. They also very much favored sweet and flavored wines, their favorite being the Muscat of Samos.

The following old recipe for quail pie exists in a Latin text, not in Greek. But many Byzantine texts were written in Latin, and the recipe's ingredients indicate its Byzantine origin.

"In pastry dough place quails split in half. Add saffron, nutmeg, white cheese, pine nuts, and pieces of fatted pork. Seal with more dough. When the pie is done, pour in Muscat wine and bring to a boil."

**NOTE:** While you can rush the cooling process in Step 1 by removing the thighs from the stock and transferring the hot liquid to an unheated container, when you allow time for a slow cool-down together, the meat becomes more tender and the stock more flavorful.

*A donkey rests after carrying in the crops, while chickens scoot by, perhaps avoiding the cooking pot.*

## CRETE'S CREATIVE PIE MAKING

Like Sicily, the large island at the base of Italy, Crete, the island at the base of Greece, has a cuisine with a personality that is noticeably different from that of mainland fare. The reasons may be several. Crete, like Sicily, is large and the variety of its landscapes supports a diversity of foodstuffs: farming and herding, olive trees, coastal seafood, mountain wilds. The range of available edible goods is staggering, and would lead inventive cooks to innovate with it all. The island has seen many rulers of many cultural traditions who have left their stamp in many ways, including the cuisine.

On top of all that, the Cretans have a character of their own that speaks of thrift, wile, creativity, and decided independence. The cooks of the island and their unique dishes, including their pies, reflect those characteristics: countless vegetable entrees bestowing on the islanders their renowned health. There are half-moon *kalitsounia* pies filled with kefalograviera cheese, orange juice, and cinnamon; *lynoi* tarts of cheese and sesame seeds; *kallitsounakia*, pies of wild greens; as well as liver pies and pies of goat marinated in orange juice, oregano, and brandy.

# lamb pie

## WITH ALMONDS, RAISINS, ORANGE, AND MINT

### ARNOPITA

**MAKES ONE 13- X 9-INCH PIE; SERVES 12 AS AN APPETIZER**

ALTHOUGH ALMOST EVERY REGION OF GREECE HAS A SPECIAL MEAT PIE—BEEF PIES IN EPIROS, PORK PIES IN THRACE, MIXED MEATS IN KEFALONIA—THE TWO MOST FAMOUS ONES COME FROM THE FARTHEST REACHES OF THE COUNTRY. CRETAN MEAT PIES ARE PACKED WITH LIVER AND CINNAMON, WITH SWEETBREADS, AND WITH BRAINS.

At the opposite end of the nation, Macedonia, succulent lamb galvanizes the appetite. As Macedonians are happy to demonstrate, meat pies are best filled with pieces and shreds of meat, not ground meat. In keeping, an opulent lamb pie where the shredded meat is tossed with almonds, raisins, orange, and mint offers a lavish chewiness, while the filo's flakiness crumbles delectably into the mix.

*2 lamb shanks, cooked as in Roasted Lamb Shanks with Garlic and Thyme (page 387), and cooled in their juices*

*2 tablespoons butter*

*1 small onion, finely chopped*

*1/4 cup raisins or dried currants*

*1/4 cup blanched almonds, coarsely chopped*

*1 tablespoon chopped orange zest*

*1 tablespoon chopped fresh mint leaves*

*2 large eggs, lightly beaten*

*1/2 teaspoon salt*

*12 to 16 sheets commercial filo dough, or 4 to 6 sheets homemade*

*Olive oil or melted butter, for oiling the filo*

*1 egg yolk beaten with 1 teaspoon water (optional)*

1 When the lamb shanks are cool enough to handle, cut the meat off the bones and chop it. Transfer the meat to a mixing bowl, along with ¼ cup of the cooking juices, and set aside.

2 Preheat the oven to 350°F. Lightly oil the bottom of a 13- x 9-inch baking dish or equivalent round pan.

3 Melt the 2 tablespoons butter in a medium-size skillet over medium heat. Add the onion, raisins, and almonds and sauté until the onion is well wilted, about 4 minutes. Stir in the zest and mint and add the mixture to the lamb. Add the eggs and salt and stir to mix.

4 Following the tips in Filo Finesse (page 87), cut the filo sheets to size. Oil and layer 6 to 8 sheets of commercial filo (or 2 or 3 sheets of the home-made filo) in the bottom of the prepared baking dish. Add the filling, spreading it out evenly. Oil and layer the remaining sheets of filo over the top. Oil the top of the pie. Tuck the filo in around the edges, and score to make 12 pieces. Oil the top of the pie, or brush it with the egg wash.

## PIE FOR THE PIOUS, NONE FOR THE POOR

Byzantine religious leaders believed that good and evil waged a continuous battle at all times and in every person. To aid the side of good, in the tenth century the Byzantine clergy decided to compile a list of human sins. They included slander and envy, fornication and usury, rancor and avarice, pride and murder. There was no hope of sinning secretly. Watchful demons kept track of transgressions, which they detailed in record books they stored between earth and heaven. Only a full confession expunged sins and released the crime from the soul.

It was also a sin not to pay taxes to the emperor. This sin—apparently among the most serious—could be canceled only by payment or by torture. Citizens who did pay taxes and were loyal, however, entered into a contract with the emperor whereby they would always be provided food. Only absolute paupers were excluded from the contract. As they paid no taxes, their food depended strictly on the charity of fellow citizens. It seems the Byzantine emperors gave nothing to those who gave naught to them. One hopes the pie makers were more generous souls.

5 Place the dish in the oven and bake until the top and edges are golden and crisp, about 35 minutes. Serve right away.

### VARIATIONS:

**Lamb Filling Fill-ups:** A lamb filling, with its touch of Byzantine ornateness, invites other possibilities. Use it to fill hollowed-out tomatoes and peppers, or make gemlike *bourekakia* (see page 108).

**Eggplant Pie:** The Greeks would certainly not skip putting the eggplant within flaky filo. Substitute 2 to 3 pounds chopped cooked eggplant for the shredded lamb (peeled, eggplant sautéed in olive oil, or unpeeled eggplant baked to a pulp, then peeled). Like most eggplant dishes, the filling benefits from letting the ingredients sit together awhile, so you might want to make it a day ahead. A splash of balsamic vinegar can be added; it moves the pie beyond simply savory toward the sweet-and-sour spectrum.

# meat and cheese bourekakia

## WITH WALNUTS

### MAKES 16 TO 18 PIECES

BOUREKAKIA IS THE TURKISH WORD FOR SMALL FILO PACKETS. THE WORD COMES FROM *BURUK*, TURKISH FOR "COIL," ONE OF THE FAVORITE SHAPES OF *BOUREKAKIA. BOUREKAKIA* ARE SO DELIGHTFUL THAT THE CRUSADERS OF THE THIRTEENTH CENTURY WROTE HOME THAT THEY DIDN'T WANT TO LEAVE THEM BEHIND.

In Greek the pastries are called both *bourekia*—or the diminutive *bourekakia*—and *pitakia*, meaning "little pies." The shapes they can come in are many: triangles, half-moons, snails, cigars or flutes, boats, or whatever other fancy the filo folder contrives. The fillings tucked inside are as varied: meat, poultry, seafood, cheese, greens, all sorts of vegetable mixes, rice, noodles, and nuts. The only "must" is that the filling be tantalizingly savory. Here the filling is meat and the little pie is cigar shaped.

*1 tablespoon olive oil*
*1 small onion, finely chopped*
*$^1/_4$ cup walnuts, finely chopped*
*$^3/_4$ pound ground beef chuck or ground lamb*
*$^1/_3$ cup dry red wine*
*$^1/_2$ teaspoon salt*
*$^1/_4$ teaspoon freshly ground black pepper*
*2 tablespoons chopped fresh mint leaves*
*1 large egg, beaten*
*$^1/_3$ cup grated kasseri cheese*
*8 to 9 sheets commercial filo dough, or 6 to 7 sheets homemade, quartered to make approximately 9- x 7-inch rectangles for commercial or 7- x 6-inch for homemade*
*Olive oil or melted butter, for oiling the filo*
*1 egg yolk beaten with $^1/_2$ tablespoon water (optional)*

1 Heat the 1 tablespoon oil in a large heavy skillet over medium heat. Add the onion and walnuts and stir until steaming, 1 minute. Add the meat and stir, using a fork to break up the chunks, until beginning to brown, 2 minutes.

2 Stir in the wine, salt, and pepper and bring to a boil over high heat. Reduce the heat and simmer until thickened, 10 minutes. Remove from the heat and let cool slightly. Stir in the mint, egg, and cheese. Set aside to cool completely.

3 Preheat the oven to 400°F. Very lightly oil a baking sheet.

4 Brush a rectangle of filo lightly with oil. Place about 1$^1/_2$ tablespoons of the meat mixture in a corner and spread it out into a 2-inch-long sausage shape, toward the other empty corner, reaching diagonally from corner to corner. Fold an unfilled corner over the meat and roll one turn. Fold the sides of the filo over the roll, toward the center, then roll up all the way to make a short, fat cigar-shaped roll. Place it on the prepared baking sheet, seam side down. Lightly oil the top of the roll and brush it with the egg wash, if using. Repeat until all the meat mixture is used.

5 Place the baking sheet in the oven and bake until the rolls are crisp and golden on top, 20 minutes. Serve right away or at room temperature.

## VARIATIONS:

**Chicken Liver:** A pie that echoes the *tzoulama* of Crete is one I sometimes hanker for when nostalgic for that island. For the filling, replace the meat with 2¹/₂ pounds chicken livers that have been sautéed in olive oil and finely chopped. Replace the dry red wine with a sweet one— Mavrodaphne or Muscat. Add ¹/₂ cup currants that have been soaked in sweet wine (see page 49), and about 1¹/₂ teaspoons ground cinnamon. When building the pie, first spread a layer of crumbled *mizithra* cheese over the bottom crust. Then spread the liver filling over the cheese and cover with the top crust.

**Sweetbread Pie:** To make pies of sweetbreads, replace the meat in either the filling on the facing page or the lamb shank on page 106 with the same amount of sweetbreads that have been soaked, peeled, and gently sautéed in olive oil.

## BOLIKA BOUREKAKIA

·················

B ourekakia can be contrived in many and plentiful *(bolika)* fashions.

They can be wrapped in pasta, puff pastry, or bread dough as well as filo.

In some places in the Middle East, *bourekakia* are dropped whole into oil and deep-fried. Other times they are steamed.

They are sometimes topped with grated cheese and bread crumbs before baking, glazed with egg, or dusted with sesame seeds. *Bourekakia* are the quintessential finger food of Greece and all the Near and Middle East, and the delight of the hors d'oeuvre table.

Try them and you will see why.

# OPULENT BYZANTIUM

AN ARGUMENT HAS RAGED FOR MANY YEARS AS TO WHETHER THE FOODS COMMON TO BOTH GREECE AND TURKEY ARE ORIGINALLY GREEK OR TURKISH.

The most likely answer is that the shared cuisine derives from a single fountain from which both have drunk, a capital and kingdom both have owned: heralded Byzantium.

## AN EASTERN CAPITAL

The Byzantine Empire was founded in 330 C.E. when Constantine the Great transferred the capital of the Roman Empire from Rome to a city he at first called "New Rome," which in time came to be called after him, Constantinople. The Goths had invaded Italy and the incursions had destroyed the confidence of the once mighty Romans. Meanwhile a new religion, Christianity, had spread across the Roman Empire, and Constantine himself had converted. The center of that new faith lay to the east, away from marauding barbarians, and so, declaring his faith, Constantine moved.

The city he chose had been founded by a colony of Greeks from Megara under their leader, Byzas, in 658 B.C.E., and was already revered as holy. Several of Christianity's first disciples had traveled there, and saints of the new faith had experienced miraculous events nearby. The city also sat like a catbird on the world's richest trade route. Rome's treasuries had shriveled as the empire lost control over commerce, but Byzantium, midway between the Hellespont and the Bosporos, held sway over all the sea traffic between the Black Sea, the Aegean, and the Mediterranean. The city lay as well on a jutting promontory that brought Europe almost within arm's reach of Asia. So positioned, the colony served as a natural crossing point between the two continents and as a terminus of the overland spice route. Byzantium was a money box.

## CONSTANTINE'S EMPIRE

The empire Constantine launched lasted more than a thousand years. At various times it stretched to Armenia and the Caucasus mountains, through Serbia, the Kievan Rus of Russia, Syria, southern Italy, Palestine, and parts of North Africa. The dominion grew from what had been the eastern part of the Roman Empire, where the language and the dominant culture remained Greek. Throughout the life of the realm, the intellectual class spoke a version of Greek, while the common people largely spoke popular Greek. The alphabet derived from the ancient Greek. It came to be known as "Cyrillic" after the Byzantine apostle Kyrillos, who converted the Slavic people to Christianity and translated the Gospels into their language.

The empire's citizens thought of themselves as Romans—*Romanoi*. They would not recognize the term "Byzantine"; historians in the West invented that name. By the seventh century, the empire had changed so profoundly from its Roman forerunner that scholars devoted to Rome wished to distinguish—and elevate—the early Roman Empire from the latter. They began to refer to the eastern Empire with a term derived from the original name of the town Constantine resettled. The city to this day retains Constantine's name, although in curiously condensed form: In Greek the capital of the empire was called *Constantino-poli*, "Constantine's City," but the city loomed so singularly that it came to be known merely as "the City," or *i Poli*. To go to the city—a mark of importance—was *eis tin Poli*. The Turkish pronunciation of that same phrase is *Is-tan-bul*.

## AN IMPERIAL CITY

Thriving on the wealth, major city centers swelled with ranks of plutocrats, each of whom might have had several hundred slaves, a retinue of servants, including a hundred eunuchs, a stable, a palace, and a princely litter. Along with the rich and aristocratic, the empire housed courtiers, multitudes of clergy, and hordes of merchants. There were scribes, doctors, lawyers, imperial guards, entrepreneurs, and shopkeepers. Education was important, so Byzantium had many teachers. Women as well as men possessed wealth and position. They appeared on the streets and took part in social gatherings and ceremonies.

Poverty was as extensive and conspicuous as the wealth. Many inhabitants of Byzantium went without daily bread, for the rich, the royal, the administrators, and the church gathered up most of the plenty. Streets held beggars, lunatics, runaways, prostitutes, outcasts, and the sick. There were so many poor that they, too, had social classes: The *penes* were the poor with no means to support themselves. The *ftohoi* had vocations but could not rise above impoverishment. So many were the poor that it was here that the institution of charity arose.

*The art of painting icons reached its zenith during the Byzantine era and set the style to follow.*

## A LAND OF SAINTS

This world was also populated by a third class of inhabitants: the spectors of saints. As real and arduous as daily life in Byzantium was, an atmosphere of mysticism, legend, and miracle prevailed. It was during the Byzantine era that great numbers of Christianity's early saints appeared and reached beatification—St. George, St. Anthony, St. Nicholas, St. Demetrios, and St. Theodore.

*A stunningly detailed Byzantine mosaic of the Virgin Mother and Child.*

Perched on vast wealth, the people of Byzantium were enamored of spectacle and ostentation. Yet at the heart of all the pomp and ceremony was religion. Churches were lavishly adorned with colorful mosaics and icons inlaid with gems and precious metals. Services involved flaming lamps, incense, spectacular robes, banners, garlands, and objects of silver and gold.

## BYZANTINE COMPLEXITY

Spurred by the riches and the potential for power, as years passed a great web of laws, regulations, statutes developed. It's not without reason that the term "byzantine" grew to describe anything unduly rife with machinations and complexity.

Despite the ostentation and intrigue, however, the achievements of the empire were striking. The Byzantines began the tradition of monasteries. The legal code of Justinian emerged, along with the legislation of Christianity. The Byzantines established the rules for entrance into the religion, the sacraments, ceremony, and Lent. Volunteer work appeared.

The wealth of the empire also led to the extensive development of arts and crafts. The depictions of the Holy Family and saints—how they were to be represented in Christian iconography—were established. Much of what became the early music of Christianity emerged—simple vocals with a cantor or psalmist. Supported by the wealthy and the church, full-time artisans brought to new heights colorful mosaics, intricate gold and enameled jewelry, and metalware. Incredible fabrics and tapestries were woven, ceramics crafted, and ivory and bone carved.

There was tremendous erudition and intellectual life. Rulers and aristocrats were obsessed with the study of literature and of military discipline. Byzantines kept the ancient Greek tales alive and passed them on, much as earlier Romans had. It was Byzantine teachers who brought classics to medieval Italy and to the scholars and courts of northern Europe, and it was they who, fleeing the crumbling empire, ignited the Renaissance.

## AN IMPERIAL MELTING POT

So, too, the assets of the empire led to the development of cooking. Constantinople alone was a prolific source of foodstuff. Long before Constantine moved there, Archestratos and other Greco-Roman writers lauded the food eaten in Byzantium, especially the fish. The empire's long reach extended to some of the richest soil in the world: the flatland of Georgia, the Danube basin, the olive-nurturing soils of Anatolia. Peasants cultivated vineyards, orchards, nut trees. They planted both winter and summer crops, among them millet, oats, barley, and rye—a medieval innovation. Though they continued to till with the simple scratch plow, they grew cabbage, onions, leeks, carrots, garlic, cucumbers, sesame, melons, citron, pear, apple, cherry, plum, fig, pomegranate, mulberry, peach, and—to them the king of fruit—quince. Even the food of the poor included numerous vegetables, many fruits, cheese, olives, onions, salt pork, cabbage, and extensive flavorings—honey, pepper, cinnamon, cumin, caraway.

Chickens were so popular that a poultry industry developed, providing eggs to everyone. Specialists raised pigeons, geese, pheasants, and peacocks. Hunting provided boar, wild donkey, gazelle, and game birds. New foods came in: the eggplant, the orange, and finally sugar. The Byzantines discovered and carried with them the dried meat *pastoumas* of the Balkans. They imported a strange new fish delicacy, a roe from the Black Sea, called *kabiari* (caviar). They exchanged fish of southern seas for kippered herring from Britain.

Bakers invented literally hundreds of breads, wheat bread now ascending over barley. The population demanded so much bread, and bread was considered so basic, that bakers paid no taxes. One, a Hellenic baker named Paxamus, invented a hard toast that is still known throughout Byzantine lands by his name, *paximadi*. Pastries both savory and sweet reached a new apex. Chefs contrived rice puddings, jams, conserves, cookies, and a veritable fountain of flavored soft drinks entailing a whole new range of tinctures—ginger grass, violet, chamomile. Cheeses crafted in many new styles, mixed with spinach and such, made their entrance. To complete the menu, Byzantines favored flavored wines, and so wines were imbued with mastic, anise seeds, and other augments that became the ancestors of vermouth, absinthe, and ouzo. Meanwhile, though the poor drank vinegar water, the richer Byzantines began to drink their wine straight—no water was added.

Daily foods became complex. One typical Byzantine dish consisted of chicken white meat marinated in wine and stuffed with dumplings. Byzantines sprinkled nutmeg on gruels of yellow split peas, stuffed leaves, used saffron and rosemary in bread and in everything else in sight. They molded specific pots and pans for specific culinary purposes—a certain one for nut cakes, another for wheat cakes. Because of the new periods of abstinence Christianity demanded, there developed a whole cuisine based on the foods that were not forbidden, such as flatbreads, shellfish, and vegetables. And in due time the diet also embraced the diverse foods of all Byzantium's conquered people. The cuisine became a "melting pot."

## THE TRIUMPH OF THE TURKS

Throughout its long course, the Byzantine Empire constantly suffered bombardment from outside forces, all considered "barbarian." They came from the west and north as Goths, Serbs, and Bulgars. They rode in from the south and east as Arabs, Huns, and ultimately Turks. At the end, the invaders also included Crusaders from the west. Besieged by surrounding populations, particularly the unrelenting drive of the Turks, at last the empire crumbled. Ottoman Turks overran the great "City" in 1453, closing a chapter of history with finality.

So vast, so wealthy, so influential was Byzantium that many thought its end would bring the end of the world. No other empire has lasted as long. By the time it ended, the empire had encompassed ancient, medieval, and modern worlds, and its cuisine reflected its greatness.

## PART TWO

# the banquet of dishes

# RIPENED FRUIT SHINES ON A WHITEWASHED COUNTERTOP. A FRYING PAN SIZZLES NEARBY. CHILDREN RUN IN AND OUT THE DOOR. FATHER HAS ARRIVED. AND ON THE WELL-USED OILCLOTH-COVERED TABLE SITS A LAVISH ARRAY OF FOODS— TRULY A "SPREAD." READY FOR THE FAMILY TO DINE ON ARE SIX, EIGHT, PERHAPS TEN DISHES, AND NO ONE BLINKS AN EYE. THE SPRAWLING LARGESSE IS NORMAL, FOR IN THE GREEK WAY OF DINING, EVERY MAJOR MEAL IS A FEAST OF MANY FOODS.

most eat a diet far more balanced than do many people with other sorts of dining customs.

A number of the dishes in the typical Greek repast can be prepared in advance; others can be simmered right up until the table is spread; others are cooked or reheated just before serving.

The delights of dining this way are wide-ranging. The taste buds get to luxuriate in flavor after flavor—the roastedness of grain, the bite of garlic and onion, the juiciness of meat or bird, the sapidity of vegetable, the richness of sauce and myriad seasonings. An equal

*The selection of dishes offered at a Greek meal can be stunning.*

Rather than a constrained triad of protein, starch, and vegetable, waiting on that table lie a stew of beans, a fresh-from-the-garden salad, a fish soup, a small cut of pan-roasted meat, a plate of greens, simmered squash, slices of cheese, a bowl of spaghetti glistening with red sauce, fried potatoes, and possibly fried eggs. Rather than making a huge amount

of one entree, the Greek cook instead adds yet another kind of dish to the array. There is no special way to serve the plates, no order or courses. The cook just lays them out for all to help themselves.

Those dining pick a bit here, a dab there, never a huge portion of any one. In the end

number of textures—crunchy, crisp, hearty, meltingly soft, pulpy, and brawny—greet the palate, while a parallel set of aromas greets the nose. Temperatures range from room-cool to steaming hot.

The foods presented are enticing to the eye. There are plates of different sizes and

*Feasters at an ancient banquet welcomed musicians, here a flutist.*

shapes, a bowl, a platter, a fish-shaped server. They are filled with compositions of tomato red, sienna morsel, ecru bread, yolk yellow. The array might include a soup of vegetables, fish, legume, meat, or poultry; almost always a salad of a freshly harvested vegetable—cabbage, lettuce, radish, cucumber, or tomato; a plate of pulses—giant beans, lima beans, black-eyed peas; certainly a vegetable—simmered greens hot and cold, eggplant, okra, green beans, artichoke; perhaps a fritter; and always bread—hearty, crusty, plain, or seeded. There might be a garlic *skordalia* or a walnut sauce made from ground walnuts and pan juices. For dessert, always fresh fruit, perfectly ripe, sweet, dripping juice.

All told, every meal is an Epicurean adventure in the true sense of the Greek philosopher Epicurus. The table presents not an unwise or intemperate indulgence, but rather a lovely range of sensations, each one leading to pleasure, that pleasure leading to happiness. Epicurus expounded his thoughts from a garden in ancient Athens, and every Greek meal offers a garden's sort of variety back.

To dine at the Greek table is to dine both back in time and forward, for a range of foods and flavors were what ancient Greek philosophers and doctors advised Greeks to eat. Atheneaus states there were seventy sorts of bread alone. Socrates advised that simple grains should be gilded with all matter of tasty side dishes, from cheese to spice to piquant herbs. Ananos described meats by the season, similar to the year's round of seasonal vegetables. It is the way we modern Americans have also come to prefer: an assortment of choices and tastes at our table, an appetizer; a soup; a salad; a good grainy bread; a bit of fish, bird, or meat; a panoply of vegetables; a tasty grain or potato, perhaps studded with savories and herbs.

Two main meals are served, the greater one between one o'clock and three—perhaps earlier in the countryside. It is called *yeuma,* or simply *mesimeri,* meaning "midday." A smaller meal is served in the evening, after work is done, the shops have closed, and the sun has set—anytime between eight and eleven. This is *deipno,* and for it the array is less extensive. In order to tarry over the range of taste, texture, and color, the style of eating is utterly relaxed. Greeks take time to browse among the offerings, to talk, sit back, and enjoy. Along with the complement of foods, Greek meals feature a certain timelessness. Should you be invited to a dinner, no time is specified. Neither is an end set. People will lazily start anyway whether you are there yet or not. If you overstay, people will drift off to sleep. A meal, Greek etiquette seems to say, is not only a time to take in the abundance offered by the earth but also a time to disconnect from life's hustle and work's bustle. Dining is unto itself; meals are living life. I like the implication.

# bread
# THE STAFF OF LIFE!

ACCORDING TO PYTHAGORAS,
WIZARD OF MATHEMATICS,
THE ADVENT OF BREAD MARKED
THE BEGINNING OF THE WORLD.
TO HOMER, MASTER OF THE TALL
TALE, BREAD EATING WAS THE ACT
THAT MADE HUMANS HUMAN:
THOSE WHO KNEADED AND BAKED
THE LOFTY LOAF—AS THE GREEKS
DID—DREW BREATH IN A CIVILIZED
MANNER; THOSE WHO WERE
STRANGERS TO CRUST AND CRUMB
CARRIED ON IRREDEEMABLY AS
BARBARIANS.

Let the bins
be full and the
dough always
overflow the
kneading trough.

—HOMER, EPIGRAMS

*Baking bread in rings is as ancient as the banquets in Sparta.*

Bread was held to be so essential that the Greeks believed it was the first food that was cooked. *Mageireivo,* "to cook," arose from *masa,* both a type of flatbread and the verb for kneading. The most common bread made by the ancient Greeks was a plain leavened loaf they called *artos,* which in time became the term for all bread.

Other people had the knowledge and skill to make bread—the Egyptians and Hebrews were probably the first to develop leavening— but the early Greeks turned bread making into an art and an industry. By the fifth century B.C.E., Greeks were baking dozens of kinds of bread, some say hundreds. By the third century, bread was the subject of treatises by authorities and medical writers, such as Dilfilos of Sifnos, and later Galen. Athenaeus describes seventy-two varieties of bread. Greeks contrived bread from barley and wheat, from coarse groats to fine meal. They kneaded in poppy, flax, sesame, and anise seeds, honey, milk, cheese, pepper, raisins, wine, olives, pulses, and olive oil. Some breads were sour, some sweet, some flat, some risen. Some were free-form, others shaped, some domed, some round, and some twisted in rings.

Bread remains so basic a food that no Greek would think to have a meal, nor even a snack, without the sustaining loaf. Though the modern term for bread is *psomi,* bread stores are still called *artopoleions,* and Greeks still bake a ravishing array of breads. To the ancient flours modern Greeks have added rye, corn, and rice. They have extended flavorings to ouzo, *mahlepi, mastiha,* and a spirited variety of out-of-the-ordinary herbs and spices. The basic breads still range from the rougher to the more refined, from whole wheat and semolina to those made of silky white flour. In the countryside breads span the spectrum from slightly sour, dense, and earthy rustic loaves to specialty cakes containing corn, raisins, and olives. In the city, the granivore can find fine white bread, sesame rings, and smooth cake-style breads.

As well as continuing all the shapes and styles from ancient times, holiday breads bear holy stamps and decorations, hide coins, and proudly cushion dyed red eggs. As in ancient times, each holiday boasts a special bread, adding another reason for celebration.

Modern time constraints and ease of transportation have nibbled away at home baking in Greece, and except for holidays, when the baking of specialty loaves is a sentimental imperative, the breads of Greece now mostly come from the local commercial baker. The sampler presented here offers a selection of Greek-style breads. Some are traditional, others recontrived in innovative fashion.

# country bread

**MAKES TWO 1½-POUND LOAVES**

THOUGH PROFESSIONAL BAKERS HAVE ALWAYS THRIVED IN GREECE, UNTIL RECENTLY GREEKS MADE MOST OF THEIR OWN BREAD AT HOME. IN THE COUNTRYSIDE ESPECIALLY IT WAS THE WIFE'S CHORE TO PRODUCE THE BREAD NEEDED BY THE FAMILY—AND FAMILIES ATE POUNDS OF BREAD EACH DAY. IN SOME VILLAGES EACH HOUSE BOASTED ITS OWN SMALL COURTYARD BEEHIVE OVEN IN WHICH THE "LADY OF THE HOUSE," THE *NOIKOKYRA,* BAKED HER LOAVES. OTHER VILLAGES FEATURED A NUMBER OF LARGER, THOUGH SIMILARLY SHAPED, DOMED OVENS WHERE GROUPS OF RELATED WOMEN—SISTERS, AUNTS, AND COUSINS OF SEVERAL GENERATIONS—BAKED COMMUNALLY. THE WOMEN WOULD USE FLOUR GROUND FROM THEIR OWN WHEAT AND BARLEY, OR WOULD PURCHASE FLOUR GROUND AT LOCAL MILLS.

Now, generally, small local bakeries have taken over what was once the wife's chore, but the bread they produce is still the sort village women used to turn out. Utilizing a mix of coarse flours, it is what fancy bakeries label "peasant bread." But the countryside bread of Greece tastes like no other peasant bread. Rather than gaping with holes, it is dense. Rather than sporting a thick, chewy crust, its crust is thin and as crunchy as a cracker. Greek country bread is not highly risen, the crumb is thick and doughy, the color tan. It is somewhat sour in taste. The loaves are usually hand-formed, and they beckon with a fragrance and substance like no other.

*2 packages active dry yeast*

*1 teaspoon sugar*

*2 cups whole-wheat flour*

*2 cups warm water*

*4 cups unbleached all-purpose flour, plus extra for the work surface and kneading*

*3 teaspoons salt*

*¼ cup olive oil, plus extra for coating the bowl and baking sheet*

1 Mix together the yeast, sugar, ½ cup of the whole-wheat flour, and ½ cup of the water in a small bowl. Set aside in a warm place until spongy all the way

## BREAD AND URBANITY

The ancient Greeks considered their knowledge of bread and bread baking, which they began very early, a mark of civilization that lifted them above other peoples. They called the Romans, who were unfamiliar with bread until they met the Greeks, "porridge-eating oafs." The Romans, in turn, grew to esteem Greek bread bakers so highly that almost all the bakers in the entire Roman Empire, not just Rome itself, were Greeks. Some of the breads Greeks baked for the Romans were so luxurious that Cato, the stringent Roman censor, felt they were leading to decadence. He advised the Romans to return to gruel. They refused.

through, 30 minutes to 1½ hours, depending on how sour you want your bread.

2 In a large bowl, stir together the 4 cups all-purpose flour, the salt, and remaining 1½ cups whole-wheat flour. Make a well in the center and add the yeast mixture, ¼ cup oil, and remaining 1½ cups warm water. Stir with a wooden spoon until fairly well mixed. Then use your hands to knead the mixture in the bowl until you can gather it into a crumbly ball, 1 to 2 minutes. Transfer the dough to a lightly floured surface and knead until smooth and elastic and no longer sticky, about 5 minutes.

3 Lightly coat the dough with oil, and place it in the bowl (it can be the same bowl, wiped clean). Cover the bowl with a cloth and set it aside in a warm place until doubled in bulk, 2 to 2½ hours.

4 When the dough has risen, lightly coat a baking sheet with oil. Punch down the dough and knead it on a lightly floured surface for 1 to 2 minutes. Divide it in half and form each half into a slightly flattened oblong about 15 x 4 inches, or into an 18- x 4-inch loaf. Place them on the prepared baking sheet, cover with a cloth, and set aside in a warm

place until almost, but not quite, doubled in bulk, 1 to 1½ hours.

5 When ready to bake the bread, preheat the oven to 400°F.

6 Using a sharp knife, cut three or four slits in one direction and three or four crosswise in the other direction in the top of each loaf to make a large crosshatch pattern. Set the loaves aside to rest for 10 minutes.

7 Brush the top of the breads liberally with water and bake until distinctly golden across the top, 30 minutes. Brush liberally with water again, letting some drizzle down the sides, and continue baking until the loaves are very golden brown and hollow sounding when tapped with your knuckles, 15 minutes. Remove and let cool completely on the baking sheet before slicing.

**COUNTRY OR CITY BREAD (PAGE 124) ADD-INS:** Add any of these in either recipe, Step 2, after you've added the flour.

*COARSELY CHOPPED*

*2 cups cooked carrots*

*2 cups cooked chickpeas*

*1 cup olives, pitted*

*1½ cups onions*

*1½ cups walnuts*

*1 cup raisins or dried currants*

## WHEN THE PROOF IS NOT IN THE PUDDING

For those unfamiliar with bread baking, the instruction to "proof" the yeast may be confusing. In its most particular sense, to proof means to test that the yeast is active and ready to do its job, a process that takes just a few minutes.

When the bread requires more work from the yeast, the yeast is mixed with some of the flour and a bit more liquid and is left for longer, from an hour up to overnight. During that time, the yeast mixture becomes a "sponge," a mysterious entity that somehow adds flavor and airiness along with leavening. In this book, if the yeast needs only to be tested, I call for a short activating time, about 15 minutes, until the mixture is "bubbly." If the bread needs more activation from the yeast, the time is longer, an hour or more, and the mixture is described as "spongy."

*Preserved fruit*

*½ cup commercial candied fruit*

*½ cups fresh rosemary, mint, dill, or fennel*

*YOU CAN ALSO ADD:*

*¼ cup anise, sesame, or poppy seeds*

*½ cup honey*

# THE BREAD MAN COMETH

THE DENIZENS OF THE GREEK VILLAGE WHERE I SETTLED IN HAD LONG SINCE GIVEN UP DAILY BAKING. THE ISLAND'S BIGGEST VILLAGE, CALLED "THE MARKET," HAD ATTRACTED A BAKER. HE SINGLEHANDEDLY BAKED ENOUGH BREAD FOR THE ENTIRE ISLAND, AND HE DELIVERED!

Every day except Sunday the baker dispatched great loads of bread to the island's fourteen villages. Because there were few cars and the road—should anyone wish to call it that—to the village where I lived was basically a track sunk two feet into pumice dust, the deliveryman faced a daily ordeal. He needed something that was capacious and could navigate the dust. And so the deliveryman arrived on a motorbike with two boxes strapped to the back, out of which the loaves stuck up like arrows pointing toward Orion.

Housewives could stop the bike with its courageous rider to buy bread directly, but the bulk of his delivery went to the one village store. All day busy homemakers dropped in to purchase the loaves they needed for the day. At three, when school let out, there was a quarter-hour's chaos in the shop when the children who lived in the upper part of the village stopped in to buy their family's bread before carting it up the steep mountainside to their homes.

Only one sort of bread was offered: a resolute, chewy, country bread. The loaves came in two sizes, one kilo and two. For the Saturday delivery the baker added a limited number of round loaves stamped with the holy seal, the *prosforo*, for customers to offer at Sunday service. For these there was always a rush.

I loved the bread. Throughout the years I never grew tired of it.

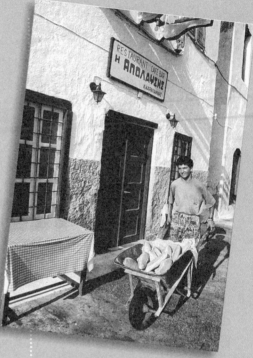

*Delivered by put-put, by truck, by wheelbarrow, fresh-baked bread arrives daily.*

It quashed the desire for variety, for all in one it was slightly sour, yet held the sweetness from its simple ingredients. It was not quite brown, yet not white; crusty, yet opened up into a crumb as malleable as marshmallow. It was heavy, but evenly textured with no gaps or holes, and very wholesome smelling. I dream about it.

Luckily for me, the island bread has remained the same despite the passing years, so upon my every return I get to savor it again. The only difference is that the baker now has a small truck instead of a dust-digging put-put.

*A rack of* prosforo *seals to stamp the sign of the cross on Sabbath bread.*

# city bread

### MAKES TWO 1¾-POUND LOAVES

I N ANCIENT GREECE CITIES ROSE TO BECOME INDIVIDUAL
CITY-STATES AND SEATS OF DEMOCRACY. BECAUSE PEOPLE
AMASSED IN CITIES, AWAY FROM AGRARIAN FIELDS,
THEY NEEDED FOOD SENT IN. A LARGE DIVERSITY OF
OCCUPATIONS SPRANG UP TO SUPPLY THE DEMAND:
IMPORTING, EXPORTING, PEDDLING, BAKING, ALL WERE
JOBS THAT NEEDED DOING AND FILLING. THE MAJOR
GRAIN IMPORTED WAS WHEAT. FILLED WITH NITROGEN,
WHEAT ALLOWED GREAT NUMBERS OF PEOPLE TO THRIVE
WITHOUT MUCH MEAT OR FISH. WHILE IN MUCH OF
RURAL GREECE THE BREADS STAYED COARSE, THE BREADS
IN THE CITIES GRADUALLY BECAME WHITER AND LIGHTER.
COARSE COUNTRY BREAD WAS OFTEN CALLED "DIRTY"
BREAD, AS OPPOSED TO WHITER, "CLEANER" CITY BREAD.

The city ways of Greece have
continued, with even the ancient
word for "bread" staying the
same. Every day, contemporary
urban Greeks travel to the
*artopouleion*—the bread shop—
for their staff of life. City bread
has also stayed much the same,
whiter and lighter than country
bread. Throughout history, just
the fact that city bread was
white made it an esteemed prize
among the rural population.
And still to this day, villagers
bring back sweeter, lighter city
bread as gifts to relatives in the
provinces.

*¹/₄ cup warm water*

*2 tablespoons sugar*

*2 packages active dry yeast*

*2 cups milk, scalded and cooled*
  *(see Notes)*

*¹/₄ cup olive oil, plus extra for*
  *coating the bowl and*
  *baking sheet*

*7 cups unbleached all-purpose*
  *flour, plus extra for the*
  *work surface*

*2 teaspoons salt*

*1 tablespoon milk, or melted butter,*
  *for the glaze*

*2 tablespoons sesame seeds*
  *(optional)*

1 Stir together the water and
sugar in a large bowl. Sprinkle
the yeast over the top and set
aside in a warm place until
spongy, 1 hour.

2 Stir the 2 cups milk and the
¼ cup oil into the yeast mixture.

## BREAD AND MUSIC

A very old, crude clay figurine
shows a row of women
kneading bread to the accompaniment
of a flute player (see photograph at
right). All the kneaders have their hair
tied similarly in wide headbands. Their
arms are outstretched; their hands are
flat, thumbs splayed out. Their heads
are bowed to their work. The loaves
they shape resemble French baguettes.

Who were the girls? Servants in
the kitchen of a wealthy household?
Slaves of a bakery owner? Both large
manors and commercial bakeries
certainly existed in ancient Greece,
and those able to keep servants or own
slaves did so. In any case, the figurine
shows that people have long matched
the motion of rhythmic, perhaps
monotonous acts—like kneading
dough—to the cadence of music.
Accompanied and coordinated by the
lilting flute, the labor of the line of
kneaders looks so pleasant one almost
wants to join them. At the very least,
one wants to partake of their
musically inspired bread.

Add the 7 cups flour and the salt and stir with a wooden spoon until well mixed. Place the dough on a lightly floured surface and knead until smooth and elastic and no longer sticky, 10 minutes.

3 Pat the dough into a ball and coat it very lightly with oil. Lightly coat a large bowl with oil and place the dough in it. Cover the bowl with a cloth and set it aside in a warm place until doubled in bulk, about 2 hours.

4 Punch down the dough and knead it again on a lightly floured surface for 1 to 2 minutes. Coat it with oil again and return it to the bowl. Cover and set aside in a warm place until doubled in bulk again, 1 1/2 to 2 hours.

5 When the dough has risen the second time, lightly oil a baking sheet. Punch down the dough and divide it in half. Pat each half into an oblong shape and place the loaves on the

prepared baking sheet. Cover with a cloth and set aside to rise a third time until almost doubled in bulk, about 1 1/2 hours (see Notes).

6 When you are ready to bake the bread, preheat the oven to 400°F.

7 Brush the top of each loaf with the milk, and sprinkle the sesame seeds over the top, if using. Bake until golden and hollow sounding when rapped, 40 to 45 minutes. Set aside on the baking sheet until completely cool, then slice and serve.

## NOTES:

■ You can, as the Greeks often do, use warm water instead of the scalded milk.

■ Be careful not to let the dough expand too much on the third rising, or the loaves will collapse as they cool after baking.

*A flutist provides rhythm for a row of bread-kneading women (see box, facing page).*

## THE RISE OF BREAD

How yeast—and what it could do—was discovered remains a mystery. Probably the ancient Hebrews were the first to stumble upon the process. They knew it well enough by the time Moses led the tribes across the Red Sea to abandon it deliberately, and for at least a week, they were reduced to flatbread. If the Hebrews were not the first to hit upon leavening, then most likely it was the Egyptians. In 500 B.C.E. Hekataeus of Miletus referred to them as the "bread eaters," and though the Egyptians left no recipes, their hieroglyphics mention some 140 types of different breads.

It was the Greeks, however, who developed bread. They mastered the techniques of separating the husks and other inedible parts of grain from the nutritious kernels. They unriddled which types of flour were suited for which breads, the fine to the rough, the white to the dark. They expanded the clay bell and griddle into the baking oven. They used all known types of grains, mixed various flours, and applied all sorts of baking methods. Many of their breads were unleavened; others they raised with starter or a kind of baking powder called *nitron*. They also contrived a wine-based yeast, eked from the fermentation of grapes.

# GREECE'S FIRST BREAD BAKERS

FOR MUCH OF ITS PRIMEVAL HISTORY, GREECE, LIKE THE REST OF EUROPE, HAD NO HUMAN INHABITANTS. SOMETIMES THE ROCKY ARCHIPELAGO WAS CONNECTED TO AFRICA, SOMETIMES NOT. EXACTLY WHERE THE VERY FIRST PEOPLE ENTERED NO ONE CAN SAY FOR SURE, BUT THEY MUST HAVE LIKED THE SUN AND SEA BECAUSE THEY CAME EARLY AND THEY STAYED.

## CAVE DWELLERS

Evidence shows that well before 200,000 B.C.E. humans had moved into a cave in three-fingered Halkidiki, near where Mount Athos's monasteries now sit. They were Neanderthal people, big-boned and heavyset. They crafted large stone tools that, over many millennia, barely altered in form. From Halkidiki they spread across Macedonia and south into the Peloponnesos, perhaps following their favorite foods. Sites in Thessaly show that these Ice Age occupants ate a trio of pachyderms—rhinoceros, hippopotamus, and elephant. They entered Kefalonia and other areas of Greece by about 40,000 B.C.E. Apparently they ate their quarry raw. No campfire ashes or charred bones remain.

When the ice receded 25,000 to 20,000 years ago, a new and larger human community appeared in Greece, now all *Homo sapiens*, people such as ourselves. On and off for some ten thousand years, they occupied a cave called Franghthi in southeastern Greece, near Argos. Some of them drifted up to the plains of Thessaly; others lived by Greece's then rushing rivers and broad lakes. By about 11,000 B.C.E. they began to make small stone tools and build permanent settlements, each exploiting very particular kinds of food. On the Klithy cliffs of Epiros, the people ate ibex almost exclusively. At Kastritsa cave, they consumed red deer. The inhabitants of Sidari cave on Corfu, then still part of the mainland, dined on cockles. No one yet lived, it seems, in the Cyclades, Dodecanesos, or Crete.

## TOOLS OF OBSIDIAN

About the time that settled villages emerged in the neighboring Near East, at Jericho and Jarmo, around 9000 B.C.E., a new group of people showed up at Franghthi cave. They made tools from obsidian found in Melos, and since the obsidian shows up all over Greece, water travel must have been established. They had fire and gathered wild grasses. They munched on wild almonds, which are poisonous if consumed raw, so they must have cooked them. They soon added wild barley and oats to their diet and also collected lentils and a pulse called bitter vetch. It seems they still followed the animals they liked to hunt, but at the same time they built permanent homes, and some

shrines. Fishing increased, as it often does when hunting decimates animal numbers. By 7000 B.C.E. the amount of wild grasses and pulses at a number of places shows they were encouraging them to grow.

## THE FIRST FARMERS

When true cultivation appears in Greece soon after, however, it came with a brand-new population. With their arrival into the Aegean region, they brought about an abrupt and drastic change. The earliest farming settlements pop up in Knossos in Crete and in Thessaly in about 7000 B.C.E. They are, indeed, the first farming sites in Europe. They occur in previously unoccupied locations, suggesting they were founded by experienced farmers who could recognize the soils that produce good crops. They involve new foods. Of the barley, wheat, sheep, and goats they ate, only barley had been eaten by people in Greece before. The tools the people used were different as well, and they came with crafts not previously seen.

These new people planted new free-threshing wheat from Asia Minor, the first sort of wheat suitable for bread. They manufactured mud bricks such as the people of Asia Minor fashioned. Because they picked exactly where they settled, they

must have known where they were headed. After their arrival, they soon took up residence in many sites around Greece: Gediki, Ahilleion, Sesklo, Argissa, Soufli, and Nea Nikomedia. There are no signs that the engaged in warfare. It seems they landed peacefully in their new homeland and found a land of plenty.

Their settlements were small, each housing perhaps a hundred people. They still gathered many foods, including wild fruit and nuts. They fished and hunted. But soon they added pigs to their goats and sheep. They used milk and made cheese.

With these people and their new foods, new cooking methods appeared. They discovered pottery, which allowed them to simmer their grains into porridge. And then, as if overnight, suddenly they developed ovens. At first they used the ovens merely to parch their precious grains for nicely roasted porridges, but shortly after that they began to bake rough grain cakes, and in no time flat . . . bread.

Are these people the ancestors of the later Greek Minoans? Probably so. By 3000 B.C.E. these same little villages begin to show all the features that the mysterious people we call Minoans had: the palaces, the thrones, the tools, the arts. Greeks call what occurred with these new people the Epoch of Copper. We call it the Bronze Age, the earliest civilization.

# Twice-baked Toasts

## PAXIMADIA

### MAKES ABOUT 40 TOASTS

CHESTNUT BROWN, SLOW-BAKED HARD TOASTS, PAXIMADIA DATE BACK TO THE FIFTH CENTURY B.C.E. THEY ARE OFTEN CALLED "RUSKS" AND LIKENED TO ZWIEBACK OR MANDELBROT. THEY COME TWO WAYS: MADE FROM REGULAR DAILY BREAD, OR FROM BREAD THAT HAS BEEN SLIGHTLY SWEETENED. EITHER WAY, THEY ARE A GREEK "KEEPER," ENSURING A BREAD SUPPLY AT ALL TIMES.

Every Greek homemaker keeps a store of *paximadia*. From their storage place, they can be pulled out for any occasion—to offer a guest with a *meze* or coffee, to sate a hungry child just home from school, to soothe a teething baby. Daily, they serve for dipping in breakfast milk or afternoon tea. The all-through crunchiness of *paximadia* is achieved by baking them twice, the second time very slowly (often overnight in the baker's still-warm oven after other baking is completed).

Without question, the best jam to smear on *paximadia* is a spoon sweet (see pages 535 to 547). The syrup will run down the sides of the thick, crisp toast and soak into the hard interior the way no sticky jelly can.

*1 recipe Country Bread dough (page 121), prepared through Step 3*

1 Preheat the oven to 400°F.

2 Punch down and shape the Country Bread dough into two loaves, each 18 inches long and 4 inches wide. Do not score the loaves. Brush the top of the loaves liberally with water, and bake until the loaves have formed a light brown crust, but are not quite done, 20 to 25 minutes.

3 Cut the bread into 1½- to 2-inch-thick slices. Allow the slices to cool completely on the baking sheet.

4 When the bread has cooled, preheat the oven to 175°F.

**5** Place the slices, cut side down and without touching, on ungreased baking sheets. Bake until completely dry and hard all the way through, 6 to 8 hours. Use right away or store in an airtight container for up to 6 months.

**NOTES:**

■ To give *paximadia* an extra-toasty finish, remove the twice-baked slices from the baking sheet, place them on the oven rack, raise the temperature to 400°F, and bake, turning once, to make the crumb even crunchier, 5 minutes longer.

■ *Paximadia* make excellent crumbs for stuffing a turkey (see page 429) or crusting meat and fish.

■ Commercially made and packaged *paximadia* can be purchased at Greek delicatessens and gourmet groceries.

■ To make quick *paximadia* from dense flatbread, see Variation, page 138.

*Using a time-honored long-handled oven paddle, a grandmother pulls just-baked crusty bread out of the oven.*

**VARIATIONS:**

**City Toasts:** *Paximadia* can also be made from the City Bread dough using the same method as for Country Bread.

**Sweet *Paximadia*:** Greeks have a sweet tooth, so *paximadia* made from sweet bread are also a pantry staple.

To make sweet *paximadia*, follow the directions using the dough for Easter Bread (page 139).

For traditional sweet toasts, substitute 1 teaspoon anise seeds for the *mahlepi* and mastic.

*Paximadia* are also often flavored with sweet wine, such as Mavrodaphne, and are sometimes sprinkled with sesame seeds.

For Greco-Italian-style toasts, add coarsely chopped almonds or pistachio nuts, dried fruit such as raisins or citron, or fennel seeds.

## THE LAST BAKER OF PYRGOS

As home bread baking dwindles in Greece, and even commercial village bakers give way to town ones, it's harder and harder to find someone who makes barley rings (page 130) or *paximadia*. But every now and then you come across a baker who still fires up a wood oven.

I found such a baker in Pyrgos, a hilltop village on Santorini, whose streets and houses wind like a spiral staircase up to a crumbling old Venetian castle. Almost buried below one of the curving lanes, Georgos, an old man missing one eye, still bakes barley rings and thick slabs of bread toast. Georgos tried the new breads from the town baker and nibbled at the packaged *paximadia* most Greeks now buy, but all they did was make him pine for the old bread. Nothing tastes like bread that has baked in a wood-heated, plaster-lined oven, he told me. The thick earthen walls capture and radiate the heat that turns the toast the color of amber, as if dipped in honey.

No sign marks the site of Georgos's shop, where he sells directly off the baking sheets. You have to know where he is or know enough to ask. If you find out, you can join the steady stream of customers scaling the slope to his doorstep. Still clad in the tweed cap and goat-hair undershirt of earlier times, old Georgos's days are ebbing. Whenever I'm in Pyrgos, I trod up the spiral pathway and get his products while I can.

# black barley rings

## MAVROKOULOURIA

**MAKES 12 RINGS**

BARLEY WAS BY FAR THE MOST COMMON GRAIN IN ANCIENT GREECE AND PROVIDED THE FLOUR OF MOST OF THE BREADS. BLACK—REALLY DARK BROWN—BARLEY RINGS REMAIN ONE OF THE MOST UNUSUAL AND RENOWNED GREEK BREADS. TRADITIONAL IN CRETE AND THE SOUTHERN CYCLADES, THEY ARE THE EPITOME OF RURAL BREADS. THEY NOURISH, LAST, AND FEED THROUGH WINTER, KEEPING HEARTS STRONG.

When I first arrived in Greece, despite the availability of soft wheat bread, homemakers had large chests full of their homemade hard barley rings to soak in coffee for breakfast. The rings were the mainstay of Santorini until recently, and part of what kept the island's residents so healthy. Barley rings are nutty, honest, truly down-to-earth. They stay crunchy even when soaked in liquid. They are the bread of choice for bread salad (page 195). They are marvelous crumbled in soup, and I still dunk them in my morning brew. Traditionally the rings are made with sourdough starter. Here I use yeast.

*2 packages active dry yeast*
*2 teaspoons sugar*
*3 1/2 cups stone-ground barley flour*
*1/2 cup warm water*
*1/4 cup olive oil, plus extra for coating the dough*
*1 teaspoon salt*
*1/2 cup water*
*Unbleached all-purpose flour, for the work surface*

1 Mix together the yeast, sugar, 1/2 cup of the barley flour, and the warm water in a large bowl. Cover with a cloth and set aside in a warm place until bubbly, 30 minutes.

2 Add the 1/4 cup oil, remaining 3 cups barley flour, the salt, and the 1/2 cup water. Stir until you can gather the mixture into a sticky ball.

3 Transfer the dough to a floured surface and knead until smooth and elastic, about 5 minutes.

## SOURDOUGH STARTER
### PROZYMI

Early bread bakers leavened their dough with a "starter," which they fermented from a bit of flour and sweetener. Once they had a starter, they could keep it going by replenishing it with a bit of unbaked bread dough. Though Greeks today can purchase packaged yeast, and many do so for the rare times they bake homemade bread, grandmothers and serious bakers still use their own starter, called *zymas, zymi, prozymi,* or, in the villages, *zoumi.* It is made without any yeast at all. It is starter that adds the alluring taste and bouquet of sourness, as well as the pithiness, to some of the world's best breads.

4 Coat the dough with oil, transfer to a bowl, cover with a cloth, and set it aside in a warm place until a bit spongy but not nearly doubled, 2 hours.

5 Divide the dough into 12 pieces. With your hands, press each piece out to form a flat oval about 12 inches long, 6½ inches wide, and ¼ inch thick. Fold in the long sides of each oval so that they overlap, forming a roll. Then pull the roll around, with the side seam on the inside, to form a ring. Squeeze the ends together and press any cracks closed.

6 Place the rings on an ungreased baking sheet. Cover with a cloth and let rest until a little spongy again, 30 minutes.

7 Preheat the oven to 400°F.

8 Brush the rings with water and bake until beginning to brown, 30 minutes. Remove from the oven and allow them to cool completely on the baking sheet.

9 When the rings have cooled, preheat the oven to 200°F.

10 Place the baking sheet in the oven and bake the rings until dry all the way through, 7 hours (overnight is fine). Store in an airtight container for up to 1 year. To use, soak the rings briefly in water, coffee, tea, or other liquid until just soft, about 5 minutes.

**NOTE:** If stone-ground barley flour is hard to find or time is short, commercially made barley rings can be purchased at any Greek specialty grocery store.

## ABOUT BARLEY AND ITS RELUCTANCE TO RISE

Barley flour is notorious for its stubborn resistance to leavening. It is low in gluten, so baked goods made from it often stay short, stout, and chewy. Most recipes for barley bread actually call for more wheat flour than barley, or add other ingredients that will push the product skyward. But in Greece, barley rings are made of just plain barley flour. Their height may be helped by the fact that the rings are folded over, but also the barley flour in Greece is different from that found in the United States; it is quite fibrous. Perhaps that explains how the bakers of southern Greece, using only their own starter, achieve barley rings as much as two inches tall. Because of the flour differences, the barley rings in this recipe, though delicious, are lighter in color and shorter in stature than the native ones.

*Rolling sweet* koulouria *rings, an Easter version of the recipe on page 132.*

# sesame and cumin bread rings

## KOULOURIA

**MAKES 16 RINGS**

A S EARLY AS 600 B.C.E., GREEKS WERE SPRINKLING LOAVES OF BREAD WITH THREE FLAVORFUL SEEDS: FLAX, POPPY, AND ESPECIALLY SESAME. SESAME IS FOUND IN THE MINOAN RUINS ON THE ISLAND OF SANTORINI. THE MYCENEANS MENTION SESAME FREQUENTLY ENOUGH TO ABBREVIATE ITS NAME TO "SA" AND REFER TO IT OFTEN WHEN WRITING ABOUT FOOD; IT SEEMS LIKELY THEY USED THE SEED FOR BOTH FLAVORING AND OIL.

Still today, rings of white city bread sprinkled with sesame seeds are considered to be so elegant, so citified (compared to rougher, unadorned country breads), that no father, mother, uncle, aunt, or cousin who travels to an urban center returns home without bearing an armload. To supply the visitors, bread hawkers swarm around piers and train stations. They stack the sesame rings up their arms from wrist to shoulder or pile them ring upon ring on long poles.

There are many versions of these popular rings. Some contain yeast, some don't; some eggs, some not. Some add orange, vanilla, brandy, or mint. A look back in time shows that sesame was sometimes combined with another seed known to the ancient Greeks: cumin. Pliny, the Roman scholar, considered cumin the spice that best wakes the appetite. A relative of parsley that grows around the Mediterranean, cumin was a popular flavoring in Byzantine times. When sprinkled on bread rings along with venerable sesame, it gives the crust a doubly ancient savor. Sesame adds toast; cumin mystery. Sesame flavors with grace; cumin with resolve.

## A SEEDY TRICK

••••••••••••••••••

Ancient Greek bakers had a use for seeds—especially sesame and poppy seeds—rarely seen today. They used the seeds to dust bowls and pans as we would flour to prevent the dough for cakes, cookies, or noodles from sticking to the sides. Take the description by Athenaeus (second century B.C.E.):

"The kneading trough is greased and sprinkled with poppy seed, over which the dough is placed, and so it does not stick to the trough while rising. When it is put in the oven, some coarse meal is sprinkled in the pottery baking pan, over which the loaf is laid, and turns it a pleasing color, like that of smoked cheese."

*1 cup warm water*

*2 teaspoons sugar*

*2 packages active dry yeast*

*3 1/2 cups unbleached
    all-purpose flour*

*1 teaspoon salt*

*2 large eggs, lightly beaten*

*Olive oil, for coating the
    baking sheets*

*1 egg yolk beaten with
    1 teaspoon water,
    for the wash*

*1/3 cup sesame seeds*

*1 tablespoon cumin seeds*

1 Stir together ¼ cup of the water and the sugar in a small bowl. Sprinkle the yeast over the top and set aside until bubbly, 15 minutes.

2 Place the flour and salt in a medium-size bowl. Add the yeast mixture, eggs, and remaining ¾ cup water. Mix with your hands, working the dough until you can gather it into a sticky ball. Transfer the dough to a lightly floured surface and knead until smooth and elastic and no longer sticky, 5 to 6 minutes.

3 Lightly grease two baking sheets with oil. Divide the dough into 16 portions. With your hands, roll each portion out on a clean, unfloured surface to make a rope about 10 inches long and ¾ inch in diameter. Form the rope into a circle, pinch the ends together, and set it on a prepared baking sheet. Repeat until all the dough is formed. Cover with a cloth and set aside in a warm place to rise for 20 minutes.

4 Preheat the oven to 375°F.

5 Brush the top of each dough ring with the egg wash. Sprinkle the rings liberally with the sesame and cumin seeds. Bake until golden, 15 to 20 minutes.

6 Let the bread rings cool on the baking sheets for 30 minutes before serving. They will keep, wrapped in plastic wrap, for several days.

## VARIATION:

**Aromatic Additions:** To make more fanciful versions, some bread bakers add to the dough any of the following:

*1 tablespoon coarsely grated orange zest*

*1½ teaspoons vanilla extract*

*1 tablespoon brandy*

*1 tablespoon chopped fresh mint leaves (or 1 teaspoon dried)*

## CIRCLING BACK, WAY BACK

The tradition of baking bread in rings, then stacking them high upon a stick, goes back at least to Sparta. There, the poor and orphaned who had no food to contribute to communal tables were required to bring long reeds to the dining halls as the token for their share. They would cut reed batons from the marshes and with them carry bread rings to the diners.

# pita bread

## MAKES TWELVE 8- TO 9-INCH ROUNDS

THE FIRST BREADS IN GREECE WERE FLATBREADS, AND THEIR USE HAS CONTINUED EVER SINCE. WE DEVOUR FLATBREADS TODAY IN THE FORM OF PITA, TORTILLAS, LAVOSH, CREPES, PANCAKES, AND SO ON. FLATBREADS ARE MENTIONED IN VERY EARLY GREEK WRITINGS. THEY WERE ENJOYED JUST AS THEY ARE NOW, ALONE AND AS A PLATE FOR OTHER FOOD.

Flatbread was so basic and so widespread that its name has remained as unchanged as its popularity. *Pita* it was and *pita* it is, a word that became the root of both "pie" and "pizza." Wherever Greeks live today, there is still pita.

Greek pita is different from Lebanese or other Near East flatbread. It does not puff up in the middle, and so it is never stuffed—not even with a gyro. Rather, Greek pita stays a single layer, like a pillowy bread pancake, and is rolled around a filling or broken into pieces to sop up food. Homemade pita wraps a hot, promising razzle-dazzle around any food.

*2 cups warm water*
*1 teaspoon sugar*
*2 packages active dry yeast*
*6 cups unbleached all-purpose flour (see Notes)*
*1 1/2 teaspoons salt*
*1/3 cup olive oil, plus extra for coating the dough*

1 Stir together 1 cup of the water and the sugar in a small bowl. Sprinkle the yeast over the top and set aside until bubbly, 15 minutes.

2 Place the flour and salt in a large mixing bowl. Make a well in the center and pour in the 1/3 cup oil, the yeast mixture, and the remaining 1 cup water. Stir with a wooden spoon until crumbly, then knead in the bowl until the dough can be scooped into a ball.

3 Transfer the dough to a lightly floured work surface and knead until smooth and elastic and no longer sticky, about 5 minutes. Lightly coat the dough with oil, return it to the bowl, cover with a cloth, and set it aside in a warm place to rise until doubled in bulk, about 1 1/2 hours.

4 Punch down the dough and let it rest for 20 minutes.

5 Divide the dough into 12 portions. On a lightly floured surface, roll out each portion to make an 8- to 9-inch round about 1/8 inch thick. Set the dough rounds aside, without stacking them, and cover them with a damp cloth so they don't dry out. Let them rest for 30 minutes to 1 1/2 hours.

6 While the dough is resting, preheat the oven to 500°F.

7 When you are ready to bake them, place as many dough rounds as will fit on an ungreased baking sheet without overlapping. Place the sheet in the oven and bake until the pitas are puffed up, 3 minutes. Check the oven, and rotate the baking sheets if the pitas are baking unevenly. Continue baking until the pitas are beginning to turn golden on the bottom but are not at all crisp, 2 minutes. Carefully

remove the pitas, being watchful to avoid the escaping steam. Stack the pitas and wrap them in a towel. Repeat until all the pitas are cooked.

**8** Serve right away, or let the pitas cool completely, wrap them in plastic wrap, and refrigerate for up to 3 days. Or freeze for up to 2 months. Reheat before serving.

## NOTES:

■ Half white and half whole-wheat flour can be used to create a more rustic pita.

■ The pita dough may be prepared in advance through Step 4, then wrapped in plastic and refrigerated for several hours or as long as 3 days. Bring back to room temperature before continuing with Step 5.

*Although headless, this ancient statue of Demeter shows the goddess's grace of form.*

# DEMETER AND THE SEED

In almost every book on Greek cooking, the bread chapter speaks of the goddess Demeter, how she was the deity of grain, how her daughter Persephone was taken by Hades—with the assistance of their brother Zeus—how in her grief for her daughter Demeter stopped all cereals from growing until the entire world was starving, how finally Zeus arranged to get Persephone back, but since Persephone ate three pomegranate seeds in the underworld, she had to return to her captor's dark realm for three months of the year: actually the summer in the myth, not the winter.

As the myth goes, during the time of Persephone's descent each year, all the fruits of the earth quit growing. Demeter's festival in autumn, at the harvest, was a celebration of Persephone's return and the new season of growing that Demeter would now allow. Demeter was the focus of the great Eleusinian mysteries and the cult at that site where four daughters and a mother cared for the goddess while she grieved for Persephone. More interesting to me, however, is Demeter's association with the hypnotic, soporific poppy.

## HONORING THE POPPY

A goddess of poppy appears early in Greece, well before the arrival of Greeks. A statue dated 1400 B.C.E. from the sanctuary of Gazi, four miles west of Heraklion, Crete, shows the goddess bedecked in the poppy's voluptuous flower. On the statue, the heads of the poppy flowers are cut the same way they are today in order to extract the opium before the pods ripen. Clearly, Minoan women of Crete understood the effect of opium and took it for suffering and despair.

A thousand years pass and there appears a poppy flower frieze from 500 B.C.E. at Eleusis. In it stands a goddess. She smiles softly and sweetly, a poppy stalk in her hand. But wait. The goddess with whom the flowers are shown isn't a wild Nereid or a besotted female version of Dionysos. It is motherly Demeter, the goddess of cereals, caretaker of food, giver of bread. Why of all flowers is the poppy associated with the goddess of grains?

## A MINOAN GODDESS?

Three possible explanations come to mind: Demeter, whose veneration stems from pre-Greek, prehistoric times, might be a Greek version of an older Minoan goddess, that same one who touted a crown of poppy-seed capsules on her head. Later, when Demeter so grieved for her kidnapped daughter Persephone that she could not sleep, it seems she turned to the poppy's hypnotic bliss for comfort. Finally, Demeter, of all the pantheon of Greek deities, represented fertility. From her came the blossoming of fruits of the earth, the kernels of grains, the seeds of life. A single poppy pod can hold two million seeds. What better symbol can there be for a goddess of fertility than the bright-petaled, poppy blossom ripe with seed?

# olive garlic bread

## WITH LEMON ZEST

### ELIOPSOMI

#### MAKES 1 LOAF

IT HAS OFTEN BEEN SAID THAT IF YOU REALLY WANT TO UNDERSTAND CYPRUS, YOU MUST GO THERE. CERTAINLY YOU MUST IF YOU WANT TO UNDERSTAND THE FOOD. THOUGH BASICALLY GREEK, MUCH CYPRIOT FOOD IS PARTICULAR TO THAT FAMOUS ISLE. IT COMES FROM PRODUCE LOCALLY, AND SOMETIMES SINGULARLY, GROWN ON THE ISLAND'S RICH SOIL.

By late classical times Cyprus was known for rich wheat and a special variety of garlic. The island's groves of olive trees and its citrus were coveted by conquerors. Even Cyprus's breads boast of its proud ingredients: wheat, garlic, and olives. Customarily, the bread includes mint, but because that herb doesn't take well to a hot oven, here it is replaced with another of Cyprus's fabulous crops: lemon.

1 cup warm water

1/2 teaspoon sugar

1 package active dry yeast

3 1/2 cups unbleached all-purpose flour, plus extra for the work surface

1/2 teaspoon salt

1/4 cup olive oil, plus extra for coating the loaf and the baking sheet

1 tablespoon chopped lemon zest

1 tablespoon minced garlic

1 1/2 cups (9 ounces) Greek olives, preferably oil-cured, pitted

1 Stir together the water and sugar in a small bowl. Sprinkle the yeast over the top and set aside until bubbly, 15 minutes.

## THE NONTRADITIONAL CHOICE

While it is easier to use Kalamata olives (they are readily available and can be bought pitted), traditional Cypriotic olive breads use only oil-cured or oil-and-salt-brined olives, never those that are cured even partly in vinegar, as Kalamatas are. Cyprus produces both green and black olives, plump to wrinkled, cured in numerous ways. Nudging tradition, I have sometimes used Kalamata olives for the olive flatbread, and have found the taste of the bread, while slightly tarter than the traditional, still excellent.

2 Place the 3 1/2 cups flour and the salt in a large bowl and mix with a fork. Make a well in the center and add the 1/4 cup oil, the zest, garlic, olives, and yeast mixture. Stir together until fairly well mixed; then use your hands to knead the mixture into a crumbly ball.

3 Transfer the dough to a lightly floured surface and knead until it is smooth and elastic and no longer sticky, 10 minutes. Lightly brush the dough with oil, cover it with a cloth, and set it aside in a warm place to rise until doubled in bulk, about 2 hours.

**4** Lightly grease a baking sheet with oil. Punch down the dough and knead it again for 1 minute. Pat the dough into a ball and flatten it slightly to make a round about 6 inches in diameter. Place the dough round on the prepared baking sheet and set it aside in a warm place until doubled in bulk again, about 1½ hours.

**5** When ready to bake the bread, preheat the oven to 425°F.

**6** Place the bread in the oven and bake until quite golden, 30 minutes. Brush the top and sides of the loaf liberally with oil and continue baking until browned and hollow sounding when tapped, 5 minutes more.

**7** Remove the bread from the oven and cool on the baking sheet until ready to serve.

## VARIATION:

**Olive Cheese Bread:** Olive Garlic Bread easily turns into another Cypriot loaf, a cheese and olive bread. Omit (or leave in) the garlic and lemon zest and add 1 cup grated cheese, preferably Cypriot *haloumi*.

# olive flatbread

## CYPRUS-STYLE

### ELIOPITA

#### MAKES ONE 10-INCH LOAF

**G**REEK FLATBREADS, LENTEN *LAGANA*, BREAD RINGS, FANCY TWISTED BREADS, AND BREADS WITH OLIVES, HERBS, AND TASTY MORSELS ALL COME TOGETHER IN A SLIGHTLY LEAVENED SPECIAL OLIVE BREAD FROM THE ISLAND OF CYPRUS.

The ancient Greeks had a form of baking powder called *nitron,* and here that tradition is followed. The bread is hand flattened after rising and "needled" with rosemary instead of the customary mint. The rosemary reminds us (as it should, being the herb of remembrance) of Sicily, that once-Greek island at the other end of the Mediterranean from Cyprus. Onions, so loved by the nearby Egyptians, are added too. While embellished and tingling in flavor, the cakey bread is still unpretentious. Thick and chewy, it calls out for a dunking in a saucer of pure and simple olive oil.

3½ cups unbleached all-purpose flour, plus extra as needed
1 tablespoon baking powder
½ teaspoon salt
½ teaspoon chopped fresh rosemary needles, or ¼ teaspoon dried
¾ cup warm water
¼ cup olive oil, plus extra for coating the baking sheet and the loaf
1 cup (6 ounces) green oil-cured or green Kalamata olives, pitted
1 medium onion, finely chopped
Pinch of whole fresh rosemary needles

**1** Sift the flour, baking powder, and salt into a large bowl. Stir in the chopped rosemary. Make a well in the center and add the water, the ¼ cup oil, the olives, and onion. Stir together until fairly well mixed, then gather the mixture into a crumbly ball.

2 Transfer the dough to a lightly floured surface and knead, working in extra flour as needed, until smooth and elastic and no longer sticky, 10 minutes. Form the dough into a ball, cover it with a cloth, and let it rest on the work surface until beginning to rise and starting to feel spongy, 15 to 30 minutes.

3 While the dough is resting, preheat the oven to 375°F. Lightly coat a baking sheet with oil.

4 When the dough is ready, flatten it out with your hands into a 10-inch-diameter round. Transfer it to the prepared baking sheet and bake until slightly golden, 40 minutes.

5 Brush the top and sides of the bread liberally with oil and sprinkle on the rosemary needles. Continue baking until quite golden, 15 to 20 minutes. Remove from the oven and cool on the baking sheet completely before serving.

**NOTES:**

■ Olives provide the acid element that is needed to activate the baking powder.

■ In this recipe, the reason for sifting the flour is twofold: to ensure that there are no clumps of baking powder in the dough (the taste is not pleasant) and to lighten the flour for the weak leavening.

## RAISIN BREAD

Throughout Greece and Cyprus, people bake rustic breads incorporating the fruit from the grapevines that wasn't eaten as a snack or pressed for wine. They prefer a raisin bread that is straightforward, combining flour and fruit without swirls of spice, and I have come to appreciate the elegance. For the leavened type, omit the garlic and zest from Olive Garlic Bread (page 136), and replace the olives with 1½ cups dark raisins. For a more cookielike raisin bread, replace the olives in Olive Flatbread (page 137) with 1 cup raisins and the onion with ½ cup chopped walnuts.

The raisins of Greece are sundried, still with their seeds (though you can certainly use seedless), and pungently winey in flavor. To simulate the taste and texture, I use older raisins, which I soak in retsina.

**VARIATION:**

**Quick Olive *Paximadia:*** Since flatbread starts out rather condensed in texture, *eliopita* makes a fine hard rusk, especially to accompany hors d'oeuvres. You can top the rusks with a pile of finely chopped tomatoes, heap them with dressed sautéed chickpeas, or spread them with *taramasalata* or other pastes. Since they are oven-toasted rather than slow-baked like traditional *paximadia,* they can be at hand quickly.

Preheat the oven to 300°F. Cut Olive Flatbread into slices ¼ to ½ inch wide and 3 to 4 inches long. Place the slices on a baking sheet and toast, turning once, until light golden on both sides, about 5 minutes per side. Remove, and brush one side of each slice with olive oil. Or, to keep for later, cool the rusks completely on the baking sheet and then store them in an airtight container. They will keep for up to 6 months.

# easter bread

## WITH RED EGGS

### TSOUREKI

**MAKES TWO 1½- TO 1¾-POUND LOAVES**

THE JOYOUS FESTIVITIES AND THE MARVELOUS FOODS OF EASTER SWEEP EVERY GREEK INTO THEIR EMBRACE. EVERY FAMILY ROASTS A WHOLE LAMB OR GOAT, STEWS A JOINT OF THE MEAT, OR SIMMERS *MAGEIRITSA* SOUP (PAGE 176). THE BAKING THAT HAS BEEN GOING ON FOR DAYS NOW MANIFESTS AS SUMPTUOUS TREATS: SWEET *KOULOURIA* RINGS, POWDERED SUGAR COOKIES, CHEESE PIES, AND THE MOST ESSENTIAL, THE EASTER BREAD. CALLED *LAMBROPSOMI* OR *TSOUREKI*, THE BREAD VARIES SLIGHTLY IN SHAPE AND FLAVORING FROM REGION TO REGION, BUT IT IS ALWAYS RICH, SWEET, AND, MOST IMPORTANT, DECORATED WITH EGGS DYED RED. THE CRUST IS HONEY BROWN, THE CRUMB AIRY AND A RICH OCHER. THE PIECES WAFT THEIR PINEY, MASTIC AROMA. NO WONDER FAMILY MEMBERS HOVER UNTIL THE BREAD IS BROKEN AND, WITH IT, MAKE COMMUNION WITH BOTH THEIR FAITH AND ONE ANOTHER.

*FOR THE DOUGH:*

*1½ cups milk, scalded and cooled to lukewarm*

*1 package active dry yeast*

*1 cup sugar*

*7½ cups unbleached all-purpose flour*

*½ teaspoon salt*

*1½ teaspoons ground mahlepi (see Notes)*

*1 teaspoon powdered mastic (mastiha; see Notes)*

*8 tablespoons (1 stick) butter, cut into small pieces, at room temperature*

*4 large eggs, beaten until frothy*

*Olive oil, for coating the dough and the baking sheets*

*1 egg yolk beaten with 1 tablespoon milk, for the wash*

*½ cup (about 2 ounces) sliced almonds*

*4 to 6 Red Eggs (recipe follows)*

## IZ XZ NI KA
### THE HOLY *PROSFORO* BREAD

As part of every Greek Orthodox sabbath service, the priest leading the devotion blesses and breaks a special bread that is impressed with a holy seal and distributes pieces to all attendees. The act takes place during the transubstantiation part of the service. The stamped center of the bread represents the Host and is mixed by the priest with wine blessed for Communion. As part of their commitment to their religion, women bring the holy bread to the service.

Essentially a simple country or city bread, it differs only in that water replaces the oil and it is generally shaped in a round, not long, loaf. The name of the bread is *prosforo*, or "offering." It is sometimes also called *antidoro*, which means "in lieu of a gift." As part of her dowry, every bride used to receive a stamp to mark the *prosforo* she would bake as a wife. Nowadays bakeries make the *prosforo* on Saturday.

The holy seal is cross-shaped and reads *IZ XZ NI KA*, the Greek insignia for "Jesus Christ Conquers." The seals, hand carved by monks, can be purchased in stores carrying Orthodox religious paraphernalia. The *prosforo* divides the bread into a cross shape, and became the model for sweet Easter bread, hot cross buns.

1 Pour ¾ cup of the milk into a bowl. Add the yeast, 1 tablespoon of the sugar, and 1 cup of the flour and stir to mix. Set aside in a warm place until lightly spongy all the way through, 30 minutes.

2 Sift the remaining sugar, 5 cups of the flour, and the salt into a large mixing bowl. Add the *mahlepi*, mastic, and butter and briefly mix with your fingers. Make a well in the center and pour in the beaten eggs, yeast mixture, and remaining ¾ cup milk. Knead with your hands until you can gather the mixture into a ball, 1 to 2 minutes.

3 Dust a work surface with some of the remaining 1½ cups flour. Transfer the dough to the floured surface and knead, dusting the surface with flour as needed, until the dough is smooth and elastic and no longer sticky, 10 minutes.

4 Lightly coat the dough ball with oil and place it in a clean bowl. Cover the bowl with a cloth and set it aside in a warm place to rise until the dough has doubled in bulk, about 2 hours.

5 Punch down the dough and transfer it to a lightly floured surface. Knead the dough again for 1 minute, then divide it in half. Cover the two portions with a cloth and let them rest until puffed up again, 20 minutes.

6 Divide one of the portions of dough into thirds. With your hands, roll each third to form a rope about 20 inches long. When you have three ropes, braid them together. Pinch the ends together, tuck them under the braid and place the braid on a lightly oiled baking sheet. Repeat with the remaining portion. Set the braids

aside, covered, in a warm place until doubled in bulk, about 1 hour.

7 When you are ready to bake the bread, preheat the oven to 350°F.

8 Brush each braid with the egg wash. Press 2 or 3 red eggs into each braid and sprinkle the almonds over the top. Bake until very golden on the top and sides, 40 to 45 minutes. Remove from the oven and let rest on the baking sheets for 30 minutes. Slice and serve while still warm, or cool completely and wrap in plastic wrap. The bread will keep at room temperature for up to 1 week.

## NOTES:

■ Mastic is generally sold in crystals. These reduce to a powder when lightly ground with a mortar and pestle or with a mallet. Both mastic and *mahlepi* can be purchased from any Greek specialty food store, from mail-order catalogs, or on the Internet. For a description of mastic, see page 143. For a description of *mahlepi*, see page 505.

*Workers sort and grade newly harvested mastic tears on Hios.*

■ If necessary, 1½ tablespoons vanilla extract can be substituted for the mastic, and the *mahlepi* can be omitted—but the flavor of the bread will not be traditional.

■ Some cooks also add about 1 tablespoon coarsely grated orange zest to the dough.

■ If you're one who loves warm bread, you can slice the loaf right after it comes out of the oven; the texture will be more spongy and cakelike than breadlike.

## RED EGGS

As much as the lamb, eggs are an emblem of the Greek Easter. To Greeks, spring eggs denote sudden wealth, the fertility of the coming summer, abundance, and above all else, joy. Announcing Christ's resurrection in a splendid splash of color, the eggs for the Easter bread are dyed red. In earlier days this was done in water tinted scarlet from beets, the first spring vegetable, or, where it was available, reddish wood. Now cooks generally use commercial packets of dye. The dyeing begins on Holy Thursday, before the solemnity of Good Friday wraps the week in black. Indeed, Holy Thursday is sometimes called *Kokkinopefti*, "the day red falls," to symbolize Christ's blood.

*3 cups water*
*2 tablespoons red wine vinegar*
*2 teaspoons red food coloring*
*4 to 6 eggs (see Note)*
*Olive oil*

1 Place the water in a saucepan just large enough to hold the eggs in one layer and bring to a boil over high heat. Add the vinegar and red food coloring. Reduce the heat to just below the boiling point, and gently, one at a time, add as many eggs as will fit in one layer. Cook for 15 minutes, adjusting the heat so the liquid simmers without boiling. Then remove the pan from the heat and set the eggs aside to cool in the liquid for at least 40 minutes.

2 Lift the eggs out of the liquid and pat them dry on paper towels.

3 Grease your hands with olive oil and rub the eggs to make them glossy. Use right away or store in the refrigerator for up to 3 days.

## EGG BEATING

In addition to decorating the Easter loaf, in Greece eggs make up part of the toys bestowed upon children and part of the games played on Easter day. With the leftovers from the bread dough, women shape small bread dolls (for girls) and snakes or other animals (for boys) and place a red egg as the head of the figure. Village children have few toys, and these bread toys delight them.

Red eggs are given in baskets and are hidden for the children to find. And both children and adults play a special game with uncooked eggs on Easter day: With egg in hand, they greet each other and hit their eggs point to point while saying "Christ is risen." One person gets hands, if not clothes, splattered—to much laughter—while the one with the stronger egg goes on to test it on another Easter reveler.

**NOTE:** The color of the eggshell affects the depth of color when the eggs are dyed. Brown eggs turn out a denser red; white eggs turn out more luminescent.

# christmas bread

## WITH SWEETENED FIGS

### CHRISTOPSOMO

**MAKES TWO 1½- TO 1¾-POUND LOAVES**

UNTIL FAIRLY RECENTLY GREEKS REGARDED CHRISTMAS AS A LESSER HOLIDAY THAN EASTER. THEY CELEBRATED THE BIRTH OF CHRIST WITH A JOYOUS MASS, BUT THE OCCASION DID NOT MERIT A FAMILY GATHERING, AND CERTAINLY NOT A TREE BROUGHT INTO THE HOME. NOR DID THE DAY INVOLVE GIFT GIVING. GREEKS GIVE GIFTS ON JANUARY 6, EPIPHANY, THE DAY WHEN THE MAGI ARRIVED, BRINGING TO THE CHRIST CHILD HIS FIRST PRESENTS.

But the culture of other countries has influenced modern Greece. Now Greeks sometimes put small store-bought trees in their homes, roast a turkey (page 429), or at the very least, bake a Christmas bread. The bread is essentially like the Easter and New Year's loaf—a sweetened braid—but with no eggs this time, and no coin. Instead the Christmas bread echoes northern Europe's traditional fruit-studded cake.

In times past, northern Europe had little fresh fruit in midwinter, so it was enormously festive to receive treats of dried or candied fruit, preserved from summer's abundance. The idea took hold in Greece, although in midwinter there are oranges and apples aplenty. Still, Greeks have adopted the idea of the Christmas fruitcake in their own way. Their bread is laden with two summer fruits of Greece that dry spectacularly—figs and grapes (raisins)—to which they add walnuts. Rather than the cardamom and nutmeg of northern Europe, Greek Christmas bread employs their beloved mastic. The bread is frequently glazed with a syrup of honey, orange juice, and almonds. The bread is a delight, offering the intense candylike qualities of dried fruit while still being airy and light. For added glow, the dried fruit here is marinated overnight before the dough is mixed.

*Rather than being stamped with a wooden seal, the cross on this holy bread has been hand formed and appliquéd with strips of dough.*

## FOR THE DOUGH

1 1/2 cups milk, scalded and cooled
   to lukewarm
1 package active dry yeast
1 cup sugar
7 1/2 cups unbleached all-purpose flour
1/2 teaspoon salt
1 1/2 teaspoons ground mahlepi
   (see Notes)
1 teaspoon powdered mastic
   (see Notes)
8 tablespoons (1 stick) butter, cut into
   small pieces, at room temperature
4 large eggs, beaten until frothy
1 cup dried golden figs, preferably
   Kalimyrna, cut into 1/4- to 1/2-
   inch pieces and soaked overnight
   or longer in 1 1/2 cups retsina wine
1 cup raisins, soaked overnight
   or longer in 1 1/2 cups
   Mavrodaphne wine
1/2 cup walnut pieces
Olive oil, for coating the dough
   and the baking sheets

## FOR THE TOP

3 tablespoons honey
3 tablespoons orange juice
1/2 cup sliced almonds

1 Pour 3/4 cup of the milk into a bowl. Add the yeast, 1 tablespoon of the sugar, and 1 cup of the flour and stir to mix. Set aside in a warm place until lightly spongy all the way through, 30 minutes.

2 Sift the remaining sugar, 5 cups of the flour, and the salt into a large mixing bowl. Add the

## MASTIC

When I was growing up, I would swoon at the aroma of cardamom wafting from the kitchen where my Swedish mother was baking. I loved the perfume so much that when I first started cooking, I would keep a tiny dish of coarsely crushed seed on the counter to perfume the air. All that changed when I discovered mastic.

*Mastiha* (mastic) is the resinous sap that is exuded from a tree of the pistachio family when it is wounded. The *Pistacia lentiscus chia* tree grows only on the Greek island of Hios. From it oozes a sap so hauntingly aromatic that people through the ages have used it to clean the teeth and freshen the breath, and also to flavor foods, particularly breads and stews.

Chian mastic growers scrupulously clean and carefully slash the bush stems. From the cuts seep small, semihard, clear globules of sap, known as "tears," which drop upon sand that has been sprinkled on the ground to catch them, or else the tears are carefully scraped from the bush. The tears, gathered in the morning when they are cool and firm, are sorted by hand for quality and then sold to plants where the drops are washed, baked, and formed into "chiclets"

(at one time before the manufacture of commercial chewing gum, it was chewed by sailors as gum). The mastic is then sold to spice dealers and to the makers of *mastiha* liqueur. In the days of the Ottoman occupation, the women of the harem, who had no way to make money of their own, were by some odd benefaction allowed to trade mastic. Through intermediaries they bought the sap from islanders and sold it to the spice merchants who thronged the bazaars and ports, thereby acquiring the pin money to purchase the little treats they desired.

I place small open jars of the sap in my kitchen to scent the atmosphere, and crumble the golden tears into my baking and many other dishes (see Grilled Whole Fish with Mastic-Flavored Bread Stuffing, page 326, and Sweet Mastic "Avgolemono" Custard, page 534.) Mastic tastes like lush piney vanilla. It smells like the perfume Shalimar, but with a conifer tinge. It is irresistible. For my Easter and Christmas baking, there is no other choice of aromatic. My habit from childhood remains, but since Greece, the spice has changed.

*mahlepi*, mastic, and butter, and briefly mix with your fingers. Make a well in the center and pour in the eggs, yeast mixture, and remaining 3/4 cup milk. Add the figs, raisins, and walnuts. Knead until you can gather the mixture into a ball, 1 to 2 minutes.

3 Dust a work surface with some of the remaining 1 1/2 cups flour. Transfer the dough to the floured surface and knead, dusting the surface with flour as needed, until the dough is smooth and elastic and no longer sticky, 10 minutes.

# COOKING BELLS AND BEEHIVE OVENS

WHEN THEY FIRST STARTED MAKING BREAD, THE GREEKS SIMPLY BAKED THE LOAVES WITHIN THE FLAMES OF AN OPEN FIRE OR ON AN UNCOVERED HEARTH. BUT WITH THE RISE OF BREAD'S IMPORTANCE, THEY SOON DEVISED A DOMED LID TO PLACE OVER THE BREAD ON THE HEARTH. THEY CALLED THE LID A *TESTUM*, AFTER THEIR WORD FOR TORTOISE SHELL. EARLY ON, THE PORTABLE *TESTA* WERE MADE OF TERRA COTTA, BUT IN TIME THEY WERE MADE OF METAL AS WELL. GREEKS ALSO CALLED THEM *KLIBANOS*. SOME OF THESE COOKING BELLS, OR BAKING COVERS, HAD FEET OR FLANGES, BUT MOST RESTED ON THEIR RIMS. THE LOAVES WERE PLACED ON THE HEARTH, OFTEN ON A COOKING TILE, THE *TESTUM* WAS PLACED OVER THE LOAVES, AND THE BAKER THEN PILED RED-HOT COALS OVER THE *TESTUM*, CREATING A SMALL, BOXY ENCLOSURE WITHIN THE FIRE.

*Testa* ovens are very efficient. They contain the heat well. Loaves placed inside their tight dimensions touch one another or touch the bell's walls, ensuring a moist and soft crust. Archaeologists have found many *testa* with small holes in the top, indicating that the Greeks had figured out air circulation—in short, convection.

Soon the Greeks advanced to a stationary appliance shaped much the same as the bell—the oven. A Greek figurine dating from 1000 B.C.E. shows a house with an oven attached. A second figurine, dating from about 600 B.C.E., shows a group of women gathered around a domed oven, much as one sees today. By the fifth century B.C.E., beehive-shaped ovens with an opening at the front were in common use. They still are. Beehive ovens range from two to six feet in diameter. They seem to last for eternity—after all, repairs require only some more brick and mud. And they are effective. The breads and other foods that emerge have a bricky, earthy quality that no other oven seems to match. What's more, they allow you to do your baking outdoors.

The construction of a beehive oven is a leisurely affair, taking several days. Bricks or terra-cotta roofing tiles, whole or in pieces, are thickly bonded together with plaster or cement. Starting from a circular base of whatever circumference the owner desires, the walls are sloped ever inward as they climb higher, until the top can be domed over. A wide, low door is formed at the front and the oven is left to dry. When it's time to bake, twigs are stacked in a pile in the center of the oven floor and set afire. Once the twigs have burned to ash and the oven floor and walls radiate high heat from the fire, the ashes are swept out and the baker uses a long, flat paddle to slide bread, pastries, and casseroles into the hot chamber. Against the oven's gaping door, the baker places a metal plate, often rather makeshift, and the plate is held in place with a big rock.

Both appliance and process might seem unreliable, and, certainly in the age of electric ovens, archaic, but in fact it's quite the opposite: The beehive oven worked so well that it spread across the Mediterranean, to North America, and into the fancy brick-oven restaurants of today.

*Dome-shaped and thick-walled beehive ovens retain intense, even heat.*

4 Lightly coat the dough ball with oil and place it in a clean bowl. Cover the bowl with a cloth and set it aside in a warm place to rise until the dough has doubled in bulk, about 2 hours.

5 Punch down the dough and transfer it to a lightly floured surface. Knead the dough again for 1 minute, then divide it in half. Cover the two portions with a cloth and let them rest until puffed up again, 20 minutes.

6 Divide one of the portions of dough into thirds. With your hands, roll each third to form a rope about 20 inches long. When you have three ropes, braid them together. Pinch the ends together, tuck them under the braid, and place the braid on a lightly oiled baking sheet. Repeat with the other portion of dough. Set the braids aside in a warm place until doubled in bulk again, about 1 hour.

7 When you are ready to bake the bread, preheat the oven to 350°F.

## BREAD LORE
..................

When I first lived in Greece I noticed that the older village women often carried a little bread in their apron pockets. The bread could be a bit of pita or country loaf, but more often was from Sunday's *prosforo*, or holy bread. Then I saw new mothers placing a smidgeon of bread under the mattresses of their babies' beds and under their own pillows.

I was told that both customs were to ward off the evil eye, for bread is holy. Bread counteracts the devil and his deeds. Bread is the cure for all illnesses and is placed with the dead for the afterlife. In a country where bread is so ancient and so important, it follows that it is imbued with many powers. It is said that to knife the *prosforo* bread is to stab Christ, for the bread is his body. That bread is always broken, never cut.

8 Bake until very golden on the top and sides, 40 to 45 minutes. Remove from the oven and let rest on the baking sheet.

9 In a small bowl, mix together the honey, orange juice, and almonds. When the bread is still slightly warm, glaze it with this mixture. Slice and serve while still warm, or cool completely. The bread will keep at room temperature for up to 1 week.

## NOTES:

■ Mastic is generally sold in crystals. These reduce to a powder when lightly ground with a mortar and pestle or with a mallet. Both mastic and *mahlepi* can be purchased from any Greek specialty food store, from mail-order catalogs, or on the Internet. For a description of mastic, see page 143. For a description of *mahlepi,* see page 505.

■ You might want to decorate the top of the bread with a few fig "flowers" (see page 529, Step 3), separated, buttered, and sprinkled with sesame or toasted almonds.

# new year's bread

## WITH CANDIED GINGER COINS

### MAKES TWO 1½- TO 1¾-POUND LOAVES

NEW YEAR'S DAY IS THE DAY OF ST. BASIL, AND ALTHOUGH BASIL IS ONE OF THE MORE IMPORTANT ORTHODOX SAINTS, HIS DAY— PERHAPS BECAUSE IN THE MODERN CALENDAR IT ALSO DENOTES THE TURNING OF THE YEAR—IS TREATED AS A DAY OF PLEASURE RATHER THAN SOLEMNITY. IT'S A TRUE HOLIDAY. GREEKS SLEEP LATE AND GO ABOUT DOMESTIC CHORES IN A DECIDEDLY LEISURELY MANNER.

Still, in all the churches a mass honoring St. Basil and the New Year takes place, and the numerous churches and chapels dedicated to the saint have their feast. All those named Basil, or Vasilis in Greek—and they are legion—also celebrate their name day. For all, though, the day's most notable feature is a very special breadlike cake. Within the cake is buried a coin, a token of good fortune. Whoever bites on it in his or her piece will have prosperity, maybe love, maybe opportunity—who knows?— during the coming year. Greeks divide good fortune into two parts: *tixi,* "luck," and *moira,*

"fate." To be the holder of an amulet over both is to walk through twelve months doubly charmed.

Traditionally, New Year's bread is baked in a shallow pan so that many pieces can be cut for all family members and guests to have their chance at the coin. The cake also turns out well when baked free-form on a sheet. In a novel rendition (that doesn't deny anyone fortune's smile), special edible coins of gingerroot ensure that everyone will garner good luck. Just to munch on a sweet and spicy ginger coin is luck aplenty.

1 recipe dough for Easter Bread
  (page 139), substituting
  2 teaspoons ground ginger
  for the mastic and mahlepi,
  prepared through Step 5
Olive oil, for coating the baking sheets
1 to 2 cups Candied Ginger Coins
  (recipe follows)
1 egg yolk beaten with 1 tablespoon
  milk, for the glaze

1 When the dough is ready, grease two baking sheets with oil.

2 Pinch a small handful of dough off each dough half and set the handfuls aside. Press 1 or 2 ginger coins into each dough half and form them into balls. Pat the balls into rounds about 1 inch thick. Place one round on each prepared baking sheet. With your hands, roll the reserved dough into long ropes, and form them into decorations on top of the loaves, without pressing them into the top.

3 Cover the loaves with a cloth and set them in a warm place until doubled in bulk, about 1 hour.

4 When you are ready to bake the bread, preheat the oven to 350°F.

5 Brush the glaze mixture over the top of each loaf, and bake until very golden on the top and sides, 40 to 45 minutes.

6 Remove the loaves from the oven and decorate the tops with the remaining ginger coins. Let rest for 1 hour on the baking sheets, then slice and serve, accompanied by the candied ginger syrup if desired. The bread will keep for up to 5 days, wrapped in plastic wrap or aluminum foil at room temperature.

**NOTES:**

■ Instead of making the candied ginger, you can purchase it, but then you sacrifice the syrup, a nice surprise accompaniment for spooning over the slices.

■ Traditionally, when only one coin is hidden in the bread, the top is sprinkled with slivered almonds.

## CANDIED GINGER COINS

### MAKES ABOUT 2 CUPS

In ancient Greece, ginger was considered an exotic aromatic and was used to induce dreams. Today ginger is little used in Greece, other than in the candied form. Still, candied ginger suits the Greek spirit—sweet but with a lively nip.

*1 pound young fresh ginger,*
*    preferably large pieces*
*3 cups granulated sugar*
*3 cups water*
*1/4 cup raw sugar crystals*

1 Slice the side nodules off the ginger and set them aside for another dish. Peel the ginger with a vegetable peeler and slice the pieces into 1/4-inch-thick rounds.

2 Place the ginger rounds, granulated sugar, and water in a large saucepan. Bring to a boil and simmer briskly until the ginger is tender and the liquid is thick and syrupy, about 40 minutes. Remove the pan from the heat and allow the ginger to cool in the syrup.

3 Drain the ginger in a strainer set over a bowl, reserving the syrup. Set aside to drip dry in the strainer for 30 minutes.

4 Spread the ginger rounds, without crowding, on wire racks or bamboo mats. Sprinkle with half the raw sugar. Turn each piece over, and sprinkle with the remaining raw sugar. Set aside to dry until no longer moist, several hours or as long as overnight, depending on the weather. Use right away or store in an airtight container indefinitely.

**NOTE:** You can also dry the ginger in a microwave oven: Spread the strained rounds, without the raw sugar coating, on a plate and microwave on high power for 2 minutes. Transfer the rounds to a large platter and sprinkle the raw sugar over them. Turn the rounds over to coat them in the sugar, then set aside to cool and firm up.

## GINGER

....................

The ancient Greeks were familiar with ginger, which they called *ziggibero*. They believed it was from Arabia, not Asia, because it came by way of the Red Sea, and the Arab spice merchants, who never revealed their sources, were content to let the Greeks believe that. The spice was very rare and very expensive, even more so than nutmeg, mace, cinnamon, or cardamom. So, while the Greeks enjoyed cooking with it—and even more making remedies for illness with it—dishes using ginger were few. The same remains true today. Both the spice and candied ginger are occasionally used in sweets and beverages—rarely in any other dish— and they are still thought exotic.

# CYPRUS: THE COPPERY ISLAND

WITH THE COAST OF ASIA MINOR IN CLEAR VIEW, CYPRUS RESTS LIKE A STEPPING-STONE BETWEEN CONTINENTS. MANY HAVE USED THAT STEP TO LEAP FROM ONE LAND TO ANOTHER.

It is the third-largest island of the Mediterranean, after Sicily and Sardinia. Because of its location, its beauty, and its richness, Cyprus has been occupied since at least 7000 B.C.E. Buried in the island's hills were the ores that the first metal tool makers required. It is from *Kypros*, Cyprus's name in Greek, that we get the word "copper." Since ancient times the island's ingneous and limestone folds have supported olive, carob, and citrus trees, as well as forests and fields of wildflowers.

## THE MYCENEANS AND THE ACHAEAN GREEKS

Following the Minoans, arriving Greeks were quick to spot the island's bounty. The Myceneans settled the island in about 1400 B.C.E. and were soon followed by waves of Achaean Greeks—the Greeks of the *Iliad*—who brought with them Greek language, reli-

*The monastery of Our Lady of the Golden Pomegranate, dedicated to the Virgin Mary of Cyprus.*

gion, and customs. By 750 B.C.E. Cyprus contained ten city-states and was the site of the cult of the goddess Aphrodite, who, myth proclaims, floated to Cyprus from her birthplace, Kythera.

## THE BYZANTINES

The lush fields of Cyprus were by then not only ripe with grain, grapes, and olives, but also with orchards of lemon and orange trees. Byzantines held the island for centuries, building grand basilicas and monasteries. Beginning in 647 C.E., Arab forces began a three-century siege of the island, lasting until the Greek emperor Nikiphoros Fokas expelled them. By then the Crusades had begun and Cyprus seemed a perfect launching pad from which to free the Holy Land. In 1191 Richard the Lion-Hearted's fleet shipwrecked near Cyprus on its way to the Third Crusade, and when the Cypriot emperor behaved harshly to the shipwrecked crusaders,

Richard seized the island. He married Berengaria of Navarre in the Cypriot city of Lemesos and proclaimed her queen of England. A year later he sold the island to the Knights Templar, who resold it to the deposed king of Jerusalem.

The Franks ruled for a while, followed by the Venetians and the Ottomans. The British assumed administration of Cyprus in 1878, annexed it in 1914, and when the Ottomans relinquished all claim to the island, made it a colony of the crown in 1925.

## A COUNTRY DIVIDED

After the Second World War, the Cypriots launched a struggle to free themselves from British rule. They campaigned for union with Greece, but eagerly accepted recognition as an independent state in 1960. Sadly, though, independence did not flow easily. Though 82 percent of the island's population was Greek, 18 percent was of Turkish descent, with a mix of Maronites, Armenians, and Catholics from the Frankish and Venetian periods. In 1974 Greece's ruling military junta attempted to assassinate the president of Cyprus, who was pro-independence, though he was both Greek and an Orthodox archbishop. Using the junta's terrible blunder as an excuse, Turkey invaded the island, taking more than one third of the territory.

## GLORIOUS FOOD

Today lovely Cyprus lies divided. But the bounty that lured all its occupants still graces its tables.

Every book on Cyprus mentions the tang of fresh lemons, the smell of fermenting grapes, the aroma of baking bread, the salty nip of olives. The food, while mainly Greek in origin, has been influenced by Turkey, Armenia, Lebanon, Syria, Italy, France, and Britain. Luxuriating in its fertile climate, the island produces figs, beans, chickpeas, herbs, olives and olive oil, dates, almonds, and lemons.

Islanders continue to produce bulgur wheat and smoke-cured pork, and bake wonderful olive breads.

This is how you might eat in Cyprus:

For *meze* with your glass of island wine—red from Mavro grapes or white from Xynisteri— you get black and green *tsakistes,* native olives in a dressing of lemon, garlic, herbs, and coriander seed, and spreads of *talattouri,* Cypriotic *tzatziki,* as well as tahini and *tarama.* Snails come next, and pickled cauliflower and dressed kohlrabi might accompany it. Grilled *haloumi* cheese comes along with smoked pork or grilled pork rissoles. Bulgur wheat is steamed with onions and stock and served with yogurt. Greens are joined with black-eyed peas and olive oil.

Cypriots continue to enjoy *moukentra,* a mix of lentils, rice, and onions. They also eat *kolokasi,* wild taro root, which resembles a sweet potato and is not found in mainland Greece. For an afternoon sweet they make *mahlepi,* a cream pudding floating in rosewater syrup.

And then they might have a glass of a sweet dessert wine found nowhere else, called Commandaria. It tastes like a sweet union of raisin and brandy. Look for it in Greek specialty stores. One good brand is Saint John.

# SOUP
# FOR HARD TIMES AND GOOD TIMES

As GREECE GAVE BIRTH TO ONE OF THE GLOBE'S EARLY CIVILIZATIONS, ALONG WITH IT CAME THIS MOST CIVILIZED FOOD. AFTER ALL, ENJOYING A BOWL OF HOT SOUP REQUIRES THAT FIRE BE CONQUERED AND RECEPTACLES INVENTED. FROM ANCIENT TIMES TO MODERN, SOUPS HAVE FIGURED ON THE GREEK MENU. TODAY IT IS FREQUENTLY THE KEYSTONE DISH ON THE TABLE, WITH OTHER PLATES OF FOOD MERELY OFFERING ACCOMPANYING DIVERSION.

He who wants no soup, gets two bowls full.

—GREEK PROVERB

While soup (with the necessary bread) has always been the fare that feeds the poor, the rustic, and the working people, everyone, including the wealthy and cosmopolitan, share an appetite for this most nutritious, sturdy, and abiding of foods.

The soups of Greece are particularly filling, often more like brothy stews than infused stocks. They contain beans and lentils, selections of meat, fish, and vegetables with noodles or rice, and thick pastes of sesame and chickpea.

Little information exists about the soups the ancients supped on. We know they simmered legumes, combined peas

and broad (fava) beans, and boiled meats into bouillons.

"No one roasts an ox foot," Athenaeus remarks when commenting on Homer's menu for Odysseus, meaning that such sinewy pieces were plopped into the boiling pot even then, when ox-thigh-eating heroes did their deeds. From the Bronze Age on, fishermen from the Hellenes, traveling from Gibralter to the Levant, cooked up their seafood catch in brimming kettles and passed their formulas on to the people they met. Visitors in Byzantine and Ottoman times tell of the filling, comforting, steaming vats of *trahanas* (sour milk noodles) that were set out as welcoming meals.

What finds its way into the soup pot today, as in ages past, spans the whole gamut of Greek fare: birds and meat from every flock and herd, fish and shellfish of every watery tract, and the whole range of their sun-blessed vegetables. Especially notable are the many and matchless vegetable soups. With their produce, their oil, their crystal water, and

*At the festival of a church's saint day, a man ladles out servings of thick fava soup to all the celebrants.*

## BRINGING IT TO A BOIL

By about 6500 B.C.E., people living in Greece had started to make pottery containers, meaning that food—and therefore soup!—could be boiled. As a result, grasses, pulses, meats, and fish came out of the coals and into a pot.

In boiling, the entire surface of the food is in contact with the heat. The cooking temperature is actually rather low compared to broiling, roasting, baking, and frying, but with the all-round contact on the food, boiling does the job in an efficient manner. The method doesn't take a constant eye or a particularly delicate touch, so it frees up the cook.

And of course there is the added value that not just the solid food becomes edible. Much of its essential nutrition is extracted into the water, and thus the water itself becomes food—hence soup.

a little sautéing, Greek cooks are able to turn out vegetable soups of stunning depth without using any meat, poultry, or fish.

If soup is the food of the poor, it is the poor in coin only, for as you will see, it is the food of the rich in spirit.

On the Cycladic islands, *manestra* is the name of their version of tomato soup, which in other parts of Greece might be called *domatosoupa*—"tomato soup." As befits a Greek dish, ancient or modern, a continuing discussion, complete with many hand gestures, surrounds how the tomato soup in the islands acquired the name *manestra* and what *manestra* means. Some claim that the name derives from the small pasta it contains, and that it is really a pasta, not a tomato, soup. Others claim that *manestra* is the Greek version of *minestra*, the simple vegetable soup of Italy also called *minestrone*—which is possible because the Cycladic islands were the possession of Venice, Genoa, and other Italian cities for five hundred years.

The two arguments, like the comic mask and the tragic mask of drama, are actually but one discourse with different perspectives. Indeed, *minestra* is used interchangeably with *zuppa* in Italy to mean soup and also some pasta dishes. The word and meanings came to Greece, so, in short, the dialog is a monolog and *manestra* is better eaten than discussed.

# manestra

**SERVES 6**

WHEN I CALLED MY FRIEND MARKELLA, ON THE ISLAND OF SANTORINI, TO TELL HER I WAS SERVING *MANESTRA* IN OUR CAFE AND EIGHT HUNDRED PATRONS WERE LAPPING IT UP, SHE EXCLAIMED, "MANESTRA! HAVE YOU NO SHAME? IT'S WHAT WE EAT WHEN WE ARE THE MOST POOR, WHEN WE HAVE NO MONEY FOR ANYTHING BETTER." "BUT MARKELLA," I RESPONDED, "IT'S SO GOOD!"

And all the points were true. When Victoria and I owned the Good and Plenty Café, which abounded with students who were both poor and often vegetarian, we ladled out Greek *manestra* by countless bowlfuls. It's also the soup the villagers in Greece make when they have no cash for finer fare. And, oh, it's so good!

*Manestra* is the prime example of Greece's remarkably flavorful soups made purely from a vegetable base. The ingredients are ridiculously few. The liquid is plain water. The depth is derived simply from sautéing onions, garlic, and crimson tomatoes in lush olive oil. Yet the soup sings with startling character and requires little preparation time.

In Greece *manestra* is sometimes served with cheese sprinkled over the top, which gives the very tomatoey mixture a pleasant milky, contrasting bite. When they were small, my children especially liked the cinnamon and mint variation on page 154.

*1/3 cup olive oil*

*1 large onion, finely chopped*

*4 large cloves garlic, minced or pressed*

*2 teaspoons chopped fresh oregano leaves, or 1 teaspoon dried*

*2 1/2 pounds ripe tomatoes, chopped into 1/4- to 1/2-inch pieces*

*1 1/2 teaspoons salt*

*2 quarts water*

*1/3 cup orzo, trahana (page 247), or other small pasta*

*1/3 cup grated kefalotyri or Parmesan cheese*

## TRAHANA SOUP
••••••••••••••••••••

Along with *manestra* and bread soup, a mix of *trahana* noodles (page 247) and water has been a sustaining pottage from at least Byzantine times. *Trahana*, in fact, provided people a sort of instant soup mix. The sour-milk noodles were dried until crumbly and then stored as a powder. When a meal was needed, water was added to the powder to form a sort of porridge. The taste for *trahana* soup is rather an acquired one, not much to the palate of those who haven't grown up with it. But it does give *some* justification for using *some* soup mixes: After all, the practice is more than two thousand years old.

1 Heat the oil in a large heavy nonreactive pot over medium-high heat. Add the onion, garlic, and oregano and sauté until the onion wilts, about 5 minutes.

2 Stir in the tomatoes and sauté until they collapse, about 10 minutes.

3 Add the salt and water, and bring to a boil. Then reduce the heat and simmer until the tomatoes are very soft and the liquid is deep brownish red, about 40 minutes.

4 Add the orzo and simmer until it is tender, about 5 minutes.

5 Ladle the soup into individual bowls. Sprinkle on a generous spoonful of cheese and serve right away.

## VARIATION:

**More *Manestra Myrodies:*** Occasionally the Greek cook will stir in one or two favorite *myrodies*—a double-pronged word meaning both "flavor" and "perfume." When simmering the soup in Step 3, add ¼ teaspoon ground cinnamon. And if desired, just before serving, swirl in 1 tablespoon shredded fresh mint leaves.

# bread soup

## WITH GARLIC, CUCUMBER, CAPERS, AND MINT

### ☀ SERVES 6

IN GREECE, WHERE BREAD IS ALWAYS SERVED WITH SOUP, BREAD SOMETIMES *IS* THE SOUP. PARTICULARLY WHEN IT IS A LITTLE OLD OR STALE, THE CRUSTY STAFF OF LIFE IS SOAKED AND TURNED INTO A PORRIDGELIKE POTTAGE.

The idea of bread soup is not unique to Greece, though it may have originated there. Italian, Spanish, and French cuisines all feature bread soups. Some serve the winning bowlful dolloped with garlic, others with herbs, others with beans or greens. Greeks consider bread soup, like *manestra*, to be a dish for sparse times and a curative for the sad or unwell. But to limit the preparation to such untoward circumstances is far too restrictive! Chilled bread soup revivifies. Made rich, not thrifty, with oil; embellished, not plain, with parsley, capers, and mint; showy, not humble, with cucumber, it takes on luxury, distinction, and fancy.

## A "MASS" OF DOUGH

Now called *zymi*, in ancient times bread dough was called *maza*, which means "mass." The term came from *masso*, "to knead." *Maza* also meant "barley cake," in contrast to *artos*, "wheat bread." From the term *maza* we still derive the words for both "dough" and "bread" in many languages, such as the Spanish *masa harina*, used in Mexico to make tortillas, and the Hebrew *matzoh*, used to make unleavened cracker bread.

In both dough and bread form, both these *mazas* are also used in soups, as breadlike dumplings or crumbled in dry.

*Like soup and sandwich, stuffed half-moon* kaltsounia *pies and other pitas pair perfectly with any Greek soup.*

1 large loaf (1 pound) very stale Greek or other crusty bread, cut into 1-inch-thick slices (see Notes)

10 cups water

12 cloves garlic

2 teaspoons salt

1 to 1 1/2 cups olive oil (see Notes)

2 tablespoons red wine vinegar

1 medium cucumber (12 ounces), peeled and coarsely grated or finely chopped

2 tablespoons chopped fresh flat-leaf parsley leaves

2 tablespoons capers, coarsely chopped

2 tablespoons finely shredded fresh mint leaves

1 Quarter the bread slices and combine them with the water in a large bowl. Set aside to soak until the bread is thoroughly softened, 5 to 10 minutes depending on how stale the bread is.

2 Place the garlic and salt on a cutting board and mince together with a chef's knife.

3 Lift the bread out of the water and squeeze the pieces lightly, leaving them quite moist. In batches, puree the bread together with the garlic mixture, oil, and vinegar, in a blender or processor. Transfer the puree to a large bowl.

4 Stir the cucumber and parsley into the bread mixture and sprinkle the capers and mint over the top. Serve right away, or cover and chill for several hours before serving.

## WHEN BREAD AND SOUP WERE LACKING

Behind the Greek preoccupation with food, and hence their fabulous cuisine, is the fact that food crises—and all too often the famine that follows—have occurred frequently since ancient days. In fact, the need to procure a steady food supply drove Greek expansion across the Mediterranean. Mythology says a seven-year drought impelled the Thirans, following the instructions of the Delphic oracle, to "send brother from brothers, chosen by lot," to found a colony at Cyrene (Kirene), probably around the eighth century B.C.E. The Halkidians from Euboea (Evia), who built Reggio on the toe of Italy, were men who were chosen to leave, one out of every ten, because of a failure of crops in their native land. According to Plutarch, drought and plague in Corinth led Archais to establish Syracuse in Sicily.

While there were no food riots in classical Greece because the constitution allowed for alternative forms of protest, as supplies got short popular indignation would turn against the grain dealers. If their conduct was not above reproach in the distribution of grain, they were punished. Grain dealers were supervised by grain wardens, and trials of both dealer and warden were frequent. Some were executed.

Greece still must import much of its grain, at considerable expense. Famine struck as recently as during World War II and the political struggles of the 1950s. So bread, by the plate or in the bowl, is precious not just symbolically, but in reality.

**NOTES:**

■ Though the original idea was to use up leftover bread in a satisfying way, you may want to make bread soup even when you don't have day-old bread. Starting with fresh bread, cut the loaf in half lengthwise and bake the halves in a 200°F oven until dry but not toasted, about 20 minutes. Cool completely, then proceed with the recipe.

■ The 1½ cups olive oil, ordinary for the Greek palate, might seem a bit much for others. If so, just use 1 cup.

# zesty lentil soup

## WITH TANGY GREENS AND HERBS

### FAKIES

**SERVES 6**

THINK OF GREEK LENTIL SOUP AS HESIOD'S SOUP. AS THE GREEK CIVILIZATION BEGAN TO BLOSSOM, HE WAS THE FIRST TO SPEAK OF THE MERITS OF HARD WORK, HUMILITY, MODERATION, AND SIMPLICITY. LENTIL SOUP SURELY REPRESENTS ALL THOSE VALUES: FUEL FOR THE LABORER, LENTILS ARE RICH IN MINERALS AND PROTEIN AND AT THE SAME TIME PRODIGIOUSLY TASTY.

Here the soup is thick and porridgy, contrived to make a solid meal, and sparked with a dash of hot pepper, as is common in certain areas of Greece. Often lentil soup is brought to its flavor peak with a dash of vinegar at the end—the forthright red wine vinegar of Greece, not sugary balsamic. But even better is a squeeze of lemon juice.

2 tablespoons olive oil

3 tablespoons tomato paste

1 onion, finely chopped

1 bay leaf, crumbled

1 teaspoon chopped fresh oregano
    leaves, or ¹/₂ teaspoon dried

¹/₂ teaspoon fresh thyme leaves,
    or ¹/₄ teaspoon dried

1 small dried red chile pepper,
    stemmed and chopped

2¹/₂ cups (about 1 pound) lentils

1 pound tangy greens, such as
    turnip, mustard, or dandelion,
    well rinsed, stemmed, and
    coarsely chopped

10 cups water

¹/₂ teaspoon freshly ground
    black pepper

1¹/₂ teaspoons salt

Lemon wedges or red wine
    vinegar

1 Place the oil, tomato paste, onion, bay leaf, oregano, thyme, and chile pepper in a large non-reactive pot over medium heat and stir until the mixture is well blended and the onion has wilted slightly, 3 to 4 minutes.

2 Add the lentils, greens, water, and black pepper and bring to a boil. Reduce the heat and simmer, uncovered, until the lentils are very soft but not quite collapsed, about 30 minutes.

3 Stir in the salt and serve right away, accompanied by the lemon wedges or a cruet of vinegar for squeezing or drizzling over.

**NOTE:** As with dried beans, in lentil soups the salt should be added only at the end. Otherwise, the lentils will not soften completely.

**SAGE ADVICE**

A wise man does all things right, including the seasoning of lentil soup.

**—THE STOIC PHILOSOPHERS, THIRD CENTURY B.C.E.**

# FAVA STORIES

**W**E ARE SITTING ON SOME STEPS OVERLOOKING THE SQUARE. AS WOMEN WE CROSS THE SQUARE, BUT WE DON'T TARRY THERE; IT'S MEN'S TERRITORY. EVERY AFTERNOON, THOUGH, WE GATHER IN GROUPS AROUND THE SQUARE TO DO CHORES AND CHAT. WE LOOK DOWN AT THE SQUARE AS IF THERE IS ACTION THERE, BUT AS USUAL, NOTHING IS HAPPENING.

Some of us hold between our legs two big, round millstones: one, on the bottom, we secure fast with our legs; the other, on top, spins around. Both have a central hole in which we put an oval stone to keep the mill together. We grind the top stone around in slow, considered circles, now and then spilling unhusked peas down the central hole. The mill takes off most of the skins on the *fava* we are preparing, and splits most of them in half, turning them from dusty brown to golden yellow. They slide out between the rotating stones and onto a ground cloth we have below. Others pour the newly split peas into great round, screen-bottomed sieves, and we shake and toss the peas as we pick out pebbles.

"You missed one," says Marousi.

"I saw it," I respond, tossing the pebble to the ground.

"Did you hear that Artemia's daughter Paraskevi got engaged?" asks Rambelia.

"No," we all reply, rapidly turning our ears to the news.

We hear about the engagement, to whom (though we know from weeks of rumor), and when the wedding will be. Who will prepare *koufeta*—the wedding honey and almonds—becomes the topic, and who will sing the wedding songs. What new items does the bride still need to get? Will Hristo, of our own village musicians, play the *bouzouki*, Spiro the *laouto*, and Ianni the *klarino* at the party?

We talk of relatives in distant places, how they are doing. We wonder how the new widow is faring. Can she make it on her own? Her children are young. And all the while we keep grinding and picking.

Last year we heard that a man in Pyrgos village had invented a *fava* cleaning and splitting machine, and we took our lentils there. He had taken a two-stroke motorcycle engine and attached it to a grinding device. He had hooked a chute for the *fava* atop, a bag to catch the skins to the side, and a basket to catch the bare split *fava* in front. But still we talked the whole way there and back, dragging our bags and picking out rocks.

Either way we grind our *fava*, we take our share and head for our kitchens. There we boil up the peas around a fat onion. We serve out bowls, pour on oil, maybe capers, maybe olives. And we eat with the joy of being able to talk and work together, sharing laughter and chores.

*Conversation and team work make kitchen chores go quickly. Here two women sort wild greens to enjoy with fava soup.*

# yellow split pea soup

## WITH MYRIAD TOPPINGS

### SERVES 6

FAVA IS WHAT GREEKS CALL THEIR OWN DISTINCT YELLOW SPLIT PEAS. IT IS PARTICULARLY RENOWNED AS THE FOOD OF SANTORINI, WHERE I HAVE LIVED AND OFF FOR MANY YEARS, AND ALL THAT IS SAID ABOUT SANTORINIANS BEING *FAVA* EATERS (A MAJOR JOKE IN GREECE) IS TRUE: WE EAT *FAVA* BY THE GALLON.

We split it, and then we simmer it up into great pots of the nuttiest, most roasty, sunniest pea porridge you can imagine. We top it with olive oil, red tomato sauce, caper buds and leaves, olives, fried onions, garlic, baked sardines, salty anchovies . . . and every creative, zesty, savory, tangy, herby accompaniment we can think of. We eat *fava* for midday meal and for evening meal. We eat *fava* on Mondays and Sundays, on common days and holy days, when it's Lent and when it's not. We eat it hot and soupy and as crisp fritters. We eat it because we have it, but mostly because we love it.

Whenever I leave the island, one woman after another gives me a going-away gift of the most important, personal remembrance she can, and it is always a bag of her own homegrown, home-shucked, home-split golden *fava*. So I always have a supply in the United States.

There is archaeological evidence that *fava* keeps for millennia, but of course it doesn't last that long for me, because back home I cook *fava* on Mondays and Sundays, common days and holy days. . . .

*FOR THE SOUP*

*3 cups (about 1 pound, 6 ounces)*
  *yellow split peas*
*1 large onion, peeled*
*3 cloves garlic, minced or pressed*
  *(optional)*
*3 tablespoons olive oil*
*3 quarts water*
*1 teaspoon salt*

*TOPPING CHOICES*

*Lemon wedges*
*Extra-virgin olive oil*
*Pickled Red Onions (page 75)*
*Olive and Caper Tapenade*
  *(page 477)*
*Skordalia (page 461)*
*Anchovy fillets, salted or in oil*
*Marides (page 59)*
*Quick Fresh Tomato Sauce (page 474)*
*Red Tomato Meat Sauce (page 472)*
*Roasted Tomato "Paste" (page 479)*
*Fried Garlic Topping (page 481)*
*Wilted Parsley or Cilantro Topping*
  *(page 481)*
*Shredded grape, caper, or other*
  *tart leaves*
*Marinated mushrooms (page 50)*
*Sausage Slices (page 58)*

1 Rinse the peas in a colander under cold running water, drain, and place in a large pot. Add the onion (whole), garlic if using, oil, and water. Bring to a boil over high heat, then reduce the heat and simmer briskly, uncovered, until the peas are almost tender and much of the water is gone, about 1 hour.

2 Partially cover the pot, reduce the heat to a gentler simmer, and continue cooking until the peas stir into almost a puree, so the texture is like a chunky porridge, 45 minutes to 1 hour more.

3 Remove the onion, stir in the salt, and serve right away, garnished with the desired topping.

## THE PEDIGREED PORRIDGE

*O*spria, the Greek word for all the dried legumes, is a relative of the ancient word *pale*, meaning "fine powder," which probably comes from the Sanskrit *palale*, for "ground sesame seed." From this root came the Greek words *poltos*, a thick porridgelike soup, and *polono*, "to pulverize"; our word "pulse," for the pea family, and "pollen," for the fine powder spores of plants; *polenta*, the ground cornmeal of Italy (the term was first used for powdered pearl barley); our verb "pulverize"; and our term "porridge," the old English word for soups made from wet powder, like, indeed, pease porridge, the old English soup of split peas.

# white bean soup

## WITH *SKORDALIA*

### SERVES 6

ARCHAEOLOGISTS HAVE FOUND BEANS, PEAS, AND LENTILS IN GREEK SETTLEMENTS DATING FROM BEFORE THE BRONZE AGE. AT FIRST PEAS WERE THE MOST COMMONLY EATEN LEGUME— SCADS OF THEM SHOW UP IN STORAGE VESSELS. THEN LENTILS—RED, YELLOW, AND PINK—TAKE OVER. ALL ALONG, THE SINGLE EUROPEAN BEAN, THE BROAD (FAVA) BEAN, APPEARS LIKE A SPINSTER AUNT HOVERING AROUND ITS DISTANT LENTIL COUSINS.

When New World pulses arrived in Greece, the story changed. The broad bean found a whole family of relatives, and today they claim pulse preeminence in Greek cuisine. Green beans, usually stewed *yiakni*, are probably the most commonly served vegetable. Giant beans and lima beans appear in soups and salads. But it is the small white bean simmered up in a tantilizing soup named after it, *fasolada*, that occupies the table again and again. Indeed, a family might eat *fasolada* as many as two or three times a week.

Here added to the thick and stalwart bean soup is a swirl of *skordalia*, Greece's favorite topping, to strike up a garlicky harmony.

2 rounded cups (1 pound) white
    beans, such as great northern,
    cannellini, or navy beans
10 cups water
$^1$/2 cup olive oil
1 medium onion, finely chopped
1 medium carrot, finely chopped
1 large rib celery, finely chopped
2 medium tomatoes, fresh or canned,
    coarsely chopped
$^1$/4 teaspoon freshly ground black
    pepper
1 teaspoon salt
$^1$/2 cup Skordalia (page 461)
2 tablespoons chopped fresh flat-leaf
    parsley leaves

1 Place the beans and 4 cups of the water in a large nonreactive pot and bring to a boil over high heat. Boil for 1 minute, then remove from the heat and set aside to soak, covered, for at least 1 hour and up to overnight.

2 Drain the beans, rinse in a colander, and return to the pot. Add the oil and remaining 6 cups water. Bring to a boil again, then lower the heat and simmer, uncovered, until the beans begin to soften but are not yet tender, about 30 minutes.

3 Add the onion, carrot, celery, tomatoes, and pepper, and continue simmering until the beans are almost disintegrating, about 45 minutes.

4 Stir in the salt and ladle the soup into individual bowls. Spoon a dollop of the *Skordalia* into each bowl, sprinkle the parsley over the top, and serve right away.

**NOTE:** Some recipes for *fasolada* call for baby lima beans rather than white beans. I have never seen limas used in the soup in Greece, and soups made with them tend to turn out bitter. White beans, on the other hand, like navy beans, are famous for their sweetness.

## VARIATIONS:

**Soup of Beans and Lentils:** Members of the same family, albeit from different branches, can swim in the same waters. In a doubling up of legumes, *fasolada* can be made with a mix of beans and lentils, using 1 cup of each. Lentils do not require the hour's soak; add them when you return the beans to the pot in Step 2.

**Smooth *Fasolada:*** For a satiny version of *fasolada*, the ingredients can be pureed after cooking. Pour the soup into a blender or food processor and blend until smooth. Swirl in the garlic paste and serve.

## THE COURTESAN AND THE CAPER

No gods of ancient Greece are associated with capers, as Athena is with the olive, but one famous courtesan was. Phryne was a quite famous "escort" around 400 B.C.E. and it is said that as well as working at her profession, she gathered, brined, and sold capers. At least she did this before she became avidly sought after; later, presumably, she didn't have the time. One wonders if in her simple soup days, she didn't throw some of the buds into her bowl; and if at the height of her career, when at banquets every night, trays of roast lamb, fruits, and nuts were brought before her, she didn't sneak in an occasional caper as she capered.

# chickpea soup

## WITH GARLIC, SAGE, AND TARRAGON

### REVITHIA

**SERVES 6 TO 8**

EARLY GREEKS ATE SO MANY CHICKPEAS THAT THEY BELIEVED POSEIDON AROSE FROM HIS WATERY HOME TO SHOW THEM THE SECRET OF COOKING THE LEGUME. WHY POSEIDON WOULD HAVE KNOWLEDGE OF SUCH AN EARTHLY PLANT REMAINS UNANSWERED, BUT IT SEEMS THAT SEAFARING GREEKS BROUGHT CHICKPEAS TO SPAIN WHEN THEY COLONIZED THERE. THE ANCIENT WORD FOR CHICKPEAS WAS *EREVYTHIA*, TODAY SIMPLY CUT SHORT TO *REVITHIA*. THE CHICKPEA'S OTHER NAME, GARBANZO, IS BUT A SPANISH TWIST ON THE OLD GREEK (*GAR* FOR THE ER, *B* FOR THE V, AND *Z* FOR THE TH). SAGE AND GARLIC ADDED DURING COOKING LEND AROMA AND DEPTH TO THE HUMBLE SOUP, AND A FINAL TOPPING OF TARRAGON ON THE BOWLFUL BESTOWS INTRIGUING DISTINCTION.

3 cups (about 1 3/4 pounds) dried chickpeas

4 quarts water

3 teaspoons baking soda

1/3 cup olive oil

1 onion, finely chopped

3 cloves garlic, minced or pressed

1 teaspoon finely chopped fresh sage leaves, or 1/2 teaspoon dried

2 teaspoons salt

1/2 teaspoon freshly ground black pepper

1/3 cup fresh lemon juice

1 1/2 teaspoons chopped fresh tarragon leaves (see Notes)

1 Place the chickpeas and 2 quarts of the water in a large pot. Bring to a boil over high heat, reduce the heat, and simmer briskly until the skins loosen, 20 to 25 minutes. Drain the chickpeas in a colander and rinse them under cold running water to cool them.

## PEELING AND PUREEING CHICKPEAS

Chickpeas will collapse into a soft and nubby puree when they're cooked, but they won't do so unless they are peeled. In my experience, the easiest way to peel them is to cook them long enough for the skins to loosen, then sprinkle them with baking soda (about 1 teaspoon per cup of chickpeas), and continue to follow the directions in Step 2 of the recipe. Many Greek cooks prefer to rub the chickpeas with their hands; I prefer to use clean dish towels.

If you dislike the slight flavor of baking soda that lingers, there is another method: Cook the chickpeas for 20 minutes or so, drain them, and then transfer them to a bowl of fresh water. Let them soak for a few minutes, then rub them vigorously (the skins will be far more stubborn about coming off completely).

If you don't want to peel the chickpeas, you can puree the soup in a food processor once the peas are cooked thoroughly soft. The result will be a little less sweet with the tougher peel blended in.

2 Spread a cloth on a counter and transfer the chickpeas to the cloth. Sprinkle the baking soda over the peas and rub the peas around to cover them with

baking soda, spreading them out in a single layer as you go. Cover the peas with another cloth, and pressing your hands firmly over it, rub back and forth to loosen as many chickpea skins as you can. With your fingers, finish removing the loose skins. Transfer the peeled chickpeas to a clean colander. (Do this in batches if you like.) Rinse the peeled peas and set them aside.

3 Heat the oil in a large non-reactive pot over medium heat. Add the onion, garlic, and sage and sauté until the onion is well wilted, 5 minutes. Add the chickpeas and remaining 2 quarts water and bring to a boil. Reduce the heat and simmer briskly, uncovered, until the chickpeas are soft enough to collapse into a puree, 1 hour.

4 Add the salt, pepper, and lemon juice and whisk vigorously to puree most of the peas while retaining some chunks. Ladle the soup into individual bowls, garnish with the tarragon, and serve right away.

## ROASTED CHICKPEAS

·················

S ome ancient Greek writings describe whole roasted chickpeas that were apparently popped in the mouth like popcorn while people sat around the fire. They do make a savory snack.

Place 1 pound dried chickpeas and 10 cups water (or enough to cover the peas by 2 inches) in a large pot. Bring to a boil over high heat, reduce the heat, and simmer briskly until cooked through but not collapsing, 50 minutes to $1\frac{1}{4}$ hours. Drain and set aside to drip dry.

Preheat the oven to 300°F. Spread the peas on a baking sheet that has been lightly greased with olive oil, and roll them around to coat them all over. Place in the oven and roast, shaking once or twice to rotate them, until a bit crunchy and golden, about $1\frac{1}{2}$ hours.

Cool and serve, lightly sprinkled with salt if desired. Or, to mix the ancient with the modern (roasted chickpeas were once served as a dessert!), drizzle honey over the peas and serve them as an ice cream topping.

**NOTES:**

■ Many cookbooks tell you to soak chickpeas overnight, like beans, before cooking them, but it is not necessary. The chickpeas cook in as short a time and as well without overnight soaking.

■ In some parts of Greece, around Florina and the north, the chickpeas are not peeled and are simply left whole.

■ I have tried many leafy herbs with chickpea soup, and sage and tarragon are my favorites, even though tarragon is not typically Greek. The tarragon should be fresh, though. If you don't have any, choose another fresh herb, such as basil, cilantro, or parsley. Or use lemon rounds.

# sesame Soup

## WITH OLIVES AND BASIL

### TAHINOSOUPA

**SERVES 6**

I N GREECE *TAHINOSOUPA* IS A FAST-DAY SOUP: IT IS SERVED DURING THE FORTY DAYS OF ABSTINENCE BEFORE CHRISTMAS; THE FIFTEEN DAYS BEFORE ST. MARY'S DAY (AUGUST 15); FOR THE TRULY DEVOUT EVERY WEDNESDAY AND FRIDAY; BUT MOSTLY FOR THE FIFTY DAYS BEFORE GREEK ORTHODOX EASTER, AND ESPECIALLY DURING HOLY WEEK. TINGED PINK FROM A SPOONFUL OF TOMATO PASTE, IT TASTES AS IF THE AROMATIC SEEDS ARE BURSTING IN THE MOUTH.

To Greeks the soup seems quite prosaic, but my guests never find it so. Along with Chickpea Soup (page 162), it is the soup I serve at dinner parties when I want to put something on the table that few have sampled, something that will be a conversation piece because it's such a palate pleaser. The additions of garlic, bay leaf, olives, and basil make one wish Lent lasted all year long.

*2/3 cup uncooked white rice, preferably Arborio*

*1 clove garlic, minced or pressed*

*2 tablespoons tomato paste*

*1 large bay leaf*

*1 teaspoon salt*

*2 quarts water*

*1 cup tahini (sesame paste)*

*1/4 cup fresh lemon juice*

*8 to 10 Kalamata or other good black olives, pitted and coarsely chopped*

*1 tablespoon thinly shredded fresh basil leaves*

1 Place the rice, garlic, tomato paste, bay leaf, salt, and water in a large nonreactive pot and bring to a boil over high heat. Reduce the heat and simmer, uncovered, until the rice is very soft, 15 minutes.

2 Meanwhile, stir together the tahini and lemon juice in a medium-size bowl.

3 When the rice is tender, add 1 cup of the cooking liquid to the tahini mixture and whisk until smooth. Pour it into the rice pot and whisk to mix well.

4 Heat the soup just until it is beginning to boil again, then ladle it into individual bowls. Sprinkle the olives and basil over the top and serve right away.

## NOTES:

■ Tahini, like peanut butter, naturally separates as it stands and needs to be reamalgamated before using. Two minutes in the microwave softens it enough to let you whisk it back into a satiny puree.

■ To make a meal of the soup, noodles are sometimes added.

## THEMIS

We know her—we see her often. She stands at the top of most of our courthouses, blindfolded, weighing the fate of people in the balance scale she holds. She is Themis, the goddess of justice.

Hesiod felt that Themis was the true keeper of the hardworking land-tiller's life, the ruler of the seasons, and the deity who ensured that no matter how hard life might be, all things were fair. Hesiod said of her in his poem *Theogony*:

*And shining Themis was Zeus's
  second wife.
She bore him the Horea—
  Order, Peace that flowers,
And Justice, who attends the works
  of humans.
And then she bore the Fates,
  to whom wise Zeus has paid
The greatest honor—
  Clotho, Atropos,
Lachesis, who give all good and bad
  to people.*

Themis was very wise and knowledgeable. Indeed, she seemed to know all that her fellow gods and goddesses knew. She told her son Prometheus many secrets, and not just about fire. With one he eventually gained release from Zeus's punishment. Themis, with her wisdom, succeeded her mother as the deity behind the oracle of Delphi. She also told Deucalion and Pyrrha the secret of how to bring people back to earth after the flood. She then warned Atlas that Zeus would one day steal his golden apples. It seems Themis wanted things fair and square.

# Summer Vegetable Soup

## HORTOSOUPA KALOKAIRINI

### SERVES 6

During the summer in Greece, the air blows gentle wafts of comfort. The baking sun sweetens everything from moods to grapes. The fields and markets are full to the brim of one vegetable after another, until suddenly they are all there together. Summer is the time for the most bountiful soup, a soup that uses every fresh tuber, stalk, pod, and leaf that is reaching out to take in warmth. Greeks everywhere make soups of squash, carrots, celery, tomatoes, peppers, beans, onions, okra, lettuce (there is a spring and summer soup of lettuce alone), and new potatoes. Strangely, when the days grow too hot for people to be in the midday sun, the summer soups refresh and cool. In a timeless version, special Greek touches include a dash of cucumber and a topping of sharp kefalotyri.

*The goddess Themis, whose hands
may well have held justice's scales.*

2 tablespoons olive oil

1 medium onion, quartered and
    thinly sliced

2 cloves garlic, coarsely chopped

1 pound tomatoes, cut into 1/4-inch
    pieces

1 rib celery, cut into 1/4-inch pieces

1 medium carrot, cut into 1/4-inch
    pieces

1 small cucumber (4 ounces),
    peeled and cut into 1/4-inch
    pieces

8 ounces zucchini or other summer
    squash, cut into 1/4-inch pieces

1 tablespoon chopped fresh dill

1 tablespoon chopped fresh celery
    leaves

2 tablespoons chopped fresh
    flat-leaf parsley leaves

1 1/2 teaspoons salt

1/2 teaspoon freshly ground
    black pepper

2 quarts water

8 ounces fresh peas, shelled

1/2 cup grated kefalotyri cheese,
    for garnish

1 Combine the oil, onion, and garlic in a large nonreactive pot and cook over medium heat until the onion wilts, 5 minutes.

2 Add the tomatoes, celery, carrot, cucumber, zucchini, dill, celery leaves, parsley, salt, pepper, and water and bring to a boil over medium-high heat. Reduce the heat and simmer until the vegetables are tender but not mushy, 40 minutes. Add the peas and continue simmering until they are tender, 10 minutes.

3 Serve hot, with a sprinkling of cheese on top.

## THYME FOR SOUP
..................

When the cicada sings her sweet note, it is a delight to inspect my Lemnian vines to see they are getting ripe, for it is a precocious plant, and I watch the fig swelling: when it is ripe I eat it avidly, singing at the same time "Friendly seasons" and I grind the thyme soup: I grow fat at that time in summer.

**—ANONYMOUS,
FOURTH CENTURY B.C.E.**

## VARIATIONS:

### Additional Choices from Summer's Garden:

■ Scallions—3 or 4, trimmed and cut into 1/2-inch lengths; add with the onion and garlic.

■ In the Pontos and in northern Greece, hot red peppers might be added with the onion and garlic.

■ Green beans—8 ounces, cut into 1/2-inch lengths; add with the tomatoes.

■ Green bell pepper—1 medium, seeded and coarsely chopped; add along with the tomatoes.

■ Leafy greens, such as chard, dandelion, or spinach—2 cups shredded; add with the tomatoes.

■ Okra—8 ounces, cut into 1/2-inch lengths, soaked in vinegar for 15 minutes, then rinsed; add with the tomatoes.

■ Potato—1 large, peeled and cut into 1/4-inch dice; add with the tomatoes.

■ Lettuce—2 cups shredded; add with the peas.

# winter vegetable soup

## WITH SAVORY

### SERVES 6

HESIOD TELLS THE GREEK FARMER TO PUT OFF HIS PLOWING UNTIL THE SUN HAS REACHED ITS WINTER TURNING POINT—THE SOLSTICE. HE CALLS WINTER THE "EVIL DAYS." ONE OF THE BEST WAYS GREEKS HAVE FOUND TO GUARD AGAINST THE EVIL COLD IS WITH SOUP. FEW ARE THE VEGETABLES OF WINTER, BUT LEEKS AND CABBAGE ABIDE, DRIED LEGUMES REMAIN, AND NOWADAYS POTATOES AND CANNED TOMATOES ARE AVAILABLE. EVEN BETTER PROTECTION IS PROVIDED WHEN A GREEK-STYLE WINTER SOUP IS ACCENTED WITH DAPHNE'S OWN BAY LEAF, ROBUST RED WINE, SHREDS OF SAUSAGE, AND SAVORY.

*2 tablespoons olive oil*

*1 large clove garlic, coarsely chopped*

*1 small onion, coarsely chopped*

*1 medium leek, white and light green parts well rinsed, trimmed, and cut into 1/4-inch-thick rounds*

*1 small cabbage (about 12 ounces), quartered, cored, and sliced into 1/4- to 1/2-inch-wide shreds*

*1 large rib celery, trimmed and cut into 1/2-inch pieces*

*9 cups water*

*1 1/2 cups dry red wine*

*1/4 cup tomato paste*

*1 bay leaf, crumbled*

*1/2 teaspoon dried savory*

*1 1/2 teaspoons salt*

*1/2 teaspoon freshly ground black pepper*

*8 ounces red, white, or russet potato, coarsely cut into 1/2-inch pieces*

*1 1/2 cups cooked small white beans (optional; see Note)*

*2 tablespoons chopped fresh dill or flat-leaf parsley leaves, for garnish*

*2 ounces dry salami, thinly sliced, slices cut into fine shreds, for garnish (optional)*

1 Heat the oil in a large non-reactive pot over medium heat. Add the garlic, onion, and leek and sauté gently, stirring from time to time, until beginning to wilt, about 2 minutes. Stir in the cabbage and continue sautéing and stirring until the cabbage sweats, another 2 minutes.

2 Add the celery, water, wine, tomato paste, bay leaf, savory, salt, and pepper and bring to a boil over medium-high heat. Reduce the heat and simmer briskly, uncovered, until the vegetables are very soft and the liquid is somewhat reduced, 30 minutes. Add the potato and beans, if using, and continue to simmer until the potato is cooked through, about 10 minutes.

3 Ladle into bowls and serve right away, garnished with the dill and the salami, if using.

**NOTE:** It takes 1/2 cup uncooked white beans to yield 1 1/2 cups cooked. If you are not using the beans, add another potato to keep the soup hearty.

## THE MYSTERY HERB

When I returned from my first long stay in Greece, I brought with me several small tins full of wild herbs. In one was *glykaniso*, anise seed. In another was *rigani*, oregano. In another was one that the people where I lived called *thrimbi*.

With my then inadequate dictionary, I figured it was thyme. Why not? The word has a *th*, an *i*, an *m*, so it made sense as a cognate. I was wrong. Thyme is *thymari*. When I learned that it wasn't thyme, I didn't care. I liked the herb and I continued to bring tins back and use it. I never found it in any herb market, and my dictionaries never illuminated what *thrimbi* was. It was my "mystery" herb, and not just mine. One day my colleague Victoria's cousin, also a chef, gave her a package of what he called a Greek mystery herb, named something like *threabe*, and she sent half to me. "It's my *thrimbi*," I cried, and with another spelling at hand I set to work. It turned out to be savory. Of course it wasn't ordinary savory. The savory we use in North America generally comes in two sorts: summer savory, with a fairly intense taste; and winter savory, which is more lightly flavored. *Throumbi* is yet another species of savory, *Satureja thymbra*, common to the Mediterranean and more nearly akin to thyme in flavor. So I wasn't all that far off! The herb was once believed to be an aphrodisiac. No wonder I was attached to my *thrimbi!* To substitute for it in cooking, you can use regular summer savory or marjoram or thyme.

# winter leek soup

**SERVES 4 TO 6**

SOMETIMES IN GREECE WHEN COLD WEATHER HAS ALMOST TURNED TO WARM BUT VEGETABLES ARE STILL SCARCE, THE SEASONAL SOUP IS MADE SOLELY WITH ONE VEGETABLE, AN OLD RELIABLE ONE— THE LEEK.

2 tablespoons olive oil
1 large clove garlic
4 pounds leeks, white and
    light green parts well rinsed,
    trimmed, and chopped
1 1/2 teaspoons salt
1 bay leaf
1/2 teaspoon dried savory
1/2 teaspoon freshly ground
    black pepper
8 cups water
1 cup cooked small white beans
    (optional)
2 tablespoons chopped fresh
    dill
1 cup whole milk
1 tablespoon chopped fresh
    flat-leaf parsley leaves,
    for garnish (optional)

1 Heat the oil in a large non-reactive pot over medium heat. Add the garlic, leeks, and salt and sauté until the leeks are soft, about 15 minutes. Stir in the bay leaf, savory, pepper, and water and bring to a boil over medium-high heat. Reduce the heat to maintain a simmer and cook until the leeks are very soft and the liquid is somewhat reduced, 20 minutes.

2 Stir in the beans, if using, and the dill and milk. Cook long enough to heat through. Ladle into bowls, sprinkle with the parsley, if using, and serve right away.

# double lemon avgolemono soup

## SOUPA AVGOLEMONO

### SERVES 6

AVGOLEMONO SOUP IS A SIGNATURE DISH OF GREEK CUISINE, MADE AND SAVORED THROUGHOUT THE LAND. FROM EARLY CHILDHOOD UNTIL WALKING CANE, ALL GREEKS DELIGHT IN LEMON EGG SOUP.

The soup is a light broth, very different from Greece's usual chock-full bowl, made with fish, chicken, or lamb stock. When the lemon and egg combination is whisked into the stock, it acquires a Midas touch. At the bottom of the bowl there usually swims a slight flurry of snowy white orzo or rice. Should the recipient of the soup have no appetite, *avgolemono* surely wakes it.

An *avgolemono* soup with more than the usual amount of lemon and egg, and that shuns any flour or cornstarch thickening, rouses full attention.

8 cups Chicken Stock (recipe follows),
   Fish Stock (page 171), or
   Lamb Stock (page 174)
*1/2 cup uncooked orzo or white rice,*
   *preferably Arborio*
*4 large eggs*
*1/3 cup fresh lemon juice*
*1/2 to 1 teaspoon salt*
*Freshly ground black pepper,*
   *for serving*

1 Place the stock and orzo in a large nonreactive saucepan and bring to a boil over high heat. Reduce the heat and simmer until the orzo is tender but not mushy, 12 minutes.

2 Beat the eggs in a medium-size bowl until frothy. Whisk in

## HESIOD AND THE SIMPLE SOUP OF LIFE

Not long after Homer regaled the ancient Greeks with epic tales, along came a poet who spoke of everyday life and rules of propriety.

Hesiod, a native of Boeotia, was a farmer whose greedy brother took the lion's share of the family inheritance. In retaliation, Hesiod took to rhyme to chastise his brother and to remind everyone about decency. In the poem "Works and Days," Hesiod spells out a code of conduct for simple living that still holds true in Greece and around the world.

The foundation of life is effort, says Hesiod. He speaks of the need for honesty and tells people to live in moderation. *"Myden agan,"* chides Hesiod: "Nothing too much." It is a maxim that Greeks still echo. "Pride is evil in a common man," he says; "even a noble finds it hard to bear." "The road to justice is a better way, for in the end justice will win the race." "Invite your friend, but not your enemy, to dine." "Be cordial to your neighbor." "Shun evil profit, for dishonest gain is the same as failure." "Add to your stores and famine will stay away." "Let wages to a friend be fixed before he does a job for you, not after." "Don't let a flattering coaxing woman take you in. She doesn't want you; she wants your barn."

"Constant attention will make your work go well; idlers wrestle with ruin all their days." "Avoid gossip, which is wicked, easy to start, then hard to get rid of." "Never pass a lovely brook without looking at the beauty of the stream and praying." "Eat cheese and meat. Drink wine."

the lemon juice, then slowly beat in 1 cup of the hot stock, whisking vigorously.

3 Remove the saucepan from the heat, and whisk in the egg and lemon mixture. Add the salt and serve right away, without reboiling. Pass the pepper separately.

**NOTE:** It is important not to reboil the soup once the lemon and egg mixture has been added, or the egg will break into clumps.

## VARIATIONS:

*Avgolemono* **Add-Ins:**

■ Instead of orzo or rice, use other tiny pasta, small pieces of vermicelli, *trahana* (page 247), or tapioca.

■ As garnish, use:

■ White pepper, cayenne, or freshly grated nutmeg instead of the pepper.

■ A pinch of chopped fresh herb, such as sage, mint, dill, or parsley.

■ Other ingredients to add in (cook them in the stock before the egg and lemon mixture is added) include:

■ Minced bits of chicken.

■ Tiny meatballs.

■ Beef tripe cut into ¼-inch dice (about 1 hour cooking time).

# CHICKEN STOCK

### MAKES 2 QUARTS

The simple stock that is derived from simmering chicken serves as the foundation for soups and sauces worldwide. It also functions universally as a curative. In the villages of Greece, I have enjoyed it both ways. Chicken "juice," simmered up from the free-ranging fowl, amended with a stir of eggs and a brisk squeeze of lemon, has opened many a name day, baptism, and wedding banquet I've attended and always seems to say to the guests, "We are all alike, for we all like chicken soup." And when I would fall under the weather (the Greeks say "to be cold" as we say "to have a cold"), friends brought cups of plain chicken stock to mend me. Like the Greeks, I prefer a rich, flavorful stock, one that really lives up to the Greek term "juicy."

*4 pounds chicken parts, including backs, wings, and giblets (excluding the liver)*
*3 quarts water*
*1 small onion, halved (optional)*
*1 carrot, quartered (optional)*
*Celery leaves (optional)*
*2 to 3 sprigs fresh thyme, or 1 pinch dried thyme (optional)*

## CHICKEN CHEMISTRY
· · · · · · · · · · · · · · · ·

In a rare reversal, the Greek word for soup, *soupa*, comes from Old English. The root of the term is *suppa*, meaning bread soaked in liquid. The bread of *suppa* was called the *sop*, and what you did with it was sop up the *suppa*. Though Greeks today call soup *soupa*, the original word for the dish was *hemos* (or *chemos*), meaning "juice" or the liquid essence of something. Their present word for broth, *zomos*, means a watered-down version of *hemos*. From *chemo* of course we get "chemical," which is elemental juice.

1 Place all the ingredients in a large pot and bring to a boil over high heat. Reduce the heat, partially cover, and simmer gently until the chicken is falling off the bone on the back and wing pieces, 1½ hours.

2 Remove the pot from the heat and set it aside until cool enough to handle. Then carefully pour the ingredients through a strainer set over a large bowl. Discard the solid ingredients and set the stock aside to cool to room temperature.

3 If using right away, skim off the fat that has risen to the top and proceed with the recipe. If storing, pour into storage containers without skimming, place in the refrigerator until thoroughly chilled, and then cover. Protected under its fat seal on the top, the stock will keep in the refrigerator for up to 5 days or in the freezer for up to 6 months.

**NOTES:**

■ The optional onion, carrot, celery, and thyme create a more complexly flavored stock. Without them, the chicken parts alone turn out a fine, light broth.

■ For any stock—poultry, meat, fish, or vegetable—salt is never added until you are ready to use the stock in a recipe. That way, you avoid the potential of turning out an oversalted dish.

# FISH STOCK

### MAKES 2 QUARTS

While in the United States we use fish stock rather rarely, Greeks use it often. It is far more commonly the base for *avgolemono* than is chicken stock. In fish stock, a sea essence and a slightly saline fragrance linger, both of which add a mouthwatering tang to the stock.

*2 pounds bones and trimmings from nonfatty white fish, such as halibut, trout, snapper, bass, or cod*

*1 large onion, quartered*

*2 ribs celery, coarsely chopped*

*3 cloves garlic, halved (optional)*

*6 sprigs fresh flat-leaf parsley*

*6 sprigs fresh thyme, or 1/4 teaspoon dried*

*6 sprigs fresh dill*

*1 bay leaf, crumbled*

*1 whole clove, stuck into one of the onion quarters*

*1/4 teaspoon cracked white or black pepper*

*7 cups water*

*1 cup dry white wine*

1 Place all the ingredients in a large nonreactive pot and bring to a boil over high heat. Reduce the heat, partially cover, and simmer gently for 1 hour.

2 Remove the pot from the heat and set it aside until it is cool enough to handle. Then gently pour the ingredients through a strainer set over a large bowl. Discard the solid ingredients and set the stock aside to cool to room temperature. Use right away, refrigerate for up to 5 days, or freeze for up to 6 months.

### CLEARLY SOUP

For a clear stock or broth, be it meat, poultry, or vegetable based, it is important to watch the liquid as it is coming to a boil and reduce the heat before it is roiling furiously. Otherwise, the fat from the meat or poultry, or the starches from the vegetables, emulsify into the liquid and make it murky.

# yogurt lemon soup

### SERVES 6

GREECE OFFERS ANOTHER VERSION OF A SASSY LEMON SOUP THAT OMITS THE EGG AND TAKES ON A SWIRL OF YOGURT. WHEN IT EMPLOYS A TRIO OF LEAFY FLAVORS—DILL, CORIANDER, AND THYME—AND WHEN IT GIVES A NOD TO TIME-HONORED BARLEY OVER IOANNI-COME-LATELY RICE, IT BECOMES AS SPIRITED AS IT IS SOOTHING. SERVE IT HOT OR COOL; WHEN COOL, ACCOMPANY IT WITH CUCUMBER WEDGES.

*1/2 cup pearl barley*
*5 cups water*
*1 1/2 teaspoons salt*
*8 cups Chicken, Fish, or Lamb*
  *Stock (pages 170, 171, and 174)*
*1 tablespoon chopped fresh*
  *dill*
*1 tablespoon chopped fresh*
  *cilantro leaves*
*1/2 teaspoon fresh thyme leaves*
*1 cup plain yogurt,*
  *or Thickened Yogurt*
  *(page 471)*
*1/3 cup fresh lemon juice*
*Freshly ground black pepper,*
  *for serving*
*2 cucumbers, peeled and*
  *quartered lengthwise,*
  *if serving cold*

*Harvesting lemons in Crete.*

1 Place the barley in a sieve and rinse it well under cold running water. Shake it dry and transfer it to a small saucepan. Add the water and 1/2 teaspoon of the salt and bring to a boil over high heat. Reduce the heat and simmer, uncovered, until the grains are soft and just beginning to open, 45 minutes. Drain and rinse the barley.

2 Place the stock, dill, cilantro, thyme, and barley in a large non-reactive saucepan and bring to a boil over medium-high heat.

3 Meanwhile, whisk together the yogurt and lemon juice in a small bowl.

4 Remove the saucepan from the heat, and whisk in the yogurt mixture and the remaining 1 teaspoon salt. Serve right away, or allow to cool and serve later. Pass the pepper separately. If serving cool, accompany each bowl with a spear of cucumber.

# beef and rice meatballs

## IN TOMATO ROSEMARY BROTH

### SERVES 6

YOUVARELAKIA ARE PILLOW-SOFT, GENEROUSLY MEATY MEATBALLS THAT GREEKS ADD TO A BROTHY SOUP. SEVERAL VARIATIONS EXIST, BUT IN MY OPINION, THE BEST IS WHEN THEY SWIM IN A SULTRY VEGETABLE BROTH MADE CREAMY WITH TANGY YOGURT. PRECOOKING THE RICE LEADS TO MOIST AND AIRY MEATBALLS RATHER THAN DENSE ONES. BROWNING THEM ADDS MORE ASSERTION TO THEIR SOUPY SURROUNDS. HERE A TOUCH OF ROSEMARY AND MINT CONTRIBUTES ANOTHER DIMENSION TO THE BROTH. FOR THE SAME MEATBALLS IN A SOUPLESS RENDITION, SEE PAGE 52.

6 cups favorite beef stock or Lamb Stock (page 174) or vegetable stock

2 cups dry white wine

2 medium tomatoes, cut into $^1/_4$-inch dice

2 tablespoons tomato paste

$^1/_4$ teaspoon chopped fresh rosemary needles, or $^1/_8$ teaspoon dried

2 tablespoons olive oil, for browning the meatballs

1 recipe Beef and Rice Meatballs, prepared through Step 1 (page 376), rolled the size of small walnuts

1 cup Thickened Yogurt (page 471)

1 tablespoon chopped fresh mint leaves

1 Place the stock, wine, tomatoes, tomato paste, and rosemary in a large nonreactive pot and bring to a boil over high heat. Reduce the heat and simmer, uncovered, until the tomatoes are soft and the wine no longer "raw," about 15 minutes.

2 Meanwhile, lightly oil a skillet with 1 tablespoon of the oil and heat over medium-high heat. When it begins to smoke, add as many meatballs as will fit in one uncrowded layer. Cook, turning once, until the meatballs are browned all over, but not well-done, 4 to 5 minutes. Continue browning the meatballs, adding a little more oil as needed, until all are browned. (You can prepare the stock and meatballs about 1 hour ahead.)

3 When you are ready to finish the soup, bring the stock mixture back to a boil. Drop in the browned meatballs, partially cover, and simmer until the meatballs are cooked through but still tender, 5 to 6 minutes.

4 Ladle the broth and meatballs into individual bowls, garnish with a dollop of yogurt and a sprinkling of mint, and serve right away.

# lamb barley soup

## WITH ORANGE ZEST

### SERVES 6

A RISTOTLE, THE GREAT PHILOSOPHER AND TEACHER, WROTE ABOUT FARMING AND UNDERSTOOD THAT ALL OF GREECE'S HERDS CAME FROM WILD ANIMALS TAMED BY MAN— AND NOT ONLY TAMED, BUT IN MANY CASES, IMPORTED. AMONG THEM WAS THE SHEEP, WHOSE TAMING HAD OCCURRED THOUSANDS OF YEARS BEFORE ARISTOTLE'S BIRTH IN LANDS EAST OF GREECE. THE BARLEY THAT WAS CENTRAL TO THE GREEK DIET IN ARISTOTLE'S TIME WAS ALSO NOT NATIVE TO GREECE AND HAD BEEN DOMESTICATED FAR EARLIER FROM WILD GRASSES.

Some things stay the same across millennia. Lamb is still a main meat in Greece and barley still a crop. The two combine into a traditional soup of ancient origin still energizing and filling.

*Woolly sheep, ready for shearing.*

8 cups Lamb Stock (recipe follows)

1 medium leek, white and light green parts well rinsed, trimmed, and coarsely chopped

1 small turnip (4 ounces), peeled and cut into $1/4$- to $1/2$-inch pieces

$2/3$ cup pearl barley

1 teaspoon salt

$1/4$ cup chopped fresh flat-leaf parsley leaves

$1 1/2$ tablespoons chopped fresh dill

1 tablespoon finely shredded orange zest

1 Place the stock, leek, turnip, barley, and salt in a large pot and bring to a boil over high heat. Partially cover, reduce the heat, and simmer until the barley is tender, about 30 minutes.

2 Stir in the parsley, dill, and zest and serve right away.

## LAMB STOCK

### MAKES 2 QUARTS

M any powers are attributed to lamb broth in the Greek heartland: It strengthens the weak, energizes the tired, cures the ailing. All could be right. The stock does bolster. It imparts a very meaty underpinning to whatever else a dish contains. Does it quicken the wit and invigorate the body? If Greece's record of thinkers and heroes is any evidence, then it surely does.

1 tablespoon olive oil

1 3/4 pounds lamb shoulder blade
    chops, meat cut into
    1/4- to 1/2-inch pieces,
    bones reserved

1/2 small onion, coarsely
    chopped

1 rib celery, cut into 1-inch
    lengths

1 large bay leaf

3 quarts water

1 Heat the oil in a large pot over high heat until it is beginning to smoke. Add the lamb meat and bones and stir until they are brown and the juices have turned golden, 6 to 7 minutes. Add the onion, celery, bay leaf, and water and bring to a boil.

2 When the liquid is just beginning to boil, skim the foam off the top. Partially cover, reduce the heat to medium, and simmer gently for 1 1/2 hours.

3 Strain the stock through a strainer set over a bowl. Remove and reserve the lamb meat for another use; discard the remaining ingredients. Allow the stock to cool completely, until the fat rises to the top. Skim off and discard the layer of fat before using.

**NOTE:** After cooling and before skimming, the stock may be covered and stored in the refrigerator for up to several days or frozen for up to 6 months. Remove the fat layer before using.

## KNITTING MY WAY IN

When I first moved into the tiny Greek village where I eventually lived for years, I was terrified. I knew no one. The village was very remote and traditional, with many women wearing black and all in head scarves. It had no electricity, no running water, practically no road, and I had promised my university I'd stay for at least a year. No one spoke English, and worst of all, I could speak no Greek.

Oh, I had studied the language. I could conjugate verbs and decline nouns. But the vocabulary I had learned was completely useless. What good was "bus station" on an island with no buses!

But on my very first day I happened upon a stroke of luck that established the warp and woof of my stay. To fight my desire to run, I dragged a chair out on my patio and pulled out my knitting. As it happens, I can knit in twists and turns and holes and cables, not because of any particular talent but because of a no-idle-hands upbringing. I had brought great balls of soft mustard-colored yarn from Athens, and I began to knit them into a sweater. The women in the village had only undyed goat yarn that they had home-spun, and they could only knit a straight knit stitch, yarn strung around their necks. Soon I had a massive audience. They watched the lacing, the holes appear and disappear, the fretting of cables. By virtue of my wool and my knitting, I instantly achieved something that could have taken months: The ladies decided I was acceptable. No woman who was going to set up shop as a lady of the night (which was what they feared) could knit like that!

Later, when she decided her hands could no longer spin, my adopted grandmother, Kouina, gave me her simple, worn *rouka*, the spindle she had used since girlhood, "Now," she said over the lamb broth I had cooked, "you don't have to buy the wool to knit—you can spin your own."

About eleven o'clock in the cold and dark of Saturday night, bells peal to beckon the Greek villagers to their joyous Easter services. One by one, family groups—mothers dressed in their best, fathers with jackets and freshly pressed pants, daughters in ruffles and white socks, sons in miniature suits—walk from their homes to the church to celebrate their faith's holiest day. Each person carries a brand-new fat candle.

Just before midnight, the sanctuary fills with incense and chanting voices, and all the lights—candle, oil, electric—are extinguished. Behind the altar screen, the priest recites the prayer and performs the act that is the year's most sacred moment: renewing the light of Christ. At the stroke of twelve, he emerges with a tiny, flickering flame in his hands. Everyone rushes forward to light a candle from the spark of Christ's reawakening. Outside, young boys set off firecrackers, making the small children wail. The devout reignite the lamps that illuminate the altar and the icons. People call "Christ is risen" to one another and wish each other many happy returns.

In kindred groups everyone now begins to trail home, where each will etch the sign of the cross above the door with the candle's burning wick and light their dwellings anew. They then turn to Easter soup. I remember well the long night, huddled with sleeping children gathered in the laps of nodding grandparents. I also remember the soup we had when at last we wandered home: the sweetness of the meat, the swirl of egg and lemon—the finishing touch of a year worked hard; the ray of hope for the year to come.

# easter lamb soup

## MAGEIRITSA

### SERVES 6

MAGEIRITSA IS MADE ONLY FOR EASTER. AS THE WORSHIPERS RETURN FROM THE JOYOUS ALL-NIGHT EASTER SERVICE, STRONG OF SPIRIT BUT WEAK OF BODY FROM LENT'S LONG ABSTINENCE, THEY LOOK TO THIS SOUP TO RESTORE ENERGY. THE NAME OF THE SOUP MEANS "SMALL COOKING" AND IMPLIES THAT AFTER A FAST A PERSON SHOULD NOT EAT A HUGE MEAL, BUT ACCUSTOM THE EMPTY STOMACH WITH SOMETHING LITTLE. STILL, AFTER LENT'S AUSTERITY, MAGEIRITSA OFFERS THE HOLIDAY'S FIRST MEATY BITES—NOW-SANCTIONED LAMB TIDBITS COMBINED WITH NOW-PERMITTED EGG MADE AIRY WITH LEMON. FOR MOST GREEKS, IF THE ANTICIPATED LAMB ON A SPIT IS THE CULMINATION OF EASTER'S FESTIVITIES, MAGEIRITSA IS THE PROLOGUE.

1 pound lamb innards, such as
   the heart, liver, and tripe
   (optional; see Notes)
3 tablespoons olive oil or butter
   (see Notes)
2 cups thinly sliced scallions,
   including green parts
1 pound lamb meat, cut into
   $^1\!/_4$- to $^1\!/_2$-inch cubes
1 cup shredded hearts of romaine or
   butter lettuce
$^1\!/_2$ cup finely chopped fresh dill

$^1\!/_2$ teaspoon anise seeds
8 cups Lamb Stock (page 174)
6 tablespoons rice, preferably
   Arborio
2 tablespoons finely chopped
   lemon zest
$^1\!/_2$ cup chopped fresh flat-leaf
   parsley leaves
4 large eggs
$^1\!/_2$ cup fresh lemon juice
Salt and freshly ground black pepper,
   to taste

## SOUP TO START AND SOUP TO END THE FAST

Soup both opens and closes Easter. The Sunday before Lent is marked with *tyrozoumi*, "cheese juice," an herby meat broth served with cheese, both of which will be prohibited for the next fifty days.

**1** If you are using the innards, rinse them well and place them in a medium-size saucepan. Cover with water, bring to a boil over high heat, and cook for 3 minutes. Drain, and set aside until cool enough to handle. Then cut the innards into small pieces the same size as the lamb meat.

**2** Heat the oil or butter in a large nonreactive soup pot over medium heat. Add the scallions and sauté until soft and translucent, about 5 minutes.

**3** Add the chopped meat, and the innards, if using, and sauté until browned, about 10 minutes. Then add the lettuce, dill, and anise seeds and sauté for 5 minutes.

**4** Add the stock and rice and bring to a boil over high heat. Cover, reduce the heat, and simmer for 20 minutes.

**5** While the soup is cooking, mix the lemon zest and parsley together in a small dish. Set aside.

**6** Beat the eggs in a medium-size bowl until frothy. Whisk in the lemon juice. Then gradually beat in 1 cup of the hot liquid from the soup, whisking vigorously.

**7** Remove the soup pot from the heat. Whisk in the egg and lemon mixture. Add salt and pepper to taste. Immediately ladle the soup into bowls, without reboiling, topping each serving with a good pinch of the parsley mixture. Serve right away.

### NOTES:

- If you don't care to use any innards, substitute another pound of lamb meat in their place.

- If you are including tripe in the soup, be sure to wash it well before using.

- Where butter is available, it is splurged on—and used in Easter soup for sautéing the scallions.

## THE EGG CYCLE

Supplied as we are with poultry-industry eggs, few realize that in the natural order of things, eggs actually are seasonal. Life in a Greek village demonstrates clearly that they are. Some months of the year, eggs abound. Other months have a dearth of eggs. The cycle runs this way:

About September or October, the free-ranging chickens react to autumn's shortening days by ceasing to lay eggs. As they slowly halt their reproduction, the Greek homemaker begins to cook chicken dinners. When they are laying, the hens are too precious to roast. Better to let them roost. The chicken owner spares the year's two best laying hens and one rooster and tends them over the winter.

Sometime in December the rooster cozies up to the two hens, and soon they lay the new year's first batch of eggs. The chicken keeper needs these first eggs to produce a new stock of laying hens for the months to follow, so she allows them to hatch. Within a number of weeks the new chicks from the first batch have met the rooster and are ready to begin laying. By Easter, the laying hens are many and there are eggs aplenty, providing the spring ritual one of its great bounties: the Easter eggs.

Throughout late spring and over the summer, the hens continue laying and the cook has plenty of eggs to fry, beat into omelets, or stir into soups and sauces. By the end of summer the first few hens again quit their laying. These are the first to find their way to the dinner table, and the egg and chicken cycle—or is it chicken and egg?—begins again.

# fish soup

## WITH LEMONY MAYONNAISE

### PSAROSOUPA

**SERVES 6**

WHILE A TOURIST MIGHT WAX NOSTALGIC OVER THE GRILLED FISH IN GREECE, IN THE TYPICAL HOME, THE FISH BROUGHT IN BY A FISHERMAN OR PURCHASED FROM A FISHMONGER MOST OFTEN FINDS ITS WAY INTO THE SOUP POT. USUALLY THE SOUP IS MADE WITH A WHOLE FISH, ALTHOUGH SOMETIMES LARGE PIECES OR FILLETS ARE USED. WHEN IT IS PREPARED, THE SOUP IS POURED INTO A LARGE BOWL AND SET ON THE TABLE FOR ALL TO SHARE. EACH EATER TAKES A PORTION OF BROTH, SOME OF THE VEGETABLES, AND A PIECE OF THE FLAKY FISH FOR HIS OR HER INDIVIDUAL DISH. THE RECIPE BELOW, A CROSS BETWEEN CRETAN AND PATMOS-STYLE FISH SOUP, EMERGES AS A TUREEN OF VELVETY SOFT AND MOIST FISH SIMMERED WITH SHALLOTS, GARLIC, TOMATO, POTATO, AND ZUCCHINI, TURNED PINK WITH TOMATO PASTE AND RICH WITH WINE AND OLIVE OIL. A DRIZZLE OF LEMON MAYONNAISE FOR DECORATION AND FLAVOR IS THE TOPPING

*1 whole white fish (2 1/2 to 3 pounds),*
*  such as striped bass or*
*  red snapper, gutted, scaled,*
*  and left whole; or one*
*  2 pound steak or fillet,*
*  1/2 to 3/4 inch thick*
*2 teaspoons salt*
*2 tablespoons olive oil*
*6 large shallots (3 ounces),*
*  cut into 1/4-inch-thick rounds*
*6 large cloves garlic, halved or*
*  coarsely chopped*

*4 fresh tomatoes (1 pound),*
*  coarsely chopped*
*1 1/2 tablespoons tomato paste*
*1 1/2 teaspoons chopped fresh oregano*
*  leaves, or 3/4 teaspoon dried*
*1 cup dry white wine*
*6 cups water*
*12 small red potatoes (about 1 pound),*
*  scrubbed and halved*
*4 small zucchini (10 ounces), cut into*
*  1/4-inch-thick half-rounds*
*1 cup Lemony Mayonnaise (page 470)*

## A SHAGGY FISH STORY

There is a comic tale that you hear across Greece. It concerns not Crete or Patmos, but the island I most often live on, Santorini, which is an active volcano.

It seems one day a fisherman is rowing along, alone in his boat, not realizing how close he has drifted toward Santorini's smoking volcano. Suddenly a fish pops to the surface, already nicely cooked. The fisherman nets it and thinks of devouring it, but decides the dish is a little too plain. No more than a few moments later, up pops a cooked onion, and a few seconds after, a stewed tomato. The fisherman now has a very nice fish soup, all without effort, thanks to Santorini's thermal waters.

1 Sprinkle the fish inside and out with 1 teaspoon of the salt and set it aside.

2 Heat the oil over medium heat in a large nonreactive pot large enough to hold the fish in one layer. Stir in the shallots, garlic, tomatoes, tomato paste, and oregano and sauté until the vegetables begin to soften, about 10 minutes. Pour in the wine and water and bring to a boil over high heat. Reduce the heat and

simmer gently until the tomatoes collapse and the liquid is brothy, about 20 minutes.

3 Add the potatoes and zucchini and lay the fish over the top. Sprinkle with the remaining 1 teaspoon salt and bring to a boil again. Cover, reduce the heat, and simmer gently until the fish is easily flaked off the bone and the potatoes are tender, 20 to 25 minutes.

4 Serve right away, drizzling 2 to 3 spoonfuls of the mayonnaise over each serving.

**NOTES:**

■ If you are using a whole fish, gently lift it out of the pot using two large spatulas, and place it on a plate. Remove the skin and

# FROM MASSALIA INTO THE NORTH

G reeks sailed everywhere around the Mediterranean, founding cities and bringing their cauldrons. Undeniably, their colonies in Sicily, Egypt, and around the Black Sea were imposing and powerful. But in terms of influencing northern Europe, perhaps their settlement of Massalia, later Marseilles, was the most significant.

Marseilles sits at the base of one of the main trade and invasion routes into Europe, the Rhine-Rhône river chain. It's clear that from early times Greeks, or at least Greek goods, made their way up that route. In fact, Greek goods seem to have answered a demand for "treasure" in lands to the north. As far up as Vix on the Seine, Seurre on the Rhône, and Hochdorf and Heuneburg on the Rhine, Greek vases, drinking cups, bowls, and cooking cauldrons—*kakaves*—have been found. If the northern folk were drinking from Greek cups and cooking in Greek pots, the question is, were they also already taking in Greek customs, ideas, and recipes?

ease off the top fillet. Being careful to remove all the small bones, return the fillet to the pot. Carefully lift the skeleton off the bottom fillet. Check for bones, scoop the fillet off the skin, and return it to the pot.

■ If you are using fish fillets or steaks instead of a whole fish, the timing will be slightly shorter.

*Lakes and quiet inlets offer abundant spots for fishing, here by two women.*

## "BURIED-IN-THE-SAND" FISH SOUP

....................

I n Aenus and the Pontos buy the sow-fish which some mortals call the "buried-in-the-sand" fish. Boil the head of this fish, adding no seasonings, but only putting in water and stirring often.

**—ATHENAEUS, SECOND CENTURY** B.C.E.

# fisherman's catch stew

## KAKAVIA

**SERVES 6**

KAKAVIA, SAY THE GREEKS, IS THE FORERUNNER OF OTHER FAMOUS MEDITERRANEAN MIXED-FISH STEWS, ESPECIALLY THE FAMOUS BOUILLABAISSE OF MARSEILLES. LIKE MANY COASTAL CITIES OF THE MEDITERRANEAN, MARSEILLES WAS ORIGINALLY A GREEK COLONY, NAMED BY THEM MASSALIA. IN THOSE DAYS FISHERMEN COOKED THEIR CATCH IN A THREE-LEGGED EARTHENWARE POT CALLED A *KAKAVE*, WHICH WAS PLACED IN THE CENTER OF THE BOAT. THEY MIXED UP A STEW FROM WHATEVER THEY CAUGHT THAT DAY—A COMBINATION OF FISH AND SHELLFISH—AND NAMED THE DISH *KAKAVIA* AFTER THE POT IT WAS COOKED IN.

When later populations took over the Greek colonies, the pot acquired a different name. In Marseilles it was converted to the French *bouillotte,* and the stew became bouillabaisse. The Catalan *suquet* is in the same tradition, as is San Francisco's Italian-American cioppino. Bouillabaisse is traditionally served with sautéed croutons. Borrowing from the borrowers, I take bread, toast it, spread it with oil and garlic, and slide it like small boats atop the *kakavia.*

*1/3 cup olive oil*

*1/2 large onion, coarsely chopped*

*1 leek, white and light green parts well rinsed, trimmed, and cut into thin half-rounds*

*4 large cloves garlic, coarsely chopped*

*1/2 large fennel bulb (about 5 ounces), halved and thinly sliced*

*4 tomatoes (1 pound), coarsely chopped*

*1 large bay leaf*

*2 large sprigs fresh thyme, or 1/2 teaspoon dried*

*1 cup retsina or dry white wine*

*5 cups water*

*1/4 teaspoon powdered saffron, or 1 large pinch saffron threads*

*1 1/2 teaspoons salt*

*1 1/2 pounds prepared squid, octopus, scallops, or shrimp, or a mixture (see sidebar, facing page)*

*1 pound mussels, clams, or a mixture, well scrubbed*

*1 pound meaty white fish fillets, such as monkfish, cod, snapper, or sea bass, approximately 3/4 inch thick, cut into 2- to 3-inch-wide pieces*

*1 1/2 tablespoons fresh lemon juice*

*2 to 3 tablespoons chopped fresh fennel fronds, for garnish (optional)*

*6 Garlic Olive Oil Toasts (recipe follows)*

1 Heat the oil in a large non-reactive soup pot over medium-high heat. Stir in the onion, leek, and garlic and sauté until slightly wilted, 3 minutes.

2 Stir in the fennel slices, tomatoes, bay leaf, and thyme. Reduce the heat to medium and sauté gently until all the vegetables are wilted, 10 minutes.

3 Stir in the retsina, water, saffron, and salt. Bring to a boil, then reduce the heat and simmer until the liquid is slightly reduced and no longer smells "raw," 10 minutes.

**4** Add all the shellfish and fish, cover, and simmer until the mussels or clams are open and the fish fillets are firm but still moist, 5 to 8 minutes. Sprinkle the lemon juice and the fennel fronds, if using, over the top. Float a garlic toast over each serving, and serve right away, discarding any unopened mussels or clams.

## GARLIC OLIVE OIL TOASTS

### MAKES 12 TOASTS

Sailed like a boat upon a sea of soup, acting like a barge under a spread like Eggplant Salad (page 32), or simply offering a crisp accent to go with any sort of salad, toasts made of good bread anointed with olive oil and garlic have a pantheon of uses. Topping them with *Skordalia* (page 461) or Roasted Tomato "Paste" (page 479) adds an extra measure of flavor.

*TO OVEN-TOAST:*
*12 slices (¹/₂-inch-thick) good Greek or other crusty, slightly stale bread*
*¹/₃ cup olive oil, plus extra for oiling the baking sheet*
*2 large cloves garlic, pressed*

**1** Preheat the oven to 325°F. Lightly oil a baking sheet.

**2** Combine the ¹/₃ cup oil and the garlic in a small bowl, stirring so the oil is well flavored with the garlic.

**3** Arrange the bread slices on the prepared baking sheet and brush the tops with some of the flavored oil. Place in the oven and bake until the slices are beginning to turn golden on the bottom, 3 to 4 minutes. Turn the slices over, brush the other sides with flavored oil, and bake until the tops are golden, about 3 minutes. Set aside at room temperature for up to 4 hours.

*TO FRY*
*Olive oil*
*2 to 3 large cloves garlic, coarsely chopped*
*12 slices (¹/₂-inch-thick) good Greek or other crusty, slightly stale bread*

**1** Pour oil to a depth of ¹/₄ inch into a heavy skillet. Add the garlic and place the skillet over medium heat. When the garlic begins to turn golden remove it with a slotted spoon.

**2** Place the bread in the oil and fry, turning, until golden all over, about 4 minutes.

## REPLICATING THE CATCH

Just as fishermen would have a hodgepodge of seafood to throw into their cauldron, a mixture of seafood—soft- and hard-shell shellfish along with white fish fillets—makes for the most exuberantly well-rounded *kakavia*. The mixture may vary, but it is mixture that is key. That means that the cook must be mindful of the various cooking times required.

For the recipe here, squid can be cut into ³/₄-inch-wide rings; octopus should be a bit thinner, about ¹/₂ thick or less. Scallops can be ³/₄ to 1 inch thick; very thick sea scallops should be cut in half. Small or medium shrimp can be left whole; giant shrimp should be cut in half crosswise or left whole and added to the *kakavia* a few minutes earlier. Mussels and clams should be in their shells, because the shells, along with the shrimp shells, add immeasurably to the flavor of the broth. As for the fish fillets, the length and weight is not as important as the thickness; the pieces should be about ³/₄ inch thick. If you have thinner fillets, add them to the pot 2 to 3 minutes later.

**3** Drain on paper towels, and use right away or set aside at room temperature for up to 4 hours.

# mussel soup

## WITH SAFFRON, WHITE WINE, AND TART CREAM

### SERVES 6

NEAR THESSALONIKI, THE CAPITAL OF MACEDONIA, WHERE THE SALT-WASHED LAND ON THE JUTTING COASTAL POINTS IS TOO BARREN FOR AGRICULTURE, THE RESIDENTS PICK MUSSELS FROM THE COVES AND HUSBAND HERDS ABOVE THE CLIFFS. ALONG WITH SHEEP AND GOATS, A FEW COWS MAY BE SET OUT TO GRAZE. ALL PROVIDE THE KEEPER WITH SOME MILK. THE MILK FROM THE SHEEP AND GOATS IS OFTEN TURNED INTO YOGURT. THE COWS' MILK PROVIDES A RARE BUT VALUED COMMODITY: CREAM. A STIR OF RICH CREAM TRULY ENHANCES A SOUP, ESPECIALLY A SOUP OF THE ABUNDANT LOCAL MUSSELS, HONORING IT WITH A DAB OF SLEEK OPULENCE. GREEK CREAM TASTES OF GRASSLANDS AND FIELDS, GIVING IT A SOMETIMES LOAMY, SOMETIMES TART, FLAVOR. TO DUPLICATE THE FLAVOR, FRENCH-STYLE CREME FRAICHE OR HEAVY CREAM TOUCHED WITH LEMON JUICE CAN SERVE THE PURPOSE.

*3 cups dry white wine*
*3 cups water*
*6 large cloves garlic, coarsely chopped*
*1 teaspoon fresh thyme leaves, or*
*¹/₂ teaspoon dried*
*¹/₄ teaspoon powdered saffron, or*
*1 large pinch saffron threads*
*¹/₂ teaspoon salt*

*4 to 4¹/₂ pounds mussels, scrubbed*
*³/₄ cup crème fraîche, or ³/₄ cup heavy (whipping) cream mixed with*
*¹/₂ teaspoon fresh lemon juice*
*¹/₄ cup fresh flat-leaf parsley leaves*
*Country Bread or City Bread (page 121 or 124)*

1 Combine the wine, water, garlic, thyme, saffron, and salt in a large nonreactive pot and bring to a boil over high heat. Reduce the heat and simmer, uncovered until the garlic is tender and the wine no longer "raw," about 10 minutes.

2 Add the mussels, cover, and cook over high heat until the mussels open and firm up slightly, about 10 minutes.

3 Using a slotted spoon, transfer the mussels to individual bowls, discarding any that haven't opened. Stir the crème fraîche and parsley into the liquid in the pot, and then ladle it over the mussels. Serve right away, accompanied by the bread to soak up the broth.

**NOTE:** Garlic Olive Oil Toasts (page 181), slipped under the mussels and broth, make for a sumptuous addition.

# THE MYCENAEANS AND THEIR BILL OF FARE

The Lion Gate, erected in 1250 B.C.E., is part of what remains of the fortress walls of Mycenae.

A S THE MINOAN CONTROL OF GREECE AND THE MEDITERRANEAN CAME TO AN END, THEIR PLACE WAS TAKEN BY THE PEOPLE WE CALL THE MYCENAEANS (MYKIVAIKOS). EARLY SPEAKERS OF THE GREEK LANGUAGE, THEY HAD COLONIZED A NUMBER OF CITIES ACROSS GREECE DURING THE MINOAN REIGN.

Their towns were largely centered in the eastern Peloponnesos, in and around the Argolid.

Within that cluster sat the great citadel town of Mycenae itself, which Homer tells us was the home of Agamemnon. From the name of that town, we call them Mycenaean. What they called themselves isn't known, but there are a few hints.

## HOME OF THE HEROES

Theirs is the era of the great legends of early Greece and the exploits of the legendary heroes. It is from an alliance of Mycenaean cities that the Greek heroes set sail to launch the Trojan War. Among them were Menelaus—Agamemnon's brother and husband of Helen—Achilles, Ajax, Heracles, and Odysseus. On the other side were Hector and Aeneas. Rather than to reclaim a stolen wife, no matter how beautiful, the war was probably a battle for the control of the Dardanelles, at the entrance of which sat Troy. The Dardanelles leads to the Sea of Marmara, the Bosporos, and the Black Sea, with all their seafood, and to the fertile lands beyond. Odysseus, returning home from the war, sailed from Mycenaean colony to colony across now-Greek lands. From Argos, another Mycenaean city, many soldiers of the Trojan War, including Heracles, sailed with Jason on the *Argo*, on a quest for the Golden Fleece.

## MYCENAEANS AT WAR

Though Troy had first been established by non-Greek

# Theirs is the era of the great legends of early Greece and the exploits of the legendary heroes.

people, by the time of the war it, too, was Mycenaean. The tale of the Trojan War depicts just how bellicose the early Greeks were. They arrived as bands of raiders, probably closely related; group loyalty continued within the cities they occupied. From their separate cities, they engaged in almost continuous conflict, plundering one another's towns, fields, and herds. Unlike earlier Minoan cities, Mycenaean towns, like Tiryns, Corinth, Pylos, and Mycenae itself, were surrounded by huge fortresslike walls. All

were also built on easily defensible hilltops. Troy, in particular, is famous for its many defensive walls, and rather than resting at water's edge on the Dardanelles, the city is sited on a hill nearby that gives long views in every direction to observe any approaching army, and high ground from which to conduct battle.

## MYCENAEANS AND MINOANS

Remains within Mycenaean towns tell more of their story. The temples, tablets, and tales they left behind reveal that they worshiped the same pantheon of gods that later Greeks venerated—Zeus, Athena, and the other ten Olympians. Their writing in Knossos and other Minoan cites shows they were in communication with the Minoans, and the fact that their artifacts show up as far away as Egypt, Persia, and Italy indicates that it was the Mycenaeans who began the great Greek sail across the sea and march over land.

*A funerary mask, known as the mask of Agamemnon, from 1660– 1500 B.C.E.*

*The Trojan horse, a masterful military tactic, allowed the Greeks to defeat Troy.*

If the story of Theseus gives any indication, the Mycenaeans were at first under Minoan subjugation. (Theseus is taken to Crete to ride bulls, indicating that children were sent as tribute to Minoan overlords, and the description of the labyrinth that Theseus escapes from eerily echoes their great tiered palace at Knossos.) Homer's tales suggest that the city of Mycenae held some overall dominance over what must have been the beginnings of the surrounding city-states. In their time of rule, the Mycenaean leaders clearly were rich enough to build grandiose and massive lodgings. They buried their aristocrats in elaborate tombs filled with jewels, chariots, and the bodies of wives, slaves, and horses. They could pay artisans for frescoes,

pottery, and amazing goldwork that only devoted craftspeople, free from agricultural chores, could have produced. The golden objects unearthed at Mycenae—masks, collars, bracelets, cups, vases—are dazzling. The cities had scribes who wrote down much about trade and economics. From them we know that the sovereigns collected taxes, exacted tribute from those they conquered, and carefully distributed grains and other goods, especially scarce metals, to the lesser population. They also gave away gifts from their treasuries—golden objects and woven robes—to seal alliances and guarantee loyalty.

## DISHES FOR HEROES AND WARRIORS

What the Mycenaeans ate is also clear from the ruins of their fortresses. Their diet was lively and diverse, a bill of fare we could still admire. Archaeology in the Argolid shows that in September they had pears, soon followed by ripe grapes, blackberries, and acorns. In November they had honey, leafy greens, mushrooms, wild olives, and snails. December began their marine gathering, and the olive harvest was on. By April they

had buds, shoots, wild vetch, and bulbs. May gave them capers. In June they began to reap and thresh grain and to harvest pulses. The chamomile was blooming. It was then that they picked green almonds. August brought figs, carob, chickpeas, and oregano. All the animals later known in Greece—sheep, goats, cattle, oxen, mules, and donkeys—are mentioned in Mycenaean tablets, which tell of a concern with animal husbandry, raising herds, using their milk and wool, eating their meat. The Mycenaeans also devoured wild and domestic birds and game. How much of their many foods went into the soup pot is unknown, but they left behind soup pots by the thousands.

## THE DORIANS ARRIVE

The Mycenaeans reached the pinnacle of their prosperity between 1200 and 1000 B.C.E. By then local conflicts and economic disruptions had weakened them and something else happened to end their reign. A new and fierce warrior group of Greeks entered the land: the Dorians, ancestors of the Spartans. Soon after, the Mycenaeans, almost like the Minoans before them, disappear. In fact, they vanish in a cloud of mystery, just as the Ionians did. Indeed, the Mycenaeans quite likely *were* the Ionians!

# salads
# A VERITABLE BOUNTY

WHILE THE TERM *SALATA* IS A RELATIVELY NEW ONE—ADAPTED FROM THE *SALADE* BROUGHT SOUTH BY THE FRENCH IN THE NINETEENTH CENTURY—THE GREEKS HAVE LONG ENJOYED TOSSES OF FRESH GREENS AND VEGETABLES. AFTER ALL, WHO COULD WANDER OVER THOSE FRAGRANT HILLS AND ALONG THOSE LOAMY SHORES WITHOUT GRABBING A HANDFUL OF FERNY CHICORY AND SOME WATERCRESS?

Let it rain a shower . . . Let them sprout and let them flower.

—FROM A 19TH-CENTURY GREEK SONG

So popular were salads in classical times that Athenaeus wrote a chapter on them. He especially mentions lettuce and mustard greens. Theophrastus adds beets, arugula, spinach, cilantro, dill, and cress, touting them in particular because they sprouted more than once a year. Greeks also ate chives, nettles, parsley, cabbage, and wild chicory, which they called *intybos,* a word we turned into "endive." Biting watercress was the passion of Artaxerxes and was recommended by Aristophanes to build character. The shoots of wild asparagus were avidly devoured. Wild thistles, the ancestor of the cardoon and the artichoke, were picked, despite the way they picked back. Cucumber, fennel, radishes, beet greens, onions, leeks, carrots, lovage, and all sorts of field greens found their way to the plate, as did sorrel, basil, hyssop, and rue.

Modern Greeks have greatly expanded the list of salad stuffs, adding New World

## THE YEARLY ROUND OF SALAD VEGETABLES

A plate of shredded cabbage, the first green to appear in the garden in late February. Sharp, crisp radishes, coming in May, tossed with onions, oil, and crumbled feta. Tomatoes, tomatoes, tomatoes, the juicy rubies of August, quartered and sprinkled with olives, touched with salt.

Greeks don't go to market with a fixed list of what will go into their salad. They make salad from whatever has just come in from the field. The first vegetable to spring up in the new year, as the winter's cold turns ever so slightly warmer, is cabbage, so the first salad—gleefully, giddily greeted— is *lahano,* that tender tasty cabbage, shredded, lightly oiled, and sprinkled with pepper. The second salad green to appear, right after cabbage, is spring's baby lettuce leaves, *marouli.* Again the leaves are shredded and dressed simply. Then, should they survive the cropping of their tops for cooked greens, come the beets. Arugula, scallions, and fennel's first shoots give way to summer's plethora. In come tomatoes, scarlet as cherries, juicy as any orange; they are the matter of summer salad feasts for week upon week. And so it continues with peppers, zucchini and artichokes, cucumbers and cauliflower, and a host of other summer-to-fall offerings, until the world and the growing season turn to rest.

Whether the choice is summer's array or the one or two vegetables available in the cold months, the Greek rule is a good one: Make a salad not from a fixed notion or a recipe's list of ingredients, but from what is fresh, crisp, bright, and redolent of the season.

tomatoes, potatoes, peppers, and squash. Often a single, utterly fresh vegetable is the feature. At other times, a lively medley is accented with olives and capers, frequently highlighted with cheese. The plentitude of the Greek salad bowl is stunning, and inventiveness imbues each plate.

# the single vegetable salad

### SERVES 4 TO 6

IN GREECE, THE MOST COMMON SALAD IS NOT AN ASSEMBLAGE OF RAW VEGETABLES, BUT RATHER A SINGLE VEGETABLE—SOMETIMES RAW, SOMETIMES COOKED. IN ANCIENT TIMES THE SALAD WAS DRESSED WITH *OXIMELI*, A MIXTURE OF HONEY AND VINEGAR (SEE NOTE). TODAY IT IS SHOWERED WITH AN EXCELLENT OLIVE OIL OR A JAUNTY OLIVE OIL DRESSING. EITHER WAY, THE SINGLE VEGETABLE SALAD OFFERS SIMPLE ELEGANCE.

## ALMOST SALADS

At the Greek table, side dishes of cooled cooked vegetables often function much like salads. The most popular of these are cooked greens, then zucchini. Greeks also serve cooked beets and potatoes, cauliflower, artichokes, giant beans, and black-eyed peas. In short, when it comes to salad, what is a salad or a vegetable side dish is a little hard to define.

Other "salads" on the Greek table are the appetizers we would call "spreads." Eggplant Salad (page 32), Russian Salad (page 36), and *Taramasalata* (page 43) frequently appear as side dishes.

*FRESH VEGETABLE CHOICES*

*4 to 6 cups shredded cabbage*

*4 to 6 cups shredded lettuce*

*4 to 6 cups torn spinach leaves*

*4 to 6 cups torn chicory or endive*

*4 to 6 cups watercress*

*4 to 6 cups sliced cooked beets*

*4 to 6 cups thinly sliced fennel*

*4 to 6 cups thinly shredded young artichoke hearts*

*1 pound thin asparagus*

*1 pound tomatoes, quartered*

*1 pound cucumbers, halved and thickly sliced*

*1 pound cooked cauliflower florets*

*1 pound zucchini, halved and sliced*

*1 recipe Greek Salad Dressing (pages 190 to 191)*

## HORTA SALADS
......................

In Greece *horta*, the wild greens that are so esteemed, begin to show their leaves aboveground in spring and continue until autumn's heat and winds make them wither away.

Cooked, cooled *horta* make unusual smoky, tart, ruddy, verdant salads. Dress them with oil, lemon, or vinegar. Mix them with onions; top them with crisp garlic. Try chilled cooked dandelion, chard, turnip tops, mustard greens, or purslane.

Gently toss the single vegetable in the dressing. Serve in a large bowl or on individual plates.

**NOTE:** The ancient Greeks had one salad dressing that they zealously poured over their vegetables. It was a mixture of honey with vinegar, called *oximeli*. Practically every food writer, poet, and playwright raved about it.

Galen, the famous Greek physician and food writer, gave a recipe for *oximeli*, which even today isn't hard to follow:

"Simmer honey till it foams, discard the scum, add enough vinegar to make it neither too sharp nor too sweet, boil again till it is mixed and not raw. For use, mix with water, just as you would mix wine with water."

Today, substitute good olive oil for the water.

## GREEK OLIVE OIL

Smooth, green to golden Greek olive oils were once hard to find outside their native land. Other olive-growing countries had claimed the market.

That is changing. Greek olive oils are appearing more and more, and I prefer them. Why do I think Greek olive oil is the best? Virtually all of the packers are family corporations gathering their product from family-owned orchards in tiny regional areas. They produce almost entirely extra-virgin olive oil. The association of Greek olive oil producers is extremely concerned with preserving ancient traditional methods, from cultivating the olive tree to extracting the oil from the fruit. Members of the association consider themselves artisans.

Greece produces four grades:

■ Greek extra-virgin olive oil, from the cold first pressing of the olives. It has an extremely fine taste and an acidity level of not more than 1 percent.

■ Virgin olive oil, again from the cold first pressing of the olive. It has an exceptionally fine taste and an acidity level not exceeding 2 percent.

■ Olive oil obtained by mixing refined and virgin olive oil, with an acidity of up to 1.5 percent.

■ Olive pomace oil, obtained by mixing refined oil from olive stones with virgin olive oil. It has an acidity level of up to 1.5 percent and is generally used for lotions and soap.

# greek salad dressing

THE TYPICAL DRESSING FOR A FRESH SALAD IS AS UNCOMPLICATED, FUNDAMENTAL, AND UNFETTERED AS THE SALAD ITSELF. GREEKS USUALLY DRESS THEIR SALADS WITH A DOUSING OF OLIVE OIL AND NOTHING MORE. BUT THE OIL THEY USE IS THE BEST, THE GREENEST, THE GRASSIEST, THE MOST PERFECTLY PRESSED, AND THE DOUSING IS NEVER TIMID. EVERY SALAD MAKER KEEPS A SPECIAL BOTTLE OF PRECIOUS, COSTLY OIL JUST FOR TOPPING SALADS AND HOT VEGETABLES. FROM TIME TO TIME A DRESSING INCLUDES A DASH OF LEMON. LESS OFTEN, A SPLASH OF VINEGAR IS ADDED.

Whether you choose to be a purist or to add such flavors as capers, garlic, or herbs to your dressing, be sure not to let the dressing overwhelm the freshness of the salad's ingredients. Each dressing that follows makes enough for 4 to 6 cups salad.

## OLIVE OIL ONLY

*¹/₄ to ¹/₂ cup good-quality, extra-virgin olive oil*

Pour the oil over the salad and toss gently. Serve right away.

## OIL AND LEMON

### LADOLEMONO

*1 tablespoon fresh lemon juice*
*3 tablespoons good-quality, extra-virgin olive oil*
*Pinch of salt*

In a small bowl, whisk together the lemon juice and the oil. Stir in the salt and use right away.

**NOTE:** Oil and Lemon dressing does not keep overnight.

# OIL AND VINEGAR

## LADOKSIDO

*1 tablespoon red wine vinegar*
*3 tablespoons good-quality,*
*    extra-virgin olive oil*
*Pinch of salt*
*Dash of freshly ground black pepper*

In a small bowl, whisk together
the vinegar and oil. Stir in the
salt and pepper. Use right away,
or set aside at room temperature
for up to 5 days.

### DRESSING ADD-INS

Possible extras that can be added
to the plain oil, lemon, or vinegar
dressing:

# THE SEASONS

The Greek word for "the seasons," *oi epohes* (epochs), conveys the sense that each is a prolonged and languid era, as indeed each feels as the sun turns about that aged land. Quite beautifully, the name for each of the "epochs" vividly portrays its particular character. Spring, *anoixsi*, means "the opening." Summer, *kalokairi*, translates to "good weather" and aptly also to "good time." Fall, *ftinopero*, my personal favorite, comes from two linguistic roots that together essentially mean "decaying into ruin." Only *xeimonas*, winter, seems to have no direct translation, although it is an ancient word whose stem also leads to the words "snow" and "ice." Winters in Europe in ancient times were cold, leading people to wait for the "opening," followed by the "good time" with its surfeit of summer vegetables and the sparkling dishes that could be made from them, before the bounty's decline approached, bringing the cold again.

■ Thyme, marjoram, or especially oregano—1 teaspoon of chopped fresh or a pinch of dried. Let the mixture steep for a few minutes before using. Instead of flavoring the dressing, however, many Greek cooks sprinkle the herbs—almost always oregano—over salads.

■ A pinch of spice, such as cumin or dry mustard. Or, straying farther from the Mediterranean, paprika or cayenne.

■ Two to 4 cloves garlic, finely minced.

■ A generous teaspoon of chopped capers, chopped olives, or minced shallot.

■ A whisper of honey, about 1/2 teaspoon, to add an ancient touch.

*Always useful, here a donkey is carrying the twigs and branches used to fire up a beehive oven.*

# greek village salad

## HORIATIKI SALATA

**SERVES 6**

IN THE NINETEENTH CENTURY, FOLLOWING THE FRENCH IDEAL, THE SALAD PREFERENCES OF COSMOPOLITAN GREEKS TURNED TO PLATES OF PRISTINE SOLO EDIBLES. NOT SO IN THE COUNTRYSIDE, WHERE, AS ALWAYS, VILLAGERS WERE COMBINING GLORIOUS ARRAYS OF FRESH OFFERINGS FROM THE GARDEN. THESE FABULOUS MIXES, PARTICULARLY THE ONE FEATURING THAT AMAZING NEW VEGETABLE, THE TOMATO, CAME TO BE KNOWN AS "VILLAGE" SALADS, *HORIATIKI*—FROM *HORIO*, FOR "VILLAGE"— MEANING RUSTIC AND RURAL. THE DESIGNATION WAS SOMEWHAT PEJORATIVE BECAUSE IT SIGNALED A LACK OF REFINEMENT.

Now Greeks think quite the other way. They have rebounded to the love of their own rural heritage, and with it to their glorious village salad—which in fact has followed Greeks around the world. The Greek village-style salad crops up in restaurants from French to Indian, from Frankfurt to Singapore. In a village salad, the goods are a select choice of fresh pickings (tomatoes, bell pepper, cucumber, onions) coupled with some of the pantry's best stock (olives, feta cheese, capers, oregano). The Greek-American version adds a few springy greens.

*2 small or 1 large green bell pepper, cored and sliced into thick strips*
*1 cucumber, peeled if preferred, sliced into thick half-rounds*
*1 small red or white onion, sliced into thin slivers*
*3 medium tomatoes (12 ounces total), cut into 1/2-inch-thick wedges*
*18 to 24 Kalamata olives*
*1 tablespoon capers (optional)*
*4 ounces feta cheese, coarsely crumbled*
*Salt and freshly ground black pepper, to taste*
*1/3 cup fruity olive oil*
*2 tablespoons fresh lemon juice or red wine vinegar (optional)*
*2 teaspoons dried oregano*

## GOATS AND THE GARDEN

While goat cheese blends spectacularly well with radishes and other salad vegetables, there is one thing a goat does not pair well with: a flower garden. As much as I love the goats of Greece—I will talk to them, pet them, feed them—I show considerable temper when one of my rather casual neighbors lets her goat loose to chance upon my patio. To add some color to the starkly whitewashed house, I fill the patio flower boxes with lilies, carnations, and the like. Indeed, I do this over and over because, time and again, some free-roaming goat chews up my flowers. Never will any of my neighbors accept any blame; my flowers are not taken seriously, not like a vegetable garden. Goat and garden? Not a good pairing. Goat cheese and salad? Fabulous!

Place the peppers, cucumber, onion, tomatoes, olives, capers, if using, and cheese in a large bowl. Sprinkle lightly with salt and pepper, then with the oil. Add the lemon juice, if using. Crumble the oregano over the top, toss gently, and serve.

## NOTES:

■ Because a good Greek village salad depends on whatever is fully ripe and crisp in the market, any of the secondary elements, such as the cucumber or bell pepper, can be omitted if they aren't at their best and other ingredients either substituted or increased. What must stay are the tomatoes, onion, olives, and cheese.

■ In Greek towns, the village salad is dressed with oil. In Greek cities, a touch of lemon may be added. Internationally, the dressing often incorporates vinegar. The choice of rustic or refined is yours.

## VARIATION:

**The Greek-American Rendition:** As a *horiatiki* salad depends on good fresh produce, Greek Americans were faced with a quandary. American tomatoes are often picked well before ripening and are decidedly pale in comparison to their Greek counterparts. Besides, Americans had a fixed notion that salad means lettuce, and supermarket vegetable sections almost always have some crisp fresh lettuce available to accommodate that notion. Ever adaptable, Greeks in the States altered their village salad to include lettuce. In addition, scallions are often substituted for bulb onions. As the new version traveled west, the salad picked a new appellation. In a nod to its origin, it is often called not a village salad, but a "Greek" salad.

To make the Greek-American version, add 3 cups romaine, red lettuce, baby spinach, or arugula, and reduce the amount of the other vegetables accordingly. Substitute 6 scallions, trimmed and cut into 1-inch lengths, for the red or white onion.

## LETTUCE—THE LEAVES OF LOVE

Strange as it may seem, the word "lettuce" stems from the Greek term for "milk," because the sap of lettuce oozes white and milky. The ancient Greeks considered lettuce and its milky sap to be a love potion. After all, the plant puts out new leaf after new leaf though receiving numerous cuts—just like love.

The story begins with a young boatman, Faon of Mitilini. One day Faon ferried the goddess Aphrodite from the island of Lesbos to the mainland. When he refused payment for his service, Aphrodite gave him a flask of perfume that made him irresistible to any woman of his choice. Hearing of his attractiveness, the poet Sappho pursued him, and when he scorned her, threw herself off a cliff into the sea. Aphrodite was so angered at the death of her literary idol that she turned Faon into a lettuce. Why she chose a lettuce is not explained, nor is the fact that Sappho really lived while mythological Aphrodite did not, and anyway, Aphrodite seemed more interested in other nighttime activities besides bedtime poetry reading.

In truth, the Greeks did think that the leaves were soothing, if not love-provoking. Galen called lettuce the herb of the wise and recommended eating it before bedtime to induce a good slumber. Was he right? Lettuce contains magnesium, so perhaps the Greeks discovered the first stomach-settling "milk of magnesia."

# THE TOMATO REVOLUTION

**A**S IS THE CASE WITH ITALIAN FOOD, IT IS ALMOST IMPOSSIBLE TO CONCEIVE OF GREEK FOOD WITHOUT THINKING OF THE PLUMP, RED TOMATO. YET TOMATOES ARE A RECENT RECRUIT TO GREEK COOKING, AS TO ALL EUROPEAN COOKING, A RECRUIT THAT PRACTICALLY REVOLUTIONIZED THE CUISINE.

*Richly flavored small Cyclades tomatoes dry to an even more concentrated taste. Threaded like grapes on a string, they can be plucked midwinter to spark up* mezedes *and salads.*

Tomatoes arrived in Greece only within the last two hundred years, and did not become common until after World War II. Today they enhance almost every stew, sauce, and casserole. They are stuffed, baked, simmered, and turned into preserves. And they are cut into chunks for eating with bread and for a profusion of salads.

## SANTORINI'S TERRIFIC TOMATOES

While tomatoes are grown almost everywhere across the country, Santorini, my home base in Greece, is famous for its particular variety. Perhaps it's because of the gravelly, porous volcanic soil, the arid climate where the only moisture the plants receive is from the overnight dew, the intense Cycladic sun, or the closeness of the sea around such a narrow comma of land, but for whatever reason the tomatoes of Santorini never grow beyond the size of an apricot and are imbued with an extraordinarily deep flavor. So many are grown that in July the fields turn crimson, as if lit with fire. During harvest, the village square turns into a weighing station, with a parade of tomato-laden donkeys lining up to wait their turn at the scales.

## HARVEST TIME

It is a time when I join Markos, Averkios, and Mattheos to help out. Other women do as well. We swaddle our arms in burlap and old shirtsleeves for protection, don huge hats held on with wide scarves wrapped under our chins, step into men's pants under our dresses, pull on long, sloppy socks, and slip on bedroom slippers to accommodate shuffling in the rocky pumice soil. We head into the long rows of short twiggy bushes that we know will resist our invasion. All day long, we pluck the Ping-Pong balls of fruit and toss them into bushel baskets. At least we don't have to haul the baskets back: The men shoulder them to the assemblage area, and then the donkeys ferry the baskets to the square. The square becomes all men and all mathematics, while we draw water to wash the dust off our faces. In the square, every kilo is calculated. In the evening, a caravan of trucks and donkeys conveys the day's pickings to the tomato paste factory.

Back in the village we keep our eating share. Our tomatoes are too small to stuff, but they make great salads, whether plain, or in mixed *horiatiki*, or lavishly matched with black barley rings or sourdough slices into indescribably lush bread salads. We need little else for supper, except perhaps another prize that we also gathered from its vine—a fat, pink watermelon.

# tomato and bread salad

## WITH FETA, BASIL, AND CAPERS

### SERVES 6

S INCE MUCH OF GREECE'S DENSE, CRUSTY, GRAINY, WONDERFUL BREAD HAS ALWAYS BEEN DRIED TOASTLIKE FOR KEEPING, IT STANDS TO REASON THAT THE GREEKS WOULD ALSO HAVE A NUMBER OF WAYS OF SOAKING THE BREAD TO RESTORE ITS MOIST, CHEWY SOFTNESS. BREAD SALADS ARE PROOF OF HOW THE PLAINEST, SIMPLEST OF FOODS CAN BE UTTERLY MATCHLESS. WHAT IS MORE COMMONPLACE THAN BREAD, MORE ORDINARY THAN A TOMATO, SOME OIL, SOME VINEGAR? BUT WHEN A HEARTY BREAD BECOMES IMBUED WITH TOMATO AND DRESSING, THE HUMBLE INGREDIENTS BECOME SENSATIONAL. A SPRINKLING OF SALTY ELEMENTS—OLIVES AND CAPERS—BRINGS THE DISH TO LIFE.

One Greek restaurant I go to uses dried barley ring to soak up the essence in their bread salad, just as they do in the Cycladic islands. I always order it before I even sit down.

*4 cups barley ring chunks (page 130; about 4 whole rings), very stale Country Bread (page 121), or other crusty bread, cut into 1/2-inch chunks*

*6 ripe tomatoes (about 2 pounds total), cut into large chunks*
*18 olives, preferably Kalamata, pitted and halved*
*2 tablespoons capers, drained*
*1/4 teaspoon salt*
*2 teaspoons red wine vinegar*
*1/2 cup crumbled feta cheese*
*Freshly ground black pepper*
*2 tablespoons fruity olive oil*
*8 to 12 fresh basil leaves, shredded*

## BRINING FETA AND FLOATING OLIVES

· · · · · · · · · · · · · · ·

I f you have leftover feta, or if it came wrapped in paper rather than floating in brine, you can brine it yourself to keep it soft.

Place the feta in a glass or plastic container and cover it with a solution of salt and water. An old Greek culinary adage says the amount of salt in the water is correct when an olive placed in the water floats. But that's much too much salt—about 2 teaspoons for 1/2 cup of water! For today's commercial feta, which comes quite salty, 1/2 teaspoon of salt to 1/2 cup of water will do.

1 Place the bread on a platter or in a large bowl. Sprinkle with water and set aside until partially softened, 3 to 5 minutes.

2 Arrange the tomatoes, olives, and capers over the bread and sprinkle with the salt and vinegar. Add the cheese and pepper to taste, and drizzle with the oil. Top with the basil and set aside to marinate for 15 to 30 minutes.

3 Toss, and serve right away.

# chicory salad

## WITH TOASTED WALNUTS, GOLDEN RAISINS, AND SHAVED KEFALOTYRI CHEESE

### SERVES 6

WILD CHICORY WAS A COMMON SALAD VEGETABLE IN ANCIENT GREECE, AND APPARENTLY SO MUCH SPROUTED THAT SALAD MAKERS MERELY MEANDERED ABOUT TO PICK IT, ESCHEWING ITS CULTIVATION. TODAY CHICORY IS WIDELY CULTIVATED AND MANY VARIETIES EXIST—SOME OF WHICH WE DON'T NECESSARILY RECOGNIZE AS CHICORY. ENDIVE, BOTH FLAT AND CURLY, IS A CHICORY COUSIN THAT THE ANCIENT GREEKS GREW. RADICCHIO, ESCAROLE, AND FRISEE ARE ENDIVE/CHICORIES. AND ALL THE CHICORIES ARE BUT A BRANCH OF A LARGE FAMILY THAT INCLUDES LETTUCE AND DANDELIONS. IN A NOD TO INVETERATE TASTES AND WILD GREENS, THE SALAD BELOW MINGLES THE BITTERSWEET LEAF WITH MEATY NUTS, SWEET RAISINS, AND HARD CHEESE.

*1/2 cup walnut halves*

*1/4 cup olive oil, plus some for toasting the nuts*

*2 tablespoons golden raisins*

*1 clove garlic, minced or pressed*

*2 tablespoons red wine vinegar*

*1/4 teaspoon salt*

*8 cups chicory leaves, rinsed and spun dry*

*2 ounces kefalotyri cheese, shaved*

*1/4 teaspoon freshly ground black pepper*

1 Toast the walnuts in a lightly oiled skillet over medium heat until they are beginning to turn golden and aromatic, about 5 minutes. Set aside.

2 Place the raisins, garlic, vinegar, 1/4 cup oil, and salt in a small bowl and stir to mix.

3 Spread the chicory on a platter. Sprinkle the walnuts over the leaves, and spoon the raisin mixture over all. Distribute the cheese shavings across the top, sprinkle with the pepper, and serve right away.

**NOTE:** Radicchio, Belgian endive, or a mixture of the two can be substituted for the chicory.

## THE FRUITLESS SALAD

Greeks almost never mix a sweet element in their savory foods, and they never put sweet fruit in their salad. The only "fruit" ever found in a truly orthodox Greek composition are the olive and the tomato, neither of which we think of as a fruit. In ancient times there was, however, one exception: Ancient Greeks scattered pomegranate seeds over their shredded cabbage salads. Pomegranates ripen late in the fall, almost at the beginning of winter. Cabbage comes up early in spring, as winter ends; so the two often overlap, and the combination must have seemed natural. Adding the raisins to chicory salad or dried figs to carrot (page 199) echoes this tradition. It is well worth the effort of peeling a pomegranate and separating the seeds to add to a shredded cabbage salad or coleslaw. The union of the two is as delightful as it is intriguing. For a dressing, I suggest *oximeli* (see Note, page 189).

# beet salad

## WITH BEET GREENS, SINGED ONION, AND SIEVED EGG

### SERVES 6

A S SOON AS SPRING IS IN FULL BURST, GREEKS GATHER BARELY BULBED BEETS FOR THEIR TENDER, STILL UNFURLED LEAVES. I SHARE THEIR LOVE OF FRESH BEETS, BUT PREFER THE LARGE, EARTHY GLOBES WITH THEIR ALMOST CANDYLIKE SUGARINESS. I EXHORT MY GREEK FRIENDS TO BE PATIENT AND LEAVE THE BEETS AND THEIR GREENS LONG ENOUGH TO PRODUCE WHAT I CONSIDER THE REAL TREAT—THE FULLY GROWN UNDERGROUND ORB. WHEN GREEKS DO GATHER THE ROOTS, THEY BOIL, SLICE, AND BARELY DRESS THEM. PERFECT! I SHOW UP AT ANY HOUSE WHERE I HEAR THEY ARE IN THE POT. SUCH A SALAD IS FOR BOTH THE PATIENT AND THE IMPATIENT. AND WHEN IT INCLUDES THE GREENS AND THE ROOT, GARNISHED WITH SINGED ONION AND ANOTHER SPRING FOOD, SIEVED EGG, THE MIXTURE IS BEAUTIFUL TO BEHOLD.

2 bunches beets (about 1 1/2 pounds total), greens removed and set aside

1 small white or red onion, halved and thinly sliced

1/4 cup olive oil, plus some for oiling the skillet

1 large egg, hard-cooked and peeled

Salt and freshly ground black pepper, to taste

3 tablespoons red wine vinegar

1 Scrub the beets, place them in a pot, and add water to cover. Bring to a boil over high heat, then reduce the heat and simmer briskly until tender but not mushy, 35 to 45 minutes depending on the size.

2 Meanwhile, coarsely chop or shred the beet greens. Rinse and drain them and set them aside.

3 When the beets are done, lift them into a colander, leaving the water simmering in the pot, and set them aside to cool.

4 While the beets are cooling, add the beet greens to the cooking water, stir to submerge them, and then immediately use a slotted spoon to transfer them to a separate colander. Set the greens aside to cool.

5 Using your fingers, slip the skins off the beets. Slice them into thin rounds or half-rounds, depending on their size, and arrange them on a platter.

6 Place the onion in a lightly oiled skillet over high heat and stir until wilted and browned in spots, about 3 minutes.

## CARE FOR THE TOP OR THE BOTTOM?

The Greek preference for beet greens over the root has a long history. In the gardens of classical Greece, beets were grown for their greens rather than for their roots. The roots were considered medicinal, suitable only for the sick or else tossed away for animal fodder. Not until varieties with large globes were developed did the root become the more desired part of the vegetable.

7 Distribute the onion over the beets, and arrange the beet greens around the edge. Press the egg through a sieve, or chop it very fine, and sprinkle it over the beets and onion. Sprinkle lightly with salt and pepper, then drizzle the vinegar and ¼ cup oil over all. Serve right away.

**NOTE:** The beet salad may be assembled and chilled if desired. Add the egg garnish just before serving.

## RESTORATIVE BEET WATER

In Greece, the red beet cooking water is considered a bonus. At Easter it is used to tint hard-cooked eggs, signifying the blood of Christ. At other times it is used as a restorative and tasty drink, taken warm as you would tea, with a twist of lemon.

# cauliflower salad

## WITH LEMON ZEST, CHIVES, AND CHIVE FLOWERS

### SERVES 4 TO 6

CAULIFLOWER IS A TYPE OF CABBAGE WHOSE FLOWERS STOP GROWING AT THE BUD STATE. GREEK FOLKLORE HAS IT THAT THE FLOWERY EDIBLE COMES FROM CYPRUS. ALTHOUGH THE ANCIENTS ATE THE VEGETABLE, IN LATER TIMES IT FELL INTO DISFAVOR UNTIL IT WAS REINTRODUCED BY THE ARABS. SINCE THEN, BLANCHED AND LIGHTLY DRESSED, IT AGAIN HAS HELD A VENERATED SPOT AS A STANDARD SALAD DISH. IN A LIVELY RENDITION, A CONFETTI OF GREEN CHIVES AND THEIR ROSY PURPLE FLOWERS TURN THE DISH INTO A BRIDAL BOUQUET.

1 medium cauliflower
    (about 1 ½ pounds), tough
    outer leaves and stem
    trimmed off
Oil and Lemon dressing (page 190),
    made with ¼ cup oil
2 teaspoons coarsely chopped
    lemon zest
2 tablespoons chopped fresh chives or
    green scallion tops
Several chive flowers, torn apart
    (optional)

1 Bring a pot of salted water to a boil over high heat. Place the cauliflower, top side up, in the pot and cook for 3 minutes. Turn the cauliflower over and cook for another minute. Drain and set it aside to cool.

2 When you are ready to serve it, place the cauliflower in a bowl or on a platter. Pour the dressing over it and sprinkle the zest, chives, and flowers, if using, over the top. Serve warm or at room temperature, cutting it into portions as you serve it.

# carrot salad

## WITH FRESH FENNEL, DRIED FIGS, AND PRESERVED LEMON

### SERVES 6

THE ANCIENT GREEK WORD *KERAS* MEANS "A HARD OR BONY PROJECTION," ANYTHING SHAPED LIKE A HORN, AND FROM THAT WE GET "CARROTS" AND "CAROTENE." APPARENTLY THE EARLY GREEKS THOUGHT CARROTS LOOKED LIKE UNDERGROUND ANTLERS. THEY TOSSED AWAY THE ROOT AND ATE THE LEAVES AND SEEDS. MODERN ORANGE CARROTS—SWEET, FAT, AND CRUNCHY—ARE THE PRODUCT OF CULTIVATION.

When I first lived in Greece, carrots were still fairly puny and quite rare. Now they are as abundant there as here, and the carrot salads contrived from them are as sunny as Greek food can be. Feathery fennel, carrot's cousin, adds the aroma of licorice. Joined with Greek figs, a very Mediterranean alternative to the raisins usually used, the salad radiates.

6 large carrots (1 ½ pounds total)
1 small fennel bulb, very thinly
    sliced, fronds finely chopped
12 dried figs, preferably Kalimyrnas,
    thinly sliced
½ cup fresh lemon juice
6 slices Preserved Lemons
    (recipe follows)
Extra-virgin olive oil, for serving

1 Coarsely grate the carrots in a food processor or through the large holes of a hand grater. Transfer them to a bowl, add the fennel bulb slices, figs, and lemon juice, and toss to mix.

2 When you are ready to serve the salad, transfer the mixture to a platter. Sprinkle the fennel fronds over the top, and arrange the lemon slices around the edge. Serve right away, accompanied by a cruet of oil to drizzle on as desired.

# PRESERVED LEMONS

## MAKES 16 PRESERVED LEMON QUARTERS

Though the Greeks had long had citron, the lemon didn't reach their provinces from its home, India, until the first century C.E. Lemon trees were planted wherever Arabs sailed, especially from the seventh century on. (Greek *lemoni* derives from the Arabic *leymun*.) Here and there, on the mainland and in the islands, Greeks make a pickled lemon preserve much like the long-cured lemons of North Africa. (Many island Greeks traveled back and forth to North Africa, working there and returning with new tastes.) An irresistible savory combination of lemon and salt, put together in a quick, 1-week pickle, will add a highlight to most any dish. Keep a supply on hand for a last-minute accent for vegetables, grains, meats, poultry, or fish.

*4 large lemons, preferably organic*
   *(see Note)*
*1/2 cup kosher or fine sea salt*
*1/2 cup fresh lemon juice*

1 Rinse the lemons, pat them dry, and cut them lengthwise into quarters. Place the quarters in a bowl and toss them with the salt.

## TOUSA AND *KAPPA*

I have a goddaughter in Greece. Her name is Marketousa, shortened to Tousa. I held her for her baptism when she was just an infant. She was one of the first village girls to go to high school, and now she runs a tourist travel agency. We get along like sisters, despite our age difference (I am old enough to be her mother). I take her disco dancing. She takes me Greek dancing.

In Greece, being a godparent creates a web of indelible connections. I became *kumbara*, co-parent, with her mother and father, as if we share her raising. Her sister and brother treat me as an aunt; her aunts and uncles treat me like a sister. We do favors for one another and share a special warmth. My duty to her has involved giving her gifts, usually crosses in ever larger sizes as she grew older. I counsel her. I have pushed for her education. Lately I have hit upon a novel gift: I send her great books translated into Greek. In turn she cooks me dinners. Her family is my family and, in kind, looks out for my well-being.

Since her toddlerhood, Tousa has had a certain predilection. She likes foods with names that begin with *kappa*. At first it was *karameles*, Greece's hard candies. She ate so many I feared her adult teeth would never see the light of day. Whenever someone had a funeral or memorial for the dead, Tousa showed up to grab handfuls of *kolyva* (sweetened barley kernels). Luckily, as she grew her tastes changed. Lately she has turned her desires to *karota*: She has fallen in love with carrots. The island doesn't grow any, but they come in by ship and Tousa buys them by the kilo. Tousa grates the vegetable by hand into a tall heap, and dresses the stack of shreds with oil and lemon. A few years ago I taught her the American way of adding raisins, and she turned the idea Greek by adding dried figs instead. The innovation, of course, slightly changed Tousa's habit. The best dried figs are fat golden Kalimyrnas, and that starts with *kappa*. But figs are *sika*, a word that begins with *sigma*.

2 Add the lemon juice and toss again. Transfer all to a wide-mouthed 1-quart jar, and cap it with a screw-on lid. Set aside at room temperature for 3 days, shaking and turning the jar once a day to remix the ingredients.

3 On the fourth day, place the jar in the refrigerator and let it rest for 2 more days before using. The lemons will keep for up to 2 months, covered, in the refrigerator.

**NOTE:** If you don't have organic lemons, scrub the skins.

# radish salad

## WITH PICKLED ONIONS AND FETA CHEESE

### SERVES 4 TO 6

BEFORE THE GREEKS HAD TOMATOES TO PUT IN THEIR VILLAGE SALAD, THEY HAD RADISHES. IN FACT RADISHES WERE SO ENJOYED THAT GOLDEN REPLICAS OF THEM WERE OFFERED TO THEIR SUN GOD, APOLLO. TRIBUTES OF TURNIPS WERE FORGED FROM LEAD AND BEETS FROM SILVER, BUT GOLD, THE RAREST AND MOST VALUED PRECIOUS METAL, WAS SAVED FOR FACSIMILES OF RADISHES. THE FORAGERS WHO GATHERED RADISHES AND OTHER ROOTS HELD A SPECIAL TITLE: *RIZOTOMOI*, OR "ROOT CUTTERS." MANY OF OUR VEGETABLE WORDS COME FROM GREEK "ROOTS," AND "RADISH" IS NO DIFFERENT. IT DERIVES FROM *RIZI*, MEANING "ROOT," WHICH FILTERED INTO LATIN AS *RADIX* AND TO OUR "RHIZOME."

The ingredients here are those typical of a *horiatiki* salad (page 192), but the combination is unusual and outstanding. Feta softens the radish's bite with its milky contrast, and the pickled onions add a vinegary nip. Radish Salad is such a different and noteworthy dish on the table that it is the one I almost always make for dinner parties. The radish leaves are added for their color and special flavor.

*Two reclining goddesses from an ancient temple frieze.*

## OTHER SALAD ROOTS AND BULBS

For salads, Greeks are as fond of the parts of plants that hide underground—the bulbs and tuberous roots—as they are of the leaves, seeds, and flowers. Besides radishes and carrots, two other choices are wild grape hyacinth bulbs and wild daylily tubers. In ancient times asphodel bulbs were eaten too. Greeks also enjoy the crunch of turnips and parsnips. Any of these can be substituted for the radishes.

*4 large bunches radishes, with leaves*
*1/4 teaspoon salt*
*Pinch of freshly ground black pepper*
*4 ounces feta cheese, coarsely crumbled*
*1/2 cup Pickled Red Onions*
    *(page 75)*
*1 tablespoon red wine vinegar*
*3 tablespoons fruity olive oil*

1 Trim off the tops and the root ends of the radishes, reserving the tender young leaves. Cut the radishes into thin rounds and set them aside. Wash the leaves and pat them dry.

2 Spread the radish slices and leaves on a platter. Sprinkle with the salt and pepper. Top with the cheese, then spread the onions over all. Sprinkle the vinegar over the top, generously drizzle oil over all, and serve right away.

# PERICLES, THE FATHER OF DEMOCRACY

GREECE BORROWED THE ZUCCHINI AND OTHER FOODS FROM THE AMERICAS, BUT THE UNITED STATES BORROWED SOMETHING PERHAPS MORE PRECIOUS FROM THE GREEKS. WHEN EARLY AMERICANS INSISTED THAT THEIR NEW NATION BE A DEMOCRATIC ONE, THE IDEA THEY EMBRACED EMANATED FROM GREECE, AND PARTICULARLY FROM ONE MAN, PERICLES.

Pericles was born to an aristocratic, but not wealthy, Athenian family. He never rose to an office higher than general, of which there were ten in the government. In the fifth century B.C.E., Athens was a small but vibrant democratic city-state, ruled by its citizens—but the citizens were a limited group. Pericles rose to power on a platform of egalitarian activism. He radically expanded the boundaries of citizenry and voting rights. Democracy had been a kernel of an idea before; with him the idea and form blossomed. He was elected to office by the populace time and time again, while many of his rivals were ostracized by the same voters.

Under Pericles' leadership, the Athenian people achieved great vitality and strength. The city's commercial and political expansion created the first Greek empire. Athens became the center of the world, home of a cultural and artistic outburst that set a standard for millennia to come. From his youth, Pericles followed the teachers of the new natural

*Pericles, with laurel branches, speaking to the denizens of Athens in the* Agora *(marketplace).*

philosophy—he was a friend of Zeno, Anaxagoras, Herodotus, Sophocles, Aeschylus, and the great sculptor Phidias—and he also led in promoting the Greek enlightenment. He drew the connection between democracy and rational thought that still affects our politics today. And in a strange way, he led the way to the acceptance of women as equals. After his first marriage failed, Pericles took into his house a courtesan, Aspasia, a woman of great intelligence. She was not sheltered or repressed, but freely and independently circulated among Athens's ruling circles. He discussed all his works with her. She conversed with Socrates and Plato, who jokingly claimed she wrote Pericles' speeches. He openly kissed her tenderly in the doorway of his house every time he left and returned, a sight no Athenian had ever seen.

Probably his belongings and his diet were international and democratic too. From descriptions of the times, we know Athens had silphium (an herb) and ox hides from North Africa and mackerel from the Dardanelles. There was salt and beef from Egypt, also the source for sails and rope for ships. Frankincense was imported from Syria and cypress from Crete. From Carthage there were cushions and rugs, while Libya provided ivory. For the palate, Rhodes sent raisins and figs, Euboea pears and apples. From Paphlagonia arrived dates and almonds, and from Phoenicia more dates and wheat flour. But as a great democrat, Pericles no doubt also ate the foods of the masses: bread, barley gruel, simple greens, and though not zucchini, certainly gourd salads.

# zucchini salad

## WITH ZUCCHINI FLOWERS

### SERVES 6

THE GREEK KITCHEN QUICKLY AND EXUBERANTLY ADOPTED MANY OF THE FOODS THAT ARRIVED FROM THE NEW WORLD—TOMATOES, BEANS, BELL PEPPERS, AND, AS MUCH AS THE OTHERS, THE NEW WORLD'S SQUASH.

Greek cooks stuff squash large and small (page 300), pickle squash (page 72), stew squash (see *briami*, page 282), boil it and oil it, and slice it raw into salad. They also fill and fry the cadmium-yellow squash blossoms (pages 298 and 308). A salad of the two together— squash and flower—makes for a matchless treat. The trick is to steam them together very quickly so that the color and flavor of each is preserved, then dash them with lemon, olive oil, and a not-too-shy pinch of garlic.

1 pound baby summer squash (zucchini, crookneck, pattypan, or a mixture), cut lengthwise into 1/4-inch-thick strips
12 squash blossoms, rinsed inside and out, cut lengthwise into halves or thirds
2 tablespoons fresh lemon juice
3 tablespoons olive oil
1 clove garlic, minced or pressed
1/2 teaspoon salt
1 tablespoon chopped fresh chives

1 Place the squash and blossoms, still moist from rinsing, in a vegetable steamer or in a microwave-safe dish. Cover and steam, or microwave on high, until wilted but still brightly colored, 5 minutes.

2 Without draining them, transfer the squash and blossoms to a serving bowl or platter. Add the lemon juice, oil, garlic, and salt and toss gently to mix. Sprinkle the chives over the top and serve right away.

## AN ANCIENT GREEK MARKET

There you shall at mid-winter see
Cucumbers, gourds, grapes
    and apples,
And wreaths of fragrant violets
Covered with dust, as if in summer.
And the same man will see you
    thrushes,
And pears and honey-comb
    and olives,
Beestings and tripe and summer
    olives,
And grasshoppers and bullocks'
    paunches.
There you may see full baskets packed
With figs and myrtle, crowned
    with snow.
There you may see fine melons joined
To that discovered bond, and mighty
    turnip,
So that a stranger may well fear
To name the season of the year.

—ARISTOPHANES,
"THE GOURD,"
FIFTH CENTURY B.C.E.

# potato salad

## WITH OLIVES, CAPERS, AND CARAWAY

### PATATES SALATA

**SERVES 6**

POTATOES, A NEW WORLD VEGETABLE, ARRIVED IN GREECE DURING THE OTTOMAN REIGN, SOON RECEIVED THEIR BAPTISM IN FINE OLIVE OIL, AND EVER SINCE HAVE CLAIMED UTTER DEVOTION. THEIR USE IN GREEK CUISINE IS MANIFOLD, AND GREEKS RELY ON THEM AS MUCH AS THEY ONCE RELIED ON GRAINS. THE MOST COMMON USE OF POTATOES IN SALAD IS IN *SALATA ROUSSIKI*, A FAVORITE APPETIZER (PAGE 36). BUT A SPECIAL HOMAGE IS PAID HERE WITH A MORE HELLENIC RENDITION, USING GREECE'S OWN TIMELESS OLIVES AND CAPERS.

*1 1/2 pounds red or white potatoes,
    peeled and sliced 1/4 inch thick*
*12 Greek olives, preferably Atalanti,
    pitted and coarsely chopped*
*1 1/2 tablespoons capers, drained*
*1 medium green bell pepper, stemmed,
    seeded, and cut into thin slivers*
*3 scallions, white and light green
    parts trimmed and finely chopped*
*2 tablespoons chopped fresh chives*
*1/4 cup chopped fresh flat-leaf parsley
    leaves*
*1 1/2 teaspoons chopped fresh oregano
    leaves, or 1/2 teaspoon dried*
*1/4 teaspoon caraway seeds*
*3/4 teaspoon salt*
*1/2 teaspoon freshly ground black pepper*
*1 1/2 cups Lemony Mayonnaise
    (page 470)*

1 Place the potatoes in a large pot and cover with water. Bring to a boil over high heat, then cook briskly until the potatoes are tender but still holding their shape, 6 minutes. Drain in a colander and set aside to drip dry, for at least 45 minutes or as long as several hours, at room temperature.

2 Transfer the potatoes to a large bowl and add all the remaining ingredients except the mayonnaise. Mix very gently to avoid breaking the potatoes. Add the mayonnaise and mix again. Serve right away, or cover and refrigerate for several hours or overnight.

## BRINING CAPER BUDS, BERRIES, AND LEAVES

Should you have the opportunity to gather your own capers, don't be put off by the prospect of having to brine them—it's easy. All you need is sea salt and several clean glass, plastic, or clay vessels. For caper buds or berries, narrow-necked bottles are best. For caper leaves you will want a widemouthed container.

*For the buds and berries:* Pluck off any remaining stems and most of the flowers (Greeks usually leave a few). Gently rinse off all debris and dust.

Place about a 3-inch layer of buds or berries in the container and cover with 1/4 to 1/3 inch of sea salt. Add another layer of capers and another of salt. Continue layering the capers and salt until the container is full but loosely packed—do not tamp it down. Cover and set aside in a cool pantry or in the refrigerator.

*For caper leaves:* Pluck the leaves off the stems and rinse off all debris and dust. Bring a pot of water to a rolling boil, drop in the caper leaves, and simmer until just tender, 5 to 10 minutes (depending on how young and fresh the leaves are). Drain and allow to cool.

Layer the leaves and sea salt in a widemouthed container, as described above.

The caper buds, berries, and leaves will shrink over the next few weeks and will create their own preserving brine as their liquid is released. Stored in a cool pantry or refrigerated, the buds and berries will last for 2 to 3 years; the leaves for 2 to 3 months.

# artichoke and potato salad

## WITH ANCHOVIES AND BREAD CRUMBS

### SERVES 6

THE ARTICHOKE IS A DESCENDANT OF THE CARDOON, WHICH HAS BEEN GROWN AND EATEN IN GREECE SINCE ANCIENT TIMES. ARTICHOKES ARE STILL FAIRLY EXOTIC IN THE UNITED STATES, BUT IN GREECE THEY HAVE LONG BEEN A SAVORED SEASONAL VEGETABLE. A SALAD OF ARTICHOKES, CHOPPED ANCHOVIES, GARLICKY BREAD CRUMBS, AND POTATO REFLECTS THE HEART OF GREECE. THE INGREDIENTS ARE FILLING AND SATISFYING, THE FLAVORS HAVE SOUL, AND THE COMPOSITION AS A WHOLE LIFTS THE SPIRIT.

*24 baby artichokes
   (about 2 1/2 pounds total)*
*2 medium red or white potatoes,
   scrubbed and sliced 1/4 inch thick*
*6 anchovy fillets, very coarsely chopped*
*1/4 cup fresh lemon juice*
*1/3 cup olive oil*
*1/4 teaspoon salt*
*2 tablespoons chopped fresh flat-leaf
   parsley leaves*
*1/2 cup Toasted Bread Crumb and
   Garlic Topping (page 481)*

1 Bring a large pot of water to a boil over high heat. Peel off two or three layers of the dark outer leaves from the artichokes, and cut off the thorny tops.

2 When the water is boiling, drop in the artichokes, reduce the heat to a brisk simmer, and cover the pot. Cook for 10 minutes.

3 Add the potatoes to the pot and bring to a boil again. Cover and cook briskly until the artichokes and potatoes are tender but not falling apart, 5 to 7 minutes. Drain in a colander, and set aside to cool and drip dry for up to several hours.

4 Transfer the artichokes and potatoes to a bowl or platter. Add the anchovies, lemon juice, oil, salt, and parsley and toss gently to mix. Sprinkle the topping over the salad, and serve right away or within a few hours.

NOTE: If baby artichokes are not available, you can substitute larger ones, though the whole leaves will not be edible. Simmer the artichokes in a large pot of water until tender, about 30 minutes. Drain and allow to cool, then quarter them, cut off all the outer leaves, and pull out the thistley choke. You should be left with the tender heart. (Boil the potatoes in a separate pot.) Combine the quartered artichoke hearts with the potatoes and dress as described.

*Atop an herb-covered hillside sit the ruins of an ancient building, while below, a coastal village welcomes a visiting ship.*

# cucumber boats

## FILLED WITH RICE AND CHICKPEA SALAD

### SERVES 6

IN GREEK MYTHOLOGY, THE CORNUCOPIA IS THE HORN OF THE GOAT THAT SUCKLED ZEUS. MAGICAL, IT BECOMES FULL OF WHATEVER THE OWNER WANTS. WE CALL IT THE "HORN OF PLENTY," AND USE IT AS A SYMBOL FOR ABUNDANCE. BUT BECAUSE A HORN IS NOT EDIBLE, WHAT BETTER TO HOLD A CORNUCOPIA SORT OF SALAD THAN A HORNLIKE VEGETABLE—OR AT LEAST A BOATLIKE ONE— THAT ITSELF CAN BE EATEN AS PART OF THE FARE? CUCUMBER SALADS HAVE LONG BEEN A PART OF GREEK GASTRONOMY. WHEN CUCUMBER IS THE RECEPTACLE OF ITS OWN SASSY MELANGE—RICE TO SOAK UP THE JUICES, SWEET RED PEPPER, SCALLIONS, AND LIVELY GREEN DILL AND PARSLEY—THE MIXTURE IS OPULENT.

*3 medium cucumbers (about 1 1/2*
    *pounds total), peeled*
*Salt*
*1 cup cooked rice, preferably Arborio,*
    *at room temperature*
*1/2 cup cooked chickpeas, drained*
*1/4 cup finely chopped red bell pepper*
*2 scallions, white and light green*
    *parts trimmed and finely chopped*
*1/2 tablespoon chopped fresh dill*
*2 tablespoons chopped fresh flat-leaf*
    *parsley leaves*
*1/4 teaspoon freshly ground black*
    *pepper*
*2 tablespoons fresh lemon juice*
*2 tablespoons olive oil*

1 Cut the cucumbers in half lengthwise and scoop out the seeds. Liberally sprinkle both sides of each cucumber half with salt. Place the halves, cut sides down, on paper towels and allow to drain for at least 30 minutes or up to several hours.

2 Toss the remaining ingredients together in a bowl with 1/2 teaspoon salt.

## CUCUMBER & ZUCCHINI— A RIPE STORY

Although Greeks did not have squashes, such as zucchini and pumpkin, until they were brought from the New World, they did have several other members of the Cucurbitaceae family, namely gourds, various muskmelons, and cucumbers. They also had gherkins, a small, thick, and bumpy-skinned sort of cucumber.

Cucumbers were quite beloved by the ancient Greeks. They were lauded in poems, made the fodder of off-color jokes (their shape being just too metaphoric to ignore), considered a medicine, munched on raw, and also pickled. Gherkins are picked unripe, and the root meaning of the Greek *aggouria* implies "unripe." With zucchini now frequently replacing gherkins in the Greek mind as well as in their pickle recipes, perhaps the ancient allusion to "unripe" explains the second use Greeks have nowadays for their word for zucchini, *kolokithia*. *Kolokithia!* yelled out means "nonsense!" Or, in short, something pitifully dumb and immature.

3 When ready to serve, wipe the cucumbers dry with a cloth or paper towel. Arrange the cucumber "boats" on a serving platter, fill them with the rice mixture, and serve.

# broad bean and pea salad

## WITH KEFALOTYRI AND CUMIN VINAIGRETTE

### SERVES 6

BROAD (FAVA) BEANS, THE ONLY INDIGENOUS EUROPEAN BEAN, ARE EXQUISITELY MEATY AND, WHEN COOKED FRESH, FULL OF SPRING-GREEN FLAVOR. MUCH SUPERSTITION ONCE SURROUNDED THE BROAD BEAN. THE EGYPTIANS, DESPITE BEING GREAT PULSE EATERS, REGARDED THEM AS DANGEROUS. IN GREECE, THE FOLLOWERS OF PYTHAGORAS WERE FORBIDDEN TO EAT THEM. (OF COURSE, THEY WERE FORBIDDEN TO SPEAK ABOUT THE HOLY, WEAR COLORED CLOTHES, OR HAVE INTIMATE RELATIONS AS WELL.)

Although some of Pythagoras's metaphysical and mathematical ideas were clearly off the mark, he and the Egyptians were right to be suspicious of broad beans, because they make some people ill, especially people from the eastern Mediterranean. For most of us, however, they are a wonderful springtime treat.

The salad below mixes broad beans with English peas and then travels a bit far afield to include Chinese snow peas. Pythagorianism called for the harmony of the cosmos—here three delights of the cosmos are harmoniously tossed together.

4 pounds fresh broad (fava) beans
   in their pods
1 pound fresh peas in their pods,
   shelled
4 ounces snow peas, stem tips
   snapped off
2 tablespoons fresh lemon juice
3 tablespoons fruity olive oil
1/4 teaspoon ground cumin
1/4 teaspoon salt
2 tablespoons finely chopped scallions
   (white and light green parts)
6 thin slices kefalotyri cheese,
   cut with a cheese shaver

1 Bring a pot of water to a boil over high heat. Shell the broad beans as you would peas. When the water boils, drop in the beans and cook until the water is rapidly boiling again, about 1 minute. Then, using a slotted spoon, transfer the beans to a colander and set them aside to cool.

2 Bring the water back to a boil over high heat. Drop in the peas and the snow peas and cook just until the water returns to a boil and the peas float to the top, no more than 1 minute. Drain the peas and snow peas in another colander and set aside.

3 In a small bowl, stir together the lemon juice, oil, cumin, and salt. Set aside.

4 Pinching them with your fingers, pop the fava beans out of their skins and place them in a bowl or on a platter. Add the peas, snow peas, and scallions. Pour the dressing over the top, and crumble the cheese slices over all. Serve right away.

#  big beans

## WITH FRESH HERBS AND FRUITY OLIVE OIL

## GIGANTES SALATA

### ✴ SERVES 6

APTLY NAMED *GIGANTES*, OR "GIANTS," THESE WIDE-GIRTHED, HEFTY NEW WORLD BEANS ARE POPULAR THROUGHOUT GREECE AND LITTLE SEEN ELSEWHERE. THEY ARE USED ESPECIALLY IN *BRIAMI* OR *YAKNI*, THE ZESTY GREEK VEGETABLE STEW (PAGE 282), AND THEY ARE ALSO COOKED *PLAKI*-STYLE (PAGE 286). IN BOTH PREPARATIONS, THE GIANT BEANS ARE HEARTY ENOUGH TO SUBSTITUTE FOR MEAT OR SEAFOOD. DRIED *GIGANTES* COOK QUICKLY, LIKE DRIED BLACK-EYED PEAS OR DRIED LIMAS, AND THEY ARE WITHOUT A DOUBT MY FAVORITE GREEK BEANS. A SALAD FEATURING THEIR MEATY GOODNESS IS A COMMON *MEZE*, BUT IT IS ALSO A PERFECT COMPANION TO THE DISHES ON THE DINNER TABLE. *GIGANTES* ARE HARD TO FIND IN THE UNITED STATES EXCEPT IN GREEK MARKETS, BUT THEY ARE WELL WORTH THE HUNT!

1 pound dried gigantes beans
   (see Note)
1 teaspoon salt
1/3 cup chopped fresh flat-leaf parsley
   leaves
1 1/2 teaspoons fresh thyme leaves
1/4 cup fruity olive oil

1 Place the beans in a large pot and add water to cover generously. Bring to a boil, cook for 1 minute, then remove from the heat. Cover and set aside to soak for 1 hour.

2 Drain the beans in a colander and rinse. Return them to the pot, add water to cover generously again, and bring to a boil.

## SILVER STAKES

Broad (fava) beans were often sown by ancient Greeks between grape vines to hamper the spread of the vine. The stakes of grapevines could be set closer this way, and more grapes grown. According to Hesiod, the stakes were made of silver. Doubtful, but if so, quite a precious vineyard!

Reduce the heat and simmer briskly for 30 minutes.

3 Add 1/2 teaspoon of the salt and continue to simmer until the beans are tender but not mushy and some of the skins are breaking apart, about 40 minutes. Drain, and set aside to cool.

4 Transfer the beans to a bowl and add the parsley, thyme, oil, and remaining 1/2 teaspoon salt. Toss gently to mix, and serve right away or set aside at room temperature for up to several hours.

### NOTE:

■ As a substitute for the wonderful *gigantes* beans, you can use another big, meaty, dried white bean, such as Italian cannellinis or large (not baby) limas.

# black-eyed pea salad

## WITH TOMATOES AND SHALLOTS

### SERVES 6

B LACK-EYED PEAS ARE CALLED ALMOST THE SAME THING IN GREEK: *MAVROMATI*, MEANING "BLACK EYE." KILOS OF THEM FLY OUT OF GREEK STORES. NOT BEING FROM THE SOUTHERN UNITED STATES, I WAS UNFAMILIAR WITH THEM IN MY CHILDHOOD, BUT I TOOK TO THEM IN GREECE, AND FOR MANY OF THE SAME REASONS THAT GREEK COOKS LOVE THEM: BLACK-EYED PEAS ARE QUICK TO COOK, HAVE A FLAVOR AKIN TO NUTS, AND ARE FILLING, SO A SIMPLE SALAD IS SATISFYING. THERE'S A REASON WHY I FEATURED A GREEK-STYLE BLACK-EYED PEA SALAD AT MY SON'S AND DAUGHTER'S HIGH SCHOOL GRADUATION PARTIES; AND WHY I BRING IT TO MANY A POTLUCK; AND WHY I PRESENT IT FOR NEW YEAR'S GOOD LUCK, *KALI TIXI*: THE COMBINATION IS SO TASTY IT'S GOOD FORTUNE JUST TO EAT IT.

2 cups (12 ounces) dried
    black-eyed peas
6 cups water
1 teaspoon salt
4 tomatoes (1 pound total),
    peeled, seeded, and coarsely
    chopped
1 large shallot (2 ounces),
    minced
$1/4$ cup chopped fresh flat-leaf
    parsley leaves
2 tablespoons finely shredded
    fresh basil leaves
$1/2$ tablespoon chopped fresh
    mint leaves
$1/4$ teaspoon freshly ground
    black pepper
$1/2$ tablespoon red wine vinegar
$1/8$ teaspoon sugar (optional;
    use if the tomatoes are
    more tart than sweet)
2 tablespoons olive oil

1 Place the peas in a pot, add the water, and bring to a boil. Reduce the heat and simmer briskly for 15 minutes.

2 Add the salt and continue cooking until the peas are cooked through but still firm, 17 to 20 minutes. Drain, shake, and transfer to a bowl.

3 Add the tomatoes, shallot, herbs, pepper, vinegar, sugar,

*A city-dwelling Greek homemaker grows flowers and herbs on a small balcony.*

if using, and oil and toss gently to mix. Serve right away, or cover and chill in the refrigerator for up to several hours.

## NOTES:

■ Don't be tempted to cook the peas longer, even if they seem too firm after 17 to 20 minutes. Black-eyed peas tend to become mushy and waterlogged very quickly, and they continue to cook as they cool.

■ It's important to add salt a little before the peas are done cooking. It helps them stay firm.

■ Fresh black-eyed peas can be found in early fall in produce markets. If they are very fresh (the juices in the vacuum package are clear and not murky), they are a sweet replacement for the dried ones. They take only about 7 minutes to cook.

## THE MOTHERS EARTH: GAIA AND RHEA

The Greek pantheon had not just one but two mothers of the earth. The first was the primary deity of all existence, the goddess Gaia. Before any life there was only chaos, a deep chasm in which nothing existed. Out of it rose Gaia, the broad-breasted earth. Her name is also spelled Ge, from which we get such words as "geology," the study of the earth. She bore starry heaven, Uranus, to surround her and make a home for her children. She then created the mountains, the valleys, and the sea.

Next Gaia joined with Uranus and gave birth to three mighty giants, each with a hundred arms; the Cyclops, each with one eye; and the Titans, including Oceanus, the river that circled the world. The youngest Titan, Cronos, whose name means "time," started the clock ticking. Heaven was not the best of fathers. He pushed his offspring back into Gaia, until Cronos rose up against his sire and with a sickle cut him down like so much chicory. Cronos married his sister, Rhea.

Like father, however, like son. Cronos gulped down his babies like so many tomatoes—first the goddesses Hestia, Hera, and Demeter, then his sons Hades and Poseidon. When Rhea had her next child, Zeus, she wrapped a stone in a blanket and gave it to Cronos to eat, which he devoured. She gave Zeus to Gaia, his grandmother, to raise in a cave on Crete. When Zeus was grown, with Rhea's help he released his brothers and sisters and overturned his father.

But when Zeus imprisoned his father, her baby boy, Grandmother Gaia got angry. She brought forth more giants, and created a plant that would make them immortal and invincible. Zeus foraged around, however, and located the crunchy leaf and stole it before his new uncles could find it.

Gaia went on to have more children, but Rhea was happy to give up childbearing and just remain esteemed as a goddess of plenty.

# THE SARAKATSANI, GREECE'S ROVING SHEPHERDS

**A**NYONE TRAVELING THROUGH CONTINENTAL GREECE SOON NOTICES AN UNUSUAL SORT OF COMMUNITY: SMALL CLUSTERS OF CIRCULAR DOMED HUTS OF WOOD AND THATCH.

Close to them graze great flocks of sheep and goats, guarded by shepherds dressed in rough woven black suits and sweeping goat-hair capes.

These are the Sarakatsani, the roving shepherds of Greece. They can be found across the northern stretch of the Peloponnesos and up the spine of northern Greece, largely within the rough and mountainous expanse between the Rodope range in the far northeast and the Pindos massif, including Epiros, Thessaly, Macedonia, and Thrace. From St. George's day, May 6, to St. Dimitrios's day, November 8, they take their flocks to the high mountain grasslands, where they set up their camps. During the winter months, they move down to the coastal plains. Their moves—herd, huts, and all— twice a year follow a pattern called transhumance, common to herders about the world.

The Sarakatsani speak Greek and are Greek through and through. Near them live other shepherds, the Vlachs, some of whom speak a Romanian dialect and some Albanian. The Greek the Sarakatsani speak is an old form. Their customs and values are old Greek as well. No one knows exactly how long they have lived as they do; no ancient or medieval historian thought they were important enough to record. To this day they do not marry with the nearby non-Greek shepherds, and they bear a strong antipathy toward their settled neighbors and any who live in a village or city.

## A FAMILY BUSINESS

The Sarakatsani provide the milk for most of Greece's cheese. To do so requires large herds, which in turn need many people to guard and handle them: for each herd, at least four adult men and fifteen to fifty other persons of all ages. To manage the labor, the Sarakatsani collect in families related by blood and marriage to form a company. Each person has specific duties on which all others depend; each must bow to the interest of the group and the animals' well-being.

Winter is an anxious time. Even in the lowlands, the days are cold and the grazing pastures are sparse and far from camp. During the last days of December and the first ten days of January, most of the lambs are born. Two by two, each ewe and lamb are brought to a fold close to the shepherds' huts. By mid-January the yield of milk becomes the main concern, and cheese making occupies the next six months.

The ewes are given the best grassland and are fed extra rations of corn, oats, and cakes pressed from cotton plants.

On February 1, the cheese merchant arrives and sets up

> . . . it is the path of their fathers and forefathers, righteous and the only way to live.

nearby. He builds two structures: one for the cauldrons, churns, and cream separator, the other below-ground, with a carpet of ferns on the floor, to store the newly formed cheeses. The shepherds wean the male lambs at only four weeks, to sell as Easter approaches. The Sarakatsani supply much of Greece's spring lamb.

Meanwhile, the Sarakatsani women and men build a milking pen near the cheese maker. At first the men take only a little milk; then, as the male lambs are sold and the females grow, they take more. No ewe lambs are sold unless a family is in great financial difficulty. Nor are the ewe lambs weaned early. The Sarakatsani's future depends on healthy ewes.

In two years these lambs will bear the new ones for the herd. In early March, when the lambs are weaned, the flow of milk becomes copious. Saving some of the cream for butter, the cheese maker makes

hard kefalotyri from the milk. From the remaining whey, he forms soft mizithra.

The goats are giving milk too. Goat kids are born at the end of December and are kept in warm pens built by the Sarakatsani women; the mother goats are turned out to graze by day and return at night. In March they are weaned, the male kids sold, and the goat's milk brought in ever-increasing quantities to the cheese maker for feta and mizithra.

Soon the group moves to summer pastures, where the rams are sent to the high grasslands and the goats, who can eat anything, are sent even higher. The shepherds build a fold of brushwood and branch, while the cheese merchant sets up a station within sight of four or five different families' milking pens.

At the same time, the women build temporary huts, collect wood and brush for fire, carry water, wash clothes, watch goats, gather wild vegetables and herbs, tend small gardens, keep hens for eggs to eat and sell, and make the family's cheese. They divide and spin wool, dry it and card it, knit, weave, and make all the clothes.

In June the rams are allowed to run with the milking ewes, and finally by the end of July, when the cheese maker leaves, the shepherds enjoy the few weeks during which they can relax.

## THE CUISINE OF THE SARAKATSANI

With the first milk in February and the milk brought in during the rough journey to the high mountains, the families make their own stores of rough feta. From July through August, they do the same again. For their meals they forage for wild greens and buy vegetables, fruit, olives, and flour from their farming neighbors. They also hunt. A typical Sarakatsani meal might be a rabbit stew with onion, should the shepherd have had a lucky hunt, or a casserole of leeks and celery in lemon-and-egg sauce. They might add a salad of chicory topped with their own kefalotyri. They purchase raisins and nuts from the vineyards and orchards they pass. Their bread is hearty country style, or if money is short, cornbread, perhaps flavored with wild fennel. Dried figs finish the repast. When they are watching the flocks, the men lunch on a hunk of cheese, bread, olives, and perhaps berries from a nearby mulberry tree.

## WOOL FOR RUGS

Just before the migration back down to the lowlands, the sheep are shorn and the wool is sold or woven into Greece's famous white flokati rugs. The final day of shearing is celebrated with a great feast, with meat, wine, music, and dancing.

To the Sarakatsani, shepherding is neither an occupation nor a profession; it is the path of their fathers and forefathers, righteous and the only way to live. Modern life pressures on the land have diminished the Sarakatsani numbers, yet the people and their culture remain. Having recognized them decades ago, the Greek government has given them summer grazing rights in the hills in perpetuity. Their continued presence provides Greece with ongoing richness in its ancient folkways, its lamb, and cheese for every table.

*The younger Sarakatsani shepherds travel with the goatherd to the highest pasture, while the older shepherds mind the herds below.*

# eggs
# THE DAILY GIFT

IN ANCIENT GREECE EGGS WERE SUCH A UBIQUITOUS FOOD, SO ORDINARY AND AT HAND, THAT EARLY AUTHORS, STATESMEN, AND PHILOSOPHERS HARDLY MENTION THEM. FROM ALL INDICATIONS IT SEEMS THEY PROBABLY ATE THE EGGS OF MANY FOWL— NOT JUST CHICKENS, BUT ALSO QUAIL, PROBABLY GEESE, DUCKS, AND DEFINITELY PEAHENS (THOUGH THEIR EGGS WERE APPARENTLY COSTLY).

## LOVE AT FIRST PEEL

"I would treat her like an egg, the shell of which we remove before eating. I would take off her mask and kiss her pretty face."

—SAID BY A CHARACTER WHO WAS FALLING IN LOVE, IN ARISTOPHANES' *THE BIRDS*, FIFTH CENTURY B.C.E.

But while Homer uses cocks as models of courage and hardiness, he never talks of eggs. Sybaris banished roosters in 720 B.C.E. so their crowing would not wake late sleepers, but he offers no allowance that a supply of eggs requires the presence of at least one lucky rooster. Aristotle carefully notes that pigeons lay only two eggs in a season, whereas domestic hens produce on an almost constant basis, but he issues not a cackle about eating eggs. However, we know that at least one Greek ate eggs: Philoxenos ate them—for dessert.

In the modern Greek kitchen, the egg occupies the place it has long held: ever present and ready, much enjoyed, but with little fanfare. No Greek homemaker would be without eggs, for eggs are the Greek "fast food." Eggs are served to the child or worker who has just come home. Eggs are whipped up whenever the hostess thinks the array of midday or evening foods does not offer quite enough. The cook might fry an egg in a bath of pricey oil or she might fork together an omelet, plain or with a bit of cheese, tomato, onion. Countryside homemakers still keep poultry for the supply of eggs far more than for the meat. Though ordinary, eggs are a precious offering, a hospitable welcome for both family and visitor.

## HOW GREEKS GREET THE DAY

Have you ever wondered why the breakfast offered in Greek hotels is so haphazard? It's because Greeks themselves don't actually eat what we call breakfast.

Typically, upon rising a Greek will sip coffee from a large cup brimming with hot milk, something like a French *café au lait* or an Italian *caffè latte*. Perhaps a few hard rusks of bread are dunked into the coffee to quell incipient hunger pains. Less typically, a Greek might breakfast on a plate of olives, cheese, tomatoes, figs, fresh bread, and fresh fruit.

Eggs? Never eggs. Eggs are a real food intended for a real meal, and those meals come later in the day.

*The day's fresh eggs, ready to be fried in rich olive oil or made into an omelet.*

# the greek fried egg

**SERVES 1**

I WAS INTRODUCED TO GREEK FRIED EGGS DURING MY FIRST LONG STAY ON SANTORINI. I GREETED THE EXPERIENCE WITH HORROR, THEN WITH ADORATION. I WAS USED TO MY MOTHER'S FRIED EGGS—GENTLY SIZZLED IN BUTTER, TURNED OUT EITHER WITH A GOLD YOLK OR BASTED WITH THE PAN BUTTER UNTIL THE YOLK TURNED PINK. I WAS EVEN MORE USED TO MY OWN FRENCH-STYLE FRIED EGGS—NOT ONLY FRIED IN BUTTER BUT DRIZZLED ROUND THE EDGE WITH WATER AND THEN COVERED, SO THE YOLK TURNED PERFECTLY SOFT AND PINK FROM THE STEAM.

Then I watched my generous Greek hostess pour more than a soupçon of olive oil in a pan and heat it so hot that when she cracked in the egg, it almost jumped back out. Furiously, the egg fried in about one minute, oil bubbling up, the edge of the egg turning as brown and crisp as the pages of an old book. Just before taking the egg off the heat, she spooned some of the oil over the top. She slipped the egg, oil and all, into a cereal bowl and set it down before me.

I ate it. And I ate hundreds more in days to come—and could go on relishing Greek-style fried eggs for another century. Already a lover of cold olive oils, I became a connoisseur of hot and sizzling oil. Around the egg I could taste the olive tree's age and every herb that grew beneath its branches. The crunch of the crisp edges replaced my love of potato chips. The yolk became, like the cherry on a sundae, a treasure delayed to the last bite. When I overhear tourists in restaurants, horrified as I was at first, complaining about "eggs swimming in oil," and sending them back to the kitchen, I chuckle. Ah, those doubting Thomases; they don't know what they are missing. And ah, that oil. I never had more glowing skin or shinier hair than during my years in Greece.

Here's how to make a Greek fried egg.

*¼ cup olive oil*
*1 large egg*
*Pinch of sea salt*
*Dash of freshly ground black pepper*
*1 or 2 slices hearty country bread,*
*    for serving*

1 Pour the oil into a small frying pan over high heat, and heat until hot.

2 Add the egg and fry it fast and furiously until the edge of the egg white is crisp and the yolk is yellow and firm, 1 to 3 minutes depending on how hard you like the yolk. Using a teaspoon, spoon several splashes of the hot oil over the egg.

3 Remove the pan from the heat. Slide the egg, with the oil, into a shallow bowl. Season with the sea salt and pepper. Serve hot or at room temperature, with slices of bread to sop up the runny yolk and scrumptious oil.

# OREGANO, DILL, AND MINT

**T**HREE HERBS RULE THE GAMUT OF GREEK GASTRONOMY: OREGANO, CALLED *RIGANI*, DILL, *ANITHO*, AND MINT, *DIOSMOS*. OTHER HERBS MIGHT BE USED, BUT THE REIGNING TRIO ARE FIRST AT HAND FOR ALMOST EVERY PREPARATION. DRIED OREGANO, USUALLY PICKED BY THE COOK, USED TO SIT BY EVERY GREEK STOVE IN AN EMPTY NESCAFE TIN. NOW MORE LIKELY IT IS STASHED IN A PLASTIC CONTAINER. IN SPRING AND EARLY SUMMER, THE OMELET MAKER GATHERS HANDFULS OF DILL; FOR FALL AND WINTER, THE COOK MAKES DO WITH SUMMER'S DILL DRIED. MINT IS ALMOST ALWAYS GROWING IN A POT JUST OUTSIDE THE KITCHEN DOOR.

Oregano is perhaps the Zeus of the herbs, the king. The word means "mountain joy." It is a member of the marjoram family, and the variety that grows in Greece is heady, smoky, aromatic, and richly flavorful. When I first gathered oregano on the hills and asked my companions how to dry it, they looked at me in great perplexity. "Dry it?" they asked, looking at the clusters in their hands. "Can't you see it's already dry?" And they were, of course, right as always, as right as the rare rain. Oregano in Greece grows low on the ground, on such arid hills that it requires no drying. It is both fresh and dry in one picking. *Rigani* is absolutely, no questions asked, the herb used in the marinade for steaks and kebabs. It is almost always the herb of meat and

*Enjoying a chance to sit and talk, two Greek women sort through fragrant oregano.*

vegetable stews and casseroles, especially those with tomato sauce or involving eggplant, and it is usually the herb of choice for an omelet. For any Greek cooking you must have a supply, and the best is the real Greek wild oregano, available at Greek markets.

Dill, like its cousin fennel, grows like a feathered weed across the Grecian landscape. Both the seed and the leaves have been used since antiquity. It is a member of the parsley family and native to southern Europe. Dill is used in soups, salads, and sauces—especially *avgolemono*. It is often added to lighten cheese dishes, is crucial in *tzatziki*, and is important in stuffed grape leaves. The leaves are used more than the seed in modern Greek fare. Because the leaves don't keep their grassy taste well when dried, it's best to always use fresh dill.

Mint, along with basil, is considered so perfumelike by the Greeks that many tuck a sprig behind the ear so the scent wafts across the nose throughout the day. The ancient Greeks thought the herb cooled the blood and woke up a tired mind, and considering that the variety most often grown and used in Greece is spearmint— probably the most aromatic and strongly flavored of all the mints—they may have been correct. The name, *diosmos*, comes from "two" and refers to the twin sons of Zeus, Castor and Polydeuces. Mint is used, often in combination with dill, in minced meat dishes, in yogurt sauces, on lamb in every preparation, in pies and some sweets, and to lift the density of stuffing.

# the greek omelet

## APLO

### SERVES 2

GREEKS MAKE QUICK-FIRE OMELETS—CALLED BOTH *OMELETA* AND *SFOUGATO*, OR "SPONGE"—AS AN ADDITION TO MEALS AND ALSO AS THE DINING CENTERPIECE WHEN, FOR LACK OF TIME OR MONEY, NO MEAT, FISH, OR MAJOR VEGETABLE DISH IS IN THE OFFING. THE GREEK OMELET IS RARELY PLANNED; RATHER IT IS THE BEST OF "SCAVENGER" CONTRIVANCES. A HOMEMAKER WILL MAKE IT PLAIN, OR ADD WHATEVER SHE HAS IN THE KITCHEN: TOMATO, CHEESE, ONION, SQUASH. MY FAVORITES, THOUGH, ARE THE EVER-SO-CRISP AND FILLING FRENCH FRIED POTATO OMELET AND THE FRIED CHEESE CHIP OMELET (SEE VARIATIONS).

*4 large eggs*
*3 tablespoons water (optional)*
*Pinch of chopped fresh oregano,*
*    mint, dill, or basil leaves*
*    (optional)*
*Pinch of salt*
*Pinch of freshly ground*
*    black pepper*
*2 to 3 tablespoons olive oil*

1 Beat together the eggs, water, if using, oregano, if using, and salt and pepper in a medium-size bowl until well mixed but not foamy.

2 Heat the oil in an omelet pan or medium-size skillet over medium-high heat. Pour the egg mixture into the pan and cook for 2 minutes, pushing the edges toward the center with a spatula and tilting the pan to allow the moist center of the egg mixture to spill toward the edges without disturbing the bottom.

3 Cover the pan and reduce the heat to medium. Cook for 3 minutes more, until the top is no longer runny and the bottom is golden. Fold over to make a half-moon shape, and serve right away.

## THE TWO-PAN TRICK

In northern Greece omelets are sometimes made in two same-size frying pans. The omelet's eggy mixture is poured into hot oil in the one and cooked until the bottom thickens and sets. The second pan, lightly oiled, is then placed facedown over the first, and the two together are flipped over so that the omelet falls top down from the first pan into the second. The second is put over the heat so that the undone top of the omelet, now on the bottom, cooks until firm. Many households in the United States used to have double-sided, hinged omelet pans that folded over to perform this same maneuver. Without any stirring, you could cook the omelet until half done on one side, close the empty half over the filled side, invert the whole shebang, and cook the other side. An omelet cooked in either two skillets or the hinged variety rises fluffily, much like an oven-baked frittata.

**NOTE:** I add water because it makes the eggs more tender (while milk makes eggs tougher). Greeks usually simply use eggs with no additions.

## VARIATIONS:

**French Fried Potato Omelet:**
Make ½ batch French Fried Potatoes Greek-Style (page 281). As they finish frying, pour in the egg mixture and cook the omelet as described.

**Fried Cheese Chip Omelet:**
Slice 3 to 4 ounces strong, firm mizithra or manouri cheese into "chips" 1 inch wide, 2 to 3 inches long, and ¼ inch thick. In an omelet pan or skillet, fry the cheese "chips" in 3 tablespoons olive oil over medium-high heat until browned on both sides, about 3 minutes. Then add the egg mixture and cook the omelet as described.

## OTHER GREEK OMELET COMBINATIONS

- Tomato, especially cherry tomatoes, coarsely chopped or sliced

- Bell pepper, especially green bell pepper, coarsely chopped

- Onion, coarsely chopped or sliced

- Cheese, especially kefalotyri, but also feta or kasseri

- Cooked vegetables: zucchini, artichokes, spinach or other greens, mushrooms, asparagus, fried eggplant, cauliflower

- Small bits of meat, such as sausage, liver, or kidney

- Small bits of fish, especially dried cod that has been soaked until soft

- Herbs: thyme, marjoram, savory, sage, parsley

# THE ORIGIN OF THE CHEESE CHIP OMELET

When I first went to Greece, I lived in a tiny village on Santorini where I rented a four-room cave house dug into a ravine. (Almost all houses of the island were cave houses tunneled into the volcanic ash layer of the island's dramatic caldera or into the ravines running down the island's back slope.) I used only two rooms: the large, warm front room that opened onto my patio garden, and the small narrow kitchen. As the kitchen was burrowed quite deep into the hill, it contained only a shoulder-height half-window at what was ground level outside. At first I was dismayed when, at about 5:30 almost every morning, I was awakened by a knocking on that window. There would crouch a village woman bringing me a gift of her homemade goat cheese or a bottle of moments-old goat's milk. But I soon recognized what precious gifts these were, examples of Greece's famous hospitality, the product of the giver's labor and time.

The trouble was, both cheese and milk were so strong, as a consequence of the goat's weedy diet, that I could hardly down them. Like all Greeks I resisted wasting any food, and I believed one should honor all gifts. Finally I discovered how to handle my ethical and culinary problem. One day, having no other kind of milk, I used the goat's milk to make crème caramel—and found it to be sweet-tart and compelling. To this day, goat's milk is my preferred flan-making liquid.

Another day, when I was low on other food, in a desperate attempt to make the cheese more palatable, I threw it in the frying pan as a substitute for fried potatoes in an omelet. Eureka! What a discovery! The cheese became mellow and crunchy, and the eggs softly blanketed the chips. Five thirty in the morning became an anticipated, not dreaded, hour and the omelet became my breakfast.

# eggs with yogurt and greek salsa

## ON A BED OF CAPER LEAVES AND PITA

### AVGA GEORGIKA

✦

#### SERVES 4

GREEK INGREDIENTS USED IN AN INNOVATIVE WAY BECOME A GREEK ANSWER TO *HUEVOS RANCHEROS*, WITH PITA TAKING THE PLACE OF THE TORTILLA. A GREEK "SALSA" EASILY COMES TOGETHER WITH CHOPPED GARDEN TOMATO, ONION, RADISH, AND POSSIBLY GARLIC AND A GREEN BELL PEPPER OR CHILE PEPPER. YOGURT IS AS SOOTHING A SAUCE AS SOUR CREAM. BUT WHAT MAKES *AVGA GEORGIKA* ("FARMER'S EGGS") GREEK AND SPECTACULAR IS THE LAYER OF PIQUANT CAPER LEAVES SLIPPED UNDER THE SUNNY EGG. THE NUMBER OF BRUNCHES AT WHICH I'VE SERVED *AVGA GEORGIKA* IS CLIMBING TOWARD COUNTLESS. SHUNNING TIRED HOLLANDAISE, FINDING *RANCHEROS* A LITTLE HEAVY, MY ACQUAINTANCES SEEM TO WANT TO SAY A SUNDAY *KALIMERA* (GOOD MORNING!) IN A NEW GREEK WAY.

*1 tomato, finely chopped*
*1 radish, finely chopped*
*1/4 small onion, finely chopped*
*2 cloves garlic (optional), minced*
*1/4 green bell pepper, or 1 small mild*
    *chile (optional), finely chopped*
*1 teaspoon fresh oregano leaves, or*
    *1 tablespoon shredded basil leaves*
*Salt*
*4 tablespoons olive oil*
*4 pita breads*

*4 large eggs*
*1/2 cup caper leaves*
    *(see Note and box, page 222)*
*1/2 cup plain yogurt*

1 Toss the tomato, radish, onion, garlic, if using, and bell pepper, if using, together in a bowl. Add the oregano and season with salt to taste. Set the salsa aside.

## HESTIA

The ancient Greeks worshiped a goddess of the hearth, where their daily bread was baked, named Hestia. Every meal began and ended with an offering to her. Every newborn child was carried around the hearth and presented to her before being received into the family. Every city had a public hearth with an everlasting flame, never allowed to flicker out, dedicated to her. Hestia symbolized the home, both city and abode.

Yet, poor dear, Hestia was so matter-of-fact, so humble, that no mythology exists about her. She was Zeus's sister, a virgin. In Rome six virgin priestesses, called Vestals (in Latin, Hestia's name was Vesta), served her, but she had no stories, no adventures, save her constant presence at the home fire.

She was, it seems, so day-in-and-day-out present, and so ordinary, that like the egg, she scarcely gets mentioned.

2 Heat 2 tablespoons of the oil in a large skillet over medium-high heat. Place 2 pitas in the skillet and toast until brown on both sides, about 30 seconds per side. Transfer the pitas to a dish and cover to keep warm. Brown the remaining 2 pitas and add to the dish.

3 Add the remaining 2 tablespoons oil to the skillet and gently fry the eggs over medium heat, until the whites are set and the yolks slightly runny. Place a warm pita on each plate. Cover the pita with a thin layer of caper leaves, and slide an egg over the caper leaves. Place 2 to 3 tablespoons of the salsa and about 2 tablespoons yogurt next to the egg. Serve right away, while still warm.

## NOTES:

■ Bottled caper leaves are available from Greek specialty grocers. Their brine often includes vinegar, not just salt, so rinse them well.

■ If caper leaves cannot be found, add ¼ cup capers to the chopped tomato mixture. Or use ½ cup shredded brined grape leaves.

■ The eggs can be poached or fried Greek-style, as on page 217.

## CAPER LEAVES

For many years the buds and berries of the caper plant have been available in specialty markets and good grocery stores in the United States. But the buds and berries are not the only edible part of the caper bush. The leaves and tender spring sprigs are too. In Greece, when we go caper picking, we always gather a supply of the heart-shaped leaves and a few of the bush's new green twigs. We brine them in sea salt as we do the buds, and that way have them for salads, for adding to omelets, for sprinkling on fish dishes, and for slipping under eggs.

The leaves are about the shape and size of an aspen leaf, a deep forest green. While the preserved leaves are salty from the brine, they don't have the bud's piquant nip. Rather, they are a sparkling combination of an almost tobacco flavor and wake-up saltiness. Their texture is a little tough and chewy. Greeks brine them whole and use them whole in salads and as a topping. They also shred them.

As caper-gathering time goes on, we also pick some open flowers for a dash of white color among the green. I find that I now plan at least one of my yearly trips to Greece to coincide with the caper-gathering season. When I can't, I rely on my village friends to share their supplies with me. They share the caper buds with open-handed generosity, but as for the leaves, each housewife eyes her supply, eyes me, and calculates. How many does she need to last until next summer, and how many can she spare? I, in turn, with the precious stock she gives me, try to determine how many salads and how many *avga georgika* I can cook. And I plan to arrive a little earlier next year!

*Artemios carries in a bushel of just gathered wild capers balanced on his back with one hand.*

# the other feta

## EGG BREAD

### SERVES 3

FOR THE FINAL COURSE OF A DINNER, PHILOXENOS WAS SERVED EGGS—WE DON'T KNOW HOW THEY WERE COOKED—ALONG WITH ALMONDS, WALNUTS, AND SWEET CAKES OF SAFFLOWER, HONEY, AND SESAME. WE KNOW THAT THE BYZANTINES ALSO SERVED EGGS AS A FINALE TO THE MEAL. ONE OF THEIR DISHES REMAINS ON THE GREEK BILL OF FARE AS A SWEET.

A later Byzantine dish, called *feta*, however, makes a fine Hellenic-style American breakfast or, better yet, brunch entree. The bread and egg preparation mimics French toast (the Italian word *feta* probably first referred to a slice of bread). Made the Greek way, though, the syrup consists of sugar and honey spiced with cinnamon, cloves, and lemon juice. To me, the spice-laden Greek-style syrup makes the otherwise humble combination so notable and different that oared ships, colorful markets, and caravans bearing bolts of brilliant silk come to mind.

*FOR THE SYRUP*
*1 cup water*
*1/2 cup sugar*
*1/2 cup aromatic honey, such as*
  *Hymettus (see page 501)*
*1 piece (2 inches) cinnamon stick*
*2 whole cloves*
*1 tablespoon fresh lemon juice*

*FOR THE FETA*
*4 large eggs*
*2 tablespoons water*
*Pinch of salt*
*6 slices (1/2-inch-thick) Country*
  *or City Bread (pages 121 to 124)*
  *or other good bread*
*3 tablespoons butter*

1 Mix all the syrup ingredients together in a small saucepan and bring to a boil over medium-high heat. Reduce the heat and simmer until the mixture has thickened into a syrup that coats a spoon, about 12 minutes. Keep warm.

2 Beat the eggs, the 2 tablespoons water, and the salt together in a small bowl. Pour the egg mixture into a shallow dish. Place the bread in the egg mixture and let it soak, turning once, until saturated, about 3 minutes.

3 Melt the butter in a large frying pan over medium heat until it begins to bubble. Slide in as many bread slices as will fit in a single layer (this may take two batches), along with any egg mixture not soaked up. Fry, turning once, until brown on both sides, 2 to 3 minutes per side.

4 Transfer the slices to a plate, pour the syrup mixture over the top, and serve.

**NOTE:** *Petimezi* (page 500) provides a specially sweet and fruity Greek sauce as an alternative to the honey. However, to my mind, the best way to serve egg-coated fried bread is to spread it with a spoon sweet (pages 535 to 547).

# THE GREEK DIASPORA AND THE DENVER OMELET

GREW UP IN DENVER, AND EVEN IN THOSE LONG-AGO DAYS, THE TOWN HELD A QUITE SIZABLE GREEK COMMUNITY. HOW ODD, ONE MIGHT THINK, TO FIND GREEKS LIVING IN SUCH AN ISOLATED, INLAND, COWBOY CAPITAL.

war, conquest, or massacre, but other circumstances can make a population blow like leaves across the planet. Greeks have, in fact, experienced three diasporas.

But it wasn't odd at all. As a gateway to the Rockies and the west, Denver has always been a bustling business center. Since frontier times, out of Denver have moved wagons and railroad trains loaded with every sort of trade good. Into Denver came gold, silver, and other ores, coal, and oil. And pretty much wherever a mercantile center thrives around the world, there live Greeks.

## AWAY FROM THEIR HOMELAND

Most are representative of the Greek diaspora, the spreading of the people away from their homeland— an experience common to many groups. The word "diaspora" is Greek. It means the "passing through" or "separating" (*dia*) of the "seed" (*spora*). Usually the dispersed souls are driven out by

In ancient days, as Greek communities grew too large for their surrounding environments to support them, they would send out settlers to start a colony. As early as 800 B.C.E., Greeks emigrated to Sicily and southern Italy, to Spain and France, to the Sudan, North Africa, Anatolia, and the shores of the Black Sea.

The colony maintained strong ties to the "metropolis," the mother city, in terms of continued loyalty, military support, and trade.

## Greek culture is one of emboriko, the "emporium," of trade and exchange.

After the fall of Byzantium, many Greeks of the empire, particularly the more educated, fled before the oncoming Ottomans into Italy and northern Europe. Some, to escape the Ottoman overlords, emigrated. All, as before, maintained ties to the homeland, and held strongly to Greek customs, religion, and identity.

Within the last hundred years, Greeks have undergone a third diaspora, this time spurred by poverty. Even as Greeks reestablished their nation after 1822, many found themselves forced to leave. Greece has no strong rivers to drive machinery, no mother-lodes of ore to fuel an industrial base. The soil is scratch-thin poor and the climate arid. Many can live on the land, but not necessarily live well. Seeking a better life, thousands of Greeks drifted away. In the twentieth century, with its wars and upheavals, the wave of those leaving became almost tidal.

Few of the emigrants sought a rural life or farming again. Only occasionally—as in central and northern California—did they plant orchards and vineyards. More often, they sought to follow another great Greek cultural tradition: to begin a business of their own. Greek culture is one of *emboriko,* the "emporium," of trade and exchange. Greeks covet the independence of being store owners. They identify some needed product and contrive ways to sell to customers. Following that mind-set, Greeks settling around the world targeted the commercial centers: New York, Boston, Toronto, Ontario, London, Paris, Munich, Sydney, Alexandria, Johannesburg, Melbourne, Singapore, Buenos Aires, Mexico City, and countless smaller mercantile cities.

Today Greeks flourish on every continent and keep to their native customs and maintain their identity. Greeks educate children in Greek, attend Greek churches, and journey to Greece as often as possible.

By and large the oldest sons were the first to depart. They sent money home to provide doweries for their sisters, educate their brothers, and support their parents. Cousins and nephews followed. With frugal living and hard work, they amassed enough to open a small business. Very often that business was a restaurant. Modest restaurants of home-style cooking require little capital, little special training. Everyone must eat, so potential customers are plentiful, and Greeks, like other groups, believe their food is irresistibly good and that all their mothers are great cooks. Besides, a restaurant can be family run: no strangers necessary. And so Greek eateries sprout wherever Greeks reside.

## THE EPONYMOUS OMELET

My father, who grew up in Denver long enough ago to have been a supernumerary in Buffalo Bill's Wild West Show, all his life nurtured fond memories of the Greek diners he had known as a boy. He remembered that the diners served omelets chock-full of tomatoes, onions, and green peppers, quite unlike any egg mixture to be had in his home or in other restaurants. Somehow they gained the appellation "Denver Omelet." Perhaps they were Denver's, but more so they were Greek, a dish of the Greek diaspora.

# sustaining grain

## BARLEY, WHEAT, RICE & NOODLES

**S**ITON—PLATES HEAPED HIGH WITH GRAINS UPON WHICH TASTY BITS OF VEGETABLES, FISH, AND MEAT WERE STREWN—WAS THE PARAMOUNT MEAL OF ANCIENT GREECE. IF IT SOUNDS A LOT LIKE PILAF, AND RESEMBLES THE WAY WE SERVE PASTA, IT ONLY GOES TO PROVE A PAIR OF OLD CLICHES: "THERE'S NOT MUCH NEW UNDER THE STARS"

A man who has not put away a year's food, including Demeter's grain, has little interest in quarrels and courtrooms.

—HESIOD, "WORKS AND DAYS,"
EIGHTH CENTURY B.C.E.

and "The more things change, the more they stay the same." If the things under the stars and lingering on are delicious, the truisms can only be good things.

In ancient times, grains, the fruits of Demeter, were considered to be the element that separated men from wild animals. Philosophers praised grains as being healthy, humble, and the basis of happiness. In contemporary times the quantity of robust grains in the Greek diet has been lauded as one of the reasons for the population's good health and low rate of heart disease.

At first, like other early agriculturalists, the Greeks ate their grains—barley, some millet, and wheat—in the form of simple porridges and gruels. Later they learned to manufacture bread from crushed kernels and to dry a mix of ground seed and water into what became the noodle. Bread holds grain's first place in the diet today, but grain seed and meal also appear under, next to, or mixed with other foods and in stuffings for poultry, vegetables, and leaves. As for noodles, they muster together in dishes ranging from the liquid to the firm. Noodles appear in soups, on plates, even make their way into pies.

The grains of yesterday still play a part in Greek cuisine. Barley, the grain that swirled most often in ancient Greek porridge, now pops up only sporadically. As cracked bulgur and soft semolina, wheat also makes rarer appearances than in times past. The ancient Greeks knew of rice, but its cultivation started only in the early part of

the twentieth century and its use was rare. Now its use has expanded enormously. Rice sops up flavors and sates appetites from Epiros to Crete.

As for our favorite grain, corn, it's no joke to most Greeks. Though the Italians when first introduced to cornmeal turned the grain into polenta, Greeks more or less eschew the johnny-come-lately New World grain. There are two reasons. The first importers of cornmeal to Greece brought the grain with the intention of peddling it as a new and inexpensive animal feed, not human food, and so Greeks initially became acquainted with corn as animal provender. When Greeks did turn to corn as human food, it was in association with two factors they would just as soon forget, poverty and war, and the terrible starvation both wreaked upon them. Peddlers roast sweet corn on braziers on city street corners and those singed ears are considered a treat. Here and there Greek bakers make wonderful crunchy corn breads. But for most, corn breads or corn gruels comprised the only food available during long hardships. Corn may taste good, but it smacks of bitterness. It holds little favor in Greek opinion and is rarely on any Greek menu.

*In Greece, where life-sustaining foods ripen only once a year, deities like Demeter who protect the harvest are of critical importance.*

# barley pancakes

### MAKES 24 CAKES

ARISTOTLE CLAIMED THAT BARLEY WAS THE OLDEST CEREAL, AND IT CERTAINLY WAS THE GRAIN MOST REVERED AND GLORIFIED IN ANCIENT GREEK SACRIFICES. EVERY ATHENIAN BRIDE WAS REQUIRED BY LAW TO TAKE TO HER WEDDING A BARLEY ROASTER, CALLED A *PHRYGETRON*, BOTH TO FEED HER NEW FAMILY AND TO MAKE OBLATION. ALTHOUGH IN LATER TIMES THE MAJOR GODS SEEMED TO HAVE THEIR HEADS TURNED BY FANCIER GIFTS, THE MINOR GODS, LOCAL SPIRITS, AND PAN AND DEMETER NEVER CEASED TO APPRECIATE HUMBLE BARLEY CAKES.

Those cakes were made by soaking barley kernels in water, draining them, and leaving them to dry overnight. The next day they were roasted, then ground into meal. The meal was then soaked in olive oil and patted into cakes that were cooked on griddles and served on laurel leaves. A modern-day version is less labor-intensive but no less pleasing to gods and mortals.

6 cups cooked pearl barley
   (recipe follows)
3 scallions, white and light green
   parts trimmed and finely
   chopped
4 large eggs, lightly beaten
1 cup unbleached all-purpose flour
2 teaspoons salt
Olive oil, for frying

1 Mix the barley, scallions, eggs, flour, and salt together in a large bowl. Knead the mixture until the barley is somewhat mashed and the mixture is quite sticky. Cover and set aside in the refrigerator for at least 30 minutes or as long as several hours.

2 With moist hands, form the barley mixture into 24 pancakes, each about 3 inches in diameter and 1/4 inch thick.

3 Pour oil to a depth of 1/8 inch into a large skillet over medium-high heat. Place as many pancakes as will fit in one uncrowded layer in the skillet and fry them, turning once, until golden and crisp

## WHERE TO GO FOR BARLEY

·············

First I shall recall the gifts of fair-
   haired Demeter to humankind,
   friend Moschus: Take them to
   your heart.
The best one can get, the best of all,
of rich barley, all cleanly hulled from
   fine ripe ears,
comes from the wave-washed breast
   of Eresos on Lesbos,
whiter than snow from the sky.
   If the gods eat barley-meal,
then Hermes must go there and
   buy it for them!
There is satisfactory barley-meal in
   seven-gated Thebes,
and in Thasos and some other cities,
   but theirs are grape-stones
compared to those of Lesbos.
Understand this clearly!
   —ATHENAEUS,
   **SECOND CENTURY** B.C.E.

on both sides, 2 to 3 minutes per side. Transfer them to a serving platter and repeat with another batch until all the pancakes are cooked. Serve as soon as possible.

**NOTE:** Though hot-off-the-fire is best for barley cakes if you like them crisp, for large gatherings they will hold at room temperature for a short time without any sacrifice of flavor.

## BILLY GROATS GRUEL

In the second century B.C.E., the poet Nicander of Colophon wrote down the recipe for his favorite barley pudding: "Boil a small amount of goat kid or capon. In a mortar, pound two or three handfuls of barley groats until it becomes fine meal. Mix in a little olive oil. Remove the meat from the boiling broth and pour in the barley meal. Cover the pot and let the groats swell. When the gruel has cooled, eat it using hollow pieces of bread as a spoon."

# PEARL BARLEY

### MAKES ABOUT 6 CUPS

Though barley puddings were a daily food in ancient times, they now appear only in grandmothers' kitchens or remote villages. The few I have had make me rue the loss and so I still include the nourishing kernels in much of my Greek cooking. The qualities that plumped barley delivers to a dish evoke for me antiquity, nourishment, satisfaction, honesty, fruitfulness, sun. The pearls can be used in pancakes, puddings, and pilafs, combined with other grains, or served solo. Echoing ancient times, however, whole boiled barley is also still offered at services honoring the deceased (see page 559).

*With accordion, fiddle, and* laouto *in hand, three village musicians play for a wedding party.*

*1 heaping cup pearl barley*
*9 cups water*
*1 teaspoon salt*

Place the barley in a colander and wash it well under cold running water. Shake it dry and transfer it to a medium-size saucepan. Add the water and salt and bring to a boil. Reduce the heat and simmer, uncovered, for 45 to 50 minutes, until the grains are soft and beginning to open. Drain, rinse, and use right away; or cover and refrigerate for up to several days.

# Two essential pilafs

THOUGH POTATOES HAVE USURPED SOME OF THE PLACE GRAINS ONCE HAD, THERE'S NO DOUBT THAT MODERN GREEKS STILL EAT *SITON* IN THE FORM OF PILAFS, OR *PILAFIA*. SOME OF THESE ARE ON THE MOIST SIDE, IN ESSENCE MIXTURES OF GRAIN AND LIQUID INVOLVING SPINACH, GREENS, LEEKS, SNAILS, POULTRY, OR NUTS. OTHERS ARE PLAIN FLUFFS OF CARBOHYDRATE OFFERED AS A COMPLEMENT TO MEAT AND POULTRY.

The two grains usually cooked into stirs and pilafs are wheat—in the form of *pligouri,* or bulgur—and *rizi,* rice. Occasionally pearl barley sits beneath a roast, shows up in a vegetable mix, or becomes part of a pancake (page 229). Bulgur pilaf appears most commonly in northern Greece, rice virtually everywhere across the nation.

## BULGUR PILAF

### SERVES 4

*2 tablespoons olive oil*
*1 cup medium or coarse ground bulgur*
*1/2 medium onion, finely chopped*
*1 1/2 cups Chicken Stock (page 170) or meat, or vegetable stock, or a mixture of 1 1/2 cups water and 1 1/2 tablespoons tomato paste (see Note, page 232)*
*Salt and freshly ground black pepper*

1 Heat the oil in a medium-size skillet over medium-high heat. Add the bulgur and onion and sauté until both are translucent, about 5 minutes.

2 Stir in the stock, bring it to a boil, then reduce the heat and cover the pan. Simmer until the bulgur is just tender and all the liquid is absorbed, 20 to 25 minutes. Add salt and pepper to taste, then cover and let sit for 5 minutes. Fluff with a fork and serve.

**NOTE:** If you wish to increase the quantity, just remember that you need 1 1/2 times as much liquid as bulgur. Be sure also to increase the amount of olive oil and onion as you increase the bulgur and stock.

## RICE PILAF

### SERVES 4

*2 tablespoons olive oil*
*1 cup white rice, preferably Arborio or other short-grain rice (see Note, page 238)*
*1/2 medium onion, finely chopped*
*1 1/4 cups water, stock, or a mixture of 1 1/4 cups water and 1 heaping tablespoon tomato paste (see Notes, page 232)*
*Salt and freshly ground black pepper*
*Pinch of ground nutmeg, preferably freshly grated (optional)*
*1 tablespoon finely chopped fresh parsley leaves (optional)*

1 Heat the oil in a medium-size skillet over medium-high heat. Add the rice and onion and sauté until both are translucent, about 5 minutes.

2 Stir in the water, bring to a boil, then reduce the heat to low and cover the pan. Simmer until the rice is just done, 20 minutes. Add salt and pepper to taste, and the nutmeg, if using. Sprinkle with the parsley, if desired. Fluff with a fork and serve.

## NOTES:

■ Not caring much for the flavor of plain water, a Greek cook who does not have stock on hand will usually flavor the water with tomato paste: about 1 tablespoon tomato paste to 1 cup water. This can be used for bulgur pilaf as well.

■ As with bulgur pilaf, the quantity can easily be doubled, tripled, or more: Use 1¼ times as much liquid as rice. Be sure to increase the amount of olive oil and onion as you increase the rice and liquid.

# steamed rice

## GREEK-STYLE

### SERVES 4

MOST OFTEN THE RICE IN GREECE IS COOKED LIKE BULGUR: SAUTÉED IN OIL, THEN SIMMERED UNTIL TENDER. OCCASIONALLY, HOWEVER, RICE IS STEAMED. EVEN SO, IT IS NEVER LEFT JUST STARCHLY PLAIN BUT IS FLUFFED AND OILED UNTIL EACH GRAIN HAS A DEPTH OF FLAVOR.

2 cups water
1 cup rice, preferably Arborio or
    other short-grain rice
    (see Note, page 238)
Salt and freshly ground black pepper
2 tablespoons olive oil

1 Place the water and rice in a small saucepan and bring to a boil over high heat.

2 Reduce the heat to very low and cover the pan. Let simmer without lifting the lid for 17 to 20 minutes, until the rice is just done.

3 Remove the pan from the heat and add salt and pepper to taste. Then add the oil and fluff with a fork until the grains are slightly oiled and nicely separated. Serve immediately.

## KYKEON— THE ANCIENT GRUEL

The word for "gruel" or "porridge" in ancient Greek, kykeon, seems to have also meant "to thicken" or "churn," as one would churn milk to make butter. The porridges were light, something between a thick drink and a runny pudding, and often contained combinations we would consider conflicting—onion and honey, cheese and sweet wine, or all these. Gruels were also dotted with fresh or smoked fish, vegetables, garlic, and legumes, and they were sauced, particularly with a fermented fish sauce called garos.

Kykeons are referred to so often in early literature that clearly they were as common as our mashed potatoes.

# bulgur wheat and walnut pilaf

**SERVES 4 TO 6**

WHEAT, ONE OF THE TWO CROPS THAT MADE POSSIBLE THE FIRST AGRICULTURAL SETTLEMENTS IN GREECE, HAS HAD SO LONG A HISTORY IN THAT LAND THAT ITS USES ARE LEGION. BULGUR, WHICH THE GREEKS CALL *PLIGOURI*, IS WHEAT KERNELS THAT ARE SATURATED WITH STEAM UNTIL PLUMP, BAKED DRY, AND THEN GROUND INTO CHUNKS. THE CHUNKS RANGE FROM FINE TO MEDIUM TO COARSE, BUT EVEN FINE-GRAIN BULGAR IS PEBBLY. BECAUSE BULGUR HAS ALREADY BEEN PROCESSED, IT REABSORBS LIQUID—WATER, BROTH, WINE— READILY AND COOKS RAPIDLY.

The process of making bulgur is now usually a commercial endeavor, but I can envision centuries of Greek homemakers soaking their wheat, spreading it out in the sun until dry and bronze colored, then grinding it between two round grinding stones. Here the wheaty chunks are joined by other time-honored ingredients: walnuts, onion, butter, and the lush oil of the olive. The dish conjures up the simple sowing, reaping, and gathering of life on terra firma and blends with almost any other food.

*1 1/2 tablespoons olive oil*
*1 tablespoon butter*
*1 medium onion, finely chopped*
*1/2 cup chopped walnuts*
*1 cup medium or coarse ground bulgur*
*1/2 cup dry white wine*
*1 cup water*
*1 bay leaf*
*1/4 teaspoon salt*

1 Heat the oil and butter in a medium-size saucepan over medium heat until the butter melts. Stir in the onion and walnuts and sauté until the onion wilts, about 3 minutes.

2 Add the bulgur and stir to coat. Then add wine, water, bay leaf, and salt. Bring to a boil, reduce the heat to low, and cover the pan. Cook until the bulgur is just tender and all the liquid is absorbed, 20 to 25 minutes. Stir, cover again, and set aside for 5 minutes. Remove the bay leaf, fluff with a fork, and serve.

# AN ISLAND HARVEST

**F**EW WHO STUDY A SECOND LANGUAGE HAVE A VOCABULARY THAT INCLUDES SUCH WORDS AS "SICKLE," "DONKEY SADDLE," "PLOW," "MULE TEAM," "REAP," "THRESH," AND "WINNOW." IN MY VILLAGE LIFE IN GREECE, I ENDED UP LEARNING NOT ONLY THESE GOLDEN KERNELS OF GREEK LANGUAGE BUT ALSO THE CORRESPONDING ACTIVITIES. DURING HARVEST IN THE GREEK COUNTRYSIDE, WOMEN WORK IN THE FIELDS AS MUCH AS MEN, AND WHEN I AM IN THE VILLAGE, I OFFER MY PAIR OF HANDS ALONG WITH EVERYONE ELSE.

It is not a lightweight offer. As in much of Greece, the fields on the island where I live are small parcels tiered into the hillside and separated by rock walls, so bringing in the grain must be done by hand. Yet harvesting in this fashion is truly halcyonic, as tranquil and idyllic as only an activity as ageless as time itself can be.

## A MID-JUNE HARVEST

Harvest starts when the shafts of grain have turned the color of toast and are straw-dry, about mid-June. I know the steps for reaping barley best, because barley remains the only grain that is hardy enough to grow on the arid and often chilly islands. We harvest by cutting away with hand sickles, a chore that truly merits the description "backbreaking." With sickles we can sever the sun-baked stalks as close to the ground as possible. We leave carefully arranged handfuls of the shafts upon the stubble trailing behind us. The next day or so, we return to gather the shafts into stacks just high and wide enough to make a double armload.

## ON THE THRESHING FLOOR

The stacks lie atop stubbled fields for days, drying in the sun, until the day arrives to start the threshing. Armload by armload and donkey load by donkey load, we haul the wizened, scratchy blades to the threshing floor. All across Greece, every few fields or so, lie curious circular depressions paved with stone. These are threshing floors. Their design—and probably many of the actual floors—is as ancient as the Bronze Age. You can thresh by trampling grain, but praise be to Demeter, we no longer do so. We use a mule team.

As no farmer has the four animals required to span the radius of the threshing circle, much borrowing and lending takes place until each man procures the team needed to crush the stalks. As the sun rises, every family member dons his or her oldest clothing, for nothing raises cyclones of straw and dust like threshing. We will be combing straw from our hair and washing grime from our faces for days. Women who never wear pants borrow trousers from husbands. Scarves appear from hidden repositories. Even men veil face and head. As the four animals circle hour after hour, driven by snaps from a long whip, they drag a flat crushing device behind them. We throw the stacks of grain stalks under the feet of the circling animals. Slowly all the stalks get trampled, their kernels knocked to the floor, the stripped shafts pushed to the rim of the threshing floor. By the armload we again gather up the crushed shafts to use as precious animal fodder. The fallen kernels we heap into a towering pile to await the next step, winnowing.

## WAITING FOR THE WIND

Winnowing needs the wind. We wait for a day when the breezes sharply billow. Then it's off to the floors again, now for work that breaks our arms, not our backs. Equipped with large, flat forks, we scoop up the kernels of grain and toss them into the air, relying upon gusts and gravity to do their work. The thin shell-like skin that protects the precious inner kernel of the grain, the chaff, is light, but the rich, oily inner kernel is heavy. By tossing the kernels into the wind, the chaff flutters away with the breeze while the kernel drops like a stone. We toss scoop after scoop toward the sky. We have accomplished the proverbial: We have separated the chaff from the grain.

This is why, despite its seeming uselessness in today's modern world, I prize my antiquated vocabulary. Together with other anachronisms, such as "knit" and "embroider," my harvest words shine like badges of my Greek life. I may falter linguistically when discussing urbane topics—gross national product, political coalition, and the like—but who among my Athenian friends has reaped, threshed, and winnowed?

# bulgur and vegetable pilaf

## WITH HERBS AND WHITE WINE

### SERVES 6

A FRUGAL, FILLING PILAF OF GRAIN AND VEGETABLE HEEDS AN OLD GREEK CREDO: EXTEND YOUR FOOD AS BEST YOU CAN. USE IT SLOWLY YET NOURISHINGLY, CAUTIOUSLY YET DAZZLINGLY, AND YOU WILL NEVER WANT FOR A MEAL NOR SUFFER LACK OF FLAVOR. THE HOMESPUN BUT BOUNTEOUS PILAF IS THE EPITOME OF PEASANT FOOD, WHICH IS WHY I LOVE IT SO. THE SPLASH OF WINE GIVES THE MIXTURE EXTRA VIVACITY.

*1/4 cup olive oil*

*1 small onion, coarsely chopped*

*3 cloves garlic, coarsely chopped*

*1 cup medium or coarse ground bulgur*

*1 to 1 1/2 cups mixture of 3 or 4 vegetables, such as coarsely chopped zucchini, coarsely chopped crookneck squash, coarsely chopped red or green bell pepper, cauliflower florets, cooked broad (fava) beans, chopped artichoke bottoms, cooked chickpeas*

*1 1/4 cups Chicken Stock (page 170) or vegetable stock*

*2 medium tomatoes, or 4 plum tomatoes, coarsely chopped*

*1/4 cup dry white wine*

*1 teaspoon fresh oregano leaves, or 1/2 teaspoon dried*

*1/2 teaspoon salt*

*1/4 teaspoon freshly ground black pepper*

*1 tablespoon chopped fresh dill*

1 Heat the oil in a large non-reactive skillet over medium-high heat. Add the onion, garlic, bulgur, and vegetable mixture and sauté until the bulgur is translucent and the vegetables are wilted, about 10 minutes.

2 Stir in the stock, tomatoes, wine, oregano, and salt and pepper and bring to a boil. Reduce the heat, cover the skillet, and simmer until the bulgur is just tender and all the liquid has been absorbed, 20 to 25 minutes. Remove from the heat and stir in the dill. Cover and set aside for 5 minutes. Fluff with a fork and serve right away.

**NOTE:** Other fresh herbs can be substituted for the dill: Use 2 tablespoons slivered basil leaves, or 1 teaspoon chopped savory leaves, or 1/2 teaspoon chopped tarragon leaves.

*Vegetables fresh from the fields, some of which will join bulgur or rice in a succulent pilaf.*

# THE SIN OF OPSOPHAGIA

**T**HE ANCIENT GREEKS ENJOYED THEIR REPASTS IN TWO SETS OF COURSES: THE FIRST COURSE, IDENTIFIED AS THE DINNER, OR *DEIPNON* (THE WORD IS STILL USED IN MODERN GREEK), AND A SECOND COURSE CALLED THE *SYMPOSION*, OR DRINKING COURSE. DINERS MANAGED BOTH WHILE RECLINING ON COUCHES. AS PART OF THE FIRST COURSE, BREAD AND SMALL DISHES WITH STRONG FLAVORS, LIKE OUR PRESENT-DAY APPETIZERS, WERE SERVED. THEY WERE FOLLOWED BY A SERIES OF MAIN DISHES, WHICH CONSTITUTED THE CORE OF THE REPAST.

The second course saw an entirely different set of foods, much like our desserts—dried fruits, nuts, cheese, cakes, and sweetmeats—served along with *poton*, much wine. The plates of both courses reflected a crucial distinction between edibles: Of primary importance were foodstuffs based on grain. They were called the *sitos*—the word for "cereal" and also "wheat"—and included gruels and breads based on both wheat and barley. The *sitos* was the central food of the meal, the staple. More flavorful elements, added to perk up the *sitos,* were called the *opsa* and ranged from fish and meat, to salads of bitter herbs, to cheese and onions.

## EVERYTHING IN MODERATION

Greeks had strong ideas about what comprised proper eating. People were supposed to eat mostly *sitos*. Greedy people might eat too much *sitos*, but what was truly wasteful, sinful, and thoroughly ostentatious was to eat too much *opsa*. It was particularly bad to tuck away too much fish, which was highly prized. The discussion of what was *sitos* and what was *opsos*, and how much of either was acceptable, raged in philosophical discussion. Since the ancient Greeks were concerned with the perfection of society, what people ate and in what quantity—some sages envisioned a golden age almost thoroughly vegetarian—was of overriding concern. Just where did the sin of *opsophagia*, eating too much of the goodies, begin, and what were the consequences?

## UTOPIAN MEALS

What exactly constituted a perfect meal, and what was frivolous embellishment? Socrates himself participated in the argument as part of his musing over utopia, and his concern was amusingly detailed. As described by Plato, Socrates one day blithely outlined the perfect human existence. In utopia, he said, people would produce *sitos*, wine, clothes, and shoes, and would feast on gruels laid out on rushes while reclining on couches of myrtle and moss, drinking, wearing garlands, and singing. In the midst of his fancy, though, Socrates' friend Glaukon interrupted, saying that Socrates was making these unfortunate people dine without *opsos*.

Of course, corrected Socrates, they would have *opsos*, too: salt and oil and cheese and vegetables. At which Glaukon, outraged, declared that Socrates was now describing a city of uncivilized pigs. Actually Glaukon was criticizing Socrates for not giving the people fine enough *opsos*, to which Socrates replied that Glaukon wrongly thought that utopia should be luxurious.

*A full clay crock of* makaronada *and a liter of barrel wine to the side, join other dishes on the dinner table.*

On another occasion Socrates sent spies out to see if certain persons in his acquaintance might be overdoing on *opsos*. Were they treating their *sitos* as *opsos* or their *opsos* as *sitos*? Were they secretly indulging in *opsophagia?* To do so was a reprehensible vice. In particular, politicians were scrutinized for the offense. One Aischines labeled one Timarchos a revolutionary, for he squandered a large inheritance with the most awful of sins, *opsophagia:* expensive dinner parties, flute-girls, courtesans, dice, and other pleasures, all those things a free and noble man should not let overwhelm him.

## *SITOS* AND *OPSOS* TODAY

Bulgur and Vegetable Pilaf (page 235) and Grilled Squab over Bulgur and Walnut Pilaf (page 449) are, I think, properly utopian meals that Socrates, Aischines, and even Glaukon would approve of— a sprinkling of garden produce or a rather petite bird bedded on a heap of worthy grain. In general, though, I fear the citizens of my time, myself included, have declined into malfeasant behavior. We are quite unabashed lovers of the tasty and expensive bit over the gruel of grain. We are flagrant *opsophagians*.

# rice and lentil Pilaf

## CYPRUS-STYLE

### SERVES 6

MANY OF THE REGIONS WHERE ALEXANDER THE GREAT TROD, WHERE LATER THE BYZANTINES EXPANDED, AND EVENTUALLY THE OTTOMAN PASHA PRESIDED, HAD TWO STAPLE FOODS: RICE AND LENTILS. IN THOSE LANDS, THE TWO MAINSTAYS WERE FREQUENTLY MIXED TOGETHER, AND THE COMBINATION STILL TURNS UP. OFTEN THE SCRAMBLE IS TOPPED WITH A VEGETABLE THAT WAS PREVALENT EVEN IN HERODOTUS'S DAY—THE HUMBLE ONION. WHEN FRIED CRISP, IT ADDS AN ALLURING SWEETNESS TO THE MIXTURE.

I add to the congenial trio another accent from its native turf: fresh coriander, usually called cilantro. Though fresh coriander was used aplenty in the past, Greeks—except on Cyprus—use it rarely now. But with a sprinkling of vinegar on the leaves, the herb turns the age-old pairing from humdrum to drumroll.

*1/4 cup olive oil*

*3 medium onions, cut in half and then into 1/4-inch-thick slices*

*1 cup (6 ounces) lentils*

*1 cup rice, preferably Arborio or other short-grain rice*

*2 cups water*

*1 teaspoon salt*

*1/4 teaspoon freshly ground black pepper*

*1/2 cup fresh cilantro leaves tossed with 1/2 teaspoon red wine vinegar*

1 Heat the oil in a large nonre-active pot or skillet over medium heat. Add the onions, stir to coat with the oil, and sauté, stirring occasionally, until well browned, 10 minutes. Remove from the heat and set aside.

2 While the onions are cooking, place the lentils in a medium-size saucepan and cover with water by 1½ inches. Bring to a boil, then reduce the heat and simmer briskly until the lentils are tender but not collapsing, 20 minutes. Drain and set aside.

## SHORT-GRAIN RICE

Strangely, the rice that ultimately gained hold in Greece and throughout much of the Mediterranean was not the long-grain rice of India and Persia, as one would expect, but rather the shorter-grain rice of far Asia. Italians developed super-absorbent Arborio rice from the Mediterranean short-grain rice, and because Greek foods employ rice much as Italian foods do—to absorb flavorful stocks and juices and to provide pillowing for succulent morsels like shrimp and snails, currants, and pine nuts—most modern Greek dishes benefit greatly from the use of Arborio rice. Lacking Arborio, it's best to use another short- or medium-grain rice, but if necessary, long-grain rice, which has become more available and more widely used in Greece, can be substituted. Arborio cooks creamier than regular short-grain rice and is done in a shorter time; long-grain rice needs a few more minutes than short; so if you are using other varieties of rice, you may need to slightly lengthen the cooking time.

3 Remove half of the onions from the skillet and set aside. Place the rice, the 2 cups water, salt, pepper, and the remaining onions in a medium-size saucepan. Bring to a boil. Reduce the heat to the barest simmer, cover the pan, and cook until almost dry, about 20 minutes.

4 Gently stir in the lentils, cover the pot again, and set aside off the heat to steam dry for 10 minutes.

5 Top the pilaf with the remaining onions, garnish with the vinegared cilantro, and serve right away.

# spinach pilaf

## SPANAKORIZO

### SERVES 6

RATHER THAN SERVING A HILL OF PLAIN RICE SITTING NEXT TO A SCOOP OF UNADORNED GREENS, MEAT, POULTRY, OR GAME, GREEKS OFTEN MIX THE TWO TOGETHER. IN THIS WAY THE TWO ENLIVEN ONE ANOTHER. SUCH A MIXTURE INVITES FURTHER FLAVORING WITH HERBS AND SPICES. ALMOST ALL GREEK PILAF MERGERS ARE MADE IN THE SAME WAY. SPINACH RICE IS THE *PARADIGM*, THE GREEK WORD FOR "EXAMPLE." THE CHOICE OF INGREDIENTS TO MIX WITH THE RICE IS YOURS.

3 tablespoons olive oil

1 medium onion, or the white part of 3 leeks, finely chopped

1 cup rice, preferably Arborio or other short-grain rice

1 cup chopped tomatoes with their juices (about 2 medium-size tomatoes)

3 pounds fresh spinach, well rinsed, trimmed, and torn into large pieces

1/2 to 3/4 cup water

2 tablespoons chopped fresh dill

2 tablespoons chopped fresh mint leaves

2 tablespoons chopped fresh flat-leaf parsley leaves

1 teaspoon finely chopped lemon zest

3 tablespoons fresh lemon juice

Pinch of ground nutmeg, preferably freshly grated

1 teaspoon salt

1/2 teaspoon freshly ground black pepper

1 Heat the oil in a large skillet over medium heat. Add the onion and rice and stir until both are translucent, about 7 minutes.

2 Stir in the tomatoes, spinach, and 1/2 cup water. Cover, reduce the heat, and cook until the rice is soft and the liquid has been absorbed, about 12 minutes. Add more water if the liquid is absorbed before the rice is cooked.

3 Stir in the remaining ingredients and remove from the heat. Fluff with a fork and serve.

## VARIATION:

**Rice Pilaf with Shrimp, Squid, or Snails:** To make a seafood or snail pilaf, instead of the spinach use 1 cup raw small shrimp, 1 cup cleaned squid cut into rings, or 2 cups canned snails. Cook the rice as described, stirring in the tomatoes and water as described in Step 2. Stir in the shrimp during the last 3 minutes, or the squid during the last 5 minutes of cooking time. If using snails, add them to the skillet with the onion and rice.

# SAFFRON

GREEKS HAVE LONG VALUED SAFFRON FOR ITS THREEFOLD OFFERINGS— FLAVOR, AROMA, AND COLOR. ZEUS IS SAID TO HAVE SLEPT ON A BED OF IT. PERHAPS HE CONSIDERED THE SPICE AN APHRODISIAC, FOR HIS BED WAS CERTAINLY LUSTFULLY USED. BEFORE HE CAME TO STRETCH OUT ON THAT YELLOW COUCH, A FAMOUS MINOAN FRESCO SHOWS WOMEN GATHERING SAFFRON CROCUS. THE *HETAERAE* (COURTESANS) REVERED SAFFRON AS PERFUME AND USED IT IN POTIONS. HOMER SPEAKS OF THE SPICE, AS DOES HIPPOCRATES.

*Following a tradition that goes back four millennia, a young woman gathers saffron crocuses.*

Happily for the Greeks, the flower that produces saffron, the crocus (*krokos*)—which means "egg yolk"—comes from their own hills, as well as those of Asia Minor. Two Greek myths speak of the flower and the spice's origin. In one, Crocus is the name of a beautiful youth whom Hermes loves but accidentally kills. Where the lad's blood runs into the earth, the first crocus flower springs up. In the other, a youth named Crocus so loves the nymph Smilax that the two refuse to part one another's company nor to cease their billing and cooing. The gods, tired— and perhaps jealous—of their endless courtship, separate them forever. They change Smilax into a vine and Crocus into a flower.

## A POPULAR SPICE IN ANCIENT TIMES

Many were the dishes the ancestral Greeks sprinkled and spiced with saffron. They served brilliant saffron-colored breads with the wine course after the main meal. They also used the golden spice in fish stews. The French use of saffron in their famous *bouillabaisse* very likely comes from the Greek colony at Marseilles and the fish stew that employed the spice, *kakavia* (page 180).

## MITHRIDATES' MEDICINE

Saffron was also believed to be a palliative for many ills and was taken as an antidote for venom. Mithridates, the tyrant of the Pontos, was so afraid of being poisoned that every day he drank an elixir of saffron dissolved in honey. Greeks also wove the crocus blossom into floral diadems as a way to add the sheen of gold to honorific halos when real gold was too pricy.

*With years of experience and still-nimble fingers, an older woman separates saffron threads from crocus petals.*

## SAFFRON IN GREECE TODAY

Today the native crocus and its vibrant stamen is used less in Greek cooking, although at times cooks still sprinkle the glorious golden threads into certain dishes. For one, as in ages past, they utilize the spice to give special breads a topaz hue. When Greeks do use the spice, they prefer to gather it from the wild crocuses that continue to dot the fields and poke out from rocky hideaways, rather than purchase it. Even in Greece saffron is expensive. Saffron crocuses bloom for only two weeks in the autumn. The flowers must be picked early in the day, before the sun warms them. Pickers then separate the stigmas and styles. It takes nine flowers to make one grain of the spice; a day's gathering procures perhaps 1/4 cup. It takes only a dash, though, to turn an ordinary pilaf an incandescent ocher.

# rice and noodle pilaf

## WITH ARTICHOKES, PINE NUTS, AND SAFFRON

### SERVES 6

PILAFS OF RICE WITH SPINACH, LEEKS, SNAILS, SHRIMP, AND OCTOPUS ARE CLASSICS IN THE GREEK PARADE OF FOOD. BUT WITH THE ABUNDANCE OF GREEK INGREDIENTS, THE PILAF IDEA CAN BE TAKEN FURTHER, TO CAULIFLOWER, ZUCCHINI, QUAIL, OR TO ARTICHOKES AND PINE NUTS.

The foundation of the pilaf can be taken another step too. Greeks do not usually mix noodles and rice, but peoples in lands that were once Greek do. The combination makes for a more intriguing pilaf, with a contrast of textures and shapes. Greeks, who appreciate both types of dishes, would endorse the combination. You will too. The hint of saffron brings sunshine to the table.

*1/4 cup olive oil or butter, or a mixture*
*1/2 cup broken vermicelli*
*1 small onion, finely chopped*
*1/4 cup pine nuts*
*2 cups rice, preferably Arborio or other short-grain rice (see Note, page 238)*
*4 cooked artichoke hearts, or 8 cooked baby artichokes, very coarsely chopped*
*4 cups water*
*Large pinch of saffron threads*
*1/2 teaspoon salt*
*1/4 teaspoon freshly ground black pepper*

1 Heat the oil in a medium-size heavy saucepan over medium-high heat. Add the vermicelli, onion, and pine nuts and stir until the vermicelli turns golden, 2 to 3 minutes.

2 Add the rice and continue stirring until it turns translucent, about 1 minute. Add the artichokes, water, and saffron and bring to a boil. Reduce the heat to the barest simmer, cover the pan, and cook undisturbed until the water is gone and wells have begun to form on top of the rice, 20 minutes.

3 Add the salt and pepper and gently fluff the rice with a fork. Cover the pot again and set it aside for 20 minutes. Fluff with a fork and serve.

## OTHER PILAF OPTIONS

Other possible flavorings for classic Greek rice pilafs include:

- 1/4 fennel bulb, chopped
- 1 to 2 cloves garlic, finely chopped
- 1/4 cup chopped celery leaves
- 1/2 cup cooked chickpeas or lentils
- 1 1/2 pounds any wild green
- 2 cups shredded cabbage (called *lahanorizo*)
- 2 cups chopped tomatoes flavored with 1/8 teaspoon ground cinnamon and 1 teaspoon fresh oregano (called *bourani*)
- 1 cup coarsely chopped cooked octopus or shelled mussels
- 4 cooked small birds, such as quail
- 1 cup cooked bits of poultry or meat (called *atzen*)

To finish the pilaf, sprinkle on:

- Toasted bread crumbs
- Cheese
- Toasted pine nuts

# homemade noodles

**SERVES 6**

TODAY IN THE HOMES OF GREECE, ONE CAN HARDLY ESCAPE THE NOODLE. IT SOAKS UP THE JUICES OF ROAST MEATS AS IN *YIOUVETSI* (PAGE 363), FLOATS ABOUT IN SOUPS LIKE *MANESTRA* (PAGE 153), AND FORMS THE MAIN MATTER OF TWO DISHES THAT ARE NEAR AND DEAR TO MOST GREEK HEARTS: *PASTITSIO* (PAGE 255) AND *MAKARONADA* (PAGE 250). IN GREECE, AS IN SO MANY COUNTRIES, NOODLE DISHES ARE HOMEY FOODS, CHEAP AND FILLING. THEY ARE THE ONES CHILDREN BECOME ATTACHED TO, AND THAT ADULTS YEARN FOR.

Nowadays, most Greeks buy dry pasta. The most commonly used sorts are orzo, which is generally used in soups; elbows, the pasta of casseroles like *pastitsio;* and spaghetti, used in *makaronada.* Until recently, though, homemakers made noodles. They are called *xilopites,* which means "one thousand pies." To make Greek noodles you can use either water or egg or thickened yogurt, or a combination of the three.

*7 large eggs, or 4 large eggs and ²/₃ cup thick yogurt*
*3 ¹/₂ tablespoons water if using all eggs, or 2 ¹/₂ teaspoons water if using yogurt*
*¹/₄ teaspoon salt*
*¹/₈ teaspoon freshly ground pepper, preferably white*
*¹/₈ teaspoon ground nutmeg, preferably freshly grated*
*4 ¹/₂ cups unbleached all-purpose semolina flour or wheat flour (see Notes), plus extra for dusting the work surface and rolling pin*
*2 tablespoons olive oil*

## HOW TO COOK THE NOODLES

Greeks prefer their pasta softer than the popular Italian style, *al dente.* The noodles for Greek dishes should not be overcooked, but they should be tender all through.

1 Beat the eggs, water, yogurt, if using, salt, pepper, and nutmeg together in a large bowl until well mixed.

2 Stirring with a fork, slowly begin to add the flour, 1 cup at a time and then in decreasing amounts until you cannot stir the dough with a fork anymore and it forms a sticky ball. Place the ball on a floured surface.

3 Kneading with your hands, continue to add flour slowly until the dough no longer clings to your fingers. Divide the dough into baseball-size balls.

4 Flatten and press each ball with your hand, lightly sprinkling the dough with flour as you go, until no sticky spots open up as you flatten it. Stop kneading when you reach this point.

5 Dust a rolling pin or dowel with a little flour. Lightly dusting the surface with flour again, and also the rolling pin as necessary, roll out the flattened dough as you would a piecrust. Work a little flour into any more sticky spots. Roll it out as thin as you can. Hang the rolled sheets over a clothesline or chair back to dry a little, about 20 minutes.

6 Fold the slightly dry but still pliable dough sheets over and over as you would a bolt of cloth. With a sharp knife, cut across through the folded dough every ¼ to ½ inch, depending on the size of noodle desired.

7 Cook immediately in a pot of boiling water. Or for dry noodles, scatter them on a tray and leave them to dry—outdoors in the sun, indoors at room temperature, or in a gas oven with only the pilot light on—until completely dry.

## NOODLE NOMENCLATURE

The oldest Indo-European word for "noodle" is the Greek *itrion*. At first the *itrion* was a dough that was made into a flatbread and fried. Sometime during the fourth century B.C.E., instead of frying the flattened dough, people began to boil it in water. Apparently the noodle was used in soups and mixed with lentils, and little would be known of it except that it raised a dietary question for the early Jews of Greece: Was this flat mash of grain and water unleavened and therefore all right to eat during Passover, or not?

At about the same time as that controversy, references to *itrion* become *itria*—the plural. It seems the dish was no longer made and served in the singular, just as there's never one *spaghetto*. Galen describes two kinds of *itria*, the better kind called *ryemata* (which means "flowing out," presumably from a batter) and the poorer kind called *lagana* (meaning "wafer"). It seems that *itria* had also come to mean a sweet, for Athenaeus comments that the dish was made with honey and sesame.

**NOTES:**

■ The amount of flour called for is somewhat approximate. You might need a little less or a little more, depending on the egg size and the quantity it takes to eliminate all sticky spots.

■ The noodles can also be made with chickpea flour.

# THE OLYMPIC GAMES

**F**OR THOSE WHO DEVOUR NOODLES IN READINESS TO COMPETE IN THEIR FAVORITE SPORT, HERE IS SOME BACKGROUND ON HOW AND WHERE ATHLETIC GAMES BEGAN.

Two myths depict why Olympia was chosen as the site for the Panhellenic sporting games that took place in ancient Greece every four years. In one story Heracles founded the games to commemorate his completion of the most odious of his tasks, the cleaning of the foul Augean stables. To do so, he diverted one of Olympia's two rivers, the Alfios, to wash away the filth. In the second, the hero Pelops claimed a local girl as bride when he won a chariot race, a triumph he managed by unscrewing the linchpin of his opponent's wagon. His opponent was the girl's father. A sculpture depicting both stories crowned Olympia's Temple of Zeus and it is now in the museum.

## FROM RELIGIOUS FESTIVAL TO SPORTING EVENT

The choice of Olympia as a sports capital was a good one. Olympia, in the western Peloponnesos, is surrounded by hills that are covered with abundant groves of trees. There was plenty of water for contestants to drink. Originally the site was a religious sanctuary where a sacred festival was held every four years. The earliest remains date from about 2000 B.C.E. and the sanctuary from about 1000.

Central to the town was a sacred precinct called the Altis. At first the site was dedicated to both Zeus and his wife, Hera, and the first temple there honored the two, but as Zeus gained ascendance, a separate temple to him was built and the old one left to Hera. The Temple of Zeus was by

*An earthquake shattered Olympia's Temple of Zeus in the fifth century B.C.E., centuries after it was built.*

# Olympia was the Olympics. To take the gold was as important then as it is now.

*A victorious chariot racer receives a crown of laurel leaves.*

far the most important building of the city. Doric in style, it was richly decorated with sculptures, many of which have survived. Within the temple was a great gold and ivory statue of Zeus, a work of the incomparable Phidias. In the statue, Zeus sat in an elaborate throne and held the goddess of victory in his right hand, a scepter in his left. The statue was made in Phidias's workshop just outside the Altis, where archaeologists have unearthed mounds of statue fragments, ivory, bone, and glass, along with molds for shaping faces and limbs and a cup inscribed "I am Phidias's." In ancient days, the temple with its magnificent statue was considered one of the seven wonders of the world.

A great altar to Zeus stood outside the temple. Heaped next to it rose a pile of ashes left from the bones sacrificed to the god. Beyond that lay a row of twelve treasuries that various Dorian states, from Byzantium to Gela,

Cyrene, Sicyon, and Megara, erected in gratitude for Olympic victories. Two other temples, one to the hero Pelops and one to the Great Mother of the Gods, were located in the precinct, as was a round building that Philip of Macedonia erected to commemorate his victory over the southern Greeks. It held gold and ivory statues of himself, his son Alexander, and other family members.

In the northwest corner of the Altis sat a building that contained a perpetual fire and a banquet room in which the athletes feasted. Across from it stretched a row of Zanes, bronze statues of Zeus erected with money from fines imposed on those athletes who violated the rules of the games. Nearby

stood a double building, the *ouleuterion*, where between the two wings the athletes took the oath not to play foul in the contests.

## THE OLYMPIC STADIUMS

Then came the stadium. In the early days the track ran right by the great altar of Zeus. Eventually so many athletes came that the stadium had to be moved and enlarged. From the Altis to the stadium, athletes and umpires passed through the *Krypte,* a covered entrance. Inside lay a track separated from the viewing area by a low stone wall. The course was marked by stone starting lines, and the width allowed for twenty runners at a time. Surrounding the track were embankments of earth where spectators perched. Beside the track ran a water channel with basins every few feet, providing drinking water.

## A TIME OF TRUCE

During the games a truce was declared throughout the Panhellenic world so that athletes could come from Asia Minor, North Africa, Sicily, and perhaps Greek cities in what are today Spain and France. The "Olympic village" that housed the athletes was composed of many tents, and when the games took place, the streets must have been jammed with fans, for the stadium held thirty to forty thousand persons. Foot races of one and two lengths took place, as well as a long-distance one of about 3 miles. Contestants ran races both naked and in full armor. They threw javelins, hurled the discus, wrestled, leaped, and broad-jumped. In one event, called the *pankraton,* or "all strengths," athletes performed a set of sports. Horse and chariot races took place in a hippodrome beyond the stadium.

## OFFERINGS BY THE VICTORIOUS

When an athlete won a contest, he and the city he represented dedicated an offering. Olympia today remains overflowing with statuary, urns, bronzes, and wine kraters. Within the embankments many votive offers were buried—bronze and terra-cotta statues, arms and armaments. The largest collection of ancient Greek weapons is housed at Olympia, including a Persian helmet inscribed "The Athenians dedicate this helmet to Zeus, having taken it from the Medes."

To keep in shape and to practice, athletes followed a circuit around other cities where lesser games were held, but Olympia was the Olympics. To take the gold was as important

*Nike, winged goddess of victory, crowns a winning athlete with a laurel wreath.*

then as it is now.

And contestants had to eat. They too "carbed up," for most of their foods were grain. One can imagine the pyramids of wheat berry, barley groat pudding, *trahana,* and noodles they ate. Definitely they celebrated after the events, for the ground of Olympia is littered with wine carafes and drinking cups.

According to tradition, the actual games were founded as part of the Olympian religious festivity in 776 B.C.E. and were held every four years until 393 B.C.E. The modern revival of the games was launched in Athens in 1896. Women were first allowed to compete in 1912. Winter games were added beginning in 1924.

The original Olympic games fell into disfavor because of professionalism. A hundred years after the start of the modern games, the same complaint is heard.

# sourdough noodles

## TRAHANA

TIMES OF PRIVATION IN GREECE TAUGHT PEOPLE TO TURN EVEN A SPLASH OF MILK GONE SOUR INTO SOMETHING EDIBLE. MIXED WITH A DUSTING OF FLOUR, THEN DRIED, THE TWO CREATED NOT ONLY AN IMMEDIATE FOOD, BUT ONE THAT COULD BE KEPT FOR MONTHS AND USED IF HUNGER LINGERED. MIXED TOGETHER, THE TWO MADE A NOODLE.

*Trahana*, sour milk noodles, are as old as old can be in Greek history. If nothing else, the dish provides a way to keep both grains and dairy products over winter without spoiling. Some claim *trahana* is Turkish, Persian, or Slavic, not Greek. I side with those who point to *trahana*'s long history in Greek and Roman cooking, where the name for the food has remained practically unchanged through the ages.

Made into coarse pebbles, *trahana* historically were simmered into a wheat and sour milk porridgelike soup—a gruel not unlike Cream of Wheat. As such the food can be likened to couscous, risotto, a Chinese congee, or grits. The noodle pebbles, though, do not have to be used in gruel-like fashion. They can sit like a pilaf under stews, sauces, or relishes.

As in ancient times, *trahana* today is made with sour milk or yogurt. When fresh milk is used, the dish is called "sweet" *trahana*. In days past, *trahana* was dried in the sun. Nowadays most Greeks buy *trahana* rather than make their own. Those who do make them usually use coarse wheat flour (semolina), and dry the noodles in the oven. I find that the use of sour noodles, whether strips or orzo shaped, adds a different and distinctive element to many dishes. *Trahana* is not your normal noodle, and for some it is an acquired taste. Different as they are, the noodles offer many innovative possibilities.

## HOMEMADE TRAHANA

### SERVES 3 OR 4

*1 large egg*
*1/2 cup sour milk or yogurt for sour trahana, or fresh milk for sweet trahana (see page 248)*
*Large pinch of salt*
*1 1/2 cups semolina flour*

1 Preheat the oven to 200°F.

2 Beat the egg, milk, and salt together in a bowl until frothy. Slowly add the semolina until mixed in. Transfer to a lightly floured surface and knead until a smooth, stiff dough is formed, about 5 minutes.

3 At this point there are two ways the noodles can be formed: Break the fresh dough into small pieces and press them through the holes of a colander. Or roll the dough out thickly and cut it with a paring knife into any size strips or pieces you want. Spread the noodles on a baking sheet and dry them in the sun or in a slow oven (200°F), turning them several times, until completely dry.

# WHENCE COMETH TRAHANA?

THE QUESTION OF *TRAHANA*'S ORIGIN IS A STICKY ONE, BECAUSE IT INVOLVES THE ORIGIN OF THE NOODLE. DID MARCO POLO BRING THE FOOD FROM CHINA? HAD THE ROMANS STIRRED FLOUR AND LIQUID INTO PASTE LONG BEFORE? DID THE GREEKS GET *TRAHANA* FROM THE PERSIANS, WHO GAVE IT TO THE BYZANTINES, WHO PASSED IT TO THE TURKS, THE VLACH SHEPHERDS, OR OTHERS WHO WANDERED INTO GREECE? OR HAD THE GREEKS LONG HAD THE DISH?

The ancient Greek word *trakton* is awfully close to *trahana*. In Latin the same word, *tracta*, is often translated as "pastry." Some have contended the word comes from *traho*, which means "to draw out," as a dough would be, but Apicius calls dough *tractogalatus*, a word that is decidedly Greek and means "milk *tracta*." Besides, the ancient Greek word *traktaizo* also means "handle" and "draw out" and precedes the Latin version. Athenaeus has the word as *taracta*.

## CATO TELLS ALL

Cato, the great statesman of Rome, described how semolina was made into *tracta*: It involved first making a dough, forming it into balls, drying it, then layering the dough in what seems to be a cheese pie, like lasagna. Apicius said *tracta* was used in thick soups and porridges and often accompanied lamb, a meat that is still a common companion of *trahana*. He also used *tracta* to thicken chicken stew. Lord knows, noodles are a thickener; ask any soup maker.

*Cato and other Romans were avid fans of Greek cuisine, and most of the chefs of Rome were Greek.*

## TARHANA AND TRAHANA

*Tracta* was first made from triticum, or emmer wheat, which first grew in the Greek area of Pontos. Emmer wheat is still the sort that Pontian Greeks use to make *trahana*. The Turkish word for *trahana* is *tarhana*, and the balls of

dough are made from emmer and are dried in the sun. In Persian the word is *tarkhana*, a simple twist of two letters, but there is no reference to the dish in Persian writing until the fourteenth century, when the Persians were as much influenced by the Turks as the opposite, both having been influenced by Greeks. A tenth-century Byzantine recipe tells how to soak and dry nodules of *traganos* to make a porridge. In the fifth century Hesychius, the Alexandrian, told how to make a gruel he calls both *hondros* and *tragos*. *Hondros* means "thick," and the Cretan word for *trahana* to this day is *hondros*.

## KASHI, KISHK, AND KASKI

Sliding onward with this line of thought, the word and the dish as gruel may well have turned into the *kashi* of Russia with a few not uncommon linguistic switches from the root word *tracta*. Likewise the *kishk* of Lebanon and *kaski* of Persia. All are grain gruels. Clearly the mystery has many strands. All we know for sure is that the ancient Greeks were porridge eaters long before they were bread eaters, and the porridge was made from grain and liquid. All and all, it is a pasta puzzle.

# COOKING TRAHANA

### SERVES 4 TO 6

Eat cooked *trahana* as a hot cereal, add it to soup, or use it under any vegetable *briami* (page 282) or any meat or chicken stew.

4 cups water, Chicken Stock
    (page 170), or meat stock
2 tablespoons olive oil or butter
1/2 teaspoon salt
1 cup sour or sweet trahana,
    homemade (page 247) or
    purchased

1 Bring the water to a boil in a medium-size pot over high heat. Add the oil and salt and slowly stir in the *trahana*. Cook over medium heat, stirring frequently, until creamy, about 25 minutes. Remove from the heat and set aside for 10 minutes, until fluffy and tender.

## NOTES:

■ To make a soupy meal of plain *trahana*, add kefalotyri cheese at the end of the cooking time.

■ *Trahana* is also often sautéed in olive oil until just soft, sometimes with chopped onion or garlic, before it is added to the water.

■ Plain *trahana* goes well with fresh leafy herbs like cilantro and flat-leaf parsley, especially when the leaves have been dipped in salt water.

## HERA THE HOMEMAKER

Zeus found Hera, his lovely older sister, wandering in a woods near Argos. He brought about a rainstorm and, in the guise of a cuckoo, hid within her skirt. There he assumed his true form, embraced her, and promised to make her his wife.

This he did, and she became the queen of the Olympian gods. Her name, the feminine of *heros*, or "hero," means "gentle woman" or "lady," and in her position as wife of Zeus she was the patroness of women and all they did—tend the home, mind the children, plant the garden, and cook the grains, just as Greek women do today.

Hera stood for marriage and for the family, which she protected zealously, and women all over ancient Greece worshiped her. Though she is no longer the worshiped patroness of those who clean houses and make the foods, she seems to be hovering about the Greek home and its keeper today. As fiercely loyal to marriage and family as she was millennia ago, she lurks in every noodle ever prepared.

# makaronada times six

WHENEVER THE PANTRY OFFERS NO OTHER OR NOT ENOUGH MAIN DISHES FOR THE TABLE, A GREEK HOUSEWIFE WHIPS UP A HEAP OF SPAGHETTI WITH RED SAUCE. I CAME TO RELISH THE DISH AS MUCH AS A NATIVE, FOR ALTHOUGH ON THE ORDINARY SIDE, MAKARONADA IS INFUSED WITH THE DEPTH OF FLAVORS THAT ALL GREEK FOOD HAS. I OFFER A RECIPE FOR TRADITIONAL MAKARONADA, THEN, BECAUSE GREEK FARE OFFERS SUCH A SPHERE OF POSSIBILITIES; I OFFER SOME MODERN MAKARONADAS INSPIRED BY THE GREEK CORNUCOPIA.

## TRADITIONAL MAKARONADA

### WITH RED SAUCE

#### SERVES 4

*1 pound dry spaghetti, or*
*1 pound fresh noodles*
*2 cups Red Tomato Meat Sauce*
*(page 472) or Quick Fresh*
*Tomato Sauce (page 474), warm*
*3/4 to 1 cup grated hard cheese,*
*preferably kefalotyri*

1 Bring a large pot of water to a boil over high heat.

2 Add the spaghetti to the boiling water and cook until just tender, 11 to 12 minutes for dry, 5 to 6 minutes for fresh.

3 Drain the spaghetti and heap a generous portion onto each plate. Top each serving with the sauce and a generous sprinkling of the cheese. Serve immediately.

## HOW SWEET THE OLIVE TREE

Besides its production of fruit for the oil to use in cooking and to pour on salads, vegetables, eggs, and bread, the Greeks have other uses for the olive tree and its fruit. They crush the olive pits to make *sporelaion,* "seed oil," which, although edible, is of a low grade. It is often mixed with other sorts of edible oils or used as lamp oil. They also make olive oil soap from the lowest grade of oil pressed from the pulp or the seed oil saponified with lye. (In the countryside, the big, blocky green bar of olive oil soap that leaves the skin moist and smooth is a common sight, whereas in this country it is a luxury soap.)

Greeks also use the oil to treat burns, wounds, and aches. The crushed olive leavings after the oil is pressed are used to make compost for gardens and fields. Small twigs and branches from the trees are used for fuel, and the trunks and larger branches are used in house building and furniture making. Ever proclaiming the mysterious powers of the olive, all Greeks have stories of olive tree rafters and olive branch chairs sprouting new growth.

Indeed, the amazingly useful trees rarely seem to die. When they grow very old and no longer turn out new greenery, they are cut and turned back into the ground. Soon after, they almost inevitably sprout a new tree from the old roots.

# GREEK PASTA PRIMAVERA

### SERVES 4

*1/4 cup olive oil*
*1 small onion, coarsely chopped*
*4 cloves garlic, minced*
*1 1/2 cups cauliflower florets*
*2 zucchini, coarsely chopped*
*1 1/2 cups diced eggplant*
*2 teaspoons fresh oregano leaves*
*3 tomatoes, coarsely chopped*
*1/2 cup dry white wine*
*Salt and freshly ground black pepper,*
*    to taste*
*1 pound dry spaghetti, or*
*    1 pound fresh noodles*
*3/4 to 1 cup freshly grated hard cheese,*
*    preferably kefalotyri*
*1/2 cup shredded fresh basil leaves*

1 Heat the oil in a large non-reactive skillet over medium heat. Add the onion, garlic, cauliflower, zucchini, eggplant, and oregano and sauté until well browned, about 20 minutes.

2 While the vegetables are cooking, bring a large pot of water to a boil over high heat.

3 Add the tomatoes, wine, and salt and pepper to the skillet. Bring to a boil, reduce the heat, and simmer until the wine is absorbed and the tomatoes soften, about 5 minutes.

4 Meanwhile, cook the spaghetti in the boiling water until just tender, 11 to 12 minutes for dry, 5 to 6 minutes for fresh.

5 Drain the spaghetti, and heap a generous portion onto each plate. Top with the sauce and a generous sprinkling of cheese. Scatter with basil and serve.

# SPAGHETTI

### WITH ZUCCHINI AND CAPER SAUCE

### SERVES 4

*1/4 cup olive oil*
*1 small onion, coarsely chopped*
*2 cloves garlic, minced*
*2 medium zucchini, coarsely*
*    chopped*
*1/2 medium carrot, coarsely*
*    chopped*
*1/2 medium green bell pepper,*
*    coarsely chopped*
*2 tablespoons capers*
*4 tomatoes, chopped*
*1/2 cup dry red wine*
*2 teaspoons fresh marjoram leaves*
*1 small bay leaf*
*Salt and freshly ground black pepper,*
*    to taste*
*1 pound dry spaghetti, or*
*    1 pound fresh noodles*
*3/4 to 1 cup freshly grated*
*    hard cheese, preferably*
*    kefalotyri*

1 Heat the oil in a large non-reactive skillet over medium heat. Add the onion, garlic, zucchini, carrot, bell pepper, and capers and sauté until well browned, about 15 minutes.

2 Add the tomatoes, wine, marjoram, bay leaf, and salt and pepper. Bring to a boil, reduce the heat, and simmer until sauce-like, about 45 minutes.

3 While the sauce is cooking, bring a large pot of water to a boil over high heat. Add the spaghetti and cook until just tender, 11 to 12 minutes for dry, 5 to 6 minutes for fresh.

4 Drain the spaghetti and heap a generous portion onto each plate. Top with the sauce and a generous sprinkling of the cheese, and serve.

## SPAGHETTI

### WITH FRIED SNAILS AND "ALL"

#### SERVES 4

*1/3 cup coarsely chopped walnuts*
*1/4 cup olive oil*
*12 cloves garlic, coarsely chopped*
*32 canned snails, drained and rinsed*
*1 pound dry spaghetti, or*
  *1 pound fresh noodles*
*1/4 cup coarsely chopped*
  *fennel bulb*
*1/2 cup dry white wine*
*Salt and freshly ground black pepper,*
  *to taste*
*1 cup heavy cream*
*3/4 to 1 cup freshly grated hard cheese,*
  *preferably kefalotyri*
*1/3 cup chopped fresh flat-leaf parsley*
  *leaves*

**1** Place the walnuts in a large, ungreased skillet and toast over medium-high heat, stirring once, until well browned, 3 to 4 minutes. Transfer the walnuts to a plate.

**2** Heat the oil over medium-high heat in the same skillet. Add the garlic and snails and sauté, stirring, until the garlic is soft, about 5 minutes.

## OTHER MAKARONADA SAUCES

···············

**■ LEEKS, OLIVES, AND OLIVE OIL:** Sauté chopped leeks and olives in oil, toss with warm spaghetti, and top with toasted bread crumbs.

**■ SCALLOPS, TARAMA, CREAM, AND BASIL:** Sauté scallops, then stir in *tarama* and cream and simmer until the sauce is slightly thickened. Toss with warm spaghetti, and top with shredded fresh basil leaves.

**3** Bring a large pot of water to a boil over high heat. Add the spaghetti and cook until just tender, 11 to 12 minutes for dry, 5 to 6 minutes for fresh.

**4** When the snails are just cooked, add the fennel, wine, salt, and pepper. Simmer until the wine is almost evaporated, about 2 minutes.

**5** Stir in the cream and simmer for 2 minutes more.

**6** Drain the spaghetti, and heap a generous portion onto each plate. Top with the snails and sauce, a generous sprinkling of the cheese, then some parsley, and serve.

## SPAGHETTI

### WITH "LITTLE BIRDS" AND OLIVES

#### SERVES 4

*4 grilled fresh quail (page 448)*
  *or 2 squab (page 449)*
*1/2 cup olive oil*
*6 cloves garlic, coarsely chopped*
*5 ribs celery, coarsely chopped*
*1/4 cup celery leaves, coarsely chopped*
*1/2 cup dry red wine*
*1/4 cup pitted olives, preferably*
  *Kalamata or other good*
  *Greek olives*
*1/2 teaspoon chopped fresh sage leaves,*
  *or 1 teaspoon fresh thyme leaves*
*Salt and freshly ground black pepper,*
  *to taste*
*1 pound dry spaghetti, or 1 pound*
  *fresh noodles*
*3/4 to 1 cup freshly grated hard cheese,*
  *preferably kefalotyri*
*1/3 cup chopped fresh flat-leaf*
  *parsley leaves*

**1** Cut the grilled quail or squab into quarters and set them all aside on a plate.

**2** Bring a large pot of water to a boil over high heat.

3 While the water is heating, heat the oil in a large skillet over medium-high heat. Add the garlic, celery ribs, and celery leaves and sauté until the celery ribs are softened, about 5 minutes.

4 Add the wine, olives, sage, salt, and pepper. Bring to a boil, then reduce the heat and simmer until almost all the liquid has evaporated, about 5 minutes. Add the quail pieces, and stir until heated and well coated.

5 While the sauce is cooking, cook the spaghetti in the boiling water until just tender, 11 to 12 minutes for dry, 5 to 6 minutes for fresh.

6 Drain the spaghetti and heap a generous portion onto each plate. Top with the quail pieces and a spoonful of the sauce. Scatter the cheese and then the parsley over all, and serve.

# SPAGHETTI
## WITH WHITEBAIT "AND SO ON"
### SERVES 4

*1 recipe Little Fried Fish in a Lemon*
*    and Retsina Bath (page 59)*
*1/4 cup pine nuts*
*2/3 cup olive oil*
*1 small onion, coarsely chopped*
*6 cloves garlic, minced*
*1/3 cup tomato paste*
*6 medium tomatoes, chopped*
*1/2 cup chopped fennel fronds*
*    and stalks*
*3/4 cup dry white wine*
*1 pound dry spaghetti, or 1 pound*
*    fresh noodles*
*1/2 cup retsina-soaked currants,*
*    with their liquid (see page 49)*
*3/4 to 1 cup freshly grated hard cheese,*
*    preferably kefalotyri*
*1/3 cup chopped fresh basil, flat-leaf*
*    parsley, or watercress leaves*

1 Bring a large pot of water to a boil over high heat.

2 While the water is heating, break each fish into two or three pieces and set aside.

3 Toast the pine nuts in a small dry skillet over medium-high heat, turning them until brown on all sides, about 3 minutes. Set aside.

4 In a large skillet, heat the oil over medium heat. Add the onion and garlic and sauté until translucent, about 5 minutes.

5 Stir in the tomato paste, tomatoes, fennel, and wine. Bring to a boil. Reduce the heat and simmer until the fennel is softened and the tomatoes have become saucy, 10 to 15 minutes.

6 Meanwhile, cook the spaghetti in the boiling water until just tender, 11 to 12 minutes for dry, 5 to 6 minutes for fresh.

7 Add the fish, currants and retsina, and pine nuts to the sauce. Stir gently until well mixed and warmed through, 3 to 5 minutes.

8 Drain the spaghetti and heap a generous portion onto each plate. Top with the sauce and a generous sprinkling of the cheese. Scatter the basil over the cheese, and serve immediately.

# ALEXANDRIA, GREEK CITY BY THE SEA

I N 332 B.C.E., HAVING SWEPT INTO AND TAKEN EGYPT, ALEXANDER THE GREAT LEFT HIS ARMY IN MEMPHIS AND WENT TO EXPLORE THE MOUTH OF THE NILE. ALONG ONE OF THE RIVER'S CHANNELS THROUGH THE DELTA, HE LOCATED WHAT HE SOUGHT: A GOOD ANCHORAGE WITH ACCESS TO THE MEDITERRANEAN. THE PLACE HAD A DOUBLE HARBOR, ONE SIDE FACING WEST, THE OTHER EAST, PROTECTED BY A LONG SLIM ISLAND. IT WAS IDEAL FOR A TOWN THAT WOULD CONTROL COMMERCE BETWEEN EGYPT, THE LEVANT, AND GREECE. AND SO ALEXANDRIA, THE FIRST AND MOST FAMOUS OF THE CITIES NAMED FOR ALEXANDER, WAS BORN.

Alexander oversaw every detail in planning the new city. It would have two wide avenues lined with colonnades. The market square would hold public offices, a school, gymnasium, and temple. Soon the city grew so in size and power that it commanded all the vibrant trade on the Levantine coast.

When Alexander died, his general, Ptolemy, returned to the splendid seaport and crowned himself king of Egypt. His descendants, including Cleopatra, ruled for centuries from the island. On the eastern tip, Ptolemy built one of the seven wonders of the ancient world, the Pharos of Alexandria, the prototype of the lighthouse. The city became a focal point of Hellenistic and Semitic learning. It held a museum and a library reputed to contain half a million volumes. Euclid and Archimedes accomplished their studies at Alexandria's academy. When the Romans captured Alexandria, it remained a Greek city with its own government, second only to Rome itself. But the city was famous for other than academic pursuits. It was in Alexandria that Cleopatra courted Caesar and seduced Mark Antony.

## A CENTER OF THEOLOGY AND COMMERCE

With the coming of Christianity, the city garnered renewed importance, becoming a center of theology and church government. The Old Testament was translated from Hebrew to Greek there. The Persians captured the city in 616 and the Arabs took it in 642, but still it remained a Greek center of scholarship and commerce. The city flourished as a terminal of the spice trade.

By the time Turkish forces entered in 1517, the channel to the Nile had silted up and the original city was deserted, but the city experienced yet another rebirth. Mohammed Ali Pasha dredged out a new channel to the Nile, building new docks and an arsenal.

## THE COMING OF THE SUEZ CANAL

Another rebirth came with the Suez Canal. The opening of the canal and a railroad linking Suez to Alexandria ensured the city's reascendancy. More Greeks came to join the ones who had remained. But in 1882 the city was bombarded by Britain and was made a British colony. Only in 1946 did British forces leave and turn the city over to the Egyptians. Even today, two millennia later, Alexandria remains Egypt's chief harbor.

In the modern city lie several large Greek quarters, one where Alexander's ancient city stood, though many Greeks have left in the last three decades. A grand square, customs buildings, and warehouses surround ancient churches and mosques. Import and export continue to animate the city. New wharves for the grain trade were built in the 1960s. Cereals travel from Alexandria by rail and road to the rest of Egypt. Cotton travels down the Nile.

Alexander never returned to his glorious city, but Ptolemy brought his body to be entombed there. Recently, it appears, his tomb has been found, along with dozens of Greco-Roman buildings, temples, columns, and statues that were lost beneath the sea as the result of a series of violent earthquakes. And, in recent years, with huge international backing, the great library of Alexandria has been revived. A new library has been built, designed to house 4 million electronic and bound volumes, and it will be open to all the world's people regardless of origin.

# Pastitsio

PASTITSIO—THE WORD MEANS "MADE FROM PASTA," AND THE DISH ENTERED GREEK CUISINE THROUGH ITALIAN-HELD ISLANDS—IS THE FIRST WORD THAT SPRINGS TO A GREEK'S LIPS WHEN DISCUSSING GREEK FOOD, THE FIRST DISH THAT SPRINGS TO MIND WHEN TALKING OF HOME, THE FIRST DISH THAT SPRINGS TO HEART WHEN LONELY. PASTITSIO HOLDS THE GREEK SOUL. HERE YOU WILL FIND A NEOCLASSIC VEGETARIAN VERSION WITH A HINT OF ORANGE ZEST, A MORE TYPICAL MEAT VERSION, AND SOME NOT-AT-ALL CLASSIC VARIATIONS.

Generally *pastitsio* is made in a big round pan, but any baking pan—round, square, rectangular—will do. The dish comes two ways: with noodle layers on top and bottom and a sauce between, or with sauce and noodles all mixed together. A lush *saltsa besamel* caps the top.

## NEOCLASSIC VEGETARIAN PASTITSIO

### SERVES 6 TO 8

1 tablespoon olive oil

1 1/2 pounds ziti or zitoni macaroni

3/4 cup freshly grated kefalotyri or Parmesan cheese

2 to 2 1/2 cups Quick Fresh Tomato Sauce (page 474)

1 tablespoon finely chopped orange zest

1 teaspoon chopped fresh oregano leaves, or 1/2 teaspoon dried

2 cups Saltsa Besamel (page 459)

2 large eggs, lightly beaten

## LASAGNA AND RAVIOLI: MADE IN GREECE

Ancient Greeks had a pan called a *lasana*, which, according to Homer, was used to bake flat sheets of dough. The Greeks brought that pan and the flat dough with them wherever they colonized, and one of the main areas they colonized was Italy. Taken into Italian, that word and the dish, as *lagana*, became *lasagna*. To this day, lasagna features flat sheets of dough that are arranged in layer-cake fashion with foods between. In modern Greek, *lagana* generally means the wide, low pan and flat, unleavened Lenten breads that are baked in it; but in Macedonia, *laganes* refers to a thin noodle pie layered with sausage, sauce, and greens, topped with cheese. Sound familiar?

By Byzantine times, the Greeks had become great "stuffers," and stuffing pasta is not something they missed. In particular the Pontians created many sorts of stuffed pasta, their preferred shape being the half-moon.

1 Preheat the oven to 350°F. Coat the bottom and sides of a 13- x 9-inch baking dish or equivalent round pan with the oil.

2 Bring a large pot of water to a boil over high heat. Add the macaroni and cook until just tender, 12 to 14 minutes.

3 Drain the macaroni and add half of it to the prepared dish. Sprinkle half the cheese over the macaroni, then spread the tomato sauce over the cheese. Sprinkle the zest and oregano over the sauce. Distribute the remaining macaroni evenly over the top.

4 In a mixing bowl, combine the *besamel* and the eggs. Whisk until smooth. Spread the mixture over the top layer of macaroni, and sprinkle the remaining cheese over all. Bake until golden on top and crisp around the edges, 55 minutes.

5 Remove the dish from the oven and let it rest for 15 minutes, then serve.

**NOTE:** For a tarter note, use the yogurt white sauce variation (page 460) instead of regular *Saltsa Besamel.*

## VARIATION:

**Classic Meat *Pastitsio*:** For a traditional rendition of *pastitsio*, omit the orange zest and substitute Red Tomato Meat Sauce (page 472) for the Quick Tomato Sauce.

# PASTITSIO PIE

### SERVES 6 TO 8

M y friends the Navon family, Greek Jews living on one of the Princes islands in the Sea of Marmara within view of Istanbul, made *pastitsio* in an ornate Byzantine pie fashion, something like an edible mosaic in a gilded frame. To make it requires several steps beyond the usual, but the result is quite a statement: macaroni baked in a pie with a flaky filo crust.

*12 sheets filo dough, commercial*
  *or homemade, cut to fit a*
  *13- x 9-inch pan*
*Olive oil, for oiling the filo*
*1 recipe Neoclassic Vegetarian Pastitsio*
  *(page 255) or Classic Meat*
  *Pastitsio (variation, this page),*
  *sauce and noodles mixed together*
*2 cups Saltsa Besamel (page 459)*

1 Preheat the oven to 375°F.

2 Following the tips in Filo Finesse (page 87), oil and layer one third of the filo in a 13- x 9-inch baking dish. Cover the filo layer with half the *pastitsio*, and spread half the *besamel* over the *pastitsio*.

3 Repeat the layers of oiled filo, *pastitsio*, and *besamel*.

## ALTOGETHER NEW *PASTITSIOS*

....................

M aking *pastitsio* in the layered style, replace the vegetarian or meat sauce with:

■ Mussels in White Wine with Shallots and Basil (page 69)

■ Chopped cooked octopus, squid, or shrimp

■ Leek (page 97), spinach (page 92), or *horta* (page 267) filo pie filling

■ Lamb pie filling (page 106)

■ Steamed Whole Cauliflower in Lemon-Nutmeg *Besamel* Sauce (page 273), chopped

■ Sautéed mushrooms

■ Any vegetable *briami* (page 282)

■ Duck meat, especially Duck with Ouzo Orange Cinnamon Sauce (page 421)

■ Thyme-Fed Snails with Tomatoes, Spring Garlic, and Spring Onions (page 452)

4 Layer the remaining oiled filo over the top, and brush the top of the pie with oil. Tuck the filo in around the edges. Score to make 6 to 8 pieces.

5 Bake until the noodles are heated through and the crust is golden, about 1 hour. Let the pie rest for 5 minutes, then serve.

# orzo and beans

## WITH MUSTARD GREENS, OLIVES, AND TOASTED BREAD CRUMBS

### SERVES 6

HOW LONG HAVE NOODLES BEEN COMBINED WITH THE OTHER STAPLE OF THE MEDITERRANEAN, PULSES? PROBABLY SINCE POTTERY ALLOWED PEOPLE TO STEW UP A SOUP OF WHATEVER THEY HAD GATHERED.

Today on the Dodecanese islands, the combination of noodles and pulses is a common one. Otherwise, the dish seems to have left its mark more on Magna Graecia than on the mainland, for example in southern Italy's famous *pasta e fagioli*. The combination is still delightful, warming, and natural. The twosome always feels to me like a safe harbor—the tastiest, most basic of foods. On the islands, the noodles used are small seed-shaped noodles called *kritharaki*, or "little barley," also known as orzo. The bean used is often the New World white bean, but sometimes it is the Old World chickpea. Add a leafy green, as they do on the islands, and another incomparably Greek ingredient: olives.

*1 cup (9 ounces) white beans, such as great northern, cannelini, or navy beans, or chickpeas*
*³/4 teaspoon salt*
*1 ¹/2 pounds mustard greens, finely shredded (9 to 10 cups), rinsed, and drained*
*1 ¹/2 tablespoons fresh lemon juice*
*1 ¹/2 tablespoons butter*
*³/4 cup coarse bread crumbs, preferably homemade*
*³/4 pound kritharaki (orzo), cooked and drained*
*¹/4 cup Kalamata or other good Greek olives, pitted and quartered*
*¹/4 cup olive oil*

1 Place the beans in a medium-size saucepan, add water to cover by 1¹/2 inches, and bring to a rolling boil over high heat. Remove from the heat and set aside to soak for 1 hour.

2 Drain and rinse the beans, return them to the pan, and add fresh water to cover by 1¹/2 inches. Bring to a boil over high heat, then reduce the heat and simmer briskly for 25 minutes. Stir in ¹/2 teaspoon of the salt and continue simmering briskly until the beans are tender but not mushy, 5 minutes more.

3 While the beans are cooking, prepare the remaining ingredients: Bring a large pot of water to boil over high heat. Add the greens and cook for 10 minutes, until tender but still brightly colored. Drain, pressing down gently to release excess moisture. Transfer the greens to a bowl. Add the lemon juice and remaining ¹/4 teaspoon salt. Toss together and set aside.

4 Melt the butter in a medium-size skillet over medium heat until foaming. Add the bread crumbs and stir until golden and crisp, 2 to 3 minutes. Transfer to a paper towel and set aside.

5 When the beans are done, drain them and transfer them to a serving bowl. Add the greens, orzo, olives, and oil and mix together. Sprinkle the bread crumbs over the top and serve.

# ALEXANDER THE GREAT AND THE SPREAD OF HELLENISM

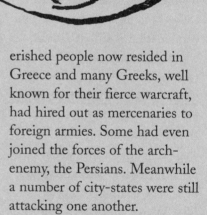

**A**LEXANDER THE GREAT WAS BORN IN PELLA, MACEDONIA, IN 356 B.C.E., THE SON OF PHILIP, KING OF MACEDONIA, AND OLYMPIAS, THE DAUGHTER OF KING NEOPTOLEMUS OF EPIROS.

From age thirteen to sixteen he was tutored by Aristotle in science, philosophy, literature, politics, governing, and medicine. He was an avid student who later would dispute the morality of slavery with his tutor, and who when he sacked Thebes in one of his first military forays spared the home where the great poet Pindar penned his odes.

## A RETURN TO GLORY

The glory days of Pericles in Athens were history, and Greece's many wars had left its cities mighty but exhausted. Though trade still flourished and brought riches, and Panhellenic festivities played on, the tribunal that governed Greece had for the first time ignited disparity and rancor. Large numbers of impov-

erished people now resided in Greece and many Greeks, well known for their fierce warcraft, had hired out as mercenaries to foreign armies. Some had even joined the forces of the arch-enemy, the Persians. Meanwhile a number of city-states were still attacking one another.

Alexander took up the mantle of Greek unification and revenge

*Alexander declared that all people were equal, regardless of race or ethnicity, and he wished all people to live in peace and harmony.*

against the Persian empire. Largely due to him, soon many of Greece's separate cities were joined and Greek culture, language, thought, and habits were dispersed across Mesopotamia to the Himalayas, down the Indus valley, and across to Arabia and Egypt.

Alexander launched his conquests from a mighty base. His father, once a prisoner in Thebes, had snared a powerful throne in Macedonia. An intelligent, educated, indefatigable man with a keen sense of battlefield and political strategy, Philip believed himself surrounded by foes on all sides. Philip began a conquest of all Greece. When he assailed Byzantium, young Alexander took up arms on his own and defeated the Thracians.

## LIKE FATHER, LIKE SON

Then Philip was assassinated. As the claims of other applicants to the throne, including the son of Philip's new Macedonian wife, came into dispute, Alexander rose. Because the orator Demosthenes was decrying him in Athens, Alexander acted swiftly. He moved against Thessaly. He then sped across Illyria to the Danube river. Returning, he cruelly crushed rebellious Thebes, to the shock of other Greek cities. As he now held all of Greece save Sparta, a council of the combined cities appointed him to lead the assault on Asia already planned by Philip.

To prepare for battle, Alexander visited the oracle at Delphi, who proclaimed him invincible. He marched forth with lightly armed troops from Crete, Macedonian archers, Thracian javelin men, thirty thousand foot soldiers, and a cavalry of five thousand. The cavalry was to be the force that struck first,

*Fertile Macedonia not only provides a major portion of Greece's produce, but also gave birth to its two great innovative kings, Philip and Alexander.*

followed by soldiers armed with spears and shields assembled in the phalanx formation that Philip had invented. The infantry would be his conquerors.

## ENGAGEMENT WITH THE PERSIANS

As Alexander crossed into Asia Minor, he stopped first at Troy to seek inspiration from Homer. At the Granicus river near the Sea of Marmara he met and routed the first Persians. Moving quickly across Asia Minor, he overthrew tyrants and installed Greek marshals and Panhellenic policy. He took Halicarnassus, and by the winter of 334–33 B.C.E., pushed on to Angyra (Ankara). He encountered Darius, king of

*. . . while conquering he spread the ideas of democracy and freedom.*

*Alexander battled Darius, the lion of Persia, and won.*

Persia, and his army at the Pinarus river and enveloped them. Darius fled.

Alexander then turned south. Planning to isolate the Persian fleet, he marched across Syria and Phoenicia. When he reached the heights of Gaza, bitter resistance halted him for two months, but in November 332, he entered Egypt.

Egypt was the breadbasket of the eastern Mediterranean. On the fertile delta of the Nile tons of grain, which Greece badly needed, sprouted each year. While securing this crop, Alexander first revealed the policies that would characterize his reign. He installed Greek commanders while leaving local administrative officials in place. He erected altars to Greek gods,

but he did not expunge traditional religions nor expel the clergy, and he founded the first of the many Hellenistic cities that came to be named after him, Alexandria.

## THE DEATH OF DARIUS

Alexander now controlled the whole coast of the eastern Mediterranean and felt ready to attack the land around the Euphrates. He breached the Tigris and occupied Babylon. He pressed on over the Zagros mountains and into Persia proper. He entered Persepolis and Pasargadae, where he burned down Xerxes' palace. With Persia's cities now his, Alexander decided to unify the Macedonian and Persian empires. He advanced to eastern Persia near Tehran and the Caspian Sea. Darius meanwhile had fled to Bactria, only to meet a brutal welcome: Bactria's ruler murdered Darius upon his arrival. Alexander retrieved Darius's body and sent it to Persepolis for burial. At this point Alexander had no hindrance to his claim that he was the one "great king." An inscription in Rhodes from the year 330 B.C.E. calls Alexander the "Lord of Asia."

But Alexander's thirst for land and conquest was not sated. He moved on across the Caspian Sea to the site of modern Kabul. Pursuing Bactria's king, he crossed the Hindu Kush. Still he continued. He advanced across Samarkand to the eastern edge of the Persian empire. Using catapults, he broke the resistance of the Scythian nomads. He met his most obstinate foe, the Massagetai people, and vanquished them. He then attacked Oxyartes in his high cliff holdout. Alexander sent his troops up the rock with ropes by night. By dawn he had humbled Oxyartes, whose daughter, Roxana, he then married.

Alexander recrossed the Hindu Kush, sending half his troops through the Khyber Pass while he marched with the others toward the Indus river. In 326 he crossed the Indus and entered Taxila. He was eager to go on, but his army refused. Stifled by heat and rain, they mutinied, and Alexander was forced to turn back. He erected altars to the twelve Olympian gods, built a fleet, and proceeded down the Indus.

## LANDS OF GRAIN AND PULSES

All the lands where Alexander forayed were hubs of early grain cultivation. All depended as well on many kinds of lentils and peas. Egyptians grew many sorts of pulses, including rich and earthy tiny red lentils. In the Levant, people thrived on chickpeas. Mesopotamia was the birthplace of most of the major cereals— millet, wheat, and barley—and as Alexander traveled east, his troops discovered and fed upon rice. As much as Alexander's story is about the spread of Hellenism, it is also about the foods of the Mediterranean diet.

Alexander himself was abstemious at meals and scolded his young officers when they indulged in too much food and wine. He seems to have had an appetite only for conquest. Aristobulus, a historian, said that while Alexander's entourage enjoyed rare dishes in each of the nations they conquered, their king ate only fruit and light food. When Queen Ada of Caria found him too thin, he told her the best appetizer was hearty exercise before breakfast. Still, it was after a banquet and night of revelry back in Babylon that Alexander took ill and died. He was thirty-two.

## THE SPREAD OF GREEK CULTURE

Alexander made fast an empire far more extensive than any before. In each place he conquered he introduced Greek customs, language, and philosophy. By the end of his marches, the area experiencing the Greek culture extended from the Indus river to the Magna Graecia colonies of Italy. He founded sixteen cities, six of which still stand. Alexander brought art, architecture, and city planning along his path. He set up coinage and consolidated a single economy. He wrote to Aristotle of each place he traveled, sent samples of plants and reports of animals, soil, geography, and weather. He brought new methods of agriculture and foods, new ideas of government in civil, military, and financial administration. He coupled conquest with tolerance, and while conquering he spread the ideas of democracy and freedom. He had Greek adopted as the universal language throughout the empire, so that Greek became the agent of unification. With Greek as the common language, the empire he conquered was ready for the entrance of the Romans and Byzantines.

Meanwhile, Alexander left yet another legacy: His troops carried olives, and all along the route they traversed, the pits sprouted trees.

*Iris, the goddess of the rainbow, in her chariot speeds Alexander in an arc across the sky, as far as he traveled the world.*

# The vegetable parade

**W**HEN PERSEUS SETS OFF TO KILL THE TERRIBLE GORGON MEDUSA, WITH HER HAIR OF SNAKES AND FACE SO FIERCE THAT ANYONE WHO LOOKS FULL UPON IT TURNS TO STONE, THE NYMPHS GIVE HIM THREE MAGICAL GIFTS TO HELP HIS ENDEAVOR. THE TWO USUALLY CITED AS MOST PRECIOUS ARE A PAIR OF WINGED SANDALS TO SPEED HIM AS FAST AS HERMES AND A CAP OF INVISIBILITY TO CONCEAL HIS ESCAPE. I, ON THE OTHER HAND,

Seek not, oh my soul, the life of the immortals; but enjoy to the fullest the resources that are within your reach.

—PINDAR, ODES, FIFTH CENTURY B.C.E.

have always thought the third gift the most valuable. It was a bag that would expand to hold anything Perseus put in it, no matter what the size.

I need that bag when I go vegetable shopping in Greece. I always start out thinking I'll buy just one cabbage, an onion or two, a few beets. But the minute I enter the market, with its array of incredible produce, I am bewitched. I end up purchasing string beans as snap-able as bread sticks, matte-finish ivory eggplant as firm as snowballs, garlic so impudent the cloves pop from their skins with a tweak of the fingers, okra so flawless they curve like commas to admire themselves, artichokes tight and snug as new-fallen pinecones, potatoes so newly dug their skins enfold them like spandex.

I am not alone in reveling in this Greek treasure trove of vegetables: The Greek diet has been essentially a vegetarian one for eons. The ancients dined mostly on grains and vegetables. Contemporary Greeks generally eat meals created almost entirely from plant foods. Meat, fowl, and fish are but occasional offerings. As a result, the Greek menu of vegetable dishes is a wonder.

On the menu are single vegetable dishes accented by oil, lemon, herbs, cheese, or savory sauces. Hand-in-hand come vegetable stews—*yakni, briami*—in which a splurge of vegetables is braised to form a complex medley. Baked vegetables, such as everyone's favorite, *moussaka*, burst out of ovens daily. Every vegetable and leaf that can serve as a container is stuffed. Leftover vegetables find themselves mixed with flour, onion, and herbs and fried into crisp coquettes and fritters. Undoubtedly the spectacular vegetable cuisine contributes to the Greeks' low rate of heart disease.

As for transporting the vegetable wealth from market to home, the loosely woven, infinitely expandable string bags that all Greek shoppers used to carry, before plastic ones arrived, could almost do. But I still declare that what the Greek vegetable eater really needs to encompass all the marvels offered at the market is a bag as voluminous as Perseus's!

# SIMMERED, SAUTEED & FRIED

## chestnuts and shallots

### SIMMERED WITH HONEY AND THYME

#### SERVES 4 TO 6

SOME SCHOLARS THINK THE GREEKS BROUGHT EUROPE'S PRESENT-DAY CHESTNUT TREE TO THE CONTINENT AFTER EUROPE'S OWN NATIVE SPECIES DECLINED. WHETHER THEY DID OR NOT, THE ANCIENT GREEKS SO ESTEEMED THE CHESTNUT, AND BELIEVED IT GAVE THEM INVINCIBLE STRENGTH, THAT ONE OF THEIR FIRST NAMES FOR IT WAS "ZEUS ACORN." THE STATELY TREES PROSPERED IN EUBOEA AND SARDIS, AND EVEN MORE ABUNDANTLY IN THE ASIA MINOR DISTRICT OF KASTANEA, FROM WHERE THE NUT ACQUIRED THE NAME GREEKS STILL USE—KASTANO.

From the dawn of Greek cooking, the most appreciated vegetables have included tree nuts, wild greens, mushrooms, the early cultivated pulses, and onions. These were usually given a treatment suitable to their simplicity; a simmering, a quick turn in hot oil, a dunk in hotter oil, or a roasting over coals. As more and more vegetables joined the inventory, many received the same time-honored, fundamental treatment; bean met bubbling water, eggplant met hot oil. Greeks today relish an almost innumerable catalog of old to new vegetables, and as before, many are plainly and elegantly simmered, some sautéed, some fried. To honor the march of history, the recipes that follow proceed from the oldest to the newest vegetables in the Greek herbaceous feast.

Throughout ancient times the chestnut remained a staple, especially in areas so harsh that cereal grasses refused to thrive. People stewed the nut, pounded it, ate it as a gruel, and mixed it with lentils, peas, and chickpeas. Breads were made with chestnut flour. To this day Greeks delight in chestnuts, though now more as a treat purchased at a street-corner brazier or stuffed in a holiday bird. In keeping with more ancient ways, here the whole morsel is simmered with other venerated ingredients, sweet shallots and honey perfumed with thyme.

2 tablespoons butter
8 ounces shallots, peeled and
    cut into 1/2-inch rounds
    or wedges
1 1/2 teaspoons fresh thyme leaves,
    or 1/2 teaspoon dried
1 pound chestnuts, peeled and
    cooked (see Notes)
1/3 cup water
2 tablespoons honey
1 1/2 tablespoons fresh lemon juice
1/4 teaspoon freshly ground
    black pepper

**1** Melt the butter in a medium-size skillet over medium heat. When it is foaming, add the shallots and thyme and sauté until wilted, 5 minutes.

**2** Stir in the chestnuts, water, honey, lemon juice, and pepper and bring to a boil. Reduce the heat and simmer gently, uncovered, until the liquid is reduced and the shallots and chestnuts are soft but not collapsing, 5 minutes. Serve right away.

**NOTES:**

■ To peel chestnuts, make an incision in each chestnut with a sharp paring knife. Place them in a pan of lightly salted water, bring to a boil, and boil for 10 minutes. (Or put the chestnuts in a baking pan in a single layer, place in a preheated 450°F oven, and roast until the skins open, 10 minutes.) Remove the chestnuts from the water (or oven) a few at a time, and when they are barely cool enough to handle, peel away the outer shell and the inner skin, exposing the beige nut. It is important to work quickly because once the chestnuts are removed from the heat, the loosened skins will re-adhere. If this happens, return the chestnuts to the water or oven briefly. Once they are all peeled,

place the chestnuts in a pot, add water to cover, and bring to a boil. Boil until the chestnuts are tender, about 20 minutes. Drain. Use immediately or store in a sealed container in the refrigerator for up to 1 week.

## THE GREEK VEGETABLE TRADITION

Since the earliest days, the Greek diet has consisted largely of cereal grains and garden and field plants. By the time Pythagorus admonished people to eschew flesh in the fifth century B.C.E., the vegetable tradition was probably already long established. Eating meat was wrong, Pythagorus declared; meat caused harm, and by shunning it people could also avoid the onus of animal sacrifice.

Still, then as today, the Greek diet cannot be called vegetarian. Ancient Greeks enjoyed the culinary gifts of animals from land, sky, and waters, but they ate those foods only now and then. The same held true until very recent times.

The reasons for the largely vegetable cuisine are probably threefold. The diet was a necessity because vegetable foods were the most available and people had to eat. It was a matter of economy because meat, fowl, and fish were costly. Besides, animals were needed to produce other foods, such as milk, cheese, and eggs. And finally, the diet was convenient. Most people lived on the land, and what the land produced was handy. In due time these three reasons led to two more: convention and taste. The dishes that came to be customary and identified as "Greek" were largely the vegetable ones, and Greeks grew to prefer vegetable meals. Many Greeks I know simply don't like meat; others pass up seafood. Recently Greeks, along with numerous other people, have added a final reason for maintaining their traditional diet: its healthfulness. Eating vegetables has served them well, and they mean to keep their amazing good health going.

■ Ready-to-use canned chestnuts are a tempting alternative to peeling your own, but they do not work for a toothsome vegetable side dish. They collapse and turn the mixture more mushy. However, you can purchase peeled, freeze-dried chestnuts in jars and in vacuum-wrapped boxes in gourmet food stores. Use them as you would fresh chestnuts.

# Warm greens

## HORTA

### SERVES 6

HEAPING PLATEFULS OF SIMMERED GREENS ARE SERVED TWO WAYS IN GREECE: STILL STEAMING HOT, STRAIGHT FROM THE COOKING POT, AND COOLED TO ROOM TEMPERATURE, ALMOST LIKE A SALAD. EITHER WAY, THE SATISFACTION AND VITALITY THEY OFFER ARE ABOUNDING. BEAR IN MIND THAT SOME GREENS NEED TO BOIL LONGER THAN OTHERS TO BECOME SOFT AND TENDER (COLLARD AND KALE TAKE LONGER THAN PURSLANE). SOME ARE BETTER STEAM-WILTED WITH BARELY ANY LIQUID (ENDIVE AND ARUGULA). SOME CAN BE FOUND AT THE GROCER'S; SOME MUST BE HUNTED ON THE HILLS.

Top a plate of hot greens just lifted from the boiling water with a sprinkling of chopped olives or a stir of pressed garlic and dash of lemon.

*3 tablespoons extra-virgin*
*    olive oil*
*2 cloves garlic, minced or*
*    pressed*
*2 pounds greens, trimmed,*
*    washed, and drained but*
*    not spun dry*
*¹/2 cup pitted Kalamata olives,*
*    coarsely chopped*
*Water, as needed*
*2 tablespoons fresh lemon juice*

1 Heat the oil in a large non-reactive pot. Stir in the garlic, then the greens and olives, mixing well. Add water as necessary (see Note, page 268), and simmer gently until the greens are very tender, 5 to 30 minutes depending on the type.

2 Stir in the lemon juice and serve right away, while still warm.

**NOTE:** Recognizing how good greens are for you, Greeks drink the cooking water as a healthful beverage.

## GREENS, WILD AND TAME

Feathery fern to sprouting bulb, leaf as broad as a plate to grasslike spear, plump shoot to prickly thistle, growing in tangles or hiding alone, some biting, some bitter, some sweet, some sour: The abundance of wild and tame greens devoured in Greece utterly defies enumeration. Most were known to the ancients—bryony, mustard, mâche, grape hyacinth. Some have more recently entered the inventory—spinach, Swiss chard. Some are widely cultivated; some still require pursuit. Some are known throughout the country; some are so local that Greeks from neighboring areas wouldn't know them.

Hardly a day goes by without some green appearing among the table's offerings. Sometimes the greens are fried; others that cook quickly are sautéed. When staunchly wild, some—like the field dandelion—need several dips in hot water. Many become the filling for a pie (pages 93, 95) or the flavoring for a pilaf (page 231). Most are simply boiled, topped with the kitchen's best pungent olive oil, and placed before the diner like a warm salad.

## GREENS IN THE OLIVE GROVES

Many wild greens are found in olive orchards, where they are often gathered and eaten by the olive pickers. Their presence in the orchards is due in part to an ancient law forbidding anyone from cutting down an olive tree. Even in the busy marketplace that was the center of ancient Athens, Plato was able to sit under an olive tree to carry on his dialogs. The tree is still there, still alive, and from time to time puts out shoots. Another historic olive tree still grows in Ephesus, beside the sacred well of Ypelaio, and another stands on Delos, under which Leto is said to have given birth to Apollo and Artemis. Because of the law, the ground around the trees lies untilled. The olive roots make the ground uneven, and the volunteer greens grow there undisturbed.

Though the hills of orchards teemed with wild greens, in ancient Greece it was considered "not civilized" to eat wild foods; what was wild was disdained. Behind kitchen doors, however, the ancients ate wild vegetables by the basketful. Rather than admit to the habit as more and more patches of wild greens disappeared from the hillsides, it was common to attribute their devouring to unknown parties.

# greens salad
## WITH HARD-COOKED EGGS AND FRIED GARLIC
### SERVES 6

GREEKS RARELY COOK UP A MERE HANDFUL OF GREENS—THEY PREPARE WHOLE ARMFULS OF THEM, AND AS A RESULT THEY OFTEN HAVE LEFTOVERS, COOLED AND READY FOR THE NEXT MEAL. THESE THEY SERVE LUKEWARM AS A SALAD. WHEN GREEKS WAX NOSTALGIC OVER THE WILD GREENS (WHICH THEY OFTEN DO!), THEY HAVE A HARD TIME DECIDING WHETHER THEY PREFER THEM STEAMING HOT OR TEPID. I PREFER THE COOL GREENS, BECAUSE THEIR FLAVOR INCREASES MORE AS THEIR TEMPERATURE EBBS.

4 cups cooked greens, such as dandelion, mustard, turnip, spinach, or chard, at room temperature (see Note)
2 hard-cooked eggs, each cut into 6 wedges
1/4 cup fresh lemon juice
1/2 cup extra-virgin olive oil
1/3 cup Fried Garlic Topping (page 481)

Spread the greens on a platter, and arrange the eggs around the edges. Drizzle the lemon juice and olive oil over all, sprinkle the fried garlic over the top, and serve right away.

**NOTE:** The amount of water to use for cooking greens is quite variable, but not really tricky. For sturdy-leaved, slightly bitter greens, such as dandelion, collard, turnip, or kale, add enough water to cover the greens so that they boil until tender. For more delicate-leaved greens, such as spinach, arugula, chard, watercress, beet greens, or sorrel, the water clinging to the leaves after washing will suffice. Purslane, Asian greens, the choys, and other stiff-leaved but not at all bitter greens lie in-between; add several splashes of water, but not enough to float them.

### VARIATIONS:

■ Add anchovy fillets for a more substantial dish.

■ Top with toasted sesame seeds instead of the fried garlic.

# green peas and pearl onions

## IN DILL OIL

### SERVES 6

PROBABLY NO COMBINATION OF VEGETABLES COULD BE MORE ANCIENT THAN PEAS WITH ONIONS. REMAINS OF PEAS HAVE BEEN FOUND IN THE EARLIEST CITY OF TROY, DATING FROM 12,000 B.C.E. THE PEAS THERE, THOUGH, WERE SOFT AND GREEN FOR ONLY A FEW DAYS BEFORE BECOMING HARD. THE BRILLIANTLY GREEN, QUICK-COOKING ENGLISH SORT WAS DEVELOPED IN THE SIXTEENTH CENTURY IN NORTHERN EUROPE. GREEKS NOW ALSO EAT THEM WITH THEIR VENERATED ONION COMPANION AND A DASH OF TOMATO PASTE, THEY ARE A FAR CRY FROM THE OFTEN BLAND VERSION SERVED "UP NORTH."

*1/3 cup olive oil*
*10 ounces pearl onions, peeled*
*1 1/2 tablespoons tomato paste*
*1 cup water*
*1 1/2 tablespoons chopped*
  *fresh dill*
*1/4 teaspoon salt*
*3 pounds fresh peas, shelled*
  *(about 3 cups)*

1 Heat the oil in a large nonreactive saucepan over medium-high heat. Add the onions and stir until well coated and beginning to soften, about 2 minutes.

2 Add the tomato paste, water, dill, and salt and stir until well mixed. Bring to a boil, cover, reduce the heat, and simmer until the onions are pierceable but not yet tender, 15 minutes. Remove the cover, add the peas, and continue simmering until the sauce has thickened and the peas and onions are very tender, 5 to 10 minutes.

3 Remove the pan from the heat and let the mixture rest for at least 5 minutes. Then serve right away, or at room temperature, or chilled.

## THE LAVISH PALATE OF THE ANCIENT PERSIANS

Intermittently at war with the Persians and always disdaining them, the ancient Greeks often contrasted their own eating habits with those of their enemy. The Greeks, said Herodotus, were modest leaf-eaters, *philotroges*, who dined on small things to the point that they could be described as a people of *mikrotrapezi*, or "small table." The Persians were said perhaps to eat better food, but to eat so lavishly as to be the object of derision. Many Greek sources describe the Persians, rich and poor alike, as eating whole beasts, in particular camel, ox, ass, hog, lamb, gazelle, and stag. And while the Greeks acknowledged that roasting such beasts might be a munificent culinary custom, it was equally a prodigal one. It demanded a ridiculous amount of fuel, when instead a judicious person could get along just fine eating such foods as peas, onions, and a hunk of bread.

# beets and turnips

## IN SWEET CAPER BUTTER

### SERVES 6

EVERY NOW AND THEN IT BEHOOVES A GREEK COOK TO ENHANCE AN ANCIENT DISH WITH A SUBSTANCE THAT ANCIENT GREEKS DID NOT ADMIRE AND MODERN GREEKS STILL RARELY USE: BUTTER. THE EARLY GREEKS RIDICULED THE BARBARIAN RAIDERS AT THEIR DOOR FOR THE GHASTLY HABIT OF EATING ANIMAL FAT INSTEAD OF LUSCIOUS, CIVILIZED OLIVE OIL. BUTTER, THEY THOUGHT, WAS BEST APPLIED AS A BODY SALVE, NOT SERVED AS A FOOD.

Still, rather surreptitiously, in this century the long-civilized Greeks have slipped a bit into the barbarian habit. Quite often they use butter in their baking. Occasionally they slather a bit onto a vegetable. That touch of the "boorish" is particularly wondrous when combined with capers and root vegetables.

*2 bunches beets (1 ¹/2 pounds total), tops removed*
*4 medium turnips, peeled and cut into ¹/4-inch wedges*
*4 tablespoons (¹/2 stick) unsalted butter*
*¹/2 teaspoon sugar*
*2 tablespoons capers*
*2 tablespoons chopped fresh dill*
*1 lemon, cut into 6 wedges*

1 Rinse the beets, place them in a saucepan, and add water to cover. Bring to a boil over high heat, then reduce the heat and simmer briskly until tender but not mushy, 35 to 50 minutes depending on the size. Drain and set aside until cool enough to handle. Peel the beets and cut them into ¹/4-inch wedges.

2 While the beets cool, bring another pot of water to a boil. Drop in the turnips and simmer briskly until tender but still firm, 5 minutes. Drain.

3 Place the butter, sugar, capers, and dill in a clean pot over medium-high heat. When the butter foams, add the beets and turnips, stir to coat, and reheat for 2 minutes. Garnish with the lemon wedges and serve.

## THOSE MUTTERING, BUTTERING BARBARIANS

It's commonly thought that the term "barbarian" originally meant "bearded one" and that it was applied to the un-suave tribes sweeping into Greece because they were a hirsute people with much fuzzy stuff upon their faces. Not so. "Barbarian" was an onomatopoeic term the Greeks applied to the strangers because they couldn't talk properly. They "bar-bared." They mumbled and stuttered. Still, they became civilized enough to give their favorite cooking medium a Greek name: In both ancient and modern Greek, the word for "butter" is *voutyro*, or "cow cheese." The Romans adopted the word as *bouteron*. In conquering the British Isles, they left the word without the ending, as *bouter*.

# sautéed mushroom caps

## WITH GARLIC AND BREAD CRUMBS

**SERVES 3 AS A MAIN DISH, OR 12 AS A MEZE**

PORTOBELLO AND SHIITAKE MUSHROOMS MAY BE NEW TO GREEK GASTRONOMY, BUT THEY LEND THEMSELVES BEAUTIFULLY TO A TREATMENT THAT HAS CHANGED LITTLE OVER THE MILLENNIA. POLIOCHUS, A THIRD-CENTURY B.C.E. COMEDIC POET, CLAIMED THAT ALL HE NEEDED TO EAT WAS A BRAISED MUSHROOM, AND IF THERE WAS A LITTLE DEW ABOUT SO THAT HE COULD FIND A SNAIL, HE WAS HAPPIER STILL.

Ancient Greeks braised their mushrooms with an abundance of garlic and sprinkled them with fresh parsley or other herbs. The treatment here does not include Poliochus's snail, but it has the same plain country ease and elegance, with the addition of butter, and is filling enough to demonstrate why Poliochus thought a mushroom constituted a perfect meal.

*3 giant mushroom caps*
*(5 to 6 inches in diameter),*
*such as portobellos, or 6 to 8*
*smaller caps, such as shiitakes*
*2 tablespoons olive oil*
*Salt*
*6 tablespoons ($^3$/$_4$ stick) butter*
*4 cloves garlic, finely chopped*
*$^1$/$_2$ cup bread crumbs, preferably*
*homemade*
*2 tablespoons chopped fresh flat-leaf*
*parsley leaves*
*2 teaspoons fresh lemon juice*

1 Trim the stem ends of the mushrooms and wipe the caps and stems with a dry cloth to clean them without moistening. Cut off the stems flush with the caps. Finely chop the stems and set aside.

2 Heat the oil in a large skillet over high heat. Place the mushroom caps, top sides down, in the skillet and cook until beginning to soften, 6 minutes. Turn, reduce the heat to medium-high, and continue cooking until the caps are tender but not soggy, 2 to 3 minutes. Transfer them to a platter, setting the caps top down. Salt lightly and set aside.

3 Add the butter to the same skillet and reduce the heat to medium. When the butter is almost melted, add the reserved chopped mushroom stems along with the garlic, bread crumbs, and parsley. Raise the heat to medium-high and stir until the stems are soft and the bread crumbs are toasted, 4 to 5 minutes.

4 Spread the bread crumb mixture over the mushroom caps and sprinkle the lemon juice over all. Serve right away.

# THE HERBS OF GREECE

HERBS, LIKE WILD GREENS AND MUSHROOMS, ARE SOMETHING GREEKS OUTSIDE THE CITIES HAVE ALWAYS GATHERED FROM THE FIELDS, HILLS, AND RIVERBANKS; A FEW, LIKE BASIL AND GERANIUM, ARE GROWN FROM YEAR TO YEAR IN LUSH POTFULS. VIRTUALLY DOZENS OF HERBS—LIKE AGRIMONY, PENNYROYAL, VERBENA, HYSSOP, LAVENDER, AND CALAMINT—ARE USED FOR HEALING, WHILE OTHERS ARE USED IN COOKING. IN THE CITIES, HERBS MIGHT BE DISPLAYED ON THE CART OF THE NEIGHBORHOOD PRODUCE PEDDLER, AND NOWADAYS THEY APPEAR MORE IN OUTDOOR MARKETS, BUT OFTEN THOSE ARE GATHERED BY THE SELLER OR HIS COHORT. HERE ARE SOME OF THE WILD AND CULTIVATED HERBS THAT GREEKS USE IN COOKING.

**ANISE,** *glykaniso,* meaning "sweet anise"—abundant everywhere

**BASIL,** *vasilikos*—rarely used in cooking, but grown in decorative pots in every household

**BAY LEAF,** *dafni* and *dafnofila*—of which the honorary wreaths of ancient Olympic victors and poets were woven; readily available

**CELERY** and **CELERY ROOT,** *selino*—sprouting all along the coast; a dark-leafed, stringy sort, it is considered more flavoring herb than vegetable

**CHAMOMILE,** *hamomili*—for flavoring and teas, and for dyeing hair blond

**CHERVIL,** *anthrismos, hairifyllon,* or more commonly *frankomaintanos* ("Frankish parsley")—occasionally used as a cooking aromatic

**CHIVES,** *krommion* or *kremidi*—used quite rightly as a combination onion and herb

**CITRON,** *kitron*—the "golden apple of the Herperides," not an herb per se, but used with sugar or honey to flavor sweetenings

**CORIANDER/CILANTRO,** *koriandroto* or *koliantros,* both seeds and fresh leaves—gathered everywhere

**DILL,** *anithos*—ubiquitous, used mostly in spring (replaced with fennel in the fall)

**FENNEL,** *maratho*—the great opportunist of every fallow field in Greece

**JUNIPER BERRY,** *iouniperos* or *agriakuparissi* ("wild cypress")—not specifically an herb, but gathered and used for flavoring

**LIME BLOSSOM,** *tilio*—used as both tea and flavoring

**MARJORAM,** *mantzourana*—like oregano and thyme, thrives on every dry slope of Greece

**MINT,** *diosmos, mentha,* or *menta*—many sorts, some sweet, some bitter, but mostly spearmint, picked by the handful

**MUSTARD,** *moustarda* and *sinaposporos*—growing in vineyards and fallow fields, the leaf also used as a green

**OREGANO,** *rigani*—absolutely abounding on every arid peak

**PARSLEY,** *maidanos*—also once a garland for the venerated, both the curly and flat-leaf varieties sprout as thick as clover. Rock celery, another stronger type of parsley, is also gathered and used

**ROSEMARY,** *dendrolivano*—the twiggy stems with needle-like leaves spill over rocks and rock walls everywhere.

**ROSE PETALS,** *triandafila*—if not in the fields, always in flowerpots; also rose and lemon geranium leaves, *geranion* or *arbaroriza*

**RUE,** *apigano*—a pungently aromatic shrub with tiny oval leaves used to flavor olives and cure illness

**SAGE,** *faskomilo, alisfakia,* or *hamosfaka*—a number of varieties sprout on the slopes; used as a curative drink Greeks call "mountain tea"

**SAVORY,** *throumbi* and *thrimbi*—a number of varieties depending on the area, found everywhere that oregano, thyme, and marjoram grows

**THYME,** *thymari*—grows so abundantly that snails are fed armloads of it as a purge before they are eaten

# steamed whole cauliflower

## IN LEMON-NUTMEG *BESAMEL* SAUCE

### SERVES 6

CAULIFLOWER SEEMS TO BEG FOR A GREEK-STYLE COMPOSITION. SOMETIMES GREEK COOKS COAT CAULIFLOWER FLORETS IN BATTER AND DEEP-FRY THEM. SOMETIMES THEY COOK THE FLORETS ALONG WITH A COLLECTION OF COLORFUL COMPANIONS INTO A *BRIAMI* (PAGE 282). SOMETIMES THEY DRAW OUT A CAULIFLOWER'S SUBLIME FLAVOR WITH A BRUSH OF OLIVE OIL AND A DASH OF PEPPER, OR CRAFT IT INTO A COLD SALAD (PAGE 189). HERE THE VEGETABLE IS COATED IN A WASH OF NUTMEG- AND LEMON-FLAVORED *SALTSA BESAMEL*. SIMPLE, BUT ELEGANT.

*2 tablespoons fresh lemon juice*
*Pinch of ground nutmeg,*
*    preferably freshly grated*
*2 cups Saltsa Besamel*
*    (page 459), warmed*
*2 small whole cauliflowers,*
*    stem ends trimmed,*
*    tender leaves left on*
*1/3 cup coarsely grated kefalotyri*
*    cheese*
*1 lemon, cut into 6 wedges*

1 Stir the lemon juice and nutmeg into the *besamel*, and set it aside to keep warm.

2 Bring a large pot of water to a boil over high heat. Drop in the cauliflower and cook just until they can easily be pierced with a fork, about 8 minutes. Drain and transfer to a platter.

3 Pour the sauce over the cauliflower and sprinkle the cheese over the sauce. Garnish with the lemon wedges and serve.

## THE A-MUSING CAULIFLOWER

When I think of cauliflower, I think of the Muses, for hardly any other vegetable is so amenable to artistry.

The Muses were the daughters of Zeus and his aunt, Mnemosyne, whose name means "memory," as does the word "muse." They were the goddesses of all the subjects we now classify as "arts" at a university; history, art, philosophy, language, and music. They were minor gods. Their importance came about from their popularity among the arty, who claimed that they were their inspiration. The nine Muses divided up the artistic turf:

**CALLIOPE** ("good voice"), the muse of epic poetry

**CLIO** ("renown"), of history

**ERATO** ("lovely"), of lyric poetry and song

**EUTERPE** ("gladness"), of music

**MELPOMENE** ("singing"), of tragedy

**POLYMNIA** ("many songs"), of mime

**TERPSICHORE** ("joy in the dance"), of dance

**THALIA** ("great good cheer"), of comedy

**URANIA** ("heavenly"), of astronomy

In ancient Greece, "diet" didn't mean quite what it does now, and it seems to me that the old meaning is perhaps better than our current one. The word *diaita*—from which we get "diet"—meant an entire regimen for living, not merely a regimen of foods, and certainly not an abstention from food. A *diaita* included not only the meals eaten but also the daily course of exercise, bathing, and self-care. A proper, well-rounded *diaita* was thought to bring health, security, and nourishment. To depart from a good diet could even cause bad politics.

Plato believed the political decadence of his fellow citizens was the result of their straying from a righteous routine and eating in too luxurious a manner. He called for a return to a humbler menu, including good vegetables. He wrote: "Clearly people ought to have salt, olives, cheese, onions, and vegetables that are the fare of rural folk. They should even be served dessert, namely figs, chickpeas, and broad beans, and they will roast myrtle berries and acorns on the coals and nibble on them while drinking in moderation."

# artichokes and celery
## IN CELERY SEED AVGOLEMONO

### SERVES 6

WILD CELERY GROWS NEAR DELPHI, AND IN A NUMBER OF WAYS, THAT IS APPROPRIATE. SOMETHING "DELPHIAN" IS SOMETHING OBSCURE, AND THE FLAVOR OF CELERY—EVEN OF THE STRONGER WILD SORT—IS OFTEN SO EVASIVE IT IS USUALLY USED TO BOOST A DISH'S TASTE IN A HIDDEN WAY. A THING DELPHIAN IS ALSO AMBIGUOUS, AND WILD CELERY CAN EASILY BE CONFUSED WITH ITS NEAR RELATIVE, PARSLEY. THE ANCIENT GREEKS MIXED UP THE TWO AND CALLED THEM BOTH *SELINO*.

Delphi is also the place sacred to the god Apollo. In the fields below the sanctuary grow artichokes, a vegetable that exhibits truly apollonian traits: harmony, order, and balance. Greeks commonly eat them young, when they are particularly delicate. Combining the two vegetables creates a subtly nuanced treat, but topping them with a celery seed sauce changes the picture greatly.

A lemon egg sauce containing just a touch of celery seed stands out sassily. Apollo had a brash side along with his harmonious one. I think he would approve.

6 medium artichokes, well trimmed, quartered, chokes removed (see Note)

4 large ribs celery with leaves, trimmed ribs cut into 2-inch lengths, leaves coarsely chopped

6 scallions, white and light green parts trimmed and cut into 3-inch lengths

1/2 teaspoon salt

6 cups water

3 large eggs

1/3 cup fresh lemon juice

1/8 teaspoon celery seeds

1 Place the artichokes, celery, scallions, salt, and water in a large nonreactive pot. Bring to a boil over high heat, cover, and simmer briskly until the artichokes are tender, 25 to 30 minutes. Using a slotted spoon, transfer the vegetables to a bowl and set it aside. Reserve the cooking liquid in the pot off the heat.

2 Crack the eggs into a medium-size bowl. Whisk until frothy, then beat in the lemon juice. Slowly whisk in $1/2$ cup of the cooking liquid along with the celery seeds. Whisk the egg and lemon mixture into the liquid remaining in the pot, place it over medium-low heat, and whisk gently, taking care not to let the mixture boil, until thickened, about 5 minutes. Return the vegetables to the pot, stir to mix, and serve right away.

**NOTE:** Because the artichokes are mixed with the sauce in this dish, all the tough outer leaves should be removed down to the tender inner ones, and the tops cut off to the tender part of the leaves, so that the diner can use knife and fork and doesn't have to labor messily with his or her fingers.

## ST. GEORGE:
### PATRON OF BOTH BATTLE AND GARDEN

Since the age of classical Greece, the common man has been both farmer and soldier. In ancient times, one god appeared sunny on the planted field and fierce on the battlefield. He was Apollo, keeper of the peaceful sun and pugnacious defender of Troy. As Greece turned to a new religion, Christianity, a figure who much resembled Apollo arose from the great era of saints. His name meant "farmer," but St. George was also an armored knight, riding a white steed, carrying a spear, and slaying a dragon.

George's origins are enigmatic. His name indicates that he was from a rural place and people, perhaps Kappadokia. The legends about him begin to arise about the fifth century and continue for centuries. The deeds he performs are the stuff of the heroes of mythology, but they, too, take place in a rustic milieu. A farmer loses a pair of oxen; the neighbors laugh at him for not being a good manager; St. George helps him find his yoke. A gaggle of poor boys promise George a cake if he helps them win at games; four merchants take the cake and eat it, so St. George locks them in a church and makes them pay a fine. A man tries to bargain down the promise he made to St. George in return for his help; George raises the price and appears in the man's dreams dressed for battle; the man slaughters an ox to feed his common fellows; George brings forth live animals from the bones. Centuries later in Cyprus, mounted on his steed, he rescues a boy from raiders.

Yet George also remains the keeper of all men-at-arms. It is said he was a soldier, and his intercession is implored in battles. He was also a rebel. Some contend it was St. George who tore down the imperial edicts commanding that all Christian churches be razed, scriptures burned, and believers jailed that were posted by Emperor Diocletian of Nicomedia, and for that he was hunted and martyred.

Greeks call him the Great Martyr, and it's not hard to see why a people with such a peasant tradition, yet so often wracked with war, would love him. Among Greeks he merits such esteem that his name day is set aside as a national holiday. If his day falls near Easter, it is delayed a month so that St. George may be celebrated separately from the rites of the holy week. Like Apollo, he merits honor on his own.

## FOUR SURVIVING RECIPES

When my home burned down with all my cooking equipment and this book half written, the instructions for only four dishes remained: One was for rice pudding (my children's favorite breakfast), one was for stuffed zucchini flowers (page 308), and two were for eggplant. They escaped because I had served them to my Greek friend Argine, and though a great cook herself, she had requested copies of the recipes.

Argine also had a contrivance that made my response immediate—she had a fax machine. The rice pudding had a creamier texture, she claimed, than hers. The zucchini flowers she wanted because her garden was sprouting its last summer offerings. The eggplant she had to have . . . because she had to have eggplant. Next to her *moussaka*, apart from her eggplant salad and eggplant slippers, she would now have fried eggplant with feta, and basil and eggplant with shallots (page 289). Several days later, when the smoke was still rising from the ashes, Argine appeared at my no-longer-doorstep with a set of cups and saucers and four flimsy faxes, my four extant recipes, including the two for Greece's beloved eggplant.

# fried eggplant
## WITH FETA AND BASIL

### SERVES 4 TO 6

THERE ARE TIMES IN GREECE WHEN WHOLE FIELDS TURN WHITE OR PURPLE FROM THE RIPENING EGGPLANTS. THEN AN EGGPLANT MADNESS OF A SORT ENSUES. PEOPLE BUY BAGFULS, SLIPPING THEIR THUMBS OVER THE SLEEK SKINS TO MAKE SURE THAT THE EGGPLANTS ARE PERFECTLY, FIRMLY RIPE, WITH NOT ONE WRINKLY DAY TOO MUCH IN THE SUN. IN ONE OF THE BEST TRANSFORMATIONS, THE SLICES ARE TURNED INTO SALVERS FOR OTHER SUNNY HELLENIC FOOD—DENSE TOMATO, BITING FETA AND KEFALOTYRI CHEESE, OREGANO, AND SOMETIMES BASIL. LIGHTLY FLOURING THE EGGPLANT SLICES GIVES THEM BETTER COLOR AND TEXTURE AND ALLOWS THEM TO COOK IN LESS OLIVE OIL.

*Olive oil, for frying*
*1 large eggplant, trimmed and*
    *sliced into 1/4-inch-thick rounds*
*Unbleached all-purpose flour*
*18 to 20 large fresh basil leaves*
    *(as many as there are eggplant*
    *slices), rinsed and patted dry*
*4 ounces feta cheese, cut into*
    *the same number of slices*
*2 medium tomatoes, cut into*
    *the same number of thin slices*
*4 or 5 Kalamata olives, pitted and*
    *quartered lengthwise*
*1/4 cup grated kefalotyri or*
    *kefalograviera cheese*
    *(optional)*

1 Pour oil to a depth of 1/4 inch in a large nonreactive frying pan and heat over medium-high heat. Dust the eggplant slices with flour and place as many slices as will fit without crowding in the pan. Fry until lightly golden on both sides, about 3 minutes altogether. Transfer to paper towels to drain, and continue with another batch until all the slices are fried.

2 Wipe out the pan, leaving it lightly greased. Place a basil leaf on each eggplant slice. Top with a slice of feta, a slice of tomato, and an olive quarter.

3 Heat the pan over medium-high heat. Add as many eggplant slices as will fit without crowding, cover, and cook until the feta melts, about 1½ minutes. Transfer to a platter and continue with another batch until all the slices are refried.

4 Just before serving, sprinkle a pinch of grated cheese, if using, over each slice.

## NO MORE EGGPLANT TEARS

. . . . . . . . . . . . . . . . . . . .

The eggplants of yesteryear had a bitter quality, and it was the practice to leach out the bitterness by salting them before cooking. As the salt seeped in, fluid bearing the acrid taste would rise to the surface like tears to be blotted off. Nowadays, eggplants lack that bitter tinge, and salting is rarely necessary, though some cooks still prefer to draw the liquid out to make the eggplant flesh firmer.

If you wish to firm the flesh, lightly salt the sliced eggplant. Let sit for 30 minutes, then pat dry.

# fresh lima beans

## WITH YOGURT, PARSLEY, AND DILL

### SERVES 6

WHEN NEW WORLD BEANS ARRIVED IN GREECE, PEOPLE TOOK TO EVERY TYPE: STRING BEANS SIMMERED UP AS A SAUCY SIDE DISH, SMALL WHITES SUBMERGED IN A SATISFYING SOUP, BIG WHITES IN COLD SALADS AND HOT ENTREES. THEY ALSO QUICKLY ADOPTED LIMA BEANS. LIMAS ARE AN ANCIENT BEAN, FOUND IN SITES SOME EIGHT THOUSAND YEARS OLD IN THE CHILCA CAVES OF PERU. THEY ARE MEATY AND FLOURY. THEIR GREEN TASTE, TOOTHSOME TEXTURE, AND QUICK COOKING HAVE TURNED THEM INTO WORLDWIDE FARE.

Assessing their size, Greeks placed limas, along with giant beans and Old World broad (fava) beans, into their category for big beans, *koukia,* as opposed to the smaller navy, pinto, or red beans called *fassolia.* With their fine sense of combination, Greek cooks chose yogurt as a sauce for such a mellow, meaty bean. Here shy dill and vivid parsley augment the creamy yogurt. In yogurt sauce, lima beans make a side dish that is complementary to everything else on the table.

*2 tablespoons olive oil*

*8 scallions, white and light green parts trimmed and finely chopped*

*2 tablespoons chopped fresh dill*

*¼ cup chopped fresh flat-leaf parsley leaves*

*1¼ pounds shelled fresh or frozen lima beans*

*1½ cups water*

*2 cups plain yogurt*

*1 teaspoon salt*

**1** Heat the oil in a large non-reactive saucepan over medium heat. Stir in the scallions and sauté until beginning to wilt, 1 minute.

**2** Stir in the dill and parsley, then the lima beans. Add the water and bring to a boil. Cover the pot, reduce the heat, and simmer briskly until the beans are tender, 5 to 10 minutes depending on the size. Drain and transfer to a serving dish.

**3** Whisk the yogurt and salt together in a small bowl. Gently stir the yogurt into the beans and serve right away.

# new potatoes

## WITH MINT AND SPRING ONIONS

### SERVES 6

A LTHOUGH THE POTATO ENTERED GREEK CUISINE DURING THE TIME OF THE OTTOMANS, IT WASN'T UNTIL THE ENGLISH TOOK COMMAND OF PARTS OF GREECE IN THE LATE 1800S THAT IT BECAME A SIGNIFICANT PART OF THE DIET.

When the potato first arrived in Greece, it was opposed by the Orthodox priests, who insisted the vegetable was the apple Eve gave Adam in the Garden of Eden and would lead any eater to sin. If that were so, all Greeks would now be bound for Hades, because the potato—with its easy growing, its tasty and filling advantages, its many ways to prepare—took over the pots, pans, and plates of Greece. As with the tomato, it's hard to think of Greek food now without the potato. Potatoes are roasted alongside meats and birds or braised on their own in sauces. They form the platforms of casseroles. They are mashed, used as a sauce base, pressed into patties, simmered and herbed, and sliced and fried. Potatoes adorn the banquet table as side dish, filler, comfort food, taste favorite. In a minty rendition, the small new potatoes of spring are combined with shallots or other offerings of the onion family.

*2 pounds (30 to 32) small red or*
  *white potatoes, peeled (see Note)*
*2 tablespoons finely chopped*
  *spring onions, scallions, shallots,*
  *baby leeks, garlic shoots,*
  *or a mixture*
*1 tablespoon shredded fresh*
  *mint leaves*
*1/4 cup fruity olive oil*
*1 teaspoon salt*
*1/2 teaspoon freshly ground*
  *black pepper*

**1** Bring a large pot of water to a boil over high heat. Add the potatoes and cook until they can easily be pierced with a fork but are not falling apart, 10 to 15 minutes depending on their size. Drain in a colander and set aside to cool and drip dry for 5 minutes.

2 Return the potatoes to the pot, add the remaining ingredients without tossing, and set over low heat just long enough to reheat without further cooking. Gently toss to mix at the last minute and serve right away.

**NOTE:** Greeks peel their potatoes. If you prefer to skip this step, just scrub the potatoes and boil them in their skins.

## THE POTATOES OF LARISA

Dimitroula, Angeliki, and I headed out by tractor one morning across the fields near their homes on the outskirts of Larisa, one of Thessaly's largest cities. Ahead of us, instead of Greece's usual spiny limestone buttes and jagged coastline, was a flat plain with fields that were big enough to plow with an American—albeit small—John Deere. In the distance we could see the hazy outline of the Pindos mountains to the west and the Kamvounian range to the north. But seeing Mount Olympus was not our goal; we were off to sack potatoes.

Months before, brothers Lefteris and Stavros, my companions' husbands, had trenched long furrows across the plots they worked. Today they were going to start bringing in the fat russet potatoes that would be taken into town for weighing, selling, and shipping. We were to help bag the dense tubers as they were unearthed.

For a number of hours we followed the men as by machine and hand they pulled tubers from underground. One by one the fresh potatoes came up to the sunlight. With no bruises and no blade cuts, no greening and no eyes, they would fry up into crisp fries.

At midday, we made a tent by tying a cloth to the John Deere on one side and to two sticks on the other, and broke open the repast: cool boiled zucchini, stuffed tomatoes, eggplant salad to go on our country bread, and some retsina wine. We rested in our tent for an hour or so, then absconded with the green and yellow tractor to use in the next field, part of Angeliki's dowry, where we also dug for our dinner some new little thin-skinned white potatoes. "How could we have double potatoes for dinner?" I asked. As usual in Greece my question was answered with a slightly sarcastic query: Was I watching my figure? Thank the gods on faraway Olympus, no. Give me fresh Greek potatoes—not old, not shipped, not stored, not limp—anytime in any way. I would feast on them that night— boiled, oiled, lemoned, and salted—and the gods would envy me.

*Rather than sell to middlemen, a Thessaly farmer trucks his potatoes and scale to a Larisa square.*

# oven fried potatoes

## WITH OREGANO AND LEMON

### PATATES LEMONATA

**SERVES 6**

I HAD NEVER SEEN THE LIKES BEFORE I WENT TO GREECE: BIG RUSSET POTATOES, PEELED, CUT IN LONG THICK WEDGES, PLACED IN A BAKING PAN, ANOINTED WITH FINE OLIVE OIL, DOUSED WITH LEMON, AND ROASTED UNTIL THE OUTSIDE WAS CRACKLING AND THE INSIDE FLAKY. NOW I "FRY" SUCH POTATOES IN MY OVEN ALL THE TIME. THE TRICK IS PROBABLY THE LEMON: WHO ELSE BUT THE GREEKS WOULD SEE IT AS FLAVORING FOR A POTATO? OR MAYBE IT'S THE "FRYING" WITH OLIVE OIL. AND WHO ELSE WOULD RAIN OREGANO ON FRIED POTATOES? TRY THEM. YOU'LL NEVER LOOK BACK.

*4 large russet potatoes, peeled and cut into 1/4- to 1/2-inch-thick sticks*
*1/2 cup olive oil*
*1/2 cup water*
*2 teaspoons chopped fresh oregano leaves, or 1 teaspoon dried*
*1 teaspoon sea salt*
*1/2 teaspoon freshly ground black pepper*
*1/4 cup fresh lemon juice*

1 Preheat the oven to 450°F.

2 Place the potatoes, oil, water, oregano, sea salt, and pepper on a baking sheet large enough to hold the potatoes in one uncrowded layer (or divide the ingredients between two baking sheets). Turn to mix, coating all the potatoes with oil and seasoning, and place in the oven.

3 Bake, turning twice, until the potatoes are lightly golden and beginning to crisp, 45 minutes. Add the lemon juice, turn to coat, and continue baking until the potatoes are golden and very crisp, 10 to 15 minutes more. Serve right away.

## ACRES OF FEARLESS BEAN FIELDS

The word for "field" in Greek is *horafi*. Fields are measured in *ektare*, often translated as "hectare." A Greek farmer will tell you how many hectares he owns, and how many he has planted to wheat, or tomatoes, or potatoes. From *ektare*, we get "acre," the word for the unit we measure our own fields in, and from there the many words that have to do with things that grow in fields, like acre-culture, or agriculture, and agronomy—all the terms beginning with "agro." The original Greek *ektare* also means "outside," "edge," or "margin," for fields were outside and on the edge of town. So from the same stem we have "acrobat," for someone who walks on the edge. We also get "acronym," for a name that's made up from the leading edge of several other words, and a plethora of other "acro" terms, including "acrophobic," which doesn't really mean "fear of heights," but rather "fear of the edge."

# french fried potatoes

## GREEK-STYLE

### SERVES 6

UNCOUNTABLE PLATES OF UNBELIEVABLY GOOD FRIED POTATOES COME OUT OF GREEK KITCHENS DAILY. MADE IN A WAY THAT SHOULDN'T WORK, THEY ARE DROPPED IN WATER FIRST AND NOT DOUBLE-FRIED. NO FRYER IS USED—JUST A BIG SKILLET. YET THEY COME OUT PERFECTLY COGNAC-COLORED ALL AROUND, EACH ONE CRISP, HOT, CHEWY, AND SUBLIME. THEY REMAIN A MYSTERY TO ME. WHAT DOES IT? THE QUICK WATER BATH? THE SPRINKLING WITH SEA SALT? THE SINGLE FAST HOT FRYING? THERE'S NO POINT IN WONDERING ABOUT IT—JUST MAKE THEM AND ENJOY THEM TO THE VERY LAST MORSEL.

6 medium russet potatoes,
    peeled and cut lengthwise
    into ¼-inch-thick sticks
1 teaspoon sea salt
2 cups vegetable oil

1 Place the potatoes in a large pan of water and, using your hands, toss them for a minute. Transfer the potatoes to a colander and shake off the excess water. Sprinkle the sea salt over the potatoes and toss to coat.

2 Heat the oil in a large, deep, heavy skillet or pot over high heat until it is very hot.

3 Place as many potatoes as will fit in one tight layer in the skillet. Fry over high heat for 2 minutes. Stir and turn the potatoes over, and cook until golden and crisp, another 2 to 3 minutes. Transfer them to paper towels to drain, and repeat, allowing the oil to reheat between batches, until all the potatoes are fried. Serve right away.

## WHEN IN GREECE . . .

In Greece, the more you eat, the more you are given. My son, Jesse, knows this from experience.

Shortly after he graduated from college, Jesse and two friends went trekking around the world. Naturally Jesse wanted to show his friends the Greek village he had known since childhood. As they arrived, he warned them that they would be fed, that the amount of food would be overwhelming, and that they should not—by all means *not*—ask for more. The boys were greeted with delight—Jesse was, after all, almost one of their own—and to have three strapping *levendi*, "young heroes," all over six feet tall, coming down the road was an occasion for partying. Immediately they were sat down to dinner. In front of them were placed olives, cheese, bread, *dolmades*, filo pie, fish soup, roast chicken, stuffed tomatoes, rice and spinach, Jesse's favorite *tzatziki*, his second favorite, *skordalia*, a fried egg just to make sure there was enough, and to make doubly sure, a heaping plate of fried potatoes.

As the boys ate, one pal decided to rise to the challenge. He announced to Jesse that he believed he could out-eat the Greeks, and he proceeded to eat everything. As he cleaned a plate, my friends began to prepare their usual emergency filler: more fried potatoes. The villagers were delighted with Paul's appetite: How manly of him! How courageous! How godly! And so the fries kept coming until finally Paul fatigued, Paul faltered, Paul failed. The Greeks had won again—and with the simplest of bullets, the russet potato.

# STEWED VEGETABLE STAND-OUTS

# vegetable stew

## BRIAMI

### SERVES 6 TO 8

WHEN APOLLO'S BRILLIANT SUN RIPENS THE VERDURE AND VEGETABLES POUR INTO THE HARVESTERS' HANDS, GREEK COOKS KNOW JUST HOW TO TREAT THE ABUNDANCE: THEY BLEND THE VEGETABLES TOGETHER IN DELICIOUS AND COLORFUL STEWS. THESE STEWS HAVE MANY NAMES, MOST OF WHICH REFER TO THE TYPE OF POT USED TO SIMMER THE MIXTURE. THE MOST COMMON IS THE *BRIAMI*, WHICH CAN BE STEWED ON TOP OF THE STOVE OR IN THE OVEN.

Because most often the mixture is concocted of spring and summer vegetables, that season is followed here, but almost any vegetable can be added. Classically, dill and parsley season the medley—oregano is too overbearing—and for a touch more edge, capers are added.

*1/3 cup olive oil*
*1 large onion, halved and thinly sliced*
*6 cloves garlic, coarsely chopped*
*1 1/2 pounds potatoes, peeled and cut into 1/2-inch pieces*
*1 1/2 pounds zucchini or other summer squash, or a mixture, cut into 1/2-inch rounds or pieces*
*1 medium green bell pepper, seeded, stemmed, and cut into 1/2-inch-wide strips*
*1 1/2 pounds tomatoes, peeled and coarsely chopped, juices reserved*
*1 teaspoon salt*
*1/2 teaspoon freshly ground black pepper*
*1/4 cup chopped fresh dill*
*3/4 cup chopped fresh flat-leaf parsley leaves*
*1/4 cup dry white wine*
*1 tablespoon capers*

With vegetables the primary medium the talented cooks of Greece have had to work with over the generations, it's not surprising that they can create impeccable stews out of the garden's many offerings. Juices reduce, flavors merge, until the dishes are truly inspirational. Single vegetables are simmered until pliantly tender, then blanketed in oil. Zesty mixtures of two to twenty vegetables, called *briami, tourlou,* or *yakni,* are reduced until all the various juices merge into ambrosia. *Plaki* is another name for a *briami*-like medley, usually referring to beans or peas simmered soft with a smattering of sliced scallions or onion, then swirled with oil and touched with vinegar. Vegetables are also braised *yiouvetsi,* just like meat (page 363). When simmered alone, without benefit of meat, the plate is called *tourlou yiouvetsi.*

All Greek vegetable minglings are divinely flavorful. Forget those memories of sorry, soggy stewed vegetables. Greek vegetable stews are something else altogether.

## TO COOK ON THE STOVETOP:

1 Heat the oil in a large non-reactive pot over medium heat. Add the onion and garlic and sauté gently until well wilted but not browned, about 5 minutes.

2 Add the potatoes, zucchini, bell pepper, tomatoes with their juices, salt, pepper, dill, ½ cup of the parsley, and the wine. Bring to a boil, cover, and cook over medium heat until the vegetables are very tender and the mixture is very juicy, 1 hour.

3 Remove the cover and stir the vegetables. Continue cooking, uncovered, until the liquid is reduced and the vegetables are quite soft, 30 minutes. Serve hot or at room temperature, sprinkled over the top with the capers and remaining ¼ cup parsley.

TO BAKE IN THE OVEN:

1 Preheat the oven to 350°F.

2 Heat the oil in a large nonreactive flameproof casserole. Add the onion and garlic and sauté gently over medium heat until well wilted but not browned, about 5 minutes.

3 Add the potatoes, zucchini, bell pepper, tomatoes with their juices, salt, pepper, dill, ½ cup of the parsley, and the wine. Bring to a boil, cover, and transfer the casserole to the oven. Bake until the mixture is very juicy, about 1 hour.

4 Remove the cover and bake until the liquid is reduced and the vegetables are quite soft, about 30 minutes.

5 Serve hot or at room temperature, sprinkled with the capers and remaining ¼ cup parsley.

**NOTE:** *Briami,* freshly cooked or left over, keeps in the refrigerator for up to 5 days and freezes for up to 6 months.

## OTHER VEGETABLES TO ADD TO BRIAMI

While limiting a *briami* to a small selection of vegetables highlights their individual flavors, my favorite version of the dish embraces the entire feast I find at the produce market—I add a little of everything I find, along with the oil, onion, garlic, tomatoes, herbs, white wine, and capers. Replace all or some of the bell peppers, or ½ pound of the potatoes, or the zucchini, with any of the following:

■ Eggplant—1 medium, cut into ½-inch cubes

■ Okra—8 ounces, trimmed and left whole if small or cut into 1½-inch pieces if large, soaked for 30 minutes in ¼ cup white vinegar, then rinsed

■ Squash blossoms—8 ounces, rinsed

■ Celery—3 large ribs, trimmed and cut into ½-inch-wide slices

■ Carrots—3 medium, peeled and cut into ¼-inch-thick half-rounds

■ Mushrooms—8 ounces small to medium, cleaned, ends trimmed

■ Green beans—8 ounces, trimmed and left whole if small or cut into 1-inch lengths if large

■ White beans—1 to 1½ cups, precooked

■ Chickpeas—1 to 1½ cups, precooked

■ Broccoli—8 ounces florets and thinly sliced stems

■ Cauliflower—8 ounces florets

■ Spinach—1¾ pounds trimmed and rinsed leaves

■ Leeks—2 medium, trimmed, cut into ¼-inch-thick rounds, and well washed

■ Fresh black-eyed peas or broad (fava) beans—8 ounces

■ Turnips, parsnips, or other root vegetable—8 ounces, halved or quartered and sliced ¼ inch thick

*Briami* can also be topped with grated kefalotyri or feta cheese.

# APOLLO, THE SUN GOD

FOR THE GREAT ABUNDANCE OF VEGETABLES, THE ANCIENT GREEKS THANKED APOLLO, THE MASTER OF THE SUN. WITHOUT THAT SUNNY ORB, NO VEGETABLE WOULD RIPEN.

Apollo and his twin sister, Artemis, were the children of Zeus and a young Titaness named Leda, who had caught Zeus's eye and to whom he appeared as a swan. Fearing the wrath of Zeus's wife, Hera, no place on earth would shelter poor pregnant Leda. Finally the little island of Delos, which was thought not to be earth-bound but floating, took Leda in. There Apollo and Artemis were born, and in honor of them even now, the island (evidently quite firmly attached to Earth) remains sacred. No life events like birth or death are allowed to take place there; visitors must come and leave within a single day.

## A GREAT OLYMPIAN

Apollo and his twin were probably originally gods from somewhere north, but once adopted by the Greeks, Apollo rose in stature to sit among the greatest of the Olympians. Some call him the *most* Greek of all the gods. He was not at first associated with the sun, but in about the fifth century B.C.E., Greeks began to see Apollo as the ruler of the life-giving star and to lavish him with oblations for it. They gave him a second name, *Phoebus,* meaning "bright."

Besides ripening vegetables with his sunny rays, there are other reasons why Apollo was the deity of vegetables. After his traumatic birth, Apollo, fed on nectar and ambrosia by the goddess Themis, grew fast.

At Delphi he installed an oracle to predict the fate and future of things, which would suit everyone who wonders if their garden will prosper. Apollo was the patron of the arts, and the patron of medicine, too, and Greeks still believe that certain plants bear medicinal qualities—as do we. A harvest festival honoring Apollo featured beans.

## UNLUCKY IN LOVE

Apollo sided with Troy in the Trojan War. He built the walls of Troy and gave the "gift" of divination to Cassandra. When she refused his romantic overtures, however, he punished her, declaring that although she would always know the future, no one would believe her. As lucky as Apollo was at carrots and cardoons, and as sunny as his personality was (though he had occasional flare-ups and eclipses), he was ever unlucky at love. Besides Cassandra, the nymph Daphne turned him down. So did the Sibyl of Cumae, Marpessa, and Synope. Men, too, refused his wooing. His nuzzling so harmed both Hyacinthus and Cyparissus that he turned them into plants. All told, Apollo would have been better off had he just stuck to lovage.

*In an ancient depiction, Apollo with his lyre arrives by four-horse chariot to meet his sister, Artemis, the huntress.*

# fresh broad beans

## PLAKI-STYLE WITH TOASTED BREAD CRUMBS

### SERVES 6

THE WORD *PLAKI* MEANS "TILE" OR "FLAT PAVING STONE," OR ANYTHING SIMILARLY FLAT, LIKE A RECORD, A BLACKBOARD, OR THE FACE OF A CLOCK. IT ALSO IS A FLAT DISH IN WHICH FISH AND VEGETABLES ARE OFTEN SIMMERED, AND FROM IT COMES THE ANCIENT *PLAKI* STYLE OF COOKING.

Food cooked *plaki*-style always has zesty morsels added for flavor and aroma. When they come straight from the pod, fresh broad beans, which we know as fava beans, are ready to soak up the pungent flavors. Whether you cook them *plaki*-style in a shallow skillet or in a deep stockpot, the result will be excellent.

*4 pounds fresh broad (fava) beans, in their pods*
*1/3 cup olive oil*
*1 large onion, chopped into 1/4-inch pieces*
*4 cloves garlic, coarsely chopped*
*1 small carrot, trimmed and cut into 1/4-inch-thick half-rounds*
*1 rib celery, trimmed and cut into 1/4-inch-thick slices*
*1 pound tomatoes, or 5 canned tomatoes, chopped into 1/4-inch pieces, juices reserved*
*1 bay leaf*
*1 teaspoon fresh oregano leaves, or 1/2 teaspoon dried*
*1/2 teaspoon salt*
*1/4 teaspoon freshly ground black pepper*
*2 cups water*
*2 tablespoons butter*
*1 cup coarse bread crumbs, preferably homemade*

1 Bring a large pot of water to a boil over high heat. Shell the beans as you would green peas, discarding the pods. When the water boils, drop in the beans and bring back to a boil. Cook just until the skins loosen, 2 minutes. Drain and set aside until cool enough to handle. Pinching them with your fingers, pop the fava beans out of their skins and place them in a bowl. Set them aside.

2 Heat the oil in a large nonreactive pot over medium heat. Add the onion and garlic and sauté until wilted, 5 minutes. Stir in the carrot, celery, tomatoes and their juices, bay leaf, oregano, salt, pepper, and water. Bring to a boil, then reduce the heat and simmer until the vegetables are tender, 20 minutes.

3 Add the beans and simmer until they are tender, 8 minutes. Remove the pot from the heat and set it aside while you toast the bread crumbs.

4 Melt the butter in a medium-size skillet over medium heat. When it is foaming, add the bread crumbs and stir until lightly toasted, 3 to 4 minutes.

5 Sprinkle the bread crumbs over the stew and serve.

# giant beans

## PLAKI-STYLE
## WITH HONEY AND MINT

### SERVES 6

*The stunning cliffs of Meteora. Their name means "to hang in midair."*

ON EVERY RETURN TO GREECE, WHEN I ASK FOR A WELCOMING MEAL OF *GIGANTES*, MY FRIENDS KNOW TO COOK THE GIANT BEANS *PLAKI*-STYLE TO MELT MY HEART. THERE COULD HARDLY BE A BETTER CHOICE TO RECONNECT ME WITH MY ADOPTED LAND. MY GREEK ALMOST-FAMILY WOULD LIKE TO GIVE ME A SUMPTUOUS MEAL AND GIANT BEANS ARE NOT THEIR IDEA OF LUXURY, BUT IT IS MINE. I CAN GET A CHOP ANYWHERE, BUT GREECE'S HUGE WHITE BEANS, SOFTENED AND SIMMERED WITH TOMATO AND ONION UNTIL THE SAUCE IS THE BEAN AND THE BEAN IS THE SAUCE— THAT'S AS RARE AS CAVIAR. AS A PERFECT COMPLEMENT, MY CHOICE IS NOT CHAMPAGNE BUT RATHER ORDINARY *BROUSKO*, THE VILLAGE RED, RIGHT FROM THE BARREL.

Not quite classic, my version of giant beans *plaki* is perked up with mint and, for a sweet touch, a swirl of honey and vinegar. *Gigantes,* a colossal white bean, are hard to find except in Greek markets, but you can use dried limas, small white navy beans, or black-eyed peas. The *brousko?* Well, you would have to go to a village, have them fill a bottle, and smuggle it home, so instead pick up a hearty rustic red wine.

*1 pound dried gigantes beans (see Note)*
*1/2 cup olive oil*
*2 medium onions, chopped*
*3 cloves garlic, chopped*
*1 rib celery, chopped*
*3 medium tomatoes, chopped*
*1 tablespoon tomato paste*
*1 bay leaf*
*1/2 tablespoon fresh oregano leaves, or 1 teaspoon dried*
*2 whole cloves*
*1 tablespoon honey*
*2 tablespoons red wine vinegar*
*1 teaspoon salt*
*1/4 teaspoon freshly ground black pepper*
*3 cups water*
*1/2 cup Skordalia (page 461)*
*1 tablespoon shredded fresh mint leaves*

1 Place the beans in a large saucepan and add water to cover by 2 inches. Bring to a boil over high heat, cook for 1 minute, then remove from the heat. Set aside to soak for 1 hour.

2 Drain the beans, rinse them, and set them aside in a colander.

3 Heat the oil in a large non-reactive pot over medium heat. Add the onions, garlic, and celery and sauté until wilted, about 5 minutes. Stir in the tomatoes, tomato paste, bay leaf, oregano, cloves, honey, vinegar, salt, and pepper. Simmer until the mixture is well blended and a sauce has formed, about 10 minutes.

4 Add the 3 cups water and the beans and bring to a boil over high heat. Lower the heat and simmer briskly until the beans are very tender and some of their skins are breaking apart, 1 to 2 hours, depending on the age of the beans.

5 Remove the pot from the heat, swirl in the *skordalia,* and sprinkle on the mint. Serve right away or at room temperature.

**NOTE:** If you substitute dried limas, white beans, or black-eyed peas, dried limas and black-eyed peas cook in the same time as the giant beans; smaller white beans require about 1½ hours of cooking to soften completely.

# THESSALY

**D**URING CLASSICAL TIMES, MANY FARMERS LIVED AND WORKED IN GREECE'S ONE FLAT PLAIN, THE WEDGE OF THESSALY, OR THESSALIA. A BASIN OF RICH SOIL, IT LIES BETWEEN THE ICY WINDS OF THESSALONIKI—A NAME THAT MEANS "THESSALY'S VICTORY"—AND THE WARM WINDS OF ATHENS. WITH ITS CONFLUENCE OF WINTER RAINS AND HOT SUMMER HEAT, THE PLAIN IS STILL THE SOUL OF GREEK FARMLAND.

Although wide and level, it boasts some of the most spiritual, historic, and important places in Greece. Mount Olympus looks over it from the north. To the west stand the awesome cliffs of Meteora with their Byzantine monasteries precariously clinging to them. East lies the hook-shaped Mount Pilio peninsula, which served to protect the mainland of northern Greece from many invasions. Several of Greece's main rivers—including the Aliakmon to the north and the Pinios to the center—drain through Thessaly, and within the plain lie the bustling cities of Larisa, Trikala, and Volos.

## A FRUITED PLAIN

The abundance of fruit, grains, and vegetables that grows in Thessaly is nearly immeasurable. In the amazingly fertile Mount Pilio peninsula, home of the mythological centaurs, thousands of herbs and wild greens flourish on its steep slopes. Orchards and vineyards frame its coast. Across the breadth of the province, the farthest inland of any part of Greece, flat enough for myriad tractor furlongs, fields vibrate with okra, peppers, eggplant, artichokes, and beans.

## AN EATER'S PARADISE

Few tourists explore Thessaly. Its cities have become boisterous transportation centers. Cargo ships dock in Volos. Roads bring in cargo and carry goods of all kinds up and down the country, and Thessalia's cities are main arenas for manufacturing. Compared to Greece's foamy shore and wild highlands, the plain seems dull, although some still climb to the remaining monasteries of Meteora, scaling the cliffs—now easier with stairs carved in stone than in the days of pegs stuck in rocks or rope ladders.

Yet Thessaly is an eater's paradise. Refugees from Asia Minor turned Volos into the *ouzeri* ("ouzo bar") capital of Greece, though the usual drink is *tsikoudia* or *tzipouro,* the clear brandy made from grape pulp. Appetizers of Thessalian produce—fried, roasted, and stewed—come with every tiny glass. The small town of Zagora grows most of Greece's apples. In Trikeri, people wear traditional costumes on holidays and serve traditional fare to visitors, while near the ancient theater of Larisa, sophisticated restaurants serve glorious contemporary fare based on the surrounding cornucopia.

Yes, Thessaly is the place to eat. Alexander the Great once said that to own Thessaly is to own Greece, for with it one could feed an army. To visit it now is to devour some of Greece's best, for much of it continues to flower there.

# string beans

## WITH SHALLOTS, WHITE WINE, AND FENNEL SEEDS

### FASOLAKIA

✹

### SERVES 6

I F I COULD STRING TOGETHER THE NUMBER OF GREEN BEANS I HAVE EATEN IN GREECE, I'D HAVE A CORD LONG ENOUGH TO PULL ME BACK WHENEVER I WANTED TO RETURN. SLIM AND TENDER STRING BEANS ARE FOUND *POUTHENA*, "EVERYWHERE," AND *PANDOU*, "ANYWHERE," AND EATEN AVIDLY ALL THE TIME IN GREECE.

The beans are served as a hot vegetable all on their own. The choice is, as with all Greek food aesthetics, excellent. Long and thin as they are, green beans don't easily match in texture with other vegetables, but here, Greek-style, extra verve comes from shallots, tomato, and a splash of white wine.

*2 tablespoons olive oil*
*3 large shallots, finely chopped*
*1 clove garlic, coarsely chopped*
*1/8 teaspoon fennel seeds*
*4 medium tomatoes, peeled and cut into 1/4-inch pieces, juices reserved*
*2 tablespoons chopped fresh flat-leaf parsley leaves*
*1 tablespoon chopped fresh mint leaves*
*1 1/2 pounds green beans, trimmed and left whole*
*1/3 cup dry white wine*
*2 cups water*
*1 teaspoon salt*
*1/4 teaspoon freshly ground black pepper*

1 Heat the oil in a large non-reactive pot over medium heat. Add the shallots, garlic, and fen-nel seeds and sauté until slightly softened, about 2 minutes. Stir in the tomatoes with their juices and continue cooking until the tomatoes are soft and stewed down, 5 minutes.

2 Stir in the parsley, mint, green beans, wine, water, and salt and pepper and bring to a boil. Then reduce the heat, partially cover the pot, and simmer until the beans are very tender and the liquid is reduced by half and saucelike, 45 minutes. Serve right away.

## PEPPER

Theophrastus, philosopher and botanist of the fourth century B.C.E., distinguished two kinds of pepper, which he called the long and the black. Long pepper was the fruit of a plant that grew in northern India. Black pepper came from a plant of southern India. He considered long pepper superior and more valuable than black.

Greeks longed for their pepper, and the trade in the spice flourished. Like us, they pulverized the dried berry. Greeks also mixed pepper into milk, added it to wine, and kneaded it into dough. The pepper we grind into our dishes is the black pepper. Long pepper continues to be used in the Far East, but is rarely seen outside those realms today.

# eggplant

## WITH SHALLOTS, WINE, AND BASIL

### SERVES 6

JUST AS TOMATOES GROW MORE COMPACT AND MORE FLAVORFUL IN GREECE'S BLAZING SUN, SO DO ONIONS. COMMON YELLOW ONIONS GROW ONLY TO PEACH SIZE AND PACK A BLAST THAT EXPLODES LIKE A SMALL VOLCANO. THEIR FLAVOR IS BOTH NIPPY AND HONIED. SO WHEN I WANT TO REPLICATE THE POWER OF GREEK ONIONS, ESPECIALLY WHEN COMBINING THEM WITH SOMETHING AS MARRIAGEABLE AS EGGPLANT, IT IS ALWAYS A QUANDARY. WHAT TO USE?

The answer is shallots, which impart a vibrant onion essence, while their sugars make them as mellow as satin. Eggplant, when simmered in wine, also softens, though more like fleece. Basil adds a balmy hint, and red wine pulls it all together like a long-cooked ratatouille. Like many Greek dishes, a stew of vegetables tastes even better when it has aged a day or so—though this one rarely gets the chance.

1 cup olive oil

2 medium eggplants, trimmed
    and cut into 1-inch cubes

12 medium shallots (12 ounces total),
    peeled and left whole

6 to 8 cloves garlic, slivered

4 medium tomatoes, coarsely chopped

3/4 cup dry red wine

1 bay leaf, crumbled

1 teaspoon salt

1/2 teaspoon freshly ground black
    pepper

1/4 cup shredded fresh basil leaves

6 whole fresh basil leaves, for garnish

## BASIL

Vasilikos means "royal," and the name tells it all. If ever there was a regal herb, commanding yet delicate, perfumed yet brimming with character, it is basil.

Basil is the crowning herb of Greece. A member of the mint family (native to India, Southeast Asia, the Near East, and Africa), it flourishes in the sun, and so abounds in Greece. It grows as an annual, and comes in a number of slightly different flavors and colors, with leaves sometimes large, sometimes small, blooming as it goes to seed in spears of little white flowers. It was once cooked and eaten commonly in Greece. From Socrates to Galen, basil was deemed a major *opsa*. Dioscorides, an ancient physician and herbalist, declared that too much was hard on the stomach, but in moderation when taken with wine, basil was good for the eyes. Greeks still grow the herb in abundance—pots of it sit on almost every Greek veranda, yet it is rarely used in today's traditional Greek cooking. Somewhere along the way, its use in Greek fare, though not the Greek love for its aroma, diminished.

Still, innovative cooks in villages everywhere sometimes surreptitiously slip sprigs of basil into their stews and soups. It is part of their "secret ingredients." Occasionally cooks add it to bread starter; others apply it to quince jam. Happily, its use is having a revival. Basil was definitely good with the ancient gruels, but the modern vegetables— eggplants, tomatoes, squash—cry for the ancient herb. I never let them pine. I add it.

**1** Heat the oil in a large non-reactive skillet over medium heat. Add the eggplant, shallots, and garlic and sauté, stirring frequently, until the eggplant wilts, 10 to 12 minutes.

**2** Stir in the tomatoes, wine, bay leaf, and salt and pepper and simmer without stirring until the oil rises to the top and the eggplant is very soft and beginning to stick to the bottom (but not burning), 45 to 50 minutes.

**3** Remove the skillet from the heat and let the mixture cool for 10 to 15 minutes. Then stir in the shredded basil and serve, warm or at room temperature, garnished with the whole basil leaves.

**NOTE:** It's tempting, but do not reduce the amount of oil. If you do, the eggplant will absorb too much wine and will taste sharp.

## THE CULTIVATED MONTHS OF THE AGRICULTURAL CALENDAR

From the Byzantine era until recent times, the farmers of Greece had their own names for the months of the year, and those names told the story of the yearly round of agriculture.

The name for January is *Gennaris*, from *yeno*, "to give birth," the month when goats and cows drop their kids and calves.

February is *Flevaris*, which has to do with veins, and probably with the running of sap; it also means "cleansing."

The name for March is *Anoiksiatis*, "the opening."

April is *Vrohi*, "the rain."

May has several names: *Kerasaris*, "cherry," *Triandafilas*, "roses" (a word that means "thirty petals"), and *Louloudas*, "flowers," for a month when Greece's hills are covered with blossoms.

The name for June is *Theristis*, which means "the harvesting"; it is the month when wheat and barley are reaped with sickle and scythe.

July is *Alonaris*, which means "the threshing."

In some places August is called *Trigos*, for the grape harvest, although that is early for grapes. In other places September has that name.

September is sometimes called *Stavros* for the festival of the Holy Cross, an important day in the calendar. It is also called *Trigos* or *Trigitis*,

a term meaning "bringing in the grapes to press into wine."

October also has several names. In ancient times, it was *Pyanopsia*, the term for harvesting *ospria*, or all the legumes. The name is also close to the word for "germinating." October was the month when many festivals celebrating the broad (fava) bean, the lentil, and chickpeas took place. Such festivals are still held occasionally, and where they occur, great cauldrons of the still staple and still sustaining beans are cooked, usually *plaki*-style. Bands of village musicians play. Men dance, kicking high while the women circle in line. The glory of all the produce, the fresh and those dried to last, is venerated. October's later post-Byzantine names are *Aidimitriais*, for the festival of St. Dimitrios.

November is called *Sporias*, *Sporiatis*, *Spartis*, and *Spartaris*, all referring to sowing seeds. It is also called *Krasominas*, meaning "wine month," for it is then, forty days after pressing the grapes, that the barrels of new wine are opened. In other places November is called *Trigominas*, again "grape month," and *Vroharis*, or "rain."

December's names were various versions of *sitari*, or "wheat"—in this case winter wheat, a fall-sown crop that lies in the ground all winter to be harvested in late spring.

# okra stew

## WITH TOMATOES, WHITE WINE, SAFFRON, AND CILANTRO

### BAMIES

#### SERVES 6

OKRA, AN AFRICAN VEGETABLE, CAME INTO GREEK COOKING BY WAY OF THE MANY GREEKS WHO SETTLED IN ETHIOPIA. ITS AFRICAN NAMES, *NKRUMA* AND *NGAMBO*, BECAME THE GREEK *BAMIA—BAMIES* WHEN MANY, NOT JUST ONE, ARE PILED INTO A COOKING POT. AND THE CLEVER GREEKS FOUND A WAY TO ENJOY OKRA WITHOUT ITS OFTEN OBJECTIONABLE GUMMY JUICE: THEY SOAK THE OKRA PODS IN A VINEGAR BATH, THEN SET THEM IN THE AIR—OR BETTER YET, THE SUN—FOR A BIT. THE OKRA COMES OUT STURDY, YET STILL SOFTLY FELTLIKE. AS A RESULT, AND BECAUSE OF ITS OPEN-FIELD TASTE, OKRA IS ONE OF THE MOST COMMONLY COOKED VEGETABLES OF GREECE.

Greeks fry the pods so they crunch like roasted nuts, surround roast meats with a chorus of them, and submerge them in incredible stews. Many are the guests who, usually disdaining okra, try them Greek-style and fall forever under their spell. Combined with onion, tomato, saffron, and the ancient herb cilantro, okra stew hints of the many exotic places Greeks have wandered.

*1 1/2 pounds small, fresh okra, stems trimmed off*
*3/4 cup white vinegar*
*1/2 cup olive oil*
*1 large white onion, halved and thinly sliced*
*2 medium tomatoes, peeled and very coarsely chopped, juices reserved*
*1/4 teaspoon saffron threads*
*1 teaspoon salt*
*1/2 teaspoon freshly ground white pepper*
*1/2 cup dry white wine*
*2 tablespoons chopped fresh cilantro leaves*

1 Place the okra in a large non-reactive dish, add the vinegar, and toss to mix. Set aside for at least 45 minutes or up to 1 hour (but no longer). Drain and set aside.

2 Heat the oil in a large non-reactive skillet over medium-low heat. Stir in the onion, tomatoes with their juices, saffron, salt, and white pepper and cook until the vegetables are wilted but not browned, about 5 minutes.

3 Stir in the okra and the wine, raise the heat to medium-high, and bring to a boil. Reduce the heat to medium-low again, partially cover the skillet, and cook until most of the liquid is gone and the okra is tender but still crunchy, about 35 minutes.

4 Remove the skillet from the heat and stir in the cilantro. Serve right away, at room temperature, or chilled.

### OKRA-PEDICS

When Greeks first adopted okra, they ascribed nonculinary uses to the strange vegetable. Perhaps because of its gummy juice, okra was believed to make a good soaking solution for poultices for aching muscles, broken bones, and burns. And in times of poverty, okra seeds were used as a substitute for coffee.

# CRISP CROQUETTES AND FRITTERS

# santorini fava croquettes

## SUSANNA-STYLE

### FAVA KEFTEDES

**MAKES TWELVE 2- TO 2½-INCH CROQUETTES; SERVES 3 OR 4 AS A MAIN DISH, OR 6 TO 8 AS A *MEZE***

NOT WILLING TO LET A DROP OF PRECIOUS GOLDEN *FAVA* (PAGE 159) GO TO WASTE, SANTORINIANS TURN THE THICK SOUP OF YELLOW SPLIT PEAS INTO DINNER CROQUETTES. LIKE THE CHILDREN IN THE VILLAGE, I ALMOST CAME TO PREFER THE *KEFTEDES* OVER THE SOUP. NOW I EYE THE SIMMERING POTS TO CALCULATE WHETHER (AS IS USUAL) TOO MUCH IS BREWING, IN THE HOPE THAT THERE WILL BE LEFTOVERS. AND IF THERE AREN'T ANY, I COOK UP A POTFUL JUST FOR CROQUETTES. THE SOUP IS COMFORTING AND RESTORATIVE, BUT THE CROQUETTES . . . YOU CAN CHEW!

These *keftedes* are as thick and munchy as a hamburger. The insides are soft, the outside crisp,

*The old harbor of Santorini, from which 600 stairs lead to the top of the cliff.*

Greeks are true believers in the adage "Waste not, want not." In keeping with that maxim, they never waste any food. To use up vegetable leftovers they continue a tradition they have enjoyed since time immemorial. They concoct two types of marvelous fried treats: If the vegetable can be pureed, they puree it, add savory bits of garlic, onion, tomato, and herbs, a little flour and perhaps some egg to bind it all together, and form it into patties. Or they take pieces of eggplant, onion, squash, squash flowers, and the like, dip them in a light batter, and fry them. In short, they make fritters and croquettes—which they call *keftedes*, the same word they use for "meatball." Either way, never a bit of vegetable wealth is wasted.

and every bite is full of sunny flavor. There are taste surprises in the croquette package too. Santorinians add chopped onion and vibrant Cyclades tomato, which I match at home with chives, shallots, and cherry or plum tomatoes. Sometimes the islanders add spinach, but the leaf I like best, if I have any, is a bit of caper leaf. Bottom line, though, the frills don't matter. *Fava keftedes* persuade me that Gaia is still the nurturing mother.

*2 cups leftover Yellow Split Pea
Soup (page 159), at room
temperature*

*1/2 medium tomato, cut into
1/4-inch dice*

*1 1/2 tablespoons finely chopped
shallots*

*1 tablespoon chopped fresh
chives*

*3 tablespoons shredded cooked
spinach, or 1 tablespoon caper
leaves (optional)*

*1/2 tablespoon finely chopped
fresh oregano, mint, or
dill leaves (optional)*

*1 large egg, lightly beaten (see Notes)*

*1/2 cup unbleached all-purpose
flour*

*3/4 teaspoon salt*

*1/4 teaspoon freshly ground
black pepper*

*Olive oil, for frying*

*1 recipe Wilted Parsley Topping
(page 481)*

*1 recipe Skordalia
(page 461; optional)*

**1** Combine all the ingredients except the oil, topping, and *skordalia* in a medium-size bowl and blend thoroughly. The mixture should be quite dry but moist enough to hold together. If it is too wet, add a little more flour.

**2** Shape the mixture into patties, using 1/4 to 1/3 cup for each.

**3** Pour oil to a depth of 1/4 inch in a heavy frying pan and heat it over medium-high heat. Add as many croquettes to the pan as will fit without crowding. Fry, turning once, until crisp all the way through, 4 to 6 minutes per side. Transfer the croquettes to paper towels to drain, and repeat with another batch, adding more oil as needed, until all the croquettes are fried.

**4** Arrange the croquettes on a platter and garnish with the topping. Serve warm or at room temperature, accompanied by the *skordalia*, if using.

### NOTES:

■ If the *fava* mixture is moist enough, Santorinians don't use egg in their *keftedes*. They simply add flour, a little at a time, until the mixture binds together just well enough to be formed into patties.

■ You can substitute 4 scallions, white parts and green tops finely chopped, for the shallots and chives.

## OTHER PATTY MATTER

The Greeks love fried food and deftly turn many a pulse and other vegetables into gorgeous croquettes. Here are some typical combinations:

**LENTILS**—pureed, usually with chopped carrot and a swirl of *skordalia* added to the mixture

**CHICKPEAS**—leftover soup (page 162) or pureed, with mint or basil and a little lemon zest

**POTATO**—mashed, preferably with bits of fennel

**TARAMASALATA** (page 43)—made thicker with more potato or with bread crumbs, turned into patties and fried

**LETTUCE, SPINACH, TOMATO, CAULIFLOWER, BROCCOLI, ASPARAGUS,** and just about any other small vegetable bits mixed in a flour dough, as in Markella's Crispy Croquettes (page 295)

# THE WELCOME PARTY

**S**OME MONTHS AFTER I HAD SETTLED IN MY GREEK VILLAGE FOR THE VERY FIRST TIME, THE VILLAGERS DECIDED THAT, SINCE MY HOUSE WAS LARGE AND MY FURNITURE SPARSE (A BOOKCASE CONTRIVED OF CINDER BLOCKS AND BOARDS, A SINGLE BED, A TABLE, A TWO-PERSON DIVAN), I SHOULD HAVE A PARTY. I FIGURED I'D MEET ALL THE VILLAGERS I HADN'T YET MET. I KNEW BY THEN THAT EVERYONE CAME TO EVERY FESTIVITY AND I'D ANNOUNCE MYSELF AS ONE OF THEIR OWN.

The words were no sooner out of my mouth than the event spun out of my hands. "Don't worry," said my neighbors, "we'll take care of everything." Within minutes the news was out and the invasion began.

Over the next days my door—never a barricade anyway—became a free-swinging turnstile. A parade of party planners entered at will and held committee meetings huddled on my *divani*. It seems I bought a barrel of Dimitri's wine. (He had plenty, I was told, and besides, this barrel was ten years old. I took that to be an asset, not a liability, and indeed the wine, which tasted almost like figs, was fantastic.) I learned as well that I had hired musicians—old Bagalos to play the *klarino*, his sons Loukas also to play *klarino*, and Averkios the *laouto*, plus his brother Patanas to play . . . I don't even remember what Patanas played! What would a party be without live music? The invitation was all-encompassing, so there was no need to bother with any formal notification. The hours were understood by everybody (except me): The party would begin whenever it got dark and would last until everybody left. Now all that remained was the menu. With all the wine and music, food was, after all, a must.

The trouble was, it was Lent. Because of the religious restrictions, all the ladies had pots of *fava* on their stoves, so the solution was clear: I would serve *fava kefthedes*—whatever those were! Again the fateful "don't worry" was declared. On the day of the party, thirty or more women stormed my door, bearing their portable gas stoves and pots of cooked *fava*. They chopped onion and tomato, added flour and argued over egg. And then the patting began. We slapped and shaped and pressed until a mound of patties as high as a hillock rose in my kitchen. Soon there were sizzling frying pans everywhere. The patties were fried, and fried, and fried, until our eyes watered. They were laid out on waxed paper, *skordalia* was made, plates were washed, small wineglasses were assembled. The sun set and the musicians arrived.

I discovered *fava kefthedes*. The village discovered that I could dance. Line after line of dances formed, handkerchiefs held between hands, leaders spinning. People passed around plates stacked high with *kefthedes*, a perfect fuel. Wineglasses were filled and presented to dancers, the men downing theirs, the women sipping a swallow and daintily spilling the remainder. We had enormous fun, spinning and twirling and eating our croquettes until every *kefthe* was gone and everyone drifted off. And when was that? When Apollo, the sun god, had started a new arc across the sky.

*Young and old, men and women, costumed or not, Greeks are ever ready to join hands and hankies in a line dance.*

# markella's crispy croquettes

**MAKES SIXTEEN 2-INCH CROQUETTES;
SERVES 4 AS A MAIN DISH, OR 8 AS A MEZE**

MY FRIEND MARKELLA KNOWS ABOUT FOOD FOR HARD TIMES. SHE KNOWS BECAUSE SHE LIVED THROUGH WORLD WAR II AND THE OCCUPATION OF THE ISLAND, WHEN ALL THE PRODUCE WAS TAKEN AWAY. SHE LIVED THROUGH THE POSTWAR UPHEAVALS. SHE LIVED THROUGH THE ISLAND'S DEPOPULATION AND DECLINE. DURING MUCH OF THIS TIME, FOOD WAS SO SPARSE THAT EVERY MORSEL WAS STRETCHED. BUT AS MARKELLA POINTS OUT, THAT FOOD WAS ALSO ESPECIALLY ZESTY. IT INCLUDED SOUPS OF THE MOST PROSAIC VEGETABLES, AND SMALL GARDEN TIDBITS MIXED WITH FLOUR AND FRIED UNTIL CRUSTY. AS A RESULT OF THAT FLAVORFUL COOKING, THE CHILDREN OF THOSE TIMES HAVE NOSTALGIC AND PALATE-FRESH MEMORIES OF THE "POOR" FOOD.

Markella still takes the last of her garden lettuce and spinach and turns the leaves into tasty croquettes. Tomato and *fava* croquettes are the most common ones on Santorini—available even in restaurants—and Markella cooks those, too. Her grown children flock to the table like kids when she serves them, crisp yet vegetal, like salad-filled pancakes.

1 large head romaine lettuce,
　finely chopped
12 ounces spinach, well rinsed
　and finely chopped
1 medium onion, finely chopped
$1/4$ cup chopped fresh dill
$1/8$ teaspoon ground nutmeg,
　preferably freshly grated
1 teaspoon salt
$1/4$ teaspoon freshly ground
　black pepper
$1/2$ cup unbleached all-purpose
　flour
$1/2$ teaspoon baking powder
Olive oil, for frying
$1/2$ cup freshly grated kefalotyri cheese
12 Kalamata olives
1 lemon, cut into 6 wedges
1 recipe Skordalia
　(page 461; optional)

1 Rinse the lettuce and spinach in plenty of water, and transfer them to a colander to drain. Shake off the excess moisture, and transfer the greens to a large nonreactive pot. Cover and cook over medium heat, stirring once or twice, until well wilted, 10 minutes. Drain again and press lightly to release the excess moisture without drying the greens completely.

2 Transfer the lettuce and spinach to a medium-size bowl. Add the onion, dill, nutmeg, salt, pepper, flour, and baking powder and mix well. The mixture should be quite dry but moist enough to

# ORACH: MOUNTAIN SPINACH OF THE MEDITERRANEAN

In the poor soil around the Mediterranean, and as far north as Siberia, there grows a leafy edible that hints of dandelion and spinach, but differs from those more familiar greens in two ways: The leaves aren't green, at least not on both sides. The bottom of the leaf may be as verdantly dark as laurel, but the top is brilliantly violet. And though growing like a green, the taste of the plant is somehow un-green. In English the plant is called "orach" or sometimes "mountain spinach," though it isn't a relative of spinach at all. As well as growing wild, it is now being cultivated, and like dandelion, it is becoming available in more and more markets.

The leaves of orach are velvety, and their taste is staunch, sometimes slightly bitter—especially the wild variety. Like spinach, its leaves release considerable juice when cooked, but orach's liquid is fuchsia-hued and colors everything that is cooked with it Day-Glo pink. The mature leaves of orach have a heft that spinach lacks, but they can easily be substituted or added to anything in which cooked spinach appears: rice and spinach pilaf, spinach pie, the leaf in lentil soup. The baby leaves are shaped like quarter-size coins and can offer a bright replacement for watercress or mâche in salads. Indeed, orach and much Greek food make a happy pairing: Try the leaves sautéed in olive oil, chopped in a pesto to top lamb, stuffed in fish, and combined with lettuce in Markella's Crispy Croquettes (page 295).

## NOTES:

■ The chopped spinach and lettuce together measure 10 to 11 cups before cooking and about 2 cups when cooked.

■ Markella and the other women in the village use self-rising flour, which already includes baking powder. If that's what you have, use it and omit the 1/2 teaspoon baking powder. The croquettes are much crisper and lighter, however, when made with all-purpose flour and baking powder.

■ Markella kneads the croquette mixture with her hands, not with a machine or even a utensil, just until the dough is thoroughly mixed. The method produces lighter croquettes.

## OTHER CROQUETTE-ERY

■ In place of the spinach and lettuce, use one of the following:

  2 cups grated raw zucchini

  2 cups finely chopped tomatoes, adding more flour if the mixture is too wet to form into patties

  2 cups other finely chopped cooked greens

■ Chopped mint and parsley can be substituted for the dill or added to it.

form into a patty. Shape the mixture into patties, using about 1/4 cup for each one.

3 Pour oil to a depth of 1/4 inch in a heavy, nonreactive frying pan and place it over medium-high heat until hot. Add as many patties as will fit in the pan without crowding and fry until crisp all the way through, 4 to 6 minutes per side. Transfer them to paper towels to drain, and repeat with another batch, adding more oil as needed, until all the patties are fried.

4 Arrange the patties on a platter, sprinkle the cheese over, and garnish with the olives and lemon wedges. Serve warm or at room temperature, accompanied by the *skordalia*, if using.

# okra fritters

**SERVES 6 TO 8 AS A MAIN DISH, OR 12 TO 16 AS A MEZE**

THOUGH THE ITALIANS ARE PROBABLY MORE FAMOUS FOR THEIR GLORIOUS PLATTERS OF VEGETABLE FRITTERS, GREEKS HAVE LONG APPLIED THE SAME JUBILANT TREATMENT TO THE PROFUSION OF MEDITERRANEAN VEGETABLES. AND WHILE BOTH DIP ZUCCHINI, EGGPLANT, ARTICHOKES, AND MUSHROOMS INTO BATTER FOR FRYING, GREEKS ALSO GIVE THEIR EXTRAORDINARY OKRA THE SAME TREATMENT. SOAKED IN A FIRMING VINEGAR BATH, DIPPED IN A DELICATE BATTER, SLIPPED INTO SIZZLING OIL, THE PODS COME OUT A TRULY WONDERFUL MORSEL.

1 1/2 pounds fresh okra pods,
    preferably small, tops trimmed off
3/4 cup white vinegar
2 large eggs
1/4 cup water
3 tablespoons sifted unbleached
    all-purpose flour
1/2 teaspoon salt
1/2 teaspoon freshly ground black
    pepper
1 cup olive oil, for frying
Lemon wedges
Tzatziki (pages 465 to 469),
    Skordalia (pages 461 to 464),
    or Roasted Tomato "Paste"
    (page 479), for dipping
    (optional)

1 Toss the okra with the vinegar in a large bowl. Set it aside to soak for at least 45 minutes but no longer than 1 hour. Rinse the okra and pat the pods dry.

2 Beat the eggs and water together in a medium-size bowl. Then beat in the flour, salt, and pepper and set the bowl aside near the stove.

3 Heat 1/2 cup of the oil in a large, heavy frying pan over medium-high heat. Coat a batch of the okra in the egg batter.

## OTHER FRITTERS TO FRY

Greeks love crunchy okra fritters, but they do not limit their pleasure to the one vegetable. Nor should we! Just remember to pat the vegetables dry so the batter will adhere:

**TINY BABY ARTICHOKES**—outer leaves removed, tips cut off, parboiled until almost tender

**ASPARAGUS**—just the tips

**CARDOONS**—outer stalks removed, thorns and fibers removed, cut into 2-inch pieces, boiled until soft

**EGGPLANT**—baby eggplants trimmed and cut in half, or larger eggplants trimmed and sliced 1/4 inch thick

**ZUCCHINI**—cut lengthwise 1/4 inch thick

**MUSHROOMS**—wiped clean and stem ends trimmed

**WHOLE SMALL CHILE PEPPERS**—washed, stems left on

**BELL PEPPERS**—cut into chunks 1 inch wide and 2 to 4 inches long

**ONION**—cut into pieces or wedges 1 inch wide

**JERUSALEM ARTICHOKES**—peeled and cut into 1-inch chunks

**BROCCOLI** or **CAULIFLOWER FLORETS**—blanched for 1 minute

And if you have a scattering of leftover vegetables, or you want to make a confetti of fritters for a celebration, make a mixed fritter platter—the batter is the same for all.

## FRITTER DIPPING
......................

Like chips in dips, vegetable fritters become more alluring when given a dab of a contrasting sauce. Among the sauces to try are:

■ Traditional (page 465), Beet (page 467), or Radish *Tzatziki* (page 469)

■ any of the *Skordalias* (pages 461 to 464)

■ Roasted Tomato "Paste" (page 479)

■ or even a touch of one of the *meze* spreads: *taramasalata* (page 43), either of the Eggplant Salads (page 32, 33), or Eggplant and Yogurt Spread (page 35).

4 Fry the okra—as many pods as will fit in the pan without crowding—until just golden and crisp, about 1½ minutes. Drain on paper towels, and repeat the coating and frying process, adding more oil to the pan as needed, until all the okra is fried.

5 Transfer to a platter, garnish with the lemon wedges, and serve right away, accompanied with a dipping sauce, if using.

# zucchini flower fritters

## STUFFED WITH CHEESE

### SERVES 4 OR 5 AS MAIN DISH, OR 7 TO 10 AS A MEZE

THE ANCESTORS OF ALL THE MANY SORTS OF SQUASH—ZUCCHINI, CROOKNECK, PATTYPAN, SPAGHETTI, ACORN, BUTTERCUP, AND SO ON— ARE NATIVE TO CENTRAL AND SOUTH AMERICA. OVER THE PAST CENTURIES, ONE VARIETY AFTER ANOTHER HAS MADE ITS WAY TO THE MEDITERRANEAN, WHERE THEY ALL HAVE FOUND A CLIMATE MUCH TO THEIR LIKING.

In fact, they grow there in such furious profusion that there's no need to let all the millions of blossoms turn into the fully ripened vegetable— the flowers themselves can be eaten. The flowers of all the varieties are much alike: brilliant ocher yellow in color, almost salaciously alluring in shape, lettucelike in texture. They open magnanimously, as if asking to be filled. Greek cooks quickly spotted how perfect they are for a special sort of fritter. With curdy Greek cheese tucked inside, petals closed, the flower battered and fried, squash blossom fritters are a Grecian delight.

*Happy with her handiwork, a Greek homemaker displays her rack of homemade* hlorou *cheese.*

2 large eggs

¼ cup water

3 tablespoons sifted unbleached
    all-purpose flour

½ teaspoon salt

½ teaspoon freshly ground
    black pepper

4 ounces kasseri, or other tasty
    melting cheese, coarsely grated

2 ounces manouri, or ricotta salata
    cheese, coarsely grated

2 tablespoons minced scallion,
    white and light green parts

1 teaspoon chopped fresh oregano
    leaves, or ½ teaspoon dried

20 large squash flowers, lightly
    rinsed and patted dry

1 cup olive oil, for frying

Lemon wedges

**1** Beat the eggs and water together in a medium-size bowl. Beat in the flour and salt and pepper and set the bowl aside near the stove.

**2** In another medium-size bowl, mix together the cheeses, scallion, and oregano.

**3** Gently pry open the squash blossoms and fill each with about 1 tablespoon of the cheese mixture. Gently pinch the tops of the blossoms together to enclose the mixture.

**4** Heat half the oil in a large, heavy frying pan over medium-high heat. Coat a batch of the squash flowers in the egg mixture. When the oil is hot, add as many to the pan as will fit without crowding and fry them, turning once, until lightly golden, about 1½ minutes. Drain on paper towels and repeat the coating and frying process, adding more oil as needed, until all the flowers are fried.

**5** Transfer to a platter, garnish the platter with the lemon wedges, and serve right away.

## GATHERING—AN ART I WILL NEVER TOTALLY MASTER

As small children following their mothers, Greek girls in the countryside learn which wild plants and herbs are edible or aromatic, which to gather for food or flavoring. Little boys learn the art too, for as small children they are constantly in their mothers' company; later, as farmers, they often bring home armfuls of wild plants they spot sprouting in patches as they go from field to field. I can recognize the kinnikinnick of my native Rocky Mountains, but I was a blank page when I first arrived in Greece. Taking me by the hand, as they did in so many ways, my Greek companions slowly began to show me the leaves and roots, the stalks and flowers that I could add to my larder.

I am now almost accomplished when it comes to Greek herbs. I can spot all the obvious—oregano, marjoram, sage, and definitely dill, fennel, and anise—but I still miss the rarer varieties, the various sorts of savory, the mountain teas with no American equivalent. But I shall never master all the greens. When pouncing on a carpet of chicory, my eyes bypass the salsify. When scooping up amaranth greens, I never notice the chenopodium. Some greens I just don't recognize. My companions jump upon a thicket of some chartreuse shoot I have no knowledge of—I see nothing but weed. My knowledge grows with each visit, but the bounty is so enormous that I am resigned to remaining forever botanically challenged. The good side is that I don't have to master total recognition because my friends are so generous. Whether I pick the greens or they do it, I get to enjoy them all—pennyroyal mint to thistle, sow thistle to burdock.

# STUFFED VEGETABLES

## vegetable stuffings

### THE TWO BASICS

IN GREEK COOKING, TWO BASIC STUFFINGS ARE USED TO FILL ALL THE EDIBLE CONTAINERS, BE THEY LEAF, TOMATO, ZUCCHINI, PEPPER, OR WHATEVER. GENERALLY, THE CHOICE BETWEEN STUFFINGS FOLLOWS A CERTAIN RULE: MEAT STUFFING IS USED FOR HOT ENTREES; MEATLESS RICE AND NUT STUFFING IS USED IN APPETIZERS, SERVED WARM OR COOL.

But the rule is by no means absolute. Tomatoes and bell peppers, perhaps the most common vegetables stuffed, are often packed with the meatless stuffing, and sometimes with meat. Squash and quince can be filled with either. As with all Greek cooking, it's a question of whimsy and what tastes best.

The containers sometimes have dual roles as well. Grape leaves filled with rice serve as the world-famous *dolmades* appetizer (for the traditional stuffing, see page 47). Filled with meat, sauced with egg and lemon, and placed on the table piping hot, they are a magnificent dinner dish (page 311). The meat stuffing that

follows is the classic, the meatless is a neoclassic variation. Aristotle, who sorted out all matters hot or cold, would probably call the general stuffing rule system sensible. To the rest of us, it doesn't matter. Stuffed hot or stuffed cold, stuffed vegetables are delectable.

*Stuffed tomatoes, peppers, and other vegetables are ubiquitous offerings at Greek tavernas.*

The custom of filling foods with other foods goes back so far in Greece that its beginnings are as obscure as a Delphic oracle's prophesy. We know that birds were stuffed and that large animals were baked with small ones inside. But all along, the most common foods filled with other foods were vegetables, flowers, and leaves.

Early Greeks stuffed fig, mulberry, and hazelnut leaves. They scooped out and refilled gourds and fruit. Tucked inside the edible packages were meats, grains, and miscellanies of other vegetables. The idea continued. Byzantine flourishes were embraced, New World foods adopted. Today, along with grape leaves, cabbage leaves, lettuce leaves, and quince, eggplants, artichokes, tomatoes, peppers, and squash provide a vessel for rice, bulgur, chopped meat, olives, capers, and their own inner pulp seasoned and reinserted. Stuffed foods offer a use for small amounts of leftovers and make for added largesse on the dinner table.

To prepare stuffed tomatoes with either of the following recipes, see page 303, Steps 1, 4 and 5; bell peppers, page 304, Steps 3 through 6; grape leaves, page 47, Steps 4 through 10, adding 1 1/2 tablespoons lemon juice to the water as instructed in Step 8.

# MEAT AND RICE STUFFING

## MAKES 5 CUPS

The stuffing mixture will fill 8 tomatoes or bell peppers, or 65 grape leaves.

*1/2 cup cooked short-grain rice, preferably Arborio*
*1/2 pound ground beef or lamb*
*1 medium onion, finely chopped*
*1 tablespoon coarsely chopped lemon zest*
*1 cup chopped fresh flat-leaf parsley leaves*
*1/4 cup chopped fresh mint leaves*
*1/8 teaspoon ground nutmeg, preferably freshly grated*
*1 1/2 teaspoons salt*
*1/2 teaspoon freshly ground black pepper*
*2 tablespoons tomato paste*
*1/2 cup dry white wine*
*1 tablespoon fresh lemon juice*

Place all the ingredients in a medium-size bowl and mix together. Use right away, or allow to cool, then cover and refrigerate for up to 48 hours.

## YES, QUINCE TOO

The ancient Greeks were not at all hesitant to seize the vessel-like advantage of the "golden apples" of mythology that they loved—quince—and fill them with other foods. The dish is luscious, meaty with the meat stuffing, nutty with the rice, and will have guests clamoring for more. Just as eggplant must be softened and scooped out first, so must quince: Parboil whole quince for 10 minutes, skin on; drain, and slice around the top to make a lid as you would a tomato or bell pepper. Scoop out the pulp, being careful not to split the sides or skin. Separate and discard the core and seed. Place the pulp on the bottom of the baking pan. Stuff the quince with your choice of filling and place on top of the pulp layer. Pour in 1 cup water mixed with a little sugar and a small piece (1 to 2 inches) cinnamon stick. Bake in the oven as in Step 5, page 303.

# RICE AND ALMOND STUFFING

## MAKES ABOUT 5 CUPS

The stuffing will fill 8 tomatoes or bell peppers, or 65 grape leaves.

*1/4 cup dried currants*
*1/4 cup golden raisins*
*1/2 cup retsina wine (omit if using presoaked currants; see page 49)*
*1/2 cup olive oil*
*1 cup uncooked short-grain rice, preferably Arborio*
*1 large onion, finely chopped*
*1/2 cup slivered almonds, chopped*
*1 tablespoon finely chopped lemon zest*
*1 teaspoon salt*
*1/4 cup chopped fresh dill*
*2 tablespoons chopped fresh marjoram leaves*

1 Combine the currants and raisins with the retsina in a small bowl. Cover and let stand at room temperature for at least 1 hour, or preferably overnight.

2 Heat the oil in a medium-size skillet over medium heat. Add the rice, onion, almonds, zest, and salt. Sauté until the onion is translucent, about 5 minutes.

3 Drain the currants and raisins, reserving the retsina to soak another batch, if you like, and add them to the skillet. Continue to sauté until any liquid is almost completely evaporated, about 3 minutes. Remove the skillet from the heat and stir in the dill and marjoram. Use right away, or allow to cool, then cover and refrigerate for up to 48 hours.

# fresh tomatoes

## STUFFED WITH ANCIENT INGREDIENTS

### SERVES 6 TO 8

IN TRADITIONAL GREEK RESTAURANTS THE CUSTOM IS TO SELECT YOUR MEAL BY TAKING A LOOK AT WHAT IS COOKING IN THE KITCHEN. CLEVER COOKS PROMINENTLY DISPLAY HUGE ROUND PANS FILLED WITH JUICY STUFFED TOMATOES FOR THREE GOOD REASONS: FIRST, STUFFED TOMATOES ARE SO FLAVORFUL, SO SATISFYING, AND SO AROMATIC THAT NO MATTER HOW OFTEN YOU SEE THEM, YOU ALWAYS WANT THEM. SECOND, THEY ARE GLORIOUSLY COLORFUL, ADDING A VIBRANT SPLASH OF CRIMSON TO ANY ARRAY OF FOODS IN THE KITCHEN. AND FINALLY, THEY ARE AS EXPECTED AS BREAD!

Big, round, sun-sweetened tomatoes filled with either of the basic fillings (page 301) are always worth the anticipation. Filling them with ingredients from ancient annals gives an unexpected twist: bulgur instead of rice to soak up simmered juice; chickpeas to awaken memories of when earthy legumes were daily sustenance; mint and cilantro to remind us that Greece is ever an Eden. A touch of chile pepper gives the slight bite the ancients relished. The new-old combination is sure to become a new favorite.

6 to 8 large summer-ripe tomatoes
1 tablespoon olive oil
1 small onion, finely chopped
1 large rib celery, with leaves, finely chopped
1 large mild fresh chile pepper, such as Anaheim or poblano, seeded and finely chopped
1 cup medium or coarse ground bulgur
1/4 cup dry white wine
1/2 cup cooked chickpeas
1/2 teaspoon salt
1/4 teaspoon freshly ground black pepper
1 cup Thickened Yogurt (page 471)
6 sprigs fresh cilantro, or 6 fresh mint leaves

1 Prepare the tomatoes: Cut off the tops, making a 1/4-inch-thick slice. Set the caps aside. Using a paring knife, carefully cut the cores and pulp out of each tomato, leaving a 1/4-inch-thick shell. Discard the core. Finely chop the tomato pulp and place it in a strainer over a bowl to collect the juice. Strain any juices that have accumulated in the shells into the bowl as well. You should have a pile of tomato caps, a pile of tomato shells, a pile of chopped tomato pulp, and the bowl of tomato juice.

## PUTTING A CAP ON THINGS

Most Greek cooks take a 1/4- to 1/2-inch tomato slice off the stem end, sometimes with the stem still intact, to make a cap. Naturally, each cap is a little different. Others reverse the picture and cut their cap off the rounded bottom end of the tomato. That way all the caps on the stuffed tomatoes look like uniform beanies and not disparate berets. Still others take a tiny slice from the bottom to make a flat platform for the tomatoes so they don't tilt in the pan, then cut off the top ends for caps. I don't care for the last method because having both ends open allows too many juices to flow out. I'm happy to have my tomatoes sit a little atilt.

**2** Heat the oil in a medium-size saucepan over medium heat. Add the onion and stir until it wilts, 5 minutes. Add the celery, chile pepper, and chopped tomato pulp. Stir and continue to cook over medium heat until the vegetables soften, 3 minutes.

**3** Mix in the bulgur, wine, chickpeas, and salt and pepper. Remove the pan from the heat and let the mixture cool, stirring from time to time, for at least 10 minutes, or as long as 45 minutes.

**4** Stuff each tomato shell with a heaping ½ cup of the bulgur mixture. Arrange the stuffed tomatoes in a large wide pot or baking dish so that they are tightly packed in one layer. Place a tomato cap on top of each stuffed tomato. Carefully pour all of the strained tomato juice into the pan (but not over the tomatoes).

**5** *If cooking on the stovetop:* Bring the liquid to a boil over medium-high heat. Reduce the heat, cover, and simmer until the tomato shells are beginning to soften, 10 minutes. Set the lid ajar, and continue simmering until the bulgur is fluffy and the tomato shells are quite soft, 10 minutes more.

*If baking in the oven:* Preheat the oven to 375°F. Place the baking dish in the oven and bake the tomatoes, uncovered, until the tomato shells are soft and the rims and cap edges have begun to brown, 30 to 35 minutes.

**6** Remove the pan from the heat or oven and set aside to cool for 15 minutes before serving.

**7** When you are ready to serve them, gently lift the tomatoes onto a serving platter. Set the tomato caps to the side of each tomato. Spoon about 2 tablespoons of the yogurt over the top of each tomato, and place a cilantro sprig or a mint leaf on top. Serve warm or at room temperature.

## VARIATION:

**Bulgur and Chickpea Side Dish:** The bulgur stuffing can be served as a salad side, like *tabouli,* on its own. Replacing the wine with water, mix together the bulgur, water, chickpeas, salt, pepper, and ¼ cup strained fresh tomato juice or tomato paste thinned with water. Allow to stand for 15 minutes before serving.

## NICANDER'S BRIAMI

While cooking vegetables in a sumptuous stew was as common in times past as now, the ingredients have changed. Nicander, a Greek poet of the second century B.C.E., details his vegetal *briami* recipe as including alexanders (also known as angelica, tasting like a combination of juniper, celery, and asparagus), cuckoo-pint arum (one of a number of curiously named European arums), star of Bethlehem (a lily that some say is edible and others claim is poisonous), and hound's tongue (named for its hairy leaves and a direct translation of the Greek *kynoglossos*). These Nicander stewed in a mélange with chicory, asparagus, carrot, and fennel.

For a modern version of *briami*, see page 282.

# bell peppers

## STUFFED WITH EGGPLANT, OLIVES, AND CAPERS

### SERVES 6

WHEN BELL PEPPERS ARRIVED FROM THE NEW WORLD, GREEK COOKS TOOK TO THE VEGETABLE WITH GUSTO. IN GREECE, BELL PEPPERS ARE ROASTED, SAUTEED IN OIL, AND CUT INTO SALADS, BUT MOST OFTEN THEY ARE STUFFED. SO BRIGHTLY HUED, PEPPERS PERFECTLY COMPLEMENT THE GREEK SENSE OF VIVIDNESS. SO PIQUANT IN TASTE (GREEK BELL PEPPERS HAVE MORE CHILE TO THEM THAN THE AMERICAN ONES), THEY SATISFY THE GREEK DESIRE FOR BITE. SO FILLABLE IN SHAPE, THEY ABSOLUTELY INVITE THE EXPERTISE OF THE GREEK COOK. IN THIS SIGNATURE DISH, THE PEPPERS ARE TANTALIZINGLY FILLED WITH EGGPLANT, OLIVES, AND CAPERS.

*1/2 cup olive oil*

*2 medium eggplants, cut into 1/4-inch dice*

*1/2 teaspoon salt*

*1/2 cup dry white wine*

*24 black olives, preferably Kalamata, pitted and chopped*

*1/3 cup capers, drained*

*2 large cloves garlic, minced or pressed*

*2 teaspoons coarsely chopped lemon zest*

*3 tablespoons tomato paste*

*2 teaspoons chopped fresh oregano leaves, or 3/4 teaspoon dried*

*6 medium bell peppers, preferably a mixture of colors*

*1 cup water*

1 Heat the oil in a large skillet over medium-high heat. When it is hot, reduce the heat to medium, add the eggplant, and stir to mix. Add the salt and wine and stir to mix. Cook, stirring frequently, until the eggplant is well wilted and juicy, 10 minutes.

2 Stir in the olives, capers, garlic, zest, tomato paste, and oregano. Cook over medium-low heat, stirring frequently, until the eggplant is very soft, 5 minutes. Remove the skillet from the heat and set it aside to cool for 5 minutes.

3 While the mixture is cooling, slice the tops off the peppers to make 1/4-inch-thick caps and set them aside. Remove the cores and seeds from the peppers.

4 Fill the peppers with the eggplant mixture and arrange them in one tightly packed layer in a wide pot or baking dish. Top the peppers with the caps. Carefully pour the water around (not over) the peppers.

## PARCHED VEGETABLES

The earliest chronicles of Greek life mention that vegetables were parched, or dry-roasted. Presumably the roasting was done over an open fire or on clay griddles placed above the flames. Fire-roasting, or grilling, is still a favored technique. Take whole, halved, or sliced vegetables—such as beets, zucchini, eggplants, bell peppers, potato—and dab them with oil and herbs; then slide them onto a grill or griddle over coals or flame. Cook until slightly charred and tender. The time will vary according to the size, thickness, and delicacy of the vegetable. Or wrap the vegetables, whole or in large pieces, in foil and slip them into the coals of a fire. Remove them when a peek inside the foil lets out steam and the vegetables are soft. Again, the time will vary.

**5** *If cooking on the stovetop:* Bring the water to a boil over high heat, then reduce the heat and cover the pan. Simmer until the peppers are soft but not collapsing, 25 minutes.

*If baking in the oven:* Preheat the oven to 375°F. Place the baking dish in the oven and bake the peppers, uncovered, until the pepper shells are soft and the rims and cap edges have begun to brown, 30 to 35 minutes.

**6** Serve the peppers right away, at room temperature, or chilled.

**NOTE:** The eggplant stuffing mixture becomes a delicious appetizer when wrapped in a lettuce leaf *dolmada*-style or used as a lively topping for small toasts, or as a side relish for meats and poultry.

# MANY-HUED COSTUMES

**WHEN I FIRST ARRIVED IN GREECE THIRTY YEARS AGO, WOMEN GATHERING VEGETABLES FROM THE FIELDS OR BRINGING RIPE TOMATOES TO MARKET WERE STILL SOMETIMES DRESSED IN THE TRADITIONAL COSTUME OF THEIR PROVINCE. INDEED, THE DRESSES WERE STILL THE DAILY WEAR OF WOMEN IN THE RUGGED NORTHERN REACHES OF GREECE, AND IN EVERY AREA, OLDER WOMEN HERE AND THERE CLUNG TO THEIR UPBRINGING, THEIR CUSTOM, AND THEIR COMFORT.**

The costumes ranged from rough black wool skirts with white lacy overblouses, to vests of dense, polychromatic embroidery, to wide hems of bead and embroidery that dangled below simple smocks, to kaleidoscopically patterned aprons, scarves of lace, hats shaped like Alexander's helmet, and wildly multihued woven belts. The colors of the costumes were as variegated as the vegetables the women might be preparing: red as big lush tomatoes; orange, gold, and green as peppers; white and purple as eggplant; yellow as squash. Amid the colors, blue beads to protect against the evil eye winked out.

In the Peloponnesos, women sported skirts and belts loosely woven from strings, similar to the string skirts carved on prehistoric figurines. The belief was that the strange, macramé-type tangling confused the devil and thwarted the jealous arrows of the evil eye. In Macedonia aprons swung with great red fringes and tassels. And everywhere most rural women, even in modern dress, still covered their heads with scarves tucked over their ears and tied beneath their chins.

## EVERY OUTFIT TELLS A STORY

The dresses and aprons and scarves told more than just what region a woman came from; they told the woman's story. Only a young unmarried woman might don a bodice with golden sleeves. A tasseled apron announced a young wife still of childbearing age. Past midlife, a woman's ornamental clothing and fringed garments were laid in a trunk and she took to dressing in plain attire. By old age, the dress might be a white or black chemise with no embroidery, black overdress, apron, and head scarf.

Where I lived, the contemporary clothing continued to bespeak a woman's stage in life. Only young unmarried girls and new brides wore red. Young mothers donned blue. As her children grew, brown became a woman's appropriate dress color. Any family death—parent, sibling, cousin—put a woman in black for a month to three years, and the loss of a husband garbed her in black for the rest of her life. All women wore white scarves until a death changed the hue.

Dress has changed now, though older women still shy from red and white, and widows still mostly wear black. Meanwhile, their chores have little changed. They still keep house, glean from the fields, shop the markets, and prepare for their families pans full of tomatoes stuffed with grain.

## BEYOND THE CLASSICS
............

The beef or lamb filling for *Bourekakia* (page 112), with its touch of Byzantine ornateness, can be used to fill tomatoes, peppers, eggplant, squash, and quince in a jewel-like manner. The Stuffed Chicken-Neo-*Plaka*-Style (page 418) offers a stuffing mixture more influenced by the spice route. Large vegetable containers are sumptuous when filled with the Pork, Chestnut, and Fig Stuffing (page 430), and grape and cabbage leaves filled with dabs of yellow lentil stuffing (page 427) make a dainty and unusual entree or *meze*, with chicken liver substituted for the goose liver. The stuffing for squash blossoms (page 308) offers a choice of a meatless filling.

Also beyond the commonplace vegetables Greeks stuff are leeks (sliced lengthwise), mushrooms, onions, potatoes, lettuce leaves, the leaves of other greens, and edible flowers. For a most distinctive plate, rather than a single vegetable, a variety of vegetables can be stuffed and served.

# eggplant slippers

## PAPOUTSAKIA

### SERVES 6

UPON REFLECTION, IT BECOMES CLEAR THAT THE GREEK DEVOTION TO BOTH EGGPLANT AND OLIVE OIL IS REALLY JUST A SINGLE ONE. EGGPLANTS SOAK UP SO MUCH OLIVE OIL THEY SOMETIMES SEEM BUT A CONDUIT FOR THE GOLDEN LIQUID. ON THE OTHER HAND, EGGPLANTS REALLY BURST INTO FULL FLAVOR WHEN SATURATED WITH THE STUFF. THERE ARE, HOWEVER, TWO DRAWBACKS TO THE OTHERWISE SUBLIME UNION. EGGPLANT DISHES CAN BECOME VERY EXPENSIVE AS THEY LAP UP THE PRICEY OIL. AND TO TODAY'S TASTE, SO MUCH OIL CAN SEEM A LITTLE WEIGHTY ON BOTH THE PALATE AND THE TORSO.

To assuage these predicaments, here is a meaty eggplant slipper that uses less oil than the original meatless version it is based on, *imam bayaldi*. *Imam bayaldi* means "the reverend of the mosque faints," and the dish supposedly got the name because an imam, upon asking his new bride to cook eggplant every day, discovered that her entire dowry of olive oil had been used up in a single week! (Another version has it that the imam was so taken with the prepared dish, he fainted from joy.)

The trick in preparing the slippers is to allow the eggplant to soften in oil in a first brief frying, thereby enhancing the flavor, then to bake the filled slippers surrounded by a little water. Greeks—whose eggplants are longer and narrower than ours—call such stuffed eggplant halves "little shoes."

3 medium eggplants

1/2 cup olive oil

2 medium onions, finely chopped

10 to 12 cloves garlic, finely chopped

1 1/2 pounds lean ground beef
   or lamb

3 tablespoons tomato paste

1 1/2 tablespoons chopped
   fresh oregano leaves,
   or 2 teaspoons dried

1/2 teaspoon salt

Freshly ground black pepper, to taste

1 cup dry red wine

1/2 cup freshly grated kefalotyri,
   Parmesan, or other hard
   grating cheese

1 Cut the eggplants in half lengthwise. Scoop out the center of each half, leaving a 1/4- to 1/2-inch-thick shell. Set the eggplant shells aside. Coarsely chop the pulp.

2 Heat 1/4 cup of the oil in a large skillet over medium heat. Add the onions and garlic and cook until wilted, 5 minutes. Add the meat and cook, stirring to break up the chunks, until it is browned, 5 minutes. Stir in the eggplant pulp, tomato paste, oregano, salt, pepper, and wine and bring to a boil.

3 Reduce the heat and simmer until the juices are deep reddish brown and bubbling up from the bottom of the skillet, 45 minutes.

## SUN . . . STROKE

The sun that ripens eggplants to plumpness and grapes to sweetness can also bring about a certain weakness, an ailment the Greeks simply call "the sun." The ailment causes general dizziness and debilitation and the victim, usually someone who has labored too long in the fields or at the laundry line, is treated to an elaborate cure.

I had spent a long, dusty morning gathering eggplants and other vegetables on a brilliant day with Rambelia, Zafiroula, and old Antonia when suddenly Rambelia felt weak. "It's the sun," said Antonia, by which she meant the affliction, not the fiery orb beating down on us. Antonia directed me to take Rambelia to the shade of a nearby tree while Zafiroula ran for a chair and a pitcher of water. When Zafiroula returned, Antonia sat the victim in the chair. She took a white scarf and measured from Rambelia's fingers to her elbow three times, knotting the scarf at each measure. By making the knots in the scarf, she bound the sunstroke, for what is bound cannot follow its course. She placed the scarf over Rambelia's head umbrella-style, with Rambelia holding out the scarf's tips. While reciting a special chant specifically to heal the weakness, she drizzled water from the pitcher upon the scarf and over Rambelia's head. The brain was thereby cooled, the sun's damage fended off. Rambelia gave a heavy sigh, stood up, and, color returned, flashed us a beautiful smile. "I wonder," she said, "if the *blorou* cheese I made yesterday is ready to go on these eggplants."

4 Meanwhile, in another large skillet, heat the remaining 1/4 cup oil over medium-high heat. When it is hot, place as many eggplant shells as will fit in one layer in the skillet and cook, turning once, until browned and wilted, 10 to 12 minutes. Transfer them to a baking dish large enough to hold them in one tightly packed layer, cut sides up. Continue with another batch, adding more oil if necessary, until all the shells are wilted. Set aside until ready to use.

5 Preheat the oven to 350°F.

6 Fill the eggplant shells with the meat mixture. Sprinkle the cheese over the top. Pour water around (not over) the shells to a depth of 1/4 inch.

7 Place the dish in the oven and bake for 1 hour, until the shells are soft and the filling is bubbling in the center. Remove and set aside until cool enough to handle. Serve right away, at room temperature, or chilled.

## HOT EGGPLANT TIPS

M ost eggplant dishes share two traits, and Greek-style eggplant concoctions are prime examples: They improve with a wait, and they hold heat for a long while. Both features make them good dishes to prepare ahead. You can let them linger on the stove for several hours until tepid, when they will be more flavorful; or you can prepare the dish a day ahead and reheat it. Whether it is served right away or reheated, be aware that eggplant stays burning hot longer than most foods.

## NOTES:

■ Originally in Greece the terms *imam bayaldi* and *papoutsakia* referred to both a meat-filled and a meatless version of stuffed eggplants. In recent years, the name *imam bayaldi* has come to refer to only the meatless version, in which eggplant halves are topped with sautéed onions and a fresh tomato sauce such as that on page 474, then baked, while *papoutsakia* has come to mean the meat-filled version.

■ Eggplant Slippers keep uncooked for up to a day and after cooking for up to 5 days. Cooked, they can also be frozen for up to 6 months.

# squash blossoms

## STUFFED WITH RICE, CURRANTS, AND HERBS

### SERVES 6 TO 8

THE ANCIENT GREEKS WRAPPED LEAVES AROUND THE NUTTY GRAINS THEY KNEW BEST, BARLEY AND WHEAT. THEY CONTINUED THE CUSTOM WITH SOFT, PLIABLE RICE WHEN THEY ACQUIRED IT. OVER TIME, THEY ALSO CHANGED THE WRAPPING FROM GRAPE AND FIG LEAF TO LETTUCE AND CABBAGE. THEY APPLIED THE SAME STUFFING TO DIFFERENT LEAVES AND FILLED THE SAME LEAF WITH DIFFERENT STUFFINGS. WHEN SQUASH BLOSSOMS ARRIVED, THEY OFFERED GREEK COOKS A STELLAR NEW WRAPPING. NOT ONLY WERE THE LEAFY PETALS BIG, NOT ONLY WERE THEY AS INCANDESCENTLY YELLOW AS GRAPE LEAVES WERE GREEN, THEY WERE ALREADY TIED TOGETHER AT THE BOTTOM! RATHER THAN FOLDING AND REFOLDING, THEY COULD JUST BE FILLED.

And so throughout Greece, in summer and autumn, you will find filled squash blossoms. The unique flavor and texture of the flower's petals—not green like leaves, not firm like pepper, tomato, onion, or eggplant, but

*A spine of an old marooned ship sits on a cliff-framed beach in Zakinthos.*

poignantly floral—adds a fragrant top note to the stuffing inside.

*1 1/2 tablespoons dried currants*
*About 1/4 cup retsina wine*
 *(omit if using presoaked*
 *currants; see box, this page)*
*1 tablespoon olive oil*
*1/2 cup uncooked short-grain rice,*
 *preferably Arborio*
*4 scallions, white and light*
 *green parts trimmed and*
 *minced*
*1 large clove garlic, minced*
 *or pressed*
*1 teaspoon tomato paste*
*1/2 cup water*
*1 tablespoon chopped fresh*
 *flat-leaf parsley leaves*
*1 tablespoon chopped fresh dill*
*Small pinch of ground cinnamon*
*1/4 teaspoon salt*
*18 to 20 large squash blossoms,*
 *lightly rinsed and patted dry*

1 Combine the currants with the retsina in a small bowl. Cover and let stand at room temperature for at least 1 hour, or preferably overnight. Drain the currants, reserving the retsina to soak another batch, if you like.

2 Heat the oil in a small saucepan over medium heat. Stir in the rice, currants, scallions, and garlic and sauté until the rice becomes translucent and

is well coated, about 2 minutes. Add the tomato paste, water, parsley, dill, cinnamon, and salt and stir to mix well. Cover and cook until the water is absorbed and the rice is beginning to soften, about 5 minutes. Remove the pan from the heat and set aside until cool enough to handle.

3 Fill each squash blossom with about 1 tablespoon of the filling, leaving room for the rice to expand as it finishes cooking. Stack the filled blossoms closely

in one or two layers in a medium-size saucepan. Add water barely to cover and bring to a boil over medium-high heat. Reduce the heat, cover the pan, and gently simmer until the rice is done, 20 minutes. Remove the pan from the heat and let rest for 10 minutes.

4 To serve, lift the stuffed blossoms out of the liquid and transfer them to a platter. Serve hot, at room temperature, or chilled.

## KEEPING CURRANT

Black and sugary, tiny dried currants are not the same as the black, red, and white fresh currants of the *Saxifraga* bush of northern Europe, used to make cassis liqueur, jellies, tarts, and game sauces. Rather they are a special variety of miniature grape first grown in the Peloponnesos. Indeed, the word "currant" comes from the ancient Peloponnesian city and area of Corinth. When the Venetians conquered the coast and islands of western Greece, they were charmed by the tiny dried Corinthian grapes. They imported scads of them to sprinkle in many of their fancy dishes, especially the ones using their new food, sugar. The two together made seductively sweet treats.

When the Ottomans started to encroach across the Greek mainland,

the Venetians, zealous to guard their dulcet tidbit, transplanted the currant vines to their Ionian islands, especially to Zante, now called Zakinthos. From there the dried grapes took the name "Zante currants." The export of the miniature dried grapes became so profitable that it helped line the coffers of Venice and the dried currant went on to become one of Greece's main trade goods. Most of the world's dried currant supply is still grown in its original homeland. I always keep a supply of them on hand, as well as a special supply soaking in retsina and in Mavrodaphne in the refrigerator (page 49). Retsina gives a wondrous piny depth to the currant and Mavrodaphne adds a haunting sweetness.

# stuffed cabbage leaves

## MACEDONIAN-STYLE

### LAHANODOLMADES

#### SERVES 6 TO 8

THE GREEK WORD *DOLMADES* REFERS TO OTHER STUFFED LEAVES AS WELL AS GRAPE LEAVES. AND IT IS SAID THAT IN ONE OF THEIR VERY EARLY FORAYS INTO GREECE, ABOUT 600 B.C.E., THE CELTS NOT ONLY STOLE CABBAGE BUT TOOK THE IDEA OF STUFFING CABBAGE LEAVES FROM THE GREEKS AS WELL. THOSE CELTS WALKED ALL OVER EUROPE, APPARENTLY SPREADING THE IDEA OF STUFFED CABBAGE, BEFORE BEING PUSHED BACK BY THE ROMANS, THE GERMANIC TRIBES, AND THE SLAVS.

Cooks often don't wait for the first tender grape leaves to appear in early summer to make *dolmades*—they make them as soon as the late-winter cabbages appear. Caraway bolsters the flavor of the leaves with a subtle clarity. Traditionally the filling for cabbage *dolmades* contains beef or lamb, but pork, as is used here, is a late-winter choice. Cabbage *dolmades* often include egg, and in Macedonia the leaves might be braised with a little butter as well as oil. Lemon egg sauce often tops them, but I think yogurt is more refreshing.

1 large head green cabbage

8 ounces ground pork

$^1/_2$ cup uncooked short-grain rice, preferably Arborio

1 medium onion, finely chopped

1 large egg, lightly beaten

$^1/_4$ cup chopped fresh flat-leaf parsley leaves

2 tablespoons chopped fresh dill

1 teaspoon caraway seeds

1 teaspoon salt

$^1/_4$ teaspoon freshly ground black pepper

6 tablespoons ($^3/_4$ stick) butter, cut into pieces

2 cups Thickened Yogurt (page 471)

1 Bring a large pot of water to a boil over high heat. Cut out the core of the cabbage, and slide the whole head into the pot. Cover and boil until the cabbage is soft enough to separate the leaves without tearing them but not cooked all the way through, 10 minutes. Drain and set aside until cool enough to handle.

2 Gently pull the outer leaves off the cabbage, removing as many as you can without breaking them, and set them aside. Coarsely chop the smaller, less soft center leaves. Set them aside.

3 Mix the pork, rice, onion, egg, parsley, dill, caraway seeds, salt, and pepper together in a medium-size bowl.

4 Fill and roll the cabbage leaves to make packets as you would grape leaves (page 48). Place half the butter pieces and the chopped cabbage in the bottom of a large flameproof casserole. Arrange the cabbage rolls in two or three (at the most) tightly packed layers over the chopped cabbage. Dot the top with the remaining butter, and add water to almost, but not completely, cover. Place a plate over the cabbage rolls to keep them submerged during cooking.

When Greeks think someone is conceited, they invoke a vegetable metaphor: "Important," they say, "as the cabbage." "My sweet leek" is a term of endearment. A mess is often called "a salad." When a person is dull or a conversation bland (we would say without any "meat"), Greeks say it is "saltless." And the word that means something so hotly fried it jumps and sputters, *petahti*, is the term applied to a lively person, especially a woman. She is sometimes called a *petahtoula*, a "little spitfire."

5 Bring to a boil over high heat, then lower the heat, cover the casserole, and simmer gently until the leaves are very tender, 1½ hours. Serve hot or at room temperature, accompanied by a bowl of yogurt.

## VARIATIONS:

**For More Traditional Cabbage Dolmades:** For a more standard stuffed cabbage, substitute beef or lamb for the pork.

■ Use the Rice and Almond Stuffing on page 301.

■ Instead of yogurt, serve the cabbage rolls with *Avgolemono* Sauce (page 457) made with the *dolmades* cooking liquid.

# stuffed grape leaf dolmades

## LAMB, RICE, AND APRICOT WITH *AVGOLEMONO* SAUCE

### MAKES 40 TO 42 DOLMADES; SERVES 6

THE MOST FAMOUS GREEK DISH, *DOLMADES* OF GRAPE LEAVES, IS FIRST MENTIONED WHEN ALEXANDER THE GREAT CONQUERED AND DESTROYED THE CITY OF THEBES. THE SCORCHED-EARTH FORAY LEFT PROVISIONS SO SCARCE THAT THEBANS TOOK TO ROLLING BITS OF MEAT IN GRAPE LEAVES. CLASSICAL GREEKS CONTINUED TO USE GRAPE LEAVES AS ENVELOPES FOR THEIR GRAINS AND OTHER TASTY MORSELS. IN LATER TIMES, THE BYZANTINES MADE THE FILLING MORE ORNATE WITH CURRANTS, NUTS, AND EASTERN SPICES.

Today Greek *dolmades* are made in two versions. One is meatless and served as an hors d'oeuvre (page 47). The other version, more filling, includes meat, rice, usually raisins or currants, and a sprinkling of dill and parsley. These *dolmades* are served hot, blanketed in an *avgolemono* coating. The special *dolmades* here owe a bit of a bow to Victoria's background, having, as they do,

a flare of Greece's longtime close affiliation with Armenia, where apricots thrive. Such *dolmades* sing a song of the deep past while truly melting in the mouth.

*Even before classical times, when temples like this were built at Corinth, Greeks knew of and traded with the Armenians.*

8 ounces ground lamb or beef

1 cup uncooked short-grain rice,
   preferably Arborio

1 medium onion, finely chopped

12 sun-dried apricots, finely diced

2 tablespoons chopped fresh
   dill

1/2 cup chopped fresh flat-leaf
   parsley leaves

1 1/2 teaspoons salt

1/2 teaspoon freshly ground
   black pepper

1/4 cup fresh lemon juice

40 to 42 large grape leaves
   (see page 48)

2 cups Avgolemono Sauce
   (page 457)

1 Place all the ingredients except the leaves and the sauce in a large bowl and mix thoroughly.

2 Fill and roll the grape leaves as described on page 48. Arrange them in tightly packed layers in a large, heavy pot. Add water to cover by 1 inch, and place a heavy or weighted plate directly on top of the leaves to keep them sub-merged. Bring to a boil over high heat, then reduce the heat, cover the pot, and simmer until the rice is tender, about 50 minutes.

3 Remove the pot from the heat. When the *dolmades* have cooled slightly, carefully pour off the liquid, while gently pressing down on the plate. Arrange the *dolmades* on a platter. Pour the sauce over the top, and serve warm or cold.

**NOTE:** The apricots can be replaced with currants or dark or golden raisins. As always, any of these are much tastier when presoaked in retsina (see page 49).

## GREECE AND ARMENIA

Invaders speaking a language related to Greek arrived in the lower Caucasus mountains and into eastern Anatolia in about 1400 B.C.E. Greeks called the area "greater Armenia" and recognized the language as close to their own. Herodotus said Armenian was a variety of Phrygian. Relations between Greece and Armenia were constant, with merchants and settlers traveling up and down the Bosporus, across the Black Sea and Anatolia.

Greeks from Byzantium brought Christianity to Armenia around 300 C.E., and with the new faith, the Armenians developed a rich liturgical and literary tradition. One of the Christian bishops, Mesrop Mashtots, took the Greek alphabet and used it as the basis of a unique Armenian alphabet. With a common religion, ties between Greece and Armenia remained strong, and when the Ottomans swept across the region, first taking Armenia, then Greece, the bond was strengthened in the face of a common foe.

Through all the eras—classical, Byzantine, Ottoman, and still today—Armenian merchants resided in Thessaloniki and Athens. Armenia adopted much Greek food, but the trade went both ways. In Greek food today are Armenian fruits, especially dried apricots. Both have, seemingly forever, processed grapes into wine and fine brandy and wrapped grape leaves around fillings to make *dolmades*. Whenever we are cooking together, Victoria and I compare: How alike are the Greek meatballs and the Armenian? How equally sublime are Armenian *dolmades* and Greek? We always agree at least enough to perfect the recipe.

# THE RENOWNED CASSEROLE

# moussaka

### SERVES 8 TO 12

GREEKS PREPARE MOUSSAKA WITH LOVING CARE: EACH SLICE OF EGGPLANT IS LAID IN THE PAN AS IF PLACING A BLANKET OVER A BABY. THE MEAT SAUCE IS STIRRED AND SAMPLED ANY NUMBER OF TIMES UNTIL THE BALANCE OF HERBS AND SPICES ACHIEVES PERFECTION. THE WHITE SAUCE TOPPING IS WHISKED UNTIL IT IS THE COLOR OF OLD IVORY AND SWELLS UPWARD LIKE A CLOUD. ONLY THEN, AS THE CASSEROLE IS TIERED LAYER BY LAYER, IS THE COOK HAPPY.

There are numerous variations on the triumph, of course. Some cooks use a bottom layer of potato. Some add green peppers or a layer of sautéed or softly boiled greens. Some put raisins or currants in the meat sauce to add a sweet touch. Some use a dusting of cinnamon or bread crumbs on top, instead of nutmeg. Some varieties of *moussaka* are made with squash slices, artichoke hearts, or even rice.

I prefer a *moussaka* of only eggplant and more eggplant. No sweetness in the sauce for me— a savory blend couples best with the olive oil and eggplant. To make the sauce truly outstanding, I use a combination of white wine and brandy. The eggplant slices are baked to achieve the smoky taste that never develops in frying. As for the topping, redolent nutmeg cannot be bettered as the spice to accent curdy kefalotyri cheese. In return for its loving preparation, the queen of all Greek dishes comes out of the oven a pleasure garden of flavors.

In the taste quartet of renowned Greek dishes, Greek salad is the violin, filo pie is the viola, *dolma* is the cello, and the depth of the bass sings out in *moussaka*.

To enter a Greek restaurant is to think *moussaka*. To sample Greek cuisine for the first time is to bite into *moussaka*. To enjoy Greek food is to fall in love with *moussaka*. It comes in two versions: with an inner tier of saucy and succulent meat between layers of vegetable, and purely vegetarian. The two versions, of course, have many small variations, almost as many as there are Greek cooks. More white sauce, or less. All eggplant with no potato, or a layer of potato as the foundation. A long-simmered meat center, or a quick dash of meat and spices. It doesn't matter, though. To dive into the casserole in any of its versions is to dive into divinity. It is reason alone to know Greek cooking: A life with no *moussaka* is desolate indeed.

### FOR THE EGGPLANT
### AND FILLING
*3 medium eggplants*
*1 cup olive oil, or more as needed*
*1 1/2 pounds lean ground beef or lamb*
*1 large onion, finely chopped*
*3 cloves garlic, finely chopped*
*3 tomatoes, finely chopped*
*1 tablespoon tomato paste*
*2 teaspoons chopped fresh oregano*
    *leaves, or 1 teaspoon dried*
*1/4 teaspoon ground allspice*
*Small pinch of ground cinnamon*
*1/4 teaspoon freshly ground*
    *black pepper*
*2 tablespoons Metaxa or other brandy*
*1/2 cup dry white wine*
*Salt, to taste*

# TWO GREEK COOKS, TWO GREAT MOUSSAKADES

O F ALL THE *MOUSSAKADES* I HAVE EATEN IN GREECE— AND I ORDER IT INEVITABLY EVERYWHERE I GO— TWO STAND OUT BEYOND ALL OTHERS.

Poulakis *Taverna* on Panos Street, in the Plaka district of Athens, is what one would call a "hole in the wall." Hemmed in by other restaurants on either side, it boasts only a stretch of asphalt with a few tables outside the door and a few scattered tables in a dark, not-too-well-kept interior. The kitchen is the size of a hatbox. But it has something no other Plaka *taverna* has: it has Kyria Dina.

## THE BEST IN ATHENS

Poulakis *Taverna* was started by Dina's beloved husband, Ioannis. He hand-painted the murals, oversaw the tables, called out to passersby, and if they stopped to eat, kept them returning with his secret weapon: His wife, Dina, was his cook, and he knew how good she was. Sadly, Ioannis died young. But Dina carried on, and throughout the years, she has refused to turn the kitchen over to anyone else—a decision that has the taverna thriving, for everything Dina cooks is stellar. Oh, she has some steaks and chops at hand, a fish or two to grill, but Dina specializes in the baked dishes that make Greek food so notable. Every day on her tiny counter she lays out a number of grand achievements, including stuffed tomatoes, beans *plaki*, a vegetable *briami*, and because the area is a tourist attraction and *moussaka* is such a famous Greek dish, *moussaka*. Dina's *moussaka* has a very thin layer of potatoes on the bottom. She claims they're only to make the pieces cuttable, not for filling or taste. Over those she layers eggplant slices at least an inch and a half high, with a center layer of meat sauce that she has cooked for hours. Her *besamel* topping is a pale caramel color, still jiggling soft, unadorned, unelaborate, but fluffed up and crusted to perfection. When she cuts a great rectangle for a serving, the juices run across the plate. Dina's midday *moussaka* never lasts until evening.

## A BEACHSIDE CONTENDER

On Kamari Beach on Santorini, Kyria Eirini set up a little restaurant after an earthquake destroyed her village and it was rebuilt down by the sea. No one else had opened a *taverna*, and Eirini knew a few stragglers were bound to come to the black-sand beach, at least on Sundays. Now the beach is packed with people year-round, and at least half of them lunch at Eirini's. She sits there in the quiet morning, preparing the garlic, washing the parsley, chatting, and then attacks the cooking. Each dish, like Eirini herself, is unassuming, the best of Greek cooking. She offers seafood caught on the beach, octopus that she beats against a rock, grilled red mullet, and shark. But like Kyria Dina, she also prepares a number of oven dishes from whatever produce the island provides, and always *moussaka*. Hers has no potatoes. Eirini insists that it be all eggplant. Her middle layer of meat is more like a ribbon than a stratum, merely giving a burst of meat flavor to the surrounding vegetable, and she always adds a central strand of fresh tomatoes. Her *besamel* is more a filigree than a crust, but she never spares the nutmeg or cheese.

Both cooks have changed some dishes through time. Kyria Dina, catering to tourists, offers more meat roasts, *yiouvetsi*, *stifado*, meatballs. The last time I was at Eirini's she offered fried clams; cheese balls; chicken salad; pork chops in wine, parsley, and garlic; rice with onions, peppers, and parsley; and a *horiatiki* salad with potatoes and black-eyed peas. While changing with the times, though, both have kept to the secret that makes their fare so fine: They've kept their cooking homespun, which with Greece's fantastic ingredients can't be beat.

*Here I am with Kyria Dina, pointing at a picture of myself taken at the* taverna *thirty years earlier.*

**FOR THE TOPPING**
*3 cups Saltsa Besamel (page 459)*
*1 tablespoon fresh lemon juice*
*⅛ teaspoon ground nutmeg,*
*    preferably freshly grated*
*⅔ cup freshly grated kefalotyri cheese*

**1** Preheat the oven to 450°F. Lightly oil several baking sheets.

**2** Trim the stem ends off the eggplants, and cut them into ¼-inch-thick lengthwise slices. Coat each slice on both sides with oil. Arrange the slices in one layer, without overlapping, on the baking sheets. (You may need to do this in several batches, depending on how many baking sheets you have and the size of your oven.) Bake for 10 minutes, turn them over, and continue baking until well wilted and slightly golden, another 8 to 10 minutes (see Notes).

**3** Remove from the oven and set aside until cool enough to handle. Reduce the oven temperature to 350°F.

**4** While the eggplant is cooling, prepare the filling: Place the meat in a large nonreactive skillet. Turn the heat to medium-high and cook, using a fork to break up the chunks, until the meat is browned, 10 minutes. Add the onion and garlic and continue cooking and stirring until well mixed, 3 minutes. Add the remaining filling ingredients and mix well. Cook over medium heat, stirring from time to time, until the mixture is fairly dry and crumbly, 20 minutes. Remove the skillet from the heat and set it aside to cool.

**5** Prepare the topping: Stir the *besamel,* lemon juice, nutmeg, and 2 tablespoons of the cheese together in a mixing bowl. Set it aside.

**6** To assemble the *moussaka,* cover the bottom of a 13- x 9-inch baking dish with an overlapping layer of eggplant slices. Spread one third of the meat mixture over the eggplant, and then sprinkle 1 tablespoon of the remaining cheese over the filling. Repeat the layers of eggplant, filling, and cheese. Arrange the remaining eggplant slices over the second layer (don't worry if there are not enough slices to cover the filling completely), and spread the remaining filling over them. Spread the topping over the meat, and sprinkle with the remaining cheese.

**7** Place the dish in the oven and bake until the *moussaka* is bubbly, golden on top, and slightly browned around the edges, 1 hour. Remove it from the oven and let it rest for at least 20 minutes before serving.

**NOTES:**

■ The easiest way to coat the eggplant slices with oil is to pour about 1 cup olive oil in a bowl and use your hands to "brush" each side. You may need a little more oil; the idea is to coat them well without saturating.

■ To streamline the process, the meat filling and the topping mixture can be prepared in advance and refrigerated, covered, for up to 2 days. It is best, however, to proceed with the assembling and cooking of the *moussaka* once the eggplant preparation is under way.

■ You can also fry the eggplant slices as is done in the Vegetable Moussaka, Step 2, page 316.

■ In both versions of *moussaka*—with and without meat—a layer of greens, such as spinach, kale, chard, or dandelion, simmered until soft and then fried until lightly crisp, makes the dish more complex, unusual, and leafily enchanting.

# vegetable moussaka

## WITH POTATOES

### SERVES 6 TO 8

T HE WORD MOUSSAKA REFERS TO ANY VEGETABLE CASSEROLE—ONLY WITH TOURISM HAS THE TERM BECOME SYNONYMOUS WITH THE MEAT AND EGGPLANT VERSION. ALL ACROSS GREECE, IN THESSALY AND THRACE, IN ATTICA AND MANI, MEAT STILL IS NOT EATEN DAILY. VEGETABLES RULE. CONSEQUENTLY, MANY OF THE *MOUSSAKADES* GREEKS EAT ARE BUILT OF WHATEVER VEGETABLES ARE FRESH, CAN BE SLICED TO LAYER, AND WILL BAKE UP JUICY AND ZESTY.

What defines it as *moussaka* is that the sliced vegetables, acting like wide pasta, are stacked in strata. Potatoes are a favorite building block; so is zucchini, and always eggplant. Some *moussakades* boast a layer of beans, others artichokes. Sliced celery with a few of its chewy leaves provides an appealing tier. Punctuated with cumin, crunched with bread crumbs, mellowed with a dab of butter, the towering *moussaka* here features eggplant, tomatoes, and potatoes. The result is a humble pie giving tribute to the many tastes of Greece's garden.

2 medium eggplants
Olive oil
2 pounds white potatoes, peeled and
    sliced into ⅛-inch-thick rounds
¼ cup bread crumbs
2 large tomatoes, thinly sliced
3 egg yolks
¼ teaspoon ground cumin
4 cups Saltsa Besamel (page 459),
    at room temperature
½ cup coarsely grated kefalotyri
    cheese

1 Trim the stems off the eggplants, and cut them into ¼-inch-thick lengthwise slices.

2 Pour oil to a depth of ⅛ inch in a large nonreactive skillet over medium heat. When the oil is hot, add as many eggplant slices as will fit in one layer and sauté, turning once, until wilted and beginning to turn golden in spots, 2 to 3 minutes. Transfer the slices to paper towels to drain, and continue with another batch, adding more oil as you go, until all the slices are fried.

3 Fry the potato slices in the same way, making sure to drain them well on paper towels also.

4 Preheat the oven to 350°F. Grease the bottom and sides of a 13- x 9-inch nonreactive baking dish. Sprinkle the bread crumbs over the bottom.

5 Arrange half the potato slices in an overlapping layer over the bread crumbs. Place a sparse layer of tomato slices over the potatoes. Top the tomatoes with half of the eggplant slices in an overlapping layer. Repeat the layers of potatoes, tomatoes, and eggplant.

6 Stir the egg yolks and cumin into the *besamel*, and pour it over the vegetables. Sprinkle the cheese over the sauce.

7 Place the baking dish in the oven and bake until the *moussaka* is bubbling and golden all across the top, 1 hour. Remove the dish from the oven and let it rest for 15 to 20 minutes before serving.

## VARIATIONS:

**Varying the Vegetable Layers:** Other vegetables choices to layer in a *moussaka* are:

■ Zucchini, sliced lengthwise or cut into rounds and lightly fried in olive oil

■ Carrots, thinly sliced lengthwise or in rounds and parboiled until slightly soft

■ Turnip, sliced and parboiled until slightly soft

■ Chestnuts, parboiled until softened, then sliced

■ Artichoke hearts, parboiled until softened

## RED ROOTS, BLUE LEAVES, YELLOW STIGMAS: VEGETABLE DYES

Plant products were not only used as food in ancient times. The colored juices of fruits, flowers, roots, leaves, and stems were also used to stain the wool and flax woven into elaborate togas and tunics, pleated draperies, and intricate robes. Homer mentions that leather, as well as textiles, was colored. Some of the vegetables used were edible; some were used only as dye. Those that gave the deepest and most brilliant hues were particularly valued.

Beet juice, still used to dye eggs, imparts a dark garnet. Saffron, still used to color the robes of Tibetan priests, was gathered for its intense yellow. Madder root produced red-based pigments from red-blue to brown, crimson, carmine, pink, yellow, and violet. The word "indigo" comes from the Greek word *indigos*, the plant that was the main source of blue coloring. Edible safflower, sometimes called in English "dyer's thistle," created a range of yellow and red hues. Certain sea snails were also used, as was a kind of lichen, both producing shades of purple.

Fixing the color to last and to avoid fading was the real problem, as it still is, but the process used to dye fabric was much the same as it is today. Wool, usually in the raw state before spinning, or linen in the form of thread before weaving, was dipped into vats of densely tinted liquid. The Greek word for "dyeing," which also means "to dip," is *bafo*, and from it we derive the word for another sort of dipping, "baptism."

# CLASSICAL GREECE— A TIME OF PHILOSOPHERS AND FARMERS

AS THE MYCENAEAN CIVILIZATION FADED AWAY, GREECE SLIPPED INTO A LONG DARK SPELL. LITTLE IS KNOWN ABOUT THAT SHADOWY ERA, BUT A GREAT GESTATION MUST HAVE BEEN OCCURRING, FOR WHEN THE GREEKS EMERGED TO THE LIGHT AGAIN, THEY LAUNCHED A CIVILIZATION UNPARALLELED IN WESTERN HISTORY.

That civilization reached full blossom in Greece's classical period.

During the classical age, 750 to 200 B.C.E., ideas on how to live, on mathematics and science, on art, teaching, governing, and philosophy that still influence us sprung forth as if from a well-tended garden. The classical period nurtured some of history's greatest architects and artists, astute politicians, and most brilliant thinkers. Thucydides and Pericles lived and led during this time. Socrates, Plato, and Aristotle taught and argued. Phidias and other great designers built towering temples that still enthrall the viewer. Artists chiseled statues whose beauty takes the breath away millennia later. Great playwrights— Aeschylus, Sophocles, Euripides, Aristophanes—penned dramas and comedies that are frequently performed today. Athletes established sports that would be at the heart of competitions for centuries to come.

## THE RISE OF GREAT CITIES

The great cities of Greece grew into glowing metropolises. Athens, Sparta, Corinth, and Thebes became important centers, and their shape and features still characterize what

*Central squares with their marketplaces are still the vibrant hubs of Greek communities.*

we think of as urban life today. Throughout the dark ages, Greek people had lived in small villages situated on high ground—*acropoleis*—where they could defend their settlements. As the classical age unfolded, the high grounds with their graceful temples became entirely sacred places, sites of ritual and religion. Meanwhile, people flocking to the cities built rows of houses along lanes leading to the sacred sites and erected walls enclosing their towns. In Athens these walls extended to the port of Piraeus. More and more people squeezed within the walls, until the populations became a mix of citizen and foreigner, aristocrat and laborer, servant and slave.

## THE MARKET'S MANY ROLES

In the center of the cities, sitting under the shadows of commanding temples and surrounded by a scramble of burgeoning neighborhoods, was the hub: the market, or *agora*. Every great Greek city featured a large central area that was dedicated to commerce, talk, and hubbub. The market was surrounded by colonnaded walks behind which stood the narrow stalls of peddlers. Peasants from the countryside brought beans, peas, beets, turnips, cabbage, cardoons, greens, onions, garlic, olives, and capers to sell in the stalls. Other peddlers opened booths to forge pots and pans, fix shoes, and

paint amphorae. Others flipped pancakes, roasted chestnuts, sizzled fritters, stewed legumes, and concocted herbal remedies. In a nearby area, fishermen brought in swordfish, tuna, grouper, squid, and octopus. Butchers peddled beef, lamb, goats, pigs, and birds of many sorts. In the center of the market stood an altar for sacrifice, a fountain, and an area for memorials. Here, while their servants and slaves bought the needed utensils and provisions, the lords of the household discussed the news, voted on war and peace, elected or ejected leaders. It was in the market that

*In every town and village, rowed houses stretch out along narrow, paved, crooked lanes.*

Socrates was condemned to death and put hemlock to his lips, that Plato taught, that Pericles was ostracized. The cities were also home to hospitals, government houses, lecture halls, gymnasiums, and theaters.

## TOWN AND COUNTRY

All these developments rested on the labor of the common folk, most of whom owned and worked family farms. Each city-state depended on its citizen farmers, landowners living within the city or out on the land. Most of those who were citizens of the city-state—not servants or slaves—held farms on the outskirts; many others lived on their farms, traveling to the urban capital only to vote. They lived quite well. Both the town residences and the country houses of the landowners might have had as many as seven rooms, though the homes of smallholders and workers were far less grand. The large houses often featured an entrance hall, porter's lodge, court, porch, inner hall, office, bedchambers, and outside patio. There might be a number of small kitchens for baking breads and stewing vegetables. Each house had an upper floor reserved for the women. Wives and daughters in classical Greece were confined to the home. The women on the streets and at the grand banquets were servants, slaves, or courtesans.

## THE CITIZEN-FARMER

Socrates describes a farmer of his time: As was the custom, the man had just married a girl, not yet fifteen, whose only domestic skill was weaving. He tells his new bride that her path to success lies in managing the household well. She is to supervise all domestic tasks and in so doing to be economical. She is to oversee the weaving, ensure that the grain is always ready for making food, and tend to any servants who are ill. The better she does over the years, the more the farmer will honor her in her old age. He wants her to be orderly, explaining that order is beauty. He tells her how to store the various kinds of foods and how to keep the cooking utensils separate from those for spinning and those for bathing. He asks her opinion: Should he deal with people honestly or trick them?

A good farmer, Socrates says, rises early and attends to his town business first. Then he walks back to his farm to supervise the day's labors. Returning home, he washes and has a meal of only bread and wine. He must then check on his household managers, his slaves and bailiffs; he punishes them if disobedient, rewards them with food if good. Happy men work well, and if they work well they deserve a higher reward—better clothes and shoes. Meanwhile, the farmer works in partnership with nature. He must know the quality of the soil, when and where to grow barley, when and where to grow wheat. Agriculture is an art.

## THE FARMER-FATHER

For his children the farmer provides toys of hoops and knuckle bones. He sees that his daughters learn to embroider, that his sons learn to train cocks and quail for fighting. For amusement, like Greeks today, the farmer of classical Greece indulges in much talk. Conversation is his joy. With other men, he attends symposia after dinner, and is entertained there by musicians and dancers.

## THE FARMER-SOLDIER

At some point in the day the farmer must practice his martial arts to keep himself ready to be a soldier. The common farmer of ancient Greece was not only a tiller of the land, he was also a soldier. As a warrior he is called upon to fight for his city whenever war looms. (Only the Spartans had a professional army.) The farmer-soldiers carried a short sword for cutting, a cavalry sword for downstroke, a spear for thrusting. Each wore a helmet, body armor, leg covers, and a round or oval shield. The farmer must make sure that his horse is always ready for cross-country forays, for the troops also had cavalry, horse-drawn chariots, and cart-drawn flame

**The great cities of Greece grew into glowing metropolises . . . their shape and features still characterize what we think of as urban life today.**

throwers. As soldiers, Greek citizens fought to preserve the life of their particular city-state and its customs. The goal of war was to return to the farm and the life of sowing grains and harvesting vegetables.

## A DIVERSE HARVEST

It was because of the family farmer—growing grains and vegetables, fighting when called upon—that democracy developed in classical Greece. The farmers of Greece grew different crops to ensure independence and autonomy. They raised grains, fruit to make fresh and dried products, olives for eating and cooking and lamp oil, grapes for raisins and wine, livestock for meat, cheese, milk, and hides, and vegetables and greens from the garden. All these allowed them not to depend on a monarch and to provide enough to subsidize and pamper artists, writers, and thinkers.

*In a line-up of ancient Greek philosophers, Plato sits in the center—a student of Socrates and a teacher of Aristotle.*

# fish and shellfish

THE SEA DOES NOT MERELY
SURROUND GREECE, IT PERMEATES
IT. IT LAPS UPON THE CLIFFS AND
BEACHES OF THE ISLANDS, SWIRLS
IN FOAMY INLETS DEEP INTO THE
MAINLAND, AND CARVES SALTY
CHANNELS BETWEEN PROVINCES.
AS MUCH AS GREECE IS THE LAND,
IT IS THE SEA, AND THE SEA HAS
ALWAYS FED THE GREEKS.

*Each thing
in its time
and mackerel
in August.*

—GREEK PROVERB

Greeks partake of all the sea's offerings—fish with and without fin, shellfish that curl about themselves or fan out in crenulation, cephalopods that reach out from watery nook to wrap tentacles around floaters-by. Every Greek knows how to tell if a sea creature is fresh: Is the fish's eye clear, the mussel shell closed, the squid still firm and glistening? And wherever Greeks dwell, they show a deft hand at cooking seafood. Seafood *tavernas* occupy the narrow tips of practically every half-moon-shaped beach. They top every jutting point; some sit on stilts right in the water. In Greek eateries from Athens to Adelaide, smoky grills spin out the aroma of sizzling swordfish, roasted John Dory, and seared tuna. You know that seafood is the house specialty by the restaurant's name: "Aegean," "Hydra," "Hellespont," "Samos," "Ithaca," and "Corfu." Many are called

> *"Hunters of the deep sea,*
> *Pray, have we caught anything yet?"*
>
> *"All that we have caught we left behind, and*
> *all that we didn't catch we carry home."*

—HOMER, EPIGRAMS, CIRCA 800 B.C.E.

"Meltemi" for the wind that blows across the Mediterranean in July and knocks both boat and fish *anakatameno*—"upside down."

Ancient Greek writers wrote more about fish than about any other food. Archestratos and Athenaeus detailed not only in which city the best of almost every fish was found, but from what bay or stretch of coastline. Ananios recorded fish by season, while Antiphanes, so familiar with their habits and wares, satirized fishmongers and fish markets.

The appetite for fish remains unchanged today. Each rosy-fingered dawn, from every

shipping port in Greece, a fleet of fishing boats sallies forth to bring home a watery catch. In seaside villages by the light of late afternoon, weary workers take to the soothing waters in hopes of snagging the evening's meal. On sandy shoals Greek men spread nets and, using both hands and feet, repair tears to ensure a continued catch. Wading in the soft waves on languid Sundays, women gather periwinkles, sea urchins, and limpets.

With the same flair as their forebears, modern Greek cooks create seafood dishes that are as numerous, varied, and magnificent as the ocean's inhabitants.

# grilled whole fish

## IN GRAPE LEAVES

### SERVES 6

AS MUCH AS AMERICANS DELIGHT IN FISH FILLETS AND FISH STEAKS, GREEKS RELISH THEIR FISH WHOLE. COOKS EYE THE ARRAY THE FISHERMEN HAVE BROUGHT IN, PICKING THE ONE THEY WILL SLIDE BEFORE KIN OR CLIENT. WAITERS EXHIBIT TRAYS OF THE WHOLE FISH OFFERED THAT DAY AS SOON AS DINERS SIT. OTHER RESTAURANTS DISPLAY THE CATCH IN GLASS CASES. IN THE LINEUP THERE MIGHT BE A RED MULLET, GEM OF THE AEGEAN—FAMOUS FOR ITS FLAVOR AND ITS HIGH PRICE—STRETCHED NEXT TO A MACKEREL, A BREAM, OR A SEA BASS. THE GREEKS ARE ABSOLUTELY RIGHT: THERE'S NOTHING QUITE LIKE AN ENTIRE FISH, COOKED BONE-IN, OPENED ON THE PLATE, FRAGRANT STEAM RISING.

Any whole fish can be wrapped in tangy grape leaves. Set on the grill and broiled, it cooks to aromatic and moist perfection. Mackerel is the choice here, but small red snapper, herring, mullet, striped bass, large sardines, or trout from inland waters would also work beautifully.

6 whole mackerel or other small, whole, bone-in fish (8 to 10 ounces each), scaled and gutted
Salt
1/4 cup fresh lemon juice
24 to 30 grape leaves (see box, page 48)
Olive oil
Lemon wedges, for garnish

## AN ICHTHYO-GOURMAND

Antiphanes, a writer of the fourth century B.C.E., makes it clear that seafood was abundant and that the ancient Greek appetite was, to put it mildly, lusty. Certainly Antiphanes' appetite was. He lists a veritable plethora of fish, and it seems he planned on eating them all at one sitting: "Let us have a sliced mullet," he said, "a simmered electric ray, a filleted perch, a stuffed squid, a baked smooth-tooth fish, the first slice of grayfish, the head of a conger eel, the belly of a frog that fishes, the flanks of a tuna, the back of a ray, the loin of a spotted fish, a bit of sole, a sprat, a shrimp, a red mullet, and a hogfish."

Somehow, that final entry, "hogfish," seems apt.

1 Remove the heads from the fish or leave them on, as you prefer. Liberally salt the fish inside and out and rub them inside and out with the lemon juice. Gently squeeze the excess liquid out of the grape leaves without wringing them dry. Wrap enough grape leaves around each fish to enclose it completely, head to tail. Place the wrapped fish on a platter, cover with plastic wrap, and set aside in the refrigerator for at least 30 minutes or up to several hours.

# MENU

## OTHER DISHES FOR THE TABLE

CRUSTY BREAD, OLIVES, AND CHEESE

CHICORY SALAD
WITH TOASTED WALNUTS,
GOLDEN RAISINS,
AND SHAVED KEFALOTYRI
CHEESE
page 196

FRENCH FRIED POTATO
OMELET
page 220

FRESH FRUIT TO FINISH

2 When you are ready to cook the fish, heat a grill to medium. Lightly coat the grape leaf wrapping with the oil.

3 Place the fish on the grill and cook until the leaves are lightly charred all around and the fish flakes easily when pierced with a fork, 8 to 12 minutes. Serve right away, garnished with the lemon wedges.

**NOTE:** Meaty fish steaks such as swordfish or snapper can also be wrapped in leaves before cooking, and in addition to grape leaves, fig leaves can be used.

# grilled whole fish

## WITH MASTIC-FLAVORED BREAD STUFFING

### SERVES 6

FISH APPEAR AS A FREQUENT DECORATIVE MOTIF ON MINOAN MURALS AND POTTERY, AND BY MINOAN TIMES SMALL, UNFIRED CLAY CHARCOAL BROILERS WERE MADE TO GRILL THE CATCH, AS WELL. FISH SWIM ACROSS THE LIPS, HANDLES, AND BORDERS OF EVERY TYPE OF GREEK MYCENEAN CLAY VESSEL, TOO, AND BY CLASSICAL TIMES, THE EVEN LARGER NUMBER OF PLATES DECORATED WITH FISH TRULY TESTIFIES TO THE GREEK ARDOR FOR FISH. IDENTIFIABLE ON THE PLATES ARE SNAPPER, PARROT FISH, BREAM, PORGIES, AND OTHERS. AMAZINGLY, BOTH THE PLATES AND THE BROILERS ARE STILL MADE!

One of the advantages of grilling whole fish is that once opened and cleaned, they almost beg to be stuffed. The ingredients can be many—some basil leaves, chopped vegetables, small shellfish, bread crumbs. A stuffed grilled fish is always enticing and different, but to make the fish still more dazzling, here a bread stuffing is flavored with mastic. *Mastiha*, or mastic, is usually used as a

*An afternoon prize. It will be on the grill within an hour.*

flavoring only for sweet, festive breads, but it's a pity to make use of it so infrequently. It can impart a welcome piney note to vegetables, soups, salad dressings, and poultry as well as fish.

1 1/2 tablespoons olive oil,
    *plus oil for coating the fish*
*2 small ribs celery, including*
    *leaves, finely chopped*
*1/2 cup finely chopped onion*
*1/2 cup finely chopped tomato*
*1 1/2 tablespoons chopped fresh*
    *flat-leaf parsley leaves*
*1 1/4 teaspoons powdered mastic*
    *(see Notes)*
*3 ounces country-style bread,*
    *cut into 1/4-inch cubes*
    *(2 packed cups)*
*3/4 teaspoon salt*
*1/2 teaspoon freshly ground*
    *black pepper*
*6 medium whole fish*
    *(8 to 10 ounces each),*
    *such as mullet or trout*
    *(see Notes)*

1 To prepare the stuffing, heat the 1 1/2 tablespoons oil in a medium-size skillet over medium-high heat. Stir in the celery, onion, tomato, parsley, and mastic and sauté until the vegetables are wilted and the mixture is piney-smelling, 2 minutes. Remove the skillet from the heat, stir in the bread cubes and salt and pepper, and set it aside to cool a bit.

2 When you are ready to cook the fish, heat a grill to medium.

3 Rinse the fish inside and out and pat them dry. Fill the cavity of each fish with about 1/2 cup of the stuffing. Use toothpicks to close and secure the cavities. Rub the outside of each fish with a little oil and set it aside at room temperature until the grill is ready.

4 Place the fish on the grill and cook for 4 minutes. Turn and cook on the other side until the flesh flakes easily when pierced with a fork, but is still quite moist, 3 to 4 minutes depending on the heat of the fire and the size of the fish. Serve right away.

**NOTES:**

■ Mastic generally comes in the form of crystals, which can be reduced to powder with a pestle or mallet. For a description of mastic, see page 143. It is available at Greek specialty food stores.

■ In Greece, the prized *barbounia* (red mullet) would be a first choice for this dish, but trout, small snapper, and other white-fleshed medium-size fish swim well with the woody freshness of mastic.

■ Whole stuffed fish can also be pan-fried over medium-high heat or baked at 375°F. The timing is about the same.

## THE TRAIL OF THE OLIVE

A spiny, indigenous variety of olive was already growing in Greece when the first people began to live there. The tree was native to the Levant as well, and people in both places were quick to realize the value of the fruit and, soon, to cultivate it. Olive pits are found in many Neolithic and Bronze Age sites. The Bible mentions olives and olive oil many times. Orchards of olive trees were quickly thick enough for raiders to use the wood to burn down besieged towns.

Though the wild olive yields little oil, the Minoans on Crete developed the domestic olive enough for the unctuous liquid to play a vital part in their economic command of the eastern Mediterranean. They had the plant under cultivation by 2500 B.C.E., and by late Minoan times had invented oil presses. They also had settling vats for extracting the oil from the olive fruit, much like those still used in Crete.

When the Greeks took over from the Minoans they embraced the Minoans' olive legacy. By the classical period, from about 800 to 300 B.C.E., Greeks were breeding many new varieties of olives. Orchards of olive trees were grown wherever Greeks spread. Olives need coastal semiarid land, and that is where Greeks settled—in places where the tree could grow.

# THE *FOUFOU*

ALONG WITH MY LITTLE TWO-BURNER GAS HOT PLATE, THE ONLY OTHER KITCHEN "APPLIANCE" I USED ALMOST DAILY WHEN I LIVED WITHOUT ELECTRICITY OR RUNNING WATER DURING MY FIRST STAYS IN GREECE WAS MY PRECIOUS *FOUFOU*.

A *foufou* is a small, ancient-style terra-cotta charcoal broiler. The modern models are the same design as those two millennia old. Made of red clay, about fifteen inches tall, they look like large, wide, and welcoming wine cups on thick, hollow stems. At the bottom of the cup lie several incisions leading into the stem. At the bottom of the stem is a triangular cutout. Two small curlicued handles sit on opposite sides of the cup's broad lip.

## A VERSATILE TOOL

To use a *foufou,* you put a small heap of charcoal in the cup, perhaps with a bit of paper underneath, and light it. When the coals have burned to a red glow, you place the food you wish to cook—two or three *souvlaki,* one or two small chops, or a whole fish—into a long-handled, two-sided grill basket and set the device, with food encased, on the lip of the *foufou* cup over the coals. When one side of the food is cooked, you flip the grill basket over to cook the other side.

As the coals burn, the ashes drop through the cup's incisions and pile up at the bottom of the hollow stem, to be easily dumped out later through the triangular slot. The slot, in the meantime, has acted as a fire-feeding airhole. The design is of pure neatness and utter efficiency.

*A narrow street in Sifnos provides both brilliant sun and inviting shade.*

I never had a charcoal grill more versatile or handy, certainly none quicker to heat or easier to clean. The small pile of coals in a *foufou* is fiery ready in a flash, or as the villagers would say, *mani-mani.* The grill basket turns over a steak, vegetables, or fish without spillage, no utensils needed. When the cooking is done and the cinders are cold, you pick up the *foufou* by its handles and dump the detritus over garden soil or into a trash can. Then you perch the brazier back on a shelf, where its shape and terra-cotta color make a decorative statement.

## A THING OF BEAUTY

I so appreciated my *foufou* for its lovely form as well as its function that I brought it home to the States with me. It was sitting on a shelf when my house burned down but miraculously it survived—only with a twist, a literal one. My *foufou* of unfired clay emerged fired, but shaped, alas, in a figure-eight. Sadly, it's become harder to find *foufous* in Greece now. They are made and sold on only the island of Sifnos. I intend to go there on my next visit to procure a new, untwisted one. I have lots of fish to grill in my future.

# fish plaki-style

## WITH ZUCCHINI AND SAGE

### SERVES 6

COME LUNCHTIME, INNUMERABLE PANS OF FISH BAKED *PLAKI*-STYLE POP OUT OF OVENS IN GREECE. *PLAKI* IS THE GREEK TERM FOR OVEN-BRAISING IN A FLAT PAN. USUALLY THE SAUCE CONSISTS OF TOMATOES, THE VEGETABLE IS POTATO, AND LOTS OF GARLIC SIMMERS ALONG.

But just as the pizza has undergone a highbrow revolution in recent years, so can fish *plaki*. The fish can be "baked" in the skillet to ensure that it doesn't overcook. The vegetables can move from the customary onion and potato to leek and zucchini. Most notably, the sauce can become a combination of the usual tomato and lemon egg, resulting in an enticingly different pink *avgolemono*. Tinged with sage, rather than oregano, the large amount of garlic is omitted out of respect for the rosy *avgolemono*. The result: a sophisticated palette of tastes.

*2 1/2 pounds cod, snapper, bass, halibut, or salmon fillets or swordfish steaks, in 3- to 4-inch-wide pieces, or whole fresh sardines, anchovies, or small mackerel*

*Fresh lemon juice*

*Salt*

*2 tablespoons olive oil*

*1 medium leek, white and light green parts trimmed, well rinsed, and thinly sliced*

*2 medium zucchini, thinly sliced*

*3 medium tomatoes, coarsely chopped*

*1/2 teaspoon chopped fresh sage leaves, or 1/4 teaspoon dried*

*1/4 teaspoon salt*

*1/2 cup dry white wine*

*4 egg yolks, whisked until frothy*

*1/4 cup fresh lemon juice*

*Shredded fresh sage or chopped fresh parsley leaves, for garnish*

> ### PLAKI— FROM FLAT GRIDDLE TO FLAT OVEN TO FLAT PAN
> ·····················
> The word *plaki* comes from *plax* or *plak*, which originally meant "broad" or "flat" and was the name of a flat griddle stone on which ancient Greeks cooked food. From it we get our words "plate," "placid," and "platitude"—all still meaning "flat" in one sense or another, a description that never applies to the flavor of food cooked *plaki*-style.

1 Place the fish in a nonreactive dish and sprinkle lemon juice and salt over both sides. Set the dish aside.

2 Heat the oil in a large non-reactive skillet over medium heat. Add the leek and stir until wilted, about 1 minute. Stir in the zucchini, tomatoes, chopped sage, 1/4 teaspoon salt, and the wine. Sauté until all the vegetables are wilted, about 5 minutes.

3 Place the fish in the skillet and spoon some of the vegetables and liquid over them. Cover and cook until the fish is beginning to flake but is still moist, 10 to 15 minutes depending on the type of fish. Remove the skillet from the heat and, using a slotted spoon, lift the

fish and vegetables onto a serving platter. Set it aside in a warm place.

4 Whisk the egg yolks and ¼ cup lemon juice together in a small bowl. Slowly whisk the egg and lemon mixture into the juices in the skillet. Return the skillet to low heat and continue whisking for 2 minutes, then turn off the heat, whisking gently until the mixture is thickened, about 3 minutes. Pour the sauce over the fish, sprinkle the shredded sage over the top, and serve right away.

## UTTERLY FRESH FISH

When you walk into a Greek fish market, there are scores of choices: Whatever is displayed that day is clear-eyed, firm-fleshed, sweet-smelling. They have to be or the poor fishmonger is sure to suffer abuse. Greeks are adamant that their fish be utterly fresh and for three millennia have suspected the deceitfulness of the fish peddler. "Who knows," they mutter, "what the sly fishmonger has done to make his fish seem as if they just swam out of the sea." So to cook fish Greek-style, keep the same credo and use a specimen just plucked from Poseidon's brine.

# baked white fish fillets

## WITH BLOOD ORANGE, SWEET WINE, AND BAY LEAF

### SERVES 6

WERE ODYSSEUS AND JASON TO MEET AND SHARE A FISH DISH, IN ALL LIKELIHOOD IT WOULD THIS ONE. ODYSSEUS TRAVELED WEST TO A LAND WHERE ORANGE TREES BLOSSOM. JASON WENT EAST TO A WOODED REGION WHERE DARK STREAMS RAN AND BAY TREES FLOURISHED. GREEKS OF THOSE HEROES' ERA DRANK FRUITY WINES FULL OF NATURAL SUGARS.

Many an ancient sailor must have been famished for a fish fillet adorned with gatherings from the shores where they landed (although they rarely knew where they were). Here, a Greek-style baked fish with elements from east and west honors them. The orange to use is not the sweet juice oranges of Florida or California, but rather the semisweet juice of blood or Seville oranges.

*2 to 2½ pounds white fish fillets or steaks, such as halibut, cod, or swordfish in 3- to 4-inch pieces*
*Fresh lemon juice*
*Salt*
*3 tablespoons olive oil*
*2 medium leeks, white and light green parts trimmed, well rinsed, and cut into 2-inch-long shreds*
*12 kumquats, sliced into thin rounds*
*⅓ cup Seville or blood orange juice*
*½ cup Mavrodaphne or light port wine*
*1 large or 2 small bay leaves, crumbled*
*2 tablespoons chopped fresh chives*
*Freshly ground black pepper*

## THE BEAMING BREAM

To go with the orange flavoring and the golden era of Greek mythology, the choice of fish here might be bream. The gilt-headed bream of the Mediterranean, according to Greek legend, wears a gold moon-shaped medallion upon its brow because, like the dove that told Noah when his ship neared dry land, the bream led Deucalion's ark to safety during a flood. Deucalion, upon reaching land, was told by the oracle at Delphi to throw the bones of his mother (the stones of the Earth) over his shoulders, and from them sprang human beings to repopulate the world. In thanks, the bream was honored with its metal-colored medal.

1 Place the fish pieces on a plate that is large enough to hold them in one layer and sprinkle them liberally on both sides with lemon juice and salt. Cover and set in the refrigerator for 1 to 2 hours.

2 When you are ready to cook the fish, preheat the oven to 450°F. Transfer the fish to a large nonreactive baking dish and set aside.

3 Heat the oil in a medium-size nonreactive skillet over medium heat. Add the leeks and kumquats and stir until slightly wilted, 1 minute.

4 Stir in the orange juice, wine, and bay leaf and bring to a boil. Cook over medium heat until the leeks and kumquats are well wilted, 2 minutes. Pour the sauce over the fish, spreading the leeks and kumquats out evenly.

5 Place the dish in the oven and bake until the liquid is bubbling and the fish flakes easily when pierced with a fork, 15 minutes. Sprinkle the chives and some pepper over the top and serve right away.

**NOTE:** You can also use swordfish steaks in this recipe.

## ARCHIMEDES' GIFT TO FISHERMEN

Though Archimedes is not thought of as a hero to fishermen, he was. As well as having devised a mathematical method that prefigured calculus and having perfected the understanding of the relationship among geometrical objects, he wrote the laws of flotation that influenced the design of ships. He called the work simply "On Floating Bodies." To top it off, he deduced the concept of specific gravity, explaining why both sailor and landlubber didn't lift off into space.

Archimedes lived in Syracuse, a Greek community on the island of Sicily that was famous for its fish. The city still basks in the glory of its prodigious seafood. There Archimedes also died, slain by a Roman soldier when Rome sacked the city in 212 B.C.E. The original texts of Archimedes' works, written on vellum, survived the raid. The Byzantines, not knowing what they had, wrote over them, but enough was found underneath for Poseidon's children ever to thank the great thinker.

# swordfish steaks

## WITH *SKORDALIA*

### SERVES 6

JUST AS WE CALL THE FISH "SWORDFISH," IN GREEK THE BEHEMOTH SWIMMER IS CALLED *KSIFIOS* (OFTEN SPELLED *XIFIOS*), THE WORD FOR "SWORD." THE FISH WON ITS METAPHORIC TITLE NOT JUST FOR ITS JAW'S PROMINENT SHAPE BUT ALSO FOR THE WAY IT USES THAT PROJECTION. THE SWORDFISH LIKES TO STAB BOATS AND WHATEVER ELSE FLOATS BY WITH ITS PROBING JAW, SO MUCH SO THAT BEACHED FLOTSAM AND JETSAM OFTEN BEAR SWORDFISH BEAKS EMBEDDED IN THEM. THE TRAIT HAS GIVEN THE FISH A FEARSOME, IF PROBABLY UNDESERVED, REPUTATION AS AN OCEANGOING GLADIATOR.

As a fish to eat, the swordfish offers meat that is firm, sweet, and non-"fishy." For that alone, Greeks particularly favor it, and I admit, it is my very favorite ocean fish. In Greece, swordfish steaks almost always come grilled, slathered with the classic garlic paste *skordalia*. I see no reason to change a good thing.

1 cup Lemon and Oil Marinade (page 482)

6 swordfish steaks (3 pounds total), each ¹/₂ inch thick

1 recipe Skordalia (page 461; see Note)

1 Place the marinade in a dish that is large enough to hold the steaks in one layer. Add the swordfish and turn to coat it in the marinade. Marinate for 20 to 30 minutes at room temperature, or cover and refrigerate for up to 2 hours. Turn the steaks once or twice while they are marinating.

2 When you are ready to cook the fish, heat a grill to medium-hot.

3 Place the swordfish on the grill, coat the top side of each piece with a thin layer of *skordalia*, and cook until grill marks appear on the bottom, 4¹/₂ to 5 minutes.

4 Turn the steaks over and coat the grilled top side with a thin layer of *skordalia*. Cook until firm and still a tiny bit pink in the middle, 4¹/₂ to 5 minutes.

5 Remove the fish from the heat and let rest for 3 minutes for the juices to settle. Serve with the remaining *skordalia*.

**NOTE:** While in the classic version swordfish is served with bread or white potato *skordalia*, other versions, such as Sweet Potato *Skordalia* (page 463), accompany the fish equally well.

## MENU
### OTHER DISHES FOR THE TABLE

CRUSTY BREAD, OLIVES, AND CHEESE

GREEK-AMERICAN VILLAGE SALAD
page 193

GIANT BEANS *PLAKI*-STYLE
page 286

POTATO CROQUETTES
Box, page 293

FRESH FRUIT TO FINISH

## SHARK AND OTHER FIRM WHITE FISH
......................

A long with swordfish and eel, Greeks esteem steaks of Mediterranean sharks. The meat is treated and served exactly like swordfish. I often choose shark over swordfish when the shark is pink and fresh, and both Atlantic and Pacific shark take beautifully to Greek-style cooking.

Add bonito, cod, and bass to the list of fish with firm white meat for grilling, baking, or skewering like swordfish. And on any of them, don't forget the *skordalia!*

# swordfish kebabs

## WITH BAY LEAF AND OLIVE AND CAPER TAPENADE

### SERVES 6

OCCASIONALLY GREEKS LIKE TO COOK MEATY SWORDFISH WITH HERBS INSTEAD OF GARLICKY *SKORDALIA.* THE PREFERENCE—AN UNUSUAL AND COMPELLING CHOICE FOR FISH—IS BAY LEAF. TO TAKE FULL ADVANTAGE OF IT, THE SWORDFISH IS PLACED ON SKEWERS WITH BAY LEAVES AND ONION SLICES BETWEEN THE PIECES. THE HERB GIVES THE FISH AN ENIGMATIC ACCENT, AND PIECES OF SWORDFISH ARE A LOT CHEAPER THAN WHOLE STEAKS. INSTEAD OF RELYING SOLELY ON THE MARINADE, A TOPPING OF OLIVE AND CAPER TAPENADE ON THE KEBABS ROUNDS OUT A TREASURE CHEST OF FLAVORS.

*1 cup Lemon and Oil Marinade (page 482)*
*8 to 10 bay leaves, cut into 1-inch pieces*
*2 1/2 pounds swordfish, cut into 1 1/2-inch chunks*
*1 large onion, quartered, layers separated*
*2 cups Olive and Caper Tapenade (page 477)*

1 Place the marinade and the bay leaves in a dish that is large enough to hold all the swordfish chunks in one layer. Add the swordfish and onion and turn to coat it in the marinade. Marinate for 20 to 30 minutes at room temperature, or cover and refrigerate for up to 2 hours. Turn the fish once or twice while it is marinating.

2 When you are ready to cook the swordfish, heat a grill to medium-hot.

## BAY LEAF

Bay leaves are the dark green, silvery foliage of an evergreen tree, called *daphne* in Greek and *laurus* in Latin, native to the Mediterranean and Asia Minor. Though usually small, the tree can grow to a height of fifty to sixty feet. It prefers damp, murky forests and riverbanks, and its long, pointed, glossy leaves are intoxicatingly fragrant.

Because of their intense aroma, the leaves have long been used in many ways: They were burned as incense to perfume temples and suspended in bouquets to freshen households. As a token handed down from the god Apollo, wreaths of bay leaves were given to the wise and honorable to wear as diadems. (Many of us, all those with bachelor's degrees, still sport crowns of bay, at least metaphorically. The term "bachelor" comes from "baccalaureate," which means "bay berry.")

With its musky tinge, *daphne* became an essential culinary flavor enhancer in early Greek cooking as well and is still much used. Scarcely a meat stew, vegetable casserole, or fish *plaki* or *kabob* is cooked without bay leaf.

The tree plays a role in Greek legend. Apollo teases Eros that his arrows are silly, at least compared to Apollo's mighty missiles. So Eros takes two of his disparaged projectiles and with the one made of gold for love, shoots Apollo. With the other, made of lead for disdain, he shoots Daphne, a comely nymph and huntress. Smitten, Apollo chases after Daphne relentlessly. She flees with all her might. Finally the god nearly catches Daphne on the edge of a river. Her father, a river spirit, is filled with mercy, and just as Apollo reaches Daphne turns her into a silvery bay tree. Apollo, grieved, has to abandon his pursuit but decrees that ever after, bay garlands should decorate his lyre, his quiver, and the heads of minstrels. (Nothing was said about poets.)

In the sense of the bay tree's biology, though, perhaps Apollo did catch Daphne: A single bay tree can be both sexes.

5 Arrange the skewers on a platter and serve right away, accompanied by the tapenade.

**NOTE:** To give contrast to the bay leaf, I sometimes add ½ tablespoon Dijon mustard to the marinade, or 2 tablespoons grated kefalotyri cheese.

## FISH, SHIPS, SWORDS, AND BEAKS

As they turned into ocean travelers and warriors, the Greeks began to read more and more imagery into the sea. They saw swords in the noses of fish, and in the bows of ships they saw beaks.

They soon realized the advantage in a ship having a pointed prow and began to fit the prows with ramming devices. They called these *rostra*, from *rhis*, the word for "nose," "beak," and "to peck" (*ramfos* was a curved beak and meant "to probe"). Very early, around 340 B.C.E., the encroaching Romans thought it a fine trophy to take the *rostra* from enemy vessels they subdued and carried them back home to demonstrate their prowess. The *rostra* were displayed in front of the speakers' platform in the forum. In due course the entire platform became known as the "rostrum."

3 String an onion section, a piece of bay leaf, and then a swordfish chunk on a skewer. Repeat, in that order, until the skewer is filled, ending with a piece of onion. Fill all the skewers in this fashion. If there are extra onion sections left over, thread them on a separate skewer and cook them along with the others.

4 Place the skewers on the grill and cook, turning once, just until white curds form on top of the fish and the centers are still a bit pink, 7 to 8 minutes. Transfer the skewers to a platter and let them sit for the juices to settle, 5 minutes.

# stewed salt cod

## WITH POTATOES, CURRANTS, SAFFRON, AND RETSINA

### SERVES 6

"APOU TRON ANAPAMENA, TRON EFTA KATARAMENA," IS A FAMOUS GREEK PROVERB THAT TRANSLATES AS "HE WHO EATS OUT OF WELL-BEING EATS SEVEN CURSES." IT WARNS US THAT A PERSON WHO DOES NOT WORK FOR HIS KEEP BUT LIVES OFF WEALTH MEETS MANY MISERIES, AND IT REFLECTS A FUNDAMENTAL CULTURAL CODE THAT MAY EXPLAIN WHY EVEN WEALTHY GREEKS CONTINUE TO LABOR ALL THEIR LIVES.

Salt cod is humble fare, costing but a few hard-earned drachmas (or Euros), but in Greece it is never considered a deprivation. Rather it is exalted as a succulent and filling mainstay. Dried cod is sold all around the Mediterranean in long, flat planks as hard as Bakelite. Most village grocery stores keep the planks under the oilcloth-covered table that serves as a counter, as no shelf can hold the unruly stack. Generally, once the salt is soaked out and moisture has replumped the cod, Greeks stew the fish with potatoes, onion, and tomato. The dish is a notable example of how good inexpensive foods can be. With a scattering of Greece's candylike currants, a dash of flowery saffron, and a resiny retsina to give it a lift, the poor man's dish becomes princely.

1 1/2 pounds salt cod

1/3 cup currants or golden raisins

1 cup retsina wine (omit if using pre-soaked currants; see page 49)

1/4 cup olive oil

1 medium onion, halved and thinly sliced

Large pinch of saffron threads

1/2 teaspoon freshly ground white pepper

4 medium potatoes, peeled and cut into 1/4-inch-thick slices

1 tablespoon chopped fresh flat-leaf parsley leaves

1 lemon, cut into 6 wedges

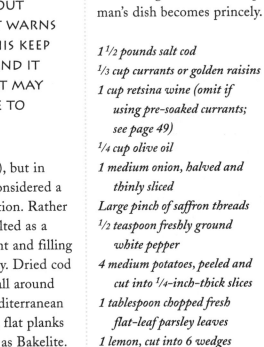

*Salt cod for sale for both drachmas and Euros.*

# SALT COD, THE FISH THAT FEEDS IN HARD TIMES

I WANDERED INTO THE STORE ON ONE OF MY FIRST EVENINGS IN GREECE TO FIND MARKOS HOLDING FORTH BEHIND THE TABLE THAT SERVED AS THE COUNTER. AS HAPPENED NIGHTLY, A GROUP OF MEN HAD GATHERED TO DISCUSS AFFAIRS OF THE SOIL AND OF THE WORLD. NO WOMEN WERE THERE. WHEN DAY DEPARTED AND DARKNESS FELL, THEODOSIA, MARKOS'S WIFE, AND ALL THE WOMEN SHOPPERS WOULD DISAPPEAR AND THE STORE BECAME THE DOMAIN OF HER HUSBAND AND HIS FRIENDS.

Nonetheless, privileged by being a new, unknowing foreigner, I decided to join their company. Because all the chairs were occupied, I pulled out what looked like a cruddy old board from under the table to sit on. "Careful," said Markos, "you're sitting on a codfish." A codfish? It certainly didn't look like a fish to me. It was shaped like a lath, colored like timber, as hard as siding, and as dry and brittle as bark. It had no fin, no tail, no water, no smell. Surely it was wood.

## THE GREAT SUSTAINER

Codfish, *bakaliaros*, is the "meat and potatoes" fish of the Mediterranean, a great sustainer. Overfished now, once it existed in great quantities. But more than its vast numbers, its great importance comes from the fact that at some point it was discovered that cod could be dried out like a sponge, kept for long periods, and later remoisturized to cook up lavishly. As a result, when no other fish, nor possibly meat, was available, people all across the Mediterranean and up and down the Atlantic could sustain themselves with its nourishing protein. Cod slaked the hunger not just of Greece, but of much of the Western world.

## A PRECIOUS PRIZE

In the United States, salt cod comes in small boxes as if it were a precious prize, but in Greece and the rest of southern Europe, the fish comes unwrapped, in great dry planks. Either way, the flaky flesh must be reconstituted and, for succulence, desalted. With soaking and rinsing, salt cod provides tender, pulpy meat that absorbs sauces and the flavors of herbs and vegetables so readily that stews of it offer taste sym-phonies. As well as making a silken fish spread, it fries up crisp on the outside and velvety on the inside in fritters that beg for a topping. In Greece, the customary zesty garnish is *skordalia*.

Some people still believe that cod's use in folk cuisine makes it a less-than-worthy dinner. Quite the opposite. Poseidon must have much loved cod to let it proliferate so profusely, and if anyone knew a good fish, Poseidon did.

*Top: Picking out a still pliable salt cod. Some are dried much firmer for even longer keeping. Bottom: Restaurants along the water receive daily deliveries of the freshest fish.*

# MENU

## OTHER DISHES FOR THE TABLE

CRUSTY BREAD, OLIVES, AND CHEESE

*SPANAKOPITA*
page 92

BEET SALAD
WITH BEET GREENS,
SINGED ONION,
AND SIEVED EGG
page 197

FRESH LIMA BEANS
WITH YOGURT, PARSLEY,
AND DILL
page 277

FRESH FRUIT TO FINISH

1 Rinse the salt cod well, rubbing off as much salt as you can. Place it in a dish and add water to cover amply. Let soak in the refrigerator for 24 hours, changing the water three or four times. Drain and rinse again before using.

2 Place the raisins and retsina in a small container, cover, and set aside to soak for at least 1 hour, preferably ovenight (see page 49).

3 When you are ready to cook the cod, heat the oil in a large nonreactive sauté pan over medium heat. Add the onion and cook, stirring, until well wilted, 2 minutes.

4 Stir in the saffron, the white pepper, and the raisins and retsina. Arrange the potato slices over the top. Place the fish pieces over the potatoes, bring to a boil, and reduce the heat to a gentle simmer. Cover the pan and cook until the potatoes are almost but not quite tender, about 20 minutes.

5 Remove the cover and turn the fish pieces over. Raise the heat slightly and cook briskly until the potatoes and fish are tender and the sauce has thickened, 5 minutes.

6 Sprinkle the parsley over the top and serve right away, garnished with the lemon wedges.

## THE GREAT AEGEAN CONGER EEL

In the opinion of many Greeks, the meatiest of all the fish in the sea is the famous conger eel, and I cannot disagree. While similar in taste to swordfish and shark, the texture of its thick, round steaks is compactly dense yet flakily delicate, and beautifully amenable to grilling and baking. The flavor rings clear, with barely a hint of salt. To top off these splendid qualities, there is only a single central bone—no prickly maze of fish bones to hunt through.

Though eels do not appear to be fish—they look like some strange sea snake—they are fish indeed, and they are plentiful in the seas surrounding Greece. Besides grilling and baking, Greeks bread and fry them, roast eel steaks in brown paper, and wrap the steaks in grape or fig leaves (see page 48). Eel can also be oven-stewed *plaki*-style (see page 329), added to *kakavia* (page 180), or in a classic technique, stewed in a wine and tomato sauce (see Octopus in Red Wine, page 349). When eel is marinated and grilled in the same fashion as swordfish, the sauce of preference is *skordalia*.

If you come upon sea eel in your fish market, try it. In the United States eel often comes with the skin already peeled and sometimes boned, though eating around the bone is no trial. Steaks can be as much as four to five inches in diameter and two inches thick—the filet mignon of seafood.

# salt cod

## WITH SWEET POTATO *SKORDALIA* AND SPINACH-OREGANO PESTO

### SERVES 4 TO 6

NUGGETS OF SALT COD—BATTERED, FRIED IN OLIVE OIL, AND SERVED WITH TWO SAUCES, *SKORDALIA* AND PESTO—SETTLE FOREVER THE QUESTION OF WHETHER FRIED FISH IS PEDESTRIAN OR EXTRAORDINARY. ALABASTER AND SILKY ON THE INSIDE, BURNISHED AND CRISP ON THE OUTSIDE, THE SMARTLY COOKED FISH MAY NOT COME FROM A SHELL, BUT THEY ARE PEARLS SENT FROM THE OCEAN TO THE DINNER PLATE.

## MENU

### OTHER DISHES FOR THE TABLE

CRUSTY BREAD, OLIVES, AND CHEESE

TRADITIONAL *MAKARONADA* WITH RED SAUCE
page 250

ROASTED BELL PEPPERS

SIMPLE ZUCCHINI SALAD WITH GREEK SALAD DRESSING
page 189

OLIVES AND ORANGES
Box, page 492

*1 pound salt cod*
*³/4 cup unbleached all-purpose flour*
*¹/4 teaspoon baking powder*
*¹/2 teaspoon salt*
*¹/4 teaspoon freshly ground black pepper*
*¹/2 teaspoon fresh lemon juice*
*³/4 cup water*
*Olive oil*
*1 ¹/4 cups (¹/2 recipe) Sweet Potato Skordalia (page 463)*
*1 cup Spinach-Oregano Pesto (recipe follows)*

1 Rinse the salt cod well, rubbing off as much salt as you can, and place it in a dish. Add water to cover it amply. Place it in the refrigerator and let it soak for 24 hours, changing the water three or four times.

2 When you are ready to cook the cod, mix the flour, baking powder, salt, pepper, lemon juice, and ³/4 cup water together in a large bowl. Set it aside for 30 minutes.

3 Drain and rinse the cod again, then cut it into ¹/2-inch nuggets. Pat them dry.

4 Stir 1 tablespoon of the olive oil into the batter, add the cod,

and stir a bit to coat the nuggets. Pour oil to a depth of ¾ inch in a heavy skillet over medium-high heat. Use a slotted spoon to transfer a batch of nuggets from the batter to the skillet—as many as will fit without crowding. Fry, turning once, until golden all over, about 6 minutes. Transfer the nuggets to paper towels to drain, and repeat with another batch until all are fried.

5 Serve right away, accompanied by the *skordalia* and the pesto.

*1/2 cup drained cooked spinach*
*2 scallions, white and light green parts trimmed and cut into pieces*
*1 teaspoon fresh oregano leaves, or 1/2 teaspoon dried*
*1/4 cup red wine vinegar*
*1 tablespoon fresh lemon juice*
*3/4 cup olive oil*
*1/4 teaspoon salt*
*1/8 teaspoon freshly ground black pepper*

1 Combine the spinach, scallions, and oregano in a food processor, and process until pureed.

2 Add the vinegar, lemon juice, oil, salt, and pepper and blend well. Use right away or set aside at room temperature until ready to serve.

**NOTE:** The pesto is best served within several hours. Though it remains flavorful if refrigerated overnight, it loses its bright green color.

## SPINACH-OREGANO PESTO

### MAKES 1 CUP

The abundant spinach that grows in Greece perks up filo pies, swirls in soup, and adds jaunty munificence to pilaf. Following that tradition, but giving the leaves a more central role, I pulverize them into a fine union of pesto and vinaigrette. As well as enlivening cod nuggets, the pesto adds exuberance to grilled fish dishes, grilled chicken, and vegetable fritters.

*On a day when the sea is calm, a fishing fleet of filled kaikis sits moored along a quay.*

## FOUR FISH RECIPES FROM ARCHESTRATOS

"The thymnia or female tuna is found in Byzantium in particular. Take the tail of it, cut it in pieces, and roast it until thoroughly done. Sprinkle it with nothing but salt, moisten it with oil, and soak it in a strong brine. If after that you wish to eat it without a sauce, it is excellent enough to give the gods an appetite, but if you serve it moistened with vinegar you take away its merits."

"When Orion disappears from the sky and the mother of the grape that bears wine sheds its hair [when the vines lose their leaves], get yourself a roasted sar, well garnished with cheese. Let it be big and hot, sprinkle it with vinegar since it is naturally dry. . . ."

"I praise every sort of eel, but those that are taken at Regio, in the strait, are by far to be preferred. . . . One eats them cooked in beet leaves."

"Any sort of whitebait, except from Athens, especially that of spawning season which the Ionians call 'sea foam,' . . . add to them sea anemones, of the sort that have hairs all over. Season them together with aromatic flowers of vegetables crushed in oil, and fry them whole in a frying pan. They should no more than glimpse the fire; they are cooked in the same time that it takes the oil to crackle."

# POSEIDON

IN THE GREEK PANTHEON, THE GOD WHO RULED OVER THE WATERY REALM OF THE SEA, RIVERS, AND LAKES WAS FIERCE POSEIDON. LIKE ZEUS, HIS YOUNGER BROTHER, HE WAS THE SON OF CRONOS AND RHEA. STRANGELY, THOUGH, CONSIDERING HIS WATERY PURVIEW, POSEIDON'S NAME MEANS "HUSBAND OF EARTH." IN SOME DESCRIPTIONS HE IS ALSO CALLED "EARTH HOLDER" AND "EARTH SHAKER," AND HE WAS WORSHIPED AS THE PERPETRATOR OF EARTHQUAKES. TRUTH BE TOLD, HE WAS THE FICKLE CAUSE OF MOST DISASTERS. IF IRKED, HE COULD LASH OUT FLOODS AND DROUGHTS AS WELL AS TREMORS.

Poseidon lived in an underwater palace where neriads, his daughters, attended him. He sped across the sea in a mighty, frothy chariot accompanied by dolphins—so quickly that he could pass from the north to the south of the Aegean in a matter of moments. When he took part in battles, earthquakes rattled under his footsteps, although to the fish who lived in his watery kingdom, these were only waves.

## A VIOLENT SORT

The earlier sea gods of the Mediterranean had been peaceful, but Poseidon was a violent sort, more swordfish than sole. He is always portrayed bearded, rising from a roiling sea, carrying his signature weapon, the trident, and wearing a stormy expression. His bride, Amphitrite, a daughter of Oceanus, ran away before the wedding. In the form of a horse, he ravaged his sister Demeter, the earth goddess, who had changed herself into a mare to escape him. She bore him the sacred horse Arion and a daughter, Despina, whose name later came to mean "young miss"

and to refer to the Virgin Mary, an evolution in etymology I dare not take up here.

## POSEIDON AND THE MINOANS

For whatever reason, Poseidon had a love-hate relationship with the Minoans. Though the Minoans were sea people and the Greeks at first land-lubbers, and though Poseidon quarreled

*Poseidon announces his rise from the sea, trident in hand and at the the ready.*

violently with Minos, the king of Crete, Poseidon promised and sent him a bull that arose from the sea. Minos found the bull so perfect that he kept it rather than sacrificing it as he should have. In revenge Poseidon caused Minos's wife to love the bull and with it to bear the monster Minotaur. Poseidon then dispatched his son Theseus to kill the Minotaur. Later he roused yet another bull from the sea to kill Hippolytus, the son of Theseus and the Amazon queen, Hippolyta, although the lad was his grandson.

For all his inconsistencies, though, Poseidon fervently supported the Greeks over all their enemies—certainly over the Minoans; wily Theseus escaped his Minoan sea captors. He also gave the Greeks their first horses , and provided them much sustenance. His wine-dark realm—as Homer described the sea—teemed with the food they grew to love, and when they presented him gifts of golden bulls, he filled their nets with fish.

# pan-fried skate

## WITH VINEGAR, DILL, SHALLOTS, AND TOMATO

### SERVES 4 TO 6

SKIMMING ACROSS BOTTOM SANDS LIKE GREAT AQUATIC PARAGLIDERS, SKATE—ALSO CALLED RAYS— ABOUND IN GREECE'S SEAS, AND GREEKS HAVE BEEN SAVORING THEM THROUGH THE CENTURIES. THE WINGS OF THE SKATE, ATTACHED BY LIGHT CARTILAGE, NOT BONE, TO THE TORSO OF THE FISH, UNDULATE IN THE WATER AND ALLOW THE FISH TO TURN AND TWIST EFFORTLESSLY WHILE SWIMMING, AS IF WINDBLOWN.

Rays, in fact, have no bones at all. Though they are so camouflaged in coloring that often only their movement reveals their presence, fishing nets do claim the bottom skater. In markets, the willowy wings come already skinned. A soaking in acidulated water firms the meat, after which the flesh tastes like a collection of prized shellfish. Athenaeus called for dousing skate generously with silphium. We have no silphium—we're not even sure what it was—but we do have other enliveners: vinegar and tomato. Shallots and dill add to the savor and make this a favorite recipe.

*2 pounds skinned skate wings*
*1/4 cup white wine vinegar*
*1/4 cup olive oil*
*2 large shallots, thinly sliced*
*1/4 cup chopped fresh dill*
*1/4 cup red wine vinegar*
*1 small tomato, minced*

1 Place the skate in a large non-reactive dish. Pour the white vinegar into the dish and add enough water to cover. Cover and set aside in the refrigerator for at least 2 hours, and up to overnight. When you are ready to cook the skate, drain it and pat it dry.

2 Heat the oil in a large non-reactive skillet over medium-high heat. Add the skate wings without overlapping them and sauté until golden on the bottom, 5 minutes. Turn and sauté until golden on the bottom and beginning to flake into sections, 3 minutes. Transfer to a platter and set aside in a warm place.

3 Stir the shallots and dill into the skillet, along with a bit more oil, if necessary, to moisten the shallots. Pour in the red wine vinegar and continue stirring over medium-high heat until the liquid is bubbling and saucelike, 1 minute.

4 Pour the sauce over the fish. Sprinkle the tomato over the top and serve right away.

**NOTE:** As a substitute for skate, you can use tuna belly, the tail section of a small salmon, a meaty sole, or a squid or cuttlefish steak.

# classic shrimp and tomatoes

## BAKED WITH FETA CHEESE

### SERVES 6

HARDLY A DISH EXISTS ON THE HONOR ROLL OF GREEK CUISINE WITH MORE NAMES THAN SHRIMP BAKED WITH TOMATOES AND FETA. YOU HEAR THE DISH CALLED *GARIDES YIOUVETSI* AND ALSO *YIOUVETSAKI*. SOMETIMES IT'S DUBBED *GARIDES ME FETA* AND SOMETIMES *GARIDES KOKKIYIA ME FETA*. HERE AND THERE IT SHOWS UP ON MENUS AS *GARIDES ME SALTSA*, BUT EQUALLY OFTEN AS *GARIDES ME FETA SALTSA*. THE PROLIFERATION OF NAMES GIVES TESTIMONY TO ONE THING: A DISH SO POPULAR, WIDESPREAD, AND CLASSIC CERTAINLY MUST SING WITH FLAVOR. AND IT DOES.

Few cheeses go with shellfish, but sheep's-milk feta blankets the tender shrimp with a sharp tang the way a wash of lemon juice cannot. The cheese also echoes the sea's lightly salty bath. The tomatoes create a sauce with zest and body, with carmine hue and vegetable warmth, and a touch of brandy offers a hint of a blazing fire. Serve plenty of crusty bread to sop up the sauce.

*The shrimp being sold by this fishmonger are so fresh they're still in the cart that brought them from the dock.*

## MENU
### OTHER DISHES FOR THE TABLE

CRUSTY BREAD, OLIVES, AND CHEESE

WHITE BEAN SOUP WITH *SKORDALIA*
page 160

SIMPLE ASPARAGUS SALAD WITH GREEK SALAD DRESSING
page 189

MARKELLA'S CROQUETTES
page 295

*TZATZIKI*
page 465

FRESH FRUIT TO FINISH

1/4 cup olive oil

1/2 medium onion, finely chopped

3 cloves garlic, minced or pressed

6 medium tomatoes, coarsely chopped

1/2 cup dry white wine

2 tablespoons Metaxa or other brandy

1 tablespoon tomato paste

2 tablespoons chopped fresh dill

1/4 teaspoon freshly ground black pepper

2 pounds medium shrimp (about 42), peeled and deveined

8 ounces feta cheese

1 Preheat the oven to 400°F.

2 While the oven is heating, heat the oil in a large nonreactive flameproof casserole over medium heat. Stir in the onion and garlic and cook until slightly wilted, 1 minute. Stir in the tomatoes and cook until they soften, 5 minutes.

3 Stir in the wine, Metaxa, tomato paste, 1 tablespoon of the dill, and the pepper. Cook briskly until the tomatoes are collapsing, 10 minutes. Add the shrimp and cook, stirring from time to time, until they begin to turn pink, about 2 minutes.

4 Crumble the cheese in large chunks over the top and place the casserole in the oven. Bake until the cheese has melted, about 3 minutes. Sprinkle the remaining 1 tablespoon dill over the top and serve.

# THE BEST SHRIMP I EVER ATE

**I DECIDED TO TAKE A LITTLE VACATION FROM MY WORK AND TRAVEL TO A PART OF GREECE I HADN'T YET EXPLORED. WHAT CALLED TO ME WAS THE IONIAN SEA AND AN ISLAND WITH A RATHER DIFFERENT HISTORY—CORFU.**

Corfu, called Kerkyra in Greek, departs in its story, looks, and way of life from other parts of Greece. While other areas struggled with the Ottoman empire, Corfu was ruled by Venice, then Naples, then France. While the rest of the land fought for independence, Corfu was taken by the British. Long after the rest of Greece announced sovereignty, Britain still clung to the western island. Her stamp remains evident in stately buildings laid out in a grid, monuments to an English sense of order.

Countering those buildings are others with French colonnades. Here and about stand statues of lions, the emblem of Venice; Neapolitan dishes are still cooked, sometimes to be eaten on a cricket ground. Socially the island is unusual too. Venice rewarded those who took on Roman Catholicism, and many Catholics remain. There was a great deal of Italian and Greek intermarriage, and because the well-off were educated in Venice or Padua many island people to this day are bilingual in Greek and Italian or Greek and English. Yet, beyond the capital, the island remains largely rural and lushly agricultural.

## THE SHRIMP FISHERMAN

I headed away from the capital one day in search of solitude and soon came upon the perfect spot, a tiny fine-sand beach curved in a classic arc. At each tip of the crescent, typically, sat a little seaside *taverna*. I found an olive tree to lie under just up from the lapping waves, rolled out my towel, and opened a novel.

Suddenly, I was startled by the approach of a man. Dressed in country fashion—open rough-weave jacket over goat-hair knit undershirt, soft billed cap in hand—very shyly and very sure that the foreigner would not understand a word, he said in Greek, "Excuse me, but I've just pulled some shrimp up in my trap and I wonder if you'd like some."

"Shrimp?" I asked in Greek, springing to my feet and totally amazing him. "Did you say shrimp? Just out of the sea? Where?" "At my tavern," he said, and pointed to one of the *tavernas*. I tossed my towel around me and scurried after him.

At the *taverna*, I watched as he heated some olive oil in a frying pan, threw in the shrimp, shells and all, cooked them for a brief moment, then splashed on some Corfu wine and a shower of dry wild herb. Just as the shrimp turned pink, he slid them onto my plate.

To say I have never forgotten those shrimp sounds trite, but it's true. The key was their utter freshness, and that, no matter how I cook, I cannot re-create until I live on the beach on Corfu.

# WHERE DID THE NAME "GREEK" COME FROM?

**GREEKS HAVE LONG LIVED WITH A DOUBLE APPELLATION. THEY CALL THEMSELVES *ELLENES*, OR *HELLENES*, WHILE OTHER PEOPLE CALL THEM GREEK. TO ITS CITIZENS, THE LAND IS *ELLAS*; TO OTHERS IT IS GREECE. THE FARE THE PEOPLE EAT IS *ELLENIKO FAIGITO*; TO ENGLISH SPEAKERS GREEK CUISINE.**

How did the double nomenclature come about? The answer has long been the topic of discussion; the opinions are many, the argument lively, and probably no one will ever know for sure.

## ONCE UPON A TIME

Originally, when Greeks streamed into the land, they came as many tribes, each with a different name, each settling in a different area. One group called themselves the Graikoi, and it seems they found the region near the town of Cumae in Italy to their liking, perhaps having first lived near the town of Kyme on the Greek island of Euboea. (Maybe. Aristotle later said the Graikoi tribe lived in Epiros, in northwestern Greece.) Though there were many Greek-speaking tribes—the Ionians, the Dorians, and more—it seems it was the Graikoi that the Romans first encountered when they filtered into Italy, or before the Roman arrival perhaps it was the Etruscans or Illyrians. At any rate, the Romans began to dub all Greek-speaking people with the name of the first ones they had met: All Greek speakers became *Graikoi* and the land *Graeci*.

At the time none of the early Greek speakers called themselves *Ellenes*, the name they all later took, though Homer says a certain area near Phthia in Thessaly was called *Ellas*. Aristotle says it was the *Graikoi* who, indeed, became the *Hellenes*. Meanwhile, the great Greek general Thucydides spoke of *graike ge*, meaning "Greek earth."

*Graikoi* wasn't the only name that was applied to the Greeks. The first Greek-speaking people that the ancient Persians, then the Arabs and Turks, came across were the Ionians, who by then lived in Asia Minor. To this day the Turks call the Greeks *Yunan*, their version of "Ionian," while they call Greece Yunanistan. They also sometimes refer to Greeks as *Rum*, from their link to the eastern Roman Empire, which we call "Byzantine." What is clear is that after the death of Alexander the Great, the words *Graikos* and *Ellenes* start to become synonymous and were used by both the Byzantines and the Ottomans. At the same time, while the Byzantines called themselves "Roman," western Europeans called the Byzantine Empire the "Greek Empire," and they called one of the Byzantine provinces in what is now central Greece *Ellada*.

*Three columns from the Temple of Olympian Zeus, the tallest temple built by the ancient Greeks.*

## A GREAT NORTHERN LIGHT

As for the words *Ellada* and *Ellenes*, some scholars say the terms originally come from *seles*, an ancient word for "light" or "shine," and might have referred to the Northern Lights, since the arriving Greeks came from the north. Another surviving word from the same root is *Selene*, the name of the goddess of the moon. Other scholars scoff at the idea, but if it is so—and it is a stretch—*Ellenes* just might mean "the northerners" or, fittingly for their sun-filled and fruit-ripening land, "the people of the light."

# skewers of shrimp

## BATHED IN TARRAGON AND FRUITY OLIVE OIL

### SERVES 6

GARIDES IS THE GREEK NAME FOR SOME TWO THOUSAND SORTS OF CRUSTACEANS WE GROUP TOGETHER AND CALL "SHRIMP." SHRIMP APPEAR IN ALL OCEANS; THEY TEEM IN PROFUSION IN THE AEGEAN, IONIAN, AND MEDITERRANEAN SEAS. SINCE FIRST ENCOUNTERING THEM, GREEKS HAVE BEEN TRAPPING, NETTING, AND JUST PLAIN PLUCKING THEM FROM THE WATER.

Because shrimp cook so quickly, among the best of Greek culinary treatments is to toss the shrimp in hot olive oil and splash on herb, wine, and maybe garlic for just a moment. Equally glorious is to marinate, then skewer the shrimp on *souvlas* and barely wave them over a grill. Tarragon is not used much in Greece, but it offers a leafy version of ouzo's essence, perfect for a dish so marine.

2 pounds jumbo shrimp (28 to 32 total), peeled and deveined
2 tablespoons fresh lemon juice
2 cloves garlic, minced or pressed
1 teaspoon salt
1 tablespoon ouzo, or 2 teaspoons chopped fresh tarragon leaves
3 tablespoons fruity olive oil

1 Place the shrimp in a large nonreactive bowl. Add the lemon juice, garlic, salt, the ouzo or 1 teaspoon of the tarragon, and 2 tablespoons of the oil. Toss to mix, cover, and set aside in the refrigerator to marinate for at least 2 hours or as long as overnight.

2 When you are ready to cook the shrimp, heat a grill to hot or preheat the broiler.

3 String the shrimp on skewers, 3 or 4 per skewer. Broil or grill, turning once, until they are pink and firm but still moist, about 4 minutes.

4 Place the shrimp skewers on a platter and sprinkle the remaining 1 teaspoon tarragon, if using, and 1 tablespoon olive oil over them. Serve right away.

## MENU
### OTHER DISHES FOR THE TABLE

CRUSTY BREAD, OLIVES, AND CHEESE

EGGPLANT SALAD COUNTRY-STYLE WITH PITA
page 33

HORTOPITA WITH TURNIP GREENS
page 93

BEEF AND RICE MEATBALLS IN TOMATO ROSEMARY BROTH
page 173

ZUCCHINI SALAD WITH ZUCCHINI FLOWERS
page 203

FRESH FRUIT TO FINISH

# shrimp

## WITH FENNEL, GREEN OLIVES, RED ONION, AND WHITE WINE

### SERVES 6

HOW TO MAKE SHRIMP STAY DELICATE YET COAX THEM TO EXUDE A BOLD FLAVOR FOR FAMILY AND FRIENDS TO SAVOR? COMBINE THE SHRIMP WITH FEATHERY FENNEL, SO FRESH-TASTING IT MIMICS THE SEA'S CLEAR BLUE-GREEN WATER. ADD CRUNCHY RED ONION TO MATCH THE RUBICUND SHRIMP, AND TOSS IN GREEN OLIVES, SALTY AS SEAWATER. THE HAPPY "SCHOOL" OF INGREDIENTS SWIM TOGETHER AS HARMONIOUSLY AS DO THE MANY SUBJECTS OF THE GREAT SEA GOD OKEANOS, POSEIDON'S UNCLE, FROM WHOSE NAME WE GET "OCEAN."

## MENU
### OTHER DISHES FOR THE TABLE

CRUSTY BREAD, OLIVES, AND CHEESE

MARINATED LAMB'S LIVER
page 57

CHICKPEA SOUP WITH GARLIC, SAGE, AND TARRAGON
page 162

FRIED EGGPLANT WITH FETA AND BASIL
page 276

FRESH TOMATOES STUFFED WITH ANCIENT INGREDIENTS
page 302

FRESH FRUIT TO FINISH

*Every afternoon fisherman must mend his nets. Why not in the sun?*

2 pounds medium shrimp (about 42), peeled and deveined, shells reserved
2 cups dry white wine
1 cup water
1 teaspoon salt
1/2 medium red onion, coarsely chopped
3/4 cup coarsely chopped fennel stalk
8 large green olives, pitted and coarsely chopped
1 tablespoon olive oil
1 tablespoon minced fennel fronds

1 Place the shrimp shells, wine, water, and salt in a large nonreactive pot. Bring to a boil and simmer until the shells turn pink, 2 minutes. Remove and discard the shells.

2 Add the onion, chopped fennel, olives, and oil to the pot. Bring to a boil again and simmer until the onion is soft, 5 minutes. Stir in the shrimp and simmer just until they begin to turn pink and firm, 1 1/2 to 2 minutes. Transfer to a serving dish, sprinkle the minced fennel fronds over the top, and serve right away.

# boiled lobster

## WITH WATERCRESS MAYONNAISE

### SERVES 6

THE LOBSTER OF THE IONIAN AND AEGEAN SEAS IS NOT THE COLD-WATER CREATURE WE KNOW IN NORTHERN CLIMATES; IT IS THE SPINY LOBSTER OF THE MEDITERRANEAN. WE SOMETIMES CALL IT *LANGOUSTINE* OR SALTWATER CRAWFISH (NOT TO BE CONFUSED WITH THE FRESHWATER CRAYFISH, WHICH THE GREEKS ALSO EAT).

Athenaeus talks of the Greek delight in all the antenna-ed sea creatures—crawfish, shrimp, and lobster. He and his gourmet comrades liked to cook them in honey with parsley and mint. Greeks also eat a fan-shaped sea lobster called a slipper or shovel-nose lobster, which makes a noise like a cricket in its underwater concert hall. These can be found around Corfu. The good news in all this is that any lobster, including large cold-water ones, finds noble harbor when cooked Greek-style: with herbs from the rocky shores, a stroke of zesty pepper, and an extra-lemony mayonnaise laced with watercress.

*1/4 cup mixed chopped fresh herbs, such as thyme, oregano, bay leaf, marjoram, savory, and/or dill, or 2 tablespoons dried*

*2 tablespoons salt*

*2 small dried red chile peppers, cut in half (optional)*

*6 small live lobsters (1 to 1 1/4 pounds each; see Notes)*

*1 large bunch tender watercress sprigs*

*2 cups Watercress Mayonnaise (recipe follows)*

1 Fill two large pots two-thirds full with water. Divide the herbs, salt, and chiles, if using, between the pots and bring to a boil over high heat.

2 Drop 3 lobsters into each pot, cover, and bring to a boil. Reduce the heat to maintain a boil without overflowing, and cook until the lobsters are bright red and the small legs pull off easily, 9 to 11 minutes. Drain and set aside until cool enough to handle.

## SHELLFISH AND DEMOCRACY

The link between democracy and poor, mute shellfish might seem a bit fantastic, but it's there. In ancient Greece all the members (only men in those days) of the town, or *demos*, had the right to cast a vote on keeping or expelling a leader (*demo-kratos*, the rule by the people). Few could write, and paper for ballots was not at hand, so each voter was given the shell of a shellfish—generally an oyster—upon which to mark his opinion. Voters inscribed their yea or nay with a sharp stylus on the mother-of-pearl side of the shell and "cast" them (a term we still use) in a pile for counting. From this we gained the word "ostracize," meaning to expel, kick out, or "give someone the oyster shell"—a legacy of the Greek *ostrakon*, for oyster.

3 Pull off the lobsters' claws and small legs and set them aside. Break the bodies at the joint between the head and tail and set the heads aside. With scissors or a knife, split the underside of the tail shell down the center without cutting the meat and remove the meat.

4 Cut the lobster tail meat into thick medallions. Crack the shells of the claws, but leave the meat in the shells. Spoon the green part (the liver or tomalley), the marrowlike white part, and the pink-to-orange coral (if any) from the lobster heads into a small bowl. Place the watercress sprigs on a serving platter, mound the lobster meat over the watercress, and arrange the claws around the platter. Serve, accompanied by the mayonnaise and the bowl of tomalley, marrow, and coral.

**NOTES:**

■ Spiny lobsters, if you are using them, have no claws, so what we consider a most desirable morsel is missing; but the succulent body more than makes up for the pincers.

■ River-dwelling crayfish (5 to 6 pounds for six) can be substituted for the lobster.

# WATERCRESS MAYONNAISE

### MAKES 2 CUPS

K ardamo, which means "cress" as well as "watercress" in Greek, creates some confusion. Cress, like cardamom, came originally from Persia and was known by the ancient Greeks. Watercress, on the other hand, grows along the banks of rivers and lakes all over Europe, including Greece, and has been picked and devoured as a wild green in Greece since ancient times. The two, however, are often mistaken one for the other. Whatever the name, what counts is watercress's bite. Since ancient times Greeks have loved peppery greens, such as mustard greens and watercress, to quicken silky fare. On lobster or crawfish a watercress mayonnaise does exactly that—gives the sleek meat some sass.

*1 1/2 cups Lemony Mayonnaise
   (page 470)*
*1 1/2 cups chopped watercress leaves*

Stir the mayonnaise and watercress together in a small bowl. Use right away or refrigerate for up to several hours.

# A SEA CREATURE FOR MOPPING UP

G reece holds the crown for another gift from the sea, one that is not edible but whose uses are countless: the sponge. Since ancient times, sponge fishing was particularly the industry of the island of Kalymnos. The strange creature—black when gathered, golden and foamy when cleaned—covered the underwater sands circling the island, and as those were depleted, the Kalymnian fishermen followed them to farther reaches.

At first they dove weighted down by rocks and holding their breath. When iron diving suits were invented, the Kalymnian sponge divers rapidly took to their use. With them they were able to dive much deeper and stay underwater longer, but many young men were lost to accidents or became crippled from the bends. Nowadays the sponge divers use scuba gear, but alas, the island's industry has dwindled due to the scarcity of real sponges and the proliferation of synthetic ones. Still, fat, glorious, golden sponges are sold all over Greece and especially on Kalymnos. They are plump, sea-scented, and perfect for mopping up after a great seafood supper.

# octopus in red wine

## WITH OLIVES AND THYME TOASTS

### SERVES 6

ARISTOTLE, ENUMERATING THE SPLENDID SEAFOODS OF GREECE, LUMPED TOGETHER OCTOPUS (*OKTOPOUS*, SOMETIMES CALLED *POULYPOUS*, OR "MANY FOOT"), *SEPIA*, OR CUTTLEFISH, AND *TEUTHIS*, OR SQUID. HE CALLED THE GROUP *MALAKIA*. WE LUMP THEM TOGETHER TOO, AND CALL THEM CEPHALOPODS—MEANING QUITE DESCRIPTIVELY "HEAD FEET." WHAT CHARACTERIZES THE BUNCH IS THE CURLING FOOTLIKE TENTACLES THAT GROW STRAIGHT FROM THEIR HEADS. WHAT ALSO CHARACTERIZES THEM IS THEIR RICH MEAT AND LUSCIOUS TASTE.

By far the most famous cephalopod is the octopus (meaning "eight foot"). Since ancient times, hardly a fisherman could pull in his net without finding at least one entrapped. They are savored as a true prize, and should a fisherman bring his wife one, she is thrilled. Octopus are cooked in a number of ways: doused with lemon and oil and served as an appetizer (page 65), pickled, served with rice or pasta, in salad, stewed, or in the most famous treatment, simmered in wine, usually with their ink. Certain Greek restaurants serve *only* octopus in wine! The spicing is key. Here mace adds a touch of warmth and sweetness, while vinegar and wine add a bit of tang. It's rare to obtain the ink in market-bought octopus— it's generally sold separately for coloring pasta and the like. It's not essential for a fine octopus stew, but should you have it, by all means add it.

## MENU
### OTHER DISHES FOR THE TABLE

CRUSTY BREAD

FRIED CHEESE CUBES
page 40

PEARL BARLEY
page 230

SAUTEED MUSHROOM CAPS WITH GARLIC AND BREAD CRUMBS
page 271

LAMB, RICE, AND APRICOT *DOLMADES* IN *AVGOLEMONO* SAUCE
page 311

FRESH FRUIT TO FINISH

1 medium or 2 small fresh octopus (about 3 pounds total)
1/4 cup olive oil
1 large onion, finely chopped
2 cloves garlic, minced or pressed
12 green olives
2 tablespoons tomato paste
2 teaspoons red wine vinegar
3 cups dry red wine
1/4 teaspoon ground mace
1/2 teaspoon salt
24 Thyme Toasts (recipe follows)

1 Rinse the octopus and place it whole in a large pot. Cover the pot and set it over very low heat. Let the octopus "sweat," turning it once, until pink all over and firm, 20 minutes. Drain and set the octopus aside until cool.

# THE AEGEAN AND THE IONIAN—
# THE "FISHING PONDS" OF GREECE

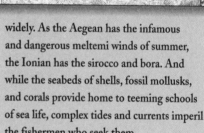

GREECE IS CRADLED BETWEEN TWO GIANT WINGS OF THE MEDITERRANEAN SEA, EACH SO LARGE THAT IT HAS ITS OWN NAME. TO THE EAST, REACHING CLEAR TO THE KALKIDIKI PENINSULA, SWIRLING ABOUT THE DODECANESE AND CYCLADIC ISLANDS TO THE SHORES OF CRETE, IS THE AEGEAN (AIGIO) SEA. LIKE A GREAT BAY, THE AEGEAN WASHES BETWEEN THE GREEK PENINSULA ON THE WEST AND ASIA MINOR ON THE EAST. IT STRETCHES 380 MILES LONG AND 186 MILES WIDE AND IS CONNECTED TO THE BLACK SEA THROUGH THE STRAITS OF THE DARDANELLES, THE SEA OF MARMARA, AND THE BOSPOROS.

Despite its jagged shoreline, the Aegean acts like a big bowl. When waves come up on it, they lift within the sea's boundaries as if smacking up the sides of a basin, reaching higher and higher until they are daunting.

## A TEMPERATE BATH

I have never seen such waves or gotten so seasick as when sailing across the Aegean. The deepest part of the sea lies east of Crete, where the depth reaches some 11,600 feet. The rocks of the ocean floor are mainly limestone, but two old volcanos sit at the bottom. North winds generally prevail in the Aegean, although from late September to late May, during the mild winter, the winds alternate with southwesterlies. With a temperature range of 75° to 77°F in August and 50° to 52°F in February, a wide variety of fish get exactly the temperate bath they desire.

The islands that dot the Aegean are the peaks of a submerged land mass called the Aegeis. Not only do the islands facilitate contact and travel, but the almost infinite number of inlets, beaches, bays, ports, and sheltering coves give harbor to seaman and land lover alike. Yet the sea is characterized by violent and uncertain currents that have perplexed researchers since Aristotle studied them. The sea is not often smooth, and men wanting to fish face a constant challenge.

## THE WATERS TO THE WEST

The Ionian Sea lies to the south of the Adriatic Sea, bound by Greece on the east and southern Italy on the west. Its waters lap the shores of the most westerly of the Greek islands—the Ionian—from Corfu in the north to Zakinthos (also called Zante). Again the coastline is marked by inlets, and the temperature of the water varies widely. As the Aegean has the infamous and dangerous meltemi winds of summer, the Ionian has the sirocco and bora. And while the seabeds of shells, fossil mollusks, and corals provide home to teeming schools of sea life, complex tides and currents imperil the fishermen who seek them.

## FULL OF LIFE

Marine life abounds in both seas, although curiously the waters of the two are the most impoverished of the world. Both have low nutrient and high saline contents. Neither derives much replenishment from continental rivers. Their saving grace is their warmth, which acts like an incubator, giving the creatures that dwell within time to reach maturity and spawn. It could be said that the Aegean was the cradle of Greek civilization while the Ionian was the avenue of Greek expansion. Together they gave the Hellenic people food and liberty. Upon them Greeks spread their way of life, their thoughts, and their recipes.

2 Cut the head of the octopus in half. Pull out and discard the interior elements, reserving any inky juices in a bowl. Slice the head meat into 1-inch-wide strips and place them in the bowl with the juices. Cut the tentacles crosswise into 1-inch-thick rounds and add them to the bowl. Set aside.

3 Heat the oil in a large nonreactive saucepan over medium heat. Stir in the onion and garlic and cook until beginning to turn golden, 5 minutes. Add the octopus pieces, their juices, and all the remaining ingredients except the toasts.

4 Bring to a boil, cover, reduce the heat, and simmer until the octopus is chewable but not yet tender, 45 minutes. Remove the cover and continue simmering until it is quite tender and the liquid is thickened and saucelike, 15 minutes. Garnish with the toasts and serve.

## THYME TOASTS

### SERVES 6

The winy sauce of octopus stew needs something to soak up every drop. A toast serves the purpose. To season the toast, thyme pairs beautifully with the red wine, and a brush of olive oil adds richness.

*1 baguette, cut into ¹/₂-inch-thick slices*
*Several sprigs fresh thyme, or ¹/₂ teaspoon dried*
*2 tablespoons olive oil*

1 Preheat the oven to 450°F.

2 Arrange the bread slices in one layer on a baking sheet and bake until barely golden around the edges, 5 minutes.

3 Using the thyme sprigs as a brush, rub one side of each toast with oil. (Or, if using dried thyme, stir it into the oil and use a pastry brush to rub the toasts.) Use right away or store in an airtight container for up to 2 days.

## OCTOPUS ON THE ROCKS

The sight became familiar. As I watched fishermen return with them, or a scuba diver with one on a harpoon, or Eirini at her beach restaurant preparing one for a stew, I saw Greeks take an octopus fresh from the sea, walk to the nearest rock outcrop, and with great swings bash the beast again and again against the stone.

Was this some strange ritual? An ancient hatred trickled down from the visage of Medusa's head to the look-alike cephalopod? Was I watching cephalo-abuse?

No, it was a cooking necessity. Octopus, especially those over fifteen inches in length, come out of their watery home very tough, and the meat needs serious tenderizing. Who knows when the ancient method was developed, but rocks are handy, the tentacles provide a handhold, and so Greeks tenderize octopus by smashing them on rocks.

Market-purchased octopus, even in Greece, are already softened and the cook usually need not worry about this step. But should you spear your own or buy one untenderized fresh from the sea, you need to take the blunt end of a cleaver or a meat hammer, or find a rock and pound away until the octopus's tendons give way and soften.

# squid

## BAKED IN A BROWN BAG
## WITH TOMATOES, MINT, AND GARLIC

### SERVES 6

THE GLOBAL RESTAURANT TERM FOR SQUID, "CALAMARI," COMES FROM THE GREEK *KALAMOS*, MEANING "REED." FROM "REED" THE TERM CAME TO MEAN "WRITING PEN." SQUID HAVE INK, AND ALSO A LONG PENLIKE CENTRAL BONE THAT WAS USED AS A WRITING INSTRUMENT. TO THIS DAY SCHOLARLY GREEKS ARE CALLED *KALAMARI*. IT'S ALSO STILL COMMON TO COMMIT SQUID TO PAPER, BUT IN ANOTHER FASHION—COOKING.

In the traditional preparation, squid is baked in a brown paper bag. Cuttlefish are just as likely to be used. Both come out juicy, steeped in flavor, and with a toasty air from the baked paper wrap. Cuttlefish is fleshier and has a smoother texture than squid. If you use cuttlefish, they need a little more time to cook tenderly, about 30 minutes.

*4 pounds squid, cleaned
(see box, this page)*
*4 medium tomatoes, peeled and
coarsely chopped*
*6 large cloves garlic, finely chopped*
*1 tablespoon chopped fresh mint
leaves*
*1 1/2 teaspoons salt*
*12 to 18 small toasts, such as Thyme
Toasts (page 351), for garnish*

1 Preheat the oven to 450°F. Prepare a brown grocery bag for baking (see Note).

2 Place the squid in the center of the prepared bag. Top with the tomatoes, garlic, and mint, and then sprinkle the salt over all. Fold up the bag envelope-style to enclose the ingredients. Place the bag, seam side up, on a baking sheet.

3 Bake until the bag is puffed out a bit, 20 minutes. Transfer the bag to a platter and ease it open, taking care to avoid the escaping steam. Arrange the toasts around the squid and serve right away.

## PREPARING SQUID

While already cleaned squid are an excellent time-saver and, ounce for ounce, a good buy, too much of the flavor of the sea is washed away in the commercial cleaning. I recommend buying whole squid and preparing them yourself.

With a paring knife, sever the tentacles from the squid body just above the eyes where you feel a hard ball. With your fingers, push out the hard ball from the center of the tentacles and discard the ball. Gently pull out the inside material, trying to avoid tearing the bodies. Rinse the prepared tentacles and bodies in a colander.

To cut cleaned squid bodies into rings, slice crosswise to the thickness desired. If the tentacle section is small, leave it whole; if large, halve it lengthwise through the area where the hard ball was located.

If stuffing the whole squid bodies, fill the squid, close, and secure with toothpicks.

**NOTE:** To prepare a brown bag for baking, cut it lengthwise and open it out. Coat the face-up side (inside) with a thin film of olive oil (about 2 tablespoons for a large grocery bag). The oil will seep through to the other side and will prevent the bag from crumbling or burning in the oven during baking.

# sautéed squid

## WITH OUZO-SOAKED LEMON ZEST AND SHREDDED GRAPE LEAVES

### SERVES 6

SQUID HAVE TEN "FEET"—TWO MORE THAN AN OCTOPUS—AND AN ARROW-SHAPED BODY RANGING FROM A FEW INCHES TO MANY FEET IN LENGTH. THEY SWIM BOTH FORWARD AND BACKWARD, PROPELLING THEMSELVES WITH A JET OF WATER THROUGH AN INTERNAL FUNNEL, AND LIKE OCTOPUS, THEY HAVE INK, SO THEY CAN SQUIRT A DARK CLOUD INTO THE WATER AND DISAPPEAR. SOME "FLY" ON THE WATER'S SURFACE RATHER THAN PUMP THROUGH IT. THE ONLY SEA THEY DO NOT SWIM IN IS THE BLACK SEA.

For eons Greeks have cooked squid in a grand array of ways, the most famous being their fried *kalamari* (page 62). In an innovation employing classically Greek ingredients, rings of squid are sautéed with ouzo-soaked lemon zest and topped with a garnish of shredded grape and parsley leaves. Ouzo's anise hint, hidden in the zest, imbues the squid with intrigue. Enraptured diners will ask you what that unknown allure—so ancient, yet so new—could be.

*1/4 cup ouzo*
*Zest of 2 lemons, cut into thin strips*
*1/4 cup olive oil*
*5 pounds squid, cleaned, bodies cut into 1-inch-wide rings, tentacles left whole or halved (see box, facing page)*
*1/3 cup fresh lemon juice*
*1 1/2 teaspoons salt*
*3/4 cup shredded jarred grape leaves*
*1/4 cup chopped fresh flat-leaf parsley leaves*

1 Place the ouzo and zest in a small bowl and set it aside.

2 Heat the oil in a large non-reactive skillet over high heat. Add the squid and stir until it is beginning to turn pink, 1 minute.

3 Add the lemon juice, salt, and ouzo and zest mixture. Continue to stir over high heat until the liquid is reduced and slightly thickened, 2 to 3 minutes. Transfer to a platter, sprinkle the grape leaves and parsley over the top, and serve right away.

## MENU

### OTHER DISHES FOR THE TABLE

CRUSTY BREAD, OLIVES, AND CHEESE

ZESTY LENTIL SOUP WITH TANGY GREENS AND HERBS
page 157

SIMPLE TOMATO SALAD WITH GREEK SALAD DRESSING
page 189

STEAMED WHOLE CAULIFLOWER WITH LEMON-NUTMEG *BESAMEL* SAUCE
page 273

CABBAGE LEAVES WITH RICE AND ALMOND STUFFING
page 301

FRESH FRUIT TO FINISH

# ARCHESTRATOS AND HIS FISH

No cookbook survives from ancient Greece. Apparently, though, a few existed. Plato mentions one called the *Mithaikos*. An expert in fish named Erasistratus wrote one, as did a man named Archytas and two men, both named Heraclides, from Syracuse. Hegesippus from Tarentum penned something of the like as well. There also existed cooks of some repute. Nereus from the island of Chios was said to cook eel so sublimely that it was fit for the gods—which back then was not yet a cliche. A cook named Lamprias invented blood stew. One named Aphtonitas created blood sausage. A few of these men's efforts and recipes are known because Athenaeus, an Egyptian archivist from Naucratis, wrote a book in the third century b.c.e. called *Deipnosophistai* (*The Sophisticate's Dinner*), full of quotations from writers, eaters, and cooks.

It is in that book that a smattering of recipes and numerous opinions from the famous cook and gourmet Archestratos are recorded. Archestratos lived much earlier than Athenaeus, in the time of Pericles. He was a native of Fela, a Greek colony in Sicily, and was more a traveling food commentator than a cook. He tried and critiqued food from almost every territory known to Greece, and certainly fish from every inlet and cove along the Adriatic, Aegean, and Mediterranean, and he was clearly more than willing to list what he deemed "the best."

Archestratos was very thin, had a high enough metabolism to eat massive amounts, and wit enough to write his comments in mock imitation of the style in which serious poets and historians then wrote. His writings reveal not only that fish held the top spot in Greek cuisine but that, along with the season, the *exact* place a fish, meat, vegetable, or fruit came from—down to the very beach, copse, garden, and orchard—was believed to determine the food's flavor and quality. The gustatory detail might chagrin any food maven today. The ancients, it seems, had such acute palates that they could discern the tiniest taste difference between neighboring tide pools.

Here are a few of Archestratos's pithy comments:

Get yourself the parrot fish of Ephesus, but in winter eat the mullet taken at Trichontus. Or, roast a great parrot fish from Chalcedonia, which is on the other side of the sea. . . . You will notice very good ones at Byzantium.

Sturgeon should be eaten principally at Rhodes, and if you see one in the market, it is necessary to haul it off by force, even at the price of later having to face arrest for kidnapping.

In vast and sacred Samos you will find an extremely large tuna called *orcin*. . . . Buy some promptly, no matter what the price.

When you go to Miletus, buy a mullet of *capiton* from lake Geson or a sea perch—that offspring of the gods—for these fish are excellent there. . . . Take care not to entrust the dish to a Sicilian or an Italian, for they do not know how to season fish in such a way as to cause them to be eaten with pleasure, but rather they spoil everything by mixing in cheese heavyhandedly or by sprinkling it with vinegar or their briny infusion of sylphium. They are the cleverest, though, at preparing . . . a great variety of delicious little noodle dishes.

# grilled shellfish

## WITH *TARAMA*, LEMON ZEST, AND BREAD CRUMB GARNISH

### SERVES 6

LONG BEFORE APHRODITE SAILED ASHORE UPON HER SCALLOP SHELL, GREEKS WERE DEVOURING THE TREASURES FOUND IN ALL SORTS OF SEASHELLS. EARLY DWELLING SITES IN GREECE ARE LITTERED WITH THE DETRITUS OF SHELLFISH FEASTING, AND WHEN GREEKS BEGAN TO WRITE, THEIR POEMS AND PLAYS TOUTED THE DELIGHTS OF EATING OYSTERS, MUSSELS, LIMPETS, SCALLOPS, COCKLES, AND MANY KINDS OF VENUSES.

Then as now, many shellfish were enjoyed raw, but some were simmered and sizzled. A collection of several sorts of shellfish, as someone gathering them from the sea or shore might find, can be grilled right in their shells. Topping sea with sea, a garnish of Greece's beloved fish roe, *tarama*, tossed with lemon and bread crumbs, is irresistible.

*1 1/2 pounds large mussels,*
*scrubbed and debearded*
*1 1/2 pounds large clams,*
*well scrubbed*
*12 large oysters, scrubbed*
*1/2 cup Tarama with Lemon Zest and*
*Bread Crumbs (recipe follows)*

1 Heat a grill to high.

2 Place the shellfish directly on the grill rack, cover, and cook just until they open, about 10 minutes for the mussels, 12 minutes for the clams, and 15 minutes for the oysters.

3 Using tongs, transfer the shellfish to a platter. Discard any that haven't opened. When they are cool enough to handle, twist off and discard the top shell, taking care to retain the juices in the bottom shell with the edible portion still intact. Arrange them on a serving platter as you go.

4 Sprinkle the garnish over the top, and serve right away.

## TARAMA

### WITH LEMON ZEST AND BREAD CRUMBS

#### MAKES 1/2 CUP

Robust *tarama*, so fragile in color and so vivacious in flavor, can be used as a garnish or topping in place of more expensive caviar and decorates a plate with its rosy hue. One of its best uses is in a topping. With lemon and bread crumbs, it adds fancy and zest to other seafood.

*1 tablespoon tarama*
*2 teaspoons finely chopped*
*lemon zest*
*2 teaspoons bread crumbs*
*1 tablespoon chopped fresh*
*flat-leaf parsley leaves*
*1/4 cup fresh lemon juice*

Mix the *tarama*, zest, bread crumbs, and parsley together in a small bowl. Just before serving, stir in the lemon juice.

# THE MINOANS— INHABITANTS OF GREECE BEFORE THE GREEKS

A BRILLIANT FRESCO ON THE WALL OF A HOUSE IN THE BURIED CITY OF AKROTIRI DEPICTS A NUT-BROWN MAN HOLDING A STRING OF FRESHLY CAUGHT FISH IN EACH HAND. ON EACH STRING HANG SEVEN OR MORE FISH. THE MAN'S ELBOWS BEND TO BEAR THE WEIGHT.

He is smiling, as well he should be with such beautiful trophies.

Are the fish gar? Gray mullet? More likely they are dolphin fish, still common today. The man is a Minoan. Akrotiri was a great Minoan city on the island of Santorini,

though the now crescent-shaped island was round when the man lived there.

## THE MYSTERIOUS MINOANS

No one knows what the Minoans called themselves. The name we call them was

*A fisherman with his catch, from the Minoan city of Akrotiri.*

given to them in honor of King Minos by Sir Arthur Evans, who first discovered evidence of their existence. They lived in Greece before Greek-speaking people arrived. Most likely they were the descendants of the settlers

and chalices. They had elaborate architecture with sprawling, multichambered buildings, intricate enough to earn the description "labyrinth." They created striking art and enjoyed a taste for luxury. They had

seem to have brought grains with them when they came, in Greece they found other foods to supplement those: almond, cherry, pear, pistachio, walnut, wild strawberry, sorb apple, wild garlic, onions, edible greens, basil, mint, oregano, rosemary, sage, thyme, and saffron, with which they cooked and made perfume. They added celery, lettuce, cumin, sesame, thistle, flax, and white mustard from their trading partners. They grew a range of cereals and pulses, developed orchards and vineyards. They had goats and sheep for milk and wool, along with ducks, bees, and pigeons. But although they had horses and donkeys, they used them only as pack animals. Only when the Greeks came did horses with riders appear.

> Clearly . . .
> kernels of Minoan civilization
> filtered into the Greek
> way of life.

who brought agriculture to Greece at the beginning of the Bronze Age; their cities are located near where those settlers colonized. Whoever they were, they went on to build an empire, with great palace cities largely centered on Crete and scattered on nearby Cycladic islands and mainland harbors. Their complex and powerful civilization dominated the Mediterranean for thousands of years.

The Minoans were a lively people. Their language is as yet undeciphered, but they wrote—first in hieroglyphics, then in pictograms, then with an alphabet. They had metallurgy, working in gold, silver, lead, and copper alloyed into bronze. They shaped ornate daggers

bathtubs, thrones, and jewelry studded with imported gems.

They looked much like many Greeks today. Their eyes were dark, their hair deep brown to reddish. In murals their skin is depicted as brown on men and white on women. They wore their hair both long in locks or braids and short and curly. Some are shown with heads shaved and isolated tresses dangling here and there.

## BRINGERS OF GRAIN

They supported their powerful empire by growing and trading grain, olives, and oil. They cleared Crete and other areas of forest. Though they

## A PEOPLE OF THE SEA

Their means of travel and trade was the sea. They had relations with Palestine, Italy, Troy, and Egypt, where they are portrayed on temple walls bearing their trade goods. Some think the Minoans might have been the biblical Philistines, for the Bible twice says the Philistines came up from Crete. The sea was also a major source of food for them. They ate all sorts of fish and heaps of shellfish, especially

*Ruins of a Minoan palace built c. 1900 B.C.E. at Malia on the northern coast of Crete.*

sea urchins, limpets, and tritons. Tuna show up in decorations on their bowls and urns. They used mollusks to make dye.

## A VOLCANO ERUPTS

Matters apparently ran smoothly and peacefully for the Minoans for centuries; few of their settlements have fortifications. But within their realm lay a hidden menace. Santorini, where Akrotiri thrived, is only seventy-two miles from Crete, the center of the Minoan civilization, and Santorini is no ordinary mountain. It is a rare and dangerous sort of volcano that builds to a perfect cone, then erupts about once every twenty thousand years. Just such a massive explosion occurred in about 1623 B.C.E. In an eruption seven times larger than Krakatoa's, the caldera imploded and collapsed, and almost all of the island sank back into the sea.

Traces of Santorini's volcanic ash are found imbedded in distant Mediterranean cliffs, revealing that the tidal wave from its eruption rose over seven hundred feet. An accompanying blast wave and cloud of ash of incalculable power swept south and eastward. Every coastal town on the shores of the eastern Mediterranean was most likely destroyed, with only inland communities surviving. Santorini itself—what was left of it—was buried under a porous pumice crust so thick that it obscured all evidence of former occupation.

## THE PRESERVED CITY OF AKROTIRI

In recent years, with the unearthing of Akrotiri, a great deal has been learned about the Minoans. When Santorini's volcano erupted, Akrotiri was preserved almost

whole in ash forty feet deep. The city stands amazingly intact. Houses three and four stories high still stand along curving streets. Indeed, the town scarcely differs from present-day Greek island villages. Narrow cobbled lanes crisscross the settlement. Here and there are small squares. Remains of well-crafted furniture, looms, elaborate frescoes, and indoor plumbing are found. Wide stone and wood staircases lead from one floor to another and up the twisting streets. Small windows on the ground floor and large ones upstairs gave light and ventilation. The ground floors were used as stores and workshops while the people lived upstairs.

Every house also had a mill to grind grains and pulses, a large stone placed on a built-in bench, with the smaller stones used for finer grinds nearby. Inside ground-floor storerooms numerous storage jars still contain the remains of peas, barley groats and flour, and dried fish. Other jars held oil, wine, and olives. Animal pens show that the stock was reared more for milk and wool than for meat.

Many vivid wall paintings tell the story of Minoan life. Though the Minoans were thought to be a peaceful people, one fresco shows a sea battle and another warriors returning from combat. Ships triumphantly return to port, where people gather and wave. Another ship falters at sea and men plunge into the water. A fleet sails off, the flagship decorated with strings of circular and fleur-de-lis-shaped bobbles, much as lights are strung on the rigging of yachts today.

On land women collect crocuses. One sprinkles incense on a glowing brazier. The women wear long skirts; big hoop earrings dangle from their pierced ears. Two boys, complete with gloves, box. Gazelles prance; blue monkeys with sickle tails leap about branches. A river winds through vegetation, and on the bank a wildcat prepares to pounce on paddling ducks.

## WAS THIS ATLANTIS?

While the Minoan civilization continued for a while after the eruption of Santorini, it never recovered. Another people soon replaced the Minoans. Indeed, in due time the destruction and disappearance of the Minoans was so complete that by the time the Greek civilization blossomed, there existed no memory or record that anyone had lived in Greece before. Nothing was known of the Minoans until the nineteenth century. There are scientists and scholars, however, who believe that the tale of the Minoans lived on in the story of Atlantis. The

Egyptians told Solon, the first great Greek leader, that he was an ignorant bumpkin who did not know that his people lived on a land where people had lived before, a people who had disappeared in a single day and night. Solon's general told this to his grandson, who was Plato's best friend. Plato chronicled the tale as it was told to him, then went on to speculate about the place and the people. He attempted to locate the land, calculating that it was so large that it could only fit beyond the gates of Gibraltar, so he called it "Atlantis."

## CHANGING THE COURSE OF WESTERN CIVILIZATION

Atlantis or not, a people that once existed were erased. Another people with other life ways and language overtook those who survived. Many believe the cataclysm changed the course of Western society. Without the massive eruption and its devastating consequences, Indo-European speakers such as the first Greeks would never have gained a foothold against the dominant peoples of the Mediterranean. Santorini's catastrophe allowed invading groups, the Greeks and possibly those moving into Italy, later to become the Romans, to gain ascendancy.

Both peoples later expanded. Both infused the rest of Europe with their ideas. Clearly, though, kernels of Minoan civilization filtered into the Greek way of life. Minoan themes entered the arts and crafts of early Greeks. They gave rise to a system of writing. What remains unknown is what other, less material things—what notions and customs, even what foods and cooking preparations—fused into the culture of the people who became the icon of Western civilization.

*The Minoan Snake Goddess (c. 1600 B.C.E.) was discovered on Crete by Sir Arthur Evans in 1903.*

# meat
## OF EVERY SORT

MEAT HAS ALWAYS BEEN A PART OF A *PANDAISIA*— A SUMPTUOUS FEAST—IN GREECE. MEAT SYMBOLIZES GOOD LIVING, CELEBRATION, FULFILLMENT, AND GRATITUDE. WHEN A FAMILY GATHERS TO HONOR A BAPTISM, ANNOUNCE AN ENGAGEMENT, OR PUT ON A WEDDING, MEMBERS PREPARE A MASSIVE STEW OF POTATOES, GARDEN VEGETABLES, AND MEAT. WHEN A GROUP TAKES ON A FESTIVE MOOD AND GOES TO A *TAVERNA*,

Then all day long until sunset we sat dining on a bounty of meat and fine wine, and then we went to sleep on the beach.

—HOMER, *ODYSSEY*

each celebrant orders meat—most likely a grilled chop. When a relative or a wandering friend returns to Greece, Greeks welcome the roamer back with a rhapsodic meat meal. Unless it's Lent, saint's-day feasts always include meat. (Should the day be Lenten and only fava porridge served, all bemoan that

the occasion is diminished and no meat will simmer in the great church stewpots.)

But beyond its celebratory role, meat does not necessarily figure in Greek cooking on a daily basis. In fact, meat is eaten so rarely that many Greeks never develop much fondness for it. This was not the case, it seems, with the ancients. Reading Homer, one would think that hardly a bull passed by that wasn't offered as a sacrifice to the gods, then served up for dinner. Indeed, Homer's lively characters never eat fish. The ancient Greeks roasted, grilled, salted, boiled, and stewed meat. Even the spartan Spartans ate a daily after-dinner treat of meat and bread, though probably lowly farmers and laborers rarely supped on meat. Hippocrates describes Greeks regularly consuming

horse, ass, fox, hedgehog, boar, deer, and hare in addition to cattle, sheep, goats, and swine. To treat an upset stomach, dog was prescribed. Aristophanes and Aristotle praise camel as a prestigious meat. And just as they do now, in days past when a guest came to a home, the hosts hurried to slaughter an animal and serve the visitor meat.

For centuries the favorite meat of Greeks has been lamb. Second to lamb is goat. That preference over beef developed when the early Greeks changed from roving herders to small-plot farmers. Sheep and goats could be raised more easily than cattle. But because the diet of most Greeks has been largely vegetarian for thousands of years, many Greek-style meat dishes feature a modest amount of meat cooked with a panoply of vegetables and grains. The cuisine involves more stews and casseroles than whole joints, although grilled chops and kebabs are popular, and whole animals are also spitted and roasted over glowing coals.

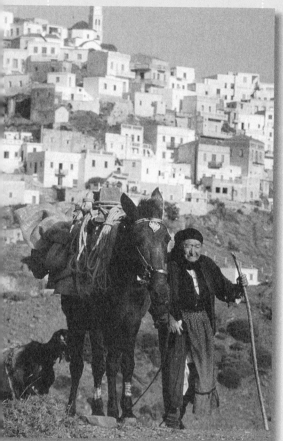

*A villager with her mule and goat packed and ready for labor head out in morning's first light.*

# pot roast

## WITH ORZO AND GRATED CHEESE

### YIOUVETSI

**SERVES 6**

IN EVERY CUISINE THERE ARE CERTAIN PAIRINGS THAT ARE ABSOLUTE, LIKE STEAK AND FRIED POTATOES IN FRANCE, MEAT LOAF AND MASHED POTATOES IN THE UNITED STATES. IN GREECE THAT PAIRING IS POT ROAST WITH LITTLE SEED-SHAPED PASTA. *YIOUVETSI* IS A KEYSTONE DISH OF GREEK CUISINE: CENTRAL, SYMBOLIC, AND BASIC. TO GREEKS OF A CERTAIN AGE OR WHO REMEMBER MOM'S HOME COOKING, THE MEAT INVOLVED IS INVARIABLY LAMB. BUT BEEF HAS RECENTLY BECOME EQUALLY FEATURED IN *YIOUVETSI*.

Tourism and political alliances have made Greek cooking more international in taste, and thus beef has taken precedence over lamb. Beef is also available more regularly. Whatever the meat, it is served on a bed of pasta variously called *sporo*, or *manestra*, but most often *kritharaki*, meaning "little barley kernels," as befits the pasta's seedlike shape. We know it by its Italian name, orzo.

I dare not fiddle with this dish—it's too close to the Greek heart. Here it is in all its rich, traditional flavor.

5 cloves garlic, finely chopped
2 teaspoons chopped fresh oregano leaves, or ³/4 teaspoon dried
1¹/2 teaspoons freshly ground black pepper
2 tablespoons olive oil
3 pounds beef top round or boneless leg of lamb (see Notes)
1 cup Quick Fresh Tomato Sauce (page 474) or canned tomato sauce
¹/2 cup dry red wine
¹/2 teaspoon salt
2 cups water
1¹/2 cups orzo
¹/2 cup freshly grated kefalotyri cheese

1 Mix the garlic, oregano, pepper, and oil together in a deep non-reactive roasting pan. Place the roast in the pan and turn to coat it with the marinade. Cover and marinate in the refrigerator for at least 2 hours, or as long as overnight. Remove the pan from the refrigerator and allow the meat to come to room temperature (still in the marinade).

2 Preheat the oven to 450°F.

3 Place the pan in the oven and roast until juices begin to exude from the meat, 20 minutes.

## MENU

### OTHER DISHES FOR THE TABLE

**CRUSTY BREAD, OLIVES, AND CHEESE**

**MUSHROOM AND RETSINA PIE**
page 100

**CAULIFLOWER SALAD WITH LEMON ZEST, CHIVES, AND CHIVE FLOWERS**
page 198

**STRING BEANS WITH SHALLOTS, WHITE WINE, AND FENNEL SEEDS**
page 288

**FRESH FRUIT TO FINISH**

4 Remove the pan from the oven, but leave the oven on. Lift the meat out of the pan and set it aside on a plate while you stir the tomato sauce, wine, salt, and water into the pan. Add the orzo and stir to mix. Return the meat to the pan, reduce the oven temperature to 400°F, and cook until the liquid is bubbling and the meat is pink in the center and more well-done on the ends, 30 minutes.

## YIOUVETSI FOR ALL THE VILLAGE

When I first lived in Greece, long before much of the countryside had refrigeration, most villages had someone who, along with farming, was a part-time butcher. Every year or so, the butcher would raise a cow, judiciously investing in its feed, and then when the animal was full-grown, slaughter it and sell portions of the meat to his fellow villagers. His neighbors gained a rare opportunity to eat fresh meat and the butcher received some extra income.

The butcher where I lived was named Lefteri. Even by village standards, he was poor—a mule driver. People believed he gave the evil eye, but that mattered little when the benefits of his sideline came ready. On that day every homemaker rushed to his home with enamel bowl in hand and money in her pocket. Lefteri's cow was never very fat. The meat was always rather stringy, and his butchering lacked finesse. Indeed, it was hard to tell if he knew what he was doing—the pieces were not recognizable as any cut of meat I knew. It didn't matter—every cook long-roasted the meat into *yiouvetsi*. There was only one drawback: As we had only one grocery store, there was never enough *kritharaki*. The store would sell out by mid-morning.

Inevitably there then began a noodle frenzy, for no one would want their *yiouvetsi* without the succulent noodle pillow to absorb all the juices. Some cooks tore their pantries apart in search of that one packet of *kritharaki* that might be hiding in some corner. Others prevailed upon sisters, mothers, and mothers-in-law, but most relatives were in the same boat. Some sent children up to town on the family donkey, hijacking the animal from field duty for this far more essential demand. Most, in final resort, broke long spaghetti noodles into pieces as small as they could manage.

Wiser cooks with discerning eyes learned a lesson in foresight. Next year, they promised, as Lefteri's new cow grew bigger and fatter, and *yiouvetsi* haunted their dreams, they would buy tiny noodles well ahead of time.

5 Remove the pan from the oven, but leave the oven on. Transfer the meat to a cutting board and set it aside in a warm place to rest. Stir the orzo in the pan and return the pan to the oven. Cook until the orzo is very tender and most of the liquid has been absorbed, 5 minutes.

6 Divide the meat into large portions and arrange them neatly on a large serving platter. Spoon the orzo around the meat. Sprinkle the cheese over the orzo and serve.

### NOTES:

■ Top round is commonly called London broil, and when cut 1½ to 2 inches thick is a good cut for *yiouvetsi*.

■ If you prefer to use lamb or goat (goat *yiouvetsi* is a rural favorite), use the lamb or goat leg and cook according to the timing in the roast lamb recipe (page 384). Because a leg of lamb is heavier than the beef roast called for here, keep your eye on the liquid while it is roasting and add more if necessary.

■ In place of orzo, you can use small macaroni, or even spaghetti broken into small pieces.

# a sacrificial dinner

## ROASTED TOP ROUND OF BEEF WITH BARLEY PANCAKES

### SERVES 45 TO 60

TO GIVE THANKS FOR A SUCCESS, A FORTUITOUS DAY, OR A LUCKY ESCAPE, TO WIN FAVOR, WARD OFF HARM, OR HONOR A GUEST, THE ANCIENT GREEKS PRACTICED THE RITUAL SACRIFICE OF ANIMALS. ONCE HAVING OFFERED HOMAGE TO THE HOLY, THEY PARTOOK OF THE ANIMAL IN A FEAST.

Today Greeks still exalt the holy with a meat extravaganza: On the day of a saint's celebration, a huge meat dinner is cooked and, after mass, served to the attending congregation. In short, for ten centuries the Greeks have recognized their link to the divine through feasts of meat.

The following roast makes for a munificent party, the top round being a grand roast that can serve forty-five to sixty people. (A smaller homage, feeding a mere four to six, is included on page 366). The ancient-style feast includes other traditional foods: wine, honey, and the ever-revered barley.

*Containers of wine for libation, and oil, water, and cloth for washing are carried to the banquet for the predinner offering to the gods.*

*1 whole top round of beef (15 to 18 pounds)*
*¹/₂ cup honey*
*3 bay leaves, crumbled*
*3 tablespoons salt*
*3 tablespoons freshly ground black pepper*
*10 cloves garlic, slivered*
*1 cup dry red wine*
*4 to 6 recipes Barley Pancakes (page 229)*

1Prepare a charcoal fire in a large grill fitted with a lid. When the fire is very hot, separate the coals into two equal piles with space in between and place the grill grate over them.

2While the grill is heating, coat the meat all over with the honey. Then pat on the crumbled bay leaves, salt, and pepper. Spread the garlic over the top of the meat.

3Place the meat on the grill rack over the space between the two piles of coals, and cover the grill. Grill, adding more coals as necessary to both piles

## MENU

### OTHER DISHES FOR THE TABLE

CRUSTY BREAD AND CHEESE

SESAME SOUP
WITH OLIVES AND BASIL
page 164

CHESTNUTS
AND SHALLOTS SIMMERED
WITH HONEY AND THYME
page 265

ARTICHOKES AND CELERY
IN CELERY SEED
AVGOLEMONO
page 274

FRESH FRUIT TO FINISH

## SMALL SACRIFICES

To make a Sacrificial Dinner for four to six, substitute these quantities:

*1 piece (2 pounds) beef top round*
*1 tablespoon honey*
*1/2 bay leaf, crumbled*
*1/2 teaspoon salt*
*1/2 teaspoon freshly ground*
*    black pepper*
*1 clove garlic, slivered*
*2 tablespoons dry red wine*
*12 Barley Pancakes*
*    (page 229)*

**1.** Prepare a regular charcoal fire and season the meat as described in Step 2.

**2.** Grill the meat, covered, until medium-rare, 20 to 25 minutes. Transfer the meat to a platter and set it aside for 15 minutes.

**3.** Pour the wine over the meat and let it sit for another 5 minutes. Then pour all the juices that have collected on the platter into a small saucepan and bring to a boil. Lower the heat and simmer until slightly reduced, about 3 minutes.

**4.** To serve, slice the beef across the grain. Arrange the slices on a platter and spoon the sauce over them. Accompany with the Barley Pancakes.

to maintain a medium-hot fire, until the meat is very rare (about 90°F) in the middle and medium-rare (about 130°F) on the ends, 2 hours (see Note).

4Transfer the roast to a large platter and set it aside, lightly covered, for at least 30 minutes to finish cooking and to allow the juices to settle.

5Pour the wine over the roast and let it sit for another 10 minutes. Pour all the collected juices into a saucepan and bring to a boil. Lower the heat and simmer until slightly reduced, 10 minutes.

6To serve, carve the roast across the grain. Arrange the slices on a large platter and spoon the sauce over the top. Accompany with the Barley Pancakes.

**NOTE:** The ruddiness of rare beef seems appropriate for a sacrifice, but Greeks prefer their meat well-done. For well-done, add another hour to the grilling time. You will definitely need more coals for the longer cooking time that well-done requires.

# beef with olives

## AND 100 CLOVES OF GARLIC

### SKORDOSTOUMBI

**SERVES 6**

GARLIC IS SUCH A PREVALENT INGREDIENT IN GREEK CUISINE THAT THE *PLINK, PLINK, PLINK* OF GARLIC CLOVES DROPPING INTO COOKING POTS RINGS OUT ACROSS THE COUNTRY LIKE THE TINKLING OF TINY BELLS. GREEK COOKS USUALLY USE THE CLOVES WHOLE, OR AT MOST GIVE THEM A FEW ROUGH CHOPS.

*Skordostoumbi*, which is the basis for the dish, means "beaten garlic," *skordo* meaning garlic, and *stoumbi* "to brush or pound," like a pesto of garlic. Greek cuisine employs a number of such pastes, and generally when *skordostoumbi* is involved the garlic is beaten to a chunky paste to be used as a garnish. Baked with beef in a clay pot, however, the garlic need not be beaten ahead of time because it dissolves into a paste on its own in the oven. Though the number of garlic cloves may seem outrageous, they melt into a sweet, mild, moist, and pulpy paste surrounding the beef chunks. Usually vinegar is splashed on the meat as a final touch in the preparation, but the addition of olives here provides a salty nip that more than meets any call for extra tang. The dish is a breeze to prepare and turns out rich and complex.

## MENU
### OTHER DISHES FOR THE TABLE

**CRUSTY BREAD AND CHEESE**

**SQUASH AND CARDAMOM PIE**
page 101

**DOUBLE LEMON AVGOLEMONO SOUP**
page 169

**SIMPLE ENDIVE SALAD WITH GREEK SALAD DRESSING**
page 189

**BULGUR AND VEGETABLE PILAF WITH HERBS AND WHITE WINE**
page 235

**FRESH FRUIT TO FINISH**

*An ancient key-trimmed plate shows a* mageiros, *who after saying a blessing will butcher a beef loin.*

*¹/₄ cup olive oil*

*3 pounds boneless beef chuck or top sirloin, trimmed and cut into approximately 2-inch chunks*

*100 cloves garlic (8 to 10 large heads), separated and peeled*

*48 Kalamata olives*

*4 cups dry red wine*

*1 tablespoon tomato paste*

*2 bay leaves*

*¹/₂ teaspoon freshly ground black pepper*

*¹/₂ cup shredded fresh basil leaves*

1 Preheat the oven to 425°F.

2 Heat the oil in a large non-reactive skillet over high heat. When it is hot, add as many pieces of beef as will fit without crowding and sauté until browned all over, about 5 minutes. Transfer the meat to a 3-quart clay pot (see Notes), and repeat with another batch until all the meat is browned.

3 Add the garlic, olives, wine, tomato paste, bay leaves, and pepper to the juices in the skillet and bring to a boil over medium-high heat, stirring to dissolve the tomato paste. Pour this into the clay pot, scraping in any browned bits; cover and place in the oven. Cook, stirring once or twice during the cooking time, until the beef is tender and the liquid is reduced to a sauce, 1³/₄ to 2 hours.

4 Remove the clay pot from the oven and let it rest for 20 minutes. Remove the bay leaves, then sprinkle the basil over the meat and serve.

## THE *HASAPIKO,* OR BUTCHER'S DANCE

Greek men dance. They snap their fingers, twirl their handkerchiefs, and in states of joy and ecstasy take solo spins across the dance floor—and dance floors can be eked out on any patio or between the tables at any *taverna.* Dancing men leap like dervishes, crouch like tigers, and lift tables full of cutlery and glasses with their teeth. Men also dance in lines. The dashing leader of the line, with the help of the second man's hand or kerchief, weaves in and out, dips to the floor, slaps his heels, and scissor-kicks high in the air. Sometimes the lines consist of all men, at times the older married men, but more often the *pallikaria,* or beautiful young lads. Frequently the center of the line is made up of women who somewhat demurely circle in a repetitive rhythm while the male leader jumps. When the line consists of women, traditionally a man holds the end position as well, enclosing the swaying women in a bound and protected moving chain.

The most famous line dance of Greece, the one you learn at your first folk-dancing class and the one seen in *Zorba the Greek,* is the *hasapiko.* The name means the "butcher's dance."

Who knows where and why the dance received its appellation. Perhaps it was from the time when those who butchered cattle were also magicians and sacrificers and they took to the floor in rapture when their duties were complete. Maybe there were simply three butchers who one day invented the steps and from their humble chore-ography a fad spread. Who knows? What is true is that every Greek from toddler to teetering knows the butcher's dance—a step to the right and one behind, a dip down and for-ward, a shuffle kick back. The dance breaks out wherever Greeks gather. As one would expect, the occasions when the dance starts up are often those festive ones where meat is served. When the lamb is on the spit, when *skordostoumbi* is in the pot, those are the times of the butcher's dance. If the affair is not exuberant, the *hasapiko* will make it so.

**NOTES:**

■ If you do not have a clay pot, use a heavy enameled or other stovetop-to-oven casserole.

■ Whole flat-leaf parsley leaves can be used in place of the basil.

# beef kapama

## WITH WINE, BRANDY, COFFEE, AND HONEY

### SERVES 6 TO 8

KAPAMA CELEBRATES THE FACT THAT GREECE WAS ONCE A TERMINUS OF THE SPICE ROUTE. IN IT, THE MEAT SIMMERS IN A RUSTIC YET ARTFUL LIQUID FLAVORED WITH CINNAMON, CLOVE, AND BAY LEAF. OFTEN THE DISH IS SERVED GARNISHED WITH PEPPERY WATERCRESS. OF ALL THE GREEK DISHES, TO ME *KAPAMA* MOST SUGGESTS—IN TASTE AND FUSION—AN AMERICAN BARBECUE SAUCE. THE BEST OF BARBECUE SAUCES ARE ALWAYS THOSE HIGHLY PERSONAL ONES, THE ONES THAT CONTAIN A COOK'S PARTICULAR "SECRET" INGREDIENTS. TWO OF THOSE SECRETS ARE TUCKED INTO THE SAUCE HERE: BRANDY AND COFFEE. BEEF *KAPAMA* VIES WITH *STIFADO*, BOEUF BOURGUIGNON, AND CARBONNADE FOR TOP HONORS IN THE BEEF STEW CATEGORY. FOR ANOTHER TRULY STELLAR VERSION, TRY USING LAMB. AND FOR A MELTINGLY TENDER CHICKEN *KAPAMA*, SEE PAGE 414.

3 tablespoons olive oil

3 1/2 pounds good beef stew meat, cut into 1 1/2-inch chunks (see Notes)

1 large onion, quartered and thinly sliced

1 1/2 tablespoons tomato paste

1 1/2 cups dry red wine

3 medium tomatoes, coarsely chopped

3 tablespoons Metaxa or other brandy

1/3 cup strong brewed coffee

3 tablespoons honey

1 piece (2 inches) cinnamon stick, broken in half

3 whole cloves

2 bay leaves

1 teaspoon salt

1/2 teaspoon freshly ground black pepper

1 1/2 cups tender watercress sprigs (optional)

1 Heat the oil in a large non-reactive pot over medium-high heat. When it is hot, add as many pieces of beef as will fit in one uncrowded layer and sauté until browned all over, 5 minutes. Transfer the meat to a bowl and repeat with another batch until all the beef is browned.

## THE BOSPOROS

In Greek, the word *bosporos* means "cattle crossing." The name of that channel of water running from the Black Sea to the Sea of Marmara, also called the Bosporus, derives from the tale of poor Io, Zeus's ill-fated lover. When Zeus's wife, Hera, discovered his infidelity, she chased Io toward the sea. To save the terrified young girl as she plunged into the water, making for the far side, Zeus changed her into a heifer.

Actually the channel had probably been a true cattle crossing for millennia, as the Greeks and their animals spilled down that natural route from the Black Sea to Anatolia. The Bosporus is a narrow channel—narrow enough almost to shout across. Through it and across it passed ordinary people and warriors, goods and spices, treasure and herds, and today the waterway still sees constant crossing.

# MENU

## OTHER DISHES FOR THE TABLE

CRUSTY BREAD, OLIVES, AND CHEESE

GREENS SALAD WITH HARD-COOKED EGGS AND FRIED GARLIC
page 268

BULGUR WHEAT AND WALNUT PILAF
page 233

CARDOON FRITTERS

FRESH FRUIT TO FINISH

**2** Add the onion to the pot and stir over medium-high heat until well coated, about 1 minute. Stir in the tomato paste and wine and bring to a boil. Add all the remaining ingredients except the watercress, along with the beef and any collected juices, and stir to mix. Bring to a boil, then reduce the heat to a simmer. Cover the pot and cook over medium-low heat until the beef is almost tender and the liquid is reduced but not thick, 1½ hours.

**3** Remove the cover and continue simmering until the meat is very tender and the liquid is thick and glossy, 35 to 40 minutes. Remove the pot from the heat. Remove the cinnamon stick, cloves, and bay leaves and let the stew rest for 10 minutes before serving. Garnish with watercress, if using, and serve.

## NOTES:

■ Excellent meats for Greek beef stews include boneless beef chuck, especially the eye of the chuck, or beef short ribs cut in 3-inch lengths.

■ If using Greek coffee, be sure to let the coffee settle and then pour it carefully so that none of the gritty dregs seep into the sauce.

■ In some fruit-growing areas, prunes are added to *kapama*.

■ For a sweet change in *kapama* or another spicy Greek stew, I sometimes replace all or part of the honey with apricot spoon sweet (page 538) or preserves.

■ To turn the *kapama* into a barbecue sauce for grilled beef, lamb, or chicken, heat the oil in a heavy medium-size saucepan. Add the onion, tomato paste, and tomatoes and sauté until the tomatoes wilt, 5 minutes.

Add the wine, brandy, coffee, honey, cinnamon, cloves, bay leaves, salt, and pepper. Bring to a boil and simmer briskly for 45 minutes. Use right away or cool, cover, and refrigerate for up to 2 weeks. Brush it on the meats while they grill or pour it on afterward.

## GREEK COFFEE AS GREEK FLAVORING

Though coffee is offered to every guest, coffeehouses stand on every square, coffee-making *brikias* hang in every kitchen, and every Greek imbibes several tiny cups of the liquid a day, Greeks rarely use their thick, rich national coffee as a flavoring. Yet so many Greek dishes, especially the savory, become all the more shaded with flavor when a tiny cup of it is poured into the stewpot. Coffee adds to a dish's complexity. Coffee adds roundness to a mixture of ingredients, pulling them into a union, and coffee imparts a mahogany hue to a sauces's color, making it look all the more luscious. Not just a drink, coffee is a flavoring, a chef's addition, a home cook's secret pal. Aromatic, pungent Greek coffee is one of the best secret ingredients of all.

# GRILLING

**I**N GREEK MYTHOLOGY, THE OLYMPIAN GODS HAD SECRETED FIRE FROM MANKIND FOR THEIR OWN ENJOYMENT. HUMANS, MEANWHILE, TREMBLED FROM THE CHILL, ATE RAW FOOD, AND COULD NOT FASHION METAL.

Prometheus, sympathetic to the humans, steals fire from Mount Olympus. Carefully wrapping some flame in a fennel stalk, he hands it over to the *hoi polloi*, the masses. Elated, the Greeks take to the precious gift and put it to immediate use. They have been using it ever since—to grill meat.

Grills are among the most commonly found cooking artifacts in Greek archaeological sites, and grilled meats are still among the most famous in Greek cuisine—marinated steaks and chops, chunks of meat skewered on small swords called *souvlas*, ground meats packed in upright loaves set to spin and broil near red-hot vertical bars, and whole animals turned on spits over hot coals.

## BRISOLES AND PAIDAKIA

**A**ny steak of beef, veal, or pork is called a *brisola*, while lamb or kid chops are called *paidakia*. To sizzle one up on a hot grill is the most common way to cook such a piece of meat. In the Greek fashion, the meat is not simply grilled plain. Before it meets the fire it receives a bath, or if time allows, a soaking in oil and lemon. The meat is then dusted with oregano before it hits the flame. Steaks and chops are cut thin, no more than $1/3$ inch thick, and cooked until well-done, but you may pick any thickness and grill them to any doneness you prefer. The trick is the treatment: Simply take a deep dish or pan, pour in a few tablespoons of good olive oil, add the juice of $1/2$ to 1 whole lemon, garlic, always oregano, and sometimes wine. Place the meat in the mixture for a few minutes to a few hours. Make sure to turn the meat to coat both sides. Either sprinkle dried oregano into the marinade, or with your fingertips dust oregano over both sides of the steak or chop after it receives its oily, lemony coating. The meat will have a characteristic Greek flavor and will be moist and aromatic.

*Tenderhearted Prometheus delivers purloined fire to humankind wrapped in a fennel stalk.*

## SOUVLAKIA

Whether it's tiny bits of meat on small bamboo skewers or large cubes on long metal ones, stringing it along a sword, then placing the sword on a grill, is perhaps the best-known Greek-style way to cook it. The preparation is called *souvlaki,* from *souvla* for "sword" and *aki,* meaning "little." Usually *souvlakia* receive the same oil, lemon, and oregano soaking that *brisoles* do. The proprietor of a good *souvlaki* stand will have great piles of skewered *souvlakia* resting in a marinade pan, ready to be cooked for the next customer. As a popular snack, a *souvla* of meat is served simply with a slice of bread pierced on the point of the skewer. In restaurants, the *souvla* may include pieces of onion, tomato, and pepper alternating with chunks of meat, all of it unstrung like a row of dominoes next to a mound of rice when it is served. The thickness of the meat pieces ranges from ¹/₂ to 1 inch. Chicken can be used as well as beef, lamb, or pork. *Souvlakia* can be made of ground meat as well (see page 391).

## GYROS

They are ubiquitous, having spun their way around the globe. Everyone thinks of them as the "Greek hamburger." *Gyros* are constructed of ground meats, herbed and spiced, patted into a tall cylindrical loaf, skewered on an upright spit, and spun in front of a standing broiler that grills the outside of the loaf as it turns. The outer layer is then sliced off, caught in a soft pita bread, spread with *tzatziki* (page 465), and topped with chopped onion and tomato. The best *gyros* also come splashed with a scoop

*With sprigs of fresh leaves for goat fodder, a man riding sidesaddle— typically—on his donkey goes home with goats following.*

of drippings from the bottom of the grill. At most *gyro* stands the pita is folded around the pyramid of fillings, and the whole roll is twisted into a square of wax paper and placed in the hand of the eater. Some stands and restaurants serve *gyros* open on a plate. Every *gyro* maker has his or her own special mix of lamb, beef, herbs, and spices, with ground lamb almost always the main ingredient. Without an upright grill, it's hard to duplicate *gyros,* but my version is on page 391. In Greece the ground meat grills are not called *gyro.* They are called *souvlaki,* just like the skewered sticks of meat. The name *gyro* comes from the "gyrating" grill.

## ON THE SPIT

Hardly any cooking method is more Greek than roasting a whole animal on a spit. *Tavernas* by the seaside sometimes have four or five animals roasting, waiting for afternoon and evening patrons. At Easter, villages may feature dozens of spits turning, one on every family patio. The meat—lamb, kid, sometimes pig—is always tenderized with one or two days of marinating before cooking.

place pans on the coals under the meat to catch the drippings. When the meat shrinks from the bone, the animal is done. The whole roasted animal rests

## Grills are among the most commonly found cooking artifacts in Greek archaeological sites.

### LONG-LASTING MEAT SAUCE

*Garos*, the original steak-and-everything-else sauce, originally from ancient Greece and made famous by the Romans, was made from fermented fish. Greeks most commonly used it on meats. It has not disappeared, however. Though few of us recognize it, Worcestershire and other popular meat sauces still use fish—now generally anchovy—as a base.

Early on the roasting day, the meat is rubbed again with the marinade. Meanwhile, the innards are made ready for *kokoretsi* and *mageiritsa* soup (page 176). After passing the spit—usually metal, but sometimes Greeks use strong tree limbs—through the animal from head to foot, the hooves are secured together with wire or strong twine. The spit should extend for six or more inches at each end so that the ends of the spit may be placed on stands.

A large fire is started in a shallow pit or in a cleared area long enough to heat the entire animal from head to foot. The fire is left to burn down to coals before the animal is placed over it.

Greeks sprinkle the meat with olive oil and lemon and brush it with thyme twigs as the roasting continues. Some

at least 30 minutes for the juices to collect before slicing. A lamb or kid takes about 3 hours to roast, a pig longer, depending on its size.

### KOKORETSI

In Greek traditional cooking, the delectable organ meats, the kidneys, liver, heart, lung, and sweetbreads of lamb or kid are cut into chunks, mixed together, and spit-roasted in a special preparation called *kokoretsi*. Wherever whole animals spin on spits, a rod or two of *kokoretsi* roasts nearby. The various organs are marinated, rubbed with herbs and salt and pepper, and strung in random fashion along a spit. The animal's cleaned intestine, rather than being used as a casing to be filled with meats, is used like a wide, edible ribbon to wind

round and round the skewered pieces, binding the meats in a tight sausagelike roll to the skewer. The whole package is then set over charcoal and slowly roasted, with frequent basting to keep the meat juicy. A pan is placed under the meat to catch the dripping juices. When the package of meats is roasted through, it is removed from the fire, the spit pulled out, and the meat sliced into thin rounds, wrapping and all.

There is a long tradition of grilling animal entrails on swords or spits in Greek history, and *kokoretsi* continues it. Individual organ meats, such as spleen, are often slipped onto small wooden skewers (the kind used for *souvlaki*) as well. These, too, are bound on with strips of intestine. They are cooked on grills in the *kokoretsi* way.

## KOINE, THE GREEK OF THE BIBLE

Koine, which means "common" or "ordinary," is the version of Greek that was spoken at the time of the Roman Empire. The Romans had taken over what had been the Greek empire, and since they admired Greek culture, they adopted the Greek of their time, along with Latin, as their empire's lingua franca. Particularly in the eastern part of their realm, they utilized *Koine* to communicate with the many peoples under their rule, and those various peoples spoke *Koine* to communicate with one another. So it was that many of the apostles and early saints of Christianity, many of whom came from cities that had once been Greek, spoke *Koine*. When they set about to record the life of Christ and the events of the New Testament, they wrote about them in that language.

They also translated the Old Testament into *Koine*. Some Old Testament stories have never been found in the original Hebrew, in fact, only in *Koine*.

As much as Greek words and concepts spread throughout the Roman Empire, coming to us in a stew of Greek and Latin roots, so did foods—particularly a stew of beef and onions. From the Greeks via the Romans, stew developed into something of a culinary lingua franca, the *Koine* of the stovetop. Everyone, it seems, speaks stew.

# beef and rabbit stifado

### SERVES 6

BY THE TIME OF *KOINE* GREEK—THE COMMON GREEK SPOKEN THROUGHOUT THE ROMAN EMPIRE AND IN WHICH THE NEW TESTAMENT IS WRITTEN—*STIFADO* WAS A FAMILIAR DISH AROUND THE MEDITERRANEAN AND BEYOND. THE CONCOCTION CONSISTS OF STEW MEAT AND OTHER INGREDIENTS, COOKED IN A POT OF SAVORY LIQUID. THE WORD *STIFADO*, WHICH BASICALLY MEANS "STEW," WAS RESHAPED BY VARIOUS LANGUAGES INTO *ESTUFADO, STUFATA,* AND . . . STEW.

*Stifado* well demonstrates the deeply flavored nature all stews should have. Greece lay so near the spice routes that cinnamon and clove were favored aromatics early on. Bay, or laurel, which is an essential ingredient of almost any luxurious stew, comes from a native Greek tree. Traditionally *stifado* included only rabbit, but beef was often used when rabbit was not available. My favorite rendition combines the two. *Stifado* is one of the crown jewels of Greek cuisine, and given its full stewing time, it fulfills its name and promise unconditionally.

$^3/_4$ cup olive oil

$1^3/_4$ pounds bone-in beef chuck roast, boned, meat cut into 1-inch cubes, bone reserved; or $1^1/_4$ pounds boneless beef chuck, cut into 1-inch cubes (see Notes)

1 rabbit (about $2^1/_4$ pounds), cut into 6 pieces

1 pound red or white pearl onions, peeled and left whole

1 pound shallots, peeled and left whole

6 cloves garlic, coarsely chopped

2 tablespoons tomato paste

1 cup dry red wine

$^1/_2$ cup balsamic or red wine vinegar

2 bay leaves

1 piece (3 inches) cinnamon stick

3 whole cloves

$^1/_2$ teaspoon salt

$^1/_4$ teaspoon freshly ground black pepper

3 Remove the bay leaves, cinnamon stick, cloves, and beef bone. Serve right away.

**NOTES:**

- By using bone-in beef chuck, boning it, and cutting your own chunks (a process that takes only a few moments), you gain a nice bone or two to add to the stew during cooking. Bones add invaluable flavor to the sauce of any long-stewing meat dish. To save time, though, you can buy pre-cubed beef chuck.

- If you prefer, use 3 pounds beef or 2 rabbits instead of combining the two meats.

- Beef and Rabbit *Stifado* can also be cooked in the oven. Place the covered pot in a preheated 400°F oven and cook for the same amount of time. No stirring is necessary.

- Rabbit does not reheat successfully—it becomes bitter and gamey. Should you have leftovers, enjoy the rabbit pieces cold, with a salad and bread.

## A STEWY CONFESSION

On one of my longest stays in Greece, when I was doing my first anthropology fieldwork, I rented a house on Santorini. Typical of that island, it had four rooms separated by thick, whitewashed walls made of pumice mixed with concrete. Though the roof was flat on the outside so rain could run off into the cistern, on the inside the ceilings revealed their house's true shape, a rounded arch. Most of Santorini's old houses were cave houses like mine, dug into the pumice strata of the island. My two front rooms had windows out under the clear, sunny sky. In the back, the rooms that burrowed into the earth were dark and dank. In the winter the moisture seeping from the soil colored the back of those two rooms the motley blue-green shade of mildew. I lived mainly in one front salon, making rapid trips through an intervening moldy room to my tiny tunnel-shaped, half-buried kitchen.

Times sometimes got quite lonesome, and cooking for one—at least anything that took much preparation—in that narrow, dank kitchen cavern, lit only by an untrustworthy kerosene lamp, became an unpleasant task. I had no refrigerator—the village had no electricity—so I couldn't cook a generous portion and save the leftovers for a second meal. Fortunately I made a happy discovery: canned *stifado*.

I had never eaten much canned anything, but for some reason the Greeks turn out canned single portions of beef *stifado* that are quite tasty and satisfying. Upon opening the small flat can, I would find a single bay leaf lying across the meat. Onions in rich broth surrounded a hefty chunk of beef, and the sauce was full of flavor. Of course I preferred the *stifados* I made from rabbits a neighbor gave me, from cuts of beef I purchased the rare times it was available, or the plates of stew bestowed on me by friends. Still, I was thankful to have *stifado* any way I could get it.

1 Heat the oil in a large non-reactive pot over medium-high heat. When it is hot, add the beef in one uncrowded layer and brown all over, about 5 minutes. Transfer the meat to a plate, and brown the rabbit all over, 5 minutes.

2 Add the beef bone, if using, and all the remaining ingredients, including the meat and any collected juices. Stir and bring to a boil. Then reduce the heat, cover, and simmer, stirring once or twice, until the meat is fork-tender, 1½ hours.

# beef and rice meatballs

## IN YOGURT-TOMATO SAUCE

### YOUVARELAKIA

**MAKES 40 TO 42 MEATBALLS; SERVES 6 TO 8**

MEATBALLS CAN BE COOKED JUST UNTIL THEY ARE STILL A BIT FIRM TO THE BITE, OR THEY CAN BE COOKED UNTIL THEY COLLAPSE INTO MORSELS. *YOUVARELAKIA* ARE THE SOFT SORT OF MEATBALL. THEY ARE UBIQUITOUS IN GREECE, A WAY TO USE INEXPENSIVE GROUND MEAT TO FEED THE FAMILY AND TO STRETCH IT EVEN FURTHER BY MIXING THE MEAT WITH RICE. EVERY GRANDMOTHER MAKES THEM. EVERY GREEK RESTAURANT SERVES THEM. *YOUVARELAKIA* APPEAR IN A SOUP (PAGE 173) AND AS A MAIN DISH. THE BALLS ARE SHAPED ROUND OR IN THICK FINGER-SIZE OVALS, PROMPTING MANY COOKBOOKS TO CALL THEM MEAT "BARRELS."

I prefer *youvarelakia* as a meat course rather than in a soup. For that, traditionally the meatballs are smothered in *Avgolemono* Sauce (page 457) or in a basic tomato sauce (page 474). Occasionally a Greek cook thickens the tomato sauce with yogurt, and that tangy, creamy twist

*Although lamb was the favored meat in Greece for centuries, beef has recently taken precedence.*

is followed here. Capers perk up the yogurt and chopped mint adds a refreshing punch. The meatballs cook much faster and softer when the rice is cooked first.

*FOR THE MEATBALLS*
*1 pound ground beef (see Note)*
*1 cup cooked rice, at room temperature*
*1 medium onion, finely chopped*
*1 large clove garlic, minced or pressed*
*1/4 cup chopped fresh flat-leaf parsley leaves*
*1 tablespoon chopped fresh mint leaves*
*1/8 teaspoon ground cinnamon*
*1 teaspoon salt*
*1/2 teaspoon freshly ground black pepper*
*1 large egg*
*2 tablespoons olive oil, for browning the meatballs*

*Youvarelakia Yogurt Sauce (recipe follows)*
*1 tablespoon chopped fresh mint leaves, for garnish*

1 Place all the ingredients for the meatballs except the oil in a medium-size bowl and mix thoroughly with your hands. Roll tablespoon-size amounts of the mixture between your palms to form walnut-size balls. Use right away, or cover and refrigerate for up to 2 days.

**2** When you are ready to cook the meatballs, heat 1 tablespoon of the oil in a heavy skillet over medium-high heat. When it is hot, add as many meatballs as will fit in one uncrowded layer. Cook, turning once, until the meatballs are cooked through but still moist, 8 to 10 minutes. Transfer them to a plate and repeat, adding a little more oil, as needed, until all the meatballs are cooked.

**3** Return the meatballs to the skillet, add the *Youvarelakia* Yogurt Sauce, and partially cover the pan. Simmer for 3 to 4 minutes, until the meatballs are heated through but still tender.

**4** Transfer the meatballs and sauce to a platter. Sprinkle the mint over all, and serve right away.

**NOTE:** Fattier sorts of ground meat, such as ground chuck, make the tenderest meatballs. Three quarters of a pound of ground lamb or veal combined with 1/4 pound ground pork can also be used.

## MENU
### OTHER DISHES FOR THE TABLE

WARMED PITA BREAD, OLIVES, AND CHEESE

BROAD BEAN AND PEA SALAD WITH KEFALOTYRI AND CUMIN VINAIGRETTE
page 207

FRIED EGGPLANT WITH FETA AND BASIL
page 276

SANTORINI *FAVA* CROQUETTES SUSANNA-STYLE
page 292

FRESH FRUIT TO FINISH

## YOUVARELAKIA YOGURT SAUCE

### MAKES ABOUT 4 CUPS; SERVES 6 TO 8

Yogurt, one of the world's oldest foods, somehow makes every dish taste fresh. Perhaps it is the hint of grassiness intermingled with yogurt's particular sourness. Perhaps it is yogurt's smooth density. Yogurt-based sauces are airy, not weighty.

1/3 cup olive oil

6 medium tomatoes, peeled and coarsely chopped

3 large cloves garlic, coarsely chopped

3/4 teaspoon chopped fresh rosemary needles, or 1/4 teaspoon dried

1/3 cup capers, drained

1 tablespoon coarsely chopped lemon zest

3/4 cup dry white wine

1/2 teaspoon salt

1 cup Thickened Yogurt (page 471)

Heat the oil in a large nonreactive skillet over medium-high heat. Add the tomatoes and garlic and stir until bubbling briskly, 1 minute. Add the rosemary, capers, zest, wine, and salt. Continue cooking until the tomatoes are soft and the mixture is bubbling briskly again, 2 minutes. Stir in the yogurt and use right away or set aside at room temperature for up to 3 hours.

**NOTE:** *Youvarelakia* Yogurt Sauce may be stored in the refrigerator, covered, for up to 3 days; reheat gently before using.

# THE CAPER FAMILY BUSH

**C**APPARALES, THE ORDER OF FLOWERING PLANTS TO WHICH EDIBLE CAPERS BELONG, CONSISTS OF 4 FAMILIES, 111 GENERA, AND THOUSANDS OF SPECIES. IN SHORT, THE CAPER'S FAMILY "BUSH" IS ENORMOUS.

The name of the order derives from *kapparis*, the word Dioscorides used for the tart bud, which was already popular in his time. That bud, the one we still enjoy, comes from the dominant branch of the order, which includes the brassicas (cabbage, cauliflower, turnip, radish, and mustard), the horseradish tree, and such flowers as stock, wallflower, the crucifixion thorns of America's southwestern desert, scurvy grass and shepherd's purse, the proliferous nasturtium and the tufted rose of Jericho. There are aquatic kin, marsh cress and cuckooflowers, and the sea kale. Some of the family work: The Mediterranean caper bush, besides producing edible buds and berries, produces wood hard enough to make tool handles and boat keels. Its wood also resists termite attack. Some *capparales* fruits and barks go nto curry. The brassicas provide food and are used for spice and seed oil. The pounded leaves and twigs of *Cadaba farinosa* are made into cakes and almost everywhere the leaves and seeds of plants of this order are used medicinally for wounds, rheumatism, toothache, and as a sedative.

*Capparis spinosa*, the line that produces the capers we use in cooking, doesn't much like to leave the arid Mediterranean. The shrub has been transplanted to a few places with limited success, but mostly the mother of all *capparales* likes to stay home.

## THE JOY OF GATHERING CAPERS

Going with a group of Greek women to gather capers is beyond question one of my favorite chores. Heeding how gravelly the soil is and how thorny the job, we put on our worst shoes, cover our arms in old long-sleeved blouses, and advance upon the stony terrain in search of budding caper bushes. We struggle up dirt banks and over ravines, plunking the green buds into bags slung about our waists. It was on one such outing that I learned one of the best techniques to put the curse of the eye on someone (cast a spell on a cake of soap, pitch it into the victim's cistern).

Once home, we rinse the buds and salt them down with coarse sea salt: a layer of capers, a sprinkling of salt, another layer of capers, and so on until the bottle

or jar is full. Within two weeks the volume in the containers shrinks by a third as the capers produce their own preserving brine from their leached juices. And well preserved they are. One batch I brought back to the United States kept for fifteen years.

## WHICH CAPERS TO BUY

But no matter how big the jug of capers I bring back from Greece, sooner or later I run out. Then, like anyone else, I must buy some.

The best capers to buy are those that are salt-packed. These are available in bulk in good Greek delicatessens and in jars or vacuum-sealed pouches in many gourmet markets. Depending on your taste, and how salt-covered the capers are, you might want to rinse these before using them. You can cover rinsed capers with fresh water and store them for several months in the refrigerator. Those still in salt will keep, in or out of the refrigerator, for a year or more.

More commonly found in stores are bottled capers in a vinegar brine. These are more astringent and less versatile for cooking than the salt-packed ones, but they are often the only choice. You can enhance them by soaking them in several changes of fresh water to reduce the vinegar flavor before using them.

# greek-style veal shank

### SERVES 4

GREEK STORIES, BOTH MYTH AND MODERN, ARE FULL OF COMPETITION. HEROES, ANIMALS, TRICKSTERS, SOCCER PLAYERS VIE TO SEE WHO IS BETTER. VEAL SHANK COOKED GREEK-STYLE WINS THE CONTEST FOR MEAT SIMMERED ON THE BONE. SHANK, OF COURSE, HAS NOT ONLY MEAT OUTSIDE BUT BUTTERY MARROW INSIDE, A TREAT THAT IS TRULY A TROPHY, A SUCCULENT SPOONFUL OF MEAT ESSENCE. THE MARROW IS THE MEAT OF "COURAGE," THE "MARROW" TO PERSEVERE AND WIN. OSSO BUCO, VEAL SHANK ITALIAN-STYLE, COMES WITH A WINNER'S WREATH CALLED *GREMOLATA*, A MIX OF CHOPPED PARSLEY, GARLIC, AND LEMON ZEST. FOR MY GREEK VERSION, A DIADEM OF BASIL, CAPERS, AND LEMON ZEST, STUDDED WITH CRUMBLED CHEESE, SEEMS FITTING TO CROWN THE GLORIOUS SHANK.

*1/4 cup olive oil*

*4 pieces (2 inches long; about 3 1/2 pounds total) veal shank*

*6 large cloves garlic, coarsely chopped*

*2 tablespoons chopped fresh marjoram leaves, or 1 teaspoon dried*

*3 cups dry white wine*

*3 tablespoons tomato paste*

*1 1/2 teaspoons salt*

*2 tablespoons finely shredded fresh basil leaves*

*1 tablespoon capers, drained and coarsely chopped*

*1/2 tablespoon coarsely chopped lemon zest*

*1/3 cup coarsely crumbled dry mizithra or manouri cheese*

1 Heat the oil in a large non-reactive pot over medium-high heat. Add the veal and sauté, turning once, until browned all over, 5 minutes.

2 Add the garlic, marjoram, wine, tomato paste, and salt and stir to mix. Bring to a boil, reduce the heat, cover, and simmer until the veal is tender and the liquid has thickened, 1 3/4 hours. Remove the pot from the heat, set the lid ajar, and allow to rest for 15 minutes.

3 Toss the basil, capers, zest, and cheese together in a small bowl. Sprinkle over the veal and serve with narrow spoons to scoop out the marrow.

## NOTES:

■ Greek beef, *moshari*, is from younger cattle than American beef, yet older than American veal. It is not as soft and white as our veal—actual milk-fed young veal does not exist in Greece—but it is not as full flavored as American beef, either. Since Greek beef tastes somewhere in between, for convenience's sake, in this recipe and the one for roll-ups on page 380, I call for the more available veal shank and veal scallopini.

■ For an even more tender and succulent dish, allow the veal to rest in its sauce for several hours after cooking; then reheat it just before serving.

■ Feta can be substituted for the mizithra or manouri cheese, though it is moister.

# stuffed veal roll-ups

## WITH FENNEL AND BREAD CRUMBS

### SERVES 4 TO 6

IN ALMOST EVERY CAFE IN GREECE, TOURISTS WHO WANDER IN ARE PRESENTED WITH A MENU. MENUS, HOWEVER, RARELY HAVE MUCH TO DO WITH WHAT IS BEING SERVED THAT DAY. THE PREPARATIONS IN A GREEK CAFE, AS IN A HOME KITCHEN, DEPEND ON WHAT IS IN THE MARKET THAT MORNING—WHAT VEGETABLE JUST RIPENED, WHAT MEAT THE BUTCHER ACQUIRED, WHAT ELEGANT FRUIT HAS TAKEN ON FULL FLAVOR AND COLOR. THE TRULY TRADITIONAL WAY A CUSTOMER MAKES HIS CHOICE IS TO WALK INTO THE KITCHEN, LIFT THE LIDS OFF THE SIMMERING POTS, EXAMINE THE CONTENTS, SNIFF THE WAFTING ESSENCE, AND PICK THE ONES THAT SING TO HIS OR HER DESIRES.

For whatever reason, on almost all the menus Greek restaurants hand out—especially the rural ones—there is a strange entry called beef "roll-ups." Spelled various ways—rol ups, roll ap's, rolups, rolos—the constant manifestation of this fantasy food (for I have never seen a roll-up; everywhere I order it, I'm told "we don't have it today") became one of the ongoing jokes of my many years in Greece. Victoria and I finally decided to create the mysterious "roll-up": sleek fennel and bright olives rolled up in pliant veal, cooked in an anchovy-flavored sauce and garnished with capers.

*FOR THE VEAL AND STUFFING*

6 thin slices veal scallopine (about 5 ounces each)

4 tablespoons (1/2 stick) butter

4 tablespoons olive oil

1 cup finely chopped fennel bulb

1 medium leek, white and light green parts trimmed, well washed, drained, and finely chopped

1 1/2 cup very coarse bread crumbs, preferably homemade

12 Kalamata olives, pitted and finely chopped

1/4 cup chopped fresh flat-leaf parsley leaves

1 teaspoon salt

1/2 teaspoon black pepper

2 large eggs

*FOR THE SAUCE*

2 cups dry white wine

4 medium tomatoes, coarsely chopped

4 large cloves garlic, finely chopped

4 anchovy fillets, finely chopped

2 bay leaves, crumbled

*FOR THE GARNISH*

2 tablespoons capers, rinsed and chopped

2 teaspoons finely chopped lemon zest

2 tablespoons chopped fennel fronds

1 Place each slice of veal between two pieces of waxed paper and pound it with a mallet until it is about ⅛ inch thick and 7 to 8 inches in diameter. Transfer the slices to a platter and set aside.

2 Prepare the stuffing: Melt 2 tablespoons of the butter in 2 tablespoons of the oil in a medium-size skillet over medium heat. Add the fennel and leek and sauté gently until the vegetables wilt, 5 minutes. Transfer to a medium-size bowl, add the bread crumbs, olives, parsley, salt, pepper, and eggs, and mix well.

3 To make the roll-ups, place one piece of veal on a work surface. Spread one sixth of the stuffing along one side, and roll it up into a cylinder, enclosing the stuffing. Secure with toothpicks if necessary to keep the roll from popping open. Repeat until all the veal is rolled. Set them aside.

## A CALENDAR OF MEATS

·················

"It is sweet to eat in autumn the flesh of the nanny goat, and of the adult pig, when they turn and tread the vintage. Then is the season of dogs and hares and foxes. The season for sheep is the summer when the cicadas chirp. Then from the sea comes the tuna, no mean food that, but outstanding among all fish in a sharp sauce. The fat ox, it seems to me, is sweet in the middle of the night and in the day."

**—ANANIOS, AN IAMBIC POET SIXTH CENTURY B.C.E.**

4 Melt the remaining 2 tablespoons butter in the remaining 2 tablespoons oil in a large nonreactive skillet over medium-high heat. Add the roll-ups and sauté, turning once, until browned all over, about 4 minutes. Transfer the roll-ups to a plate and set them aside while you make the sauce.

5 Add the wine to the skillet and bring it to a boil. Stir in the tomatoes, garlic, anchovies, and bay leaves and bring to a boil again. Return the roll-ups to the skillet. Reduce the heat, cover, and simmer until the veal is tender, 1½ hours.

6 Transfer the roll-ups to a plate, cover, and set aside in a warm place. Continue to cook the sauce, uncovered, until it has thickened, 15 to 25 minutes.

7 Place the roll-ups on a serving platter and spoon the sauce over them. Garnish with the capers, zest, and fennel fronds.

## NOTES:

■ To create more servings or to present the roll-ups in a dressier fashion, slice them crosswise into 1½-inch-thick rounds before arranging them on the platter.

■ If there's any extra stuffing that wouldn't quite stay in the roll-ups, add it to the sauce before returning the roll-ups to the pan.

# THE WARP AND THE WEFT: SHEEP AND THEIR WOOL

FROM ANCIENT TIMES TO MODERN, THE TRUE VALUE OF SHEEP IN GREECE LIES NOT ONLY WITH THE MEAT OF THE BEAST, BUT ALSO WITH THE HAIR OF ITS HIDE.

Sheep have wool—soft, warm, weavable wool—and from antiquity until recent times, Greeks wove their clothing, their rugs, their table spreads, and wall hangings, with the wool of their sheep.

It isn't known exactly when the weaving began, but it was early. One of the first sites where evidence is found is mighty Troy. Strewn about Troy's oldest levels lie thousands of loom weights. In Greek mythology, it is Zeus himself who originated weaving. At the beginning of time, this mightiest of gods stood before

*Ancient Greek ceramics tell of women's work, such as weaving.*

a loom and as a gift for his bride, Hera, wove a splendid mantle depicting the earth and the sea. With his gift, he began the custom of marriage among both immortals and mortals.

The metaphor of weaving appears very early in Greek writing. The many things that take interlacing are seen to be "woven." One such matter is marriage; others are politics and poetry. Plato uses "warp and woof" to describe all unions of opposites. Society is intertwined. Oracles spin prophesies. We still talk, as did the Greeks, of the fabric of human life and history.

## WOMEN WEAVERS

In ancient times the work of weaving—gathering of wool, balling it, combing it, spinning it, and weaving it—was the main occupation of women. Women spent most of their waking hours at their spindles and looms. Greek women wove figures, told stories, spelled messages in the textiles. Philomela wove in a cloth the story of how she had been raped by her brother-in-law, who had then cut out her tongue, so her kin could read the story and avenge her. Both wives, such as Theano, the spouse of Pythagoras, and concubines, such as Chrysseis, the young captive woman favored by Agamemnon, spoke of their duties in life as sharing a man's bed and weaving on their looms. Wives took pride in their skill (they probably did the ornate work, while slaves and apprentices wove plainer utilitarian items). Shrouds were important, and women could weave in such an intricate manner that their pieces could recount the deeds of families and the stories of the gods.

A single woven robe could take years to complete, and weavings were valued as highly as gold, silver, and bronze, and likewise traded as money. The goods were stored in treasure vaults, and a gift from a lord's or king's supply of well-guarded robes was both valuable and an honor.

Little, though, is known about how the weaving was done. No ancient writer describes it, perhaps because it was so familiar. Sheep were combed, the wool formed into balls, the balls separated into threads, the threads wound on a spindle, the spindle dropped to the floor, letting gravity twist the threads into yarn. The few descriptions indicate that the looms were vertical and that women wove standing up. They worked designs in intense and thrilling colors. A Minoan fresco from Santorini shows women gathering saffron, which was probably used for yellow dye. They used other plants, madder and woad, for red and blue.

## AN ENDURING TRADITION

Until just a few years ago, most rural women in Greece still wove. The regional costumes that have only recently disappeared were all home-woven from sheep's wool and featured complex geometric designs along with figures of people, plants, and animals. I own a Greek underslip, perhaps fifty years old, woven of undyed wool and sewn like a tunic, with a deep hem so intricately woven, then densely embroidered, that it was clearly meant to hang below the dress.

Fine textiles are still woven in many parts of Greece, among them the island of Mykonos, where beautiful, lacy wool panels are sold to tourists. Until recently many daughters' dowries had to include piles of woven blankets, table decorations, embroideries, and doilies. All were woven by the women of the family, and especially by that maiden daughter from her childhood to

*Knitting the wool from their sheep is also a traditional task of Greek women.*

her matrimony. Today every family treasure still includes a few antique woven pieces—cloths, rugs, bags—and these make up parts of the dowries grandmothers hand down to their granddaughters.

The metaphor of weaving is still used for cooking as well. Greek women tell me how they "weave" flavors. They twine a dish of lamb with artichokes. They braid in dill and wreath the dish with egg and lemon sauce. Food is loomed by a wife as deftly as if she were lacing fine-spun wool.

# roast leg of lamb

## WITH MUSTARD SEED CRUST

### SERVES 6 TO 8

NO MEAT BEARS MORE SYMBOLIC IMPORTANCE IN GREECE THAN LAMB, NOR IS ANY MEAT MORE BELOVED. A *KASANI* (POT) OF LAMB IN THE OVEN OR ON THE BURNER SIGNIFIES THAT ALL IS WELL. AND IT SUITS THAT LAMB IS THE EXALTED MEAT, FOR NOTHING GOES BETTER WITH THE WILD THYME, MARJORAM, AND OREGANO OF THE COUNTRY, WITH THE ROSEMARY AND MINT, WITH THE FETA CHEESE, EGGPLANT, AND BRUSQUE RED WINE.

The version of roast lamb here stays within the Greek vocabulary. The lamb is crusted with oregano, black pepper, and the seed of the mustard that covers the Greek hills. Slightly sour *trahana* porridge and pickled onions or green tomatoes offer punch and a perfect counterpoint to the rich meat.

*1 leg of lamb (5 1/2 to 6 pounds), preferably with the shank (see Notes)*
*4 large cloves garlic, slivered*
*1 tablespoon black peppercorns*
*1/2 tablespoon mustard seeds*
*1 tablespoon chopped fresh oregano leaves, or 1 1/2 teaspoons dried*
*1 teaspoon salt*
*2 tablespoons olive oil*
*1 recipe cooked trahana noodles (page 247)*
*1/2 cup Pickled Red Onions (page 75) or sliced Green Tomato Pickle (page 74)*

1. Using your fingers to find the natural openings around the bone and a small paring knife to make slits across the top of the leg, insert the garlic slivers into the lamb. Place the leg in a roasting pan.

2. Pulverize the peppercorns and mustard seeds together in a pepper grinder or with a mortar and pestle. Add the oregano and salt and stir to mix.

3. Vigorously pat the spice mixture on the lamb, coating it all over. Pour the oil around the lamb and turn to coat it all over. Set the lamb aside at room temperature for at least 30 minutes for the spices to season the meat (see Notes).

4. Preheat the oven to 425°F.

5. Place the lamb in the oven and roast until juices begin to exude, 20 minutes. Reduce the temperature to 375°F and continue roasting until the meat is done as you like, 1 hour and 10 minutes to 1 hour and 20 minutes (medium-rare will register 145°F in the thick part of the leg).

6. Remove the roast from the oven and let sit in a warm place for the juices to settle, 15 minutes.

7 Carve the lamb and serve it accompanied by the *trahana* and garnished with the pickled onions.

**NOTES:**

■ In American markets these days, one frequently finds a trimmed leg of lamb, which means with the shank cut off. Probably it's for economic reasons—why pay for the shank when it's mostly bone anyway? However, in Greece leg of lamb without the shank would be unacceptable. The shank end, though bony, offers some of the tastiest morsels of the leg.

■ You can also refrigerate the lamb, lightly covered in plastic wrap, overnight after coating it with the spice mixture and olive oil—the extra time allows the rub to season the leg further. Bring it to room temperature before cooking.

■ Spice-crusted leg of lamb is also superb when grilled indirectly over a charcoal fire. The timing is the same.

# spring lamb stew

## WITH ARTICHOKES, DILL, AND LEMON EGG BROTH

### SERVES 6

TRADITIONALLY, GREEK LAMB STEW ARRIVES BLANKETED IN A THICK EGG AND LEMON SAUCE. THAT CAN BE A BIT TOO HEAVY FOR TODAY'S TASTE, BUT THE COMBINATION OF LAMB, EGG, AND LEMON IS TOO FRESH AND TOO WONDERFUL TO LOSE. A TAKE ON A CLASSICAL GREEK LAMB STEW UTILIZING PAN JUICES FOR A LIGHT GRAVY WHIPPED WITH A FROTH OF EGG AND LEMON OFFERS A LIGHTER, MORE CONTEMPORARY VERSION. THE ADDITION OF ARTICHOKES AND DILL PROVIDES THE SWEET, VERDANT ESSENCE OF A SPRING MEADOW.

2 tablespoons olive oil
1 1/2 pounds boneless lamb stew pieces, cut from the leg (see Note)
Salt and freshly ground black pepper
2 medium onions, coarsely chopped
4 cloves garlic, coarsely chopped
5 cups water
18 baby or 6 small artichokes, trimmed and halved or quartered

1/2 cup chopped fresh dill
3 extra-large eggs
1/4 cup fresh lemon juice

## MENU
### DISHES FOR THE TABLE

CRUSTY BREAD AND OLIVES

CHEESE PIE WITH LEMON AND NUTMEG
page 89

SIMPLE WATERCRESS SALAD WITH GREEK SALAD DRESSING
page 189

RICE PILAF
page 231

TOMATO CROQUETTES
Box, page 296

FRESH FRUIT TO FINISH

1 Heat the oil in a large non-reactive skillet over medium-high heat. When it is hot, add as many lamb pieces as will fit in one uncrowded layer. Season lightly with salt and pepper and sauté until browned all over, about 5 minutes. Transfer the lamb to a dish, and repeat with another batch until all the lamb is browned.

2 Add the onions and garlic to the skillet and sauté until the onions begin to turn golden, about 2 minutes. Stir in the lamb, any collected juices, and the water. Bring to a boil, then reduce the heat, cover the pan, and simmer until the lamb is almost tender, 40 minutes.

3 Add the artichokes, cover again, and continue simmering until the artichokes are almost tender, 20 to 25 minutes. Stir in the dill and simmer, uncovered, until the artichokes are very tender and the liquid has thickened a bit, 5 minutes.

4 Whisk the eggs in a bowl until bubbly but not frothy; then slowly whisk in the lemon juice. Remove the skillet from the heat and slowly whisk in the egg and

## AN INTRIGUING RENDITION OF SPRING LAMB STEW

..................

A splendid version of Spring Lamb Stew omits the lemon and egg and adds some extra ingredients—one a mystery—that make the dish a different celebration of Greece.

■ Increase the amount of garlic to 6 cloves

■ Change the 5 cups water to 3 cups water plus 1½ cups dry white wine

■ Along with the artichokes, add 12 to 14 Kalamata olives and 5 to 6 anchovy fillets

■ Omit the eggs and lemon juice

■ Cook as directed on this page

The anchovies that abound in the Greek waters are the mystery element. They dissolve in the cooking, yet their hidden presence deepens and enriches the stew until guests will ask how you came up with such a sumptuous concoction. It's up to you whether you reveal the secret or not.

lemon mixture. Return the skillet to low heat and continue stirring vigorously until the liquid is thickened and saucelike, 1 to 2 minutes. Serve right away.

**NOTE:** It's important to use lamb chunks cut from the leg. Otherwise, the meat is too fatty for a delicate fricassee. The leg bone can be added to the stew for flavor and then removed before Step 4.

## VARIATIONS:

**Other Springtime Options:** A multitude of vegetables work well in a stew with savory lamb. Equally, there are omnifarious ways to assemble the stew.

■ Instead of artichokes, try 2 cups of broad (fava) beans or freshly shelled peas (if adding peas, add them with the dill in Step 3).

■ Oregano can replace the dill.

■ Spring Lamb Stew is also delicious when made with the artichokes and dill but without the egg and lemon addition.

■ You can also substitute ¾ cup tomato sauce for the egg and lemon mixture. Add 1 cup wine in place of 1 cup of the water.

■ Substitute cut-up chicken for the lamb.

## KOKKINISTO

There is a famous Greek meat preparation called *kokkinisto*, or "reddened" meat. In my first forays into Greek cooking I was always puzzled by it, since neither the meat nor the sauce in the preparation seemed particularly red to me. Sometimes the dish of simple braised meat was sauced with tomatoes, but then almost all Greek stews have tomatoes, and this "reddened" meat had no more than the usual. And then I realized that I was dealing with a perceptual matter that I had met in other realms. All people see the whole spectrum of color visible to the human eye, but people in differing cultures divide up the spectrum differently. Some put greens with what others think of as yellow. Some people see as red or black what others group into blue (Homer's wine-dark sea, for example). While living in Greece, I learned that what the Greeks often see as red looks brown to me.

When I first made wedding *koufeta* (see page 557), old Maria told me to cook the honey until it turned red. It never did in my view, though it got good and bronzy brown, at which point she came yelling at me to shut off the flame. Once Katina sent me on a long trek back to the village to get her red sweater, but I could not find it on the coat pegs in her house. When we returned together, it turned out that her "red" sweater was decidedly, and frustratingly to my eyes, tan. And so I came upon the clue to *kokkinisto*. In reddened meat, the meat is well seared on all sides before liquid is added to the pan. The trick isn't used exclusively in Greek cooking. In our stews, we use it often, only we call it "browning."

# roasted lamb shanks
## WITH GARLIC AND THYME
### SERVES 6

THE BOTTOM OF A LEG OF LAMB, THE SHANK, HAS SOME OF THE TOUGHEST MEAT ON THE ANIMAL. IT IS ALSO SOME OF THE MOST FLAVORFUL. THE CUT IS FULL OF CONNECTIVE TISSUE AND THEREFORE REQUIRES A LONG, SLOW COOKING METHOD, SUCH AS BRAISING OR MOIST ROASTING. THEN THE GLOSSY, RICH MEAT ON A WELL-COOKED LAMB SHANK FALLS FROM THE BONE. ANY HERB AND SPICE THOROUGHLY PERMEATES THE MEAT. GARLIC SUCCUMBS INTO A SOFT, SWEET PULP.

Oven braising mimics what a Greek country cook would do—slip the seasoned shank into a pan and then into a glowing beehive oven. Lacking an oven, the cook might give a few coins to the bread baker to make some room and roast the shank for her. By whichever method, the cook leaves the dish for hours, no attention needed, for her time is precious and her chores are many. Sound familiar?

## MENU
### OTHER DISHES FOR THE TABLE

CRUSTY BREAD, OLIVES, AND CHEESE

SIMPLE RADICCHIO SALAD WITH GREEK SALAD DRESSING
page 189

FRESH BROAD BEANS *PLAKI*-STYLE WITH TOASTED BREAD CRUMBS
page 285

SQUASH BLOSSOMS STUFFED WITH RICE, CURRANTS, AND HERBS
page 308

*TZATZIKI*
page 465

FRESH FRUIT TO FINISH

### FOR THE LAMB

*6 small lamb shanks*
   *(about 1¼ pounds each),*
   *cut in half crosswise*
*12 large cloves garlic, coarsely chopped*
*6 large branches fresh thyme,*
   *or 2 teaspoons dried thyme*
*1 piece (3 inches) cinnamon stick,*
   *or tiny pinch of ground cinnamon*
*1 teaspoon ground coriander*
*1 teaspoon salt*
*½ teaspoon freshly ground*
   *black pepper*
*½ cup dry white wine*

### FOR GARNISH

*1 tablespoon chopped fresh flat-leaf*
   *parsley leaves*
*1 tablespoon chopped fresh chives*
*1½ teaspoons chopped fresh dill*

**1** Preheat the oven to 375°F.

**2** Place the lamb, garlic, thyme, cinnamon, coriander, salt, pepper, and wine in a lidded roasting pan or clay pot that is large enough to hold the meat in a tightly packed layer. Turn to mix the ingredients and coat the lamb. Cover the pan and roast for 1 hour.

**3** Turn the shanks over and continue roasting, uncovered, until the meat is falling off the bones, 45 minutes to 1 hour.

**4** Mix together the parsley, chives, and dill.

**5** Transfer the shanks to a platter. Moisten them with some of the cooking juices, sprinkle with the herb mixture, and serve right away.

**NOTE:** If you're only serving four, prepare six shanks anyway and use the meat from the two extras in the Lamb Pie with Almonds, Raisins, Orange, and Mint (page 106).

## LAMBLESS IN GREECE

It seems irreverent to say so, but not every locale in Greece provides a home for lamb. More likely goats, even donkeys, are the prevalent beast. The presence of lamb depends somewhat on the presence of herders. Where the soil is rich, intensive agriculture takes up every inch of land with little or no soil left for animal husbandry—unless, of course, some intrepid entrepreneur recognizes the rarity of and demand for meat in the area and, as a smart businessperson, fills the need. The island of Santorini, for instance, because it has rich volcanic soil, is a thoroughly agricultural island. Every scrap of turf is walled or terraced into a patchwork of fields, all of which are farmed. Animals are few because every inch is given over to crops.

The same is generally true of Santorini's sister island, tiny Therasia. On that sliver of land, there lived a poor and fieldless woman who saw that no one on her isle, or on the larger one opposite, had extra meat animals. So she took to keeping a small herd of goats and sheep—some ten or so goats, and two or three sheep. She found fodder by walking her sheep and goats down the rock paths and along the beaches, and sometimes trading meat for pasture with a family whose fields were temporarily aban-

doned. (Most of Therasia's men earned their keep at sea; often the place seemed an island of women.) I would travel over to Therasia every now and then to listen as she waxed nostalgic over the changing way of life.

After the earthquake of 1956 destroyed most of its houses, Santorini's residents had rebuilt their dwellings in the old style, but before they had time to finish painting them, the island became a tourist center and was acclaimed for its whitewashed houses. Santorini's houses were not whitewashed before. Like the Parthenon, the Erechtheion, and other temples of ancient Greece, the island houses were painted a merry rainbow of pastel colors—yellow, blue, green, pink. Some of Therasia's buildings still sport the old hues. The church is yellow, the inn where I stayed pink. There are blue houses, green ones, and some with two or more hues. As the herding woman had never been off her tiny island homeland, she was amused by the purpose of my visits, and I was delighted to see her well-tended animals kicking up dust on the pathways. I would accompany her as she rambled about the tiny island. We would share a cheese, some sea urchins, and bread with classic white *tzatziki*.

# lamb wrapped in filo

## OUTLAW-STYLE

### ARNI *KLEFTIKO*

#### SERVES 6

DURING THE NINETEENTH CENTURY, THROUGHOUT GREECE'S PROLONGED FIGHT FOR INDEPENDENCE, BANDS OF BRIGANDS AROSE ACROSS THE LAND. LEGEND CLAIMS THAT THEY WERE THOSE DISPLACED WHEN FIERCE OTTOMAN TROOPS BURNED DOWN THEIR RESISTANT VILLAGES. REFUSING TO SUBMIT TO TURKISH RULE, THEY TOOK TO THE MOUNTAINS, WHERE THEY LIVED AS NOMADIC OUTLAWS, HIDING OUT IN RUDE SHELTERS AND PASSING THEIR DAYS RAIDING THE ENEMY.

Outflanking the advancing Ottoman platoons, they would swoop down to protect Greek towns, after which, like the mist, they would disappear into the hills again. Stealing upon Turkish settlements, they would pilfer livestock, weapons, and valuables. Although in later times a number of the brigands seem to have been nothing but common thieves, still a great mythology grew up around these bandits. In patriotic song and tale, they wear the crown of popular heroes and are idolized as Robin Hoods. They are known as *kleftes,* or robbers.

Because they could not reveal the location of their camps with smoke and often had to move swiftly, the *kleftes* also became associated with a particular style of cooking, where the food is either cooked in a tight casserole allowing no smoke to escape or, more famously, is wrapped and sealed in ready-to-pick-up-and-run packets of filo. In either case, the ingredients cook very slowly; with no steam escaping, the juices are trapped inside. When the vessel is opened, redolent aromas issue forth to reveal a succulent filling. Typically *kleftiko* dishes combine just what a bandit on the run might grab for a hasty meal—a hunk of meat, a wedge of cheese, some quickly chunked vegetables, a dash of spice. The version here gives homage to the bandit's life and what he (or sometimes she!) might forage: lamb, dandelion, wild onion, a handful of dried raisins, a drop of sweet wine.

## THE *KLEFT*'S LIFE

Night is black upon the mountains,
Snow falls in the Ravines,
Where ways are wild and gloomy,
Through rocks abrupt and gorges,
The *Kleft* unsheathes his sword.

And in his right hand naked
He bears the lightning flash,
The mountains are his palaces,
He has the sky for cover,
He has his gun for hope.

The pallid tyrants flee
Before his dreadful sword;
His bread is steeped with sweat,
He knows how to live with honor,
He knows too how to die.

In the world fraud has her way,
And injustice, so wills fate,
The wicked are the wealthy;
But here upon the mountains
Sequestered virtue dwells.

**—ANONYMOUS**

2 tablespoons olive oil

1 1/2 pounds boneless lamb stew
   pieces (1-inch cubes), cut from
   the leg (see Note, page 356)

Salt and freshly ground
   black pepper

1 medium leek, white and
   light green parts trimmed,
   coarsely chopped, and
   well rinsed

1/4 cup raisins

1 teaspoon ground cumin

1/2 cup Mavrodaphne or
   Commandaria, Vin Santo,
   Madeira, or sweet
   Muscat wine

4 packed cups coarsely chopped
   dandelion greens or arugula

12 sheets filo dough, commercial
   or homemade (see Filo Finesse,
   page 87)

Olive oil or melted butter,
   for oiling the filo

2/3 cup (about 3 ounces) crumbled
   mizithra or other sharp
   crumbly cheese

1 Heat the oil in a large non-reactive skillet over medium-high heat. Add as many lamb pieces as will fit in one uncrowded layer. Season them lightly with salt and pepper and sauté until browned all over, about 5 minutes. Transfer the lamb to a dish, and repeat with another batch until all the lamb is browned.

2 Return the lamb and any collected juices to the skillet. Add the leek, raisins, cumin, and wine. Stir to mix, bring to a boil, then reduce the heat and simmer briskly until most of the liquid has evaporated but the mixture is still moist, about 5 minutes. Remove the skillet from the heat and set it aside to cool.

3 Bring a medium-size pot of water to a boil. Add the dandelion greens and boil until wilted but still bright green, about 3 minutes. Drain and set aside.

4 Preheat the oven to 350°F.

5 Place a sheet of filo on a work surface and lightly brush it with oil. Place another sheet on top of the first, and brush it with oil. Place one sixth of the lamb mixture in the center of the top filo sheet. Place one sixth of the dandelion greens over the lamb, and top with one sixth of the cheese. Fold the filo over the lamb envelope-style to make a large packet. Brush the top and bottom of the packet with oil and set it on a baking sheet, seam side down. Repeat until all the ingredients are used and you have 6 packets, spaced at least 1 inch apart.

6 Place the packets in the oven and bake until the filo is golden and crisp, 40 to 45 minutes. Serve hot or at room temperature.

**NOTES:**

■ The *kleftes* cooking method is also sometimes called *exotiko*, or "countryside" cooking. Originally, in the casserole version, the cooking pot was placed over coals in a deeply dug fire pit, but today a slow cooker, pressure cooker, or well-sealed stew pot could be used as well. In the packet version, *exotiko* packets are wrapped in filo, bread or pastry dough, or parchment.

■ The filo packets may be prepared in advance and refrigerated, covered with a damp cloth, for several hours. Bring to room temperature before baking.

# ground lamb kebabs

## WITH SORREL AND PINE NUTS

### SOUSAKAKIA SOUVLAKI

#### SERVES 4 TO 6

WHEN WHOLE ROASTS OR CHUNKS FOR STEWING ARE TOO DEAR OR HARD TO FIND, GREEKS TURN TO GROUND LAMB. IN PARTICULAR, THEY FORM GROUND LAMB INTO LONG, JUICY "STICKS" OF MEAT. AS *SOUSAKAKIA* THESE ARE OFFERED AS AN ENTREE AMONG THE ARRAY OF DISHES ON A TABLE. THEY ARE ALSO PATTED AROUND SKEWERS, SIZZLED ON GRIDDLES, AND SERVED WRAPPED IN PITA JUST LIKE KEBABS OF WHOLE MEAT PIECES.

Grilling retains more flavor than frying, but grilled or fried, the key is that the kebabs must be as flavorful as they are juicy, so the ground lamb is always blended with onions and sometimes pine nuts. The kebabs here—shaped for ease as skewerless *sousakakia souvlaki*—are also mixed with sorrel, which adds a slightly sour note. When they are done, turn the tantalizing lamb kebabs into hot pita bread and top them with a racy, brilliant beet *tzatziki*.

*2 packed cups chopped sorrel leaves*
*1 pound lean ground lamb*
*1/2 cup pine nuts, finely ground*
*1 small onion, minced*
*2 cloves garlic, minced*
*1 large egg*
*1/2 teaspoon ground coriander*
*1/2 teaspoon salt*
*8 pita breads*
*Olive oil*
*2 cups Beet Tzatziki (page 467)*
*Several sprigs fresh mint*

1 Bring a medium-size pot of water to a boil over high heat. Stir in the sorrel and cook just until the water begins to boil again, 1 minute. Drain in a colander and set aside to cool and drip dry.

2 Place the lamb, pine nuts, onion, garlic, egg, coriander, and salt in a medium-size bowl. Add the cooled sorrel and mix well. Divide the mixture into 8 portions and shape each one into a "sausage" 4 to 5 inches long and 1 1/2 inches in diameter. Cover and set aside in the refrigerator until ready to cook (they will keep as long as overnight).

3 Heat a grill to medium-high.

4 Place the *souvlaki* "sausages" on the grill rack and cook, turning once, until barely pink in the center, but still moist, 10 to 12 minutes. Transfer them to a serving platter and set aside.

5 Lightly coat the pitas with oil. Place them on the grill rack and grill, turning once, until very lightly toasted, 1 to 1 1/2 minutes.

6 Serve the *souvlaki* accompanied by the pitas, Beet *Tzatziki*, and mint sprigs.

### NOTES:

■ If sorrel is not available, substitute the same amount of spinach tossed with 1 tablespoon fresh lemon juice.

■ The *souvlaki* may be cooked under the broiler. In this case, heat the pita breads in the oven.

# braised lamb sweetbreads

## WITH LEEKS, SPRING HERBS, AND CAPERS

### SERVES 3

SWEETBREADS ARE A TIME-HONORED OFFERING FOR POST-LENTEN FEASTING IN GREECE. ALONG WITH THE KIDNEYS, HEART, AND LIVER FROM THE LAMB OR CALF, THEY ARE WRAPPED AROUND SKEWERS, TURNED ON SPITS, AND WHEN THERE ARE ENOUGH OF THEM, THEY ARE ENJOYED ON THEIR OWN. BEING SPRING FARE, THEY ARE SEASONED WITH GLEANINGS FROM THE MEADOWS: SLIM, YOUNG LEEKS BARELY STURDY ENOUGH TO STAND UPRIGHT; TENDRILS OF SWEET MARJORAM SPROUTING OFF THEIR PARENT STEMS; MAYBE TWO TINY BAY LEAVES PLUCKED FROM THE TIP OF A NEWLY SPROUTED BRANCH; A TUMBLE OF WISPY PARSLEY SPRIGS.

3 tablespoons butter
  (see Notes)
1 pound lamb or veal sweetbreads,
  soaked and peeled
  (see box, this page)
Unbleached all-purpose flour
1 tablespoon tomato paste
2 small or 1 medium young leek,
  white and light green parts
  trimmed, well rinsed, and
  cut into thin slivers
1 tablespoon capers, drained
1 1/2 cups Lamb Stock (page 174),
  Chicken Stock (page 170),
  or favorite beef or vegetable
  stock

1 cup dry white wine
2 tablespoons Mavrodaphne or
  Muscat wine
1 tablespoon fresh marjoram
  leaves
2 tiny fresh bay leaves
  (optional; see Notes)
1 teaspoon freshly ground black
  pepper
1/2 cup fresh flat-leaf parsley sprigs
  (tender tops only)

## PREPARING SWEETBREADS

The sweetbreads served in Greece are usually lamb, though sometimes they're veal. Either type requires some soaking time before they're peeled, a process that transforms the chewy, protectively encased nodules into a tender delicacy.

Place the sweetbreads in a large bowl and add water to cover. Set them aside to soak for 1 hour or so. Rinse them, return them to the bowl, and add fresh water to cover. Set aside to soak for another hour. (If the sweetbreads are particularly fresh—for instance from an animal newly slaughtered rather than from a butcher who has already readied them for cooking—repeat the soaking process two or three more times, until the water remains fairly clear and the sweetbreads look "blanched," not tinged pink.) Peel away the outer membrane that covers the sweetbreads all around. Delicately pull away the connecting filament from the underside, which will allow you to separate each sweetbread into separate bundles of three or four nodules each.

1 Melt the butter in a large skillet over medium-high heat without letting it brown. Pat the sweetbreads dry, add them to the skillet, and sauté until lightly golden, 2 to 3 minutes.

2 Without removing the sweetbreads, sprinkle the flour into the skillet and stir until it is blended in with no lumps. Add the tomato paste, leek, and capers and stir to mix. Then add the stock, white wine, Mavrodaphne, marjoram, bay leaves, and pepper. Give everything another turn to mix well, cover the pan, and simmer gently over low heat for 20 minutes.

3 Lift the lid, stir gently, cover, and continue simmering until the sweetbreads are tender and the sauce is thickened, 10 minutes. Remove the skillet from the heat and set it aside for 20 minutes so the sauce can mellow and the sweetbread juices can settle.

4 When you are ready to serve the sweetbreads, briefly reheat them, if desired, and scatter the parsley over the top.

**NOTES:**

■ Here the butter helps emulsify the cooking liquids into a smooth, rich sauce in a way olive oil could not.

■ While dried bay leaves are a godsend for flavoring many a winter dish, for this one, with its exhalation of spring, only tender fresh leaves will do. Rather than using dried bay leaf, omit it and let the marjoram take the reins.

## ANOTHER TALL TOQUE TALE

While one story claims a French origin for the tall white hat that chefs traditionally wear, another legend gives the hat a Greek derivation. The cooks of the Byzantine empire were famous within that realm for their extraordinary talent with food, but they were no fighters—they hadn't the heart; they were as much lambs as the ones they cooked.

As the Ottomans approached and Constantinople was about to fall, the chefs, like many, fled. They took to the hills and hid out in monasteries, particularly one large one near Mount Athos. They were happy to bestow their talents on the holy monks, but in due time their clothes wore out. They had no choice but to wear the same clothes as their hosts, black garb and tall black hats. As a result they were constantly taken for monks, not cooks, yet they were barred from offering prayers, save those said over a perfect stewed hare or some such. Besides, though it was sinfully prideful, they missed their old notoriety and distinction. Finally they went to the abbot and asked if they could wear the same clothes as the monks, but in white, not black. The wish was granted. The tailors sewed tall white hats, and chefs ever after have been wearing them with great distinction.

*A Greek Orthodox priest wearing the tall black hat that may have inspired the tall, white chef's hat.*

# grilled marinated goat

## WITH LEMON, DILL, AND OREGANO

### SERVES 6 TO 10

WITH THEIR APPETITE FOR A HUGE RANGE OF FOOD AND NEED FOR LITTLE WATER, GOATS ARE A NATURAL FOR GREECE, A LAND OF THIN AND WEEDY GROUND COVER AND RIVERLESS TERRAIN.

From the earliest days, Greece's poor farmers recognized the virtue of the wily and tenacious goat. Of course it is the goat's milk that is most important—the cheese made over many months offers more food for family consumption than does the meat of one kid. To this day in rural Greece almost every industrious homemaker keeps a goat or two. Every day she makes farmer's cheese, *mizithra*, or *hlorou*. Still, every spring that homemaker has a kid goat or two to provide a festive dinner.

Goat is moist, unexpectedly delicate, silken, yet rich, yielding to stewing, grilling, roasting, and a symphony of seasonings. Many Greeks prefer goat meat to lamb, and I join in the chorus. If you agree, you can substitute it as the meat in any of the lamb recipes.

*1 kid goat (6 to 7 pounds), quartered (see Note)*
*12 cloves garlic, coarsely chopped*
*1 cup coarsely chopped fresh dill*
*1/4 cup whole fresh oregano leaves*
*2 teaspoons salt*
*1 teaspoon freshly ground black pepper*
*1/2 cup fresh lemon juice*
*1 1/2 cups dry red wine*
*1 cup olive oil*

1 Place all the ingredients in a nonreactive pan or baking dish that is large enough to hold the goat pieces in one layer. Turn to coat, cover, and marinate in the refrigerator for 12 to 30 hours.

2 Heat a grill to medium. Lift the goat out of the marinade, place the pieces on the grill rack, and cook for 20 minutes. Turn the pieces over and cook until medium-rare to medium, 15 to 20 minutes. Remove the meat from the grill and let rest for 15 minutes for the juices to settle. Carve the goat, arrange the pieces on a platter, and serve.

**NOTE:** Any butcher who caters to a Greek, Italian, Caribbean, or Mexican clientele knows how to quarter a goat and has the tools to make it easy. Just ask.

## GETTING ONE'S GOAT

Goats don't recognize private ownership and boundaries. Animals feeding off someone else's field caused fights in ancient Greece as they do today. In Eupolis's comedy *The Goats*, talking billy goats state:

"On evergreen, oak and fir we feed,
    all sorts and conditions of trees,
Nibbling off the soft young green
    of these, and of these, and of these;
Olives tame and olives wild
    are theirs and thine and mine . . ."

# roasted goat

## WITH MOUNTAIN HERBS AND POTATOES

### SERVES 6

GOAT MEAT SEEMS TO BE INNATELY ENHANCED BY HERBS, PERHAPS BECAUSE—AT LEAST IN GREECE—THE NIMBLE CREATURES NIBBLE ON OREGANO, MARJORAM, SAVORY, PURSLANE, TURNIP, CHICORY, RUE, ANISE, FENNEL, CRESS, AND SOME BULBS TO BOOT. IT FOLLOWS THAT GOAT MARRIES WELL WITH HERBS WHEN IT IS COOKED. WHILE THE USUAL DISH OF MEAT AND POTATOES MAY SEEM PLAIN, WITH GOAT, THE SAVOR IT PROVIDES IS NOT.

1 kid goat hindquarter (leg and
    loin section, 3 to 3 1/2 pounds)
6 cloves garlic, slivered
2 tablespoons chopped fresh
    thyme leaves, or 2 teaspoons
    dried
2 large bay leaves, crumbled
2 teaspoons hot paprika
1 teaspoon salt
1/2 teaspoon freshly ground black
    pepper
1/4 cup red wine vinegar
1/2 cup olive oil
3/4 cup dry white wine
4 large baking potatoes,
    peeled and sliced into
    1/4-inch-thick rounds

1 Cut the goat hindquarter in half at the joint between the top of the leg and bottom of the loin section. Make slits in the meat with a paring knife and insert the garlic slivers. In a small bowl, mix together the thyme, bay leaves, paprika, salt, and pepper. Rub this mixture all over the goat meat. Place the goat in a large, nonreactive dish or in a plastic bag, pour the vinegar and 1/4 cup of the oil over it, and turn to coat. Cover (or seal the bag) and set aside in the refrigerator for at least 4 hours or as long as overnight, turning it once or twice. Bring to room temperature before cooking.

2 Preheat the oven to 400°F.

3 Heat the remaining 1/4 cup oil in a large flameproof roasting pan over medium-high heat. Add the goat pieces and brown on both sides, about 8 minutes. Add the wine and tuck the potatoes around the goat pieces. Cover and roast in the oven until the meat shreds easily, 45 to 50 minutes. Remove from the oven and allow the meat to rest for 10 minutes for the juices to settle.

4 To serve, carve the goat and arrange the slices on a platter. Place the potatoes around the meat, and spoon the sauce over all.

## A CAPRA-ICIOUS ETYMOLOGY

It's odd that the word "goat" is hidden within one of the unhappiest words in English: "tragedy." *Tragos* means "male goat." *Ado* means "to sing," or "a song." So tragedy, in essence, means a song sung to a goat. One wonders: Did the lonely goatherd sing out his laments to his favorite goat, or did he lament that one of his herd became a stew? The word *tragos* is also possibly the root of the word *trahana*, Greece's sour milk noodles, and in keeping, the noodles are most often made with goat's milk or yogurt. *Tragos* in ancient Greek also meant "spelt," a common coarse grain.

# AN EASTER JOURNEY ON THE SEA

EVERYONE WHO HAS LIVED IN A SMALL GREEK VILLAGE HAS A FAVORITE GOAT STORY. CERTAINLY I HAVE. THE TIME WAS ALMOST EASTER AND I HAD GONE TO VISIT A FRIEND ON THE REMOTE ISLAND OF ANAFI, WHOSE NAME MEANS "THE LIT UP," BECAUSE IT IS THE ISLAND APOLLO ILLUMINATED TO HELP JASON AND THE ARGONAUTS FIND A HARBOR WHEN DARKNESS ENGULFED THEM. HAVING HAD A NICE STAY, I NEEDED TO GET BACK TO SANTORINI, BUT IN THOSE DAYS THE SOUTHERN CYCLADES HAD ONLY ONE CONNECTING BOAT, WHICH TRAVELED AROUND THE ISLANDS FOR ONE WEEK IN ONE DIRECTION, STOPPING AT SANTORINI FIRST AND THEN ANAFI, AND THE NEXT WEEK IN THE OTHER DIRECTION, STOPPING AT ANAFI FIRST AND THEN SANTORINI.

## A *KAIKI* FULL OF GOATS

The week I needed to return, the boat was going the wrong way. Luckily, as so often happens in Greece, the fates provided an unexpected solution. A butcher had traveled over from the island of Ios to buy goats on Anafi for Easter. He had engaged a wide-

*Men in traditional* fustanella *skirts dance in celebration of Easter.*

bottomed little Aegean boat, a *kaiki*, to take him back, and the captain was happy to take me along. From Ios I could catch the boat on that week's circuit to Santorini. It was

late afternoon when we boarded—150 goats, 3 calves, 1 cow, the butcher, his brother, the captain, one assistant, and me. The number of animals was such that there was not a speck of room for me, so I curled up in a coil of rope with a kid goat on my lap. So weighty was the cargo that scarcely an inch of the *kaiki*'s deck rose above seawater. When everyone and everything was on—including the cow, loaded by a makeshift crane of rope and a canvas sling—off we went.

## CELESTIAL NAVIGATION

The journey took all night. The night was moonless, the sea a vast, black, churning abyss. The Milky Way was infinite and splendid, splashed across the sky. All the captain had to aim us through the ebony depths was a sextant. He would set it, maneuver it, turn the wheel, and plow assuredly onward. The butcher and his brother were wretchedly ill. I came precariously close, saved by the stability of my rope coil. The goats bleated, and skidded and peed throughout the entire journey. About an hour before dawn, the clustered lights of Ios harbor suddenly appeared. Soon we pulled next to a dock, where men affixed the *kaiki* to the pier, all the while making hungry comments about the cargo. A few hours later, the steamer to Santorini pulled in and I boarded.

Never before had I really comprehended how huge the universe was, nor how deep, dark, cold, awesome, and forebidding the sea. I had renewed respect for those who plied it, especially those who for millennia steered using only celestial navigation. All this from one humbling night in the midst of a mass of goats on their way to becoming Easter dinner.

# almost classic pork and celery stew

**SERVES 6**

WHILE THE ANCIENT GREEKS APPARENTLY RELISHED PORK AND DEVOURED A GOOD DEAL OF IT, ONLY OCCASIONALLY ARE PIGS RAISED AND THEIR MEAT SERVED IN MODERN GREECE. RECIPES USING PORK ARE FEW AND FAR BETWEEN. WHEN PORK IS COOKED, IT IS USUALLY PREPARED IN A RATHER STANDARD FASHION, SIMMERED WITH WINE AND HERBS OR GRILLED ON SKEWERS. THERE IS, THOUGH, ONE CLASSIC GREEK PORK DISH: PORK STEWED WITH CELERY OR ENDIVE. THE RECIPE HERE IS A TAKE ON THAT CLASSIC. TRADITIONALLY THE DISH CALLS FOR *AVGOLEMONO* SAUCE, BUT HERE THAT HEAVY BLANKET IS OMITTED AND REPLACED WITH A TANGY MIX OF CAPERS AND MUSTARD.

*1 tablespoon olive oil*

*2 3/4 pounds boneless pork shoulder (pork butt or Boston butt), trimmed and cut into 1-inch chunks*

*Salt and freshly ground black pepper*

*8 ounces (6 to 8 large) shallots, sliced into 1/4-inch-thick rounds*

*2 cups water*

*1 teaspoon dry mustard*

*1/4 cup chopped fresh celery leaves*

*8 ribs celery, trimmed and cut into 1 1/2-inch lengths*

*2 tablespoons capers, drained*

*2 tablespoons chopped fresh flat-leaf parsley*

1 Heat the oil in a large non-reactive pot over medium-high heat. When it is hot, add as many pieces of pork as will fit in one uncrowded layer, and season them lightly with salt and pepper. Cook, turning, until browned all over, about 4 minutes. Transfer the meat to a plate and repeat with another batch until all the pieces are browned.

2 Add the shallots to the pot and stir to mix. Add the water

and stir to deglaze the bottom. Add the mustard and celery leaves, along with the pork and any collected juices. Bring to a boil, cover, reduce the heat, and simmer gently until the meat is almost fork-tender, 1 hour.

3 Stir in the celery and capers and continue to simmer, covered, 50 minutes more. Remove the pot from the heat and let the stew rest for 10 minutes. Sprinkle the parsley over the top and serve.

**NOTE:** For a classic pork and celery stew, when the stew is done, pour off the liquid and make *Avgolemono* Sauce (page 457) with it. Stir the sauce back into the stew just before serving.

# pork stew

## WITH OLIVES, ANCHOVIES, CILANTRO, AND WHITE BEANS

### SERVES 6

G REECE'S PANTRY OFFERS A WIDE ARRAY OF INGREDIENTS THAT CAN MAKE PORK STAND OUT. WHEN OLIVES AND ANCHOVIES JOIN WITH THE MEAT, THEY ADD THE KICK THAT PORK SOMETIMES CALLS FOR.

1 tablespoon olive oil
3 pounds boneless pork shoulder
    (pork butt or Boston butt),
    trimmed and cut into 1¹/₂-inch
    chunks
Salt and freshly ground black pepper
1 cup dry red wine
6 anchovy fillets, coarsely chopped
6 cloves garlic, coarsely chopped
¹/₂ teaspoon fresh thyme leaves,
    or ¹/₄ teaspoon dried
2 cups water
18 Kalamata olives
¹/₂ cup Wilted Cilantro Topping
    (page 481)
4 cups cooked Big Beans (page 208)
    or other white beans

1 Heat the oil in a large non-reactive pot over medium-high heat. When it is hot, add as many pieces of pork as will fit in one uncrowded layer, and season them lightly with salt and pepper.

Cook, turning, until browned all over, about 4 minutes. Transfer the meat to a plate and repeat with another batch until all the pieces are browned.

## FOOD FOR THOUGHT

A esop, the Greek slave and teacher who wrote the fables—as famous and moral today as they were almost three millennia ago—was asked by his master Xanthos to go to the market and buy food for a dinner party Xanthos was giving that night. The guests were all philosophers. Aesop, wanting to please his master and help him impress his guests, chose the tongues of sacrificed pigs. The guests were euphoric over the choice and complimented Xanthos, saying, "Congratulations, Xanthos. You have given us a meal full of philosophy."

2 Add the wine to the pot and stir to deglaze the bottom. Add the anchovies, garlic, thyme, and water. Add the meat and any collected juices. Bring to a boil, cover, reduce the heat, and simmer gently for 1 hour. Set the cover ajar and continue simmering, partially covered, for 20 minutes. Stir in the olives and cook until the meat is fork-tender, another 30 minutes.

3 Remove the pot from the heat and carefully pour the liquid into a bowl. Allow it to rest for 10 minutes, then spoon the fat off the top and pour the juices back into the pot. To serve, arrange the cilantro sprigs over the top, and serve accompanied by the beans.

**NOTE:** If you have the bone from a pork shoulder roast, include it for extra flavor.

**VARIATION:**

A *Halkidiki* Version: Substitute ¼ cup capers or 12 lightly crushed juniper berries for the olives.

## ARCADIA

The term "arcadian" has became synonymous with images of petticoated shepherdesses bearing crooked staffs, with very, very white sheep frolicking by the riverside, with lush green glades and simple, happy folk playing pipes of Pan. However, the real Arcadia, while stunningly lovely, is not one bit like the fantasy of it. Yet the romanticized vision of the supposed Arcadia held such allure for eighteenth-century Europeans that people dressed in shepherds' costume, tripped about the woods on idylls, and wrote odes about rustic virtue.

Arcadia, perched as it is in the heart and at the height of the Peloponnesos, is brown, dry, and covered with scree. Only a rare tree or bush breaks through; thistles are more common. What few rivers run give scant water. One can see how an impish, surefooted, half-goat god who played a shepherd's pipe became the beloved deity of the region.

Arcadia hasn't even been particularly peaceful. Although its remote mountains remained largely untouched in ancient battles (despite the nearby presence of the martial Spartans), at the start of the Greek war of independence in 1821, General Kolokotronis massacred ten thousand Turkish inhabitants when he liberated Tripolis, Arcadia's capital. The Turks retaliated when they retook the city three years later; and when they withdrew a hundred years later, they burned the city down.

There are, however, plenty of goats in Arcadia. During my travels—on hardly discernible dirt roads—I passed through medieval villages still crowned with Frankish castles and bestudded with Byzantine churches. I saw the most remote of Greece's ancient temples. One time I stopped in Andritsena at a square miraculously lined with shade trees, and went to a *taverna*. The worried owner shuffled up, mumbling, "Oh, no, a foreigner. I'm in trouble. What to say. What to say?" Obviously afraid we could never communicate, he was overjoyed when I spoke to him in Greek. In five minutes there appeared on the table a glass of retsina, a plate of appetite-tingling salty cheese, and shortly after, a big dish of roasted goat. "This is Arcadian," he pronounced over it, as if giving a blessing. "Because of the rocks and the mountain air, our food is the most flavorful in Greece." Pan could not have produced better.

# homemade pork and veal sausage

## WITH ORANGE, CORIANDER, AND RED PEPPER

### LOUKANIKA

**MAKES EIGHT TO TEN
3-INCH SAUSAGE LINKS OR PATTIES**

GREEK CUISINE OFFERS ONE UNIQUE AND WONDERFUL PORK SAUSAGE, WHICH IS MADE FROM COAST TO COAST. IT IS A BLEND OF PORK AND BEEF—HERE VEAL—AND IS REDOLENT OF ORANGE. GREEK SAUSAGE IS EASY TO DUPLICATE IN THE HOME KITCHEN, ESPECIALLY IF YOU MAKE PATTIES RATHER THAN FILL SAUSAGE CASINGS. ALONG WITH THE ORANGE AND A SPRINKLING OF CRUSHED RED PEPPER, A DASH OF RETSINA ENLIVENS THE ALREADY AROMATIC SAUSAGE WITH THE ESSENCE OF PINE.

1 pound ground pork

8 ounces ground veal

1 clove garlic, minced or pressed

1 teaspoon finely chopped
    orange zest

1/2 teaspoon ground coriander

1 teaspoon crushed red
    pepper flakes

1 teaspoon salt

1/2 teaspoon freshly ground
    black pepper

1/3 cup retsina wine

Pork casings, well rinsed, or caul
    (veil) fat (optional)

Olive oil, for cooking the sausages

1 Place all the ingredients except the casings and oil in a medium-size bowl and mix well.

## MENU
### OTHER DISHES FOR THE TABLE

CRUSTY BREAD, OLIVES,
AND CHEESE

RUSSIAN SALAD
WITH CAPER MAYONNAISE
page 36

YELLOW SPLIT PEA SOUP,
WITH PICKLED RED ONIONS
pages 159 and 75

ZUCCHINI FRITTERS
Box, page 297

BELL PEPPERS STUFFED
WITH RICE AND ALMOND
STUFFING
page 301

FRESH FRUIT TO FINISH

2 *To form sausages:* If using the casings, use a sausage stuffer, a pastry bag fitted with a large tip, or a large funnel to fill them with the meat mixture; twist at 3-inch intervals to make individual sausages. Alternatively, cut 4-inch squares of caul fat and wrap them around 1/3-cup portions of the meat mixture; press to flatten to about 3/4 inch thick.

*To form patties:* Pat 1/3-cup portions of the mixture into individual patties.

Set the sausages or patties aside in the refrigerator, well wrapped, for several hours or up to 5 days.

3 When you are ready to cook the sausage, lightly oil a heavy skillet and place it over medium heat. When the oil is hot, add the sausages or patties and sauté, turning once, until cooked through but still moist, about 20 minutes. Serve them right away.

**NOTES:**

■ Fresh sausages develop more flavor if allowed to rest in the refrigerator for at least several hours before cooking.

■ The sausages may also be grilled on a medium-hot grill.

*The proprietors of Restaurant Bella Vista wait out the pause between midday dinner and evening supper.*

## PASTOURMAS

T hough Greeks have little in the tradition of preserved meats of their own, they have one they hold dear—a very garlicky preserved beef called *pastourmas*, which they adopted from the Koutsovlachs. Romanian-speaking Koutsovlachs came to Thessaly in the eleventh century. They were mainly sheep and goat herders, though many of them lived in settled villages. Occasionally they kept cattle, and when they slaughtered an animal as large and as scarce as a cow, they sought to keep all its precious bounty. Hence their hot, spicy preserved *pastourmas*.

*Pastourmas* looks like a side of unsliced bacon covered with red pepper. It is sliced and eaten cold or quickly fried.

# WHO WERE THE FIRST GREEKS?

STARTING SOMETIME AROUND 4000 B.C.E. AND OVER THE COURSE OF 3,500 YEARS, PEOPLE WHO SPOKE A NUMBER OF RELATED LANGUAGES THAT WE HAVE COME TO CALL INDO-EUROPEAN STRAGGLED FORTH FROM A HOMELAND THAT PROBABLY LAY ON THE STEPPE BETWEEN THE CASPIAN SEA AND URAL MONTAINS.

Among the first to wander out were those who spoke a form of early Greek. They traveled south and west, fanning out until they claimed parts of what is now western Turkey and the rocky-shored and many-islanded land a bit beyond, Greece.

That they overran a territory already occupied by other people is clear. They had reached as far south as Crete by about 3000 B.C.E., as evidenced by thousands of Greek-inscribed clay tablets, yet many of their words for foods growing in that land are not of Greek origin; nor are the names of many of their gods and heroes (Odysseus, Achilles, Theseus, Athena, Hera, Aphrodite, Hermes); nor are many of their place names (Corinth, Knossos, Samos, even Olympus). All these were borrowed from those who lived in the land before.

What were they like, these invaders? And how did they come to prevail?

## CATTLE AND SHEEP

Their early language indicates that they came from a land of mountains and plains, rivers and lakes. They had scant knowledge of the sea. They knew seasons, especially winter. They buried their dead with care. They made battle axes and corded pottery. But most important of all, they possessed three items of crucial value.

They had cattle. Their vocabulary concerning cows was large and detailed: They had words for cow, ox, and steer, along with meat, marrow, and herd. They must have used their oxen for traction, for they had a word for yoke. They also had sheep—they wove with sheep's wool, and they probably had goats and pigs. But it was cattle that they prized. Their word for "sacrifice" implies that the honored victim was an ox.

## A CRUCIAL BREED

They also possessed another animal, perhaps even more crucial: the horse. Among their artifacts are reins and bits. Among their legends are many stories of horses, and the horses are imbued with special powers. The horses have names, wings, and magical abilities. The keeping of a horse, the riding of a horse, winning contests with a horse, all were important, and horses were so revered that many early Greek names incorporate *(h)ippos*, the word for horse—for example, Hippolyta, queen of the Amazons.

To go with the horses, the invaders had yet another signifi-cant item: They had wheeled vehicles—carts, wagons, and chariots. It is quite possible that it was the combination of the domestic horse and the wheeled vehicle that allowed the Indo-Europeans to expand over so much territory. With this vastly superior technology, for the first time in human history a people could move en masse. Their vehi-cles were probably pulled both by oxen and by horses.

## WANDERERS AND WARRIORS

Thus it seems the early Greeks arrived as wander-ing herders—mounted, driving cattle, pulling wagons—from somewhere in the wintery north. It's not that these herder-invaders didn't practice agriculture—they did. They had a word for field: *agros,* root of our "agriculture." They knew the plough and sickle. But growing foods and the settled life didn't interest them at first. Keeping livestock was far more attractive. In their early language, all types of grains are lumped in one term. Millet, bar-ley, wheat? Compared to meat, they were an undifferentiated and apparently uninteresting muddle.

Rovers they were. The term has a second meaning, one that also applies to the early Greeks, and that is "warrior." The arriving Greeks had the bow, bowstring, and arrow. Motifs in ancient lore speak of the migrating Greeks not only as cattle keepers but also as scrappers and battlers. Their sagas exalt conquests, sieges, and plundering. They calculated wealth in terms of the number of animals they held, which spurred them into raiding the herds of others. We read in the *Iliad:* "We brought back much booty from the plain, driving it in front of us: fifty herds of cattle, as many flocks of sheep, as many herds of swine, as many wide-roaming goats, one hundred fifty bay horses, all mares, and many with their foals under them." The heroes of their tales are, to say the least, bellicose.

*Arriving with wheeled vehicles and horses, the bands of roaming warriors who were to become the Greeks came from the north.*

*A modern-day Greek still harvests his grain with a sickle.*

became Zeus's sisters, wives, and daughters. The most stalwart of them, Athena, was said to have sprung full-grown from Zeus's head.

## THE FIRST SETTLEMENTS

At first the Greek terms for "house" and "small settlement" seem to be the same, *polis*. It meant a fortified enclosure, safely placed on a high spot or with a high wall, an *acro-polis*. Later the term came to mean "city." Symbols give hint to three social classes living in these fortresses: leader-priests, warring-military, and herder-cultivators. Some Greek myths indicate that the chiefs and warriors conquered the cultivators, giving credence to the theory that the Greeks over-whelmed an already settled people. Other tales indicate that their advance was slow, that they were not instantly successful. The people who lived on the land before them had their own superior technology: metallurgy. The story of Theseus seems to say that the early Greeks paid homage to the people living on Crete and that they were required to send them payment of gifts, goods, and possibly children.

They started to grow food. Still, for a long while one of their

In time the bands of roving Greeks settled down, but the warrior culture continued. Settlements were independent states ruled by powerful commanders who enriched themselves by conducting raiding expeditions near and far. The inhabitants of each city shared a sort of brotherhood. Early Greek edifices have huge meeting rooms with ceremonial hearths and thrones, indicating large councils. Belonging to the tribe meant so much that the Greek word, ancient and mod-ern, for "freedom," *eleutheros,* comes from the word for "people" or "clan," *laos*. Freedom, in short, came from belonging.

## A PATRIARCHAL PEOPLE

Men ruled. The early Greeks were patriarchal, with the head of the family and tribe being the ranking male. Who and what a man was, was clarified by the recitation of his father's and his father's father's names. It is Oedipus, son of Laius; Telemachos, son of Odysseus, son of Laertes. The primary god the early Greeks worshipped was also male, a powerful father god. He was called "Zeus the father," *Zeu-patera*, or as the Romans transliterated it, "Ju-piter." This stern deity was a sky god, a "striker," likened to lightning and with thunderbolts at his command. In the original home-land of the Greeks, he had probably been a god of weather. As the Greeks moved into their new land and took over, their father god overrode a veritable pantheon of former deities, among whom were some power-ful goddesses. In resolution, they most important religious activities remained the burnt offering of their favored food, meat. To augment the burnt offering, the Greeks included in their supplication the first drops of wine, a drink they had learned about as they moved south.

Once settled, the Greek-speaking people flourished. They took up the cultivation of barley, wheat, pulses, and vegetables. They grew grapes and pressed wine. When a cataclysm destroyed most of the Minoan cities, Greeks repopulated them, and soon after that Greek towns experienced a great burst of development. Mycenae rose as a mighty citadel, as did Argos, Corinth, and many others. Athens appeared; then as the Dorian Greeks arrived, Sparta. The various Greek-speaking groups remained disunited for many centuries, continuing to attack one another with ferocity. Troy, after all, was a Greek-speaking city.

Nonetheless, these people, speakers of this complex tongue, went on to develop a culture that is the emblem of Western civilization. They wrote, philosophized, and advanced physics, mathematics, architecture, and art. One of their later kings

*The Parthenon, built by the early Greeks as a tribute to Athena.*

established a great empire extending from northern Greece to Egypt and India. They introduced their alphabet to other Indo-Europeans who had similarly migrated into Italy. Centuries later, descendants of those people, the Romans, turned about and invaded them.

## CONTINUITY AMID CHANGE

Today Greeks continue to live on the land they settled. Some still live in the land they first came from, their original Ural, or Pontian, homeland. They have suffered conquest by other Indo-Europeans—the Latin-speaking Romans, the Germanics, the Slavs, all of whom came in much the same manner as the Greeks themselves had. They fell to the conquests of non-Indo-European people also. Yet they still speak Greek and still hold firm to the country they first viewed as splendid. They raise cattle, plow the ground, write, philosophize, worship, and cook.

. . . these people . . . went on to develop a culture that is the emblem of Western civilization.

# birds
# FROM THE COOP

Birds—LARGE ONES, SMALL ONES, EBONY ONES, DUN ONES, ONES WITH DAZZLING PLUMAGE—HAVE FLOWN THROUGH THE VIBRANT GREEK SKIES AND SPARKLED ON GREEK SALVERS SINCE ANCIENT DAYS. HOMER WAS SO DELIGHTED WHEN HE WAS GIVEN A BRACE OF FAT THRUSHES TO GRACE HIS ROASTING SPIT THAT HE COMPOSED A POEM, "EPIKICHLIDES," ABOUT THEM. ARISTOTLE WAXED EXUBERANT OVER MEALS OF CRANE,

*Beneath her fostering wing, the hen defends*

*Her darling offspring, while the snow descends;*

*And through the winter's day unmoved defies*

*The chilling fleeces and inclement skies;*

*Till vanquished by the cold and piercing blast;*

*True to her charge she perishes at last.*

—FROM AN ANCIENT GREEK EPIGRAM

swan, francolin (a relative of the pheasant), and peacock. He wrote of barnyard fowls and pigeons domesticated for the table. Ancient Greeks, particularly on the island of Samos, raised peacocks and peahens to sup upon, although keeping them was so expensive that Anaxandrides, clearly putting life's true essentials above alimentary frivolity, asked, "Why raise peacocks when, for the price of keeping them, one could have two statues?"

To this day Greeks savor a bevy of birds. Where ponds allow, they keep geese and ducks. They relish turkey, which for some reason they call "French chicken,"

so much so that in northern towns the gobbler has become their traditional holiday fare, especially for Christmas dinner.

Far and away, the bird consumed beyond all others is the common chicken. Chickens well outnumber people in villages across Greece. Almost every rural homemaker has a coop from which she gathers eggs and, when their laying fails them, selects a hen for a family repast. Chickens are

given as gifts for favors done and cooked into lush ragouts for guests. They are roasted and grilled, boiled, and turned into soups, often with an embellishment of their own eggs.

The small household chicken flocks cannot possibly meet the demand, so a large chicken industry has arisen. As a consequence chickens are available in markets, shops selling spit-roasted birds have appeared everywhere, and the imaginative Greek cook has at hand the bird for any flight of fancy.

*A baking pan brimming with chicken and potatoes is shuffled into a hot beehive oven.*

# chicken neo-avgolemono

**SERVES 4**

AT EIGHTEEN, KOKO SPEAKS ENGLISH AND HAS A LITTLE HOUSE AND A LITTLE CAR. SHE HAS A CAREER AT A HOTEL, YET HER PROUDEST POSSESSION IS HER FLOCK OF CHICKENS. AS THE CARETAKER OF HER WIDOWED FATHER, SHE DEEMS HERSELF A HOMEMAKER AND SHE WANTS BOTH THE DAILY EGGS AND THE OCCASIONAL CHICKEN DINNER. IT'S THAT DINNER THAT WE CONSULTED ABOUT. KOKO, LIKE ALL GREEKS, LOVES *AVGOLEMONO* SAUCE (PAGE 457), BUT FINDS IT A BIT TOO "SAUCY." COULD WE COME UP WITH A LIGHTER, MORE MODERN VERSION WITH THE SAME SUNNY ELEMENTS—A "NEO"-*AVGOLEMONO*?

## A DASH OF LEMON ON THE CHICKEN

Many Greek cooks rub a little lemon juice all over a chicken before cooking it. The fragrance on the chicken skin is fresh, and the slight zing imparted to any dish is tangy and typically Hellenic. I don't add that step in all of the chicken recipes here, but you easily can: Place about 1 tablespoon fresh lemon juice in a shallow bowl and toss the chicken pieces in it. Set the pieces aside while you prepare the other ingredients, or refrigerate them until ready to use.

We could and we did. The answer is a new light but lustrous version of the classic. Here the chicken is cooked in a lemony mixture, then topped with a wine-doused sauce and a garnish of hard-cooked egg. All the flavors are there, but in a new and buoyant form.

2 tablespoons olive oil
1 large chicken (about 4 pounds), rinsed, patted dry, and cut into pieces
2 tablespoons fresh lemon juice
2 shallots, finely sliced into rings
1/4 teaspoon chopped fresh rosemary needles, or a pinch of dried
1/2 teaspoon salt
1/4 teaspoon freshly ground black pepper
1/3 cup dry white wine
1 tablespoon finely chopped lemon zest
1 tablespoon chopped fresh mint leaves
1 large hard-cooked egg, chopped

1 Heat the oil in a large non-reactive skillet over medium-high heat. When it is hot, add the chicken pieces and sauté until browned all over, about 6 minutes.

2 Add the lemon juice, shallots, rosemary, and salt and pepper and stir to mix. Reduce the heat to medium and cook, turning, until the chicken is cooked through but still moist, about 20 minutes.

3 Transfer the chicken pieces to a platter and set it aside in a warm place. Add the wine to the skillet and bring it to a vigorous boil over high heat. Stir in the zest and mint and remove the skillet from the heat. Spoon the sauce over the chicken and garnish with the chopped egg. Serve right away.

# CHICKEN AND THE CHANGING SQUARES OF ATHENS

**W**ITHIN THE CORE OF SPRAWLING ATHENS, BETWEEN GREAT AVENUES AND NARROW ALLEYS, BESIDE ANCIENT RUINS AND AROUND STATUES OF MODERN HEROES, BY FANCY BOUTIQUES AND HUGE GOVERNMENT EDIFICES, LIE MANY, MANY SQUARES.

Few are actually square—rather they are triangles, circles, and trapezoids, formed, it seems, almost haphazardly where winding, unplanned streets intersected. Some are major and monumental—Omonia, Syntagma, Atikis, Kaningos, Vathis, Karaiskaki. Some were perhaps originally the center of what was once a separate village until the city swallowed them, or are simply the commercial nubs that spring up in little neighborhoods, like Egyptou, Kiriakou, Varnava. Each has a distinct personality, although over the past few years the character of many has abruptly evolved, and food is part of the reason.

## THE CHARACTER OF THE SQUARE

Take Kolonaki Square. Tranquil, shady Kolonaki sits at the center of one of the posher areas of the city. Until recently it was a square where wealthy older gentlemen paused to have a smoke and watch attractive, impeccably dressed women emerge from the shops of Parisian designers. Now throngs of affluent young mob the square day and night, spending hours in chat and flirtation, as if work were the furthest matter from their minds.

Or take Exarchia Square. Ten years ago a quiet neighborhood hub with kiosks, dry cleaners, a clock shop—it was very much a local residents' convenience center. Now students of a political bent hang out there. The walls of the surrounding buildings sport anarchist signs and the milling clientele dress in universal anti-fashion.

## HOME-RANGE CHICKENS

**I**n rural Greece the chickens are home-raised and if not exactly free-range, at least free to range in their pen and coop. They are plucked by hand after a quick dousing in boiling water (never soaked in ice water and left to drain as are American supermarket chickens). Their flavor is magnificent. True, industrially raised chickens are now available, and every Greek grocer has a stock of frozen ones. Still, for the best flavor in any country, I recommend organic, free-range, or kosher chicken.

Or Monastiraki Square. Once it was the crumbling locus of the ragtag. It contained the old clothes market and used pots and pans trade. Workers from nearby tool and welding shops bustled through on their way to the subway or set aside their blowtorches to visit the surrounding *gyro* vendors for a bite to eat. Today Monastiraki boasts hundreds of tourist venues, all plying much the same ware. More sneakers than work boots stroll through.

## ENTER ROTISSERIE CHICKEN

Yet all the squares of Athens have one change in common, a change I must admit I readily enjoy. Next to the pricy outdoor cafés of Kolonaki sit several stands selling Athens's new version of fast food: rotisserie chicken. Dotted about Exarchia, similar stands offer up inexpensive roasted drumsticks with a few fried potatoes thrown in for the starving students. Down at Monastiraki, chicken *gyros* spin next to the traditional beef and lamb. Other versions of chicken spin, turn, and sizzle in Omonia, Atikis, Vathis.

Chicken has come to roost in the squares of Athens as if the plazas were so many coops. The backyard fowl is now a paramount food, a fast food, an inexpensive food. It is enjoyed by rich and poor, foreign and local alike, and by harried cooks and anthropologists.

# sautéed chicken

## WITH SHALLOTS, TOMATOES, CAPERS, AND SAGE

### SERVES 4

THOUGH BYZANTINE GREEKS ENJOYED A BIRD SIMMERED IN A PUNGENT, VINEGARY, AND OFTEN FISHY SAUCE, MODERN GREEK COOKING DRIFTED AWAY FROM SUCH PUCKERY INGREDIENTS TOWARD MANY VARIATIONS ON TOMATO SAUCES. NONETHELESS, THE INGREDIENTS USED BY THE EMPIRE'S COOKS ARE STILL FOUND IN EVERY KITCHEN. HERE THEY ARE COMBINED ONCE AGAIN, WITH SALTY CAPERS STANDING FOR THE SALTY FISH SAUCE. THE RESULT IS SUBTLY BYZANTINE, AND DEFINITELY TEMPTING.

1/4 cup olive oil
1 chicken (about 3 1/2 pounds),
    rinsed, patted dry, and
    cut into pieces
8 medium or 4 large shallots,
    halved if large
1/3 cup dry red wine
1/3 cup balsamic vinegar
3 medium tomatoes, coarsely
    chopped
1/4 cup capers, drained
1 teaspoon chopped fresh sage leaves,
    or 1/2 teaspoon dried
3/4 teaspoon salt
1/2 teaspoon freshly ground
    black pepper

1 Heat the oil in large nonreactive skillet over medium-high heat. When it is hot, add the chicken and shallots. Cook, stirring and turning, until the chicken and shallots are browned, 10 minutes.

2 Add all the remaining ingredients and stir to mix. Bring to a boil, partially cover the skillet, reduce the heat, and cook over medium heat for 15 minutes. Turn the chicken pieces over, raise the heat, and continue to cook, uncovered, over medium-high heat until the chicken is tender and the liquid is thickened and sauce-like, 10 minutes. Serve right away.

## THE "DAY SOUNDER"

The image of a fighting cock on an Athenian drinking cup from about 450 B.C.E. tells us that the ancestors of the domestic chicken were present in ancient Greece, probably introduced from Persia. There is little indication, however, that raising chickens was of much importance, at least for the purpose of dining—no husbandry advice, no hints of preparations, no odes to the avian. Wild birds were probably so abundantly available for eating that chickens were raised more for sport than for supper. The cock, in fact, was considered a symbol of potency and power. It also had a certain practical value. Called *emerofonos*, or "day sounder," the rooster was lauded for knowing the difference between night and day and, at sunrise, awakening people to begin their day.

## THE "KAMINETO" WAY TO COOK

Only quite recently has almost every Greek kitchen acquired an electric range with its built-in oven. Before, the preferred way of preparing a chicken—by roasting—was saved for special company.

Roasting, you see, was difficult. It required gathering twigs and firing up the outdoor oven, which was always an effort. To cook a chicken (and anything else) in the kitchen, the household chef had either a single or double stovetoplike burner hooked to a bottle of gas, called a *petrogazi*, or more commonly, a single-burner contraption perched over a smaller bulb-shaped container of alcohol, called a *kamineto*, from the Italian for "chimney."

Most housewives usually had two such *kamineti*—it was the only way to cook in two vessels at the same time. The flames of these bizarre devices, which looked like miniature Eiffel Towers, burned so high and hot that any food quickly simmered and sizzled. Most rural Greek cooks still have one and still use it frequently. When only one dish needs to be heated or one guest must have the required cup of hospitality coffee, the device, now often battered almost beyond recognition, pops out from the cabinet.

When a chicken was cooked *kamineto*, it was almost always simmered in a sauce—in sweet spices *kapama*, in tomato *kokkinisto*, in walnut sauce *karydia*. These juicy chicken dishes come out swirling in a liquid rich in flavor, aromatic and warming. No dry fried chicken for me. Give me one that swims over a chimney.

# chicken baked in yogurt

## WITH RED ONION AND GRAPE LEAVES

### SERVES 6

IT SEEMS NO ONE IN THE WORLD CAN QUITE RESIST THE IDEA OF COATING CHICKEN IN SOMETHING CREAMY. THERE IS AMERICAN-AS-APPLE-PIE MILK GRAVY TO SPILL ONTO THOSE MASHED POTATOES, BELGIAN CREAMY CHICKEN STEWS, FRENCH CREAM-AND-BUTTER-BASED SAUCES SLATHERING THE BIRD.

In countries almost devoid of cream and even butter, Greek, Indian, and Persian cooks turned to yogurt instead. In Thessaloniki, yogurt is used in a silken, milky, yet tart sauce that tenderizes the bird beneath. There, turmeric, coriander, and cumin are a traditional part of the cooking vocabulary. Grape leaves from the nearby Halkidiki vineyards, an innovation here, add a sharp green bite to the yogurt's tang. To duplicate the treatment, use the thickest plain yogurt you can find.

1 cup plain yogurt, or Thickened Yogurt (page 471)
¼ cup chopped fresh mint leaves, or 1 tablespoon dried
1 bay leaf, finely chopped
2 teaspoons ground cumin
1 teaspoon ground coriander
½ teaspoon ground turmeric
1 teaspoon salt
1 teaspoon freshly ground white pepper
2 chickens (about 3 ½ pounds each), rinsed, patted dry, cut into pieces, and partially skinned (see Note)
1 large red onion, quartered and cut into ¼-inch-thick slices
6 large or 10 small grape leaves (see page 48), cut into 1-inch-wide shreds
2 teaspoons finely chopped lemon zest

1 Preheat the oven to 450°F.

2 Whisk the yogurt, mint, bay leaf, cumin, coriander, turmeric, salt, and white pepper together in a bowl.

3 Place the chicken pieces in one or two nonreactive baking dishes so they are tightly packed in a single layer. Add the onion, grape leaves, and the yogurt mixture, and turn to coat the chicken pieces. Cover with aluminum foil and bake until the liquid is bubbling and the chicken is almost tender, 40 minutes.

4 Remove the foil, stir gently, and continue baking, uncovered, until the chicken is very tender, 20 minutes. Sprinkle the zest over all, and serve right away.

**NOTE:** To skin a chicken partially, use your fingers to pull away whatever skin comes off easily and leave the rest.

## MENU

### OTHER DISHES FOR THE TABLE

CRUSTY BREAD, OLIVES, AND CHEESE

WINTER VEGETABLE SOUP WITH SAVORY
page 167

PLUMP BULGUR PILAF MADE WITH ROASTED TOMATO "PASTE"
pages 231 and 479

SANTORINI FAVA CROQUETTES SUSANNA-STYLE
page 292

FRESH FRUIT TO FINISH

## GREEK YOGURT

Greek culinary legend credits the rough-hewn Bulgars to the north with introducing to the Greek menu that luxuriously thick, milky, yet pungent balm we call yogurt. And maybe they did. But other people might have as well. Food clues point to central Asia as the place of origin. Food mythology, indeed, claims that yogurt developed when milk packed in the saddlebags of Genghis Khan's raiders jiggled and slowly cooked into a thick curd. From the Mongols, the Indians and then the Persians picked up the yen for yogurt. Turkic nomads from the Ural mountains adopted it next. They arrived in the Balkans not long after the various Slavic tribes, including the Bulgars, descended from the north. From there somebody brought the ambrosia to Greece.

Whoever brought it, the arrival of yogurt was a boon to sheep herders from the north on down to Crete. It is from those two areas that the best Greek yogurt still comes, for those are the realms of the sheep, and yogurt made from sheep's milk is the best and the thickest. I'll never forget the first time I saw "real" yogurt; that is, Cretan yogurt. I was sitting at an outdoor café in Athens near a *galaktopouleion*, a dairy store. A truck pulled up, and from the back the driver unloaded great round pans of stuff so thick, so creamy, that it looked like cheesecake. I had to know. A cake? A sweet? "Oh no," the driver answered, "this is Cretan yogurt. Get a knife and I'll cut you a slice." A knife? A slice? How do you slice yogurt? I tried it, with Hymettus honey. Rapture. I later sampled the yogurt of Thrace, Epiros, Macedonia, and the thinner sorts from other parts of Greece. Heaven, all of them.

How much is yogurt used in Greek cuisine? With honey it serves as a common breakfast. It moistens the batter of numerous cakes. With garlic, salt, and cucumber, it becomes *tzatziki*. It is doused on fruit and shaken in fruit shakes. It smoothes potatoes, tangs up meatballs, dresses salads, cools eggplant, fills cucumbers, pulls together pilafs, and serves as the base of sour noodles.

Fewer and fewer shepherds are tending woolly herds in Greece, and stiff-as-cheesecake yogurt is becoming harder to find. Still, canny dairy suppliers are making sure that the heavenly yogurt needed for sweets, meats, treats, and sauces stays available.

# chicken kapama

**SERVES 6 TO 8**

THE KAPAMA SAUCE THAT CREATES A SATINY BEEF STEW (PAGE 369) LENDS ITS ENCHANTING FLAVORS TO CHICKEN. NO RECIPE OF MINE IS BORROWED SO OFTEN, AND NO OTHER DINNER I COOK HAS SO MANY GUESTS ASKING FOR A REPEAT PERFORMANCE. SOME OF THE RECIPE BORROWERS HAVE REPLACED ONCE-FAVORED BARBECUE SAUCES WITH KAPAMA. OTHERS HAVE STREWED LEFTOVERS ON PIZZA CRUST. COFFEE, BRANDY, HONEY, CINNAMON, CLOVE, TOMATO, RED WINE—THE DISH TRULY SHIMMERS WITH AN AURORA OF FLAVOR. MAKE SURE YOU SERVE BREAD ALONGSIDE TO SOP UP THE SAUCE.

3 tablespoons olive oil
1 large chicken (4 to 5 pounds), rinsed, patted dry, and cut into pieces
1 large onion, quartered and thinly sliced
1 1/2 tablespoons tomato paste
1 1/2 cups dry red wine
3 medium tomatoes, coarsely chopped
3 tablespoons brandy
1/3 cup strong brewed coffee
3 tablespoons honey (see Note)
1 stick (2 inches) cinnamon, broken in half
3 whole cloves

2 bay leaves
1 teaspoon salt
1/2 teaspoon freshly ground black pepper
1 1/2 cups tender watercress or basil sprigs (optional)

## MENU
### OTHER DISHES FOR THE TABLE

CRUSTY BREAD, OLIVES, AND CHEESE

MUSSELS IN WHITE WINE WITH SHALLOTS AND BASIL
page 69

ZUCCHINI SALAD WITH ZUCCHINI FLOWERS
page 203

BLACK-EYED PEA SALAD WITH TOMATOES AND SHALLOTS
page 209

NEW POTATOES WITH MINT AND SPRING ONIONS
page 278

FRESH FRUIT TO FINISH

1 Heat the oil in a large non-reactive pot over medium-high heat. When it is hot, add as many chicken pieces as will fit in a single layer. Sauté until browned all over, about 5 minutes. Transfer the chicken pieces to a bowl and repeat with another batch until all the chicken is browned. Set the chicken aside.

2 Add the onion to the pot and stir over medium-high heat until well coated, about 1 minute. Stir in the tomato paste and wine and bring to a boil. Add all the remaining ingredients except the watercress. Add the chicken and any collected juices, and stir to mix. Bring to a boil, then reduce the heat to a simmer. Cover the pot and cook over medium-low heat until the chicken is tender and the liquid is reduced but not thick, 45 minutes to 1 hour.

3 Remove the cover and continue simmering until the meat is very tender and the liquid is thick and glossy, 35 to 40 minutes. Remove the pot from the heat and let the chicken rest for 10 minutes before serving.

4 Remove the cinnamon stick, cloves, and bay leaves, garnish with the watercress, if using, and serve right away.

**NOTE:** As with Beef *Kapama*, I sometimes substitute apricot preserves for all or part of the honey.

*A narrow road winds past a typical farm on Crete.*

## FOOD PHILANTHROPY

I n places where the food supply is a little precarious, a surfeit of provisions often becomes connected to respectability. I am reminded of a family I met on Anafi long before the island enjoyed electricity. To my surprise, the family boasted a gigantic refrigerator-freezer stuffed with supplies. Lacking current, they ran the big, boxy appliance off a generator driven by bottled gas. The device was the talk of the island's one and only town, and was treated something like one of the seven wonders of the world.

When I first lived on the islands, boats might not appear for weeks at a time, and tiny, scrappy, poor Anafi was visited only by a single, weekly, decrepit and unpredictable boat named the *Despina*. Yet one family, headed by a comely and efficient woman named Sofia, was never reduced to *Manestra* soup (page 153), as other island dwellers were. The refrigerator-freezer held lamb for simmering with rice or barley, Easter cookies waiting for their day, bread from the city, cheese pies, *dolmas*, and most of all, chickens.

Still, though the monster machine gave Sofia great prominence, her true status derived from her absolutely Greek hospitality. She began life poor (who on Anafi hadn't?) as an eloped bride, and she simply, unabashedly gave food away. The more she stored, the more she gave. *Manestra*-free and chicken-wealthy Sofia, so very Greek in her behavior, performed the alchemy of changing food into philanthropy.

# sesame-crusted roast chicken

## IN TAHINI AND CAPER SAUCE

### SERVES 4

IN GREECE SESAME, BOTH AS SEED AND IN TAHINI PASTE, HAS BEEN APPRECIATED THROUGH THE AGES, WHILE CAPERS ALWAYS SPARK UP A DISH. I ADMIT I HAVE NEVER SEEN SESAME-CRUSTED CHICKEN IN TAHINI AND CAPER SAUCE IN GREECE. THE DISH IS AN ORIGINAL, BUT THE ALLURING PREPARATION IS TOTALLY IN CHARACTER.

1 chicken (about 3 1/2 pounds), rinsed and patted dry inside and out
2 tablespoons sesame seeds
2 tablespoons fresh lemon juice
1 teaspoon olive oil
1 teaspoon salt
1/4 cup tahini (sesame paste)
2 tablespoons capers, drained

1 Preheat the oven to 450°F.

2 Stir the sesame seeds, lemon juice, oil, and salt together in a small bowl.

3 Place the chicken in a baking dish just large enough to hold it snugly. Rub the sesame seed mixture over the chicken, inside and out. Cover the dish, place it in the oven, and roast until the juices are no longer pink and the breast is beginning to turn golden, 55 minutes.

4 Remove the cover, pour the juices into a small saucepan, and set the saucepan aside until the fat rises to the top, 15 minutes.

5 Meanwhile, return the chicken to the oven and continue roasting, uncovered, until it is browned and crusty on top, 10 minutes. Transfer the chicken to a platter and set it aside in a warm spot.

6 Spoon the fat off the top of the juices in the saucepan. Add the tahini and capers and whisk until smooth. Bring to a boil, whisk again, and pour the sauce over the chicken. Carve the chicken and serve, spooning some of the sauce over each portion.

## THE CAPER'S LOVELY BLOSSOM

The flowers of the caper plant are drooping, four-petaled, the size of wild roses. The petals are white or pink and have a tassel of long purple stamens extending from the center. They are quite blowsy looking, unbridled in their profusion and tempestuous in their allure. But they are very short-lived—blossoms that open in the morning are often gone within a day. The oft-quoted line from Ecclesiastes, "The flower shall wither and beauty shall fade away," could well refer to them, as they grow in wild abundance not only in Greece and Italy, but throughout the Holy Land, around the Dead Sea, across the Levant, and up to the steppes of Iran. While collecting the buds, Greeks often snag a blossom or two. I always delight in finding a caper flower in the jar, captured in time, still white, purple, soft, and madly unkempt.

# clay pot chicken

## WITH EGGPLANT, GARLIC, AND GREEN OLIVES

### SERVES 6

PICTURE EL GRECO SNIFFING A CAPON AS IT SIMMERS IN A CERAMIC *OLLA*. IMAGINE A GRANDMOTHER, A *YIAYIA*, ON CYPRUS ADDING GARLIC, ONIONS, PEAS, TOMATOES, TO A HEN, NOW READY FOR LONG STEWING, IN AN OLD CLAY *CASSAROLA*.

As sailing vessels circled the Mediterranean, so did the clay pot. Clay has been the medium for the pots that cooked Greek food since time immemorial until, alas, the unbreakable machine-made metal versions hit the Grecian shores over the last fifty years. If ever a pot made the meal, clay pots do. Clay pots offer porous walls that release vapor yet hold all the flavorful liquid within. They add a red-brown taste and color to the foods within. A typical Greek clay pot–roasted chicken might include tomatoes, peas, and perhaps potatoes, but any garden vegetable will do. A venture with eggplant and olives, the one soft, the other firm, result in a dish both poetic and earthy.

2 medium eggplants, peeled and cut into 1-inch cubes
18 large cloves garlic, peeled and left whole
1/2 cup small green olives, pitted if possible
3 tablespoons olive oil
2 teaspoons fresh thyme leaves or 1/2 teaspoon dried
1 teaspoon salt
2 chickens (about 3 1/2 pounds each), rinsed, patted dry, quartered, and partially skinned (see Note, page 413)
1 bay leaf, crumbled
1/2 teaspoon freshly ground black pepper
1 tablespoon chopped fresh flat-leaf parsley leaves
1/2 tablespoon coarsely chopped lemon zest

1 Preheat the oven to 475°F.

2 In a large clay pot or other heavy ovenproof casserole, toss together the eggplant, garlic, olives, oil, 1 teaspoon of the thyme, and 1/2 teaspoon of the salt. Arrange the chicken pieces, skin side down, in one tight layer over the vegetables. Sprinkle the bay leaf, pepper, remaining 1 teaspoon thyme, and remaining 1/2 teaspoon salt over the top.

3 Cover the pot, place it in the oven, and bake for 50 minutes. Remove and stir gently, loosening the vegetables from the bottom and turning the chicken over. Continue baking, uncovered, until the chicken is lightly browned and tender, 15 to 20 minutes. Garnish with the parsley and zest, and serve right away.

## CHICKEN SCRATCHES

The comparison between the way chickens scratch for food and bad handwriting is an ancient one. "By Heracles, do hens also have hands? For a chicken wrote this," says a character in Plautus's *Pseudolus* looking at a badly penned love letter.

# stuffed chicken

## NEO-PLAKA-STYLE

### SERVES 6 TO 8

**W**HILE STUFFING A CHICKEN IS NOT THE MOST COMMON WAY OF PREPARING THE BIRD IN GREECE, VERSIONS OF STUFFED CHICKEN SHOW UP EVERYWHERE FROM DELPHI, TO CORINTH, TO THE PLAKA DISTRICT OF ATHENS. EACH PLACE INCORPORATES PARTICULAR LOCAL PRODUCTS IN ITS STUFFING.

In cool and mountainous Delphi, pine nuts, and nutmeg embellish the rice. In Corinth, the rice holds almonds and cinnamon. In the Plaka, with its collection of singers, musicians, shopkeepers, and all manner of wanderers, naturally the stuffing contains every nut and every spice. Whatever the locale, the stuffing always includes currants and chicken liver.

When I make this dish, usually I roast two chickens and incorporate the liver into the stuffing of only one bird in deference to those who dislike it. Soaking the currants in retsina brings out the tang of the currants, while the alcohol's extra sugars give them a still sweeter touch. Depending on the season, I sometimes substitute red bell pepper for the celery. Like the lively Plaka, the filling will draw your guests to the table.

*Spreading grapes to dry into sweet, tangy raisins and currants.*

## MENU

### OTHER DISHES FOR THE TABLE

CRUSTY BREAD, OLIVES, AND CHEESE

SHRIMP-FILLED FILO ROLLS BYZANTINE-STYLE
page 103

STRING BEANS WITH SHALLOTS, WHITE WINE, AND FENNEL SEEDS
page 288

ONION FRITTERS
page 297

FRESH FRUIT TO FINISH

*1/3 cup dried currants*

*1/2 cup retsina wine (omit if using presoaked currants; see page 49)*

*4 tablespoons olive oil*

*1/3 cup pine nuts*

*1/3 cup slivered almonds*

*2 chicken livers*

*1/2 cup uncooked long-grain rice*

*1 medium onion, finely chopped*

*2 tablespoons chopped fresh flat-leaf parsley leaves*

*1/4 cup finely chopped celery, red bell pepper, or a mixture*

*1/4 teaspoon ground cinnamon*

*1/8 teaspoon ground nutmeg, preferably freshly grated*

*Dash of ground allspice*

*1/2 teaspoon salt*

*1 cup water*

*2 chickens (about 3 1/2 pounds each), rinsed and patted dry inside and out*

1 Place the currants and retsina in a small bowl, and set it aside to soak.

2 Prepare the stuffing: Heat 3 tablespoons of the oil in a large skillet over medium heat. When it is warm, add the pine nuts and almonds. Stir until golden, about 2 minutes. Transfer the nuts to a medium-size bowl and set it aside.

3 Add the chicken livers to the skillet and sauté over medium heat, turning once or twice, until cooked through but not hard, about 4 minutes. Cool, then chop finely and set aside.

4 Add the rice, onion, parsley, celery, cinnamon, nutmeg, allspice, and salt to the skillet and stir over medium heat until the onion is translucent, about 5 minutes. Add the water, along with the currants and retsina, and simmer until the rice is partially cooked, 10 minutes. Transfer the mixture to the mixing bowl containing the nuts. Add the chicken livers to the bowl (or if you want to exclude the livers from the stuffing in one of the birds, divide the mixture between two bowls and add the livers only to one of them). Toss to mix, and set aside to cool to room temperature.

5 Preheat the oven to 375°F.

6 Fill the chest and neck cavities of the chickens with the rice mixture. Set the chickens, breast side up, in a baking pan and drizzle the remaining 1 tablespoon oil over the top of the chickens and any exposed stuffing. Roast until the chickens are tender and the juices no longer run pink when the thigh joint is pricked with a knife, about 1¼ hours.

7 To serve, spoon the stuffing onto the center of a platter (or two platters if keeping the liver stuffing separate). Carve the chickens, and arrange the pieces over the stuffing. Serve right away.

**NOTES:**

■ With this stuffing, pack the cavities somewhat loosely to leave a little room for the rice to expand. It isn't necessary to truss stuffed chickens. A little stuffing spilling out collects tasty juices and turns nicely crisp.

■ Four large or six small game hens can also be stuffed with the filling. They take a little less time—about 1 hour.

## A FAVOR ALWAYS REPAID

In Greece, no favor ever goes unrepaid. Greeks have a keen sense of the value of labor, of a courtesy performed, and are determined to keep every good deed compensated for so that the playing field is equal at all times. This golden standard of return also holds Greeks together. When reciprocity is continual, it serves to link people in a chain of endless, intertwined commitment. There are three sorts of exchanges that take place: There is the exchange of people in marriage, the most valuable; the exchange of words, the most fluid and the cheapest; and the swapping of goods and deeds.

In country villages, two commodities more than any others are used to repay a favor: eggs and chickens. If one sister does the shopping for another, the next morning she likely receives two or three fresh-laid eggs from the receiving sister's hens. Should a son-in-law fix a broken wall, the next evening he finds on his doorstep a chicken all plucked and ready for the pot.

I have received many such eggs and chickens. Resistant at first—I had considered any favors or gifts I proffered to have no strings attached—I was graciously brought to understand the wider social meaning of exchange. I write letters in English for village friends, send bed linens from America, and bring back motor boat engines. I get back eggs and pullets, capers, *fava*, and tomato paste. These mean I am a member of a circle, the ever-rolling wheel of reciprocity that holds the village together.

**M**edlars grow on a small tree that has been widely cultivated throughout Europe since ancient times. In northern Europe, medlar was often the only fruit available through the Middle Ages; most serfs could manage to keep one medlar tree by their cottage to provide fruit to add to their austere diets.

In southern Europe, the short, applelike medlar tree grew in large groves across the terrain. In the United States, the European medlar is mostly unknown, although we are familiar with a distant relative, the loquat, sometimes called a Japanese medlar. Lucky Greece still has groves of the native European medlar, particularly in the northern areas of Macedonia, Thrace, and Epiros. In addition, cultivators introduced the loquat a hundred years ago or more. Both fruits are called *mousmoulo* and both are widely used as the base of preserves. They ripen in early spring, which permits the cook to create a fruited Passover or Easter dish. The native medlar from Macedonia is considered the juiciest. Medlar has a milder flavor than a third Rosaceae fruit, the apricot, and apricots can easily be substituted for medlars. European medlars are hard to find here, but Japanese loquat appear in many better produce markets during the spring. As summer rolls around and they disappear from the market, Fruited Chicken can also be prepared with apricots and cherries.

# fruited chicken

### SERVES 4 TO 6

**E**XCEPT FOR CURRANTS IN A STUFFING, IN TRADITIONAL GREEK CUISINE FRUIT IS RARELY ADDED TO A POULTRY DISH. COOKING CUSTOMS ARE DIFFERENT, THOUGH, AMONG THE GREEK JEWS OF PERSIAN, PALESTINIAN, AND IBERIAN ORIGIN. THEY BROUGHT WITH THEM A VARIETY OF DISHES THAT EMPLOY EXOTIC SPICES AND FRESH FRUIT.

They also brought a tradition of weekly Sabbath dinners, which means frequent preparation of more intricate and celebratory meals. Hot paprika, coriander seeds, seasonal fruit—all end up in the cooking pot and the Friday-night Sabbath table. Here the fruit I'd prefer to use is medlar, but because they are not commercially available in the United States, I substitute a distant Asian relative, the loquat, or apricots. Sweetly and splendidly seasoned, the bird will cause all diners to offer thanks.

*5 1/2 pounds chicken pieces, rinsed and patted dry*
*Salt and freshly ground black pepper*
*2 tablespoons olive oil*
*1 pound loquats or apricots, cut in half and pitted (see box, this page)*
*1 large onion, quartered and cut into 1/4-inch-thick slices*
*4 large cloves garlic, coarsely chopped*
*1 cup dry red wine*
*2 teaspoons hot paprika*
*1/2 teaspoon coriander seeds*
*1/4 teaspoon fresh rosemary needles, or a pinch of dried*

**1** Season the chicken with salt and pepper and set it aside. Heat the oil in a large nonreactive skillet over medium-high heat. When it is hot, add as many chicken pieces as will fit in a single layer. Sauté until browned all over, about 5 minutes. Transfer the chicken pieces to a plate and repeat with another batch until all the chicken is browned.

**2** Add the loquats, onion, garlic, wine, paprika, coriander, and rosemary to the skillet and stir. Sauté until the onion wilts, about 3 minutes.

**3** Return the chicken to the skillet, along with any collected juices, and cook, partially covered, over medium to medium-high heat for 20 minutes. Turn the chicken over and continue cooking, uncovered, until it is tender and the sauce is thick and deeply colored, 15 minutes. Serve right away.

# MENU
## OTHER DISHES FOR THE TABLE

CRUSTY BREAD, OLIVES, AND CHEESE

WATERCRESS SALAD WITH GREEK SALAD DRESSING
page 189

PEARL BARLEY
page 230

FRESH LIMA BEANS WITH YOGURT, PARSLEY, AND DILL
page 277

EGGPLANT SLIPPERS
page 306

FRESH FRUIT TO FINISH

# duck
## WITH OUZO ORANGE CINNAMON SAUCE

### SERVES 4

**D**UCK SHOWS UP ON GREEK PLATTERS LESS OFTEN THAN PHEASANT, QUAIL, PIGEON, OR THE SURPRISINGLY POPULAR TURKEY, BUT WHEN ONE DOES, IT IS OFTEN PREPARED WITH INGREDIENTS THAT BEFIT ITS RARITY.

Ducks are stewed with pomegranate, walnut, cognac, or other posh touches, or they—especially wild duck—might be braised in the heady wine, brandy, and spice mixes of *stifado* (page 374), *kapama* (page 369), or *salmi* (page 424). Other times they are simmered with delicate celeriac or basted with honey and lemon.

The same sort of flavors that Greeks employ in their exceptional duck stews can be reassigned to a marinade and sauce while keeping the duck crisp by grilling or baking. Ouzo is the nation's savored aperitif, while cinnamon is the spice of cherished *baklava*. Their combination, joined with the aromatic orange of Greek citrus groves, makes for an innovative but truly Greek preparation befitting the singularity of luxurious duck.

*FOR THE DUCK AND MARINADE*
*1 duck (4 to 5 pounds), with giblets*
*1/2 cup ouzo*
*2 tablespoons finely chopped orange zest*
*3/4 cup fresh orange juice*
*2 bay leaves*
*1/8 teaspoon ground cinnamon*
*1/2 teaspoon freshly ground white pepper*

*FOR THE SAUCE*
*(see Note)*
*1 small carrot, coarsely chopped*
*1/2 small onion, coarsely chopped*
*1 small bay leaf*
*1 sprig fresh oregano*
*2 sprigs fresh thyme*
*3 cups water*

*1 tablespoon butter, to cook the liver*
*8 sprigs watercress, flat-leaf parsley, or cilantro, for garnish*

1 Remove the giblets from the cavity of the duck. Rinse the duck inside and out and pat dry. Cut into quarters, removing and reserving the backbone and wings as you go. Trim off and discard the excess fat. Place the backbone, wings, and giblets, minus the liver, on a plate and set aside. Reserve the liver separately.

2 Combine the ouzo, zest, orange juice, bay leaves, cinnamon, and white pepper in a large nonreactive dish and stir to mix. Add the duck quarters and duck liver and turn to coat. Cover and marinate in the refrigerator for at least 2 hours or as long as overnight. Bring to room temperature before cooking.

3 While the duck is marinating, prepare the stock for the sauce: Place the reserved backbone, wings, and giblets in a medium-size saucepan. Add the carrot, onion, bay leaf, oregano and thyme sprigs, and water. Bring to a boil over high heat, reduce the heat, and simmer briskly, uncovered, for 1 hour. Check the water level from time to time, and if it gets too low add a bit more.

## VESSELS

Formed by supple fingers shaping moist, dense clay, most ancient Greek cooking utensils were earthenware. Potters worked both with and without a whirling wheel, and the variety of the cookware they spun out is amazing. Some of the pots and pans were intricately decorated, meant for show and entertaining. Some were only slightly decorated—good, charming kitchen or serving pieces, meant for pleasing family meals. Some were unadorned, quickly made and meant for wear and tear. A few of the same sort of clay cooking vessels are still used today, and cooking with them reminds us how easily they were to use millennia ago.

**KYLIX:** a two-handled, widemouthed stemmed drinking cup

**LEKANI:** a two-handled, bowl-shaped basin

**SKYPHOS:** much like a *lekani*, but taller

**KANTHAROS:** much like a *skyphos* but with ornate, spindly handles

**HYDRIA:** a three-handled, bulbous water pitcher

**OINOCHOE:** a one-handled, necked wine pitcher

**PSYKATERS:** a mushroom-shaped wine cooler

**AMPHORA:** a two-handled, necked wine jar

**OLPE:** a tall, narrow pitcher

**AMIS:** a hooded pitcher with pour lip on the side and a handle on top

**KADOS:** a large, wide, open water storage basin

**LOPAS** or **LOPIDA:** casseroles, or covered cooking pots

**TEGANON** or **TEGANI:** frying pans; flat, rimmed round platters to place over the fire

**CHYTRA:** a kettle for boiling water

**CHORUS:** mugs for pitchers

**TRIVLYION:** a stemmed dish, like a cake plate; large ones for fruit and olives; smaller ones for salt, vinegar, and silphium

**KANE** and **PAZOPSIS:** large two-handled platters; when embellished with fish designs, they were called *ichthuai*

**LYKYTHOS:** a delicate vase with a long slender neck for pouring oil slowly

4 Strain the stock through a fine-mesh sieve into a bowl, and set it aside for 30 minutes for the fat to rise to the top (or cover and refrigerate as long as overnight). Spoon off the fat before using.

5 Heat a grill to medium or preheat the oven to 375°F.

**6** Lift the duck quarters out of the marinade, reserving the marinade and liver, and set them on the grill rack or place them in a baking pan in the oven.

# MENU

## OTHER DISHES FOR THE TABLE

**CRUSTY BREAD, OLIVES, AND CHEESE**

**LITTLE HERBED MEATBALLS**
page 52

*SKORDALIA* WITH PISTACHIO OR WALNUT
page 464

**BULGUR AND VEGETABLE PILAF WITH HERBS OR WHITE WINE**
page 235

**EGGPLANT WITH SHALLOTS, WINE, AND BASIL**
page 289

**FRESH FRUIT TO FINISH**

Grill, turning the pieces every 10 minutes, or bake without turning, until the skin is golden, the breast meat is still a little rosy, and the leg meat is no longer pink, 35 to 40 minutes.

**7** While the duck is cooking, pour the stock into a large skillet and cook over high heat until reduced almost to a glaze, about 15 minutes. Add the reserved marinade and continue simmering briskly until the sauce is thick enough to coat a spoon, about 12 minutes. Set the sauce aside in a warm place.

**8** Transfer the duck to a platter and set it aside in a warm place.

**9** Melt the butter in a small sauté pan over medium-high heat. Add the duck liver and sauté until firm but still rosy in the center, about 8 minutes. Slice the liver.

## POT PARADOX
......................

"When I wish to say 'pot' to you,
 'pot' shall I say?
Or: 'hollow-bodied sphere formed
 by the whirling wheel,
Clay fashioned, baked in a cover of
 mother earth,
Engendering the succulent stewing
 forms
Of a milk-nursed, newborn flock?'"
"Heavens, enough.
Why don't you say quite simply,
 'a pot of meat'?"

**—ANTIPHANES,** *APHRODISTOS,* **FOURTH CENTURY** B.C.E.

**10** Spoon the sauce over the duck, garnish with the sliced liver and the watercress sprigs, and serve right away.

**NOTE:** You can substitute prepared chicken stock for the duck stock to save time. You'll need $1\frac{3}{4}$ cups.

# ano-kato duck salmi

### SERVES 6

AT LEAST AS OFTEN AS THEY ROAST THEM, GREEK COOKS PREPARE DUCK, GEESE, AND WILD GAME BIRDS IN THE *SALMI* MANNER. A TYPICAL *SALMI* FOLLOWS THESE STEPS: FIRST THE CAVITY OF THE BIRD IS SEARED WITH AN EMBER OR HOT INSTRUMENT; THEN AN APPLE, ONION, OR CELERY ROOT IS PLACED IN THE CAVITY. THE DUCK IS FRIED IN HOT OIL OR ROASTED UNTIL WELL BROWNED ALL AROUND AND ABOUT HALF DONE; THEN STOCK IS ADDED AND THE DUCK IS SIMMERED UNTIL THE LIQUID HAS NEARLY EVAPORATED.

The result is a wonderfully tasty sauce, but this is not my favorite way to cook duck because it emerges stewed and too soft. However, when the *salmi* steps are turned *ano-kato*—upside down—by stewing the duck first and then browning it, *salmi* produces a wonderfully crisp bird, particularly with domestic duck. *Ano-kato* is a much-used word referring to any perturbation or upheaval of events, any time the *omega* comes before the *alpha*. But the duck cooked *ano-kato salmi* is the alpha *and* the omega of delicious.

2 ducks (about 4 pounds each),
    preferably Muscovy ducks,
    with giblets (see Notes)
Olive oil, for coating the pan
2 large onions, coarsely chopped
4 large cloves garlic, coarsely
    chopped
Several sprigs fresh thyme, or
    1 teaspoon dried
Pinch of ground allspice
2 cups Chicken Stock
    (page 170)
Salt and freshly ground
    black pepper
4 tablespoons (1/2 stick) butter
2 cups dry red wine
1 cup fresh orange juice

1 Remove the giblets from the cavity of the ducks. Rinse the ducks inside and out and pat dry. Cut into quarters, removing and reserving the backbone, wings, and neck for another use. Trim off and discard the excess fat as well as the gizzard. Chop the hearts and livers and set them aside.

2 Lightly oil a large pot or skillet and place it over medium heat. When it is hot, add as many duck pieces, as will fit in one

## ALLSPICE

Allspice, called *bahari* in Greek, is a newcomer in the cast of Greek flavorings. A native of the West Indies, allspice didn't reach Europe until a few hundred years ago. It received its English name because the cooks who first sampled it thought it encompassed the flavors of most of the ancient Asian seasonings and could replace them all. In Greece, where its name simply means "spice," it sometimes does replace a mix of other spices. When the busy Greek cook doesn't want to bother with dashes from several jars, or doesn't have all she needs, she uses a pinch of allspice. Allspice is now commonly used in *saltsa besamel*, in red macaroni sauce, on wild game, and in stews, and is perfect for crisped stewed duck.

layer. Sauté until browned all over, about 3 minutes per side. Transfer to a plate and repeat with another batch until all the duck pieces are browned.

3 Return the duck to the pot and add the onions, garlic, thyme, allspice, stock, and salt and pepper to taste. Bring to a boil, cover, reduce the heat, and simmer until the duck is partially cooked and still rare in the breast, 15 minutes. Transfer the duck to a dish and set it aside.

4 Strain the cooking liquid into a bowl and set it aside for the fat to rise to the top. Skim off the fat before using.

5 Preheat the broiler or grill to medium-high.

6 Melt the butter in a large saucepan (see Note). Add the reserved livers and hearts, and stir. Add the skimmed cooking liquid, the wine, and the orange juice. Bring to a boil and simmer briskly until the liquid is reduced and thickened and a deep red-brown color, 20 to 30 minutes.

7 While the sauce is simmering, place the duck pieces, skin side up, on a rack in a broiling pan or on a grill. Broil or grill until golden brown and crisp, 5 to 8

minutes. Transfer the duck to a serving platter and set it aside for the juices to settle, 5 minutes.

8 Pour the sauce over the duck, and serve.

## THE DUCKS OF MIKRI PRESPA

In the mountainous northwest corner of Greece, at an altitude of 2,500 feet, lies the largest lake in the Balkans, Megali (Big) Prespa, and, separated by a reed-thin strip of land, its companion lake, Mikri (Little) Prespa. Megali Prespa, with its sheer cliffs and purple-blue water, touches on three countries, but little Mikri Prespa falls almost entirely within Greece. It is very much Greece's own retreat. Foreign tourists rarely visit, though that baffles me. Many generations of Greeks have enjoyed the pleasures of the site, and in 1977 the Greek government declared the area a national park because of its spectacular beauty.

Around the lakes sit many Byzantine churches, three of them what the Greeks call *askitiria*, sites so spiritual that they are intended only for solitary prayer. Anchored to a peninsula that juts between the little lake and the big one stands the unique village of Psarades. Bound by the Greek National Trust to preserve the old ways, its streets are lined with stone houses. Its fishing boats are all constructed of wood from local oak and cedar. The cattle that feed nearby all belong to a miniature breed particular to the village. Among the thick reeds that border both lakes, and out in the open waters, herons, ibis, egrets, pelicans, cormorants, and ducks feed.

Mikri Prespa is a perfect place to grill duck. No, not the wild ducks swimming on the lake—those are only for visual pleasure—rather the ducks raised on the farms nearby. There is enough water in this area for householders to fabricate small duck ponds, and both restaurant and butcher feature the birds.

Throughout the thick copses surrounding the lake, picnic tables are positioned where visitors can eat and even roast the succulent fowl. Glasses of ouzo, of course, are a necessity at such a picnic, where the smell of bark and leaves permeates the crisp mountain air as one feasts on grilled duck.

## NOTES:

■ If you use the more common, slightly larger and fatter Peking duck instead of the leaner, wilder-tasting Muscovy, add a little extra cooking time in Step 2.

■ When making the sort of sauce *salmi* calls for, it is important to use a deep, wide saucepan so that the liquid reduces in good time.

# Penelope's goose

### SERVES 6 TO 8

IN HOMER'S *ODYSSEY*, TWO REFERENCES ARE MADE TO DOMESTIC GEESE: WHEN ODYSSEUS'S SON TELEMACHUS IS ABOUT TO DEPART FROM HIS VISIT WITH KING MENELAUS, AN EAGLE SWOOPS BY, CLUTCHING IN ITS TALONS A WHITE GOOSE THAT HAD BEEN FATTENED UP FOR DINNER. IN THE OTHER INSTANCE, PENELOPE DREAMS THAT AN EAGLE KILLS THE ENTIRE FLOCK OF GEESE SHE HAD BEEN FEEDING.

Today geese are kept in small enclosures, in much the same manner that Penelope kept hers. Greek men also hunt wild geese, especially in the wetlands near Thessaloniki and in Thrace. Considering the goose's history, it seems fitting to prepare the bird with ancient ingredients: yellow lentils, studded with what was considered the prize, the goose liver; and a glaze of grapes infused with flowery chamomile and reduced to a honeylike syrup.

*1 goose (8 to 10 pounds)*
*Yellow Lentil and Goose Liver*
*    Stuffing (recipe follows)*
*¹/₂ cup Chamomile Petimezi Glaze*
*    (page 428)*

1 Rinse the goose inside and out and pat it dry. Reserve the liver and heart for the stuffing.

2 Prepare the Yellow Lentil and Goose Liver Stuffing.

3 Preheat the oven to 350°F.

4 Fill the goose cavity with the stuffing and truss it closed. Place the goose, breast side up, on a rack in a roasting pan. Place the pan in the oven and roast the goose for 3 hours, drawing off the rendered fat once an hour with a bulb baster. Reserve the fat for another use (see Note).

5 Meanwhile, make the Chamomile *Petimezi* Glaze and set it aside.

## FEATHERED OMENS

Woven through the myths of gods and sagas of heroes, the sudden appearance or dream of a bird signaled events about to happen. Which bird appeared foretold the character of the event—whether it would be good or bad, bold or dreadful. The sighting of an eagle gave a warrior direction; Zeus or Ares was with him. Athena, as support, was signified by an owl, ever wise. The eagle clutching a goose tells Telemachus that enemies lie in wait for him, and geese killed by an eagle tell Penelope that Odysseus is about to return to take revenge on the villainous suitors who have bedeviled her and her household for twenty years.

6 After the goose has roasted for 3 hours, pour the glaze over it and continue roasting until the thigh wiggles freely, the juices run clear without any pink, and the breast is golden on top, 30 minutes. Remove the pan from the oven and set it aside for the juices to settle, 20 minutes.

7 Carve the goose, and serve it right away.

**NOTE:** The fat rendered from roasting a goose can be put to good use: Fry your potatoes in it, as the French and Belgians do, or shine your boots with it, as the Greeks do.

## ATHENA, THE GODDESS WITH A BIRD ON HER SHOULDER

The great goddess Athena, for whom Athens is named, was the daughter of Zeus, and one of the twelve ruling deities of lofty Mount Olympus. Next to Zeus and perhaps Poseidon, she seems to have been the most powerful. In art and literature she appears clad as a warrior in full armor, with helmet, round shield (her father's, decorated with a frightful Gorgon's head), and goat-hide breastplate with tassels. Virgin though she was, she loved men, or at least manly deeds. She came to the aid of every intrepid adventurer—Jason, Perseus, Heracles, Bellerophon, Odysseus. Her power brought the raiding Greeks to victory over Troy.

But for whatever reason, she was also represented by a bird and carried one along—an owl. That big-eyed night flyer sits upon her shoulder. Some believe the owl represented Athena's wisdom. But was it wise to fight her uncle Poseidon or to help spear her brother Ares? Perhaps the owl reflected her aid to those wily and mischievous heroes who often flew by night on their impish deeds. Or maybe the owl told how spooky she was to carry the Gorgon shield. No one knows.

She did protect civilized life, handicrafts, and agriculture. She invented the bridle to tame the horse. But she chose a wild bird, one never tame or domestic, one not eaten, so she remains a bit enigmatic. She did see all, as the owl is thought to see roundabout, and she liked to interfere. Perhaps as her father was the eagle, the less high-flying, still well-taloned, often fierce owl was all that was left her.

*Powerful Athena, without owl, but with helmet.*

## YELLOW LENTIL AND GOOSE LIVER STUFFING

### MAKES 6 CUPS

The yellow lentils of the Mediterranean are as ancient a food as barley and wheat. A stuffing of them is wonderfully textured, soft yet a bit crunchy, flavorful, nutty, and nourishing, a captivating change from fillings of bread or rice.

*1/2 cup golden raisins*
*1/2 cup retsina, Mavrodaphne, or Muscat wine (omit if using presoaked raisins; see page 49)*
*2 1/2 cups yellow lentils*
*1 1/2 tablespoons olive oil*
*Goose liver and heart, coarsely chopped*
*1 large onion, finely chopped*
*1/2 teaspoon dried thyme leaves*
*1 teaspoon salt*

1 Place the raisins and wine in a small bowl and set aside to soak for 30 minutes or up to several days.

2 Rinse the lentils and pick out any stones. Place the lentils in a medium-size saucepan and add water to cover by 1 1/2 inches. Bring to a boil, reduce the heat, and simmer, uncovered, until tender and chewable but not mushy,

# MENU

**CHRISTMAS BREAD
WITH SWEETENED FIGS**
page 142

**OLIVES AND CHEESE**

**FISH SOUP
WITH LEMONY
MAYONNAISE**
page 178

*BRIAMI WITH CELERY*
Box, page 283

**A SELECTION OF PICKLES**
pages 72 to 75

**FRESH FRUIT TO FINISH**

12 minutes. Drain and set aside to cool for 15 minutes.

3 Heat the oil in a medium-size saucepan over medium-high heat. Add the goose liver and heart, stir, and then add the onion, thyme, raisins and wine, and salt. Sauté until the onion is well wilted, 5 minutes.

4 Place the lentils and the giblet mixture in a bowl and stir to mix. Use right away or cover and set aside for 1 hour.

**NOTE:** The goose gizzard should not be included in the stuffing. It toughens to a stony texture when cooked.

# CHAMOMILE PETIMEZI GLAZE

**MAKES ½ CUP**

Grapes, so important in ancient Greek culture, can be reduced to syrup as sweet as honey. Depending on the grape, the color of the syrup ranges from amethyst to topaz. Here that syrup is combined with aromatic, grassy chamomile (*hamomili*), a plant with tiny yellow blooms that scents the air throughout Greece. It grows in wild profusion but is seldom used as a cooking herb. Since ancient times it has been used to brew a soothing tea and also used as a rinse to make hair blonder. No reason exists, though, not to use its herbal essence for flavoring. Ancient Greeks thought the flowering plant that covered their land like a green, white, and yellow blanket so smelled like their beloved apples that they named it "ground" *(hamo),* "apple" *(milo).*

*½ cup Petimezi (page 500)*
*2 tablespoons dried chamomile flowers (see Note)*

Heat the *petimezi* in a small saucepan over medium heat. When it is beginning to boil, stir in the chamomile flowers and remove it from the heat. Allow it to steep for 5 minutes. Then strain the syrup and use it within 1 hour, while the fragrance is still fresh.

**NOTE:** Bulk chamomile tea includes whole flowers, which flavor the glaze best. Tea bags of nearly powdered chamomile are too bitter to use here.

# roast turkey

## WITH PORK, CHESTNUT, AND FIG STUFFING AND SWEET POTATO *SKORDALIA*

**SERVES 12 TO 14**

M Y ONE ATHENIAN CHRISTMAS TOOK PLACE ON A PROPERLY COLD DAY. AT THE HOME OF FRIENDS, WE WORE TWO SWEATERS AND THREE PAIRS OF SOCKS TO BUFFER THE CHILL FROM THE TERRAZZO FLOORS.

I, as the American, was put in charge of the turkey. I cooked it almost as I do at home, but in a very Greek style: I slathered the bird in Sweet Potato *Skordalia*, and rather than an American-style bread stuffing that would perplex my Greek friends, I filled the bird with a forcemeat of pork, for a slightly baconlike flavor. Chestnuts, which were roasting on every street corner in Athens, dried figs, and anise completed the dressing's autumnal composition. Since that day, I have cooked this turkey every Thanksgiving and Christmas. The bird, infused with garlic and spice, spilling out juicy figs and meat, draws an ever greater crowd every year. I served it, of course, with the Christmas Bread.

*1 turkey (10 to 12 pounds)*
*Pork, Chestnut, and Fig Stuffing*
*    (recipe follows)*
*2 1/2 cups Sweet Potato Skordalia*
*    (page 463)*
*Christmas Bread (page 142)*

1 Rinse the turkey inside and out and pat it dry.

2 Prepare the Pork, Chestnut, and Fig Stuffing.

3 Preheat the oven to 450°F.

4 Fill the turkey body and neck cavities with the stuffing and truss them closed. Place the turkey, breast side down, on a rack in a roasting pan. Rub the back of the turkey with 1/4 cup of the *skordalia*. Place it in the oven and roast for 30 minutes.

5 Reduce the oven temperature to 350°F, and continue roasting for 45 minutes. Then turn the turkey over, breast side up, and spread 1/2 cup of the *skordalia* over the breast and legs. Continue roasting until a meat thermometer inserted in the thigh meat registers 185°F, 1 to 1 1/2 hours more. Remove the turkey from the oven and set it aside for the juices to settle, 20 minutes.

6 Carve the turkey and serve, accompanied by the stuffing and the remaining *skordalia* and the Christmas Bread.

## MENU
### OTHER DISHES FOR THE TABLE

**OLIVES AND CHEESE**

**RADISH SALAD WITH PICKLED ONIONS AND FETA CHEESE**
page 201

**RICE PILAF WITH SHRIMP, SQUID, OR SNAILS**
Box, page 239

**BRIAMI WITH MUSHROOMS**
Box, page 283

**FRESH FRUIT TO FINISH**

## NOTES:

■ For a nonmeat stuffing, see Stuffed Chicken Neo-Plaka-Style (page 418) and increase the quantity accordingly, or use the lentil stuffing (minus the liver) from Penelope's Goose (page 426).

■ Stuff the turkey just before roasting it, not in advance.

# PORK, CHESTNUT, AND FIG STUFFING

**MAKES 3 POUNDS (7 CUPS), ENOUGH FOR A 10- TO 12-POUND TURKEY**

In Greece, poultry stuffings usually incorporate meat, which makes the meal particularly lavish. The use of figs is unusual, but it offers a burnished flavor. A dollop of brandy makes the stuffing warmer and toasts the harvest. Any bird with such a filling becomes sensational.

*³/4 cup dried golden figs, preferably Kalimyrna, coarsely chopped*
*¹/4 teaspoon anise seeds*
*³/4 cup brandy*
*3 tablespoons butter*
*2 medium onions, finely chopped*
*³/4 cup chopped celery leaves*
*1 ¹/2 pounds coarsely ground pork*
*¹/2 cup pine nuts*

*³/4 pound (about 18 large) chestnuts, peeled and coarsely chopped (see Notes, page 266)*
*1 ¹/2 cups coarse fresh bread crumbs*
*³/4 cup chopped fresh flat-leaf parsley leaves*
*1 ¹/2 teaspoons chopped fresh sage leaves, or ³/4 teaspoon dried*
*1 ¹/2 teaspoons salt*
*¹/2 teaspoon freshly ground black pepper*

1 Place the figs, anise seeds, and brandy in a covered bowl or jar and set it aside, covered, in the refrigerator overnight, or for several weeks. Drain, reserving both the fig mixture and the liquid.

2 Melt the butter in a medium-size saucepan over medium-high heat. Add the onions, celery leaves, and the drained figs and anise seeds. Sauté until the onions are well wilted, about 3 minutes. Remove the pan from the heat and set it aside.

## SAVORING MEMORIES

All people "contextualize" their memories. That is, they paint a mental picture of what was going on at the time of the event. The pictures both evoke the remembrance and give the details that enrich the story. Americans tend to contextualize memories in terms of what we were wearing and who was present. Greeks paint their remembrances with what they were eating: recalling the meats, pies, or syrup-soaked sweets, and just how divine it all tasted. The difference is significant.

Our important matter, the stuff that gives events their marker, is external—how we may have looked or seemed to the other. Greek memory is marked by what was internally enjoyed, the sensory and sensual experience. On the few occasions we mark by food—Thanksgiving, Hanukkah, Christmas, Passover, Easter—we like the foods repeated, so the event is always the same. It's the predictability, not the particulars, that imparts the pleasure.

It is a small cultural difference, but I have made a concerted effort to become more Greek in my memory. I prefer to say "I remember because the cook added a dollop of ouzo to the snails," or "It was the time the goose was galantined," or "Yes, yes, I recall because there were chestnuts in the filling, rather than "I remember because I wore that black skirt."

3 Place the pork, pine nuts, chestnuts, bread crumbs, parsley, sage, salt, pepper, and reserved brandy in a medium-size bowl. Add the onion mixture and mix well. Use right away, or cover and store in the refrigerator for as long as overnight. Bring to room temperature before using.

**NOTES:**

■ When stuffing chickens, game hens, or geese with this stuffing, the Greek cook would traditionally include the bird's liver, sautéed and chopped. I find turkey liver a bit too bitter, but I do add the liver when using other birds.

■ Although fresh chestnuts are a bother to peel, the effort is worth it. Peeled canned chestnuts disintegrate and become mushy in the stuffing.

■ For a game hen, reduce the amount of stuffing to make about 1 cup.

## SILPHIUM, THE ANCIENTS' MUSTARD AND THEN SOME

By far the preferred spicy seasoning used by the ancient Greeks, and by the Romans after them, was a mysterious plant called *silphium*. At one point silphium grew abundantly around the Mediterranean. Cyrene, a kingdom where Libya now sits in North Africa, was settled by colonists from Santorini solely to gather the herb that had earlier been transplanted there, and they became fabulously rich exporting it. Hunted, picked, shipped out, the plant was devoured into extinction. (The herds may have contributed to its disappearance. Sheep feeding on it, Theophrastus said, became fat and tender and tasty.) Emperor Nero is said to have eaten the last stalk.

Silphium seems to have been a relative of carrot, celery, and fennel—at least it seems so from depictions on coins, vases, and murals. It was pulverized in *garos* and almost every other sauce, tucked into jars of nuts to flavor them, added to pastes and toppings. Alexander's soldiers found a source of an inferior version in Iran that was most likely asafoetida. Whatever it was, it was used in two forms: the sap, which was taken from the fat stem and the root; and after the sap was drained, the stalk of its celerylike flower. The sap, which was translucent, spoiled easily and had to be carefully preserved; the stalk had to be stripped of its black skin.

Its taste, from all reports, was quite strong. "Pungent" is perhaps not even an adequate description. Many say that silphium is best duplicated by asafoetida, an herb eaten in many places today, whose sap is extremely bitter, whose flavor is more pungent than garlic, and whose aroma is like decaying meat.

Since no one has tasted silphium since Nero, no one knows exactly what it was like nor why it was so avidly pursued. But when silphium was sprinkled in sauces, so were cumin and coriander, and so was mustard, which still flourishes everywhere that silphium did.

*The Erechtheion in Athens features a porch supported by caryatids, statues of* kore *(young women) in place of columns.*

# THE JEWS OF GREECE AND THEIR JOSEPH'S COAT CUISINE

**S**OME OF THE MORE FANCIFUL POULTRY DISHES IN GREEK CUISINE, THOSE THAT INCLUDE LESS COMMONLY USED HERBS, LIKE ROSEMARY, OR ARE GLAZED WITH FRUITED SAUCES, WERE BROUGHT TO THAT LAND BY THE JEWS.

The first Jews arrived in Greece as far back as 600 B.C.E., when they were expelled from Babylon. The ancient Greeks were quite intrigued by the new settlers and quickly learned Jewish lore and writings. They esteemed Moses as a hero and even adapted some of Moses's story in their own epics. A few

*Many synagogues in Greece are restored and in good condition.*

centuries later, when Alexander the Great broke the spine of Persian rule, Greek colonists poured into many cities that had once been Jewish. Among

them was Jerusalem, where they built an acropolis above Solomon's temple. The two peoples were perhaps not compatible religiously and ideologically, but they found considerable meeting of the minds in other matters—in science, mathematics, and commerce.

## UNDER ALEXANDER THE GREAT

**A**fter Alexander's death, Greeks and Jews continued to live together under the rule of his generals and their dynasties. Jews adopted many Greek notions and customs; Greeks maintained their admiration for Jews. The Roman leaders who followed, since they idolized Greece, by and large were as tolerant as their predecessors. The Virgin Mary's husband, Joseph, it is said, had dealings with the Greco-Roman administrators of Egypt and traveled there on business.

It was apt, then, that a second set of Jewish refugees, fleeing the Maccabean wars between 170 and 161 B.C.E., found safe harbor in many Greek cities. They were joined by a third emigration when, during the civil wars that broke out in Egypt in Cleopatra's day, the Jews of Alexandria left to inhabit the newly founded city of Thessaloniki. Strabo, the Greek geographer of the first century C.E., noted that large numbers of Jews were living throughout mainland, island, and Levantine Greece. Jewish communities in Athens, Crete, Corinth, Thessaloniki, Veroia, Filippi, along the coast of Asia Minor, on Rhodes, and in the Aegean islands were well documented. The Apostle Paul, who spoke Greek as fluently as Hebrew, preached to Jews and Greeks alike in Thessaloniki, Athens, and Corinth.

## THE DESTRUCTION OF JERUSALEM

The numbers of Jews in Greek cities expanded again when more refugees arrived, escaping the destruction of Jerusalem in the second century C.E. Like Paul, all the Jews who resided in the Greek-speaking world had adopted the Greek language along with Roman citizenship, but as the Roman empire embraced Christianity, the Jews grew apprehensive. Still, under Roman law their rights were protected and the Jews greatly valued their Roman citizenship. When the Roman empire was reestablished in Constantinople, the Jews of Greece continued their allegiance and considered themselves Romans. Relying on the freedom and status they had under Rome's dominion, they referred to themselves as "Romiotes," and they remained the main body of Greek Jewry until the fifteenth century.

## THE BYZANTINE PERIOD

During the Byzantine era, some of the emperors tried to force the Jews to convert to Christianity, often by brutal means, and Jews were deprived of certain rights, but the Greek Jews continued to thrive. They traded in the spices they were acquainted with from distant countries. They marketed furs from the Balkan mountains. They became renowned as silk manufacturers. The Jewish silk makers of Thebes were, in fact, so famous that they were kidnapped by King Roger II and brought to Sicily. Jews also became glassblowers, pottery makers, and boatmen. Some worked as bureaucrats, teachers, and scholars. Others were farmers.

When the Byzantine empire disintegrated, Jewish centers found themselves falling under different regimes. The Jews of Euboea and the Ionian and Aegean islands came under Venetian rule and developed strong ties with the Jews of northern Italy. The Jews of Mani, in the southern Peloponnesos, an area long noted for rugged isolationism, established a stubborn independence. A number of scholars claim, in fact, that the original Maniots were Jews. But as the Ottoman empire enveloped region after region, the majority of Greece's Jews fell under Ottoman dominion.

## PEOPLE OF THE BOOK

Since Muslim law defined Christians and Jews equally as "people of the book," under Ottoman rule Greece's Jews once again began to enjoy the same standards and treatment as their Christian neighbors. Perhaps because of the fierce animosity between Muslims and Christians, most Ottomans actually felt closer to the Jews. Jewish men held major positions within the regime. Jewish women enjoyed special privileges within the courts. Free of the restrictions limiting Muslim women, they served as messengers for wives and concubines secluded in harems. In time, Greek Jews, like the Greek Christians, incorporated aspects of Turkish dress and appropriated many Turkish dishes into their cuisine, as the Jews had adapted Greek dress and food before. The Greek Jewish versions of Turkish food are considered by many experts more authentic than the renditions that filtered into Greek cooking. Yet Greek Jewish food always retained a distinctiveness derived from their ancient foodways.

At about the same time as the Ottomans were expanding their dominion, the next great influx of Jews arrived in Greece. They came in flight from Spain and Portugal, where Ferdinand and Isabella were attempting to rid the Iberian peninsula of all but Christians. Declaring that

*A family that plays together . . .*
*A Greek Jewish family in Thessaloniki.*

the Catholic monarchs' loss was his gain, Beyazid II, then sultan of the Ottoman empire, opened his borders to the new Jewish refugees. In truth, he desperately needed experienced administrators to help govern the suddenly large and unwieldy realm he had acquired from Greek Byzantium. Eager for a new homeland, large numbers of Iberian Jews emigrated to Ottoman-controlled Greek cities, particularly Constantinople, Edime, Smyrna, and Thessaloniki. Others settled in Corfu and Rhodes.

## A REFUGE FROM SPAIN AND PORTUGAL

The Jews from Spain and Portugal, known as Sephardic Jews, were quite different from the ones whose ancestry hailed from Greece and Asia Minor. During their centuries in Spain, the Iberian Jews had adopted fifteenth-century Castilian Spanish mixed with Hebrew and Arabic, to which they now added

words from Greek, Bulgarian, French, and Turkish. Their speech developed into a distinct language known as Ladino, or *djidio*, which they spoke in contrast to the Greek spoken by the already established Jews. The Sephardic Jews also brought with them a cultured demeanor from the high social positions they had known under Arab rule in Iberia. Their religious ceremonies continued to reflect the customs of the Babylonian Jews from which they, too, were descended, while Greece's Romiote Jews kept a ritual life more in keeping with the exiles who had arrived from Palestine.

Nonetheless, the two communities of Jews, the one descended from the Roman empire and speaking Greek, the other with Sephardic origins and speaking Ladino, lived side by side in Greece for the next four hundred years. Adding to the mix, Jews expelled in the fifteenth and sixteenth centuries from southern Italy and Sicily sought refuge in Greece. They were joined by Jews from Provence, Livorno, Naples, and finally, at the end of the seventeenth century, Russia and Poland. Each distinct group constructed and attended its own synagogue. At one point Thessaloniki, the Greek city with the largest Jewish population in the Mediterranean and Asia Minor, had thirty-two synagogues.

## THE END OF OTTOMAN RULE

As the Ottoman empire started to crumble and Greece began the struggle for independence, the Jews of Greece were caught in the mesh. In the early days of the turmoil, almost all the Jewish communities of the Peloponnesos were destroyed. The later Balkan wars left other Jewish centers under the control of differing emerging states, though in the end the large Jewish population of Thessaloniki came back under Greek domain. The Romiote Jews, who spoke Greek, took more easily to their new Greek citizenship. The Ladino-speaking Jews, whose ties to their Ottoman rescuers were stronger, suffered more ambivalence. Meanwhile, Christian Greeks reclaiming Thessaloniki found their former city more Jewish than Greek. Commerce stopped on Friday evening as Jews attended the synagogues. Ladino was more in use than Greek. In response, the nascent nation of Greece launched an aggressive campaign to return Thessaloniki to Greek custom that was particularly hard on the Sephardic population. That, plus a huge fire that destroyed much of the Jewish section of Thessaloniki, and the plebiscite of 1922, which brought large numbers of repatriated Greeks back into Greece, sadly caused many of Greece's Jews to emigrate to other lands.

> The cuisine of the Jews of Greece embodies all the diversity... from the rich and varied heritage of the populace.

## WORLD WAR II AND BEYOND

Still, it was only World War II that truly changed the long history of Jews in Greece. When Mussolini invaded, the Jewish community sent six thousand young men to help defend the border against the Italians. But while Mussolini was deterred, Hitler was not. The Germans invaded Greece in April 1941, and though Greece is famous for the efforts some made to save its Jewish citizens, by 1945 more than seventy thousand Jews had been deported, mostly to extermination camps in Poland. More than 90 percent of the Jews of Thessaloniki, Rhodes, and Corfu were killed. After the war a number of Jews from northern Europe settled in Greece, but of the twelve thousand Greek Jews who survived World War II, more than five thousand emigrated to Israel. At present, the once enduring and flourishing Jewish population of Greece stands at a mere six thousand.

Though their numbers have declined, a heritage of fabulous Greek Jewish cooking remains. The cuisine of the Jews of Greece embodies all the diversity one would expect from the rich and varied heritage of the populace. Greek Jewish dishes incorporate influences from Persia, ancient Greece, Rome, Byzantium, Arabia, Turkey, Spain, Italy, and northern Europe. Together they celebrate every grain and fruit spanning from the Middle East to Iberia.

Special holiday foods and traditions, from Friday Sabbath to Passover dinner—which Greek Orthodox Easter always follows— give rise to ornate meals, delicate sweets, and ritual specialties. Among the foods are fruited birds such as chicken, noodle pie with olive sauce, eggs cooked all night long in their shells, beef with matzo and walnuts, a yogurt salad combining hazelnut with the usual cucumber, figs and plums in mastic, and a fondant of lemon. All of the dishes are Jewish and all of them are Greek.

# Wild game
## FROM THE
## WOODS AND SKY

GREEKS MIGRATING INTO WHAT BECAME THEIR HOMELAND PENINSULA ENERGETICALLY PLUNDERED THE FORESTS FOR EDIBLE WILD GAME AND FOWL. MYTHS AND SAGAS VIVIDLY DEPICT THEM CHASING STAG, BOAR, WILD ASS, AND GAZELLE. THE GREEK LOVE OF THE HUNT PERSISTED AS THEIR WAY OF LIFE BECAME MORE SETTLED. BYZANTINE GREEKS HUNTED REGULARLY. FOR THE ROYALTY IT PROVIDED A FORM OF ENTERTAINMENT, THOUGH IT WAS

Then let's have a cock, a tender pigeon, a partridge, and a few such other things. And if a wild hare be offered, grab it.

—ATHENAEUS, SECOND CENTURY B.C.E.

a dangerous one—three emperors died of injuries received while stalking game. Byzantine peasants enjoyed supplementing their daily fare with wild hare, the copious wild fowl that flew across their skies, and an occasional deer.

Despite thousands of years of agriculture and animal husbandry, Greeks today still love the hunt and savor the flavor of the wild: boar over pig, pheasant over barnyard hen, and the wily hare instead of domestic rabbit. In the Greek view, the wild birds and animals are part of the free food God provides, and the call of the hunt is a call for action, symbolizing strength and bravery.

Sadly, many of the beasts and birds hunted by the ancients, the Byzantines, and even Greeks of only two decades past are gone from the land and the firmament. Deer, wild boar, and large game birds are scarce. On Corfu and in the north, wild duck occasionally convene. The mountains of the north sequester some deer. On the Cyclades islands and almost everywhere else, village men gleefully track down hare and take aim at a plethora of small game birds. Virtually every village swain knows how to construct a bird pond and a blind. Meanwhile, the women wait for the rain to bring out the snails.

*Small game birds, such as quail, have been enjoyed by the Greeks in pies and as roasts throughout their history.*

# grilled rabbit

## WITH SAVORY, JUNIPER, AND GRILLED FIGS

### SERVES 6

ALL GREEK TOWNS AND VILLAGES POSSESS A *PERIFERIA*—AN AREA IN THE ENCIRCLING OUTSKIRTS THAT IS SHARED BY THE COMMUNITY'S INHABITANTS. THOUGH THE FIELDS IN THE *PERIFERIA* ARE MOST LIKELY PRIVATELY OWNED, THE AREA IS UTILIZED BY ALL FOR GATHERING WILD PLANTS, FORAGING FOR WOOD, AND TAKING A STROLL.

It also provides the hunting grounds, for it is within these outskirts that the men build bird blinds, women gather snails, and everyone picks greens. Walking in Greece, a visitor is liable to run across men with shotguns roaming the rolling hills by twilight, or to startle women with baskets rustling about the brush. The terrain seems open, and it is, but it is also exploited by its "holders" for culinary purposes.

It is in the commons that Greece's copious hare population cavorts, and hunters pursue them with good reason. Not only do hares provide a free meal, but the hare of Greece's redolent fields is lean and robust, even without additional seasoning.

Naturally compatible with the wide variety of Greek herbs and spices, domestic rabbit preprations can duplicate the Greek in both refined and rustic manners. Here, following the rustic vein, a savory and juniper seasoning with a garnish of fresh figs render the rabbit into an Arcadian feast.

## THE RULES OF THE GAME

In the ancient Greek view, animals killed in the hunt had already met sacrifice in the process, so they were not suitable as an offering to the gods. The sentiment continues: Only domestic animals are slaughtered for festivities. Wild animals are gathered for human benefit alone.

*2 small rabbits (about 2 1/4 pounds each), including livers and kidneys, each rabbit cut into 6 pieces*
*1 teaspoon dried savory*
*8 juniper berries, smashed and then chopped*
*1 1/2 teaspoons salt*
*1 teaspoon freshly ground black pepper*
*1 tablespoon fresh lemon juice*
*2 tablespoons olive oil*
*Quick Juniper Glaze (recipe follows)*
*9 firm fresh green figs, cut in half lengthwise*

1 Rinse the rabbit pieces, liver, and kidneys and pat them dry. Place in a nonreactive dish that is large enough to hold them in one tightly packed layer. Add the savory, juniper berries, salt, pepper, lemon juice, and oil, and toss to coat the pieces. Cover and refrigerate for at least 4 hours or as long as overnight. Bring to room temperature before cooking.

2 When you are ready to cook the rabbit, heat a grill to medium.

3 Place the rabbit pieces on the grill rack. (Reserve the livers and kidneys.) Grill, turning once, until the meat is golden on the outside and firm but not dry, 35 to 40 minutes. Coat the meat with the Quick Juniper Glaze during the last 5 minutes of cooking.

4 Transfer the rabbit to a platter and set it aside in a warm place. Place the figs, livers, and kidneys on the rack and grill, turning once, until the figs are slightly softened and the liver and kidneys are firm but still rosy in the center, 3 to 5 minutes. Arrange the figs, liver, and kidneys around the rabbit and serve right away.

# MENU

## OTHER DISHES FOR THE TABLE

# QUICK JUNIPER GLAZE

### MAKES 1 CUP STRAINED GLAZE OR 2 CUPS UNSTRAINED SAUCE

The air in the Greek countryside always smells fresh, largely because the breeze is perfumed by the country's carpet of aromatic plants and shrubs. Here the air smells a bit more of savory, there a bit more of juniper, somewhere else of chamomile, oregano, or sage, but always some subtle scent wafts from the land.

Such an evanescence cannot be bottled and added to food, but a glaze of wine reduced with a bouquet of herbs can capture the sweet scent of Greek air. Use the glaze with rabbit, fowl, venison, pork, or beef or serve it as a sauce.

## JUNIPER

Juniper, with its densely meshed prickly leaves and hidden berries, grows wild all over Europe. In Greece the bush, called *agria kyparissi,* or "wild cypress," makes paths to mountain sanctuaries difficult to venture along, guards monasteries, perhaps hides the homes of nymphs and sprites. The berry and leaves of the shrub—though we usually use just the berry—add an awakening burst to foods. Greeks use the berry to heighten flavor, particularly of game, such as boar and venison, wild fowl, and hare, as well as pork and pork sausage. Juniper berries vary considerably in strength; the farther south they grow, the more essential oils they contain and the stronger the piney flavor and aroma. Only the ripe berries, which take three years to mature and by then have turned blue, are used as a seasoning. Greeks gather the ripe berries from the hillsides during last Sunday outings in October, before the rains and the onset of winter.

2 tablespoons olive oil
1 medium onion, finely chopped
1 1/2 tablespoons crushed juniper berries
1 teaspoon chopped fresh savory, thyme, or oregano leaves, or 1/2 teaspoon dried
2 cups dry red wine
1/4 teaspoon salt
1/4 teaspoon freshly ground black pepper

1 Heat the oil in a medium-size saucepan over medium-high heat. Add the onion and sauté until wilted, 2 to 3 minutes.

2 Add the juniper berries, savory, wine, salt, and pepper and bring to a boil. Reduce the heat and simmer briskly until the mixture has reduced enough to coat a spoon lightly and has taken on a glossy shine, 10 to 15 minutes.

3 Strain the glaze and use it to coat the meat or fowl you are roasting or grilling during the last 5 minutes of cooking time. Or, use the unstrained mixture as a sauce, spooning it over the meat or fowl just before serving.

## WAYS TO VARY THE GLAZE:

■ For a touch of sweetness, stir in 2 teaspoons Hymettus honey or a good splash of Mavrodaphne wine while the glaze is reducing.

■ If a sweet-tart fruity accent is desired, add 1/4 cup crushed blackberries while the glaze is reducing.

■ If the glaze is to be used on roasted meat or poultry, stir 2 or so tablespoons of the drippings into the glaze before applying it.

# FLAVORING THE GOLDEN OIL

The olive, and especially the luxurious oil the olive provides, figured as the consummate symbol of culture and civilization to the ancient Greeks. It was Athena's gift of the olive tree, rather than Poseidon's gift of a spring of fresh water, that made the Athenians choose the goddess as their protector over the powerful water god. The contest had been over which gift was the most valuable to humans. Poseidon's offering ensured one of the necessities for life. But the olive tree, with its demand for tending, harvesting, and pressing or brining, not only produced an invaluable treasure but also required community, custom, and endeavor. It signified society and social arts.

In honor of such cultivated arts, I bring a touch of civilized refinement to every wild dish in the use of olive oil. I use the green-gold liquid in game recipes in a way particularly beneficial to wild beasts and birds: to give moisture. (Game meats tend to be lean, dark, and a little dry because the animals are highly active.) And although you can use a good-quality plain olive oil in game dishes, I suggest that you add a sylvan touch from time to time by employing an olive oil infused with wild herbs and flavors. Here's how:

To 1 cup extra-virgin olive oil, add one of the following and allow it to sit at room temperature overnight. Use right away or, if keeping longer, store, covered, in the refrigerator. Bring to room temperature before using. Refrigerated, the oil will keep for no more than 2 weeks. After 2 weeks, discard the oil.

■ 1 small bay leaf

■ 1 sprig fresh winter savory

■ 1 sprig fresh marjoram

■ 1 small sprig fresh rosemary

■ 1 small sprig juniper bough

■ 2 hazelnuts (filberts)

■ A few chamomile flowers

■ A few pine needles

■ 1 small mace blade

■ 2 shavings of black or white truffle

■ 1/4 teaspoon crushed juniper berries

# oven-stewed rabbit

## CORFU-STYLE

### SERVES 6

2 small rabbits (about 2¼ pounds each), including livers and kidneys, each rabbit cut into 6 pieces
1 rib celery, coarsely chopped
1 medium carrot, coarsely chopped
1 small onion, coarsely chopped
2 bay leaves, crumbled
1 small sprig fresh rosemary
5 whole cloves
8 allspice berries
½ teaspoon freshly ground black pepper
1 teaspoon salt
½ cup balsamic vinegar
3 cups dry red wine
2 tablespoons olive oil
2 tablespoons chopped fresh flat-leaf parsley leaves

ON THE ISLAND OF CORFU THE *STIFADO* IS DIFFERENT THAN IN OTHER PARTS OF GREECE. IN ADDITION TO THE USUAL ONION AND BAY LEAVES, CORFU COOKS ADD A SERIOUS SPLASH OF VINEGAR. THE MAINLAND VERSION OF *STIFADO* (PAGE 374) IS THE MOST FAMOUS WAY OF PREPARING BOTH BEEF AND RABBIT IN GREECE, AND WHILE IT IS NEVER ORDINARY (QUITE THE OPPOSITE—IT IS DIVINE), I SOMETIMES YEARN FOR A CHANGE.

Here is a rabbit *stifado* that is extraordinary and yet quite true to the Hellenes. The onion is chopped, eliminating the step of peeling boiling onions. The traditional cinnamon has been replaced with allspice berries. The cloves and bay leaves remain, but rosemary makes an appearance. The tomato, almost always found in Greek stews, is not present. Rather there is wine, celery, and carrot, and in keeping with Corfu's style of cooking, vinegar. The gusto is enough to send the traveler sailing to Corfu, to follow the path of epic hero, romantic poet, battling kings and emperors. Was it Corfu they sought – or hares?

*Corfu's modern name, Kerkir, comes from Korkyra, a daughter of a river god Poseidon brought to the island.*

1 Rinse the rabbit pieces, livers, and kidneys and pat them dry. Place them in a nonreactive dish that is large enough to hold them in one tightly packed layer. Sprinkle all the ingredients except the oil and parsley over the rabbit. Cover the dish and marinate in the refrigerator for 2 to 4 hours, turning the ingredients once. Bring to room temperature before cooking.

2 When you are ready to cook the rabbit, preheat the oven to 325°F.

3 Heat the oil in a large heavy skillet over medium-high heat. Remove the rabbit from the

## SATISFYING EVERY APPETITE

In rural Greece it is believed that a pregnant woman should be given a taste of any aromatic food the instant she might smell it. The taste is for the baby, not the mother, for any food aroma wakens the baby's appetite, and that appetite must be satisfied or the baby will become ravenous. I know this custom firsthand, for on one extended visit to Greece I was pregnant—very pregnant—with my first child. I could hardly walk a step without someone forcing a tidbit on me, and many times I was in no mood for a tidbit.

One occasion was different. My husband and I were about to leave the island when Averkios, the tavern keep, came running up to present us with a hare he had just stalked and killed. "It's for the baby," he said. I was thunderstruck. How could we deal with a hare? It would spoil on a twelve-hour boat trip, and in an Athenian hotel there was no way to cook it. But Averkios said, "You don't understand. Give it to the ship's cook. He will cook it for you so you eat well on your trip. Just offer him a piece and he will gladly do it." And it was true. We asked to see the ship's chef. He appeared, scowling. I presented him with the bag containing the hare and, following Averkios's instructions, asked if he would cook it for us as it was a gift and wouldn't keep, and to please keep a good piece for himself. The scowl turned into the biggest grin I have ever seen, and a few hours later, he delivered to us a bubbling casserole of hare *stifado*. The sauce was as thick as molasses. The aroma wafted cinnamon, clove, and bay. The meat was white and tender as a pullet's. A leg and thigh were missing, no doubt devoured by a man whose days were so water-spent that a taste of wild land animal was almost as alluring as a Siren's song. We, too, were ecstatic while savoring our hare. And if my son-to-be indeed had desired that flavorful hare, that day he had his fill.

marinade and pat the pieces dry, reserving the marinade. Add as many pieces to the skillet as will fit without crowding, and sauté, turning once, until browned on both sides. Transfer the meat to a large nonreactive baking dish, and repeat with the remaining rabbit. Add the livers and kidneys to the skillet and brown on both sides, about 3 minutes, then transfer to the baking dish.

4 Pour the reserved marinade into the skillet and bring to a boil. Pour the marinade into the baking dish, cover, and bake until the rabbit is fork-tender and the liquid is reduced and saucelike, 1½ hours.

5 Transfer the rabbit to a serving dish. Stain the sauce and pour it over the rabbit. Sprinkle the parsley over the top and serve right away.

**NOTES:**

■ Oven-Stewed Rabbit can also be cooked on the stovetop. Follow the same steps, but return the browned rabbit and the marinade to the skillet and simmer, covered, for 1½ hours.

■ This dish can be made with beef as well: Use 2½ to 3 pounds chuck roast.

## TAKING A TIP FROM AN EXPERT

Archestratos traveled the ancient world, surveying the best of foods and noting his opinions. He recommended that hare be served during the *symposium*, or drinking section, of the meal. Here is how he cooked it:

"The hare. There are many ways and many laws for the preparation of it. Now the best way is to bring the meat roasted to each guest during the drinking. It should be hot, simply sprinkled with salt and taken from the spit while it is still a little undercooked. Do not let it worry you to see the divine *ichor* [in Greek mythology, this is the blood of the Olympian gods] dripping from the meat, but eat it greedily. All other methods are mere diversions to my mind, thick sauces poured over, cheese melted over, too much oil over—as if preparing a tasty dish of dogfish."

# braised rabbit

## MACEDONIAN-STYLE

### SERVES 6

IN ANCIENT GREEK, AS IN LATIN, AN UNDERGROUND MINE OR DRAIN WAS CALLED A *KNIKLOS* (*CUNICULUS* TO THE ROMANS), MEANING "RABBIT BURROW." IN ENGLISH, FROM THE SAME ROOT STEM, COMES "CONEY," ANOTHER TERM FOR RABBIT. (NOW YOU KNOW WHAT CONEY ISLAND WAS ONCE FAMOUS FOR!)

Macedonia is home to a mix of peoples who speak a variety of Indo-European languages, Greek, Slavic, Romanian, Albanian, and some who speak Turkish. Indeed, the place contains such a medley of people, each with their own dress, language, and customs, that the term *macedoine* in cooking came to mean a medley of ingredients.

In keeping with that, and the fact that the wild hare of Macedonia are both wily and sweet, the braised rabbit here has a brisk yet honied liveliness. The bell peppers of Greece, slightly hotter than the American ones, are simulated with the combination of orange bell and poblano peppers. The taste of the concoction is so enchanting that it will appeal to as wide a variety of diners as Macedonia holds.

*Braising Greek-style over wood adds a delicious smoky flavor to a dish.*

## MENU
### OTHER DISHES FOR THE TABLE

**CRUSTY BREAD, OLIVES, AND CHEESE**

**RADISH *TZATZIKI* WITH PITA**
page 469

**_PASTITSIO_ PIE**
page 256

**DOUBLE LEMON *AVGOLEMONO* SOUP MADE WITH CHICKEN STOCK**
page 169

**FRESH FRUIT TO FINISH**

2 small rabbits (about 2 1/4 pounds each), including livers and kidneys, each rabbit cut into 6 pieces

2 tablespoons olive oil

3 cups dry red wine

1 1/2 tablespoons honey

12 ounces portobello, porcini, chanterelle, or morel mushrooms, stems trimmed, caps wiped clean and thickly sliced

1 large orange bell pepper, stemmed, seeded, and sliced into 1/4-inch-thick strips

2 poblano peppers, stemmed, seeded, and thinly sliced

6 cloves garlic, minced or pressed

5 whole cloves

1 large bay leaf

1 1/2 teaspoons salt

3/4 teaspoon freshly ground black pepper

1 Preheat the oven to 375°F.

2 Rinse the rabbit pieces, livers, and kidneys and pat them dry. Heat the oil in a nonreactive flameproof casserole over medium-high heat. When it is hot, add the rabbit pieces and sauté, turning, until browned all over, 6 to 10 minutes.

3 Add all the remaining ingredients except the liver and kidneys and bring to a boil. Stir to mix, cover the pot, and bake in the oven for 1 hour and 15 minutes. Add the liver and kidneys and continue baking, uncovered, until the rabbit is tender, about 15 minutes.

4 Remove the casserole from the oven. Discard the cloves and bay leaf and serve.

# pan-seared quail

## CLOAKED IN GRAPE LEAVES

### SERVES 6

GAME BIRDS HAVE LONG BEEN AN IMPORTANT PART OF THE SPLENDOR OF GREEK FOOD. WOODCOCKS, PIGEONS, THRUSHES, PARTRIDGES, PHEASANT, FIGPECKERS, SNIPES, DOVES, BLACKBIRDS—ALL HAVE MADE THEIR WAY TO THE TABLE. IN THE OLD DAYS, THE GREEKS ALSO COOKED THE EUROPEAN ROBIN; A PIE CALLED *ROUVELLOPITA* TOOK FIFTY OR SO OF THESE SMALL RED-BREASTED FLYCATCHERS.

Game birds provided welcome variety to the daily fare. And there were, as the Greeks would say, *bolika* (plenty) of birds. *Ortikia* (quail) are readily available to the non-hunting shopper. Pan grilling in a grape-leaf wrapping imparts a very Hellenic tang to delicate quail meat, creating a simple and simply engaging dish.

*6 quail*
*1 teaspoon chopped fresh thyme leaves, or ¹/₂ teaspoon dried*
*2 teaspoons coarsely chopped lemon zest*
*3 tablespoons olive oil*
*Salt and freshly ground black pepper*
*12 to 18 jarred grape leaves*

1 Using kitchen shears, cut along the backbone of each quail to open them butterfly-style. Rinse, pat them dry, and place them in a nonreactive dish that is large enough to hold them opened out in one layer. Sprinkle with the thyme, zest, oil, and a liberal amount of salt and pepper, and turn to coat. Wrap each quail in 1 or 2 grape leaves. Cover and set them aside to marinate in the refrigerator for several hours or as long as overnight.

2 When you are ready to cook the quail, heat a heavy, ungreased skillet over medium-high heat until hot.

3 Without removing the grape leaves, add as many quail to the skillet as will fit in one uncrowded layer, breast side down, and cook for 8 minutes. Turn, and cook until the meat is medium-rare, 5 to 7 minutes. Transfer to a platter and repeat with another batch until all the quail are cooked. Serve right away or at room temperature.

## LITTLE BIRDS BAKED IN CLAY

......................

W hen I'm camping out in the mountains, I season quail with olive oil, red wine, and whatever I find in my knapsack pantry—or, better yet, with foraged sage, wild onion grass, or dandelion. Then, if the soil is suitable, I pack clay around the birds and pop them into the coals of the fire. The method is as old as Mount Ossa. As the clay dries and heats in the fire, the quail roast inside. Then I roll the clay "eggs" out of the coals, crack them open, and sup upon the bird inside. It is as satisfying as sleeping under the *gala axia*, in Greek quite literally "the Milky Way."

# grilled quail
## ON A BED OF BUTTER-BRAISED CABBAGE

### SERVES 6

W ITH A MARINADE TO START AND A CABBAGE NEST TO END, GRILLED QUAIL STAY AS MOIST AS WHEN THEY ARE QUICKLY PAN-SEARED. THE PERFECT SIMPLICITY—A SPARTAN WOULD APPROVE—PREVAILS SO THAT TENDER MEAT, A DASH OF PEPPER, AND A SPLASH OF OIL AND LEMON RESULT IN A DISH THAT IS DELECTABLE.

6 quail
1 teaspoon chopped fresh sage leaves,
   or $1/2$ teaspoon dried
1 teaspoon freshly ground
   black pepper
$1 1/2$ tablespoons olive oil
$1/2$ cup fresh lemon juice
1 medium cabbage (1 pound),
   quartered, cored, and cut into
   $1/4$- to $1/2$-inch-wide shreds
4 tablespoons ($1/2$ stick) butter
Salt

1 Using kitchen shears, cut along the backbone of each quail to open them butterfly-style. Rinse, pat them dry, and place them in a nonreactive dish that is large enough to hold them opened out in one layer. Sprinkle with the sage, pepper, oil, and 3 tablespoons of the lemon juice and turn to coat. Cover and marinate in the refrigerator

for several hours or as long as overnight.

2 When you are ready to cook the quail, heat a grill to medium-high.

3 Place the quail on the grill and cook, turning once, until no longer pink at the thigh joint but still pink in the center of the breast, 10 to 12 minutes.

4 While the quail cook, bring a large pot of salted water to a boil over high heat. Stir in the cabbage and bring to a boil again. Immediately drain in a colander and shake off any excess moisture. Melt the butter in a large nonreactive saucepan over medium heat. Add the cabbage and stir until well wilted but still "squeaky," about 7 minutes.

5 Spread the cabbage on a platter and sprinkle with the remaining lemon juice and salt to taste. Arrange the quail over the top and serve right away.

## VARIATION:

**A Different Vegetable Nest:** Instead of the cabbage, rest the birds on white beans dresed with olive oil and sage.

# grilled squab
## OVER BULGUR AND WALNUT PILAF

### SERVES 6

PIGEON WITH PEAS, PIGEON WITH OLIVES, PIGEON IN WINE AND IN PIE, PIGEON IN LEMON SAUCE OR ROASTED ON SPITS—THE VARIETY OF WAYS IN WHICH GREEKS COOK PIGEON GIVES AN INDICATION OF JUST HOW POPULAR THE BIRD IS.

Greeks have always kept pigeons. In classical times they built pigeon coops, but archaeological evidence shows that even very early Greeks used caves in which to breed the bird. As much as pigeons have been used for ornament, sport, or messengers, they have also been raised for food. Young pigeons, full-grown and ready to fly but still unfledged, are also a part of our cuisine, known to us as squab.

Squab meat bears the same dark hue and dainty succulence that all small game birds share, but the taste is reminiscent of larger, fatter fowl. To nestle such a small but tasty bird on a bed of cracked wheat is to heed the time-honored principle of serving a modest *opsos* with *siton*. To complete the feast, a third element would be added: the *poton,* or drink. Straight, watered, or honied, that drink should be wine.

*6 squab, well rinsed and patted dry*
*2 tablespoons olive oil*
*1 teaspoon fresh thyme leaves, or*
    *1/2 teaspoon dried*
*Salt and freshly ground black pepper*
*4 cups Bulgur Wheat and Walnut*
    *Pilaf (page 233), warm*
*1 cup watercress sprigs*

## ANOTHER REASON TO FEAST ON GAME BIRDS

Ancient Greeks hunted and ate small birds for a reason other than their savor. The avians of the Mediterranean were so numerous and hungry that they were a bane to early agriculturalists, swooping down to feast upon the fruit of tree and vine, and worse, upon the newly sown wheat and barley seeds before they had a chance to sprout.

Birds, in fact, were considered as damaging a blight as frost and drought. Hesiod, an early poet and distributor of no-nonsense maxims, advised farmers to have a young boy follow behind a spring sower to scatter dirt over the seeds in the hope of deterring the raiding birds. Farmers also cast honey cakes in fields to lure birds away from freshly sown seeds, and they spread sticky birdlime on fruit tree branches. Flourishing on the seeds of cultivation, the birds of Greece were as quick to exploit human ways as humans were to exploit them, and to this day they foster and feed each other.

## MENU
### OTHER DISHES FOR THE TABLE

OLIVES AND CHEESE

OLIVE FLATBREAD
CYPRUS-STYLE
page 137

*MANESTRA WITH MINT*
page 153

BELL PEPPERS STUFFED
WITH EGGPLANT, OLIVES,
AND CAPERS
page 304

FRESH FRUIT TO FINISH

# grilled venison
## WITH SOUR CHERRY SAUCE
### SERVES 6

THROUGHOUT BOTH ANCIENT AND MODERN GREEK STORIES, DEER LEAP BEFORE THE HUNTER'S ARROW AND MEET RUSTIC CULINARY FIRES. APOLLO HUNTS THE LEAPING STAG, AS DOES HIS SISTER ARTEMIS. PERSEUS, THESEUS, AND ODYSSEUS FLUSH HART (FULLY ANTLERED EUROPEAN RED DEER) AND HIND (THE NON-ANTLERED GROWN FEMALES) FROM THEIR SYLVAN RECESSES, AS DO BANDS OF SOLDIERS AND RAIDERS.

Greek warrior and bandit tales speak of how a meal of venison was relished. To this day, the imprint of venison remains on the Greek palate, largely whetted by saga and ancestral memory rather than actual taste. As scarce as forests are in Greece today, even scarcer are deer. Some remain in timbered areas, and recipes linger on. Here the memorable meat is cooked with sour cherries and bay leaves. Together, meat and flavorings convey the arboreal magic of the animal-filled thickets that once covered the land.

*3 cups dry red wine*
*1/2 cup balsamic vinegar*
*1 medium onion, coarsely chopped*
*2 cloves garlic, minced or pressed*
*2 bay leaves, crumbled*
*4 large sprigs fresh thyme, or*
*    1 teaspoon dried thyme leaves*
*1/2 teaspoon salt*
*1/2 teaspoon freshly ground*
*    black pepper*
*2 1/2 pounds bone-in loin of venison*
*1 cup sour cherries in syrup*
*    (see Note), drained*

1 In a large nonreactive dish, stir together the wine, vinegar, onion, garlic, bay leaves, thyme, and salt and pepper. Add the venison and turn to coat. Cover and marinate in the refrigerator overnight, turning three or four times. Bring to room temperature before cooking.

1 Place the squab, oil, and thyme in a large dish. Turn to coat, and sprinkle the birds liberally with salt and pepper inside and out. Cover and set aside at room temperature for 30 minutes, or refrigerate for as long as several hours. Bring to room temperature before cooking.

2 When you are ready to cook the squab, heat a grill to medium.

3 Arrange the squab on the grill rack, cover, and grill, turning once, until the outside is golden and the juices are no longer pink, 35 minutes.

4 Mound the pilaf on a platter and place the squab on top. Garnish with the watercress and serve.

2 When you are ready to cook the venison, heat a grill to medium-high.

3 Lift the venison out of the marinade, reserving the marinade, and place it on the grill. Grill, turning once, until medium-rare on the outside and rare in the middle, 40 to 45 minutes. Transfer to a platter and set aside for the juices to settle, 20 minutes.

4 While the venison is cooking, strain the marinade into a medium-size nonreactive saucepan. Add the cherries, bring to a simmer over medium heat, and cook briskly until reduced and thickened into a sauce, 30 to 45 minutes.

5 To serve, cut the loin into chops and arrange the pieces on the platter over the collected juices. Pour the cherry sauce over the chops and serve.

### NOTES:

■ Sour cherries in syrup are available in Greek and Turkish markets. If you have fresh sour cherries, pit them and add a little sugar (1 tablespoon per 1 cup cherries) when you cook them in Step 4.

■ You can also roast the venison with equally divine results: Preheat the oven to 450°F. Sauté the venison in a heavy skillet that has been lightly greased with olive oil until it is browned, about 10 minutes. Transfer the meat to a roasting pan, place it in the oven, and immediately reduce the oven temperature to 375°F. Roast, turning once, for 30 to 35 minutes.

*Swift, aloof, sometimes dangerous, Artemis seems not to care for fellow god or mortal, but only for the woods and the chase.*

## HOW NOT TO GO STAG

P erhaps the most famous hunting story in Greek mythology involves the pursuit of venison and takes place when deer hunter Actaeon meets deer huntress Artemis, one of the twelve great gods of Mount Olympus. In a valley thick with cypress and pine, Actaeon (grandson of Cadmus), and his friends decided to rest after a successful chase that had netted them many prizes. Nearby, Artemis—huntress, virgin, sister of Apollo—had finished her deer hunt, and with her handmaidens attending, she thought to have a bath. Unlucky Actaeon happened to step into Artemis's bathing grotto just as she slipped off her apparel. Dashing water in his face to force him to close his eyes, Artemis dared him to tell what he had seen. As he stammered for an answer, from out of his head stretched antlers, his neck lengthened, and his skin changed to hide. Artemis transformed him into a magnificent stag. Voiceless, hoofed, and burdened with a heavy rack of horns, Actaeon was besieged by his own hunting dogs and run to ground— fit punishment quite possibly, but hardly fair for such an innocent offense. Still, who can measure the ire of a not very game virgin goddess?

# thyme-fed snails

## WITH TOMATOES, SPRING GARLIC, AND SPRING ONIONS

### SERVES 4 TO 6

WHEN MY ADOPTED GRANDMOTHER, KOUINA, MADE A DISH SHE CALLED *BOURBOURISTA*, I ASKED WHAT THE WORD MEANT. SHE SAID, "YOU KNOW, HOW THE SNAILS *BOURBOURISTAN* WHEN THEY HIT THE PAN." SO I ASSUME THE TERM MEANS SOMETHING LIKE "CRACKLING" SNAILS.

Greek has many onomato-poeic terms, words that sound like the thing they are describing. After all, the word *onomatopoeia*, meaning "name poetry," or "name maker," is Greek. The spring rains of May occur when garlic and spring onions are sprouting, and bring forth the snails. Many Greek snail dishes employ thyme, but the innovation here is mastic, which imparts a mysterious allure. If you can't buy spring garlic or spring onions, use scallions and the freshest garlic you can find.

*36 canned snails, rinsed and drained (see Note)*

*1 1/2 teaspoons fresh thyme leaves, or 1/2 teaspoon dried*

*1/2 teaspoon mastic, pulverized (see page 143)*

*1/2 cup olive oil*

*2 spring onions or scallions, including tops, trimmed and finely chopped*

*10 heads spring garlic, including tops, trimmed and finely chopped*

*6 medium tomatoes, finely chopped, juices reserved*

*1/2 cup dry white wine*

*1/2 teaspoon salt*

*1/4 teaspoon freshly ground black pepper*

*Freshly grated nutmeg to taste*

## THE ABUNDANT FOREST

The woods, dark yet sun-streamed, alluring yet wild, threatening yet teeming with life, appear as a constant motif running though Greek heroic myth and contemporary folktales. Wooded hinterlands are scarce in Greece now. But once woodlands were plentiful, and much that they offered enriched the labor-filled existence of the Greek commoner as well as the nobleman.

From the forests came the timber for building houses, pine wine barrels, and twigs to feed the fire. Among the thickets grew berries, laurel, and juniper with which to flavor foods. The woods provided refuge and a place to let animals graze free. Within the woods were flowing rivers, waterfalls, lakes, and ponds. The woods sequestered edible creatures—stag, hare, boar, fierce tusked pig, wild goats, dove, and other fowl. Without slaughtering a valuable cow or goat, a person could find meaty food in the forest. It offered game for sport as well—wolf, bear, fox, and eagle.

And lest we forget, in the woods lived nymphs. I was told that if I came upon a band of them dancing, I must strip off my clothes and join their circle until the sun appeared and three cocks crowed. Fortunately (or unfortunately), I never came upon a band of sylvan sylphs, for I do get chilly.

1 In a medium-size bowl, toss together the snails, thyme, and mastic. Cover and set aside to marinate for at least 30 minutes, or refrigerate for up to several hours.

2 When ready to cook, heat the oil in a large nonreactive skillet over medium heat. Add the onions and all but 2 tablespoons of the garlic and stir until beginning to wilt, 2 minutes. Add the tomatoes and their juices, the wine, salt, pepper, and nutmeg and bring to a boil. Reduce the heat and simmer until the tomatoes begin to collapse, 5 minutes.

3 Stir in the snails, cover the pan, and simmer gently until tender, 20 minutes. Remove the cover and continue simmering until the liquid is slightly thickened and saucelike, 5 minutes. Sprinkle the reserved garlic over the top and serve right away.

**NOTE:** Canned snails are almost as good as fresh and far less trouble.

## DRUNK ON RAIN, MAD FOR SNAILS

The spells between rainfalls on the Greek islands can be long indeed, and I had lived there many months before a shower occurred. When water did pour from the sky, it produced the most bizarre behavior I had yet seen: The whole village seemed to go mad. People began to run about in a frenzy, collecting buckets, finding old sandals, gathering in gangs, laughing, yelling, cheering, swirling—I thought it might have rained ouzo. Had Dionysos reappeared? Could raindrops alone produce such a bacchanal? Well, not exactly. What the rainfall did was to flush the snails out of their hiding places into full daylight where they could be spotted and collected. The unbounded joy was over the ensuing snail hunt and the snail feast to follow.

In their oldest footwear, bare-ankled in readiness for splattered mud, the villagers took off to gather the shell-encased morsels. For the next several days every courtyard held a grain-filled bucket full of snails, munching away as they purged themselves. Then the feasts began: snails in tomato sauce, snails in herbs and oil, snails in rice. The revel—a spontaneous collective madness—went on for days, all for the gustatory pleasure of the little garden creature we most often revile.

# AESOP'S WILD KINGDOM: MORALS WITH THE MEAL

THE WORLD OF ANCIENT GREECE WAS FAR MORE CRUEL THAN THE WAY WE LIKE TO PICTURE OUR OWN WORLD. IT WAS A PLACE OF CONNIVING, WICKEDNESS, MURDER, TREACHERY, DECEIT, MOCKERY, AND CONTEMPT.

Compassion was not honored. On the contrary, the code of conduct involved total self-reliance (never trust the motives of a helper), taking advantage of the one who is down (never show weakness), being cunning and always aware that cunning might be played upon you (to be foxy is still an esteemed trait in Greece, after all!).

Or so the rules seem as presented by Aesop in his fables. Among Aesop's animal adventures—mostly misadventures— are displayed sharply cutting humor, trickery, treachery, one-upmanship, disparagement of all frailty, and a ton of mockery. Aesop juxtaposes the poor but canny peasant against the aristocracy and lets the lowly address the mighty. Even the bees get to approach Zeus with their complaints.

*One fox treed. Another near to being caught, but according to Aesop it may yet have some tricks left.*

## EAT OR GET EATEN

The ancient Greeks lived closer to nature than we do today, and satire, jokes, and telling characterizations in the form of familiar birds and beasts gave Aesop's tales universal potency. Almost every beast in every fable reveals some shiftiness of purpose, and every story spins a moral that shiftiness merits. Many of Aesop's crew are after a full belly. Eat or get eaten is one of the major themes. If not pursuing a hearty meal, the animals seem to be avoiding becoming some other creature's dinner.

The wolf tries to eat a kid, but the kid tricks him. The wolf is by profession a butcher, but the kid lures him into acting as a musician. He strikes a raw note when the kid escapes (stick to what you know).

The wolf then tries to eat a dog, but the dog asks the wolf to wait until he's fattened up. The smart dog never lets the wolf get close again (don't delay your dinner).

The raven seizes a snake to eat, but the snake twists around and bites the raven (some treasures threaten your life).

An ambivalent dog tries to eat a hare and lick its chops at the same time. Says the hare,

*Many of Aesop's crew are after a full belly. Eat or get eaten is one of the major themes.*

*Aesop surrounded by his fabled inspiration.*

"Bite me or kiss me, so that I can know if I'm your enemy or friend" (don't sit on the fence).

A fox sees footprints going into a lion's cave, but not coming out (heed signs of danger!).

When the lion and bear fight over food, the fox steals it (pay attention!).

A human eats a neighbor's harvest, so Zeus changes the pilferer into an ant (action, not form, reveals character).

The country mouse learns from the city mouse that it isn't worth fear to eat luxuriously (desires have a price).

An overconfident, self-assured hare loses a race to a slow but determined tortoise (we all know the moral to that one).

## A MASTER COLLECTOR

The tales go on and on and include a cast of creatures not always native to Greece, such as camels, jackals, and elephants. Quite likely animal fables were a way to depict vice and villainy all around the Mediterranean, and Aesop was a master collector of such parables. In Greece, of course, he knew hares as well as tortoises—not only how they behaved, but also how delicious they tasted.

# sauces, toppings, and marinades

FROM THE FIRST STEPS—A FEW LEAVES PERCHED ON A BOWL OF GRAIN, A GARLIC CLOVE MASHED IN A FLATBREAD, AN EGG TO THICKEN A BROTH—THE LEAP TO THE CREATION OF SAUCES WAS NOT A GREAT ONE IN EARLY GREEK COOKING. NOR WAS TOPPING THE DISH WITH A CONDIMENT, OR SOAKING FOOD IN A ZESTY SOLUTION BEFORE COOKING IT. IN GREEK CUISINE THE TRADITION OF ENLIVENING FOOD WITH A SAUCE, A GARNISH, A MARINADE, IS, IN FACT, A VERY OLD ONE.

Know that in cooking, no seasoning is equal to the sauce of impudence.

—ATHENAEUS, SECOND CENTURY B.C.E.

The first white sauce, some say, was invented by a chef named Ariades of Athens, though others say the chef was named Orion. A Greek called Lamprias created a brown pan sauce thickened with cooked flour. When Hector was a pup, the people who lived on the shores of the Black Sea began to make a salty extraction of dried fish that added dash, and ancient Greeks were mad for a splash of *oximeli*, their vinegar and honey dressing.

The first sauces were few and not especially ornate. Greeks made blanketing gravies that they seasoned with herbs, spices, and flower petals. For flavoring, they particularly favored silphium, saffron, and rue. They blended marinades of vinegar, grape must, oil, cheese, onions, garlic, fish paste, eggs, honey, and tidbits such as raisins.

A notable change came about when the Romans adapted Greek cuisine, adding their own gusto. They threw in a veritable hodgepodge of herbs, spices, nuts, dates, fruit syrup, and milk. Their taste for sauces with highly elaborate flavorings and satiny textures in turn influenced Greek cooking.

A second change came about in modern times, when new foods met up with traditional ingredients and preparations. Yogurt now soothed the bite, tomato replaced vinegar, potato rather than bread was used as a thickener. Meats and fish were bathed in citrus-laden marinades. Hot peppers garnished pilaf; sugar garlanded cakes.

But, in fact, Greek cooking makes use of relatively few sauces. The main quartet consists of the much-loved lemon-egg blend, an updated white sauce, garlic spread, and a yogurt splash. As important are pan juice sauces, also called *saltas*, which are developed in the cooking vessel and reduced to a syrupy consistency. There are also a few special sauces made for particular dishes.

Meanwhile, crusts and toppings have grown in number, and almost no grilled food hits the fire without a suitable marinade. All go to make the banquet of Greek dishes yet more inspired.

# THE SAUCES

## avgolemono sauce

**MAKES 2 CUPS**

S INCE CHICKENS BEGAN TO SCRATCH THE DIRT IN THEIR YARDS, GREEKS HAVE USED EGGS—IN WHEAT AND BARLEY CAKES TO HOLD THEM TOGETHER, IN STUFFINGS TO MOLD THEM, AND IN LIQUIDS TO THICKEN THEM INTO A SAUCE. IN BYZANTINE TIMES, WHEN LEMONS BECAME PART OF THE HORTICULTURE, THE BRIGHT NEW CITRUS JUICE WAS ADDED TO THE THICKENER. THE COMBINATION HAD EVERYTHING: IT WAS AT ONCE CREAMY AND ZINGY.

L ike Iris's rainbow with its span of colors, Greece's menu of sauces spans a wide range. Some are creamy mantles, others zesty and jazzy. Some provide a shimmery wash, others sit atop like jeweled ornaments.

All perform the job at hand: They exalt the food they accompany, giving it a mellow medium or a burst of sass. The word "sauce" comes from the Latinization *sal*, for the Greek *al*, meaning "salt," and Greek sauces salt in every way. They add piquancy, wit, and counterpoint.

And so it remains. *Avgolemono* —that fusion of egg and lemon— is the quintessential sauce of Greece. It does more than coat food; it perks it up, brightens it, and at the same time makes it more lavish. At its best the sauce is like a luscious culinary eiderdown. *Avgolemono* can be made with just egg yolks (very rich) or with egg and cornstarch (too gluey). I prefer to use the whole egg, white along with yellow.

*Avgolemono* is traditionally served on lamb, goat, chicken, vegetables, and Greece's ever-cherished meat-stuffed *dolmades*. Two cups will sauce 5 to 6 pounds of meat; 2 chickens; enough fish or vegetables, such as cauliflower, to serve 6; 40 to 45 stuffed grape leaves (page 47); or 20 stuffed cabbage leaves.

*1 cup meat, poultry, fish, or vegetable stock (see Note and pages 170, 171, and 174)*
*3 large eggs*
*1/4 cup fresh lemon juice*
*Salt*

1 Heat the stock in a medium-size nonreactive saucepan over medium-high heat. When it is just beginning to boil, remove the pan from the heat.

2 Beat the eggs in a bowl until frothy, about 2 minutes. Whisk in the lemon juice. Then very slowly add the stock, whisking vigorously.

3 Pour the mixture back into the pan and set it over low heat. Cook, whisking gently, until it has thickened, 8 to 10 minutes. Immediately remove from the heat and stir in salt to taste (depending on the saltiness of the stock). Use the sauce right away, or set it aside in a warm place for up to 30 minutes.

**NOTE:** *Avgolemono* sauce is usually served while still warm. However, if you wish to serve it at room temperature as more of a dressing, you can make the sauce with stock in advance, cool it, and store it in the refrigerator for as long as overnight. Be sure to

# GAROS—INFAMOUS SAUCE OF ANCIENT GREECE AND ROME

IN ANCIENT TIMES, GREEKS LIVING ALONG THE BLACK SEA COAST BEGAN TO MANUFACTURE A LIQUID FROM FERMENTED FISH, CALLED *GAROS*. THAT CONCOCTION BECAME ONE OF THE MAIN SAUCES OF ANCIENT GREECE, AND LATER *THE* SAUCE OF ANCIENT ROME. THE DEMAND FOR IT WAS SO GREAT THAT PRODUCTION OF THE STUFF SPREAD CLEAR TO SPAIN AND FRANCE.

Yet *garos* at first was probably created simply as a way to avoid wasting fish. Animals could be driven to the market alive, and almost all their parts became food or other products. Reaching port with live fish was another story: While their flesh was readily marketable, their innards were routinely discarded, and the fish also rotted easily. To solve both problems, the people on the Black Sea began to salt both fish and innards. They put the bits into a jar, waited for it to ferment, then strained the fish and collected the fermented liquid. It was this liquid that became the famous *garos*. (Not that such frugal fisherpeople threw away the solids! Those they sold to the poor to season their otherwise dull porridge.) The manufacture of *garos* and the trade in it made many a Greek, and Greek colony, rich. Of course, it had one drawback: The process of making the stuff was so odorous that laws all over Greece set forth just how far away from any settlement a *garos* plant must be.

Greeks adored the sauce and passed the dish on to their conquerors. The Romans, who called it *garum* or *liquamen*, went wild for it. It became the sauce of all sauces for them, put on everything.

They ate it in its original form and pumped it up with yet more seasonings. They used it not only as a sauce by itself, but as a way to add salt to other sauces. *Garum* was their ketchup, their mustard, and their soy. Their conquests of Gaul and other Atlantic coast areas were in part impelled by their need for anchovies and mackerel to turn into *garum*. Both Greek and Roman amphorae of *garos* are found all over the western Mediterranean and up the Atlantic coast.

But by the end of the later Byzantine epoch, *garos* began to fade from use. It had already died away in western Europe; now it disappeared in the eastern regions. Orchards of lemons and other citrus fruits had spread all around the Mediterranean. Squeeze by squeeze, their juice began to overtake the sourness of fermented fish. Salt had become inexpensive and commonplace. With these items in hand, the combination of egg and lemon became the new Greek sauce to season many a dish.

Yet the ghost of *garos* abides. The ubiquitous fish sauce of Southeast Asia has a similar base, and some of our old standards, Worcestershire and the like, still contain salt fish.

remove it from the refrigerator at least 30 minutes before using so it can come to room temperature, then whisk to smooth it again before serving. If you would like to have the *avgolemono* warm again after refrigerating, bring it to room temperature, then reheat it carefully in a microwave oven on high for 1 minute—no longer or the sauce might curdle.

## VARIATIONS:

**Mustard, Sage, and Rosemary** *Avgolemonos: Avgolemono* needs no other seasoning, but it does take in other flavors with velvet ease, each subtly changing the sauce's tone. Mustard *avgolemono* offers broccoli, cauliflower, and other raw, blanched, or cooked vegetables a snappy blanketing or dip. Sage *avgolemono* adds an intriguing mystery to soups, and rosemary *avgolemono* awakens lamb, goat, pork, and poultry. The flavored sauces can also be a binder of scalloped potatoes or a topping for meat-filled grape leaves.

Prepare the *avgolemono* as described above. Just before serving, whisk in either 2 teaspoons Dijon mustard, $1/2$ teaspoon chopped fresh sage leaves, or $1/2$ teaspoon chopped fresh rosemary needles.

# saltsa besamel

## WHITE SAUCE

### MAKES ABOUT 2 CUPS

SINCE THEIR EARLIEST DAYS, GREEKS USED THE FLOUR THEY GROUND FROM WHEAT TO MAKE A SIMPLE THICKENED WHITE SAUCE. THE ELEMENTARY, USEFUL INNOVATION SPREAD ACROSS EUROPE AND BEYOND. IN RECENT TIMES IT RETURNED TO GREECE—ALTHOUGH IT NEVER LEFT COMPLETELY—USING BUTTER AND MILK RATHER THAN OIL AS ITS EMOLLIENT AND LIQUID AND CALLED BY ITS FRENCH NAME IN GREEK, *BESAMEL*. IT IS ALSO SOMETIMES CALLED *SALTSA ASPRA*, OR "WHITE SAUCE."

In Greek cooking the sauce is essential for blanketing the top of *moussaka* and *pastitsio*, for enfolding many vegetables, and for adding soft hints of such flavors as nutmeg and lemon to many preparations. Without added enhancements, the recipe here is *Saltsa Besamel* at its most basic. Two cups of white sauce is enough to cover 6 servings of a simple vegetable dish. Two to 4 cups (1 or 2 batches) is enough to cover 1 recipe of *moussaka* or *pastitsio*, depending on how thick you want the white-sauce topping.

3 tablespoons butter
3 tablespoons unbleached
  all-purpose flour
1 1/2 cups milk
1/4 teaspoon salt
Generous pinch of nutmeg,
  preferably freshly grated

1 Melt the butter in a medium-size saucepan over medium-high heat until foaming. Add the flour, whisk until the mixture is smooth, and reduce the heat to medium. Cook, stirring, until the mixture begins to turn golden, 2 minutes.

## AN ANCIENT SWEET *BESAMEL* AND ITS CURIOUS COUSINS

Fancy sauces were considered rather immoral by upright ancient Greeks, but such sauces were part of the cuisine from early on. Two in particular entered the cuisine from Lydia, early Greece's rich and more intemperate neighbor. Both were called "lascivious comestibles" by Menander.

*Karyke*, it seems, was a sweet *besamel*. It was made of flour or bread crumbs, eggs, and honey. One could similarly sweeten and enrich today's *besamel* by adding honey or Mavrodaphne wine.

The second sauce, *kandaulos*, was so popular that it appeared in eighteen cookbooks in Athenaeus's time. Some considered it an aphrodisiac. *Kandaulos* was made up of fried or boiled meat, grated bread, cheese, dill, and broth. A few sources also included salted fish.

A third Lydian sauce, *myttotos*, was served on tuna. It consisted of garlic, leeks, cheese, honey, olive oil, and sometimes eggs.

As for immorality, or at least decline, it was thought by some that the power of bellicose Sparta began to ebb when the previously austere Spartans became enchanted with *karyke* and *kandaulos*.

2 Whisk in the milk and salt and cook over medium heat, whisking frequently, until thickened and creamy, 12 to 15 minutes. Whisk in the nutmeg.

3 Use right away, or allow to cool and refrigerate for as long as 10 days. Reheat before using, thinning the sauce with a little milk if it is too thick.

## VARIATIONS:

**Savory Accents:** *Saltsa Besamel* is also a great way to add flavor notes to food. The beauty of annexing the flavor to the sauce rather than to the dish itself is that the extra topnote lingers like the finish of a wine.

■ **For more richness:** When the sauce is done and has cooled for a minute or two, stir in 2 lightly beaten egg yolks. This is the classic version for *moussaka.*

■ **For more tang:** Add 2 tablespoons fresh lemon juice with the milk and salt.

■ **For creamier tang:** Make a yogurt white sauce, as an awakening finish to such dishes as *moussaka* and *pastitsio* or any lamb dish. Follow the recipe above, substituting ¾ cup milk and ¾ cup plain yogurt for the 1½ cups milk.

■ **For more color and mystery:** Add ¼ teaspoon saffron threads while you whisk the thickening sauce.

■ **For more bite:** Add ¼ teaspoon dry mustard or ½ teaspoon prepared Dijon mustard while you whisk the thickening sauce.

## QUICK BESAMEL

Cooking white sauce in a microwave cuts the time from about 15 minutes to 5. Place the butter in a large bowl and microwave, uncovered, on high until melted and foaming, 1 to 2 minutes. Remove the bowl and add the flour; whisk until smooth. Return the bowl to the microwave and continue microwaving, uncovered, on high until bubbling, 1 to 2 minutes.

Remove the bowl again, whisk in the milk, and microwave for 2 minutes.

Remove the bowl and whisk until smooth. Return to the microwave and cook until thickened, 1 minute.

# classic skordalia

W E ARE SITTING AROUND A TABLE AT AN OUTDOOR *TAVERNA* IN THE PLAKA DISTRICT OF ATHENS. IT IS MIDNIGHT. THERE'S NOT A FREE CHAIR TO BE FOUND, AND THE STREETS ARE HUMMING WITH PEOPLE. GEORGIOS TELLS ME HIS MOTHER MAKES IT WITH CRUSTLESS, OILED WHITE BREAD POUNDED IN A MORTAR. KOSTAS'S GRANDMOTHER STARTS WITH BOILED POTATO. ELLIE SAYS, NO, *SKORDALIA* IS MADE LIKE HER MOTHER'S VERSION, FROM EPIROS, SWEET WITH ALMONDS. KOULA USES WHITE VINEGAR—THAT'S HER FAMILY'S SECRET. NO, NO, SAYS DIMITRI, THE VINEGAR MUST BE RED. THE RESPONSES CHIME FROM TABLE TO TABLE IN EVERY PART OF GREECE AND WHEREVER GREEKS ROAM.

Who makes the best *skordalia?* How is it done? The versions are many, though only subtly different. The answer to who makes the best is "my mother," or sometimes "my grandmother."

*Skordalia* holds the heart of Greece. It is loved like mashed potatoes, remembered like warm cookies, dreamed of like a good steak—it is everyone's comfort food, although it bites. In any café you can order it by the plateful. In every household it welcomes children home from school. Nippy with the tang of crushed garlic, more a paste than a sauce, it is lavished over fried fish, poured on vegetables, spread on bread. I serve *skordalia* as a side dish with poultry, spread it over the skin of turkey, chicken, and duck before I roast them, rub it over a whole leg of pork as it grills, or put it out as a surprising appetizer dip.

Potato and bread are the two basic versions, covering almost every mother's rendition. My favorite is with potato and almond, but then Georgios, Koula, and Dimitri would beg to differ. Both recipes make enough to serve 6 as a sauce or topping crust for lamb, pork, fish, chicken, or duck, or 1 large turkey.

## WHAT TODAY'S SAUCES REPLACED

I crushed the most fragrant roses in a mortar, then added the carefully boiled brains of birds and pigs, from which the stringy fibers had been removed, and egg yolks. Then olive oil, fish paste, pepper, and wine. All of this I stirred well and placed in a new pot, giving it a gentle and steady fire.

**—ATHENAEUS, SECOND CENTURY** B.C.E.

## POTATO SKORDALIA

### MAKES ABOUT 2 CUPS

*1 large russet potato, peeled and cut into 1-inch pieces*
*1/3 cup blanched almonds*
*15 cloves garlic*
*1 cup olive oil*
*1 tablespoon red wine vinegar*
*1/2 teaspoon salt*

1 Place the potato in a small saucepan and add water to cover. Bring to a boil over high heat and cook until soft all the way through, about 10 minutes. Drain.

2 Transfer the potato to a food processor. Add the remaining

ingredients and blend until smooth. Use right away, or cover and store in the refrigerator for as long as overnight.

**NOTE:** You don't need a food processor to make *skordalia*—most Greeks make the beloved paste by hand. To do so, pulverize the nuts with a mortar and pestle, and transfer them to a bowl. In another bowl, mash the potato or bread (see below) with a fork or potato masher; add to the nuts. Press or mince the garlic and add it; then pour in the oil, vinegar, and salt. Blend well.

# BREAD SKORDALIA

### MAKES ABOUT 2 CUPS

*About 6 slices day-old bread, crusts removed, cut into ¹/₂-inch cubes (2 cups cubes)*
*1¹/₂ cups water*
*¹/₂ cup blanched almonds*
*15 cloves garlic*
*1 cup olive oil*
*1 tablespoon red wine vinegar*
*¹/₂ teaspoon salt*

1 Place the bread cubes in a large bowl, add the water, and soak until saturated, about 2 minutes.

2 Drain the bread, and squeeze all the liquid from it. Place the bread in a food processor, add the

## GREEKS AND GARLIC

How long have Greeks loved garlic? It couldn't get much longer. The oldest villages yet discovered in Europe lie on the plains of northern and central Greece. There, in sites now called Nea Nikomedia, Soufli Magoula, and Sesklo, dating back to 6000 B.C.E., people erected permanent homes and evolved from wanderers into farmers. They turned the wild grasses into crops, and they also enjoyed certain green shoots with bulbous roots that were sharp and tasty: garlic. The early settlers had placed themselves right on one of garlic's two home sites, the eastern Mediterranean (the other is central Asia).

It's clear they quickly began to cultivate the vegetable. By the time recorded Greek appears, the pungent bulb, called *skorodon* then, receives frequent mention, mostly for its flavor, but also for its value as a medicine. The physicians of early Greece claimed—as many people still maintain—that garlic is both a digestive and a potent disease preventive. Several kinds were grown, and part of the Athens market was devoted solely to *ta skoroda*, "the garlics."

In ancient times, garlic had already gathered a touch of the reputation it holds today: It was considered malodorous, and people who ate it were not allowed in the temple of Cybele. They had to eat their cloves outside.

Did the first people in Nea Nikomedia eat *skordalia?* They left no record. But in the queenly city of Athens, people of classical Greece concocted a favorite sauce of bread, oil, garlic, and a dash of vinegar that they called *skorothalmi.*

Greeks today, while acknowledging garlic's longtime odiferous reputation, give voice to a contrary opinion. They say that if you have eaten garlic and someone notices your breath, clearly *they* have not eaten properly. Had they had their share of garlic, they would never have noticed.

remaining ingredients, and blend until smooth. Use right away, or cover and store in the refrigerator for as long as overnight.

## OTHER MOTHERS' VERSIONS

■ Instead of almonds, use pine nuts.

■ Soak the bread in olive oil instead of water.

■ Instead of potato or bread, use half of each—another traditional formula.

■ Instead of potato or bread, use chickpeas, lima beans, broad (fava) beans, or another mealy legume that approximates the texture of potato when cooked.

■ Add a pinch of cayenne pepper.

■ Add 8 to 10 pitted black olives, 1 tablespoon capers, or 1 to 2 tablespoons Olive and Caper Tapenade (page 477).

# sweet potato skordalia

**MAKES ABOUT 2 CUPS**

SWEET POTATOES, LIKE WHITE POTATOES, ARE IMMIGRANTS TO GREECE. SO FAR, THEY ARE INCORPORATED INTO ONLY A FEW DISHES, BUT THEIR USE IS GROWING AS MORE AND MORE GREEKS DISCOVER THEIR UNUSUAL HONIED ESSENCE. CERTAINLY GREEK AMERICANS ARE ACQUAINTED WITH THE NUANCED SUGARINESS SWEET POTATOES INTRODUCE. A CULINARY LEAP CAN JOIN THE SWEET IMMIGRANT WITH THE ANCIENT SAUCE, TRANSFORMING THE CLASSIC INTO A ZIPPY NEW RENDITION FOR THE MODERN TABLE.

Denser and more glutinous than russet potatoes, sweet potatoes require a little extra liquid to achieve the thick but flowing consistency of perfect garlic paste. Rather than increasing the already adequate oil, a little water produces the desired fluffiness.

Sweet Potato *Skordalia* is a particularly good crust or sauce with roasted birds, and 2¹/₂ cups will cover a turkey, a large chicken, or 2 ducks. It is also enough to sauce 6 servings of pork or fish.

*2 medium sweet potatoes, peeled and cut into 1-inch chunks*
*¹/₃ cup pine nuts*
*3 large cloves garlic, minced or pressed*
*1 cup olive oil*
*1 tablespoon red wine vinegar*
*¹/₄ teaspoon salt*
*Dash of cayenne pepper*
*¹/₂ cup water*

1 Place the sweet potato chunks in a small saucepan and add water to cover. Bring to a boil over high heat, then reduce the heat and cook briskly until the potatoes can be pierced with a fork but are not disintegrating, about 8 minutes. Drain in a colander and set aside to drip dry for 5 minutes.

2 Pulverize the nuts in a food processor. Add the potato chunks, garlic, oil, vinegar, salt, and cayenne and process until pureed. Add the water and process until smooth. Use right away, or cover and store in the refrigerator for up to 2 days.

## NOTES:

■ Almonds, a more traditional *skordalia* ingredient, can replace the pine nuts.

■ Be sure to use real sweet potatoes, not yams. Yams are too pulpy.

*Plump Greek garlic adds savor to legions of Greek dishes.*

# skordalia

## WITH PISTACHIO OR WALNUT

### MAKES ABOUT 1 CUP

AEGINA, THE COUNTRY'S SECOND LARGEST ISLAND AND A VACATION DESTINATION FOR ATHENIANS, IS THE CAPITAL OF GREECE'S PISTACHIO CROP. INDEED, THE ISLAND BOASTS OF BEING THE "PISTACHIO CAPITAL OF THE WORLD."

Pistachio trees have grown all over Greece since antiquity, having arrived from their Near Eastern homeland a short step away. The pistachio is related to the shrub that produces mastic and to the ancient terebinth tree, the original source of turpentine. From nuts to oily solvent, all these products have a piney tang and aroma. The nuts are as prized today as they have been for eons, and in Aegina you can buy pistachio nuts in packages of all sizes, pistachio spoon sweets, and heavenly pistachio brittle. And so creating a *skordalia*-type sauce with them was a natural. The pistachio *skordalia* is aromatic, meatier, and less crunchy than the almond classic, slightly green of hue, and welcome on everything from fish to vegetable, especially fried eggplant slices. It is a great topping or sauce for grilled lamb or pork chops, white fish fillets or steaks, and chicken.

As for the walnut rendition, all through the ages Greeks have made a sauce with their beloved walnuts. In a *skordalia*, they offer a roasted, earthy, and noble taste and aroma.

Both nut-imbued versions of *skordalia* also garner praise when served as a *meze* dip for shrimp, raw vegetables, and toasted pita bread triangles.

The recipe makes enough for 6 portions of meat, fish, or poultry, or can be used as a topping or dip for 12 servings of vegetables.

About 6 slices day-old bread, crusts removed, cut into 1/2-inch cubes (2 cups cubes)

1 1/2 cups water

1 cup (4 ounces) shelled pistachio nuts or walnuts

8 to 10 large cloves garlic

1 cup olive oil

1 1/2 tablespoons fresh lemon juice

1/4 to 1/2 teaspoon salt (see Note)

1 Place the bread cubes in a large bowl, add the water, and soak until saturated, about 2 minutes. Lift the bread out of the water and squeeze it gently to remove some of the water, leaving the bread quite moist and reserving the water.

2 Place the nuts in a food processor and chop them as fine as possible.

3 Add the bread to the food processor, along with the garlic, oil, lemon juice, and salt. Process until pureed. Then stir in 1/3 to 1/2 cup of the reserved water, enough to make a thick but runny mixture. Use right away or cover and refrigerate for up to 3 days.

**NOTE:** If the pistachios are salted, the mixture may need no salt at all or only 1/4 teaspoon. With walnuts, up to 1/2 teaspoon salt may be needed to bring out their flavor.

## THE EVIL EYE

Among my friends in Greece are a number of grandmothers. They are loving, giving, wise, know the customs and foods like no others, and are often funny to the point of being ribald. Among them, Kouina, a widow of many years, probably holds top spot. One day in the village, as I was about to take off with a crowd of young women for a round of St. Irene's Day visits, Kouina ran up to me and stuffed into my jacket pocket a blue bead and enough garlic to make three bowls of *tzatziki*. "You must carry this," she said. "You are enviable and you could attract the eye."

"The eye?" I asked. "Whatever is that?" To which I got an immediate and thorough explanation. The eye, sometimes called the evil eye, is what flows into you when someone is jealous of you. It can cause weakness and illness. Babies and healthy farm animals are particularly prone to the malady. Few Greeks give credit to the eye now, but older Greeks strongly believe in it. I didn't think I was admirable enough to attract the evil eye. Still, it didn't seem that far-fetched—jealousy is a potent emotion.

Special blue beads ward off the eye, and since time immemorial garlic was thought to protect against evil spirits, as well as the evil eye, and also to cure ailments.

I carried the garlic in my pocket, and when I got home I made *tzatziki* with it, using what I had at hand—a combination of cucumber and radish. I have to say, of all the beliefs I encountered in Greece, the use of garlic against the evil eye was the easiest for me to swallow.

# tzatziki

### MAKES 2 CUPS

WHEN YOGURT FIRST ARRIVED IN GREEK CUISINE, GARLIC WAS ALREADY A DAILY FOOD OF LABORING PEOPLE. THE COMBINATION OF THE TWO QUICKLY TOOK ON A THIRD PARTNER, ANOTHER A COMMON FOOD: CUCUMBER. THE RESULT BECAME *TZATZIKI*, THE FOURTH IN THE QUARTET OF FOREMOST SAUCES IN GREEK CUISINE.

*Tzatziki* is part sauce, part salad. It appears on almost every *meze* table. It is drizzled over every *gyro* sandwich, spooned upon pilafs, spread over *dolmades*, dolloped into soups, slathered on fritters. I think of it as more of a "brightener" than a sauce—*tzatziki* is uplifting, cool, and bedazzling. While Greek cooks most often add dill to the mixture, mint contributes extra brightness. If you prefer, make *tzatziki* the classic way.

The recipe makes enough to serve 6 in any fashion.

*3/4 teaspoon salt*
*2 to 4 cloves garlic*
*1 1/2 cups plain yogurt*
*1 small cucumber*
*1 tablespoon chopped fresh mint*
    *or dill (optional)*
*1/4 teaspoon freshly ground black pepper*
*1 tablespoon red wine vinegar*

1 Spread the salt on a chopping board and finely chop the garlic on top of the salt (see box, page 469).

2 Transfer the garlic and salt to a medium-size bowl, add the yogurt, and stir until creamy.

3 Peel the cucumber and remove the seeds if they are large. Finely chop the cucumber. Squeeze it to remove some of the liquid, then add it to the yogurt. Stir in the mint or dill, if using, the pepper, and the vinegar. Mix thoroughly. Cover and refrigerate for up to 2 days.

# SOUVLAKI STANDS AND THE BEST TZATZIKI

AROUND THE WORLD, CITIES ONCE HAD SPECIFIC SHOPPING AND MANUFACTURING DISTRICTS—THE FABRIC SECTION, THE BUTTON STREET, THE HARDWARE AND TOOL AREA, THE BREWERY BELT, THE TILEMAKER QUARTER. BECAUSE MANY OF THESE ZONES PROVIDED SIGNIFICANT EMPLOYMENT, ENCLAVES OF THE SORTS OF PLACES WORKERS LIKED TO VISIT BUILT UP NEAR THEM. THAT INCLUDED PLACES WHERE WORKERS LIKED TO EAT, AND IN ATHENS, THAT MEANT *SOUVLAKI* STANDS—THE KIND WITH THE BIG MEAT LOAVES SPINNING AROUND ON UPRIGHT SPITS THAT WE CALL "*GYROS.*"

For working people, the food produced at the stands was perfect. It was fast enough to grab on a break, cheap enough not to tax the pocket, filling, and best of all, flavorful.

In my first years in Greece as an impoverished student, I became a connoisseur of such hidden *souvlaki* enclaves. From them I learned one thing: As well as the secret composition of the meats in the loaf and its carefully guarded spicing, the freshness of the pita, the bite of sliced onions, and the ripeness of the tomato, true perfection depended on the verve of the *tzatziki*.

## SOUVLAKI GEOGRAPHY

One of these working districts lay near the old beer factories. There the stands offered *gyros* that were like open sandwiches. A pita bread puffed on an oiled griddle was placed open on a plate, then layered with shavings of spicy lamb and beef loaf, topped with onion, cucumber, and tomatoes, the whole mound spread out so it nearly covered the plate.

Slathered over all was an incredibly zingy *tzatziki* made with village vinegar, and on top of the *tzatziki* was poured some of the meat juices that had collected in the well beneath the spinning meat. You cut into the *souvlaki* with a knife and fork.

Near the Monastiraki subway station, in the area of machine repair shops, hovered another such quarter. Here the *souvlaki* was more traditionally folded and wrapped in paper to take in hand. The lamb in the meat loaf was more seasoned, and the griddled pita was rubbed with meat juice, but what counted was the generosity of the garlic in the *tzatziki*.

Hidden around bustling Omonia Square—which is actually a circle—sat another such zone. Omonia is the people's square, noisy with traffic, filled with shoppers and workers, packed with functionary offices and inexpensive stores. The *souvlaki* there was unembellished, but the *tzatziki* was the unvarnished best—the thickest Cretan yogurt, the densest cucumber, and garlic peeled and chopped by the head just to keep up with the demand.

## THE SEARCH CONTINUES

Sadly, some of the enclaves have disappeared and some have diminished in size. Others, like Omonia's, have retreated farther into the depths of the neighborhood, away from the new hotels and gift shops. Still, I believe *souvlaki* enclaves proffering their oiled pita, their twirling meat loaves, and their brazen *tzatziki* sauces will pop up in new hubs. I look forward to the hunt.

*A souvlaki spinner shaves slices of grilled meat onto a hot pita bread.*

## NOTES:

■ Greeks do not necessarily chill *tzatziki* when adding the sauce to meat, fish, poultry, soups, or pilafs. But to use *tzatziki* as an appetizer spread or a dip for vegetables, or to add an especially cool contrast to a hot dish, chill the sauce thoroughly before serving it.

■ Greeks do not usually squeeze the liquid from the cucumber before they add it to the yogurt, but that is because their cucumbers have less moisture and their yogurt is thicker. Without the squeezing, *tzatziki* made with our traditional cucumbers can be quite watery.

## VARIATIONS:

*Tzatziki* **Add-ins:** *Tzatziki* holds its own quite well without extras, but a bit of this or that can give the sauce a different balance. Other possibilities include:

■ **Lemon or lemon zest:** Both fortify the tartness and make the sauce more fruity.

■ **Herbs:** Parsley muscles up the cucumber's green. Other possibilities include chives, shredded grape leaves, marjoram, and cilantro.

■ **Pan drippings:** A stir turns the sauce huskier.

# beet tzatziki

### MAKES 2 CUPS

HERE IS A GIFT FOR ALL WHO DREAM OF BORSCHT WITH ITS PRISTINE SPOONFUL OF SOUR CREAM FLOATING IN THE MIDDLE, OR WHO SIGH FOR BEET SALAD WITH A GLORIOUS ROUND OF GOAT'S CHEESE MELTING ON TOP. CONSIDERING GREECE'S CORNUCOPIA OF VEGETABLES, THERE'S NO REASON WHY *TZATZIKI* CAN'T FEATURE SOMETHING OTHER THAN CUCUMBER. THE COLOR OF BEET *TZATZIKI* IS BRILLIANT PINK, AND ITS EARTHY FLAVOR IS PERFECT FOR FALL AND WINTER. STILL, BEET *TZATZIKI* IS A SAUCE FOR ALL SEASONS: TART YET MOIST, PUNGENT AND TANGY, ROSILY INVITING.

Beet *tzatziki* can be used as an appetizer dip; a topping for grilled chicken or simple vegetables, especially boiled or roasted potatoes; or as a garnish for lamb barley soup. The recipe makes enough to serve 6.

*1/2 teaspoon salt*
*1 large clove garlic*
*1 1/2 cups yogurt*
*1 large beet, cooked, peeled, and finely chopped*
*1 tablespoon chopped fresh dill*

1 Spread the salt on a chopping board and finely chop the garlic on top of the salt (see box, page 469).

*Tzatziki is a top-of-the-list favorite on this Guzo bar menu.*

2 Place the yogurt in a medium-size bowl and whisk until smooth. Add the beet, the garlic and salt, and the dill and mix well. Cover and chill in the refrigerator for 30 minutes before using, or store for up to 2 days.

## VARIATIONS:

**All the Other Pretty** *Tzatzikis:* Classic *tzatziki* is creamy white with a touch of grassy green imparted by the cucumber. The flavor is springlike. But if you let your color and flavor sense run beyond tradition, it's clear that other pairings can be created. Replace the finely chopped cucumber with chopped watercress leaves, sun-dried tomatoes, pickled vegetables (pages 72 to 75), roasted red bell pepper, and pitted green olives to make novel *tzatzikis.*

## THE "AROMA" OF BEETS

Beets, as a root vegetable, have a very earthy scent, and in Greek terms, such a smell is perfume. The word "aroma," which is the same in English as in the Greek, comes from the ancient verb "to plough" and means "the scent of newly ploughed soil."

## SASSY HERMES

Of all the gods of the Greek pantheon, the saltiest, and therefore sauciest, was Hermes. From the day of his birth (which was also the day he grew to toddler-hood), he added impudence to the lives of his relatives, cheekily covering his misdeeds.

Hermes was the child of Zeus and Atlas's daughter, Maia, which infuriated Zeus's wife, Hera. He was the messenger of the gods, protector of travelers, patron of thieves and merchants. He is depicted holding a staff and wearing a wide-brimmed, winged hat along with winged sandals.

As the protector of travelers, he cleared the roads of stones, showing that no path, like no sauce, should be lumpy.

He was a trickster, altering things and enlivening them. At times he made matters more mellow, at times more spicy. He cajoled the irate Hera into loving him by cloaking himself in the swaddling clothes of baby Ares, sitting on Hera's lap, and wailing in hunger. Once Hera had nursed him, he was her "milk child," and she had to treat him as her own. He then helped his father boldly woo Io by distracting Hera's watchdog, Argus.

Hermes was a messenger and also a rescuer and inventor. He saved Odysseus from Circe and recovered his father's stolen sinews from the serpent Delphyne. He invented the lyre: As a newborn he came upon a tortoise, which he made into a musical instrument. To string the lyre, he used the skin from several cows he stole from Apollo's sacred herd. When Apollo pursued him, Hermes played so deliciously on the new instrument that Apollo begged for it. He gave the lyre to Apollo in exchange for forgiveness (but secretly stole Apollo's bow and quiver in the process).

And as a sauce blankets, so did Hermes in yet another way—amorously. His romantic exploits show just how zesty he was. Swift Hermes bedded many a "dish," from goddess to mortal, including Aphrodite and a nymph who bore him Pan.

# radish tzatziki

**MAKES 2 CUPS**

Radishes are an occasional addition to a salad for us, but in Greece the vegetable is used in a far broader fashion. In ancient times Greeks ate radishes (they had five varieties of them) as a raw snack fresh from the garden and boiled up as a dinner vegetable. They were among the foods of poor laborers.

Today, still, Greeks often munch on raw radishes as a snack, and when the gardens are full of them, consider them worthy as a centerpiece vegetable, not merely a salad complement. Like cucumbers, radishes have a crisp texture and a zesty juice. Since *tzatziki* benefits from both these qualities, it's a natural to vary the cucumber with radish. Doing so has an added advantage: With their own sort of bite, radishes combined with *tzatziki's* garlic give the sauce even more snap.

Radish *tzatziki* makes a tasty appetizer dip, especially with toasted country bread or *paximadi;* a snappy topping for vegetables, such as zucchini, green beans, or lima beans; and a refreshing condiment with rice or bulgur pilafs. The recipe makes enough to serve 12 as a dip or 6 as a topping or condiment.

*1/2 teaspoon salt*
*1 large clove garlic*
*1 1/2 cups plain yogurt*
*8 ounces trimmed red radishes,*
*    finely chopped*
*1 tablespoon chopped fresh*
*    dill*

1 Spread the salt on a chopping block and finely chop the garlic on top of the salt (see box, this page).

2 Place the yogurt in a medium-size bowl and whisk until smooth. Add the garlic and salt, the radishes, and the dill and mix well. Cover and chill in the refrigerator for 30 minutes before using, or store for up to 2 days.

## THE GARLIC-SALT CONNECTION

Chopping the garlic for *tzatziki* in salt benefits the sauce in two ways. For a *tzatziki* that is to be served immediately (before the garlic flavor has a chance to develop), it enhances the bite. For a chilled sauce, the salt abates the tendency of garlic to become acrid.

# lemony mayonnaise

## SALTSA MAYONEZA

### MAKES 1¼ CUPS

GIVEN HOW MUCH GREEKS RELISH THE COMBINATION OF LEMON AND EGG, IT'S NOT SURPRISING THAT WHEN MAYONNAISE ARRIVED ON THEIR SHORES, THEY SEIZED UPON IT. A RECENT ADDITION TO THE GREEK REPERTOIRE OF SAUCES, MAYONNAISE HAS BECOME WIDELY APPRECIATED AS A NO-NEED-TO-COOK LEMON-AND-EGG WAY TO DRESS UP COOKED VEGETABLES, FISH, CHICKEN, SALADS, AND, YES, *SANTOUITSES*—SANDWICHES!

Greek mayonnaise is more lemony than French or American mayonnaise, which befits the Greek taste bud. It is also thinner, more a sauce to drizzle than a spread. Still it is thick enough to bind a Russian Salad (page 36) or dress a lobster cold (page 70) or hot (page 347). It can be used as a salad dressing, a swirl in soup, or as a sauce for fish or shellfish, especially *kalamari*. This recipe makes enough for 6 servings of each.

*2 egg yolks (see Notes)*
*¼ cup fresh lemon juice*
*¾ cup olive oil*
*¼ teaspoon salt*

Place the egg yolks and 1 teaspoon of the lemon juice in a food processor and process until slightly thickened. Starting with tablespoon amounts, alternately drizzle in the oil and the remaining lemon juice, working up to larger amounts as the mixture thickens. Stir in the salt. Use right away, or cover and refrigerate for as long as 3 days.

**NOTES:**

■ The egg yolks in Lemony Mayonnaise are uncooked, so be sure to use very fresh, refrigerated eggs in preparing it.

■ To make the mayonnaise by hand, follow the same instructions, beating vigorously with a wire whisk.

■ If you would like a thicker, less tart mayonnaise, reduce the lemon juice to 2 tablespoons and stir in 2 tablespoons warm water at the end.

**VARIATIONS:**

**Dressing up the Dressing:** Though there are some who would decry any tinkering with a sauce that is already Hellenically perfect, there are others who cannot resist experimenting and stretching toward taste horizons. If you would like to play *saltsa iatros*, "sauce doctor," try adding any of these to *mayoneza* once the mixture has thickened.

■ Coarsely chopped lemon zest

■ Salt-chopped garlic (see box, page 469)

■ Pickles and minced onion

■ Finely chopped parsley, thyme, oregano, basil, tarragon, or chives

■ Prepared mustard

■ Anchovy paste

# thickened yogurt

### MAKES ABOUT 2 CUPS

THE GREEK WORD FOR YOGURT, *YIAOURTI*, COMES FROM THE TURKISH TERM FOR "THICKENED MILK." ALONG WITH CHEESE IT IS THE MAIN DAIRY PRODUCT IN GREECE. UNLIKE CHEESE, WHICH IS GENERALLY TREATED WITH RENNET, YOGURT IS THICKENED BY THE ACTION OF ACID-PRODUCING BACTERIA.

The first yogurt was probably eaten soon after people began to milk their cattle, goats, and sheep and utilize that milk for food. Left alone, fresh milk quickly develops the lactic acid bacteria, and if the fermentation does not go too far, it results in a thickening of texture and sharpening of taste. And "thick" is the word for Greek yogurt. We don't have any yogurt like Greece's here, but to approach it, the yogurt we have can be made denser and sharper. As a sauce on its own, a base for *tzatziki*, or a creamy thickener for other dishes, thickened yogurt has a custardlike consistency, as any Greek yogurt does.

Always welcome on the Greek table, a dish of yogurt is automatically served as a cooling side dish with almost every savory food. The recipe makes enough to serve 6.

*3 cups plain yogurt*

Place the yogurt in a colander or sieve lined with a double layer of cheesecloth and set it over a deep bowl. Set it aside until most of the liquid whey has drained off and the yogurt is thick, at least 45 minutes. Transfer the thickened yogurt to a bowl, whisk until smooth, and use right away. Or cover and store in the refrigerator for up to 1 week.

**NOTE:** The longer the yogurt drains, the thicker and more cheeselike it becomes.

## A YOGURT PREDECESSOR

Possibly contrary to the legend of Mongol hordes riding in with flasks of fermenting milk tied to their horses's hot flanks, something like yogurt was known to Greeks since classical times—a sort of thickened sour milk called *pyriate* or *oxygala*. *Oxi* meant "sour" or "vinegar"; *gala*, "milk." Galen says that *oxygala* was eaten alone with honey, just as thick Greek yogurt is today.

*While yogurt is a perfect sauce for many Greek dishes, honey is a perfect sauce for yogurt.*

## GREEK TOMATO PASTE

In the 1930s and '40s, farmers all over Greece discovered what seemed to be a fabulously lucrative new crop: tomatoes. From north to south, fields of grain and grapes gave way to tomato plants. Along every back road and near every tiny bay, processing factories sprang up to turn the new crop into sauce, puree, and paste as entrepreneurs vied to label their own brand and corner the market. Argos tomatoes were pitted against Boetian; Macedonian sold against Thracian; many labels rarely moved beyond their local region.

Meanwhile, exactly the same phenomenon was occurring in Italy, Spain, and Israel, effectively knocking out any international trade. Greeks couldn't compete with other countries, and hardly with themselves. Now many of those processing plants are barren hulks and many of the fields have returned to the old (or even newer) crops. Happily, Greece still grows abundant tomatoes, and many are still turned into *poltis domata*, tomato paste. Hard to find in the United States, Greek tomato paste is truly special. Using the small, sweet tomatoes of Greece, the paste processing plants take as long as needed to achieve an almost caramelized consistency. Any sauce made with Greek tomato paste turns brandy-brown and divine. My Greek friends laugh as they load me up with cans for my trip home. Try to find some in your nearby Greek market—it's worth it.

# red tomato meat sauce

## SALTSA KOKKINO ME KIMA

### MAKES 4 CUPS

IN NO TIME AFTER THE ARRIVAL OF TOMATOES ON THEIR SHORES, GREEKS DEVELOPED A NEW SAUCE—INDEED SEVERAL VERSIONS—THEY FITTINGLY NAMED *SALTSA KOKKINO*, AFTER THE COLOR OF TOMATOES AND THE MODERN GREEK WORD FOR "RED." GREEKS TOOK TO THE SAUCE AS THEY TAKE TO LIFE—FULLY. TODAY RED TOMATO-BASED SAUCE (WHICH COOKBOOKS OFTEN CALL *SALTSA DOMATO*) IS A MAINSTAY OF GREEK COOKING, WHETHER THE SAUCE IS MADE IN THE PAN WITH TOMATO ADDED TO THE COOKING JUICES OR MADE SEPARATELY, TO BE A BLANKET OVER EVERYTHING FROM NOODLES TO MEATS.

The most common variant is a red meat sauce utilizing *kima* (chopped meat), tomatoes, Greece's divine, dense, almost red-black tomato paste, and a handful of other touches. A splash of dry red wine brings out the full robustness, but in addition, the rendition here goes a step further. Since most Greeks add a dash of sugar, why not turn instead to one of Greece's fine sweet wines for that touch of sweetening?

In Greece the sauce is usually made with all beef, but though it's rarely used in Greece, adding ground pork creates extra richness and meaty succulence. Cinnamon, a signature fillip used from ancient times to modern, is a must.

The recipe makes enough to sauce 2 pounds of pasta, to serve 4 to 6.

2 tablespoons olive oil

1 medium onion, finely chopped

2 large cloves garlic, finely
   chopped

1 pound ground beef chuck, or
   8 ounces ground beef chuck
   plus 8 ounces ground pork

1 pound fresh tomatoes, or 1 can
   (28 ounces) tomatoes,
   finely chopped, with their
   juices

2 tablespoons tomato paste,
   preferably Greek

3/4 cup Mavrodaphne or
   Muscat wine

1/2 cup dry red wine

1 large bay leaf

1 piece (2 inches) cinnamon stick

1 teaspoon salt

1 Heat the oil in a large nonreactive skillet or pot over medium heat. Add the onion and garlic and cook until the onion begins to brown, about 5 minutes.

2 Add the meat, raise the heat to medium-high, and cook, breaking up the chunks, until it is well browned, about 4 minutes.

3 Add all the remaining ingredients and bring to a boil. Cover the skillet, reduce the heat, and simmer gently until the sauce is thick and deeply colored, 1 hour.

4 Remove the skillet from the heat and set the sauce aside for 1 hour before using. To serve, remove the bay leaf and cinnamon stick and reheat over medium heat. The sauce will keep for up to 1 week in the refrigerator, or up to 3 months in the freezer.

## THE SPIRIT OF THE OLIVE AND CAPER

Olives and olive oil have long played a part in the religious life of the Greeks. In ancient days, the olive branch signified peace, and small lamps filled with olive oil fed the sacred flames that honored the deities in the temples. The olive still symbolizes love and peace to Greeks, and olive oil remains an essential part of the solemn rites today. It is olive oil that priests use to make the sign of the cross on the child being baptized. It is olive oil that burns in the cups beneath the ikons in the church and illuminates the faces of the holy. And it is olive oil that keeps the flame alight beneath the ikons of patron saints in the small wall shrines that are a part of every Greek household.

As for the caper, it continues to blossom over the Greek land, ever tenacious and ever free, like the hearts of the Greek people.

# quick fresh tomato sauce

## SALTSA KOKKINO

### MAKES 5 CUPS

AS SUMMER TURNS THE GREEK LANDSCAPE ALMOST AFLAME WITH RIPENING TOMATOES, HOME COOKS ABANDON THE TINS OF TOMATO PASTE THAT CARRIED THEM THROUGH THE WINTER AND BEGIN TO MAKE SAUCE FROM FRESH TOMATOES. A BASKETFUL OF THE RED FRUIT, A HANDFUL OF FRESH WILD OREGANO, SOME ONION, OIL, AND SALT, AND 20 MINUTES LATER THERE IS A TOPPING FOR *MAKARONADA*, OR RICE, OR ROAST, OR EGGPLANT, OR STUFFED VEGETABLES.

Quick fresh tomato sauce can be spread on bread for an appetizer, used as a topping for yellow lentil or chicken soup; or it can serve as a sauce for fish fillets, grilled chicken, pork roast or chops, pasta, or rice or bulgur pilaf. The recipe makes enough to serve 8 to 10. Don't forget to sprinkle freshly grated rich and redolent cheese on top.

*1/4 cup olive oil*
*1 large onion, coarsely chopped*
*4 to 6 large cloves garlic,*
    *coarsely chopped*
*3 pounds ripe tomatoes,*
    *preferably plum or cherry*
    *tomatoes, coarsely chopped*
*1 tablespoon chopped fresh oregano*
    *leaves (see Notes)*
*1 small fresh green chile pepper,*
    *stemmed and finely chopped, or a*
    *generous pinch of cayenne pepper*
*1 teaspoon salt*
*1/2 cup grated kefalotyri, Parmesan,*
    *or other hard grating cheese,*
    *for serving*

1 Heat the oil in a large non-reactive skillet or pot over medium-high heat. Add the onion and garlic and cook until the onion is translucent, about 5 minutes.

2 Add the tomatoes, oregano, chile pepper, and salt. Simmer

briskly, uncovered, until the tomatoes collapse and separate from their skins and the liquid thickens slightly, 12 to 15 minutes. Use right away, or refrigerate for up to 1 week, or freeze for up to 3 months.

When you serve the sauce, sprinkle the cheese over the top.

## NOTES:

■ Fresh oregano is the key to making this sauce come alive. If you don't have some in your garden, most markets now carry fresh herbs year-round. If you have no choice but dried oregano, use about 1 teaspoon.

## WHY A GREEN CHILE PEPPER?

The small, dense tomatoes of Greece are much spicier than ours. With rarely enough moisture to grow into beefsteaks (and those that are saved to be stuffed), they hold on to every last drop of flavor. The onions, wizened by the sun, also have far more bite. I have tried many ways of duplicating the zestiness of a quick, fresh Greek tomato sauce and finally came upon the solution: One fresh green chile pepper—or lacking that, a pinch of cayenne—and the sauce takes on the spark of the Hellenes.

■ Quick Fresh Tomato Sauce might seem to benefit from a dash of wine, but its essence is its light naturalness. Adding wine makes it more "cooked." Along that line, you will find that it is more watery than a long-cooked tomato sauce.

## VARIATIONS:

**Added Temptations:** Every Greek cook likes to add her own signature to her garden tomato sauce—a *komati*, a "bit," *apo afto i ekino*, "from this or that." Every "this" and "that" comes from the heart, and every one makes the sauce all the more Greek.

■ Add one of these during cooking:

¼ teaspoon ground cinnamon, cloves, or nutmeg

1 bay leaf

1 rib celery, chopped

1 tablespoon butter

½ to 1 teaspoon sugar or honey

■ Or stir in, just as the sauce is done:

a sprinkling of shredded fresh basil, mint, or parsley leaves

## WHO SET THE TABLE, WHO CLEARED IT, AND WHO BROUGHT THE SAUCE?

Presumably in ancient Greece, as is certainly true in Greek villages today, in the homes of simple land tillers the wife, children, perhaps a sister or mother, would cook the meal, lay out basic crockery on a plank table, ladle out the grain and the *garos* sauce, and clean up after. But the story was different in the houses of the elite. There, at least for dinner parties, a troop of workers was required to get the meal on the table, each performing a specific job, not unlike the crew that oils the machinery in a modern restaurant today.

First and foremost, the grandee needed a chef. Indeed, the chef was absolutely essential if sacrificial meat was to be served. The ancient Greek *mageiros*, or "cook," was also the "magician" who slaughtered animals and performed the ceremonies involving the burnt offerings. What was not given to the gods was then braised for the guests. The *mageiros* chose the animal, the birds, and the fish, and prepared and oversaw the meal, including the vegetables, the sauces, the nuts and fruit and cheese. He and his helpers were men, and while a female servant might bring out a daily meal, for a feast the

servants had to be men. One to three might be required. They might be household servants or maybe *sklavoi*, "slaves," perhaps gained from the barbarian hordes to the north, people we still call a version of the same word, "Slav." Next and equally essential, the host needed a *trapezopoios*, a "table layer," who brought the crockery, prepared the lamps, offered the wine libations, and did the dishes. (How nice not to have to provide your own dishes!) The chef, though, was the commander. He chose the "table layer" and ordered his assistant cooks—who did much of the work—to prepare the meal as he saw fit. He might even hire the next set of workers, the entertainers who entered at meal's end. Among them were comedians, lute players, dancers. Runners were kept nearby should there be a last-minute call for a musician or courtesan.

Cooks, food preparers, table layers, slaves—all were available for hire in a particular section of the market. Some people survived just traipsing from banquet to banquet. In early Greece they were called *parasitoi*, "parasites," or "for grain-ers," and later *kolakes*, or "sticker-on-ers."

# THE DODECANESE ISLANDS— GATEWAY TO MANY SAUCES

THE DODECANESE ISLANDS, THE EASTERNMOST ISLANDS OF GREECE, ARE STRUNG LIKE PEARLS ALONG THE COAST OF WHAT WAS ONCE CALLED ASIA MINOR AND IS NOW TURKEY. THE NAME MEANS "TWELVE ISLANDS," BUT THERE ARE ACTUALLY MANY MORE.

The title stems from 1908, when twelve of the islands united against the new Turkish-led Ottoman parliament that had sharply restricted the rights of the island's citizens. Because of their proximity to Turkey, relations between the islands and the Ottoman rulers had been close. The taxes levied on the islands were less than in other parts of Greece and the people enjoyed more privileges. The curtailment of their special benefits at a time when the rest of Greece was struggling for unification tipped the scales for the islanders, and they joined the effort.

## A CULTURAL GATEWAY

The islands have been Greek since before the first millennium B.C.E. Their location, though, always made their culture a gateway to other ideas—religion, philosophy, and food. They were allied early on with the Lydians, then Persia. Later, though their distance from Athens kept them autonomous, the islands were allied with that powerful city. Alexander ruled them, and the islands then passed to his general, Ptolemy. A few centuries later, the islands' people were the first Greeks christianized as the apostles made their way up the coast of Asia Minor. In keeping that faith, the islands sheltered the Crusaders. Italians then held the islands during World War II, but the resiliant islanders once again bonded with Greece after the war.

## THE TWELVE ISLANDS

The twelve that gave the group their name are Rhodes, Kos, Kalymnos, Patmos, Tilos, Symi, Leros, Astypalea, Halki, Nisyros, Karpathos, and Kasos. Today the islands are home to some of Greece's busiest cities and ports and at the same time they embrace some of Greece's most untouched villages.

Rhodes is the largest island, so varied that a trip through its towns is like a walk through history. Its capital is the largest medieval city in Europe. Towering over it are the fortifications of the Crusaders. Paths twist by large houses with walled gardens, past small plazas and fountains. In ancient times, a hundred-foot-tall statue of Helios, called the Colossus, stood astride the harbor of Rhodes city (hence the term for anything massive). The island's second largest city, Lindos, sits on a tiny spit of land halfway down the island. Its buildings are Turkish—two-storied, made of wood, and shuttered. Around these towns stretch fertile fields and inlets that protect fleets of fishing boats.

Kos, which Homer said sent thirty ships to help conquer Troy, was a thriving center of trade in ancient times. It was a sacred center dedicated to Asclepios, the god of healing, and the home of Hippocrates, the father of medicine. In Byzantine times it was a religious capital. Today it sports Turkish minarets, Crusader fortresses, and Italian mansions.

Kalymnos was Phoenician, Doric, Persian, then Greek again. It has long been the center of the sponge industry. The island's beaches and rugged inland terrain attract many visitors.

Patmos was the home in exile of St. John the Evangelist, where he wrote his *Book of Revelations*. Tilos has walnut and almond groves and twisting villages. Symi and Leros, like the other twelve, are topped with austere monasteries. Reaching into the Aegean, bat-shaped Astypalea sports citrus orchards. On Halki copper and tin for bronze have been mined for eons. Nisyros, like Santorini, is a volcano. Stretching out farther, Karpathos fought against Sparta and was later ruled by Arabs and Italian pirates. Cave-dotted Kasos was the site of a slaughter of seven thousand by Egypt's Ottoman governor.

The wonderful foods of all twelve reveal their history. Greece's *saltsa besamel* tops English peas and Genovese pirate–inspired *pastitsio*. With native lemons aplenty, *avgolemono* abides. In the internationally influenced cities, Italian-style dishes sport Greek *kima* (an Arabic word) sauce. And everywhere, from the Turkish period, *tzatziki* flows.

# THE TOPPINGS

# olive and caper tapenade

## MAKES 2 CUPS

Greeks know about final touches, even in food, so they often add just a touch of topping or garnish to their dishes. On a salad goes a crumble of feta, onto the *meze* plate a few gleaming olives, into the lentil porridge a sprinkling of capers.

While the toppings are humble, they add a touch of glamour. And using Greece's impeccable ingredients, slightly more creative toppings can emerge: a mix of olive and caper, a mustard paste, a pesto of tomato, a crunch of garlic.

GLISTENING GROVES OF CULTIVATED OLIVE TREES STRETCH ACROSS MUCH OF GREECE. CAPER VINES THAT SEEM TO THRIVE WITHOUT A DROP OF WATER POKE OUT OF NEARLY EVERY CRACK BETWEEN STONES. HOW COULD THE TWO NOT GO TOGETHER?

Greeks have traditionally pounded olives into pastes and brined their capers—separately. Here they are combined. A touch of anchovy—an echo from the ancient *garos*—and a measure of Greece's aromatic sweet basil result in a condiment that is tangy, salty, and herby. It tops countless dishes on the Greek dinner table with gusto and aplomb.

Tapenade can be used as a dip for raw vegetables; as a spread to slather on bread or cheese slices for an appetizer; as a topping on slices of cheese, spinach, or leek filo pies; and as a condiment with eggs, beef, pork, game, fish fillets, or vegetables, especially potatoes. The recipe makes enough to serve 6 to 8 in any of these ways.

*3/4 cup pitted Kalamata or
    other Greek black olives
    (see Notes)
4 large cloves garlic
4 anchovy fillets, preferably
    salt-packed
3/4 cup capers, drained
1/2 packed cup fresh basil leaves
2/3 cup olive oil
2 tablespoons fresh lemon juice*

Place all the ingredients in a food processor and process until chopped as fine as possible. (Or use a chef's knife to finely chop the olives, garlic, anchovies, capers, and basil. Transfer the mixture to a bowl, add the oil and lemon juice, and mix well.) Use right away, or store in the refrigerator for up to 3 weeks.

## NOTES:

■ When a dish such as tapenade calls for quantities of pitted olives, there is an easy way to remove that clinging pit: With a clean wooden mallet or a hammer, tap each olive soundly enough to break it open, but not hard enough to smash the inner pit. Remove the freed pit with your fingers.

■ For a list of Greek olives, see page 30. For what capers to buy, see page 378.

# artyma

## WITH GRAPES, MUSTARD, AND PEPPERCORNS

### MAKES ABOUT 1 CUP

USTARD TURNS UP IN THE GREEK DIET BEFORE 1000 B.C.E.—ALMOST AS EARLY AS GRAPES. AT FIRST THE GREEKS KNEW IT ONLY AS A WILD PLANT THAT POPPED UP AMONG THE CEREAL STALKS AND BETWEEN THE GRAPEVINES.

Intrepid gatherers of greens and seeds—and mustard provided both—Greeks took to the biting herb and soon began to cultivate it. The job was easy; mustard flourishes in the Mediterranean climate. In due time, several types were blooming, all of which were listed, discussed, and critically evaluated by Antiphanes, Athenaeus, and other food writers. They weren't the only commentators. Pythagoras considered mustard an antidote for scorpion bites. Hippocrates thought it was good for healing wounds and for a cranky digestion and recommended the original mustard plasters.

To make a condiment, or *artyma* ("seasoning"), Greek cooks began to mix mustard with grape pulp, called must, and a little pepper, and slowly but surely it acquired the name *moustarda*. Tongue tingling and pungent, such an *artyma* is both sharp and sweet, fruity and hot. Plain or with nuts, it makes an excellent condiment with lamb, pork, game, and poultry. The recipe makes enough to accompany 6 portions.

*2 cups grapes (any color), cut in half*
*2 tablespoons mustard seeds*
*4 teaspoons finely chopped almonds or hazelnuts (optional)*
*1 tablespoon cracked black peppercorns*
*2 teaspoons fresh lemon juice*
*1/4 cup water*

1 Combine all the ingredients, including the nuts, if using, in a medium-size nonreactive saucepan and bring to a boil over medium-low heat. Cook, stirring frequently, until the grapes release their juices, about 10 minutes.

2 Partially cover the pan, reduce the heat, and simmer until the mixture is sticky and thick, about 10 minutes.

3 Serve warm, at room temperature, or chilled. *Artyma* will keep in the refrigerator, covered, for up to 3 weeks.

**NOTE:** Plain or combined with nuts, *artyma* also makes an excellent crust for meat, poultry, and game. Pat it on before grilling or baking.

## TRADITIONAL GREEK TOPPINGS

- Splash of plain extra-virgin olive oil
- Handful of plain olives—any type
- Sprinkling of capers
- Anchovies
- Good grating of sharp cheese, such as *kefalotyri, kefalograviera,* or *kasseri,* especially on anything with a tomato or white sauce
- Crumbled feta on meats, fowl, fish, game, or vegetables

# roasted tomato "paste"

## STOUMBI

**MAKES 2 CUPS**

GREEKS ONCE CALLED THEIR MASHED OR POUNDED TOPPINGS *PASTE*. TODAY THEY HAVE ANOTHER WORD FOR THEM: *STOUMBI*, WHICH MEANS "POUNDED." THEIR CUISINE INCLUDES A NUMBER OF THESE TOPPINGS: A MASH OF GARLIC AND VINEGAR; A BEAN AND GARLIC PASTE; AND A SALT OR SMOKED FISH PASTE. WHEN THE FIELDS ARE RIPE WITH FRESH TOMATOES, GREEK HOUSEWIVES ALSO MAKE A HOMEMADE TOMATO *STOUMBI*, WHICH THEY USE TO TOP MEATS, VEGETABLES, RICE PILAFS, AND NOODLES. IT CAN ALSO BE USED AS A *MEZE* DIP OR SPREAD ON BREAD OR CHEESE SLICES, OR SERVED AS AN ACCOMPANIMENT TO EGGS OR FILO PIES.

Generally, after pressing the fresh tomatoes (and, for once, extracting the peels), the *stoumbi* makers pound in only garlic, herbs, salt, and oil. I like to add an ingredient the Greeks use in *dolmades,* stuffings, and sweets— pine nuts—and to heighten the accent by roasting both the tomatoes and the pine nuts. Hot or cold, it's a paste, a topping, a relish. Call it what you will—it adds zest to grains and roasts, fritters and soup, grills and sautés. It's a *stoumbi!* The recipe will top 6 to 8 servings.

*2 pounds ripe but firm tomatoes*
*2 large cloves garlic*
*2 tablespoons pine nuts*
*1/4 cup fresh flat-leaf parsley leaves*
*1/4 cup olive oil*
*1/2 teaspoon salt*

1 Preheat the oven to 500°F.

2 Place the tomatoes on a baking sheet and roast them in the oven until the skins are split and slightly charred, 10 minutes. Remove and allow to cool.

## ROASTING TOMATOES

Roasting tomatoes adds a flavor dimension that is just right for tomato *stoumbi* and other condiments. You can oven-roast them as described on this page, or you can use one of these methods:

■ *Use a gas burner.* This method roasts the tomatoes quickly; they will be a bit less cooked and not as jamlike as when oven roasted. Set the tomatoes on a griddle or directly on the burner over high heat. Turn once, using tongs to avoid piercing the tomatoes and letting the juices escape, until the skins have split and are charred in spots, about 5 minutes.

■ *Use a charcoal or gas grill.* Grilling tomatoes produces a smoky roasted flavor. Place the tomatoes on the grill rack directly over a hot fire. Grill, turning once, until softened and charred in spots, 6 to 10 minutes.

3 When they are cool enough to handle, peel and seed the tomatoes. Place them, along with all the remaining ingredients, in a food processor and process until pureed. Use right away, or cover and refrigerate for up to 1 week.

# RHODES AND THE CRUSADERS

**I**N THE AUGUST HEAT, TOURISTS SWARMING AROUND, I AM OUT FOR A DAY'S EDIFICATION WITH MY FRIEND PETROS. HE THINKS I KNOW TOO LITTLE ABOUT THE TIME OF THE CRUSADERS AND THEIR OCCUPATION OF THE DODECANESOS. HE'S RIGHT. EXCEPT FOR SHAKESPEARE, SOME LONG-AGO HISTORY CLASSES, AND A FEW MEDIEVAL MURDER MYSTERIES, I AM FAIRLY CLUELESS ABOUT THE ERA.

Petros lives on Rhodes, near Ialyssos, a city that was named for one of the three grandsons of the sun god, Helios, who chose the island for his home. The three grandsons inherited separate sections of the island, but united in order to found the island's capital, Rhodes city. Later, in a less mythical era, that rich city was intermittently one of Athens's most feared enemies and one of its most powerful allies. Petros's library is full of books on those fevered days.

## WAVES OF RAIDERS

We have taken a bus into town. Yesterday, Petros, his wife, and I gathered tomatoes and made a *stoumbi*. Today we are carrying sandwiches of country bread slathered with the tomato paste. We will need them, says Petros, because we have a long day ahead.

Petros tells me that as the Byzantine empire weakened, wave after wave of raiders descended upon Rhodes. Persians came, then Saracens, Turks, and seafarers from Genoa. In the fourteenth century, as Constantinople fell to the Ottomans, the Knights of St. John Hospitalers arrived from western Europe, as they had earlier on the islands of Cyprus and Malta. They wanted to establish a base from which to launch their forays into Palestine. They occupied Rhodes for two centuries, until 1522, when the Ottomans regained command over the island.

## CRUSADER CASTLES

The Knights of St. John left behind marvels and edifices found nowhere else in Greece. As a religious military order, first dedicated only to helping the sick and wounded, they had grown rich and powerful. They had, in fact, bought Rhodes. Looming over Rhodes city is the crenelated fortress castle the Crusaders built. Encircling the old city are huge outer fortress walls. "Crusader" means "to mark with a cross," and to show their commitment they wore black tunics emblazoned with white crosses. But their cross was that of Western Christianity—Catholicism, not Orthodoxy—and echos of their creed still reverberate throughout the streets.

Petros shows me how they turned the small eleventh-century Byzantine Church of St. Mary into a Gothic cathedral. It represented their idea of ecclesiastic architecture: spired, not domed as the Greeks would have. They took down ancient temples and replaced them with palaces to befit the princely stature of many of the warriors. The eleventh-century palace of Armeria is now the archaeological institute, and the knights' hospital is now the museum. Petros tells me that the knights, while united in purpose and destination, were far from united in their countries of origin, their languages and customs. There were seven "tongues" in the Order of the Knights of St. John, one for every language spoken, and each built governing offices, hostels, palaces, chapels, and mess halls.

## THE OTTOMAN SIEGE

For a long while the city seemed impervious to defeat by the Ottomans, just a few miles across the sea. Sultan after sultan tried to conquer the city, only to be turned back. Finally Suleyman the Magnificent mounted a massive six-month siege and prevailed over the weary knights. The departing Crusaders left a legacy beyond their castles, however. Their arrogant promotion of their Western Christianity over Greek's Orthodoxy infuriated the Greeks and greatly contributed to the long schism between the Orthodox and the Roman Catholic church.

Rhodes seems to be emblazoned with red and passion as we bus back home. The island is known for its holy fervor. It is also known for its roses ("Rhodes" means "rose" and is the root of our word for the flower). Absorbing all Petros has told me, I think of knights on cross-mantled horses and ships with cross-festooned sails as we bump down the road. I also think of our *stoumbi* sandwiches, for I have come through two hundred years of Greece's history, and I am famished.

# three top notes

## IN THE GREEK STYLE

SINCE THE TIMES OF *OPSA* ON THE BARLEY PORRIDGE BOWL—A FEW MORSELS OF FISH, A SCATTERING OF TASTY BULBS OR TANGY LEAVES, A CRUMBLING OF CHEESE—THE SPRINKLING OF A FINAL, FLAVORFUL TOP NOTE HAS BEEN A GREEK TRADITION. USUALLY THAT TOP NOTE IS A POOL OF LUXURIOUS OLIVE OIL, A SHAVING OF SHARP CHEESE, A BROADCAST OF SALTY OLIVES. BUT WITH THE ARRAY OF TASTY GREEK INGREDIENTS, THE FINISHING TOUCH CAN GO FURTHER. THE TOP NOTE SHOULD BE SIMPLE, NATURAL, AND ELEGANT. NO FANCY FILLIPS ARE NEEDED. THEY ARE MEANT, AS OF OLD, TO ADD GUSTO. EACH MAKES ENOUGH TOPPING FOR MEATS, POULTRY, SOUP, SALAD, OR VEGETABLE FOR 6.

## FRIED GARLIC TOPPING

### MAKES ½ CUP

2 tablespoons olive oil
1 small head garlic, cloves separated, peeled and slivered or coarsely chopped
Salt

1 Heat the oil in a medium-size skillet over medium-high heat. When it is beginning to smoke, add the garlic and sprinkle lightly with salt. Reduce the heat to medium and stir until the garlic is slightly crisped, 2 minutes.

2 Transfer the garlic to a paper towel to drain. Use right away or store in the refrigerator for up to 3 days.

## TOASTED BREAD CRUMB AND GARLIC TOPPING

### MAKES ½ CUP

1 tablespoon olive oil
½ tablespoon butter
½ cup fresh bread crumbs, not too fine
2 cloves garlic, finely chopped

Heat the oil and butter in a medium-size skillet over medium-high heat. When the butter has melted, add the bread crumbs and garlic. Reduce the heat to medium and stir until the crumbs are golden and toasty smelling, about 1 minute. Use right away, or set aside for up to 1 hour.

## WILTED PARSLEY OR CILANTRO TOPPING

### MAKES ½ CUP

½ cup whole flat-leaf parsley or cilantro leaves
¼ teaspoon red wine vinegar
⅛ teaspoon salt

In a small bowl, toss together the parsley, vinegar, and salt. Use right away.

# THE MARINADES

# lemon and oil marinade

## FOR FISH

### MAKES 1 CUP

FISH PLATES IN ANCIENT GREECE WERE WIDE AND SHALLOW, A SHAPE THAT ALLOWED THE FISH TO SIT IN A MARINADE BEFORE COOKING.

Marinating fish remains a universal practice in Greek fish cookery. Allowing the fish to swim a short while in a fruity mixture of olive oil with a dash of lemon, and perhaps with some herb added, refreshes the flesh. The same sort of high-lipped plates, gaily painted with pink fish, blue fish, purple fish, can be bought in pottery and gift shops today all around Greece. What better vessel could there be to marinate a fish than a dish with a fish emblem and room to hold a bath of lemon and oil?

The recipe makes enough to marinate 2 to 3 pounds of fish fillets or shrimp.

*½ cup fresh lemon juice*
*½ cup olive oil*
*1 teaspoon salt*
*1 teaspoon chopped fresh thyme, bay, oregano, or rosemary (optional)*

Stir all the ingredients together in a small bowl. Use right away or set aside for several hours. Use the same day, as the lemon loses its punch over time.

For the Greeks, marinades are such an integral part of cooking, especially for grilling, that virtually no fish, meat, or fowl meets the fire without first having a dip, if not a soaking, in a flavor-infusing solution. The Greek cook swirls together generous amounts of oil, garlic, herbs, citrus juice, salt, and sometimes wine—the step is simply second nature. Food is sometimes cooked in a marinade as well (see Oven-Stewed Rabbit Corfu-Style, page 444), or the marinade is reduced over high heat and served as a sauce.

Marinades for fish, always containing lemon as they do, illuminate the fresh-from-the-sea essence of the fillet, steak, or whole fish. They also can begin the cooking process. For meats and poultry, marinades containing wine or vinegar tenderize by softening the surface proteins, while those containing oil moisten dry meats. But who cares about the technicalities? With their love of food, Greeks know that a marinated chop, bird, or fish is simply better.

# herb, garlic, and oil

## MARINADE FOR GRILLED MEAT

### MAKES ¾ TO 1 CUP

EVER WITH A NOSE FOR FLAVOR, GREEKS HAVE ALWAYS MARINATED THE MEAT, POULTRY, AND GAME THEY GRILL OR ROAST. USING THEIR SATINY OLIVE OIL AND ADDING TO IT SOME BITS OF GARLIC OR MAYBE ONION, A FLURRY OF HERBS, AND SOMETIMES A DOSE OF THEIR SUN-BLESSED RED WINE, THEY MIX A QUICK BATH FOR THE FARE THAT WILL SOON MEET GRILL OR BROILER. THE HERB IS ALMOST ALWAYS OREGANO, BUT GREECE'S OTHER HERBS WILL DO. THE DOUSING, GREEK-STYLE, IS SHORT—HALF AN HOUR TO TWO HOURS AT THE MOST. THAT'S ENOUGH TO IMBUE THE FOOD WITH A GREEK AURA. THE MARINADE IS ENOUGH FOR 6 PORTIONS OF MEAT.

*½ cup olive oil*
*6 to 8 cloves garlic, minced or pressed*
*1 tablespoon chopped fresh oregano, or 1 ½ teaspoons fresh thyme, marjoram, or savory leaves, or 2 teaspoons dried*
*2 to 3 bay leaves, broken in half*
*½ teaspoon freshly ground black pepper*
*1 teaspoon salt (optional)*
*½ cup dry red wine (optional)*

Stir all the ingredients together in a small bowl. Use right away or set aside for several hours.

## VARIATIONS:

■ For the herbs: Substitute or add rosemary, sage, dill, mint, parsley, chervil, finely chopped orange zest, crushed juniper berries, or, for lamb, lavender, or a mixture, keeping in mind that more pungent herbs like marjoram and rosemary should be used in smaller amounts.

■ For the garlic: Use shallots, or add celery leaves.

■ For the oil and wine: Add 2 tablespoons red wine vinegar or a dash of brandy, no more than 3 hours before cooking.

■ For the spices: Add cumin, fennel seeds, cracked or ground coriander seeds, mustard seeds, or a dash of hot paprika.

## THE GLAMOUR OF GRAMMAR

The Greeks have always believed that education makes a person beautiful. Today the word for a well-schooled soul is *morfomenos*, "well shaped." Unknowingly, we think the same: Our word "glamorous" comes from the Greek root *gramma*, "letter," or to be "lettered," the base of "grammar school." In other words, as in sprinkling a gorgeous relish on food, to go to school and become well educated adds the top note to beauty.

# GREECE'S SAUCY MINORITIES AND THEIR FOODS

JUST AS LIVELY IMMIGRANT FOODS HAVE MIXED INTO WHAT CONSTITUTES THE GLORIOUS GREEK MENU OF TODAY, A NUMBER OF IMMIGRATIONS AND INVASIONS HAVE CONTRIBUTED TO GREECE'S CURRENT ENERGETIC POPULATION.

Sicily. Among them are small pastas for *manestra* and perhaps the other pastas, fabulous pastries like *fenikia* (which means "Venice"), and hard candies. And surely the Italian red tomato sauce and the Greek one are cousins. But Greeks have never adopted sausage, bacon, and other pork products to the extent that is common in Italian cooking.

## ROMAN CATHOLICS

Greece is home to a Roman Catholic minority of Genovese, Venetian, and Frankish origin. Indeed, Greeks still call Roman Catholics "Franks." They are scattered about the country, but many live in the Cyclades and in other places that the seafaring Italian cities once held. Syros, Naxos, Santorini, and many other islands have Catholic churches and monasteries, although the number of Catholics dwelling in these places is dwindling. Several of Greece's great ship-owning families are Catholic. The Catholics from Italy brought considerable food to the Greek diet, much of which had been introduced to Italy when the Arabs conquered

## EXILES FROM BABYLON

Jews began arriving in Greece after the exile from Babylon in 600 B.C.E. The ancient Greeks accepted them, admired their faithfulness to their religion, and knew and adapted their stories. They were joined by twenty thousand more in the fifteenth century C.E., and a steady stream followed as they were ejected from Spain and Portugal. The Jews settled in Ioanina, Larisa, and Rhodes, with the majority in and near Thessaloniki. They brought new foods to Greece— meringues and marzipan, many rice dishes—while they added foods of Greek origin—bulgur, nut cakes, fish in egg and lemon sauce—to their own cuisine.

*Hagia Sophia in Istanbul was converted by the Turks into a mosque. The Turks also built mosques in the Dodecanese.*

# . . .they add a deep and valued note to the country's history, culture, and cuisine.

## GREEK PROTESTANTS

A number of Greeks belong to Protestant sects, among them Methodists, the Church of Latter-Day Saints, and Jehovah's Witnesses, and in particular, Seventh-Day Adventists, most of whom live in the Peloponnesos. Most of these groups are small but long-standing, and to all outward appearance, they live and eat as their Orthodox neighbors. A number of their concepts, such as nonviolence and non-participation in the military draft of young men—have given Greece food for thought. In addition, a number of Greeks belong to the Anglican Church, mostly in former British areas, such as Corfu, and in Athens. In areas that were British, the cuisine reflects British foods as well as religion: English puddings and pastries, northern vegetables like Brussels sprouts, French- and Swiss-style dishes such as frogs' legs.

## NOT EGYPTIANS

Gypsies started flowing into Greece in Byzantine times. No one knew who these strange people were, so because of their darker skin, the Byzantines assumed they were Egyptians. Our word "gypsy" and the Greek *gyftos* are both corruptions of the Greek *Egyptos*. They call themselves "Rom" or "Romani." Today a vibrant population of them speaking both Greek and Romani thrives in Macedonia, Thessalia, and Thrace, although many still roam as a way of life. Many are the itinerant fruit peddlers of Greece, traveling from village to village with trucks loaded with melons, apples, oranges, and for Greeks, new fruits such as bananas, papayas, and mangoes. While the men call out the names of the produce they have for sale, the wives and daughters proffer lace and embroidered linens. Their steadfastly held way of life has long added a colorful strand to Greece's rainbow of people—as has their cooking, which includes unusual preparations of red and green peppers and such dishes as chervil-flavored eggplant, spicy bean soups, and simple oil cakes.

## THE TURKS OF GREECE

Close to 500,000 ethnic Turks who were exempt from the population exchange of 1922–23 live in the western reach of Thrace. A number also live on Rhodes, Kos, and the other Dodecanese islands that Turkey held until 1947. To this day mosques tower over their villages, and the call to prayer rings out several times a day. So many of their foods are the same as the Greek—Turkish foods with Greek names and Greek foods with Turkish names—that argument will ever reign over whose cuisine is the forefather. It matters little. Whereas the Greek *souvlaki* with *tzatziki* sauce is wrapped in a pita envelope, the Turkish version, called *doner kebab*, is served on an open pita. The Turkish eat a sweet bread called *paskalya*, borrowed from the Easter pascal bread of their Christian compatriots; the Orthodox eat *bourekakia*, borrowed from the Turkish treat *bourek*. Both rhapsodize over yogurt sauce and walnut sauce.

## THE SLAVIC VLACHS

Along with the Greek-speaking Sarakatsani (see page 211), a group of non-Greek-speaking shepherds called the Vlachs herd sheep on Greek pastures. They originated in a region that is now part of Romania and speak a Slavic language along with Greek. They prospered in Greece, at one point having a separate nation. Several of Greece's most noted poets and politicians have been of Vlach origin. Like the Sarakatsani, today's vibrant Vlach groups can be seen with their flocks, winter and summer, across the mainland, and they provide much of Greece's savory cheese.

## FROM RUSSIA AND ARMENIA

Because of Greece's strong connections with Orthodox Russia and Armenia, a number of Russian and Armenian immigrants have settled there. Their origin rings out in Greek family names such as Moskopoulos. The Russians brought caviar and they bought wine. Until 1917 Odessa was a main trading port for Greek winemakers. To this day Armenian merchants run fur and spice shops in Thessaloniki and Athens, where they bargain and cajole with fellow Greek traders.

With their shared interaction and much shared history, the Armenian cuisine is almost a duplicate of the Greek. Greek *dolma* is Armenian *sarma;* Greek *keftedes,* Armenian *kufta.* Meanwhile, Greeks continue, as they have since ancient times, to relish Armenian apricots and pistachios.

*Many Greek Gypsies earn their livings as itinerant fruit peddlers.*

*In ancient times, Greece was the hub of a vast and varied empire. In modern times, it is home to a dynamic, varied population.*

## THE ALBANIAN IMMIGRATION

In the fourteenth century, when Greece had been severely depopulated by raids and invasions and local landholders needed help to work the fields, a massive immigration of Albanian settlers was welcomed to the Peloponnesos and other areas. Six hundred years later, many still speak an old form of Albanian at home or bear the family name Arvanities. They maintain many of their customs, including their music. Since 1991 they have been joined by several hundred thousand more Albanians who, suffering from terrible poverty at home, began moving south, legally and illegally. Many of them traveled down the western coast into Greece's lower peninsula. Others now live and work all around the country. To Greeks, it's as if the foods and dishes of Greece's own Epiros simply became more national—zesty lamb pies in thick crusts, rich bean soup, and garlic sauces.

## A MACEDONIAN "SALAD"

Meanwhile, the volatility of the Balkans has brought a mix of populations to Greek Macedonia. Many Greeks there are of Bulgarian and other Slavic origins, making that area a delightful and true "Macedonian salad." Legend says they brought *pastourmas,* preserved beef, to Greece. They are famous for rabbit stews cooked in a marinade and a thickened yogurt to rival Crete's.

## THE NEWEST GREEKS

Recently, Greece has become home to a number of new populations. Since the breakup of Europe's eastern bloc, the country has offered sanctuary to those heading for a brighter life and brighter sunlight. they come from Germany, Poland, the various regions of former Yugoslavia, Hungary, Bulgaria, and particularly Romania. As well, and in line with Greece's membership in the European Union, streams of immigrants from many nations of Africa, North Africa, and the Middle East—especially Iran and Iraq—have arrived. Greece has opened its doors to become the dwelling place of many a linguistic and ethnic group, all of whom are adding to the spice and savor of the country and cuisine. Indeed, the major cities of Greece today—Athens, Thessaloniki, Corinth, and others—probably more closely resemble how they were in their ancient heyday than they have for two millennia.

Greeks themselves have traveled—to France, Germany, South Africa, South America, Australia, Canada, and the United States, and have returned with fare from their wanderings: tea, toast, hamburgers, and ice cream.

# fruit
## AS THE FINALE

A FTER THE ELABORATE SPREAD OF FOODS ON THE DINING TABLE—THE FILO PIE, THE TANTALIZING SOUP AND AROMATIC BREAD, THE LEAF-WRAPPED FISH, SPICED MEATS, STUFFED BIRDS, THE NUTTY PILAF, GLISTENING GREENS, SAVORY VEGETABLE CASSEROLE, THE SIDE OF SIZZLED EGG, AND THE FINAL INSURANCE OF A MASS OF FRIED POTATOES—THE GREEK BANQUET ENDS IN ONE AND ONLY ONE WAY: WITH FRESH FRUIT.

*Every fruit is good to eat.*

—XENOPHON,
FIFTH TO FOURTH CENTURY B.C.E.

Baklava and walnut cake, spoon sweet and honeyed batter, grape must pudding—these are treats, not part of the meal. To finish a meal, to refresh the palate and face the afternoon and evening, only fruit will do. The fruit finale is an integral part of the dinner, the last bite partaken, the taste that lingers.

Many of the fruits the ancient Greeks relished were native to the country. Others came from nearby, particularly Asia Minor and Persia. The earliest apples came from the Tigris-Euphrates valley. Minoans might have brought the legendary "golden apple," the quince. Plums were found as Greeks explored the Pontos. Cherries came from Turkey and Palestine, melons from Egypt. Orchards were planted and carefully tended as far back as Homer's day. Today new fruits have arrived from tropical islands and distant continents—bananas, pineapples, prickly pears.

To leave the table refreshed with something uncooked, something as it comes from the earth, is to end the meal with the sweet taste of Mother Gaia. That is how these people of long tradition give praise and gratitude for everything the earth provides. There is no better way.

## A SPECIAL FRUIT OF THE VINE

Built upon a rock pinnacle jutting out from the southeasternmost peninsula of the Peloponnesos and connected to the mainland by only a narrow causeway, sits the fortress city of Monemvasia. The fortified town of houses winding up to a towering castle, of churches with marble doors and phenomenal ikons, is one of the most fascinating places in Greece.

Monemvasia, which means "one entrance," is where the malmsey wine immortalized by Shakespeare and Lord Byron comes from. The town was founded by the Byzantines in the late sixth century C.E. Near the site grew a particular Muscat grape that yielded a divinely sweet, heady, and aromatic wine. Monemvasia wine grew wildly popular across the empire and was exported to western and northern Europe—the most famous wine of the medieval era. Demand was such that the grape was taken to Crete, where soon most of the wine was produced. Still it was Monemvasia, with its single gateway, that grew rich on the trade.

At one point the town held fifty thousand people. With its strategic location, it became a major commercial center for the export of silks and olives and a base for pirates. At various points Monemvasia was occupied by Greeks, Franks, Turks, and Catalans. Competition for the town and the wine trade was fierce. When the Venetians took command of much of Crete, they also took control of Monemvasia. In their pronunciation the grape became known as "malvasia," later further mispronounced by the English as "malmsey."

As the ports to which the wine was sold shifted, Monemvasia became a ghost town. For many years no one lived behind its fortress walls or in its high castle. Lately, however, people have begun to reoccupy Monemvasia as a place for summer residences. A few old mansions have become hotels. The Agia Sophia church, built by the Byzantines in the thirteenth century, is open again. Bougainvillea grows up walls. Eucalyptus trees give shade. Castle turrets look directly across at mainland cliffs four hundred feet high.

As for the grape, it still grows in Monemvasia, but it was also exported to the Madeira islands, where it became the base of Madeira wine.

# greece's fruitful choices

The usual fruits served in Greece after dining today are:

*No table is complete without fresh fruit; no dinner ends without it.*

**APPLES**, *mila*, the best reportedly from Florina, a special variety from Mount Pelion called *firikia*

**APRICOTS**, *verikoka*, the best supposedly from Naoussa

**BANANA**, *mpanana*, imported

**CAROB**, *haroupia*

**CHERRIES**, *kerasia*

**DATES**, *daktilos*—both fresh and dried—have been enjoyed since early times. Their English name comes from the Greek for "digit," for they hang from the trees like fingers.

**FIGS**, *sika*, mostly large green but some black, grown everywhere, the most admired from Kalamata and Skyros

**GRAPES**, *stafylia*, grown all over, the prized eating ones from Achaea

**LOQUAT**, *mousmoula*

**LOTUS FRUIT**, *lotos*, a large mealy fruit the ancients thought could cause forgetfulness

**MANDARINES**, *mandarinia*, from Rhodes

**MEDLAR**, also called *mousmoula*

**MELONS**, *peponia*, grown everywhere, particularly prized, with the best reportedly from Methana

**MULBERRY**, *moura*

**NECTARINES**, *rodakina*

**ORANGES**, *portokalia* (meaning "Portugals"), a huge crop; blood oranges from Missolonghi

**WHITE PEACHES**, *rodakina*, and a special variety so good they are called Aphrodite, *afrodites*

## AN ORCHARD OF OLD

On the outside of the courtyard and
   next to the gates is his orchard,
A great one, four hectares, with a
   fence secured all around it,
And there is the place where his
   fruit trees are grown tall and
   flourishing,
Pear trees and pomegranate trees and
   apple trees with their shining
   fruit, and the sweet fig trees and
   the flourishing olive.
Never is the fruit spoiled on these,
   never does it give out, neither
   in winter time nor summer, but
   always the West Wind blowing on
   the fruits brings some to ripeness
   while he starts others.
Pear matures on pear in that place,
   apple upon apple,
Grape cluster on grape cluster,
   fig on fig.

—HOMER, *ODYSSEY*

**YELLOW PEACHES**, *garmades*, from Argos

**PEARS**, *axladia*

**PLUMS**, *damaskina* (prune sort) and *koromila* (big red sort), the best from Skopelos

**PINEAPPLE**, *ananas*, imported

**POMEGRANATE**, *rodi*

**PRICKLY PEAR**, *fragkosyka*

**STRAWBERRIES**, *fraoules*

**STRAWBERRY TREE FRUIT** (arbutus), *mimaikkyla*

**WATERMELON**, *karpousi*, grown everywhere, avidly loved

**WILD STRAWBERRY**, *koumara*

# the fruit

## FROUTA

### SERVES 6

IN FANCY GREEK RESTAURANTS, A SINGLE PERFECT PIECE OF FRUIT MIGHT BE SERVED ON A SMALL DISH, WITH A PARING KNIFE ALONGSIDE. THE DINER PEELS THE FRUIT, SLICES IT AS PREFERRED, AND SAVORS IT WITH PLEASURE.

At home, as the diners finish eating, the hostess takes several pieces of fresh fruit from the household's plentiful store— apples, oranges, pears, peaches, watermelon, muskmelon— whatever is ripe and in season. She pares the fruit, then cuts it into perfect wedges, drops the slices into a shallow bowl, and places the bowl at the center of the table. Diners pick up the juicy pieces with their forks and enjoy. If an eater doesn't spear enough, the hostess prompts more. But at the usual Greek meal, the fruit disappears faster than Hermes' swift sandals carried him skyward.

The same perfect, sweet, natural treat—ripe fruit, just as it is—is washed or peeled or sliced in generous amounts and offered to the group gathered in conversation in the evening, to those sitting watching the carpenter or shoemaker do his job, to friends gathered at the store for news. The variety and abundance of fruit in Greece— all perfectly ripe, lushly juicy, and so sweet that no other sugar is needed—brings the day to a sweet finale.

## OLIVES AND ORANGES— A CORFU WAY TO END THE MEAL

Greeks rarely mix sweet and salty and practically never combine fresh fruit with savory foods, but in Corfu they make an unusual fruit dish to complete the meal. Like other fresh fruit, the dish is also sometimes served in late afternoon or when sitting around chatting in the evening. The server peels oranges very carefully so that the thin inner white skin is left intact around the sections. The oranges are then sliced, and thinly slivered onion added to them, as if making a village salad. Like village salad as well, a goodly amount of olives is tossed on. The composition is dressed like a dessert salad, with a stream of good olive oil. Sweet paprika is sprinkled over the top. The orange and olive "salad" is passed to the children, who dive into the oranges until their chins are dripping, then round to the company, who take a scoop of all three ingredients, and finally back to the composer of the snack, who gets to mop up the juices.

4 to 6 apples, oranges, pears,
   or peaches
1 medium-size watermelon,
   large cantaloupe, muskmelon,
   Persian melon, or other small
   melon
2 pounds cherries or berries

1 Peel the whole fruit and slice it lengthwise into 1-inch-wide wedges.

2 Peel and separate the citrus fruit into sections.

3 Peel the melon, remove the seeds, and cut the flesh into 2-inch chunks.

4 Wash the cherries or berries.

5 Arrange the fruit in a shallow bowl and serve.

## FLOWERS AND INCENSE, TOO

Archestratos claimed that the usual after-dinner foods Greeks served—boiled chickpeas, broad (fava) beans, apples, and dried figs—were wretchedly poor fare. Rather he gives a recipe for other delights to enjoy at the meal's finale: "Festoon the head with all kinds of garland at the feasts, made with whatever the fruitful floor of the earth has in flower, dress your hair with fine, distilled perfumes and all day long toss on the fire's soft ashes myrrh and incense, the fragrant fruit of Syria."

*An ancient mosaic shows a servant carrying a bowl of many fruits to the banquet table.*

PART THREE

# confections: dulcet as ambrosia

IF YOU THINK THE SIRENS WHO USED TO LURE PASSERSBY WITH THEIR SWEET SONG NO LONGER ABIDE IN GREECE, YOU ARE WRONG. THEY HAVE SIMPLY CHANGED THEIR TUNE. THEY NO LONGER ENTICE WITH MELODY—THEY CAPTIVATE WITH THE ASTONISHING SYMPHONY OF GREEK SWEETS. AND THEY NO LONGER PIPE THEIR HARMONY FROM SOME STRANGE, FARAWAY ISLAND. THESE SIRENS CROON IN EVERY SWEET SHOP, IN THE BAKERIES, AND IN THE KITCHENS OF EVERY GREEK COOK.

honey, the natural substance that kept baby Zeus alive when his mother was forced to hide him. As their culinary arts developed, Greeks devised cakes and puddings enhanced with that amber fluid. Hecamede in the *Iliad* serves weary warriors a barley pudding sweetened with wine and honey. Aristophanes's comedies describe sweets of flour, almonds, walnuts, and honey that are similar to today's fried batter puffs, *loukoumades* or *diples*.

*Irresistible candies and nuts— a Greek specialty.*

The names of their tunes are *baklava, kadaifi, diples, rizogalo, moustalevria, glika tou koutalou, koufeta,* and *loukoumi*.

The sweets of Greece range from mellifluent pie to enticing cake, from ambrosial *baklava* to syrupy spoon sweets, to sugared cheese puffs, nectared fruit puddings, satin preserves, poached berries, sugar-crusted nuts, and taffy-soft candy.

They are not dessert. In the Greek way of dining, sweets are eaten in the late afternoon at a sugar shop, savored at festivals, indulged in when walking down the street, and appreciated as the extravagant favors at baptisms, weddings, and funerals. Late in the evening—with the last sip of ouzo, perhaps at a street café—a sweet provides the reward for a day well lived.

Sweet things have appealed to Greeks for ages. First it was

Even the god Pan preferred the lowly offering of sweet honey and sesame cakes to other oblations. The Greek love of honey comes down to us in language, as well, in the name Melissa, meaning bee, and mellifluous, meaning smooth, sweet, and honey-filled.

To further please their taste for sweets, the ancient Greeks added fruits, wines, and nuts to their cakes and pastries. They reduced their beloved grapes not just to wine, but to a thick, sugared juice to pour on their gruels and roasted meats. Indeed, to make the sweetest of the sweet wines they so loved, they added not only honey, but also the sweet grape syrup they reduced from boiling grapes.

Some of these dulcet dishes were served at the third part of the ancient Greek dinner, the *symposion,* in an atmosphere enhanced by sweet-smelling flowers: chrysanthemum, meaning blessed, or golden; thyme flowers, meaning sacrifice; dianthus, the flower of gods; fennel flowers, for victory; lavender, to scent the water for hand washing; violets to cure insomnia; and savory flowers to be an aphrodisiac. Guests and courtesans at the symposion reclined as befit the sweet part of the day, and played a game with drops of wine from their drinking kraters.

By Byzantine times mills produced more refined flour and the Greeks used it for tiered honey-soaked pastries and fried ribbons of batter. They also pounded fruits into sweetmeat and jellied berries into conserve. Like their predecessors, they flavored treats with spices from the East and with flowers and seeds at hand—cinnamon,

*Wide rolls of syrup-topped* diples—*crisp and flaky.*

clove, rose and rose geranium, sesame, and almond.

Sugar came to Greece late in the 1400s, borrowed from the Venetians. Greeks refined some of their old recipes to utilize the new granules, but they held on to honey, and many of their pastries are still sweetened with it. The treats created from the wealth of new and refined ingredients, along with Greece's incredible fruits, nuts, seeds, and cheese, received names from their ingredients and their shape: *amigdaloata* (meaning almond, for almond paste candies); *bobota* (from the word for corn, for a sweet cornmeal cake); *floueres* (meaning flutes, for pastry tubes filled with fruit or cheese); *koulouria* (meaning coils, for sweet bread rings

sometimes made with grape syrup); *finikia* (meaning Venice or Phoenician—opinions vary—for orange- and walnut-flavored honey cakes); and *kopenhagi* (meaning Copenhagen, for a filo-crusted sponge cake with nut center and honey syrup). Spoon sweets created from native fig, quince, grape, rose, melon rind, apricots, citron, and nuts were joined by ones created from bitter orange, strawberry, kumquat, and in due time, tomato, squash, and prickly pear.

Greek sweets are addictive, beckoning us to sample them again and again. The sirens, after snaring the unsuspecting with their hypnotic strains, used to turn the poor victims into beasts notorious for their overindulgence. To eat of Greek sweets is to risk the same.

*Custard-filled* galaktoboureko, *being cut into the traditional diamond-shaped pieces.*

# sweets
## IN PROFUSION

THE FIRST MEANING OF THE WORD "SWEET" WAS SOMETHING "GRACIOUS," "CHARMING," OR "PLEASING." THE WORD MOVED ON TO SIGNIFY SOMETHING "ENGAGING," "WINNING," "WINSOME," OR "FETCHING." GREEK CONFECTIONERIES ARE ALL OF THESE. UNHEARD OF IS THE PALATE THAT A GREEK CONFECTION CAN'T PLEASE. ONE HONIED CAKE IS SO WINSOME THAT IT IS CALLED *LAIS* AFTER A FAMOUS COURTESAN WHOSE LOVE WAS LUSCIOUSLY SWEET. AS FOR FETCHING, THEY FETCH YOU RIGHT IN TO PUT DOWN A FEW COINS AND PICK UP A FORK.

Forget all other desserts, there is only one— Athenian cheese cake with Attican honey from Hymettus.

—ARCHESTRATOS, SECOND CENTURY B.C.E.

# TIME-HONORED SYRUPS

# petimezi

### MAKES 2 CUPS

PETIMEZI HAS SERVED AS A NATURAL AND INCOMPARABLE SWEET THROUGHOUT THE AGES. THOUGH THE USE OF IT HAS SOMEWHAT DECLINED, IT REMAINS THE BASE FOR THE PUDDING THAT GREEKS VIEW AS NOSTALGICALLY AS WE DO APPLE PIE. ALONG WITH HONEY, PETIMEZI IS OFFERED AS A FRUITY DIPPING SAUCE FOR TIGANI, THE GREEK VERSION OF DOUGHNUTS OR FRITTERS. IT IS TURNED INTO A JELLYLIKE GRAPE CANDY AND IS ALSO USED AS A FLAVORING FOR CAKES, QUICK BREADS, AND ESPECIALLY THE COOKIES CALLED MOUSTOKOULOURA.

In my kitchen, *petimezi* has long since replaced maple as the syrup of choice for pancakes— I much prefer its unequaled fruitiness. It has taken over as the preferred ice cream topping, too— so fresh, so pure, and so unusual. I swirl it into yogurt as I would honey and drizzle it over freshly cut melon. I glaze sweets and layer cakes with it, and like the Greeks, I serve it as a sauce with fritters. I also use it as a cooking glaze when I want a sweet, fruity, authentically Greek touch (see Penelope's Goose, page 426).

I like to make my own *petimezi*. I have used palomino grapes, Thompson seedless, Red Flame, or whatever deliciously ripe grape I find at a farmer's stand or market bin. It doesn't matter if the grapes have seeds— the fruit reduction is strained. Buy the sweetest, cheapest grapes you can find. Or, lacking good fresh grapes, you can use bottled grape juice (there will be a slight boiled flavor to your *petimezi*, the result of the pasteurizing some juices receive), or use a sweet wine of the old Greek style, such as Mavrodaphne or Marsala. You can also find commercial *petimezi* in Greek food stores.

When making your own, you will need one strange ingredient: some fresh ash from your grill or

The tradition of sweet syrups in Greece goes back to the gods' own nectar and ambrosia. Mere mortals were not allowed these two heavenly treats, but it didn't matter to the Greeks below. They had two other almost divine versions: honey and *petimezi*.

Honey was so adored and so widely used that it was considered nearly a godly food. The sweet flowing stuff figures in many Greek myths. Not only was Zeus fed it, one of his two nursemaids was named Melissa, which means "honey maker." Honey was forbidden to mortals then, but intruders invaded Zeus's nursery to steal his divine quaff. The honeybees attacked the thieves, and in gratitude for their protection, Zeus clothed them in the black and ocher armor that they wear to this day.

Thousands of years before sugar arrived on their shores, Greeks added another source of sweetness to their cuisine by making a heady syrup from the grapes of their vineyards. The syrup is called *petimezi*, and I consider it one of the wonders of Greek cooking. In Roman times the same syrup was called *defructum*.

While both syrups taste truly heavenly, they don't provide quite the same results as nectar and ambrosia: "Nectar" means "overcoming death" and "ambrosia" means "not mortal." This, however, is good news. Otherwise, the demand for honey and *petimezi* would be so fierce that there would be none left to enjoy.

fireplace. This ash should come from pure wood charcoal or logs; do not use charcoal briquettes or treated wood. The ash is used to clarify the juice so that you end up with a beautifully translucent syrup. As a substitute you can use very, very dry bread. Some recipes call for the use of baking soda, but I have never tried it.

*10 pounds fresh grapes, stemmed*
*1 tablespoon clean ash, or 1 piece*
*(4 inches) very dry bread*

1 Crush the grapes in a food mill or press them through a mesh colander or strainer set over a large bowl. Extract as much juice as possible. Discard the skins, seeds, and stems and transfer the juice to a strainer lined with cheesecloth set over a large pot. Allow to drain thoroughly, pressing down on the pulp occasionally, until all the juice has collected in the pot (see Notes).

2 Tie the ash or bread in a small piece of the cloth and submerge it in the grape juice. Place the pot on the stove and bring the juice to a boil over medium heat. Reduce the heat and simmer, uncovered, for 15 minutes. Then set the pot aside and let it stand overnight. (The ash will allow the clear grape juice to rise to the top and the sediment to sink to the bottom.)

# HONEY

Although honey had been gathered around the Mediterranean since prehistoric times, beekeeping probably came to Greece from the Minoans' early contacts with Egyptians.

There were—and are—many sorts of Greek honey. Aristotle and Theophrastus critiqued honey from all over Greece, and both found that Attic honey was the best, followed by that from Salamis, Leros, Kalymnos, and Ybla. Honey from the Pontos was considered toxic, for the bees there poked their noses into rhododendron bushes. As for me, I dote on *Iymitou* (Hymettus), the most famous Greek honey, which comes from the mountain just outside Athens. But there is one special honey, gathered only in May on the island of Crete. It is called May honey, and while I've never tasted a Greek honey I didn't find exquisite, it stands out beyond all others.

In Greek cooking today honey is still as indispensable a sweetener as of old. Honey is used as the dulcet dip for fried treats like *diples* (page 513), *loukoumades*, and *svingi*. It's sweetener for cheese pies and sesame candies, the sweet soak for nut and semolina cakes, and the syrup poured over filo confections like *baklava* and *kadaifi*. It's drizzled on thick yogurt and stirred into soothing teas. In every use it is as venerated as in ancient times.

3 The next day, remove the ash, and very carefully pour the clarified grape juice into a second pot, leaving all the sediment behind in the first pot. Place the juice over medium heat, bring it to a boil, then reduce the heat and simmer until the juice reaches the consistency of maple syrup or molasses (235°F on a candy thermometer), 45 to 60 minutes. (Watch the pot and adjust the heat during the last 15 minutes of cooking so that the liquid doesn't boil over or burn, yet remains bubbling briskly.)

4 Allow the syrup to cool slightly, and then transfer it to clean glass containers. Store in the refrigerator indefinitely.

**NOTES:**

■ If your strainer isn't large enough to hold all the crushed grapes, do the draining in batches, combining the batches as the liquid drains out and the pulp reduces.

■ Since the process is a little time-consuming, I often double the amount of grapes to 20 pounds in order to make 1 quart at one

## DRESSING UP THE *PETIMEZI*

You can embroider a batch of *petimezi* with other flavors if you like. Swirl a few leaves of thyme, mint, or chamomile into the syrup. Or add a dash of nutmeg, cinnamon, or cardamom. Or for a subtle variation, stir in a few tablespoons of juice from other fruits, such as apricot, peach, or a favorite berry.

wine such as Mavrodaphne, can be used, but it produces an extremely sweet *petimezi*.

**Rosemary Grape Sauce:** You can make a thicker and more vibrantly colored grape ice cream or cake topping with a few simple changes to the *petimezi* sauce. In Step 1, crush the grapes in the colander, extracting as much juice

as possible, but don't restrain the juice through cheesecloth. Add ½ cup Mavrodaphne or other sweet wine and 4 sprigs rosemary with the ash in Step 2. Continue with the recipe as instructed. The result is a finely pulpy, aromatic, and mysteriously flavored grape topping.

time. An additional tablespoon of ash or piece of bread is needed for every 10 pounds of grapes. The cooking time for 20 pounds will be 1½ to 2 hours. On the other hand, if you want to make less, 3 pounds of grapes yields ½ cup; the cooking time is 17 to 25 minutes.

## VARIATIONS:

**Using Bottled Grape Juice:** To make *petimezi* from bottled grape juice, begin with 5 cups unsweetened grape juice, preferably white. Bring it to a boil over medium to medium-high heat and cook until 235°F on a candy thermometer, about 1 hour. The liquid should be dense but still pourable, like honey, when cooled. The yield is about ½ cup. Store as described above. Red grape juice, or sweet

## THE SWEETEST GODDESS: APHRODITE

As ancient in origin as Dionysos, god of the grape, Aphrodite, the goddess of love, was one of the twelve great deities of Mount Olympus. According to one story she was the daughter of Zeus and Dione. According to another, she arose full-grown upon the foam of the sea off Cyprus, and when she landed on terra firma, flowers sprang out of her footprints. Her name means "foam born."

Aphrodite had all the qualities of a scrumptious dessert. She was beautiful to behold. She beguiled all. She was irresistible—to the point of stealing away the wits of even the wise. She always came clad in glorious raiments and was sometimes crowned with violets. Around her there were always smiles.

Because the gods had trouble restraining themselves around her, Zeus married her off to the lame god, Hephaestus. But Aphrodite was not faithful. She was tempted as much as she could tempt. Her primary lover was

her brother, Ares, the god of war, with whom she had several children, named as would befit those who fell to her sweet enticement: Fear, Panic, and, at last, Harmony. Eros was perhaps their son too, for he was armed like his father—though with bow and arrow, not sword, and his arrows destroyed not life but willpower. Aphrodite also loved to tempt mortal men. Aeneas was her son with Anchises, and she went quite fruitcake over Adonis.

But punishment could also follow in her wake, particularly for those who trifled with her grandeur. She made the queen of Crete fall in love with a bull. She twisted Phaedra like toffee, causing her to fall in love with her own stepson. And when the muse Clio laughed at Aphrodite's passion for Adonis, she caused her to tumble like a bonbon for a mere mortal.

She even wed Dionysos. Their union, one of grapes and love, produced a son—and possibly many amphorae of sweet *petimezi*.

# FROM BEEHIVE TO OVEN

# baklava

## WITH MIXED NUTS AND *MAHLEPI* SYRUP

### MAKES 18 PIECES

THE WORD "PLANET" COMES FROM THE GREEK, MEANING "THE WANDERER," BECAUSE THE PLANETS, AS OPPOSED TO THE FIXED STARS, MOVE ABOUT THE NIGHT SKY. *BAKLAVA*, GREECE'S MOST FAMOUS HONEY-SYRUPED TREAT, DESERVES THE SAME TITLE, FOR IT IS TRULY A "PLANETARY" DESSERT. WITH ITS FLAKY CRUST, LAVISH NUT FILLING, AND DELECTABLE SYRUP, *BAKLAVA* IS THE CONFECTION THAT HAS WANDERED FROM COUNTRY TO COUNTRY ACROSS THE GLOBE. TODAY IT CAN BE FOUND AND ENJOYED ALMOST EVERYWHERE. HERE THE SYRUP IS FLAVORED WITH MYSTERIOUS *MAHLEPI*. IF YOU CAN'T FIND *MAHLEPI* FOR THE SYRUP, SUBSTITUTE THE CLOVE AND ORANGE LIQUEUR SYRUP (PAGE 512), THE METAXA HONEY SYRUP (PAGE 515), OR THE COFFEE SYRUP (PAGE 517).

1 cup (about 4 ounces) walnuts, finely chopped but not ground

1 cup (2 to 3 ounces) finely chopped almonds, or a mixture of almonds with hazelnuts or pistachios

1/4 teaspoon ground cinnamon

1 cup (2 sticks) plus 2 tablespoons butter, melted

32 sheets commercial filo dough

2 cups Mahlepi Syrup (recipe follows), at room temperature

1 Preheat the oven to 350°F.

2 Mix the walnuts, almonds, cinnamon, and 2 tablespoons of the melted butter together in a small bowl. Set it aside.

3 Brush the bottom and sides of a 13- x 9-inch baking pan with some of the remaining melted butter. Trim the filo sheets to fit the pan. Butter and layer 8 filo sheets on the bottom of the pan,

The pride of every Greek homemaker is the honied baked goods she lifts from her oven—her flour cakes and nut cakes, her holiday pastries and child-pleasing cookies, her honied fritters, and best of all, her syrup-soaked filo pastries. In her pride, she is following a timeless tradition. The art of treat baking began in Greece around the fifth century B.C.E. Soon sweet cakes were appearing in circles, squares, rectangles, shaped as animals, flowers, mushrooms, dolls, women's breasts, crowns, and wreaths. Sweet cakes were left in homage for both humble gods, such as Pan and Demeter, and high and mighty Zeus and Athena. They were also given as prizes to heroes.

By Byzantine times, professional bakers brought these sweets to new heights. Cooks concocted towers of filo dough mortared with nuts and custard. They filled rolls and nests of dough with sweetmeats.

The Greek legacy of baked sweets entices today because they are also simple to make: Cakes are composed largely of nuts and little flour, oiled sheets of dough are easily layered with goodies, candied pleasure comes from soaking in syrup, not fussing with coatings.

When baking a captivating Greek sweet, disaster—a Greek word meaning "bad star"—almost never happens. The sweet stars are all in your favor.

# THE NUTS OF GREECE

THERE IS A RICH AND VARIED MENU OF NUTS—A TERM THAT INCLUDES EDIBLE KERNELS, SEEDS, AND THE STONES OF CERTAIN FRUITS—IN GREEK COOKING, AND NOWHERE MORE THAN IN THEIR SWEETS.

**ALMONDS:** Called *amigdala* in Greek, these are the seeds of a plumlike fruit and are surrounded by both a hard shell and fleshy pulp. They are truly the favorite nut of Greece. Indeed the Greeks—that is, the Minoans, for almonds have been found in the ruins at Knossos—were the first people in Europe to cultivate them. The Romans called them "Greek nuts." They were the most common dessert nut of Greek banquets. They appear in ancient myth and recipe writing and play a symbolic as well as an edible role. No Greek wedding takes place without sugared (Jordan) almonds given as favors or almond *koufeta* (page 557) served to all the guests.

**CHESTNUTS** and **ACORNS:** *Kastana* and *velanidia* in contemporary Greek, *balanos* in ancient times, these true hard-shell nuts were gathered in prehistoric times and were eventually cultivated. Both were turned into sustaining gruels and ground into flour for breads. Hesiod wrote of their abundance. Now, though both are still used for flour, especially in hard times, acorns and particularly chestnuts are used more for treats and stuffings.

**HAZELNUTS (FILBERTS):** Called *fountouki* in Greek today, these were called *korylus* in ancient times, from the Greek word *korys*, or "helmet," due to their shape. Their tree was the first nut tree to spread across Europe after the last Ice Age, and they have been gathered in Greece and elsewhere ever since. The tree bearing them seems to have come first from the cool, forested hills above Asia Minor: They were sometimes referred to as "Pontos nut" and earlier "Herakleotic nut," for the regions west of the Black Sea. The English word "hazelnut," like the ancient Greek, comes from an early word for "headdress." "Filbert" comes from their August harvest time, which is near St. Filbert's Day.

**PINE NUTS:** *Koukounaria* are actually the seeds, enclosed in the woody cone, of many kinds of pine trees. Some of these low-growing, seed-producing pines are native to Greece, and the sweet, rich "nuts" have been used in Greek cuisine since early times. Even more popular today, they are an essential ingredient in *dolmades* and in other stuffings.

**PISTACHIOS:** Their name in Greek, *fistikia*, comes from the Persian. They have been gathered wild for three thousand years and cultivated almost as long. Though originally from Asia, they were growing in Palestine by biblical times, then borrowed by the Greeks and taken into the rest of Europe by the Romans. They are a common snack and make an unusually festive filling for *baklava* or *kadaifi*.

**WALNUTS:** Still bearing the oldest word for "nut" in Greek, *karydia*, again related to "helmet," walnuts are the second most beloved nut. Walnuts are the seed of a big, green, not very fleshy, edible (although puckery) fruit. Early Greeks cultivated a scrappy variety of the tree, but they soon discovered the better Persian sort of walnut, from which they could also press the oil. They called these "Persian" or "royal" walnuts. By Roman times, they were called "bald nuts," and our word "walnut" means "foreign nut."

*A seaside nut vendor sells small bags of nuts for strollers to nibble on.*

(see Filo Finesse, page 87). Spread one third of the nut mixture evenly over the filo. Butter and layer another 8 filo sheets over the nuts. Spread another third of the nut mixture over them. Repeat the layers once more, and end with the last 8 filo sheets. Liberally brush some of the remaining butter over the top and edges of the filo.

4 Using a sharp knife, cut through all the layers, making 15 to 18 diamond or square shapes (see page 90). Place the dish in the oven and bake for 20 minutes.

5 Pour the remaining butter over the top of the *baklava,* and continue baking until it is pale golden on top and crisp to the touch, 20 to 25 minutes. Remove the dish from the oven and set it aside until the liquid is no longer sizzling, 5 minutes.

## OIL FOR SUGARY FILO DISHES, TOO

Greeks formerly used olive oil, not butter, to moisten the filo sheets for both sweet and savory treats. Olive oil can still be used, or you can do as I often do with sweet filo pies: Use a mixture of olive oil and melted butter.

6 Pour the syrup into the cuts between the pieces and around the edges of the dish, taking care to avoid pouring it over the top (which would make it soggy). Set the *baklava* aside to cool. Then cover it and let it rest for several hours or as long as overnight, so the pastry can soak up the syrup. It will keep at room temperature for 3 days.

### NOTES:

■ There are many versions of the nut filling for *baklava.* At its most traditional, the filling is all walnuts or a combination of walnuts and almonds. But the pie filling can include hazelnuts alone, walnuts and hazelnuts, or almonds alone. Some versions combine pistachios with walnuts or almonds or are made of all pistachio. Others mix all the Mediterranean nuts, including pine nuts. An American rendition can even include pecans. Some Greek cooks add currants or raisins, an addition that I find overwhelmingly sweet. It's fun to try different nut fillings; just keep the quantity the same.

■ Some Greek bakers build *baklava* with three, not four, layers of filo and two, not three, layers of filling.

■ Sweet filo pies use more layers of dough than savory pies.

## ATHENAEUS'S BAKLAVA

Take walnuts from Thasos in the Pontos, almonds, and poppy seeds and toast them carefully. Then crush them well in a clean mortar, mix the three together, grind them while adding strained honey and pepper to them, and blend the whole together well. The mixture will become black because of the pepper. Make a flat square cake of this paste, then grind some white sesame, mix it with flour and strained honey, and make two flat cakes of it, between which you will place the preceding black paste, fastening it securely in the middle.

—ATHENAEUS, SECOND CENTURY B.C.E.

## MAHLEPI SYRUP

### MAKES 2 CUPS

*Mahlepi* is a special Greek spice. It comes from a small flowering cherry tree called mahaleb, Saint Lucie, or black cherry, which was originally native to Asia Minor. Greeks from Asia Minor and Cyprus introduced the spice into Greek cooking, and it is commonly used to flavor special sweets. The fruit is rather bitter, but the kernels impart a flavor that is subtly cherrylike, slightly flowery, slightly fruity, yet distinct and alluring. It can be found ground or in seed form in Greek markets. I find *mahlepi* so intriguing and ethereal that I use it beyond the usual ways—in sauces, gravies, stews, beverages, syrups, and more.

*1 cup sugar*
*1 cup honey*
*1 cup water*
*1 tablespoon fresh lemon juice*
*2 teaspoons ground mahlepi*

Combine all the ingredients in a medium-size saucepan. Bring to a boil and simmer briskly until thickened and reduced, about 12 minutes. Strain into a clean saucepan or bowl and set aside until ready to use. The syrup should be at room temperature and still pourable when you use it; if it has cooled too much, reheat it slightly.

# filled kadaifi nests

## WITH HONEY *TSIKOUDIA* SYRUP

### MAKES 18 NESTS

NO ONE KNOWS WHO BEGAN MAKING PASTRIES USING FINELY SHREDDED FILO DOUGH, OR WHY. MY IMAGINATION TELLS ME THAT AFTER ALL THE WORK ROLLING IT OUT SO THIN, SOME COOK COULDN'T BEAR TO WASTE A SCRAP. SO HE OR SHE GATHERED THE SCRAPS, SLIVERED THEM TO MAKE THEM ALL THE SAME SIZE, AND USED THEM AS A BIRD MIGHT TO BUILD A NEST OF DOUGH. THAT THRIFTY COOK WAS A GENIUS. CALLED *KADAIFI*, CRUSTS OF SHREDDED FILO HAVE A CRACKLY TEXTURE AND THEY ARE FILLED, SWEETENED WITH SYRUP, AND SERVED TO GENERAL ACCLAIM.

Usually the filo strands are filled with nuts, as for *baklava*, and rolled up into buns. At other times they are swirled into nest forms, then filled with nuts, usually pistachio. But with all the wonderful ingredients in the Greek pantry, the choices for fillings are almost infinite! Dates, which have been a part of Greek cuisine since before Solon sailed to Egypt, combine here with pistachio nuts for a superbly sweet and chewy filling.

*Greeks are proficient at the ancient art of weaving baskets as well as* kadaifi *nests.*

## THE SAUCEPAN FOR THE SYRUP

Greek sweets commonly employ syrups of honey or sugar to soak into the confection. To achieve the right consistency for a syrup, the size of the saucepan matters. If the pan is too wide and shallow, the solution will reduce too quickly and the syrup will be too thick to soak through the dessert. If the pan is too narrow and high, the solution can become over-cooked before it reduces the syrup stage. Use a 1½-quart saucepan for all syrup recipes.

1 cup (about 4 ounces) shelled
  pistachios, finely ground
½ cup (about 3 ounces)
  pitted dates, finely
  chopped
Zest of 1 orange, finely chopped
½ cup sugar
¼ cup fresh orange juice
12 ounces kadaifi dough
  (see Notes)
1½ cups (3 sticks) butter, melted
1 cup Honey Tsikoudia Syrup
  (recipe follows), at room
  temperature

1 Place the pistachios, dates, orange zest, sugar, and orange juice in a medium-size bowl and stir to mix. Set it aside.

2 Preheat the oven to 350°F.

3 Uncoil the *kadaifi* on a work surface and separate the strands into 18 portions. Cover the strands with a damp cloth to keep them from drying out.

4 Working with one portion of the strands at a time (and keeping the remaining ones covered), brush liberally with melted butter, enough to moisten them thoroughly. Coil the strand portion into a high round, to resemble a bird's nest. Place the nest in the palm of one hand and poke a well or depression in the center, where the filling will go. Liberally brush the top and sides with butter so the nest will keep its form, and set it on an ungreased baking sheet. Repeat with the remaining strands until all 18 nests are formed (see Notes).

5 Press about 1 tablespoon of the pistachio mixture into each nest. Place the baking sheet in the oven and bake until they are lightly golden, about 25 minutes. Remove the sheet from the oven and transfer the nests to a serving platter. Set them aside to cool to room temperature.

6 Slowly pour the syrup over the nests, coating the tops and drizzling a bit down the sides. Set the nests aside at room temperature until the syrup has been absorbed, several hours or as long as overnight, then serve.

**NOTES:**

■ Long, thinly shredded *kadaifi* dough comes boxed like filo sheets, but alas, it is not as easy to find. Most specialty Greek and Middle Eastern groceries carry it. If you can't find *kadaifi*, you can shred filo dough very, very thin yourself, being careful to keep the shreds straight for ease in working. You will have to use

## KADAIFI ROLLS

In Greece, *kadaifi* sweets, especially nut-filled, are formed into rolls as often as nests. To form rolls, cut the shredded dough into 4- to 6-inch lengths, and arrange the strands in 3-inch-wide portions. Spread 1 to 2 tablespoons of the filling along one long side, and carefully roll the dough over to make a pipe or flute (see page 87). Place them snugly in a baking pan. Or you can form long snakelike rolls of *kadaifi*, coil the roll around the pan's interior, and then cut pieces to the desired size after baking.

# TSIKOUDIA AND THE MOOR

I AM NOT ONE FOR GHOST STORIES, BUT GREEK VILLAGERS ADORE THEM. THEY COLLECT THE STORIES LIKE MODERN-DAY HOMERS, ONLY THEIR SAGAS ARE MORE TERRIFYING THAN EPIC. THEY RECOUNT THE TALES LIKE ANCIENT MINSTRELS, VIVIFY THEM LIKE RASCALLY RACONTEURS, AND—WITH RELISH—PASS THEM ON TO GENERATIONS OF WIDE-EYED CHILDREN. EACH TELLING, AS ONE WOULD GUESS, GROWS IN EMBELLISHMENT. THE TALES PROVIDE ENDLESS ENTERTAINMENT FOR FOLKS GATHERED TO PASS THE HOURS. NO GREEK TIRES OF GHOST STORIES.

I heard many of them on long, dark nights during my first stays in Greece. After all, we had no electricity.

## WHO COMES VISITING AFTER DARK?

What we *did* have were Nereids, who danced in circles in the fields. If you came upon them you had to take off all your clothes and join their dancing until they disappeared when the first cock crowed, or else they would tear you to pieces. We had *kalikantzari*, the spirits of unbaptized children, who roamed the glens after midnight, teasing travelers, stealing sausages, and playing terrible pranks. We also had the devil, who usually appeared sitting in a tree, whistling a tune, during what the Greeks call "the ugly hour," which could be midnight, but unpredictably could be any hour. Worst of all, we had the Moor. He belonged solely to our very own village, and he was horrifying!

## THE COLOSSUS OF SANTORINI

The Moor was a giant who appeared only on pitch-dark nights. He was so huge that some said he stood with one leg on each side of the village, some said one leg on each end of the island, and some said one leg on Santorini and one on Anafi. I pooh-poohed this tale, ever the nonbeliever, until one day when I was having a rare case of "village fever" (something like cabin fever) and had gone to town on my motorbike.

I had stretched my visit late, and as evening approached was enticed by friends to have an after-dinner treat in the town's most notable edifice, the looming Atlantis Hotel. The sweet offered was one of my favorites, *kadaifi* with nuts and syrup, and I was inveigled into accompanying the treat with some island-made *tsikoudia*—not swirled in the syrup but poured into a traditional small drinking glass. The one drink led to two and, I admit, to three.

By then it was edging on midnight and I had to make the trip home.

In those days, the road to my village could hardly be called a road. It was a swath cut through pumice soil so loose and dusty that tires sank down a good ten inches. It wound around strangely shaped pumice cliffs, past abandoned windmills, and virtually hundreds of caves. (Santorini is riddled with gaping, mawlike caverns.) I had to navigate it all, and as it happened, the night was moonless. It was the first time I was ever literally scared out of my mind.

*Tsikoudia*-influenced, I had visions of tripping Nereids luring me to unclothe. At any moment I was expecting a close encounter with a cloven-hoofed being. But most of all I was sure the Moor was waiting for me around every corner. I cautiously slipped around the curves, sped through the few straightaways, crept past the caverns, until the village was in view and I was almost home, when a huge shadow, long and humanlike, crossed the road.

Was it true? Was the Moor so big he could straddle the village? I looked up, almost fell over, and then Averkios, the tavern keep, swung his lantern at me. He had forgotten to bring his donkey in for the night and spotting me, gave me a good tongue-lashing. "Go home," he said. Didn't I know this was just the sort of night the Moor would be lurking?

I well knew, and now on Santorini and elsewhere I limit my *tsikoudia* drinking to a single preprandial aperitif. Any later, and I put the brandy on my *kadaifi*.

more of these short strands to make up each nest. You can also shred very thin homemade filo dough that has been rolled out to a length of about 50 inches. In that case, each nest is wound from only a few of the long strands.

■ Working with *kadaifi* the first time can be a bit awkward and difficult—ease in working with it comes with practice. Damp hands help, and it helps to keep the nests you've made covered with a damp cloth so they won't dry out while you make the rest.

■ To make more traditional *kadaifi,* fill the nests with the *baklava* filling (page 503).

## HONEY TSIKOUDIA SYRUP

### MAKES ABOUT 1 CUP

We often add cognac and brandy to foods, and give a culinary nod here and there to other fruit eaux-de-vie, like pear and peach, but we rarely think to add a splash of perhaps the world's most common fruit distillation, the one made of the pulp of the grape harvest: *tsikoudia,* or in Italy, *grappa.* Yet *tsikoudia* is hypnotically aromatic, a distinct and evocative ingredient, here in a syrup for *kadaifi.*

*1/2 cup honey, preferably flower-scented*
*1/2 cup sugar*
*1/4 cup tsikoudia or grappa*

Place all the ingredients in a small saucepan and bring to a boil. Reduce the heat to maintain a brisk simmer without boiling over, and cook until thickened, 5 to 6 minutes. Remove from the heat and cool to room temperature.

## OTHER FRUIT IN THE NEST

When I first lived in Greece, I never saw apples cooked in any way—not baked, stewed, pureed, or fried. Nowadays, though, apples appear in fillings used in pastries and atop filo layers. All Greeks do eat an abundance of raw apple. They frequently serve peeled slices to end a winter meal or to offer to family and guests who drop by, and for those purposes, apples are stocked in every larder from early fall well into spring.

I have also never seen rhubarb there, but the ancient Greeks knew it. Our name for the sweet red stalk comes from *rhu,* the ancient Greek name for a northern river, probably the Volga. The invaders from the north brought with them the strange fruitlike stalk, and our word for the tart plant still evokes the "barbarian river"—*rhu barb-arian.*

In place of the dates, 1/2 cup sweetened, cooked apple or rhubarb can tastily fill *kadaifi* nests.

# semolina custard pie

## WITH MAVRODAPHNE OR CLOVE AND ORANGE SYRUP

### GALAKTOBOUREKO

#### MAKES 15 PIECES

WHAT COULD BE A MORE DELIRIOUS COMBINATION THAN CUSTARD ENCASED IN CRISP FILO, THE DUO SATURATED WITH SWEET SYRUP? TO MY MIND, NOTHING. GALAKTOBOUREKO IS MY ALL-TIME FAVORITE GREEK DESSERT. AS A LOVER OF BOTH PUDDING AND PIE, I GET IT ALL: PILLOWY CENTER, CRISP CRUST, DULCET SAUCE. AND I PARTAKE OF THE CLASSIC ELEMENTS OF PARADISE: MILK AND HONEY. THE SEMOLINA PUDDING SETS UP IN MINUTES—NO ENDLESS STIRRING OVER A HOT PAN. THE SYRUP BUBBLES TO PERFECTION WHILE YOU LAYER THE FILO. INDEED, THE PIE COMES TOGETHER SO RAPIDLY THAT IT IS MY CHOICE TO BRING TO POTLUCKS AND CELEBRATIONS.

There are two syrup possibilities: One sings of sweet grapes and the vibrancy of deep-toned brandy; the other of clove and orange. Either saturates a pudding that is aromatic with New World vanilla.

4 cups milk

3/4 cup sugar

1/2 cup semolina flour (see Note)

1 tablespoon butter

4 large eggs

1/2 cup (1 stick) butter, melted

1 teaspoon vanilla extract

18 sheets commercial filo dough

3/4 cup Mavrodaphne Brandy Syrup or Clove and Orange Liqueur Syrup (recipes follow), cooled to room temperature

1 Preheat the oven to 350°F.

2 Heat the milk in a medium-size saucepan over medium-high heat until it is almost boiling. Stir in 1/2 cup of the sugar, the semolina, and the 1 tablespoon butter. Reduce the heat to medium and cook until thickened, about 5 minutes. Remove the pan from the heat.

3 In a medium-size bowl, beat the eggs, the remaining 1/4 cup sugar, and 1/4 cup of the melted butter together until frothy. Slowly whisk this into the milk mixture. Stir in the vanilla and set aside.

4 Brush the bottom and sides of a 13- x 9-inch baking dish with some of the remaining melted butter. Trim the filo sheets so they are 1 inch larger than the baking dish on all four sides. Butter and layer 9 filo sheets on the bottom of the pan (see Filo Finesse, page 87), making sure the bottommost filo sheets come up the sides of the dish to encase the filling. Spread the custard mixture over the filo. Butter and layer the remaining filo sheets over the top, tucking the last sheets down around the sides. Liberally brush melted butter over the top and along the edges of the filo. With a

sharp knife, score the topmost filo sheets, forming 15 to 18 square or diamond-shaped pieces (see page 90), taking care not to cut into the custard filling.

5 Place the dish in the oven and bake until the pie is golden around the edges, crisp on top, and firm in the center, 50 minutes to 1 hour. Let it cool until it is no longer piping hot.

6 Slowly pour the syrup around the edges of the pie and down the scoring. Set the pie aside for several hours, or as long as overnight, for the syrup to soak in; then serve. The pie will keep for up to 2 days at room temperature.

**NOTE:** Semolina is flour made of durum wheat, the hard wheat developed around and still common to the Mediterranean. Not as fine as our powdery wheat flour, it does not become pasty or leave a floury taste, yet it thickens a pudding rapidly and lightly. It is also the flour used to make many Greek cakes and most pasta. It is available in the baking section of most good groceries.

## MILLS AND MACHINES

An argument for the Byzantine origin of filo dough lies in the fact that the flour required to make such a delicate dough must be finely milled, and the Byzantines were the masters of mills. Throughout the Byzantine epoch, the old Mediterranean methods of harvesting, threshing, and winnowing grain continued much the same: sickles to cut the sheaves, oxen dragging threshing sleds over the stalks, forks to pitch the kernels in the wind. However, the canny Byzantine inventors considerably advanced the method of grinding grain with water mills. Indeed, the water mills were so efficient that farmers snubbed the next development, windmills, until late in the Byzantine era.

By the fourteenth century, though, windmills, too, were in great use. To this day windmills stand along almost every breeze-catching ridge throughout Greece and Asia Minor. Most are defunct and crumbling, but their silhouettes give an eerie nostalgia to the landscape.

The creativity of the Byzantine inventors didn't stop with the grinders. The citizenry consumed so much flour-based food that they desperately needed something to mix the masses of dough they baked up daily. Consequently, the canny cooks of the time invented the first dough mixer. The machine was powered by oxen—not quite practical in a modern kitchen but a particular boon to the monasteries, whose large communities of monks required considerable feeding. One of the first such mixers was devised by St. Athanasios, who oversaw a gigantic monastery on Greece's sacred Mount Athos. It is said that the monks and the teeming populations of the Byzantine cities ate so many products made from dough—loaf and flat breads, cakes and pies—that both mills and dough machines ran around the clock.

## MAVRODAPHNE BRANDY SYRUP

### MAKES ¾ CUP

Mavrodaphne wine was first created by Gustav Clauss, a Bavarian who came to Patras around 1850, began a vineyard, and in 1861 produced the first bottles of the sweet elixir he called "Mavrodaphne wine."

Next to retsina, it is probably Greece's most famous wine. In one tale it is said he named the wine for his sweetheart, Daphne, without explaining why it was called "Black Daphne."

In truth, the Mavrodaphne grape was already being used to make sweet wine, as was the "black" currant grape of the same area, long before Gustav's arrival. What he achieved was to make the wine more like Port by shortening the fermentation, adding grape spirits, which raised both alcohol and sugar content, and cleverly aging the wine in the barrel. The resulting wine, depending on the grade, is amber to mahogany in color, cherry to raisin to almost chocolate in flavor, long-lasting, complex, and hypnotically ambrosial. Combined with brandy—preferably Greece's redolent Metaxa—the two gifts of the grape reduce to a syrup that soaks seductively into the milky custard of *galaktoboureko*. The filo crust picks up beads of the sauce as if studded with rubies.

*4 whole cloves*
*1 piece (1 inch) cinnamon stick*
*³/4 cup sugar*
*¹/3 cup Mavrodaphne wine*
*¹/4 cup brandy, preferably*
 *Metaxa*
*³/4 cup water*

Combine all the ingredients in a small saucepan and bring to a boil over high heat. Stir, reduce the heat, and simmer briskly until thickened, reduced, and slightly golden, 15 minutes. Allow the syrup to cool, then remove the cloves and cinnamon stick and use.

**NOTE:** Mavrodaphne and other sugar and honey syrups can be kept, covered, in the refrigerator indefinitely, but

need to be rewarmed to runny before pouring over a filo sweet or cake.

# CLOVE AND ORANGE LIQUEUR SYRUP

### MAKES ³/4 CUP

By the first century C.E., the Greeks knew of oranges as the fruit began to spread from its homeland, China. They called them *narantsion*, which became *aurnitium* in Latin—and eventually "orange" in English. The fruit was not widely grown around the Mediterranean until the Arabs spread its cultivation around one thousand years later, just about the same time the Egyptians had developed ways to process sugar.

The union of fruit juices with sugar allowed for the formation of sweet fruit syrups and liqueurs, and sweetening the abundant, redolent juice of the orange was a natural. Orange water became a popular ingredient among late Byzantine and other cooks, used especially to flavor sweets. Orange is still a beloved enhancement for cakes, spoon sweets, and soaking syrups.

Strangely, though ancient Greeks knew of the orange, the variety that is cultivated now in such profusion is an especially

sweet type bred in Portugal, and the name for oranges today in Greece is *portokali*.

*4 whole cloves*
*1 piece (1 inch) cinnamon stick*
*³/4 cup sugar*
*¹/2 cup orange-flavored liqueur,*
 *such as Triple Sec*
*³/4 cup water*

Combine all ingredients in a small saucepan and bring to a boil over high heat. Stir, reduce the heat, and simmer briskly until thickened, reduced, and slightly golden, 15 minutes. Allow the syrup to cool to room temperature, then remove the cloves and cinnamon stick and use (see Note, this page).

## VARIATIONS:

**The Ancients' Rendition:** The ancients made a grain pudding, such as the custard that fills *galaktoboureko*, that was sweetened with sweet wine rather than sugar. Were they to use the pudding in a pie, their crust would have been thicker sheets of homemade pastry. Their syrup would have been honey thinned with water, and the top would have been sprinkled all over with a soft, mild cheese.

To make such a rendition, replace the sugar in the custard filling with ½ cup sweet wine, such as Mavrodaphne. With the added liquid, it will take a bit longer to thicken the pudding. Use commercial or homemade filo for the crust. Five minutes before removing the pie from the oven, sprinkle grated kasseri cheese over the top. Replace the sugar in either syrup with good Greek honey, lightly thinned with water.

**A Spice-Dusted Version:** Many contemporary Greek cooks do not use a syrup at all on *galaktoboureko*. Instead, they sprinkle ground cinnamon or nutmeg over the top. Some use both the sprinkled spices and the syrup.

# sweet fried pastry ribbons

## WITH METAXA HONEY SYRUP AND SUGARED ALMOND TOPPING

### DIPLES

**MAKES ABOUT 60 PIECES**

AMONG THE PARADE OF GREEK BAKED SWEETS ARE A NUMBER OF SCRUMPTIOUS FRIED PASTRIES. THERE ARE *SVINGI*, FRIED SPOONFULS OF A LIGHT, RUNNY BATTER TOPPED WITH A LIGHTER HONEY SYRUP. THERE ARE *LOUKOUMADES*, FRIED PUFFS OF BISCUIT DOUGH MUCH LIKE A FRENCH *BEIGNET*, DIPPED IN OR DRIZZLED WITH HONEY JUST BEFORE SERVING. SOMETIMES THEY ARE ALSO SPRINKLED WITH CHOPPED WALNUTS, PISTACHIOS, ALMONDS, OR SESAME SEEDS, OR DUSTED WITH CINNAMON INSTEAD OF THE TRADITIONAL CONFECTIONERS' SUGAR. YOU CAN FIND *LOUKOUMADES* BUBBLING IN VATS OF HOT OIL AT MANY GREEK FESTIVALS OR IN THE WINDOWS OF GREEK SWEET SHOPS, OR IN HOMES WHERE THEY ARE A TREAT FOR FAMILIES AFTER HOLIDAY CHURCH SERVICES.

But by far the prettiest—and to me the tastiest—of the fried pastries are *diples*. *Diples* are ribbons of thin dough, shaped into all sorts of charming forms and fried crisp and flaky. They crunch and crumble in the mouth, every morsel delivering a dab of honey. *Diples* are reputed to require considerable skill compared to the other fried treats, and they do take some work—rolling out the dough, shaping it into bow ties, rosettes, knots, or figure eights, then frying it. But the dough is actually quite easy to work, and the cut strips are very pliable. Here, sugar-coated Jordan almonds, which are given as favors at every Greek wedding, are crushed and used as a

## DIPLES ON THE DOUBLE

**A**lthough they are perhaps the fussiest Greek fried pastry to make (compared to just dripping pieces or spoonfuls of dough or batter into hot oil), *diples* are quick and easy to turn out if you know a few tricks. You'll find that the *diples*—which means "doubles," perhaps for the bow shapes and knots the dough can be twisted into—come out doubly crisp, fast, and ready to crumble in some eager mouth.

■ Give the skillet all your attention, because the frying process is very quick. The first pieces in will be ready to turn by the time you add the last of that batch, and the first turned are about ready to be lifted out by the time you finish turning the last added.

■ The best tools for cooking *diples* are tongs for turning and a slotted spoon or wire strainer for removing. Otherwise, two forks will do, but take care because the oil is hot and you need to work fast to avoid overcooking them.

■ The dough will keep, wrapped in plastic wrap, in the refrigerator for up to 3 days, so if you like, you can make the dough in advance and cook one portion at a time over 2 or 3 days.

■ You can fry the *diples* in advance and store them in an airtight container for up to 10 days, adding the warmed syrup and topping when ready to serve.

spectacular sprinkling that adds extra sweetness and crunch.

3 to 3¹/4 cups unbleached
    all-purpose flour
¹/2 teaspoon baking powder
¹/2 teaspoon salt
1 tablespoon sugar
4 large eggs
4 tablespoons (¹/2 stick) butter,
    melted
¹/4 cup fresh orange juice
Vegetable oil, for frying
1¹/2 cups Metaxa Honey Syrup
    (recipe follows), warmed
¹/4 cup Jordan almonds, finely
    chopped

**1** Sift 2¹/2 cups of the flour with the baking powder, salt, and sugar into a large bowl. Set it aside.

**2** In another bowl, beat the eggs until frothy. Beat in the melted butter and the orange juice, then beat the egg mixture into the flour mixture to make a wet dough. Transfer the dough to a floured surface and knead it, working in the remaining ¹/2 to ³/4 cup flour, until it is smooth and no longer sticky, 8 to 10 minutes. Cover the dough with a damp towel and set it aside to rest for 30 minutes.

**3** Divide the dough into three portions. Keeping the other two portions covered with a damp cloth, roll out one portion as thin as possible, and cut it into strips about 2 inches wide and 4 inches long. Tie the pieces into bows or knots, roll them up into rosettes, or leave them as strips (a mixture of different forms is the most fun). Fry these strips before rolling out the next portion of dough (or, if you have sufficient counter space, roll, cut, and shape each portion now. Keep the cut strips covered while you prepare the remaining dough portions.)

**4** Pour vegetable oil into a large heavy skillet to a depth of ¹/2 inch. Heat the oil over medium-high heat until it is hot. Then add as many dough pieces as will fit without crowding, and fry, turning once, until golden on both sides, about 2 minutes. Transfer the *diples* to paper towels or brown paper to drain, and repeat with another round until all the pieces are fried. (Make sure the oil is hot before you add each batch.)

5 If you're preparing one portion of the dough at a time, cut, shape, and fry the remaining ones as described.

6 When the *diples* are cool, gently arrange them on a large platter, stacking them two or three high. Pour the warm syrup over the top, making sure each piece gets a dollop. Sprinkle the almonds over the top, and serve (they are meant to be eaten with your hands). They will keep, loosely covered with plastic wrap, for up to 5 days at room temperature.

## SWEET PRIZES

Honey-coated fried cakes, very similar to the ones on today's menu, were offered by street vendors in the marketplace in ancient Greece. In classical times, sweet honey-dipped fried cakes were also given as prizes to winners of games. These, more similar to *loukoumades* than to *diples*, were called "tokens," *charisiou,* and the poet Kallimachos described how winning athletes were overjoyed to get them as rewards. Some of the fried cakes were presented not in honey, but with *mulsum*, a honey-spiced wine much like our mulled wine. Democritos's recipe for *mulsum* wine sauce included "finely ground peppercorns, Attica honey, and old white wine."

# METAXA HONEY SYRUP

### MAKES ABOUT 1½ CUPS

Greece's own special brandy, Metaxa, has a flavor all its own. It is sweeter than the French brandies, rounder, and softer, and has a honied top note. It offers a warm glow of a taste, rather like the aura of a candle flame. Honey is a warm substance too, and a mix of the two makes a syrup of double eloquence with a gorgeous bronze color.

*1½ cups honey*
*¾ cup Metaxa brandy, or another flavored brandy*
*1 teaspoon ground cinnamon*

Combine all the ingredients in a medium-size saucepan and bring to a boil. Reduce the heat and simmer briskly until thickened and syrupy again, about 10 minutes. Use warm. To keep, cool completely, cover, and refrigerate indefinitely.

# A GAME OF WINE DARTS

During the symposium part of the meal in ancient Greece, the diners played a game where they flung the last drop of wine in their cups at a target. The game was called *kottabos.* The cups were *krators,* broad and two-handled, so to fling the last drop required a trick.

Paintings show the clever maneuver, frequently performed by seminaked young men or party girls. The player inserted the index finger of the right hand in one handle of the cup, then balanced the cup back toward the right shoulder. The cup was then flicked over the wrist, as in an overhand softball throw, toward the target. The wine shot forward while the player held on to the cup. Tries at the target were often dedicated to certain persons, presumably lovers. The stunt was done from a reclining position, with the wine flinger resting on a pillow. Good thing it was wine and not a sticky honey syrup.

# walnut cake

## WITH COFFEE SYRUP

### KARYDOPITA

#### SERVES 12 TO 15

AMONG THE MOST COMMON ANCIENT NUT CAKES WAS ONE MADE OF WALNUTS, AND WALNUT CAKE REMAINS ONE OF THE MOST COMMON GREEK CAKES TO THIS DAY. WALNUT CAKES ARE STILL MADE ALL OVER GREECE, SOME WITH SUGAR SYRUPS, SOME WITH HONEY SYRUP, SOME WITH WINE SYRUP. HERE, THE SYRUP TO MOISTEN THE RICH, NUTTY CAKE IS BASED ON ANOTHER GREEK LOVE, COFFEE. THE COMBINATION OF COFFEE AND CAKE IS AS POPULAR IN GREECE AS IT IS IN THE UNITED STATES. TO COMPLETE THE COMBINATION (MORE AMERICAN THAN GREEK), ADD AN OPTIONAL TOUCH OF CREAM IN THE FORM OF GREECE'S THICK YOGURT.

5 tablespoons butter,
   at room temperature
1/3 cup sugar
4 large eggs, separated

2 cups (about 8 ounces) walnuts,
   finely chopped but not ground
1 cup (about 14 pieces) finely
   crumbled Paximadia (page 128),
   zwieback, or melba toast
1 teaspoon baking powder
1/2 teaspoon ground cinnamon
1/4 teaspoon ground cloves
2 tablespoons brandy
3/4 cup Coffee Syrup
   (recipe follows)

2 cups Thickened Yogurt
   (page 471) mixed with
   1/4 cup confectioners'
   sugar (optional)

*Coffee and conversation— there is never a wrong time of the day.*

1 Preheat the oven to 350°F. Grease a 9- x 7-inch baking dish (see Note) with butter or oil.

2 Combine the butter and sugar in a large bowl and beat until light and fluffy. Add the egg yolks, one at a time, beating each one in before adding the next. Beat in the walnuts, *paximadia* crumbs, baking powder, cinnamon, cloves, and brandy.

3 In a separate bowl, beat the egg whites until stiff peaks form. Fold the whites into the walnut mixture a third at a time.

4 Spoon the batter into the prepared baking dish and gently spread it out so the surface is even. Bake until the cake is pulling away from the edges and a knife inserted in the center comes out clean, 30 to 40 minutes. Set aside to cool to room temperature.

5 Cut the cake into 12 pieces, but don't remove them from the pan. Slowly pour the syrup over the cake, allowing it to seep between the slices before adding more. Set the cake aside for at least 2 hours so the syrup can soak into it.

6 Serve, accompanied by the sweetened yogurt, if using. The cake will keep at room temperature for up to 5 days.

**NOTE:** Walnut cake is traditionally cooked in a rectangular baking pan so that it may be cut into diamond shapes. An 8- or 9-inch round pan will also do, however.

## COFFEE SYRUP

**MAKES ¾ CUP**

The Greek words for "coffee" and "syrup" come from the Arab words for each—*quawah* and *salap*. So it's fitting that the bracing brew should find its way into a delectable syrup. After all, when the Arabs first brought coffee to the Mediterranean, the drink as they served it was thick and syrupy. It is similar to how the coffee that Greeks so adore remains to this day, so the step of adding such thick coffee to a *siropi*, or "syrup," is but a minor, but truly mouthwatering, reach.

*½ cup sugar*
*½ cup honey*
*½ cup strong brewed coffee*
*¼ cup water*

Combine all the ingredients in a small saucepan and bring to a boil over high heat, taking care to watch the pot so it doesn't boil over. Adjust the heat to a brisk simmer and cook until the mixture is thickened and reduced, 15 minutes. Set it aside to cool until it is thick enough to coat a spoon. The syrup may be stored in the refrigerator indefinitely.

# sesame cake

## WITH SESAME ICING

### SERVES 10 TO 12

"SESAME" IS A WORD OF ASSYRIAN OR ARAMAIC ORIGIN FOR AN INDONESIAN AND EAST AFRICAN HERB. THE PLANT'S ROSY OR WHITE FLOWERS PRODUCE OVATE, FLAVORFUL SEEDS AND A LIGHT, AROMATIC OIL. DESPITE THE DISTANT GENESIS OF THE PLANT, GREEKS HAVE PROBABLY CULTIVATED NO FLAVORING AS LONG AS THEY HAVE SESAME. FROM AT LEAST MINOAN TIMES, THE PEOPLE OF GREECE UTILIZED THE PLANT'S SEEDS FOR THEIR OIL AS WELL AS TO ENHANCE BREADS, SOUPS, HONEY, AND SYRUPS. MORE THAN THAT, THEY USED THE SEEDS DIRECTLY AS FOOD. ONE EARLY DISH WAS A PRESSED SESAME CAKE CALLED "SESAME CHEESE," *SESAMOTYRON*.

Greeks still make a wondrous cake—one of their fabulous no-egg, no-oil ones—out of sesame. The cake is rather low, rising only some 2 to 3 inches, with an indescribably moist, soft, and crumbly texture reminiscent of a carrot cake. The sesame, used here in paste form, gives the sweet cake the roasted, rich taste distinct to the seed, enhanced with spices and orange. To make the cake truly memorable, the sesame is tripled: in the cake, in the icing, and sprinkled on top. The result is a remarkable confection.

*1/3 cup unbleached all-purpose flour*
*1 1/2 cups fine dry bread crumbs*
*1/2 cup sugar*
*1 teaspoon baking soda*
*1 teaspoon ground cinnamon*
*1/4 teaspoon ground cloves*
*1/8 teaspoon ground nutmeg, preferably freshly grated*
*Pinch of salt*
*1/2 cup tahini (sesame paste; see Note)*
*1 cup fresh orange juice*
*2 tablespoons finely chopped orange zest*
*1/4 teaspoon orange-blossom water, Triple Sec, or Curaçao*
*1/2 cup water*
*1 tablespoon sesame seeds*
*3/4 cup Sesame Icing (recipe follows)*

1 Preheat the oven to 350°F. Lightly oil a 9-inch springform pan and dust it with flour.

2 Sift the flour into a large bowl. Add the bread crumbs, sugar, baking soda, cinnamon, cloves, nutmeg, and salt and stir with a fork to mix.

3 Combine the tahini, orange juice, zest, orange-blossom water, and water in the bowl of a food processor or electric mixer and process until blended. Add the mixture to the dry ingredients and blend well.

4 Pour the batter into the prepared pan and bake until the edges are pulling away from the pan and a knife inserted in the center comes out clean, 30 minutes. Remove the cake from the oven and set aside in the pan to cool completely.

5 Meanwhile, toast the sesame seeds in a small ungreased skillet over medium heat, stirring occasionally, until they are beginning to turn golden, about 3 minutes.

## BIKIBAO—A MYSTERY TERM OF REVERSE BORROWING

At my first baking session in Greece, we were going to make Lenten sesame cakes and the first batch of Easter cookies to store for the holiday. Gathered around the oven, the cooks of the village were vivaciously discussing how much of an ingredient called *bikibao* to put in. I was baffled. "What is *bikibao*?" I asked, but the bakers didn't really have an answer. *Bikibao* was *bikibao*, they said. The batter needed it.

At the next baking session, again the mysterious ingredient popped up, this time in *koulouria* and braided pascal *tsoureki* (pages 132 and 139). Once more I asked about the substance, but to no avail. Finally, on the third occasion, when we were to make cakes for relatives arriving for summer reunions, I offered, "I'll go get the *bikibao*. Just lead me to it." I went to the store to claim the needed ingredient, and after delivering the contents, I took the box to my house. There I examined it, dictionary and baking book in hand.

I didn't need to read very far, for the English appeared right on the box. *Bikibao* was merely "baking powder," and the secret additive that had me so perplexed was simply the Greek pronunciation of what to them was a tongue-tangling English term. Until relatively recently Greek cooks had only baking soda and bread starter to make baked products rise. Now, with international trade and the arrival of English and American baking powder, cake making had become far easier.

And I thought *galaktoboureko* was unpronounceable!

---

6 Remove the cake from the pan and place it on a platter, top side up. Drizzle the icing over the top and sprinkle the toasted sesame seeds over the icing. Serve right away or set aside for up to several hours. The cake will keep for up to 3 days at room temperature.

**NOTE:** Tahini is available in most supermarkets. Orange-blossom water is found in Middle Eastern and Indian markets.

## SESAME ICING

### MAKES ¾ CUP

An icing is meant to be an extra—a crown. When the icing contains the same flavoring as the cake, it intensifies the whole experience. Burnished with sugar and reduced into a flowing glaze, sesame icing makes the cake both opulent and exotic, as if the taster were visiting a silk-draped seraglio in old Constantinople.

*¼ cup tahini (sesame paste)*
*½ cup confectioners' sugar*
*½ teaspoon vanilla extract*
*1½ tablespoons boiling water*

Place all the ingredients in a bowl and beat until smooth. Use right away, or store in the refrigerator indefinitely and reheat until pourable before using.

# yogurt cake

## WITH OUZO-LEMON SYRUP

### SERVES 12 TO 16

"HE WHO GETS SCALDED IN THE PORRIDGE TRIES TO COOL DOWN EVEN YOGURT" IS A GREEK SAYING MEANING SOMETHING LIKE "ONCE BURNED, TWICE SHY." IT ALSO ALLUDES TO THE IMPLACABLE COOLNESS OF YOGURT. CHILLED OR NOT CHILLED, YOGURT SEEMS COOL. IN A CAKE BATTER, IT SMOOTHS THE MIXTURE INTO A SLEEK SATIN TEXTURE. IN GREECE, WHERE FRESH MILK IS NOT MUCH USED BUT CHEESE AND YOGURT LIE READY AT EVERY COOK'S HAND, SUCH A CAKE IS EASILY MADE. THE CAKE IS OFTEN TOPPED WITH A HONEY SYRUP, BUT I PREFER TO "FROST" IT WITH GREECE'S BRACING APERITIF, OUZO, MIXED WITH LEMON JUICE.

Butter or oil, for the cake pan
8 tablespoons (1 stick) butter, at room temperature
3/4 cup sugar
4 large eggs, separated
1 cup yogurt
1 tablespoon coarsely chopped lemon zest
1 3/4 cups unbleached all-purpose flour
2 teaspoons baking powder
Pinch of salt
Ouzo-Lemon Syrup (recipe follows)

1 Preheat the oven to 350°F. Grease and flour a 9-inch springform pan.

2 Combine the butter and sugar in a large bowl and beat with an electric mixer until creamy. Beat in the egg yolks all at once, then the yogurt and zest. In another bowl, mix the flour, baking powder, and salt together, then sift them into the bowl with the yogurt mixture. Beat to mix well.

3 In a separate bowl, beat the egg whites until stiff peaks form. Whisk half the whites into the batter mixture, then gently fold in the remaining whites.

## SESAME CAKES, HONEY MILK CAKES, AND ICED CAKES

A famous Greek text—whether fact or fiction is unknown—describes Socrates and Plato attending a literary dinner party, known today as "Philoxenos's Banquet." There, after the guests supped on eel, squid, shrimp, tuna, meat, and birds, the tables were cleared and warm water, soap, and oil were brought in for them to wash their hands. Muslin towels were provided, along with perfumes and wreaths of violets. Then came the "second table" offerings: sweet pastry shells, crisp pancakes, toasted sesame cakes soaked in honey sauce, cheesecake made with milk and honey and baked like a pie, and cheese and sesame sweetmeats fried in hot oil and rolled in sesame seeds.

In another text, Athenaeus quotes Antiphanes as raving about "iced" cakes, called *plakous*, saying: "The streams of the tawny bee [honey], mixed with the curdled river of bleating she-goats [milk], placed upon a flat receptacle of the virgin daughter of Demeter [grain] which delights in ten thousand delicate toppings. Or, shall I simply say *plakous*? I'm for *plakous*."

**4** Pour the batter into the prepared cake pan and bake until a knife inserted in the center comes out clean and the edges of the cake are pulling away from the pan, 35 minutes. Remove from the oven and set aside in the pan to cool completely.

**5** When it is cool enough to handle, invert the cake pan over a large plate and unmold the cake. If it doesn't fall free right away, use a table knife to gently pry the cake loose.

**6** Spoon about one third of the syrup over the cake and allow it to soak in for 5 to 10 minutes. Repeat this process with the remaining syrup two more times. Set the cake aside for at least 1 hour before serving. The cake will keep for several days, covered and stored at room temperature.

# OUZO-LEMON SYRUP

### MAKES 2 CUPS

Ouzo reveals its invigorating chill in the way it turns from ice-clear to frosty once water is added. Far too underused in cooking, ouzo combined with lemon in this syrup turns the slightly tart, milky yogurt cake into a very Greek and very unusual sweet.

1 cup sugar
1/2 cup ouzo
1/4 cup fresh lemon juice
1/4 cup water
1 1/2 tablespoons finely chopped lemon zest

Place all the ingredients in a medium-size saucepan over high heat and bring to a boil. Reduce the heat and simmer briskly until thickened, 10 minutes. Cool, and use right away or store, covered, in the refrigerator indefinitely.

## A BYZANTINE VARIATION:
### YOGURT CAKE WITH HIDDEN TREASURE

Byzantine bakers ornamented whatever dishes they could. One technique was to bejewel a cake with nuts and raisins, or to bury those treasures within. The best thing about the yogurt cake turning Byzantine is that its smooth, thick batter allows you to insert the filling between layers before baking! The secret cache is tucked away in one step.

#### FOR THE FILLING
1/2 cup golden raisins or dried currants, preferably soaked in Mavrodaphne or other sweet wine (see page 49)
1/2 cup chopped almonds or walnuts
1/2 tablespoon sugar

1/2 teaspoon ground cinnamon, or ground cloves, or 1/4 teaspoon ground allspice, or 1/4 teaspoon ground nutmeg, or a mix

Yogurt Cake batter, prepared through Step 3

**1.** Mix all the filling ingredients together. Pour half the cake batter in the prepared pan, and shake the pan gently until the batter lies flat. Sprinkle the filling mixture evenly over the batter. Carefully pour the remaining batter over the filling.

**2.** Bake, cool, and "frost" the cake with Ouzo-Lemon Syrup as described.

# A FINAL VALIDATION

**W**HEN I BEGAN TO LIVE IN THE VILLAGE, QUESTIONS HUNG IN THE AIR AS TO MY QUALITIES AS A *NIKOKYRA*, "HOMEMAKER." THESE QUERIES WERE FIRST QUELLED BY MY BLAZING KNITTING NEEDLES, BUT THEY WERE NOT FINALLY PUT TO REST UNTIL *MELITINIA* BAKING DAY.

I didn't know what to expect when I was hustled off by the neighboring women to my first grand baking scene. We dropped down a set of crumbling stairs and, next to Kyria Petroula's giant beehive oven, entered one of Santorini's gargantuan caverns. The island's myriad caves had been dug not only to serve as houses. In the old days many had been wine cellars, storage rooms, and stables. This one was work space. It was filled—at least that day—with a number of long flat tables, all draped in spanking clean oilcloth, and around the tables was gathered a gaggle of at least thirty women. More were entering in a steady stream, bearing armloads of kindling, boxes of matches, bags of eggs, baskets of cheeses, sacks of sugar and flour, vials of spices, food mills and graters, short round sticks, a collection of jar lids, huge bowls, and long flat baking sheets.

## SANTORINI'S EASTER SWEET

I knew it was Lent. I knew all the cheese and eggs had been stockpiled for weeks and that Easter was approaching. But I didn't yet know that Easter, called *Paska* or *Lambri*—"bright day"—was also the "sweetest" Greek holiday, nor that Santorini had its very own, very famous Easter sweet, and today was the day to make them.

Fast and efficiently, showing their years of hands-at-it, a number of the women put together the ingredients for piecrust. Others began running their highly valued home-made *hlorou* cheese through the food mills or working the rounds across graters. Others cracked eggs into bowls with abandon, whisked the eggs to form ocher ponds, ripped open sacks of flour and sugar, and dumped the contents over the eggs. Those grating the cheese added it to the mixture. All the while talk flew about. I could hardly catch a word of it, my Greek then being almost limited to phrases like "Where is the bus?" on an island without buses.

In due course, some of the women took their round sticks in hand—aha, they were rolling pins!—and began to roll out sheets of dough as thin as a drachma. Others added vanilla and mastic to the egg and cheese mixture, and whipped the vats of the brew until it looked like liquid sunshine. Still others, taking hold of jar lids, began to clamp the lids down on the rolled-out dough and cut out circles.

That's when I joined in. As one woman dropped a spoonful of the golden egg mix onto the crust circles, others began to pinch the circles to form little tartlets. Some were pinching eight flutes, some ten; some, like young Eirini, who lived behind me, had such delicate fingers that they were fluting the crusts into twenty or more scallops. "Can I try that?" I asked. "Oh, no" was the answer. "You don't know how. You're a professor." (Lowly occupation that it was!) "Just let me see," I begged, and I was offered a chair and a piecrust. Little did they know that I had come from a family of bakers and was in my element. As nimbly as I could, I pinched round the circle in tiny flutes, almost as good as Eirini's! I was offered a second crust and a third. Soon Eirini and I became the penultimate stops on a *melitinia* assembly line. (The ultimate stop was the oven.) Eirini taught me the matchstick trick, and we commenced to spin out tartlets like masters.

*Rolling out dough with a Greek rolling pin. A sawed-off broom handle or dowel can work as well.*

The *melitinia* began to emerge from the oven—cheese baked to an amber hue, wafting an aroma that had drawn all the village men to watch from the terraces above, the little pies adorned with more flutes than Aphrodite's scallop shell. Of course, more fun than the day of baking was Easter itself—when we *ate* the *melitinia!*

# easter cheese tartlets

## WITH SOUR LEMON ICING

### MELITINIA

#### MAKES ABOUT 40 TARTLETS

ON SANTORINI, THE VILLAGERS MAKE A SPECIAL EASTER SWEET THAT IS SO WINNING THAT MEN, WOMEN, AND CHILDREN HUDDLE AROUND CANISTERS OF THEM, WAITING FOR THE EASTER CHIMES TO ANNOUNCE THAT LENT IS OFFICIALLY OVER AND FOOD MADE WITH CHEESE IS NOW EDIBLE. SIMILAR SWEETS ARE MADE ON SOME OF THE OTHER CYCLADES ISLANDS, BUT NONE QUITE SO DELICIOUS AND FAMOUS AS THOSE OF SANTORINI. THEY ARE CALLED *MELITINIA,* PERHAPS BECAUSE THEY ARE SO REMINISCENT OF THE HONEY CHEESE TREATS OF ANCIENT TIMES.

Many factors make them special. First, they are made as little individual pies, so each person gets his or her own. More important, they are made like no other Greek sweet: They have a crust of dough that is fluted all around like a tart, each carefully pinched and crenelated, so that the sides stand up to hold the filling, an indescribably delectable mixture of goat cheese, eggs, seasoning, and sugar. When they are baked, the cheese turns the color of 24-karat gold and the crust becomes delightfully crisp.

Bringing the recipe home, I have added a few touches— a combination of vanilla and mastic in the filling, and a tart contrasting lemon icing that highlights the honied cheese. Because the treat is truly fit for a gala, the recipe is enough for 40, but it can be cut in half or even one quarter.

### FOR THE PASTRY
4 cups unbleached all-purpose flour
1/2 teaspoon salt
1 cup olive oil or melted butter
(see Notes)
1/2 cup water

### FOR THE FILLING
1 cup soft goat cheese (see Notes)
4 ounces feta cheese, crumbled
2 large eggs
1 cup sugar
1/2 teaspoon baking powder
1 teaspoon vanilla extract
1/2 teaspoon powdered mastic
(see Notes)
1/3 cup unbleached all-purpose
flour

### FOR THE TOPPING
3/4 cup Sour Lemon Icing
(recipe follows)
2 tablespoons finely shredded
lemon zest

1 Prepare the pastry: Sift the flour and salt into a large bowl. Add the oil and mix with your fingers or a fork until crumbly. Add the water and mix until you can gather the ingredients into a ball (add a bit more water if it's too dry). Wrap the dough tightly in plastic wrap and press into a flattened round. Set aside to rest for 1 hour or refrigerate for as long as overnight. Bring it back to room temperature before using.

## PERFECT FLUTING

Pinching the dough circles of *melitinia* into nicely shaped fluted tartlets requires a strong grip between thumb and middle finger, or you can use a wooden matchstick in one hand to press into the outside of the dough as you pinch and flute against the matchstick with the other hand. The more, the tighter, and the neater the flutes, the better. If you have trouble mastering the operation, here's another trick: Use a pastry brush to lightly moisten the outside of each dough round with water before filling and pinching. The water helps the dough hold the flutes and not collapse.

If your patience simply does not extend to this kind of cooking, you can also make the cheese tartlets in pie form. The recipe makes two single-crust 8-inch pies. The cooking time is longer, 50 to 55 minutes.

2 When you are ready to make the pies, prepare the filling: Combine the goat cheese, feta, eggs, sugar, baking powder, vanilla, and mastic in a bowl and beat with an electric mixer until well blended. Beat in the flour and continue mixing until creamy. Set the filling aside.

3 Preheat the oven to 375°F. Coat three baking sheets with oil or butter.

4 Divide the dough into 4 portions. On a floured surface, roll out one portion as thin as possible. Keep the remaining dough portions covered with a towel until you are ready to roll them out. With a 3½-inch round cookie cutter or the lid of a wide-mouthed jar (a mayonnaise jar lid is about right), cut out as many rounds of dough as you can.

5 Place a dough round on the work surface in front of you. Spoon about 1 tablespoon of the filling onto the center. Carefully working around the edge of the dough, use your fingers or a wooden matchstick and a finger to pinch the dough into upright flutes, making as many flutes as you can (see box, this page). Place the filled shell on a prepared baking sheet, and repeat with the remaining rounds. Then roll out, cut, fill, and flute the remaining pastry portions, until all the tartlets are made. Be sure to gather up the pastry scraps and re-roll them to get as many pastry shells as possible.

6 Place the baking sheets in the oven and bake until the tartlets are golden across the top and edges and the pastry is crisp, about 35 minutes. Remove, and set aside to cool for a few minutes.

7 When they are no longer piping hot, spoon some icing across the top of each tartlet, allowing it to drizzle down the sides a bit. Decorate each with a few strands of zest, and serve. The *melitinia* may be covered with plastic wrap and stored at room temperature for up to 4 days.

### NOTES:

■ Olive oil makes a harder, more traditional crust, butter a crust more like American piecrust.

■ *Melitinia* are traditionally made with moist *hlorou*—homemade unsalted goat cheese—or with moist, not dry, *mizithra*. Both

## RENNET

There is another reason besides the festive Easter banquet for slaughtering a kid goat or a lamb in the springtime. The stomach of a suckling kid or lamb contains rennet, and rennet is needed to set the cheese made from the milk of the mother goat or sheep. Both goats and sheep generally bear two young, and since the females will bear young and produce milk, after two or three months it is the males that are sacrificed for the all-important rennet—and for the meat for the pascal holiday. Meanwhile, all year long the rennet serves in daily cheese making, and thus in the preparation of next spring's cheese pies.

are soft and quite strong cheeses. They are difficult to find here, but a combination of a goat cheese such as Montrachet and the more available feta (a little saltier and sharper) simulates the taste and texture.

■ If you don't have mastic (see page 143), the vanilla alone will do.

## SOUR LEMON ICING

### MAKES ABOUT ¾ CUP

The aroma of mastic fills the kitchen with a heady, perfumed fragrance. The scent of vanilla wafts above. One more fillip, a dab of tart lemon, brings a counterpoint to the sweet just-baked *melitinia*.

*¼ cup fresh lemon juice*
*1 cup confectioners' sugar, sifted*

1 Heat the lemon juice in a small nonreactive saucepan over medium heat until warm but not boiling. Add the confectioners sugar and whisk until the mixture is creamy white and thickened, about 5 minutes.

2 Use right away, or set aside at room temperature for several hours, whisking the icing to smooth it again before using it.

# pine nut cookies

## SHAPED LIKE PEARS

### MAKES 32 COOKIES

AT ONE TIME IT BECAME VERY POPULAR IN EUROPE TO MAKE ALMOND PASTE, OR MARZIPAN, INTO MANY SHAPES. MENAGERIES OF ALMOND PASTE ANIMALS, BOUQUETS OF ALMOND PASTE FRUITS AND FLOWERS, CHESS SETS OF ALMOND PASTE PIECES, GEOMETRIES OF ALMOND PASTE FIGURES APPEARED IN CONFECTIONERY CASES. A BIT OF THE FAD DRIFTED INTO GREEK SWEET MAKING BY WAY OF VENICE, AND AS USUAL, IT ACQUIRED A GREEK PERSPECTIVE.

In the first place, the almonds were not ground into a smooth paste but were left nubbly and nutty, coarse enough to know you were eating almonds, not candy, and the shape that prevailed among treat makers was drawn from one of Greece's favorite after-meal treats: the lovely curved form of a pear. Traditionally Greece's pear-shaped cookies are still made with almonds, but in a variation here the confection uses another of Greece's favorite nuts, one a bit sweeter: pine nuts. Pine nuts make the cookie very rich, softer in texture than when made with almonds, and evocative of the pine forests that stud the Hellenic hills.

*1½ cups (8 ounces) pine nuts*
*¼ cup sugar*
*2½ tablespoons unbleached*
    *all-purpose flour*
*2 tablespoons Triple Sec or other*
    *orange liqueur*
*32 whole cloves*
*2 tablespoons confectioners' sugar*

1 Preheat the oven to 375°F.

2 Combine the pine nuts and sugar in a food processor and grind as fine as possible. Add the

flour and liqueur and process until well processed and oily, and the mixture holds together.

3 Divide the dough into 32 equal portions, and roll them between the palms of your hands to form cherry-size balls. Place the balls on ungreased baking sheets. Pinch each ball into a pear shape. Stick a clove in the top of each cookie to simulate the pear's stem.

4 Place the baking sheets in the oven and bake until the cookies are beginning to sizzle a bit, 5 minutes. Reduce the temperature to 325°F and continue baking until they are brown on the bottom and lightly golden on top, 15 minutes. Let cool until they are no longer too hot to touch, about 3 minutes.

5 While the cookies are still warm, sift the confectioners' sugar over them. You can serve them right away, but the cookies improve with age. Store in an airtight container for up to 2 months.

## THE SWEET ART OF SHOPPING IN GREECE

In Greece you cannot buy all the foods you need from a single source. You buy your dairy products, like yogurt and cheese, from the milk store, the *galaktopoleion* (though sometimes cheese comes separately from the *tyropoleion*), meat from the meat market, wine from the wine shop, fruits from the fruit shop, sausage from the sausage man, and so on. To stuff a fish for the dinner table would take three stops: bread from the bakery, vegetables from the produce stall, and fish from the fishmonger. The most alluring of all the food stores, though, is the *zaxaropoleion,* or "sugar shop."

*Zaxaropoleia* have a particular aura. They sport bright lights, chrome tables, and case after case of cakes, cookies, and candy. Their large crystal-clear windows flaunt the most enticing and eye-catching treats, pear cookies being a best-seller. I adore both the sweet shops and the style of shopping, for the time it takes means that you have to communicate: You high-five your butcher, say hello to your baker, chat up your candlestick maker. You weave the bonds of your community. It's a value call, time versus talk, but to me it's worth eschewing the supermarket for the sewing of society.

## NOTES:

■ Just as you would pluck the stem off a pear, pluck the decorative cloves out of the cookies as you eat them.

■ The cookies can be made of ground blanched almonds and the stem made of an almond sliver.

## MACAROONS GREEK-AMERICAN STYLE

When the Greeks were introduced to chocolate, they went quite *treloi*, "crazy," for it, and now dozens of chocolate treats fill the display cases in sweet stores. Chocolate is not, however, much used in home baking. In a Greek-American touch, a drizzle of chocolate adds just enough of the rich taste without overwhelming the subtleties of the macaroons.

*2 ounces semisweet chocolate, broken up*
*1 tablespoon brandy, coffee, orange juice, Triple Sec, other liqueur, or water*
*1 batch Almond Macaroons (this page), baked and cooled*

Heat the chocolate pieces and liquid together in a small saucepan or in a microwave oven until the chocolate is soft but not bubbling, about 1 minute. Whisk to smooth the mixture and then heat it a few seconds longer until it is runny but not boiling. Brush or drizzle a little of the chocolate over the top of each macaroon. Set aside to cool until the chocolate hardens, about 10 minutes. Serve right away, or store in an airtight container at room temperature for up to 5 days.

# almond macaroons

### MAKES 36 MACAROONS

ALMOND MACAROONS—CALLED BOTH MARONHINOS AND MARTSAPADES—ARE COMMONLY MADE BY THE JEWS OF GREECE AS A PASSOVER TREAT, BEING FLOURLESS, AND FOR OTHER HOLIDAYS AND FAMILY FESTIVALS. THE COOKIES ARE PART OF A TRADITION AS GREEK AS IT IS JEWISH, SINCE TREATS OF NUTS HAVE BEEN MADE BY BOTH PEOPLES SINCE DAVID REIGNED AND DIOGENES ORATED.

To us macaroons tend to be a store-bought treat, but homemade macaroons leave commercial ones far behind. There is simply no comparison. What's more, they are among the least laborious cookies to slide into an oven: a packet of almonds, some eggs, some sugar. You can have them plain and nutty or try a Greek-American rendition—macaroons drizzled with chocolate.

*2 cups (8 ounces) sliced or slivered blanched almonds*
*1 1/2 cups sugar*
*2 egg whites, beaten until bubbly but not frothy*
*1 teaspoon almond extract*
*36 blanched almond slices, for garnish*

1 Combine the 2 cups almonds and 1/2 cup of the sugar in a food processor and grind as fine as possible.

2 Add the egg whites and almond extract to the almond mixture and process until well blended. Add the remaining 1 cup sugar and process again until a thick paste forms. Set the paste aside for 30 minutes (it will continue to thicken).

3 Preheat the oven to 300°F. Coat two or three baking sheets with oil or butter.

4 Drop tablespoon amounts of the almond paste mixture onto the prepared baking sheets, allowing 1 inch between. Place an almond slice on top of each one. Bake for 20 minutes. Raise the oven temperature to 375°F and continue baking until the macaroons are lightly golden on the bottom, 5 minutes more.

5 Remove the baking sheets from the oven and loosen the macaroons. Set them aside to cool completely on the sheets. Serve right away, or store in an airtight container at room temperature for up to 5 days.

**NOTE:** You can also pipe the almond paste onto the baking sheets through a pastry tube, as is traditionally done.

# sesame fig sandwiches

### SERVES 6

WHEN FIGS BECAME A SYMBOL OF SEXUALITY (THEIR NAME AND A GESTURE FOR THEM STILL CONSTITUTING A GOOD SOLID OBSCENITY IN GREECE) NO ONE KNOWS, BUT THEY ARE AN ANCIENT FOOD. THE ANCIENT GREEKS HAD FIG CAKES CALLED *PALAFI*, AND BY THE THIRD CENTURY B.C.E., GREEKS WERE DRYING AND STORING FIGS WELL ENOUGH TO SHIP THEM TO INDIA. ON THE GREEK ISLANDS, WE SPREAD THEM ON OUR WHITEWASHED ROOFTOPS TO AIR IN THE SUMMER SUN SO WE MIGHT HAVE DRY FIGS THROUGHOUT THE WINTER.

As a final touch when they are almost dry, we open them into three petals, sprinkle them with sesame seeds, top them with another fig, and put them in the oven to bake into Sesame Fig Sandwiches. Without butter, the sandwiches are traditional. With butter drizzled on and a dash of allspice, they are more moist and luxurious. Since store-bought dried figs are usually drier than rooftop ones, when making these from commercial figs I usually resort to a drop of butter.

*1/4 cup sesame seeds*
*1/4 teaspoon ground allspice*
*18 to 24 large, golden dried figs, preferably Kalimyrna*
*8 tablespoons (1 stick) butter, melted*

1 Preheat the oven to 400°F.

2 Place the sesame seeds in a small dry skillet over low heat. Stir slowly until brown and toasted, about 4 minutes. Stir in the allspice and set aside.

# FIG TREES AND DOWRIES

In the old days, because fathers feared their daughters would be stolen and forced into an undesirable union with a poor man, rich villagers in Greece often married their daughters off when they were very young. To maintain control of the alliance, therefore, a well-heeled man would seek a union for his daughter at age fourteen or fifteen. No one, meanwhile, sought to waylay poorer girls. Their fathers took time to find good suitors and the daughters rarely married until they were in their twenties.

Then the pattern reversed. By the time of my first visits, marriage by abduction was outlawed and economic circumstances had shifted. The richer girls in villages entertained many suitors, and their fathers, waiting for the very best prospect, often held off the wedding until the daughters were in their thirties. Poor girls, on the other hand, were seen as having little to lose.

Fearing their daughters would do something rash in the face of scant opportunity, poorer fathers rushed to marry their girls off safely before anything scandalous happened. Humble girls now married at age eighteen or nineteen.

I learned all about this as old Marketousa, her daughter Evangelia, and I made fig sandwiches and layered them in fig leaf–lined baskets. Evangelia was nearly thirty and her family was quite fortuneless. "I'll become an old, dried fig," she said laughing, holding one up for demonstration. But the figs and their fabled fecundity, or perhaps the perseverance of her father, disproved her prediction. When I returned to the village a couple of years later, Evangelia had a husband, a son, and a brightly whitewashed dowry house, rebuilt around the very fig tree we had that day plundered.

5 Bake until the figs are juicy and bubbly, 10 minutes. Serve right away, or allow to cool and then store in jars or tins as you would dried apricots or raisins.

## VARIATIONS:

**Deluxe Sesame Fig Sandwiches:** With the addition of cheese or ice cream, Sesame Fig Sandwiches become a more elaborate Greek-style sweet. Top the warm sandwiches with ice cream: vanilla, toasted almond, or butter pecan. Or give them a dollop of mascarpone cheese or cream cheese blended with sweetened whipped cream.

3 With the stem side down and the round side up, gently tear a fig open so it forms three petals, taking care to keep the petals attached at the stem. Press the petals flat. Repeat until all the figs are opened.

4 Place half the flattened figs skin side down on a baking sheet. Drizzle the melted butter over them, then sprinkle a rounded teaspoon of the sesame seed mixture over each fig. Top each fig with one of the remaining figs, open side down, as though you were making a sandwich.

# HOW SPICES GOT TO GREECE

**PEOPLE WHO EAT A DIET LARGELY BASED ON STARCHES CRAVE SUBSTANCES THAT GIVE THEIR FOODS A LITTLE VARIETY—IN SHORT, THEY LOVE HERBS AND SPICES. IT'S NOT SO MUCH THAT "VARIETY IS THE SPICE OF LIFE," RATHER THAT "SPICE IS THE VARIETY OF LIFE"!**

From ancient to modern times, the Greek diet has been primarily a cereal one. In ancient days it consisted mostly of gruel. Very early on, the addition of flavorings became important. Herbs were easy. Many, like oregano, thyme, rosemary, and sage, were native to Greek soil. Others, like sesame, were imported and took immediately to the soil. But some of the more exotic spices were a different matter. Greeks could not grow cinnamon bark, clove bushes, or nutmeg trees in their climate.

Spices were in use in the Mediterranean since around 3000 B.C.E., when donkey caravans began to bring them from Asia and Africa. At first they were used for medicine, for embalming, and as perfumes. Thorny desert bushes that grew from India to Africa, like balsam, myrrh, and frankincense, were burned for their fragrance; cumin, anise, cassia, and cinnamon were too. People also wore pellets of aromatic substances as jewelry. Soon spices were being used in the cooking of food and the flavoring of wine. More and more traders started to travel up the Nile, over to China, across to India in search of others.

## THE SPICE ROUTE

Several trade routes developed to satisfy the growing appetite for spices, many of which came from very distant places. Some routes traveled over land, some over sea, and some a combination. Among the oldest was a south-north sea route from ports along the west coast of India, through the Persian Gulf, down the Arabian coast to Aden, and up the Red Sea to Egypt. Another ran from the Persian Gulf up the Euphrates and Tigris valley to Seleucia, and from there to Antioch on the Mediterranean. From the Indian port of Barbaricon, then at the base of the Indus river, a land route led northward through the Indus valley, up the Kabul river, and over the Hindu Kush to Bactra, where it bisected the Silk Route around the Black and Caspian seas, a path later followed by Alexander the Great. Each of these brought the valued aromatics to ports and trading centers, and from there the commodities reached the avid customers in lands bordering the Aegean, Ionian, and Mediterranean seas.

At first the lucrative spice emporiums were controlled by the Persians, who sat in Babylon at the intersection of many of the routes, and then by the Arabs, who commanded the sea lanes. As the trade balance became expensive for the Greeks, and later the Greco-Romans, efforts were made to extend the empire to include the spice ports and routes. Due to losses from shipwrecks, storms, robberies, and the greed of the many middlemen, spices and perfumes were expensive. Greece conquered important terminals on the coast of Palestine and up the Dardanelles to Byzantium. Rome tried to conquer Arabia. Eventually Constantinople became the capital of many of the caravan routes, and the Byzantine empire grew wealthy on the trade of aromatics and flavorings as well as other sought-after goods. The later Muslim expansion across many of the trade routes was the spur, in part, to the great explorations westward across the ocean, to find another way to gain access to the spice lands.

*In a jumble of sacks, a Greek grocery store will set out—shoulder to shoulder—beans, grains, herbs, and spices from home and distant shores.*

# LUSCIOUS PUDDINGS

# rice pudding

## RIZOGALO

✳ **SERVES 6**

THE TRADITION OF GRAIN PUDDINGS LIVES ON IN GREECE. ONE FAMOUS ONE IS MADE OF SEMOLINA AND IS CALLED *HALVAS*, THE SAME AS THE SESAME CANDY. IT IS MUCH LIKE THE PUDDING CENTER IN *GALAKTOBOUREKO* BUT IS SWIRLED WITH SPICES, CHOPPED NUTS, AND A HONEY ROSEWATER SYRUP. GREEKS ALSO MAKE A PUDDING OF NUBBLY BULGUR, CALLED *POUTIGKA*, THE GREEK VERSION OF THE ENGLISH TERM. BUT BY FAR THE MOST POPULAR GRAIN PUDDING NOW MADE, STEMMING FROM THE DAYS OF BYZANTIUM'S MASTER CHEFS, IS RICE PUDDING.

The story of pudding in Greek cuisine starts with the legendary *kykeon*, the ancients' dish of sweetened barley. No dish, save bread itself, was eaten more often in ancient Greece, and its tradition remains. It was so honored that it was offered during the Eleusinian mysteries, which took place every autumn to praise the goddess Demeter for her life-giving grain. Greeks of classical times often flavored grain puddings with honey and also mint and grape must.

The story continues with Byzantine cuisine, in which cooks added raisins and carob seeds to the softened wheat pudding and began to make the same dish with their new grain: rice.

The puddings of today's Greek cuisine are few but matchless. Some honor the timeless combination of grain and grape. Others reflect the more recent passion for custard creams, with their own Greek accent.

The Greek rendition is a marvel, relying on spices that bring the milk mixture to its most alluring: nutmeg and vanilla. Because of the egg yolks, it comes out soft and creamy yellow. And because Greeks use a shorter-grain rice, the texture is both chewy and smooth.

*3/4 cup short-grain rice, preferably Arborio*
*6 cups whole milk*
*3/4 cup sugar*
*1/8 teaspoon ground nutmeg, preferably freshly grated*
*1/8 teaspoon salt*
*3 egg yolks*
*1 1/2 teaspoons vanilla extract*
*Ground cinnamon, for garnish*

1 Combine the rice, milk, sugar, nutmeg, and salt in a heavy saucepan. Bring to a boil over medium heat, cover, and reduce the heat to low. Simmer until the rice is tender, 25 minutes.

2 In a small bowl, beat the egg yolks with a whisk until frothy. Slowly whisk in several spoonfuls of the rice mixture until the yolks are thin and smooth. Pour the yolk mixture back into the saucepan. Continue cooking over low heat until the pudding turns creamy and is thick enough to coat a spoon, about 2 minutes.

3 Remove the pan from the heat and stir in the vanilla. Pour the pudding into individual bowls, and top each with a pinch of cinnamon. Cool to room temperature or refrigerate and serve cold.

## VARIATIONS:

**Taking the Pudding from Plain to Fancy:** Rice pudding seems such ordinary fare, but to my mind it is never so. It is my children's—and my—favorite Greek breakfast. At my home in Colorado, it's the dessert that draws my friends to drop by "unexpectedly." Still, to take the best of the ordinary and make it yet more extraordinary, you can add with the rice in Step 1:

■ Raisins, preferably golden raisins, although brown raisins and currants are used too

■ Other chopped dried fruit, such as dried apricots, pears, peaches, or dates

■ Chopped pistachios, almonds, or hazelnuts

■ Mastic, in place of the vanilla

■ A few threads of saffron

■ Or you might top the rice pudding with a fruit spoon sweet (pages 535 to 547), for an absolutely outstanding dessert, or with fresh fruit or with honey.

# wine grape pudding

## WITH SEMOLINA AND SUGARED BASIL LEAVES

### SERVES 6

F RESH GRAPE JUICE, OR MUST, WAS CALLED *GLEUKOS* IN ANCIENT GREEK, AND FROM IT WE GET OUR WORD "GLUCOSE" AND THE GREEK WORD FOR "SWEET," *GLYKA*. AND SWEET THE JUICE OF GRAPES IS.

The ancients drank the juice. They boiled it down into reductions and used it as a flavoring. They added the must to bread dough to make grape-flavored cakes and wafers, and they poured it in liberally to flavor grain porridge.

Millennia later, Greeks still make such a grape juice pudding, called *moustalevria*. It is a beloved sweet, made only when perfect fresh grapes are on the vine. Paraskevi showed me how to make it one day. The day before, she had pressed and strained grapes to get pure juice, and with a pinch of ash added, left the juice overnight to clarify. She poured the grape juice into a pan, brought it to a simmer, and slowly added semolina until the mixture thickened to a pudding.

Just before removing the pudding from the heat, she stirred in her hand-ground spice mixture—cinnamon, a bit of clove, some nutmeg, and chopped walnuts. Then she poured the pudding into small bowls.

Using only cinnamon as the spice is common, but many Greeks, like Paraskevi, have their own special formulas for spicing the pudding. Others thicken the grape juice until squares can be cut of it, almost like a candy. I prefer the pudding soft, and rather than the usual walnuts, stud the deep purple with slivered almonds—though using both kinds of nuts or a scattering of sesame seeds is also common. To give the remarkable and unusual dessert a dazzling final touch, here it is decorated with sugared basil leaves.

6 cups unsweetened grape juice
    from Concord, Muscat, or other
    wine grapes
1/2 cup semolina flour
1/2 cup sliced blanched almonds
Pinch of ground cinnamon
12 Sugared Basil Leaves
    (recipe follows)

1 Pour the grape juice into a large nonreactive pot and bring to a boil over high heat.

2 Place the semolina in a bowl and slowly whisk in 2 cups of the hot juice to make a smooth paste.

3 Whisk the paste back into the pot and bring the mixture to a boil over medium-high heat. Reduce the heat and, whisking frequently, simmer until it thickens but is still liquid, 210°F on a candy thermometer, 12 to 15 minutes.

4 While the juice is simmering, toast the almonds in an ungreased frying pan over medium-low heat, stirring occasionally, until just turning golden, about 3 minutes.

5 Stir the almonds and cinnamon into the semolina mixture and pour into a shallow serving dish. Set aside until set firm, at least 3 hours at room temperature, or cover and refrigerate for up to 3 days. Garnish with the Sugared Basil Leaves before serving.

# GRAPE-DIPPED NUTS AND GRAPE-FLAVORED COOKIES

In Greece, walnuts are sometimes dipped in *moustalevria* while it is still liquid, much as we might dip them in salt or sugar. The walnuts are then dried and kept in tins for a sweet snack.

Sweet biscuits, *kouloura*, are also often flavored with grape must, or especially with grape syrup (*petimezi*; page 500), in which case they are called *moustokouloura*.

## NOTES:

■ Some Greeks use fine white baking flour rather than semolina to make their *moustalevria*, but to my mind the pudding comes out a little too thick and starchy. I suggest staying with semolina.

■ Most grape pudding is made from purple grape juice, and the color of the pudding is stunning, but the juice of white Muscat grapes can also be used.

■ Dashes of nutmeg and clove, and walnuts and sesame seeds with or in place of the almonds, can also be used.

# SUGARED BASIL LEAVES

## MAKES 24 SUGARED LEAVES

There's no reason to stop using Greece's marvelous leaves and flowers when you get to sweets. A garnish of sugared edible leaves of both herbs and flowers transports almost any treat from prosaic to romantic, typical to exceptional—and with ease. The leaves should be large and soft, not prickly, fine, or twiggy. In addition to basil, good choices are mint, marjoram, lamb's-quarter, rose and citrus geranium, and myrtle, and petals of nasturtium and unsprayed rose. Sugared leaves can adorn puddings, ice cream, and cake and pie slices.

24 large fresh basil leaves
Superfine sugar
1 egg white
1 teaspoon water

1 Gently wipe or dust off the leaves to clean them without rinsing them. Set the leaves aside.

2 Sprinkle a thin layer of sugar on a plate that is large enough to hold all the leaves in a single uncrowded layer. Set it aside. Pour some extra sugar into a small bowl and set it aside.

**3** In a small bowl, whisk together the egg white and water until frothy.

**4** Arrange the leaves on a large sheet of waxed paper. Using a pastry brush, coat both sides of each leaf with some of the egg white mixture. Lightly sprinkle both sides of each leaf with some of the sugar from the small bowl, so they are well coated but not blanketed with sugar. Transfer each leaf to the sugared plate as you go. When all the leaves are sugared, set the plate aside in an airy place to dry. This will take 2 hours or so, depending on the humidity of the day.

**5** Use right away or store at room temperature, loosely covered with waxed paper, for several days.

**NOTE:** One egg white is actually enough to make four times the leaves called for here, should you care to sugar more.

# sweet mastic "avgolemono" custard

**MAKES ABOUT 3 CUPS**

I N THE PAST TWO CENTURIES, CONTINENTAL EUROPEAN INFLUENCES HAVE INTRODUCED A NUMBER OF CREAM PUDDINGS INTO GREEK CUISINE. CALLED *KREMAS*, THEY CONTAIN NO GRAIN; THEY ARE THICKENED SOLELY WITH EGG YOLK. SOME ARE SPOONABLE, LIKE CREME CARAMEL; SOME FLOW IN A CREAMY STREAM, LIKE *CREME ANGLAISE*.

Greece has its own unique flavoring to augment fluidy custard: mastic. Savored on its own, drizzled over fruit, or circled around cakes, the mastic-flavored custard here is dazzling. In essence it is a sweet *avgolemono* sauce made with milk.

*3 cups milk*
*3/4 cup sugar*
*1 tablespoon mastic crystals (see page 143), tied in a cheesecloth bag*
*8 large egg yolks*
*2 tablespoons fresh lemon juice*

**1** Stir the milk and sugar together in a medium-size nonreactive saucepan off the heat. Add the mastic bundle and heat over low heat until the sugar dissolves, 3 minutes. Remove the bag of mastic and set the saucepan aside.

**2** Lightly whisk the egg yolks in a medium-size bowl. Slowly whisk 1 cup of the milk mixture into the yolks. Return the egg-milk mixture to the pan and cook over medium-low heat, stirring gently and constantly until it is thick enough to coat the spoon and is beginning to turn into a custard, 20 to 25 minutes.

**3** Pour the custard into a container through a strainer lined with cheesecloth. Return the mastic bundle to the mixture and refrigerate until chilled. When ready to serve, remove the mastic and stir in the lemon juice.

# SWEETNESS BY THE SPOONFUL

## quince and pomegranate spoon sweet

### MAKES ABOUT 1 QUART

WHEN THE THREE MOST POWERFUL GODDESSES —HERA, ATHENA, AND APHRODITE—ARGUED OVER WHO WAS MOST BEAUTIFUL, MOST OF THE WISER MORTALS AND IMMORTALS ASKED TO JUDGE THE CONTEST SHUNNED THE PERILOUS JOB. WHEN HERA PROMISED TO MAKE HIM THE LORD OF EUROPE, ATHENA PROMISED HE WOULD LEAD THE TROJANS TO VICTORY, AND APHRODITE PROMISED TO GIVE HIM THE FAIREST WOMAN IN THE WORLD, SILLY PARIS AGREED. HE GAVE THE PRIZE—A QUINCE—TO APHRODITE, AND SHE GAVE HIM HELEN OF TROY.

In less mythical times, the great lawgiver Solon prescribed that a newly married couple should eat a quince together in order that their conversation might ever be sweet. Thus, as a spoon sweet, one of quince could hardly be more romantic. With pomegranate—another romantic fruit of Greece—the sweet emerges a gorgeous claret. Greeks traditionally flavor quince spoon sweet with rose geranium.

Because the taste it creates is so unusual, it's a custom worth following.

6 medium-size quinces
   (about 2 1/2 pounds)
2 tablespoons fresh lemon juice
1 pomegranate (8 to 10 ounces)
2 1/2 cups sugar
2 to 3 scented geranium leaves,
   such as rose or lemon geranium,
   or 1 large bay leaf (see Notes)

When you first enter a Greek home as a guest, you immediately receive three things: a cool, clear glass of water, perhaps the most significant libation to Greeks since time immemorial; a tiny cup of Greek coffee, so freshly made it arrives still frothy and unsettled; and on a delicate plate, a small spoonful of fruit preserves, almost floating in a glistening fruit syrup.

Fruit preserves first appeared in Greek cuisine in the Byzantine era and particularly gained a place in Ottoman times, when sugar to thicken such concoctions became readily available. Sugar brought with it a world of possibilities beyond mere sweetening: Hard candies could crystallize, edible fantasies could be spun, syrup sauces could be thickened, and fruit could be preserved in a way that made it even sweeter.

Soon syruped preserves of fruit, rinds, and sometimes tiny vegetables became a Greek specialty, and there is no sweet Greeks are more proud of. The array is endless and magnificent, and their culinary possibilities cannot be ignored. But perhaps the best way to enjoy them is as the Greeks do: Offer them to your visitors as they walk in the door. What better way to tell your guests, "How sweet it is to see you."

1 Peel and core the quinces with a paring knife and cut them into approximately ¼-inch dice. Place in a large bowl and add 1 tablespoon of the lemon juice and enough water to cover. Set aside.

2 Cut the pomegranate into quarters. Holding the quarters over a large nonreactive saucepan, use your fingers to pull the seeds away from the skin and membranes, allowing the seeds and any juices to drop into the saucepan.

3 Drain the quince and add it to the saucepan. Stir in the sugar and the remaining 1 tablespoon lemon juice. Partially cover the pan and set it over medium-low heat. Cook until the quince begins to wilt and the liquid is bubbling gently, 20 minutes.

4 Stir in the geranium leaves and cook, uncovered, over medium heat until the quince is soft and the liquid is beginning to thicken, 25 minutes. Raise the heat to maintain a brisk simmer and cook until the quince is very soft and the liquid is thick but not yet jellylike, about 230°F on a candy thermometer, 15 minutes. Watch the pan carefully, stirring from time to time so the spoon sweet doesn't burn. Remove from the heat.

5 Allow the mixture to cool to room temperature. Remove the leaves and transfer to storage jars. It will keep in the refrigerator for several months.

### NOTES:

■ On the island of Naxos, quince spoon sweet is flavored with basil. Three or 4 large leaves can substitute for the geranium or bay leaves.

■ Generally I try to make spoon sweets with less sugar than is used in Greece. The amount I use with quince is half the standard amount.

## ABOUT SPOON SWEETS

The array of fruits from which spoon sweets can be made is surprising, pleasing, many-hued, and many-flavored. But not only can fruit be the centerpiece, tiny vegetables can too. Fruits, and certainly fruit flavors, can be combined. Both fruits and vegetables can have nuts tucked in their centers. Liqueurs of many sorts can augment the luscious syrups. Spicing and flavoring can range from perfumy flower petals to exotic spices and herbs one would usually think of for more piquant concoctions.

It's not possible to give a single recipe for all spoon sweets. The sugar and liquid measurements differ according to the fruit, the amount of sweetening, and the amount of liquid. Some fruits are sweeter and take less sugar; some have more liquid, and reducing their syrup to the right consistency takes longer. Water and liqueurs add to the reduction time. But a cook who wants to experiment can follow certain principles:

■ When making a spoon sweet, the cooking depends on the amount of liquid and sugars in the fruit or vegetables. More important, so does the final temperature the syrup needs to reach to attain the right thickness. It's best to judge when a spoon sweet is done by its consistency: It should be somewhat runny, not as dense as a jam or jelly. The fruit should still sit in nice pieces in the pool of syrup; the syrup should thickly coat a spoon. The ideal temperature is about 230°F.

■ If the fruit is turning too soft before the syrup has achieved the right thickness, you can remove the fruit and let the syrup cook longer. This is most likely to happen with fruits or vegetables that have a lot of juice.

■ More or less sugar can be added, depending on the sweetness of the fruit or vegetable, the liqueurs and other additions, and the preference of the cook. Just remember that the more sugar there is, the faster the syrup will thicken. Honey is sometimes used to sweeten the fruit, and so is *petimezi* (page 500).

For the Greek bride outfitting a home, a silver service with which to serve guests doesn't have merely forks, knives, spoons, soupspoons, butter knives, salad forks, and an array of serving implements. Even a butter dish, creamer, sugar bowl, and olive and pickle plate are not adequate. The service must also include a spoon sweet server.

A spoon sweet server consists of several parts. A round silver tray holds a number of small water glasses, the glasses often enclosed in silver holders. In the center of the tray stands a crystal receptacle, taller than a bowl, wider than a jar, often with a silver base, and topped with a silver lid. Around the top of the vessel there is a silver ring with hooks, from which hangs a set of small spoons.

These are the special spoons for spoon sweets. The host brings out the tray, with the glasses filled with clear, fresh water. Guests take a glass, lift the lid of the container, and unhooking a spoon, dip the spoon in the sweet preserves. They put the spoon to mouth and savor the confection. After finishing, they place the spoon in the glass of water and let the last drops of fruit syrup flavor the refreshing drink.

I haven't taken the step yet, but every time I walk down the silver purveyors' street in Athens, I say to myself, "I know nobody at home will know what this is for, but I must have one."

# cherry and tsikoudia spoon sweet

### MAKES 2½ CUPS

CHERRIES MAKE MARVELOUS SPOON SWEETS. EVERY SORT, SOUR TO SWEET, COMES OUT SUBLIME. THE RUBY ORBS CAN BE STUFFED WITH NUTS, SPICED WITH ANYTHING FROM ALLSPICE TO NUTMEG, AND CAPPED WITH SUMPTUOUS LIQUEURS. INDEED, SIMPLE, UNADULTERATED, THE SPOON SWEET IS LUXURIOUS.

The Greeks, from whose word *kerasos* we get "cherry," had a number of varieties early on. They were said to have come originally from a city called Cerasus, in the Pontos, where the climate was so favorable that, according to Athenaeus, the trees grew to a height of 24 cubits (36 feet). To my mind there is no fruit, or spoon sweet, more heavenly. I would gladly live in a city named "Cherry."

*2½ pounds cherries, pitted*
*½ cup tsikoudia or grappa*
*2 tablespoons fresh lemon juice*
*1½ cups sugar*
*5 allspice berries*

1 Place all the ingredients in a large, heavy nonreactive pot and mix gently. Bring to a boil, reduce the heat to maintain a simmer, and cook until the cherries wilt, 15 minutes. Using a slotted spoon, transfer the cherries to a strainer set over a bowl.

2 Continue cooking the liquid for 10 minutes. Stir in the juices that have collected in the bowl under the cherries and cook until the syrup is thick enough to coat a spoon heavily, 230°F on a candy thermometer, about 5 minutes. Remove the pot from the heat and set aside to cool.

3 When the syrup is cool, stir in the cherries and any extra juices that have collected. Transfer to storage jars. It will keep in the refrigerator for several months.

## NECESSARY SPOONFULS FOR A NEW DAUGHTER-IN-LAW
......................

In the late 1800s it was customary to give a bride a spoonful of fruit preserves during the wedding ritual. These were referred to as "necessary spoonfuls," and the reason for the custom involved a play on words. It was said that the sweet was to appease the bride, or *nyfi*. But the diminutive for "little bride," *nyfitsa*, also means "weasel." If not appeased, went the story, the little nuptial "weasel" might eat too much of the wedding banquet. One wonders, however, if her new in-laws were suspicious that their daughter-in-law would never be trustworthy, that she would always eat too much food. On the other hand, along with the fruit she was also given amulets of coral and carnelian to bedeck her hands and neck, blue glass beads, and Byzantine-style ornamental earrings.

# apricot and metaxa spoon sweet

### MAKES 2½ CUPS

APRICOTS TOOK THEIR NAME FROM THE GREEK *PRAIKOKION*, MEANING "EARLY TO MATURE"— IN SHORT, "PRECOCIOUS." NOW CALLED A MODERN VERSION OF THE OLD NAME, *VERIKOKO*, THEY ARE THE FIRST SUMMER FRUIT TO RIPEN, AND IN GREECE THEIR ARRIVAL IS GREETED WITH JOY. THE EARLY GREEKS THOUGHT THAT APRICOTS ORIGINATED IN WHAT WE NOW CALL ARMENIA. INSTEAD, THEY WERE PROBABLY NATIVE TO CHINA. THE PEOPLE LIVING BETWEEN THE BLACK AND CASPIAN SEAS DISCOVERED THEM EARLY AND TRANSPLANTED THEM TO THEIR LAND.

The Greeks cultivated orchards of apricots, mainly in Asia Minor near Lydia, once the center of gold working. They treasured the fruit fresh and dried them for an all-year treat. Apricots are so honeylike that when I am out of honey, I substitute apricot spoon sweet in many Greek dishes (see Beef *Kapama* with Wine, Brandy, Coffee, and Honey, page 369).

2 pounds ripe but firm apricots, halved and pitted
³⁄4 cup sugar
2 tablespoons Metaxa or other brandy
1½ tablespoons fresh lemon juice

1 Combine all the ingredients in a large, heavy nonreactive pot and stir gently. Bring to a boil over medium-high heat, cover the pot, and simmer until some of the apricot halves have collapsed and some are still whole, 8 minutes.

2 Using a slotted spoon, transfer the apricots to a strainer set over a bowl. Continue simmering the liquid for 10 minutes. Stir in the juices that have collected in the bowl. Continue cooking, stirring frequently, until the syrup is thick enough to coat a spoon, 230°F on a candy thermometer, 5 minutes. Remove the pot from the heat and set aside to cool.

3 When the syrup is cool, stir in the apricots and any extra juice that has collected. Transfer to storage jars. It will keep in the refrigerator for several months.

# grape spoon sweet

## WITH CITRUS GERANIUM

### MAKES ABOUT 4 CUPS

GRAPES GROW SO UBIQUITOUSLY IN GREECE, AND IN SUCH ABUNDANCE, THAT ONE COULD ASSUME THAT NOT EVERY BERRY IS PRECIOUS. NOT SO. EVERY LAST GRAPE HAS A USE; EVERY LAST ONE IS ENJOYED. IN ANCIENT TIMES, IT WAS A CAPITAL CRIME TO STEAL GRAPES FROM SOMEONE'S VINEYARD. THE OFFENSE HAPPENED FREQUENTLY AT NIGHT, SO THE THIEVES WERE CALLED "DAY SLEEPERS." TODAY HOSPITABLE GREEKS, WHILE NEVER STOPPING TOURISTS WHO PLUCK AMONG THE GRAPEVINES, DO GRUMBLE ABOUT IT. GRAPES ARE ALMOST CURRENCY TO GREEKS.

## WHAT TO DO WITH SPOON SWEETS

While you may hesitate to serve family or guests a spoonful of preserves, as is the custom in Greece, the uses of spoon sweets are many. Use them to:

■ Top a serving of fresh fruit—peaches, pears, a papaya half, a bowl of berries. The effect is spectacular.

■ Fill cookies, coffee cakes, and danishes. The standards are cherry and peach, but why not use grape?

■ Pour on top of or swirl into puddings. Try stirring apricot spoon sweet into caramel pudding.

■ Top cakes instead of frosting, or use as a filling between cake layers, even more extravagant when allowed to drip sweetly down the sides. Try rose petal spoon sweet over yellow cake.

■ Drizzle over ice creams and sherbets of many flavors. Try cherry preserves over chocolate ice cream or quince preserves over orange sherbert.

■ Stir into or drizzle over other fruit compotes. Pears simmered in wine become stunning when garnished with rolled citrus peel spoon sweet.

When there is no other fruit to make a spoon sweet, almost any cook can acquire grapes. Grape spoon sweet was the first I saw made—Maria, a new bride and novice cook, simmered them so long we couldn't get a spoon into them. Now I never stay in Greece without making grape spoon sweet at least once. We use the wine grapes in the field, and the sweet turns out as purple as pansies or as magenta as plums. In the United States, I frequently use green grapes for a stunning iridescent jade sweet, perfect to put on ice cream or a cake.

# CROESUS AND HIS GOLDEN COINS

IN THE SIXTH CENTURY B.C.E., A SOMEWHAT MYSTERIOUS PEOPLE CALLED THE LYDIANS OCCUPIED A LUSH BUFFER ZONE BETWEEN GREECE AND PERSIA, ALONG THE HERMUS AND PACTOLUS RIVERS OF WESTERN TURKEY. NO ONE KNOWS EXACTLY WHO THEY WERE, THOUGH THEIR NAME SUGGESTS THEY WERE SEMITIC. IT'S CLEAR THEY HAD THEIR OWN CULTURE, ALTHOUGH THEY BORROWED SOME ITEMS—SUCH AS THEIR ALPHABET—FROM GREECE. IN RETURN THEY GAVE GREECE CERTAIN FOODS: SUPERIOR BREAD, LAKE FISH, DRIED AND BUNDLED FIGS, SNOW-WHITE ONIONS, LUXURIOUS SAUCES, WINE FLAVORED WITH HONEY AND FRAGRANT FLOWERS, AND AN INVENTION ALL THEIR OWN—MONEY. THE LYDIANS WERE THE FIRST PEOPLE TO MINT GOLD COINS. IT SEEMS THEY HAD SCADS OF THE PRECIOUS METAL AND VAULTS OF GOLDEN TOKENS. TO THIS DAY THE NAME OF THEIR GREATEST AND LAST KING, CROESUS, RINGS OUT AS SYNONYMOUS WITH WEALTH, AND APPARENTLY THE STORIES OF HIS RICHES ARE FACT.

The Pactolus river carried much gold dust in its sandy flow, but the gold was mixed with silver and copper. To withdraw the gold and refine it into treasure, the Lydians developed an innovative process: They mixed the sandy gold with lead and then melted the mixture until the lead absorbed the copper, leaving the gold and silver separated. They then ham-

*Some sources say that once captured, Croesus tried to escape his conqueror by burning himself and his wealth on a funeral pyre.*

mered out foils, particles, and granules of the gold and silver compound. They dampened these, mixed them with common sea salt, and placed them in a small clay container. They put the container in an oven and baked it for several days. Inside the pot, the salt, moisture, and clay reacted with the metal, generating a vapor that evaporated the silver. The flakes and foil of now pure gold were sifted from the pot and melted into lumps on a blowpipe. The golden lumps were then minted into stamped coins and used for trading.

## AS RICH AS CROESUS

By classical Greek times, Croesus's gold was already famous. Greeks reported that Croesus's palace was sumptuous. They evoked his name and his wealth in play and oratory. They also cited his generosity, for Croesus gave fortunes to various Greek temples—including a life-size solid gold statue of a woman baking—and often bankrolled the oracle of Delphi, whose enigmatic predictions he sought. At the time, Croesus ruled over many Greek cities, in particular Ephesus and Smyrna, but rather than battle, the Greeks preferred to trade with him. Still, in due time, despite the fact that the Lydians were dreaded warriors equipped with horses and chariots, Croesus's gold didn't save him. The Persians overran his country and sacked his city. When he asked the Persian leaders what their soldiers were doing, they answered, "They are plundering your city and carrying off your gold." "Oh, no," Croesus replied. "It's not my city or my treasure. Nothing here belongs to me any longer. It's you they are robbing."

*3 pounds seedless table grapes,*
*preferably Thompson or*
*Red Flame*
*2 cups sugar*
*2 cups water*
*1/3 cup fresh lime juice*
*1/4 cup fresh lemon juice*
*12 small (1-inch-wide) lime or*
*lemon geranium leaves, or*
*1/4 cup lime juice plus*
*2 bay leaves*

1 Pluck the stems off the grapes and rinse the fruit in a colander. Set aside to drain.

2 Combine the sugar, water, lime and lemon juices, and the geranium leaves in a large nonre-active pot. Bring to a boil over high heat and stir in the grapes. Bring to a boil again, reduce the heat, and briskly simmer until the grapes collapse and the skins loosen, 10 minutes.

3 Using a slotted spoon, transfer the grapes to a strainer set over a bowl. Continue simmering the liquid briskly for 20 minutes. Add the juices that have collected in the bowl and cook until the liquid is thick and syrupy, 230°F

on a candy thermometer, 20 to 25 minutes.

4 Return the grapes, along with any more juices that have collected in the bowl, to the pot. Simmer briskly, adjusting the heat and stirring from time to time, until very thick and syrupy again, about 25 minutes. Remove from the heat and let cool completely. Transfer to storage jars. It will keep in the refrigerator for as long as several months.

## GERANIUMS

The scented leaves of certain geraniums—which we call "rose" or "lemon" geranium and the Greeks call *arbaroiza*—are used in a number of Greek preparations, from spoon sweets to teas. The leaves are not available in the herb collections in stores, but the plants can easily be found in garden nurseries and grown at home. Geraniums have long grown in Greece, and because the seedpods of these flowers resembled the head and beak of a crane, the Greeks named the plant for that bird, *geranos*. The geranium family contains about 250 cultivars, but these do not include the very popular common garden geranium, *Pelargonium*, widely grown today. Pelargonium has been mistaken for geranium over the years and so has crept into sharing the geranium name. Its own name is also from the Greek. It means "stork," once again an allusion to the birdlike shape of the plant's seedpods.

*In Greece, a window treatment might include the family's pet birds as well as pots of flowers.*

# rolled citrus strips spoon sweet

### MAKES 48 STRIPS

WELL PRECEDING THE INVENTION OF MARMALADE, GREEKS BEGAN TO MAKE A PRESERVE OF CITRON AND OTHER CITRUS FRUITS. AS ALWAYS, NOT WASTING A SPECK, AFTER MAKING USE OF THE JUICE AND THE PULP THEY TOOK THE PEEL AND TURNED IT INTO A SPOON SWEET. IT IS ONE OF THE MOST DECORATIVE, WITH CURLICUES OF PEEL HANGING SUSPENDED IN THEIR SWEET SYRUP LIKE BAUBLES IN AN AMBER SEA.

Citrus peel spoon sweet is one of the most commonly made in Greece, where Seville, or bitter, orange is the usual choice. But the always available navel orange is a fine substitute. Most Greeks sew the citrus peel into rings with needle and

*Orange slices with their juicy pulp are also poached and candied.*

thread, but I take a quicker route, one that is easier on the hands: I skewer them with wooden *souvlas*. The resulting syruped curls are quite a treat for the eye when layered over cake or ice cream, strewn in pudding, or submerged in a drink.

6 large, thick-skinned oranges,
    3 medium-size grapefruits,
    or a mixture (see Notes)
4 cups sugar
1/4 cup fresh orange or grapefruit
    juice
1/4 cup fresh lemon juice
2 cups water

1 Cut each orange into 8 wedges and remove the pulp from the wedges. Set the pulp aside for another use. You should be left with the rind, including the orange outer layer and the whole pith.

2 Roll the rind pieces into cylinders, stringing the rolls through their centers onto bamboo skewers as you go.

3 Bring a large pot of water to a boil over high heat. Add the skewers of orange rolls, bring to a boil again, and cook briskly for 15 minutes. Drain, fill the pot with fresh water, and return the skewers to the pot. Bring the water to a boil and cook briskly until the rolls are tender, 10 to 15 minutes. Drain and set aside.

4 Rinse the pot and place the sugar, orange juice, lemon juice, and the 2 cups water in it. Bring to a boil and simmer over medium-high heat until the sugar dissolves, 5 minutes. Add the rolls, still on their skewers, bring to a boil, and reduce the heat so that the liquid just bubbles up over the rolls. Cook until the liquid thickly coats a spoon and the rolls are soft but not falling apart, 230°F on a candy thermometer, 25 minutes. Remove the pot from the heat and set it aside at room temperature to cool.

5 Remove the skewers from the syrup and pull off the orange rolls. Transfer to storage jars and pour the syrup over them. They will keep in the refrigerator for as long as several months.

## THE TRAVELS OF THE KUMQUAT

Though the name suggests a kinship with the loquat, kumquats are an entirely different fruit. They are a citrus, distantly related to oranges and lemons.

For thousands of years kumquats were cultivated in Asia, never reaching Europe, until a collector for the London Horticultural Society brought them back. In a short time the shrub-like tree with its delightful, somewhat bitter, small orangelike fruit was being planted across Europe. At the time Corfu was part of the British Empire, and certain of the British governors thought the kumquat and Corfu might make a compatible match. They brought a few samples of the shrub to the island and grafted them onto a wild variety of citrus, the *Citrus trifoliata*.

Today kumquats are a major crop on Corfu. They are preserved as a spoon sweet and pressed into a sweet, orangy liqueur that is available in tourist shops in bottles shaped like Olympian gods and kilted Greek soldiers. Since kumquats have a thick, pulpy skin and a tart tone, not unlike the long-used bitter orange, Corfu kumquats end up in many a marmalade jar all the way back in England.

## NOTES:

■ If you are using a mixture of citrus, place only one type on each skewer. Then, if some of the rolls soften more quickly than others (grapefruit seems to take half the time of orange rinds), you can pull out the softened ones while the others continue to cook.

■ If you prefer to make the rind curls the traditional way, string the rolls onto lengths of heavy-duty thread with a large darning or tapestry needle, then tie the ends of the thread together to make a "necklace."

■ In another rendition of a citrus spoon sweet, kumquats, about 2 cups, can be substituted for the orange rind. They should be cut in half the long way and not skinned, then similarly slipped onto skewers.

# PLATO, THE "COOL" PHILOSOPHER

**P**LATO WAS BORN IN ATHENS, OR POSSIBLY AEGINA, AROUND 428 B.C.E., INTO ONE OF THE MOST ESTEEMED FAMILIES IN GREECE. HE COULD TRACE HIS ANCESTORS TO THE LAST KING OF ATHENS AND BACK TO THE GOD POSEIDON ON ONE SIDE, AND ON THE OTHER TO THE LAWMAKER SOLON AND ATHENS'S EARLY MAGISTRATES. HE WAS RAISED BY HIS MOTHER AND HER SECOND HUSBAND, WHO WAS AN AVID SUPPORTER OF PERICLES, AND IN CONSEQUENCE HIS CHILDHOOD HOME WAS FILLED WITH THINKERS AND POLITICIANS. SOME WERE SUCH LONG-STANDING FRIENDS OF SOCRATES THAT PLATO MUST HAVE KNOWN THE SAGE, WHO WAS LATER TO BECOME HIS TEACHER, FROM AN EARLY AGE.

At first Plato thought to become a politician, but he was soon repelled by the violent acts among the political factions of his time. Instead he took to delving into reasoning and philosophy. When Socrates was executed, Plato and other students fled to join the cadre of another thinker, Euclid, in Megara. From there Plato traveled extensively in Greece, Egypt, and Italy. Upon return he sought to found his own school of thinking and to gather his own students. He founded his academy of philosophical and scientific research, situated under a tree in the great market of Athens, and taught there for the rest of his life, lecturing without notes. He would present problems; then he and the students, Aristotle among them, would work on the solutions jointly.

And Plato wrote. He penned his thoughts in the form of conversations, or dialogues, the most famous of which is called *The Republic*. In this and other works he expounded on ethics, politics, the aesthetic of living, the mystical, and the metaphysical.

What was justice? he asked. Could virtue be taught? What constituted right, power, and good? What was beauty? He defined virtue as self-knowledge and reflected on the nature of community. Happiness was not guaranteed by the possession of things, he said, but by the right use of the things one had—particularly the gifts of mind, body, and fortune. He believed in monogamous marriage, the utilization of a child's instinct to play, and that children should be schooled where instruction in various subjects was coordinated—the origin of our idea of grammar school. Governments should be moral. Divine judgment could not be bought by offerings. In all his thinking he showed an intense concern for the quality of human life.

No other philosopher has so influenced Western thought. Plato's precepts were based on a belief in unchanging and eternal realities, independent of how matters seem to change: It is the underlying truths alone that give meaning to things. To this day, Plato is considered the pinnacle of logic and reasoning—"cool-headedness." As for food, he, like Socrates, attended banquets where many plates were offered and where the evening ended with talk and sweets. And like his mentor, Plato believed that even sweets should sing with their simplicity.

*In a medieval drawing, Plato discusses a problem with his mentor, Socrates. In Greek legend, Plato sat beneath an olive tree— and the tree still grows.*

# green tomato and currant spoon sweet

### MAKES 1½ QUARTS

**N**OT ALL THE BUDS AND BERRIES ON VEGETABLE PLANTS HAVE A CHANCE TO RIPEN; NOT ALL CAN BE EATEN BY THE FAMILY; AND SO, JUST AS GREEKS USE EVERY PART OF THE GRAPE AND ITS VINE, SOME OF THE ABUNDANT EARLY CROP OF VEGETABLES OR THE LAST ONES LEFT WITH LITTLE CHANCE TO MATURE, ARE, LIKE FRUIT, TURNED INTO A SPOON SWEET. MOST OFTEN THE PRESERVED VEGETABLES (THOUGH, TRUTH BE TOLD, THEY ARE ACTUALLY FRUITS) ARE TOMATOES AND EGGPLANT. GREEN TOMATOES IN SYRUP HAVE ALL THE FLAVOR SENSATION OF COOKED RIPE TOMATOES, WITH A TOUCH OF ACID BEHIND THE SWEETNESS. CURRANTS ADD A WINEY COUNTERPOINT, ALMONDS A CRUNCHY HIDDEN SURPRISE. FOR A REMARKABLE DESSERT, SERVE GREEN TOMATO SPOON SWEET ON OLIVE OIL ICE CREAM (SEE PAGE 548).

1 large lemon
3 cups sugar
3 cups water
¼ cup dried currants
6 whole cloves
½ tablespoon coriander seeds
1 piece (5 inches) cinnamon stick, broken in half
3 pounds green tomatoes, rinsed, stemmed, and cut into 1-inch-wide wedges
½ teaspoon almond extract

**1** Using a vegetable peeler, peel just the zest off the lemon in ¼-inch-wide strips.

**2** Place the strips of zest, sugar, water, currants, cloves, coriander, and cinnamon sticks in a large nonreactive pot and bring to a boil over high heat. Add the tomatoes and bring to a boil again. Reduce the heat and simmer, stirring occasionally, until the tomatoes collapse, so that most are mushy but some are still holding their shape, 20 minutes. Using a slotted spoon, transfer the tomatoes to a bowl, leaving the liquid and other ingredients in the pot.

**3** Continue simmering the liquid until it is thick enough to coat a spoon lightly, 230°F on a candy thermometer, 35 minutes. Return the tomatoes to the liquid, stir in the almond extract, and set aside to cool.

**4** Transfer to storage jars. It will keep in the refrigerator for as long as several months.

# baby eggplant spoon sweet

**MAKES 1 QUART**

THE EGGPLANT WAS INTRODUCED TO THE GREEKS OF ANATOLIA BY ARAB MARAUDERS. IT WAS WELL ESTABLISHED IN GREEK COOKING BY THE FIFTEENTH CENTURY, MOSTLY FOR SAVORY DISHES. THE GREEKS HAD LONG USED SMALL BULBS, ESPECIALLY THE GRAPE HYACINTH, IN COOKING, AND THE JUST-FORMING EGGPLANT HAD A COLOR SIMILAR TO THE BULBS THEY ALREADY LOVED. THEY FOUND THEY COULD SAVE BOTH THE HUE AND THE CRUNCHY MEATINESS BY PRESERVING EGGPLANTS IN SYRUP.

But the pluses go beyond. Eggplant spoon sweet is out of the ordinary, combining earthiness with an ethereal honey-ness. Hyacinth bulbs were considered an aphrodisiac in ancient Greece. Perhaps eggplant in a spoon sweet works the same in modern times?

2 pounds (45 to 50) baby eggplants, each about 2 inches long
1/2 cup fresh lemon juice
45 to 50 blanched whole almonds
3 cups sugar
1/2 cup honey
1 piece (3 inches) cinnamon stick
6 whole cloves
2 large sprigs fresh thyme
2 1/2 cups water

1 Cut off and discard the stems of the eggplants and make a small lengthwise slit in each one. Place the eggplants in a large bowl and add 1/4 cup of the lemon juice, plus enough cold water to cover. Set a plate over the eggplants to keep them submerged and set aside to soak for 1 hour.

2 Bring a large pot of water to a boil over high heat. Drain the eggplants and drop them into the boiling water. Boil until they are squeezable but still firm, 10 minutes. Drain and plunge them into cold water to cool.

3 Insert an almond into the slit in each eggplant.

4 Mix the sugar, honey, cinnamon stick, cloves, thyme, 2 1/2 cups water, and remaining 1/4 cup lemon juice in a large nonreactive pot and bring to a boil over high heat. Add the eggplants, reduce the heat slightly, and simmer briskly until the eggplants are soft, 5 minutes.

5 Remove from the heat. Discard the cinnamon stick and thyme sprigs, and set the eggplants aside to cool. Cover the pot and set it aside at room temperature overnight.

6 The next day, strain the liquid into a large saucepan. Set the strainer with the eggplants over a bowl. Bring the liquid to a boil over medium-high heat, then reduce the heat and simmer until soft threads form, 240°F on a candy thermometer, 8 to 12 minutes. Add the eggplants and any collected juices to the pan and cook until the liquid is thick enough to coat a spoon, 10 minutes. Remove from the heat and set aside to cool. Transfer to storage jars. It will keep in the refrigerator for as long as several weeks.

# rose petal spoon sweet

**MAKES 1½ CUPS**

S APPHO CALLED THE ROSE "THE QUEEN OF FLOWERS." IN HER TIME THE FRAGRANT, VELVET-SOFT BLOSSOMS WERE CALLED *RODON*.

Today, giving heed to the feature that makes the flower as visually stunning as it is perfumed, Greeks call the rose *triandafilo,* or "thirty petals." To Greeks the rose is still the queen of flowers. Many Greeks grow roses on their patio or veranda, and in the garden. And it figures: Greeks are a people to whom aroma is as important as sight, sight as important as touch, touch as important as taste. Those petals offer more to the Greeks than an invitation to inhale—they offer a rapturous spoon sweet. Greeks suspend other edible blossoms in syrup, creating other beautiful and blissful floral spoon sweets, but the one of rose petals is the most beloved. The sweet emerges as a caress upon the tongue.

*4½ cups unsprayed red rose petals*
*2 cups water*
*Sugar*
*1½ tablespoons fresh lemon juice*
*½ cup Mavrodaphne or Port wine*
*½ teaspoon powdered mastic*
*(see page 143)*

1 Rinse 4 cups of the rose petals and place them in a medium-size bowl.

2 Bring the water to a boil in a saucepan over high heat and pour the boiling water over the petals. Without stirring, cover the bowl and set it aside. Let the petals steep at room temperature overnight.

3 The next day, strain the petals in a colander set over a medium-size saucepan. Measure the liquid (it should be 1½ to 1¾ cups), and add an equal amount of sugar. Add the lemon juice, wine, and mastic to the pan and bring to a boil over high heat. Stir in the drained rose petals, reduce the heat, and simmer, stirring from time to time, until a soft ball can be formed, 240°F on a candy thermometer, about 30 minutes.

4 Remove the pan from the heat and strain the liquid into a clean storage jar. Allow the syrup to cool completely. Rinse and drain the ½ cup fresh rose petals and pat dry. Carefully stir them into the syrup. Cover and refrigerate at least overnight. It will keep in the refrigerator for as long as 3 months.

## EDIBLE FLOWERS

T he Greeks taught the Etruscans and the Romans about aromatic flowers and about the necessity of displaying wreaths of the perfumed blossoms at gala dinner celebrations. "Rose fragrance is suitable for a drinking party, as are myrtle and quince," said Athenaeus. But as well as perfuming a dinner party, many of the flowers provided ingredients for the menu. Apple blossom, chrysanthemum, daylily, geranium, jasmine, lavender, lilac, linden, and violet were among them, as well as the flowers of many herbs: basil, chamomile, chive, clover, coriander, dill, hyssop, mint, oregano, marjoram, thyme, and savory.

# SEVEN INNOVATIVE SWEETS

# greek-inspired ice creams

## TO SERVE WITH SPOON SWEETS

THERE MAY HAVE BEEN A HINT OF THEIR ORIGINATION IN ITALY, THEN FRANCE, THEN ENGLAND, BUT THE PHENOMENON OF ICE CREAM TOOK OFF IN THE UNITED STATES, AND THE U.S. STYLE OF ICE CREAM SUBSEQUENTLY SWEPT THE WORLD. EVERYWHERE THE CONFECTION TRAVELED, PEOPLE CREATED VERSIONS WITH THEIR OWN FAVORITE FLAVORS AND NATIVE FRUITS.

Below are three American-style ice creams inspired by flavors from the heart of Greek cuisine. Because their tastes are complementary, they are perfect for topping with spoon sweets. The flavors—olive oil, mastic, and dense, sweet wine—are, in fact, so essentially Greek, they go back to the dawn of Greek history.

There is a word that Greeks use daily that defies translation: *kefi*. One has *kefi* or doesn't have *kefi* at any one moment. For example, you don't go out with friends in the evening because you don't have *kefi*. You do go out because you do have it . . . or you go out to get it. The closest equivalent would be to say that you are not in a good mood.

To me ice creams, fruit sweets, and sweets made with cheese bring instant *kefi*. The possibilities based on Greek ingredients are endless.

Here follow seven sweet treats, three ice creams, three fruit-based confections, and one made from cheese, all concocted of the foods Greeks love. They are not traditional dishes, but they are as Greek as honey-soaked cakes, spoon sweets, and festive times.

## OLIVE OIL ICE CREAM

### MAKES 1½ QUARTS

*2 large eggs*
*³/4 cup sugar*
*1 cup whole milk*
*¹/2 cup olive oil*
*1¹/2 cups heavy (whipping) cream*
*1 teaspoon vanilla extract*

1 Whisk the eggs and sugar together in a medium-size bowl until well blended. Set aside.

2 Heat the milk in a small saucepan over medium heat until it is just beginning to simmer.

3 Slowly whisk the hot milk into the egg mixture. Pour the mixture back into the saucepan, place it over low heat, and cook, stirring constantly, until it thickens to the consistency of a runny pudding, about 4 minutes. Be careful not to let it boil. Set the pan aside and let the mixture cool to room temperature.

## NOT SO SWEET

Certain women in Greek history did *not* spend their time making sweets. One of these was Rodanthi. Rodanthi was a native of the village of Kritsa in the province of Lassithious on Crete, making her a *kritsotopoula*, "daughter of Kritsa." She was educated—possibly she was an only child or the child of a priest. Perhaps it was her education that gave her her determination, or perhaps there was another reason. Rodanthi was forced into an infamous sort of wedding, a *kritiko gamo*, a "Cretan wedding," essentially an abduction, with an evil Ottoman janissary. Whatever it was, Rodanthi took up the rebellion against the Ottoman oppressors as if she had been born a warrior. The year was 1821. When the Ottomans arrived to suppress her village, she realized that due to her upcoming marriage she could infiltrate the enemy camp as no other Greek could. On her wedding night she slit the throat of her hated groom. She then dressed herself as a man and ran away. Joining the rebels, she took on the name Spanomanolis, "beardless Manolis." Only when she died did her fellow rebels realize that she was a woman.

4 Whisk the oil and cream together until thoroughly blended. Slowly whisk the oil mixture into the cooled egg mixture. Stir in the vanilla. Chill in the refrigerator for several hours or overnight, then freeze in an ice cream maker.

## MASTIC ICE CREAM

### MAKES 1½ QUARTS

*2 large eggs*
*3/4 cup sugar*
*1 cup whole milk*
*1 to 2 teaspoons finely ground mastic (see Note)*
*2 cups heavy (whipping) cream*

1 Whisk the eggs and sugar together in a medium-size bowl until well blended. Set aside.

2 Heat the milk in a small saucepan over medium heat until just beginning to simmer. Add the mastic and stir until thoroughly dissolved.

3 Slowly whisk the hot milk mixture into the egg mixture. Pour the mixture back into the saucepan, place it over low heat, and cook, stirring constantly, until it thickens to the consistency of a runny pudding, about 4 minutes. Be careful not to let it

boil. Set the pan aside and let the mixture cool to room temperature.

4 Slowly whisk the cream into the cooled egg mixture until thoroughly blended. Chill in the refrigerator for several hours or overnight, then freeze in an ice cream maker.

**NOTE:** Mastic is quite piney and pungent. One teaspoon gives the ice cream a lovely, subtle aroma and flavor; 2 teaspoons will more strongly flavor the dessert.

## MAVRODAPHNE ICE CREAM

### MAKES 1½ QUARTS

*2 large eggs*
*1/2 cup sugar*
*1 cup whole milk*
*2 cups heavy (whipping) cream*
*1 teaspoon vanilla extract*
*1/2 cup Mavrodaphne, Commandaria Saint John, Greek vin santo, or other sweet Greek-style dessert wine (see Notes)*

1 Whisk the eggs and sugar together in a medium-size bowl until well blended. Set aside.

2 Heat the milk in a small saucepan over medium heat until just beginning to simmer.

# NIGHT WINE, DAY WINE, AND THE BAREFOOT COMPRESSOR

UP AND DOWN THE HILLSIDE TERRACES LAYERED INTO ITS COARSE PUMICE SOIL, SANTORINI IS RUN RIOT WITH VINEYARDS. IN PATCHES HIGH AND LOW, NEAR VILLAGES AND FAR OUTSIDE, GRAPEVINES—SOME CENTURIES OLD, SOME NEWLY PLANTED—BRING FORTH A CROP THAT MAKES THE ISLAND FAMOUS.

To the stranger's eye, however, there doesn't appear to be any viniculture, for the wines are cultivated in an odd manner. Due to the wind that roars over the rim of Santorini, the grapes are grown in twisting circles close to the ground. The vintner twines each year's new branches round in rings. In winter, when the vines are bare, the island seems to be speckled with thousands of woody O's. In summer, the new branches creep across the soil until no earth is visible. The grapes, rather than hanging down, hide beneath the foliage on beneficial beds of pumice pebble.

The yield of these vines under the hot Cycladic sun is superabundant. That radiant sun also causes a desperate rush of work at grape harvest time. It shines so starkly that if the grapes are not pressed almost instantly, the wine turns from dry to sweet in a matter of hours. A few hours more of hesitation, and the wine turns from white to red. To achieve a dry white wine, the grapes must be juiced on the day they are harvested—which means that night. And so the white wine of Santorini is called *niktari*, "night wine." *Brusko*, the red wine, is made fast on the heels of the white, by the light of the next day.

Traditionally, women are not supposed to press wine on Santorini, for fear they will turn the wine sour. But I have pressed grapes for wine, and I will tell you why.

## BAREFOOT IN THE CAVERN

On Santorini grapes are pressed in great caverns dug into the sides of ravines and cliffs. These wine caverns are different from the island's other caves. They are huge and have pressing vats carved into their floors. As the grapes are harvested, they are gathered in bushel baskets and covered in burlap to protect them from the sun's sugar-creating heat. The baskets are taken to the pressing caves, often on donkey back, and the grapes are disgorged into the dug-out vats. To one side of each vat is a spout through which the freshly pressed juice runs into an even deeper narrow cistern. A basket suspended at the bottom of the spout filters out leaves and twigs. When the pressing is done, the grape juice is extracted in pails from the cisterns and poured carefully into colossal wooden barrels that lie in racks along the cavern walls. The barrels are sealed and the juice is left to age. But all those steps are not what possessed me to jump into the pressing rings. I jumped in because the grapes are pressed barefoot.

Who could resist? Who would not jump with unshod foot upon a massive heap of plump grapes and feel the squish? Knowing I shouldn't, I admit, I threw off my sandals and plunged in, and I stayed for hours, so delicious was the sensation. Markos, the grape owner and wine maker, was horrified. But what could he do except to trust in the fates and keep on stamping?

## THE MOMENT OF TRUTH

The next day, however, anxiety hit. The wine tester arrived to test the alcoholic content of our newly pressed wine and to see if the batch was up to snuff. Was the wine going to be good or not? Silence reigned as fifteen men and I squatted by the barrel to hear the outcome. He took a sample, put in the testing meter, grimaced, and cast his eyes to the ground. Markos groaned, stood up, and paced to the cavern entrance. All the men followed suit, standing up and throwing hands over head. "Oh, no," I thought. "It's true. Women aren't supposed to press. I ruined the wine and I'm going to have to pay for the whole barrel." But the groans and gestures were only drama. Hurrahs rung out and Markos shouted, "The wine measures fourteen percent, the highest alcohol wine can get!"

Indeed, the wine was more than fine, and I was spared the punishment for my . . . misstep. Forty days later, when we tried the barely fermenting juice, it was "cooking" just fine. A year later we broke out a small casket from the giant barrel. Two years later we siphoned more, and at four years we began to pour the vintage daily. I brought bottles back with me each year until the barrel was empty. Some I drank. Some I used to poach fruit.

## PYRAMUS AND THISBE
....................

According to Greek legend, the fruit of the mulberry once grew only white. At that time, a boy and girl dwelled next door to one another, and as they grew their friendship changed to love. But for whatever reason, their parents forbade them to see one another.

The houses where the two lived, however, shared a wall, and in the wall was a small chink. Pyramus and Thisbe discovered that they could whisper through the tiny hole, and kiss the mortar between them. One day they decided to wait until dark and run away. They chose to meet under a mulberry tree whose sweet snow-white fruit glowed like a beam of light. Thisbe arrived first, but as she approached, she came upon a lioness. She ran to a nearby cave for cover, dropping her veil on the way. The lioness, mouth bloody from a fresh kill, took up the veil, shook it, and let it fall again. Poor Pyramus, when he arrived moments later, found paw prints and the bloody veil. Thinking Thisbe dead, Pyramus plunged his sword into his side. Thisbe found Pyramus lying beneath the tree, and as the tree took up his blood, its fruit changed to dark, dark red. Thisbe, praying to the gods to keep the mulberry fruit its sanguine color in honor of their love, leapt on Pyramus's sword to join him. The gods heard her wish, and the fruit of the common mulberry has been red, and only red, ever since.

3 Slowly whisk the hot milk into the egg mixture. Pour the mixture back into the saucepan, place it over low heat, and cook, stirring constantly, until it thickens to the consistency of a runny pudding, about 4 minutes. Be careful not to let it boil. Set the pan aside and let cool to room temperature.

4 Slowly whisk the cream into the cooled egg mixture, blending thoroughly. Stir in the vanilla. Chill in the refrigerator for several hours or overnight.

5 Place the mixture in an ice cream maker and begin to freeze it. When the ice cream is almost but not quite frozen, stir in the wine, then finish freezing.

**NOTES:**

■ Many areas of Greece produce their own varietals of dessert wine and vin santo from Muscat or other grapes. Commandaria Saint John is a sweet Muscat wine from Cyprus.

■ Alcohol inhibits the freezing process of the ice cream, so it should not be added until the ice cream is already mostly frozen.

**VARIATIONS:**

Generally, when an ice cream is to have a topping of spoon sweets, fresh fruit, or syrup, it's best to keep it simple. But there are a few special Greek flavorings that can be stirred in for a jot of extra pleasure. Add them while the ice cream is being stirred in the ice cream maker.

■ 1/2 cup Mavrodaphne-soaked dried currants (see page 49)

■ 1/2 cup chopped toasted hazelnuts or sesame seeds

■ 1/4 cup crumbled Candied Ginger Coins (see page 147)

■ 2 teaspoons chopped fresh rosemary needles

# poached orange slices

## WITH BAY LEAF, CARDAMOM, AND WHITE WINE

### SERVES 6

TANTALUS, A SON OF ZEUS, STOLE THE GOD'S HEAVENLY NECTAR AND AMBROSIA TO GIVE TO HIS FRIENDS. IN PUNISHMENT THE GODS BANISHED HIM TO THE LOWER WORLD, WHERE HE WAS MADE TO STAND IN WATER UP TO HIS CHIN UNDER THE BRANCHES OF A HEAVILY LADEN FRUIT TREE. EVERY TIME HE LOWERED HIS HEAD TO DRINK, THE WATER RECEDED. EVERY TIME HE REACHED FOR A LUSCIOUS PIECE OF FRUIT, THE BRANCHES PULLED AWAY. FROM HIS NAME WE HAVE THE WORD "TANTALIZING," REFERRING TO SOMETHING DESIRED THAT IS JUST BEYOND REACH.

Luckily, the branches of Greece's fruit trees are so filled with fruit that they bend quite low. With the fruit of some I created Oranges *à la Grecque*, poached in white wine with a breath of bay leaf and cardamom. The result is so good I am led to pity poor Tantalus all the more.

4 cups white wine
1 cup sugar
1 large bay leaf
12 cardamom seeds, crushed
6 medium oranges, peeled and cut into 1/2-inch-thick rounds

1 Combine the wine, sugar, bay leaf, and cardamom in a medium-size nonreactive saucepan. Bring to a boil over high heat, reduce the heat to medium, and cook, uncovered, until the sugar has dissolved, 2 minutes.

2 Add the orange slices and cook until they are barely soft, 2 minutes. Using a slotted spoon, transfer the slices to a bowl. Discard the bay leaf.

3 Cook the liquid until it is slightly thickened but still runny, 5 minutes. Pour it over the oranges and allow them to cool, then chill thoroughly before serving.

*Along the path to Aphrodite's bath in Cyprus, a village priest refreshes visitors with oranges from his orchard.*

**NOTE:** If you don't care to crunch down on cardamom seeds, strain the liquid before pouring it over the oranges.

# pears in chamomile syrup

## WITH PISTACHIO TOPPING

### SERVES 6

PEARS ORIGINATED WHERE GREEKS DID, ON THE WEST OF THE URALS ABOVE THE BLACK SEA. THE REMAINS OF WILD PEAR ARE FOUND IN MYCENAEAN SITES. HOMER RAVED ABOUT PEARS. GREEK ORCHARD KEEPERS LEARNED EARLY ON TO GRAFT FRUIT-BEARING BRANCHES TO ROOTSTOCK, AND BY ROMAN TIMES THE GREEKS HAD A NUMBER OF VARIETIES OF PEARS. THE ORIGINAL WILD PEARS WERE BETTER COOKED THAN RAW. IT IS THAT MORE ARCHAIC TRADITION THAT IS FOLLOWED HERE, THOUGH WITH FINE, FIRM, MODERN CULTIVATED PEARS.

*1½ cups water*
*2 tablespoons chamomile tea leaves*
*6 medium-size ripe but firm pears*
*4 cups dry white wine*
*1½ cups sugar*
*2 tablespoons fresh lemon juice*
*½ cup (2 ounces) shelled salted pistachio nuts*

1 Bring the water to a boil in a small saucepan over high heat. Add the chamomile tea leaves, cover, and set aside to steep for 5 minutes. Strain the liquid into a large pot and set it aside; discard the tea leaves.

2 Peel the pears, leaving them whole with stems intact.

3 Add the wine, sugar, and lemon juice to the strained liquid and bring to a boil. Drop in the pears, reduce the heat slightly, and simmer briskly until they barely give when gently pressed, 8 to 10 minutes. Using a slotted spoon, transfer the pears to a bowl.

4 Continue simmering the liquid briskly until it is reduced by half, thickened, and amber colored, 220°F on a candy thermometer, 20 to 25 minutes. Remove the pot from the heat and let the syrup cool for 5 minutes.

5 Pour the syrup over the pears, allow to cool to room temperature, then cover and chill thoroughly before serving.

6 Heat an ungreased skillet over medium-high heat. Add the pistachios and stir until toasted, 1½ minutes. Allow to cool, and then finely chop with a chef's knife or in a food processor.

7 When you are ready to serve the pears, set them in individual bowls. Spoon the chamomile syrup over them, and sprinkle the pistachios over the top.

**NOTE:** For further festooning, a scattering of fresh berries adds splendid color and a contrasting fruit taste.

## A STOREHOUSE OF PEARS

In ancient Greece, pears were stored in cool rooms called *oporothikoi*. Today they are bought in stores called *apothikoi*. From both we get the word "apothecary."

# green figs

## POACHED IN MAVRODAPHNE WITH SHAVED *MANOURI* CHEESE

### SERVES 10 TO 12

IF YOU MUST SLEEP AFTER A PICNIC, GREEKS ADMONISH YOU NOT TO NOD OFF UNDER A FIG TREE. THE EVOCATIVE SCENT WILL LEAD YOU TO WILD DREAMS—MAYBE AMOROUS, PERHAPS WITH SPELLS OF DELIRIUM, POSSIBLY WITH VISIONS OF GORGING ON THE SUCCULENT FRUIT HANGING ABOVE YOU. BETTER TO TRAP THAT FRUIT'S ENCHANTMENT BY BRINGING SOME HOME TO POACH.

Fig trees grow everywhere in Greece—in a garden, by a road, or near a house. When their fruit is ripe it is eaten out of hand as well as dried for winter's enjoyment and for export. Barely ripe figs poached in Greek wine and topped with Greek cheese make it hard to decipher what's more enchanting—the shady tree laden with its teardrop-shaped offering, or the bowl brimming with the luscious poached treat.

*1 bottle Mavrodaphne or other*
  *sweet wine*
*2 cups sugar*
*¼ cup fresh lemon juice*
*3 bay leaves*
*2 pounds ripe but firm green figs*
*6 ounces manouri cheese (see Note)*

1 Combine the wine, sugar, lemon juice, and bay leaves in a large nonreactive pot and bring to a boil over high heat. Add the figs, reduce the heat, and simmer briskly until they puff out and are very soft, 15 minutes.

2 Using a slotted spoon, transfer the figs to a large bowl. Discard the bay leaves. Continue simmering the liquid until it reaches the soft thread stage, 235°F on a candy thermometer, 20 minutes. Then stir the syrup into the figs. Allow to cool, then cover and chill thoroughly.

3 Spoon a few figs and some liquid into each dessert bowl. Serve with a slice of cheese to the side in each bowl.

## THE FIGURATIVE FIG

Over the millennia, the fig has garnered all sorts of notoriety.

■ The god Dionysos loved figs almost as much as wine. Baskets of them were offered to him.

■ Fig trees were considered holy trees in ancient times, yet nymphs feared living in them (although perhaps they only feared Dionysos!).

■ Figs could ward off demons, but could themselves be dangerous if too much fig juice was drunk.

■ Figs have mysterious powers and even today can cause all sorts of troubles, like unrequited love.

■ Fig trees attract spirits, and sitting under one, you can hear devils boiling oil in a frying pan.

But for all the exotic and dangerous qualities figs are reputed to have, I have observed only one sort of fig fame in Greece: Greeks so adore the fruit that they could all be deemed fig fanatics.

**NOTE:** If you cannot find *manouri* cheese, ricotta salata is a good substitute.

# sweet saganaki

**SERVES 6**

WITH THEIR AFTER-DINNER COURSE OF DRINKS, THE ANCIENT GREEKS SERVED NUTS AND, IF THERE WAS ANY SWEET TREAT, CHEESE CAKES. FROM THEIR TIME-HONORED LEAD, IT'S AN EASY STEP TO TAKE GREECE'S SAVORY FRIED CHEESE APPETIZER, *SAGANAKI*, AND TURN IT INTO A DESSERT.

Dusted with confectioners' sugar, the same cheese squares gently crisped in their two-handled *saganaki* skillet make a grand finishing bite or a wonderful snack. They can be accompanied by a bowl of walnuts and a dessert wine, replicating the end of the ancient banquet. In more contemporary fashion, they can sit side by side with fresh fruit, nestle within the syrup of a poached fruit confection, or linger in the company of an array of cookies. To all, they add a whiff of cheesy curd and a touch of Greek salt air. Of course they can also stand alone in all their humble glory.

*2 tablespoons plus 1 teaspoon butter*
*8 ounces manouri cheese,*
    *cut into 1-inch cubes*
    *(see Note, previous page)*
*2 1/2 tablespoons confectioners' sugar*

Melt the butter in a medium-size skillet over medium heat. Add the cheese cubes in a single layer and sauté until the bottoms begin to brown, 45 seconds to 1 minute. Turn and continue to fry until all the sides of the cubes are lightly browned, about 3 minutes. Remove with a slotted spoon and drain on paper towels. Transfer the cubes to a platter and sprinkle with the confectioners' sugar. Serve while still hot.

## CANDY

As well as pastries and puddings, Greeks relish many sweets that we could call candy. Some are of the ancient style, often based on sesame. *Halvas* are cakes of ground sesame seed sweetened with honey, or nowadays sometimes sugar. The best commercial *halvah* comes from Thessaly and Macedonia. Greeks also make a home-made *halvah* with tahini, nuts, and a sugar syrup. The term *halvas* is also used for semolina puddings.

*Pasteli*, sesame candies, are now made as a hard candy, sometimes substituting pistachios or walnuts. Greeks buy commercial *pasteli*, but they also make it at home in flat pieces like a brittle.

Other candies that Greeks enjoy became popular when sugar began to flow into Byzantine and Ottoman kitchens. Among these, the most famous is *loukoumi*, called "Turkish Delight" in English, a semisoft gum jelly confection that is flavored with many fruit and flower essences, and often mastic. It comes in many colors and contains chopped nuts—especially walnuts and pistachios. The candy is cut into cubes and heavily dusted with confectioners' sugar.

Other favorites are *mastiha*, a sugar paste made with mastic, which is served by the spoonful in a tall glass of water, called a "submarine"—a favorite of children. The same paste is sometimes flavored with vanilla and then called *banilia. Karameles*, like our word "caramel," from the Greek for "cane" and "honey," refers to hard candies of all sorts and flavors.

# CYCLADES VILLAGE WEDDING

NO EVENT ALLOWS GREEKS TO SHOW THE LOVE THEY HOLD FOR THEIR WAY OF LIFE LIKE A WEDDING. GREEK WEDDINGS ARE ELABORATE CEREMONIES FULL OF POMP, PARADES, AND SPECTACLE, BUT THE MOST IMPORTANT, AND MOST GREEK, THING ABOUT THEM IS THAT THEY ARE SOCIALLY EMBRACING. GREEK WEDDINGS BELONG TO EVERYONE. THIS IS ESPECIALLY TRUE IN SMALL VILLAGES, WHERE WEDDINGS MOVE THROUGH THE WHOLE TOWN AND TAKE UP A WHOLE DAY.

In the Cyclades, where the groom will move into the bride's dowry house, the wedding festivities begin the day before the ceremony, when the bride's relatives collect to prepare her wedding bed. Singing marriage songs, they bounce a baby—a boy for certain, but nowadays a girl as well—on the shiny new covers to ensure that the couple has a child quickly. Then they toss wedding gifts of coins and bills upon the bed.

## IT TAKES A VILLAGE . . .

Early on the morning of the wedding day, the groom's male relatives, shooting guns in the air and led by musicians, carry the man's "dowry"—his chest of drawers— to the new home the couple will share. Meanwhile, back at her parents' home, the bride dresses in white (until fifty years ago, the old women tell me, the color of the bridal dress was pink) as the guests begin to arrive—and in a village, "the guests" means the whole community. Drinks and the first round of *koufeta* are served. Then the musicians appear and lead the procession of bride, family, and sponsors, followed by the whole village, to the church. The bride is on display. She is shy, her eyes downcast. Her life is about to change.

A long altar table has been set before the altar screen and before it stand the bride and groom. With candles burning everywhere, ikons illuminated by oil lamps, and incense billowing, the priest begins with the couple's engagement. For that, rings are exchanged—simple gold bands, one for her, one for him. The priest, donned in elaborate robes, switches the rings between the fingers of groom and bride three times, then sets them forever on the third finger of the right hand of each. Now comes the actual wedding. The sponsors (like our best man and maid of honor) produce the wedding crowns, circlets of silken leaves and white flowers, tied together with a long ribbon. The priest moves behind the couple and crowns the heads of the groom and bride, switching the crowns three times before settling them on the now linked couple. A glass of wine is poured. The best man toasts the couple, who partake of the wine three times, then breaks the glass. Now the newlyweds, led by the priest, begin a dance that circles the altar three times. During this exuberant moment called "the dance of Isaiah," the couple is pelted with rice and occasionally *koufeta* (though priests have been known to return fire when bombarded by sugared almonds!). Greeks believe that which of the pair can step on the other's foot will rule the union. Of course one stamp demands a two-footed stamp back, and so with the bride's veil and skirts held high by her attendants, Isaiah's dance becomes a hilarious jig. Finally the couple exits the church, and back at the proud parents' home *koufeta* is merrily distributed to the whole town. Moving to the bridal house, the groom carries the bride in, first smashing a pomegranate on the threshold and marking a cross on the doorjamb above.

## THE FESTIVE BANQUET

A banquet follows at the home of the bride's parents. Again the whole village, and sometimes neighboring villagers, come. The premise of the feast is that if there is abundance to share in the community, bread and wine will accompany the couple for the rest of their lives. Meatballs, *dolmades*, pita, spreads, roasted meats, potatoes, and salad are served, and then a dance follows with bouzouki, clarinet, guitar. As dawn approaches, the couple finally sneaks away to the bridal home.

Three is an important number in Greek culture. It crops up in the marriage rite many times. Where I live, the bride and groom, exhausted but happy, and full of honey and almonds, stay locked in their new home for three days.

# CEREMONIAL SWEETS

# koufeta

## FROM THE CYCLADES ISLANDS

### (WEDDING "TAFFY")

#### SERVES 10 TO 20

N O WEDDING IN GREECE IS COMPLETE WITHOUT AN OFFERING OF SWEET ALMONDS. IN EARLY TIMES, THE TRADITIONAL WEDDING OFFERING TO THE GODS WAS HONEY (AS CLOSE TO NECTAR AS HUMANS COULD GET) ACCOMPANIED BY ALMONDS BLANCHED WHITE.

Wedding cakes of the two ingredients—patted together in rural regions and baked as cakes in cities—were prepared in classical Greece, and as "tokens" for attending, the parents of the bride passed honied almonds to the crowd outside the temple or church in Greco-Roman times. Today, millennia later, the custom continues unchanged all over Greece. Almonds, sweetened in one fashion or another, are given out by the bride's family on her wedding day.

In most cities and towns nowadays, wedding guests receive sugar-encrusted white Jordan almonds, gathered in packets of white tulle tied with ribbon and decorated with tiny silk flowers. The number must be odd: usually nine almonds per packet, but sometimes seven or even five. Almonds can also be honied or sugared at home, then gathered in festive tulle pouches or passed loose in bowls. But on the Cycladic islands, in villages far from cities and lacking the sweet shops in which to purchase sugared almonds, an older version of wedding *koufeta* remains. Here, a day or so before the wedding, all the female relatives of the bride gather to make a taffylike sweet of blanched almonds cooked in honey and brandy.

First honey is simmered until it is thick enough to spin on a knife or spoon, then splashes of brandy are poured

For a Greek, three major ceremonies mark life's different stages: baptism, wedding, and funeral. On each of these occasions family members gather, friends come, and in villages, everyone attends. At each event the family of the celebrant distributes sweets and drinks to all. The gatherings are a demonstration of love, of continuity, and of faith.

On two of these occasions, the sweets are particular to that event—they are served at no other time. Every Greek wedding boasts sweet almond *koufeta*. Every Greek funeral, and even more so the memorials that follow, involves the distribution of *kollyva*, an ancient and symbolic confection of boiled wheat and pomegranate. Sweets are also passed out to all attending the joyous baptism of a new infant.

The sweets of wedding and funeral are especially beloved. They speak of largesse and an offering, joyful or sorrowful, to the Almighty. Both involve the stuff of myth, symbol, and legacy. For those of us who want to partake of Greek life, they also offer a way of participating. By enjoying them, we join a people who are proud of their heritage.

in to add an essence of luxury and antiquity, and at the end, a profusion of blanched almonds is swirled into the mix. The thick confection is poured onto platters to set. After the wedding vows are exchanged, when the guests assemble back at the bride's parents' house, the platters are passed among the crowd, with a number of clean knives and a tray of water glasses accompanying. Each person slips a knife into the soft taffy, spins out a scoopful on the knife tip, and places the confection in his or her mouth and lets it melt. The knife is returned for washing, a glass of water taken, and the platter is passed on.

I love the wedding ritual—the exchange of rings, the linked crowns passed across bride to groom and back again, the circling of the altar. But like everyone else, I also love the *koufeta*.

*1 cup honey*
*2 tablespoons brandy*
*1/4 teaspoon orange-blossom water*
*1 1/2 cups (about 10 ounces)
   blanched whole almonds*

1 Pour the honey, brandy, and orange-blossom water into a large saucepan and bring to a boil over high heat. Stir, reduce the heat, and gently boil until the mixture is the color of burnished mahogany and spins off a spoon, 240°F on a candy thermometer, about 30 minutes.

2 Stir in the almonds and bring to a boil again. Remove the pan from the heat and let the mixture

## BAPTISM

Perhaps the most important ritual in the life of an Orthodox Greek—for it offers the person admittance into the blessed community and gives the new being a name—is holy baptism. Like all Orthodox ceremonies, the rite is a beautiful one.

The ceremony takes place separately from the weekly service, on a Saturday or Sunday afternoon. The light in the incense-filled church is low, the interior cool, and the baptismal font has been brought before the altar screen. The parents have chosen someone who will take their place should they not be able to raise the child, someone who will see that the child is raised well. The role of godparent is an honor, and the ties between the true and the honorary parents, and between godparent and child, will remain forever.

The baby is naked, wrapped in blankets to keep warm. The godparent—usually one, but sometimes two—has purchased a set of clothing, oil, and most important, a cross for the child to wear. The priest fills the font with water, which he blesses and tests for warmth. The baby is then unwrapped and held on high, belly up, under the dome of the church. Anointing the baby with oil, the priest makes the sign of the cross on the baby's forehead, nape of the neck, and heart. Then, invoking the Holy Trinity, he dunks the baby in holy water three times. The child is named, and the joyous relatives now take the baby and clothe it in new finery. The priest kisses the godparent's cross and hangs it around the baby's neck.

Such a joyous occasion, such a holy sacrament, calls for a celebration. After the baby is returned, now named, to his mother's arms, the family passes out all sorts of elaborate cakes. Drinks are poured for all, usually a silken brandy or other liqueur.

cool until it is no longer bubbling. Turn it out onto a large plate, allowing the almonds to spread out evenly. Cool until the mixture is thick enough to spoon up in "globs," several hours or overnight.

3 To serve, offer each diner a clean spoon or knife as you pass the platter of *koufeta* around. Each person slides the knife or spoon into the taffy and spins the implement until a scoop of the *koufeta* takes hold. The

*koufeta* is then eaten off the knife or spoon.

## NOTES:

■ *Koufeta* will keep, covered, at room temperature for up to 2 days.

■ Some villagers add a little toasted sesame seed in the *koufeta* mixture or sprinkle it on top once the mixture is poured onto the platter.

# kolyva

### SERVES 40

IN THE MOST FAMOUS OF THE GREEK MYTHS, PERSEPHONE, THE DAUGHTER OF THE GODDESS OF WHEAT AND OTHER GRAINS, DEMETER, IS KIDNAPPED BY HADES AND TAKEN TO THE REALM OF THE DEAD. IN HER GRIEF, DEMETER CAUSES ALL THE WORLD'S PLANTS TO STOP GROWING. FINALLY, FAMINE AT HAND, ZEUS RELENTS AND ALLOWS PERSEPHONE TO RETURN TO HER MOTHER, BUT ONLY IF SHE HASN'T EATEN ANY FOOD IN THE UNDERWORLD. FOR HER LONG WALK BACK, HADES TRICKS HIS CHOSEN BRIDE AND GIVES HER A POMEGRANATE. BECAUSE SHE EATS SOME OF THE SEEDS, EVERY YEAR SHE MUST RETURN TO THE OTHER WORLD FOR A TIME, AND DURING THAT TIME DEMETER ALLOWS NOTHING ON EARTH TO FLOURISH.

Greeks remember those who have passed on with the same foods. The women relatives of the deceased make a dish called *kolyva*, which contains the wheat berries Demeter gave the world and the pomegranate seeds that Persephone nibbled. And while it is a mournful memorial food, it is also a much-loved treat, patted down in pie tins, blanketed with a thick layer of sugar, and elaborately festooned with silver dragée candies, seeds, and almonds. It is brought to the church for blessing on the third and ninth day of a beloved's passing, again at forty days, a year, and three years, and also on "Soul Saturday" twice a year. After church the *kolyva* is poured into a sack or a large bowl, mixing the sugar, decoration, and grain together, and offered around. Children wait for it, paper bags at the ready. Adults, unable to forgo the comfort and memory of it, take handfuls. It is a fine way to honor the deceased with the food of life.

*Persephone, Queen of the Underworld, portrayed on an ancient coin.*

4 cups (about 1 pound, 6 ounces) wheat berries

Salt

1/2 cup sesame seeds

1 teaspoon anise seeds

1 1/2 cups (6 ounces) walnuts, coarsely chopped

1 1/2 cups (6 ounces) slivered blanched almonds

1 1/2 cups golden raisins

1 teaspoon ground cinnamon

Seeds from 1 large fresh pomegranate (see Notes)

3 cups confectioners' sugar

2 cups whole blanched almonds, for decorating

Silver dragées (see Notes)

1 Rinse the wheat berries and place them in a large saucepan. Add enough water to cover by 2 inches, along with a few pinches of salt. Bring to a boil over medium heat and cook until the berries are tender and beginning to split but not mushy, about 1¾ hours. (Add more water to the pot when the liquid reduces to the level that the wheat no longer floats, and stir from time to time so the berries don't stick to the bottom.) Drain and set aside in the strainer to cool and dry for at least 1 hour or up to several hours.

2 Place the cooled wheat berries in a large mixing bowl. Add the sesame and anise seeds, walnuts, slivered almonds, raisins, cinnamon, and the pomegranate seeds. Sift in 1 cup of the confectioners' sugar and toss it all together.

3 Transfer the mixture to a large platter or tray. Sift the remaining confectioners' sugar over the top to coat it thickly, almost like a frosting. Decorate the top with the whole almonds and the dragées.

## EROS

Aphrodite and the war god Ares had a son. In Greek he's called Eros; in English, Cupid. At first he was the protector of love, but in due time, armed with a quiver of devastating arrows, he began to dole out sweet, inescapable passion. When Eros zapped mortal or immortal with his darts, they fell into instant and relentless desire for whoever was in front of them. In impish, sometimes vengeful, glee, he stung his poor cousin Apollo many times over. He caused Jason to fall for dangerous Medea, and made Dido melt for Aeneas.

At first Eros was depicted as a strong, handsome man, blessed with athletic prowess. But later, when the Greeks and Romans began to romanticize love, they changed Eros's image. He became a winged baby with much cuter, not so piercing, aim to his arrows. Looking out for pairs that needed ardor, he would zing them and watch them walk off in together-forever bliss. We, in our worship of infatuation, have turned Eros into the chubby spirit of Valentine's Day.

Eros himself fell in love with a maiden named Psyche. She was so beautiful that people had begun to worship her instead of Eros's mother, Aphrodite. In retaliation the livid Aphrodite ordered Eros to make Psyche fall in love with the ugliest creature alive, but Eros crumbled for Pysche. So Eros asked Apollo to help him.

Apollo led Psyche to a bejeweled cave, where Eros joined her in human form. Psyche grew to love Eros, but she also grew lonely. She asked Eros to let her sisters visit. He agreed, but warned her not to question his identity. When the sisters found out that Psyche had never seen her husband, they told her he must be a monster. Fearing they might be right, the next night Psyche shined a light on the sleeping Eros. She saw that he was beautiful, but he awoke and fled. Psyche searched everywhere for Eros, with angry Aphrodite thwarting her at every turn. At last smitten Eros appealed to Zeus to let him have Psyche, and for once a myth has a happy ending: Psyche was brought to Olympus. And, in due time Psyche bore Eros a daughter named Voluptas, meaning "pleasure."

4 To serve, present the platter of decorated *kolyva*. Then, just before eating, mix it all together.

## NOTES:

■ Pomegranate is not always in season, but there really is no substitute for the seed in taste, texture, or symbolism. If it is not available, simply omit it.

■ Dragées are available in any well-stocked large supermarket, usually in the baking aisle.

■ *Kolyva* is traditionally prepared the day before the memorial service, but the wheat berries can ferment if left at room temperature overnight and the sugar can crystallize in a refrigerator's moist environment. The best pre-preparation method is to boil and refrigerate the wheat berries ahead of time, then add the other ingredients and decorate the *kolyva* just before it's needed.

## VARIATIONS:

**Marousi's *Kolyva*:** A very special great-grandmother I know adds one old element and one new one to her *kolyva:* the ancient ingredient of 2 spoons of flour that she has toasted golden in a small ungreased skillet, and the new of ¼ cup toasted coconut.

**Parsley for Remembrance, Too:** In ancient Greece parsley was a ceremonial plant dedicated to those passed away, and tombs were crowned with wreaths of the herb. In the way that so many Greek customs have remained throughout the ages, in many parts of Greece memorial *kolyva* also includes sprigs of parsley. Should you wish to add it, include 1½ cups well-rinsed and dried small sprigs of parsley with the other ingredients.

## THE THREAD UNBROKEN

Yesterday, on "Soul Saturday," we made *kolyva* for Nikos, who died too young, three years ago now. He wife, Annoula, was there, along with their sons, Luke and Antony, and their daughter, Maria. We passed out brandy (never sweet drinks at a memorial) and took handfuls of the *kolyva* mixture to nibble on.

Today Maria's son, named Nikos for his grandfather, is being baptized. He has a new outfit in white and the sea blue that Greeks adore. We have stacks of walnut cake, *baklava,* and *galaktoboureko* to pass out to guests.

When all the guests have departed, we will have a *meze* spread to savor: *saganaki*, eggplant salad, sausage slices, and little fried fish. An array of dishes waits ready on the table for the meal to follow. We will eat bread, *horta* pie, bean soup. Annoula has made a lamb *yiouvetsi*, squash, and a village salad. On the table sit large tumblers of pure water, small glasses of red wine, capers to sprinkle on the salad, and a bowl of olives. Because my children are with me, she is planning to fry heaps of potatoes and to cook a rice pudding. Baby Nikos will be given tiny tastes. Soon he will love the same foods and flavors.

There are ends and beginnings, but like a continuous thread, Greek ideas, customs, and foods carry on. And I, a welcomed stranger, have been able to share them.

# THE OTTOMAN RULE AND THE GREEK FIGHT FOR INDEPENDENCE

IN THE MIDDLE OF THE ELEVENTH CENTURY C.E., A BAND OF SELJUK TURKS SUDDENLY APPEARED ON THE EASTERN EDGE OF BYZANTIUM'S DOMAIN AND BEGAN TO THREATEN THE EMPIRE.

They had moved westward from the far side of the Ural mountains, along with other Turkish peoples who had converted to Islam centuries before.

In 1071 they defeated a Byzantine army at Manzikert, on the eastern edge of Anatolia, and swarmed across into what is now central Turkey. At first they were weak and fell under the control of the Mongols, who were riding westward behind them. But then a second group of Turkish people, the Ottomans, arrived and rapidly expanded.

By the mid-fifteenth century, the Ottomans were attacking the Byzantine empire on all sides, and in 1453 Constantinople fell to them. They then moved farther west to wrest Greece from the Venetians. Soon all but Crete and the Ionian islands fell under Ottoman Turk rule. The great sultan Suleyman the Magnificent moved northward to the edge of Vienna. His successor, Selim the Sot, swept over Cyprus, and in 1670, after lengthy and terrible battles, Crete finally fell. Virtually all Greek lands now lay under the dark cloud of Ottoman domination.

## FROM THE VENETIANS TO THE OTTOMANS

In the beginning, the Greeks welcomed the Ottomans. The Venetians had treated them as little more than slaves, and the Greeks hoped for better. But soon Ottoman rule turned even harsher. The Ottomans imposed impossibly high taxes and exacted many abhorrent tributes. In one of the most hated practices, they demanded that one of every five Greek boys be taken to become janissaries—personal guards and soldiers—in the sultan's retine. In many places they banned Christianity. Their occupation of Greece lasted close to five hundred years.

Indeed, the Turks held sway over Greece for so long that in some areas the two cultures began to blend. The Turkish language took on Greek words, and

The OTTOMAN EMPIRE at the death of Suleiman the Magnificent 1566 A.D.

Turkish words crept into Greek. The clothing styles of both peoples mixed. The cultural intermingling was especially noticeable in their food: Influenced by Mongol and Chinese foods, the Turks had acquired dumplings and stuffed vegetables. As they passed through Persia they had picked up dishes from that land. They had yogurt and made various cheeses; they acquired *yakni* stews, kebabs, and pilafs, as well as the Arab taste for eggplant and spinach. As they spread across the Byzantine empire, they adopted a great deal from the Byzantine menu and the foods of the Greeks. They began to make honey cakes, macaroons, fritters, flower and fruit preserves. They adopted wheat and olive oil. The Ottoman sultans set up their capital in magnificent palaces in Constantinople. At one point the Topkapi Palace had almost fifteen hundred servants employed in making food, from soup men to scullions.

## FREEDOM FIGHTERS

But although the foods and cultures of the two peoples began to mix, the spirited Greeks seethed under Ottoman rule. They clung ardently to their beloved Christianity and resisted Islam. They bristled under the subordination and poverty they were forced to endure and the destruction of much of their heritage. In 1687, while battling Venice, the Turks stored gunpowder within the still-intact Parthenon. A cannonball lobbed into the powder blew up the ancient temple. Other ancient and holy sites were looted, their stones chipped away. In due time, resistance groups sprang up everywhere across Greece. *Kleftic* rebel bands roamed the mountains, attacking Ottoman soldiers. Villages began resisting edicts.

Soon Imperial Russia, long the ally of Greece with their shared Orthodox religion, joined the fray. Catherine the Great sent emissaries to the Peloponnesos and Epiros to stir up yet more rebellion. New uprisings led to more terrible reprisals. The sultans imported 100,000 soldiers from Ottoman Egypt and ordered them to lay waste to the Peloponnesos. Meanwhile, the Turkish governor of Epiros, Ali Pasha, who had set up his own kingdom, zealously repressed insurgent Greeks in the north. Catherine retaliated by banishing the Turks from the Black Sea. It was in her new city of Odessa that the first Greek independence party was founded.

Ali Pasha's rebellion against the sultan gave Greece the chance it had been waiting for. On March 25, 1821, Bishop Germanos of Patras raised the Greek flag over a resistant monastery. His act ignited the full-fledged Greek war to regain autonomy. Fighting broke out all over Greece simultaneously. The war lasted a century.

At first the Greeks made large gains, but as the Ottomans realized how widespread the

As Greece fought on, Western powers were reluctant to intervene. They feared Turkey and the turmoil that would follow if the Ottoman empire collapsed,

Greece's aid and wrote appeals in support of the Greek cause. Former soldiers and physicians arrived, and money was collected. At the same time several dynamic leaders emerged among the Greek forces. A statue of the *klef* general Theodoros Kolokotronis still overlooks central Athens. Stories of Markos Botsaris are recounted today. And with the men, a woman rebel, the famous Boubolina, rose to fame.

## Lord Byron, Victor Hugo, Shelley, Goethe, Schiller, and Thomas Jefferson came to Greece's aid.

uprising was, the battles turned savage. Soon atrocities were being committed on both sides. The Greeks massacred twelve thousand Turks in Tripoli. The Turks, in turn, massacred twenty-five thousand on the island of Hios. Still, within a year the Greeks had recaptured a number of cities in both the north and the south. With these in their hands, the Greeks declared their independence on January 13, 1822.

and they were alarmed by yet another revolution in Europe. They also sadly misjudged the Greeks, believing them to be an "orientalized" people. Help came instead from educated aristocrats of Europe and America who were philhellenes—lovers of Greece and its culture. Lord Byron, Victor Hugo, Shelley, Goethe, Schiller, and Thomas Jefferson came to

### RUSSIA, FRANCE, AND BRITAIN ENTER THE FRAY

Unfortunately, the Greek leaders were not well united, and the Turks reclaimed a number of major cities. Finally the Western powers intervened, although somewhat accidentally. Russia, France, and Britain had sent a combined fleet to Pylos to demand that the Turkish forces stop the massacres. When the Western admirals sent forward a single ship under a white flag, the Turks fired on it. The furious admirals attacked and destroyed the Turkish fleet. In response, Sultan Mahmud II declared the war against the Greeks a "holy war," which provoked Orthodox Russia to send troops. With Russian forces at the gates of Constantinople in 1829, the ruling sultan accepted Greek independence and signed the

*Goethe was among many lovers of Hellenic heritage spurred to action by the Greek struggle for freedom.*

Treaty of Adrianople, granting the Greeks autonomy.

Still the struggle to become a fully reunited nation, and a democratic one, went on. At first Greeks chose a president from Corfu, but his autocratic ways offended the rebel leaders. Britain, France, and Russia intervened. They declared that Greece should be a constitutional monarchy, and that the king should be a non-Greek. Prince Otto of Bavaria was chosen. However, Otho, as the Greeks called him, arrived with a coterie of Bavarians to whom he gave all the official posts. The offended Greeks soon deposed him. Ironically, at the same time Britain marched into and claimed the Ionian islands. So doing, Britain now chose another non-Greek monarch, despite the fact that ancient Greece had never had a king, a young Danish prince who became George I of Greece.

## CRETE AND ASIA MINOR

In 1897 the Cretans, who were still under Turkish rule, rose up. International aid brought the island independence, but not yet union with Greece. Only in 1905 did Greece regain Crete.

To join the Western effort in World War I, Greece was promised that many of its Asia Minor territories would be returned.

When the allied powers reneged, Greece itself marched into Asia Minor. By then a new Turkish leader, Ataturk, had arisen. He used the Greek invasion to overthrow the oppressive Ottoman regime and at the same time, with a massive offensive, pushed the Greeks of Asia Minor to the sea. The assault led to the infamous Treaty of Lausanne in 1923, which gave Asia Minor, eastern Thrace, and several islands to Turkey; the Greek peninsula alone to Greece; and the Dodecanese islands to Italy. The treaty also called for a massive population exchange. Almost 1.5 million Greeks left Turkey for Greece, and 400,000 Turks left Greece for Turkey.

## DEMOCRACY ONCE AGAIN

Only after World War II did Greece regain the Dodecanese from Italy. Meanwhile, Yugoslavia and Russia encroached from the north, trying to join Greece to the Soviet bloc. With the aid of the United States, Greece once more resisted. For two

*Greek again since World War II, the Dodecanese islands embrace their heritage.*

decades the country struggled to regain peace, democracy, and economic recovery. When a military coup toppled the elected government officials in 1967, the last monarch of Greece attempted a countercoup and failed. He was forced to flee. Eventually a groundswell of resisting Greeks overthrew the leaders of the lawless coup. Greece reasserted its democracy and the king was not asked back.

Greece today is once again thriving—and democratic as it was from the beginning. It is a member of NATO and the EEU, international in outlook, revitalized in its ancient cultural traditions, resplendent in its zesty ways of life, and cooking up the wonderful foods of its long and complex heritage.

# CONVERSION TABLES

## APPROXIMATE EQUIVALENTS

1 STICK BUTTER = 8 tbs = 4 oz = ½ cup

1 CUP ALL-PURPOSE PRESIFTED FLOUR OR DRIED BREAD CRUMBS = 5 oz

1 CUP GRANULATED SUGAR = 8 oz

1 CUP (PACKED) BROWN SUGAR = 6 oz

1 CUP CONFECTIONERS' SUGAR = 4½ oz

1 CUP HONEY OR SYRUP = 12 oz

1 CUP GRATED CHEESE = 4 oz

1 CUP DRIED BEANS = 6 oz

1 LARGE EGG = about 2 oz or about 3 tbs

1 EGG YOLK = about 1 tbs

1 EGG WHITE = about 2 tbs

*Please note that all conversions are approximate but close enough to be useful when converting from one system to another.*

## WEIGHT CONVERSIONS

| US/UK | METRIC | US/UK | METRIC |
|---|---|---|---|
| ½ oz | 15 g | 7 oz | 200 g |
| 1 oz | 30 g | 8 oz | 250 g |
| 1½ oz | 45 g | 9 oz | 275 g |
| 2 oz | 60 g | 10 oz | 300 g |
| 2½ oz | 75 g | 11 oz | 325 g |
| 3 oz | 90 g | 12 oz | 350 g |
| 3½ oz | 100 g | 13 oz | 375 g |
| 4 oz | 125 g | 14 oz | 400 g |
| 5 oz | 150 g | 15 oz | 450 g |
| 6 oz | 175 g | 1 lb | 500 g |

## LIQUID CONVERSIONS

| U.S. | IMPERIAL | METRIC |
|---|---|---|
| 2 tbs | 1 fl oz | 30 ml |
| 3 tbs | 1½ fl oz | 45 ml |
| ¼ cup | 2 fl oz | 60 ml |
| ⅓ cup | 2½ fl oz | 75 ml |
| ⅓ cup + 1 tbs | 3 fl oz | 90 ml |
| ⅓ cup + 2 tbs | 3½ fl oz | 100 ml |
| ½ cup | 4 fl oz | 125 ml |
| ⅔ cup | 5 fl oz | 150 ml |
| ¾ cup | 6 fl oz | 175 ml |
| ¾ cup + 2 tbs | 7 fl oz | 200 ml |
| 1 cup | 8 fl oz | 250 ml |
| 1 cup + 2 tbs | 9 fl oz | 275 ml |
| 1¼ cups | 10 fl oz | 300 ml |
| 1⅓ cups | 11 fl oz | 325 ml |
| 1½ cups | 12 fl oz | 350 ml |
| 1⅔ cups | 13 fl oz | 375 ml |
| 1¾ cups | 14 fl oz | 400 ml |
| 1¾ cups + 2 tbs | 15 fl oz | 450 ml |
| 2 cups (1 pint) | 16 fl oz | 500 ml |
| 2½ cups | 20 fl oz (1 pint) | 600 ml |
| 3¾ cups | 1½ pints | 900 ml |
| 4 cups | 1¾ pints | 1 liter |

## OVEN TEMPERATURES

| °F | GAS MARK | °C | °F | GAS MARK | °C |
|---|---|---|---|---|---|
| 250 | ½ | 120 | 400 | 6 | 200 |
| 275 | 1 | 140 | 425 | 7 | 220 |
| 300 | 2 | 150 | 450 | 8 | 230 |
| 325 | 3 | 160 | 475 | 9 | 240 |
| 350 | 4 | 180 | 500 | 10 | 260 |
| 375 | 5 | 190 | | | |

*Note: Reduce the temperature by 20°C (68°F) for fan-assisted ovens.*

# bibliography

Aesop. *The Complete Fables*. Trans. R. and O. Temple. London: Penguin, 1998.

Alexiadou, V. *Greek Cuisine*. Thessalonika: V. Alexiadou Publisher, 1989.

Algar, A. *Classical Turkish Cooking*. New York: HarperCollins, 1991.

*Amphoras and the Ancient Wine Trade*. Athens: American School of Classical Studies, 1979.

Anthimus. *On the Observance of Food*. Trans. M. Grant. Totnes, Devon: Prospect, 1996.

Archestratus. *The Life of Luxury*. Ed. and trans. J. Wilkins and S. Hill. Totnes, Devon: Prospect, 1994.

Austin, M. M., and P. Widal-Naquet. *Economic and Social History of Ancient Greece*. Berkeley: University of California Press, 1977.

Back, P. *The Illustrated Herbal*. New York: Barnes and Noble, 1996.

Barber, E. *Prehistoric Textiles*. Princeton, N.J.: Princeton University Press, 1991.

———. *Women's Work*. New York: Norton, 1997.

Barron, R. *Flavors of Greece*. New York: William Morrow, 1991.

Bennet, J. "Knossos in Context: Comparative Perspectives on the Linear B Administration of LM II-III Crete." *American Journal of Archaeology* 94 (1990): 291–309.

Bent, T. *Aegean Islands: The Cyclades, or Life Among the Insular Greeks*. London: Longsmans Green, 1885.

Blum, R., and E. Blum. *The Dangerous Hour: The Lore and Culture of Crisis and Mystery in Rural Greece*. New York: Scribners, 1970.

Brothwell, D., and P. Brothwell. *Food in Antiquity*. London: Thames and Hudson, 1969.

Broudy, E. *The Book of Looms*. Lebanon, N.H.: University Press of New England, 1979.

Campbell, J. *Honor, Family and Patronage*. Oxford: Clarendon, 1964.

Cavallo, G., ed. *The Byzantines*. Chicago: University of Chicago Press, 1997.

Chaitow, A. *Greek Vegetarian Cooking*. Rochester, Vt.: Healing Arts, 1984.

Chantiles, V. *The Food of Greece*. New York: Simon and Schuster, 1992.

Chatto, J., and W. Martin. *A Kitchen in Corfu*. New York: New Amsterdam, 1987.

Conistis, P. *Greek Cuisine*. Berkeley, Calif.: Ten Speed, 1994.

Cowan, C., and P. Watson, eds. *The Origins of Agriculture*. Washington, D.C.: Smithsonian, 1992.

Cowan, J. *Dance and the Body Politic in Northern Greece*. Princeton, N.J.: Princeton University Press, 1990.

Dalby, A. *Siren Feasts*. London: Routledge, 1996.

Dalby, A., and S. Grainger. *The Classical Cookbook*. London: British Museum Press, 1996.

Danforth, L. *The Death Rituals of Rural Greece*. Princeton, N.J.: Princeton University Press, 1982.

———. *The Macedonian Conflict*. Princeton, N.J.: Princeton University Press, 1995.

Davidson, A. *Fruit: A Connoisseur's Guide and Cookbook*. New York: Simon and Schuster, 1991.

———. *Seafood*. New York: Simon and Schuster, 1989.

———. *The Oxford Companion to Food*. Oxford: Oxford University Press, 1999.

Davidson, J. *Courtesans and Fishcakes*. London: HarperCollins, 1997.

Detienne, M., and J. Vernant. *The Cuisine of Sacrifice Among the Greeks*. Chicago: University of Chicago Press, 1989.

Dickinson, O. *The Aegean Bronze Age*. Cambridge: Cambridge University Press, 1994.

Dimen, M., and E. Friedl, eds. *Regional Variation in Modern Greece and Cyprus: Toward a Perspective on the Ethnography of Greece. Annals of the New York Academy of Sciences* 268 (1976).

Doumas, C. *Thera, Pompeii of the Ancient Aegean: Excavations at Akrotiri, 1967–79*. New York: Thames and Hudson, 1983.

Drews, R. *The Coming of the Greeks: Indo-European Conquests in the Aegean and the Near East.* Princeton, N.J.: Princeton University Press, 1988.

———. *The End of the Bronze Age: Changes in Warfare and the Catastrophe ca. 1200 B.C.* Princeton, N.J.: Princeton University Press, 1993.

Dubisch, J., ed. *Gender and Power in Rural Greece.* Princeton, N.J.: Princeton University Press, 1986.

———. *In a Different Place.* Princeton, N.J.: Princeton University Press, 1995.

Fermor, P. *Roumeli.* London: Penguin, 1983.

Fitzgibbon, T., *The Food of the Western World.* New York: Quadrangle, 1976.

Friedl, E. *Vasilika: A Village in Modern Greece.* New York: Holt, Rinehart and Winston, 1962.

Galanaki, R. *The Cake.* Athens: Kendros, 1980.

Galanopoulos, A. "Zur Bestimmung des Alters des Santorin-kaldera." *Annales Geologiques des Pays Helleniques* 9 (1958).

———. "On the Size and Geographic Site of Atlantis." *Proceedings of the Academy of Athens* 35 (1960): 401–18.

———. *Atlantis: The Truth Behind the Legend.* New York: Bobbs-Merrill, 1969.

Garland, S. *The Complete Book of Herbs and Spices.* New York: Viking, 1979.

Garnsey, P. *Famine and Food Supply in the Graeco-Roman World: Responses to Risk and Crisis.* Cambridge: Cambridge University Press, 1988.

Garrison, H., with N. Kosoni and S. Tzolis. *The Periyali Cookbook.* New York: Villard, 1992.

*The Golden Deer of Eurasia: Scythian and Sarmatian Treasures from the Russian Steppes.* New York: Metropolitan Museum of Art, 2000.

Grant, M., and J. Hazel. *Who's Who in Classical Mythology.* Oxford: Oxford University Press, 1973.

Graves, R. *The Greek Myths.* 2 vols. London: Penguin, 1956.

Gray, P. *Honey from a Weed.* New York: Harper and Row, 1986.

Grayzel, S. *A History of the Jews.* New York: Meridian, 1984.

Greene, B. *The Grains Cookbook.* New York: Workman, 1988.

Hamilton, E. *Mythology.* New York: Penguin, 1946.

Hannum, H., and R. Blumberg. *Brandies and Liqueurs of the World.* New York: Doubleday, 1976.

Hanson, V. *The Other Greeks.* New York: Free Press, 1995.

Harris, A. *The Taste of the Aegean.* New York: Abbeville, 1992.

Hart, L. *Time, Religion, and Social Experience in Rural Greece.* Lanham, Md.: Rowman and Littlefield, 1992.

Herzfeld, M. *Ours Once More.* Austin: University of Texas Press, 1982.

———. *A Place in History.* Princeton, N.J.: Princeton University Press, 1991.

Hoffman, S. *Kypseli—Women and Men Apart: A Divided Reality.* Film distributed by Extension Media Center, University of California, Berkeley, 1974.

———. "The Ethnography of the Islands: Thera." In *Regional Variation in Modern Greece and Cyprus: Toward a*

*Perspective on the Ethnography of Greece,* ed. M. Dimen and E. Friedl. *Annals of the New York Academy of Sciences,* 268 (1976): 328–40.

———. "Kypseli: A Marital Geography of a Greek Village." In *Lifelong Learning,* 45 and 58. Berkeley: University Extension, University of California, 1976.

———. "The Return of the Thief." Paper presented at the American Anthropology Association and the Modern Greek Studies Association, 1993.

———. "Ruing the Theft of History, Feeling the Rise of Nostalgia." Paper presented at the Modern Greek Studies Association Meetings, 1995.

———. "Transformation Without Memory, Change Without Nostalgia." Paper presented at the American Anthropology Association Meetings and the Modern Greek Studies Association, 1995.

———. "Bringing the 'Other' to the 'Self': Kypseli the Place and the Film." In *Europe in the Anthropological Imagination,* ed. S. Parman, pp. 44–59. Englewood Cliffs, N.J.: Prentice Hall, 1997.

———. "After Atlas Shrugs." In *The Angry Earth,* ed. A. Oliver-Smith and S. M. Hoffman, pp. 302–26. New York: Routledge, 1999.

Homer. *The Iliad.* (Many editions available.)

Homer. *The Odyssey.* (Many editions avaiable.)

Isager, S., and J. Skydsgaard. *Ancient Greek Agriculture.* London: Routledge, 1992.

Jacobs, S. *Recipes from a Greek Island.* New York: Simon and Schuster, 1991.

Jenkins, N. *The Mediterranean Diet.* New York: Knopf, 1994.

Johnson, H. *Vintage: The Story of Wine.* New York: Simon and Schuster, 1989.

Johnson, P. *A History of the Jews.* New York: Harper Perennial, 1987.

Kagan, D. *Pericles of Athens and the Birth of Democracy.* New York: Free Press, 1991.

Kiple, K., and K. Ornelas, eds. *The Cambridge World History of Food.* Cambridge: Cambridge University Press, 2000.

Klein, M. *The Feast of the Olive.* San Francisco: Chronicle, 1983.

Kochilas, D. *The Food and Wine of Greece.* New York: St. Martin's, 1990.

Konstantinides, S. *Sofi's Aegean Kitchen.* New York: Clarkson Potter, 1993.

Kremezi, A. *The Foods of Greece.* New York: Stewart, Tabori and Chang, 1993.

———. *The Mediterranean Pantry.* New York: Artisan, 1994.

Lambert-Gocs, M. *The Wines of Greece.* London: Faber and Faber, 1990.

Lefkowits, M., and M. Fant. *Women's Life in Greece and Rome.* Baltimore: Johns Hopkins University Press, 1992.

Lies, B. *Earth's Daughters.* Golden, Colo.: Fulcrum Resources, 1999.

Lissarrague, F. *The Aesthetics of the Greek Banquet.* Princeton, N.J.: Princeton University Press, 1987.

Loizos, P. *The Greek Gift.* Oxford: Blackwell, 1975.

Loizos, P., and E. Papataxiarchis, eds. *Contested Identities.* Princeton, N.J.: Princeton University Press, 1991.

Mackley, L. *The Book of Greek Cooking.* Los Angeles: HP Press, 1993.

Mallory, J. D. *In Search of the Indo-Europeans: Language, Archaeology and Myth.* London: Thames and Hudson, 1989.

Man, R. *The Complete Meze Table.* London: Ebury, 1986.

Marinatos, S. "The Volcanic Destruction of Minoan Crete." *Antiquity* 13 (1939): 425–39.

———. *About the Rumor of Atlantis.* Cretan Chronicle 4 (1950).

Marks, T. *Le Problème de l'Atlatide.* Athens: Société Hellenique d'Anthropologie, 1948.

———. *Greek Island Cooking.* Boston: Little Brown, 1972.

Martin, T. *Ancient Greece.* New Haven, Conn.: Yale University Press, 1996.

Mavor, J. W. *Voyage to Atlantis.* New York: Putnam, 1969.

McClane, A. J. *The Encyclopedia of Fish.* New York: Holt, Rinehart and Winston, 1977.

McGee, H. *On Food and Cooking.* New York: Macmillan, 1984.

McGovern, P., S. Fleming, and S. Katz, eds. *The Origins and Ancient History of Wine.* Luxembourg: Gordon and Breach, 1995.

Mintz, S. *Sweetness and Power: The Place of Sugar in Modern History.* New York: Penguin, 1985.

Morris, I., ed. *Classical Greece: Ancient Histories and Modern Archaeologies.* Cambridge: Cambridge University Press, 1994.

Moudiotis, G. *Traditional Greek Cooking.* London: Garnet, 1998.

Norwich, J. *Byzantium: The Apogee.* New York: Knopf, 1996.

———. *Byzantium: The Decline and Fall.* New York: Knopf, 1996.

———. *Byzantium: The Early Years.* New York: Knopf, 1996.

Panourgia, N. *Fragments of Death, Fables of Identity: An Athenian Anthropolography.* Madison: University of Wisconsin Press, 1995.

Paradisis, C. *The Best of Greek Cookery.* Athens: Efstathiadis, 1974.

Pellegrino, C. *Unearthing Atlantis, an Archaeological Odyssey.* New York: Vintage, 1993.

Plato. *The Republic.* (Many editions available.)

*Pots and Pans of Classical Athens.* Athens: American School of Classical Studies, 1977.

Price, T., and A. Gebauer, eds. *Last Hunters: First Farmers.* Santa Fe, N.M.: School of American Research, 1995.

Ramage, A., and P. Craddock. *King Croesus's Gold: Excavations at Sardis and the History of Gold Refining.* Cambridge, Mass.: Harvard University Press, 2000.

Recipe Club of Saint Paul's Greek Orthodox Cathedral. *The Complete Book of Greek Cooking.* New York: Harper Perennial, 1990.

Revel, J. *Culture and Cuisine.* New York: Da Capo, 1982.

Rodd, R. *The Customs and Lore of Modern Greece.* Chicago: Argonaut, 1892.

Roden, C. *A Book of Middle Eastern Food.* New York: Vintage, 1974.

———. *The Book of Jewish Food.* New York: Knopf, 1996.

Root, W. *Food.* New York: Simon and Schuster, 1980.

Rosenblum, M. *Olives: The Life and Lore of a Noble Fruit.* New York: North Point, 1996.

Rosengarten, F. *The Book of Spices.* Wynnewood, Penn.: Livingston, 1969.

Salaman, R. *Greek Food.* New York: HarperCollins, 1993.

Sandars, N. *The Sea Peoples: Warriors of the Ancient Mediterranean, 1250–1150 B.C.,* rev. ed. London: Thames and Hudson, 1985.

Sanecki, K. *The Complete Book of Herbs.* New York: Macmillan, 1974.

Savill, A. *Alexander the Great and His Time.* New York: Barnes and Noble, 1993.

Schwab, G. *Gods and Heros: Myths and Epics of Ancient Greece.* New York: Pantheon, 1946.

Seremetakis, C. *The Last Word.* Chicago: University of Chicago Press, 1991.

Simeti, M. *Pomp and Sustenance.* New York: Henry Holt, 1991.

Smith, P., and C. Daniel. *The Chicken Book.* San Francisco: North Point Press, 1982.

Spoerri, D. *Mythology and Meatballs.* Berkeley, Calif.: Aris, 1982.

Stavroulakis, N. *Cookbook of the Jewish Greeks.* Athens: Lycabettus, 1986.

Stewart, C. *Demons and the Devil.* Princeton, N.J.: Princeton University Press, 1991.

Stobart, T. *Herbs, Spices and Flavorings.* New York: McGraw-Hill, 1973.

Stubbs, J. *The Home Book of Greek Cookery.* London: Faber and Faber, 1963.

Swahn, J. *The Lore of Spices.* New York: Crescent, 1991.

Trager, J. *The Food Chronology.* New York: Henry Holt, 1995.

Thomson, J. *The Greek Tradition.* London: Macmillan, 1915.

Toussaint-Samat, M. *History of Food.* Trans. A. Bell. Malden, Mass.: Blackwell, 1994.

Tselementes, N. *Greek Cookery.* New York: Divry, 1950.

Van Andel, T., and C. Runnels. *Beyond the Acropolis.* Stanford, Calif.: Stanford University Press, 1987.

Wace, A. J. B., and F. W. Hasluck. "Laconia and Laconia II: Topograph." *Annal of the British School at Athens* 14 (1907–8): 170–82, and 15 (1908–9): 158–78.

Welters, L., ed. *Folk Dress in Europe and Anatoloia.* Oxford: Berg, 1999.

Wilkie, N., and W. Coulson, eds. *Contributions to Aegean Archaeology.* Minneapolis: University of Minnesota Press, 1985.

Wilkins, J., D. Harvey, and M. Dobson. *Food in Antiquity.* Exeter: University of Exeter Press, 1996.

*Wine in Greece.* Athens: Hellenic Export Promotion Organization, 1987.

Winn, S. M. M. *Heaven, Heroes, and Happiness: The Indo-European Roots of Western Ideology.* Lanham, Md.: University Press of America, 1995.

Wise, V., and S. Hoffman. *Good and Plenty: America's New Home Cooking.* New York: Harper and Row, 1988.

———. *The Well-Filled Tortilla Cookbook.* New York: Workman, 1990.

———. *The Well-Filled Microwave.* New York: Workman, 1996.

Wolfert, P. *The Cooking of the Eastern Mediterranean.* New York: HarperCollins, 1994.

Yanilos, T. *The Complete Greek Cookbook.* New York: Avenel, 1970.

Zane, E. *Greek Cooking for the Gods.* Santa Rosa, Calif.: 101 Productions, 1970.

Zubaida, S., and R. Tapper. *Culinary Cultures of the Middle East.* London: I. B. Tauris, 1994.

# photo credits

## Cover
Art Archive/Archaeological Museum Piraeus /Dagli Orti, bottom middle; Susan Goldman middle (both); IML Image Group: Velissarios Voutsas, top right.

## Back cover
Susan Goldman, right; Rodney Racona, bottom right.

## Color Insert
AGE Fotostock: José Fuste Raga 3 top; Susan Goldman: 2, 3 middle, 4, 5 bottom, 6 bottom, 7, 8 bottom left and right, 11, 12 top, 13, 14 right, 15, 16 top and left; IML Image Group: Roberto Meazza 5 bottom, Clairy Moustafellou 6 both, Velissarios Voutsas 12 middle, Takis Spyropoulos 9; Lonely Planet: Chris Christo, 17 bottom, John Elk III 1, Kim Grant 12 bottom, George Tsafos 14 bottom, Rodney Racona 10 both.

## Interior
AGE Fotostock: 114, Walter Bibikow xviii, Kunst & Scheidulin 463, Pixta 3, Doug Scott 2

**Ancient Art and Architecture Collection:** 356

**The Art Archive:** 228; Archaeological Museum Florence/Dagli Orti 367, 403; Archaeological Museum Naples/Dagli Orti 365; Archaeological Museum Piraeus/Dagli Orti 427; Bibliothèque des Arts Décoratifs Paris/Dagli Orti 117; Musée du Louvre Paris 540, 544

**Dietrich Gehring:** 65, 498

**Susanna Hoffman:** xvi, 44, 222, 314, 431

**Lisa Hollander:** 42, 244, 292, 311, 541

**IML Image Group:** 111, 150; Alan Benson 18, 61, 82, 84, 87, 123 top, 186, 218, 335, 336 top, 467; Spyros Catramis 142, 328; Chris Christo 69, 442, 552; Manousos Daskalogiannis xv, 194, 408; Jon Davison 112; George Detsis 471; Zacharias Dimitriadis 346; Christos Drazos 360; Marc Dubin 436; John Elk III 338, 415, 491; Christopher Groenhout 319;

Paul David Hellander 259; Stella Hellander 144; Marinela Katsini 155; Noboru Komine 494; Maro Kouri 152, 487; Thanos Labropoulos 235, 444; Stelios Matsagos 140; Diana Mayfield x, 322; Doug McKinlay 135; Roberto Meazza xi, 79, 118, 123 bottom, 172, 216, 230, 326, 342, 488, 493; Clairy Moustafellou viii, 8, 21, 22, 24, 27, 28, 98, 120, 131, 158, 179, 236, 298, 497 top, 504, 542; Massimo Pizzocaro 59, 320, 396, 497 bottom, 530; Rassias 93; Alex Rodopoulos 95; Oliver Strewe 406; Takis Spyropoulos x, 262, 308; George Tsafos 286, 565; Brenda Turnnidge 10; Aris Vafeiadakis 104; Yiorgos Ventouris 522; Velissarios Voutsas iv, 7, 14, 77, 117, 294, 362, 372, 383, 466, 496, 516; Sally Webb 67

**Hugh Palmer/Thames & Hudson LTD:** iv, 17, 50, 55, 191, 214, 300, 376, 454

**Karen Kuehn:** iv, xiv, 226, 393, 404, 506

**Mary Evans Picture Library:** 354, 452, 453

**Rodney Racona:** 36, 279

**Superstock:** Brian Lawrence 484; Colin Paterson xi, xiii, 128, 418

**United States Holocaust Museum:** 434

# index

SNAKE WRITES FOR
LIZARD THIS.
A GRACE FOR SAVING
WHEN LOSS
SWALLOWED ALL.